The Complete Statistical
History of Stock-Car Racing

The Complete Statistical History Of Stock-Car Racing

Records, Streaks, Oddities, and Trivia

By Richard Sowers

Design by Tom Morgan

 **DAVID BULL** PUBLISHING

Library of Congress Cataloging-in-Publication Data:
Sowers, Richard, 1950-
The complete statistical history of stock-car racing: records, streaks,
    oddities, and trivia / by Richard Sowers.
        p. cm.
ISBN 1-893618-06-4
        1. Stock-car racing—United States—History. 2. Stock-car
racing—History

GV1029.9.S74 S58 2000
796.72'0973—dc21

            00-031241

David Bull Publishing, logo, and colophon are trademarks of David
Bull Publishing, Inc.

Book and cover design: Blue Design (www.bluedes.com)

Printed in the United States

10 9 8 7 6 5 4 3 2 1

David Bull Publishing
4250 East Camelback Road
Suite K150
Phoenix, AZ 85018
602-852-9500
602-852-9503 (fax)
www.bullpublishing.com

Page 2: Although he never reached victory lane as a driver,
cars owned by Richard Childress earned 67 victories during
the circuit's first 51 years.

Pages 4–5: NASCAR's superspeedway boom of the early '60s
was made to order for Fireball Roberts (center), whose
amazing feats on the big tracks include capturing the first
race ever held at Atlanta Motor Speedway, the Dixie 300 on
July 31, 1960.

Right: Atlanta Motor Speedway, which opened in 1960, is
among the many Winston Cup tracks that have undergone
many changes since the sport's infancy.

Page 8: It's no coincidence that the arrival of Dale
Earnhardt (3) as the 1979 Winston Cup Rookie of the Year—
followed a year later by his first series championship—has
paralleled an unprecedented era of growth for NASCAR.

Pages 10–11: Buddy Baker, in a specially timed run at
Talladega, Ala., on March 24, 1970, clocked a lap of 200.447
mph in a Dodge Daytona to become the first driver to
break the 200 mph barrier in a stock car.

Page 12: No driver in Winston Cup history was a contender
for the Winston Cup title on so many occasions, yet failed
to win it, during the circuit's first 51 years as Mark Martin.

Dedication

This book is dedicated to motorsports journalists—
and dear departed friends—Tom McCollister and
Gary Cornwell, whose encouragement helped me
undertake and complete the project.

Table of Contents

Driver Resumes

Miscellaneous Records

Sites of Winston Cup Races During the 20th Century

Acknowledgments

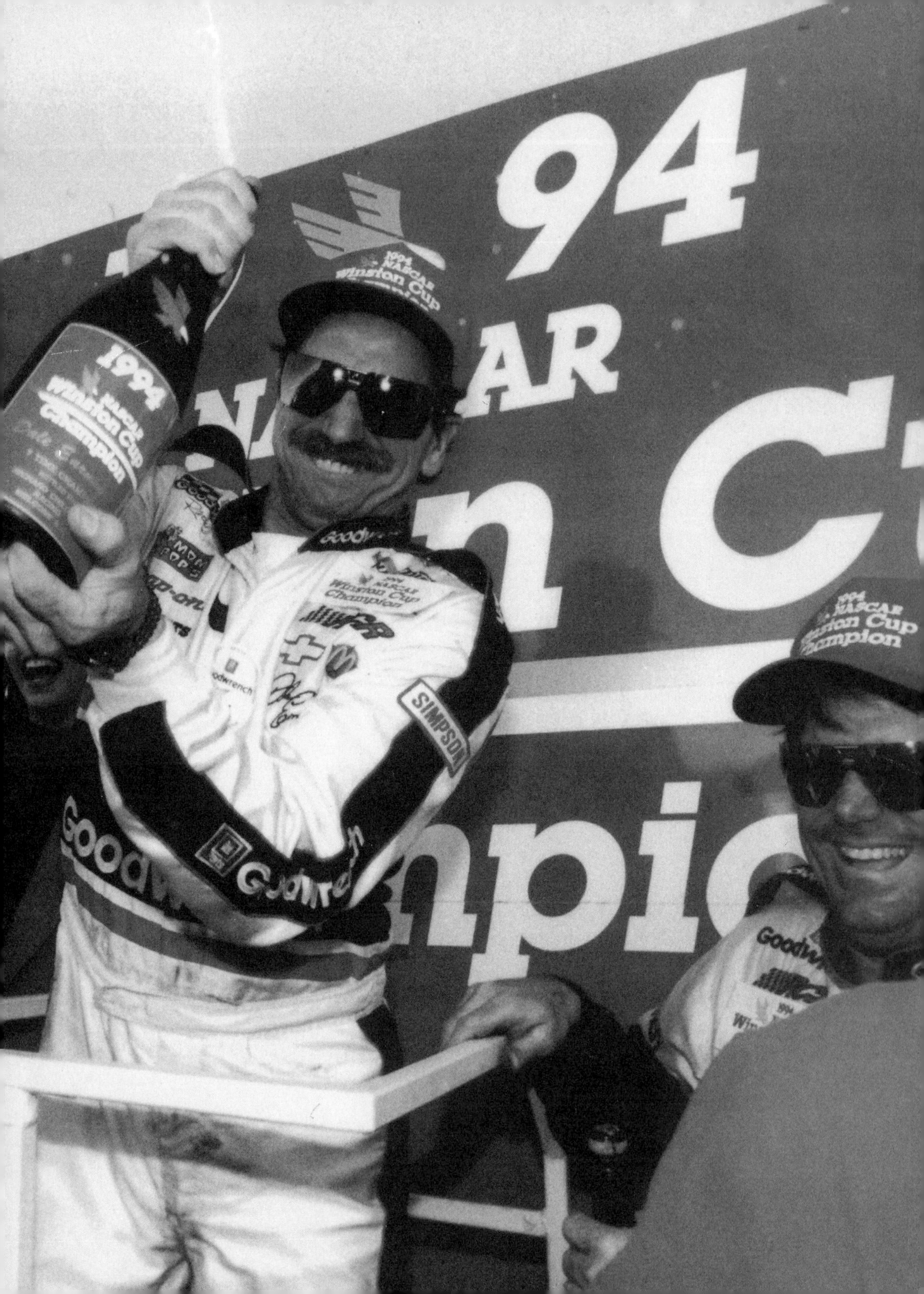

94
1994
Winston Cup
Champion
SIMPSON

Preface

There was no bigger success story in sports during the '90s than the phenomenal growth of the NASCAR Winston Cup Series.

More than 6.3 million fans—38 percent of them women—attended the 33 Winston Cup races scheduled in 1998. That's an average of more than 190,000 per event—despite ticket prices that hover in the $100 range. *The Atlanta Journal-Constitution* reported on November 8, 1998—the final day of the 50th season of Winston Cup racing—that the circuit's attendance had risen 65.5 percent from 1990-96. That's roughly the same *combined* growth the National Football League, National Basketball Association, National Hockey League, and Major League Baseball experienced during the same period.

In an era of declining television ratings for virtually every sport, NASCAR's growth as a TV staple was equally phenomenal. Every Winston Cup race is televised live on ABC, CBS, NBC, ESPN, TBS, or TNN, and new fans continue to join the sport's following. While other sports have seen their share of TV viewers diminish, network ratings for the NASCAR Winston Cup Series rose 21 percent from 1993-98, and cable ratings experienced a 40 percent increase during that period.

In fact, excluding postseason play in other sports, TV ratings for NASCAR Winston Cup races are second only to those of the NFL. And some two million radios per race are tuned to the play-by-play broadcasts of Winston Cup events. Three of the nation's largest radio networks, the Motor Racing Network, Performance Racing Network, and Indianapolis Motor Speedway Network, have some 500 affiliates apiece from coast to coast that make it virtually impossible to be at any spot in the lower 48 states and unable to receive both the telecast and the broadcast of a Winston Cup race.

Souvenir sales are approaching $1 billion per year, and it's possible to do your Christmas shopping in a NASCAR Thunder Store, then have dinner at a NASCAR Cafe.

A natural result of this growth has been a host of fans who are curious about the history of the sport and how the achievements of their heroes compare to those of the stars of yesteryear. Countless fans who now include stock-car racing among their favorite sports have been frustrated by the relative lack of in-depth historical data and records available about the sport, particularly from the years when NASCAR was merely a blip on the sports world's radar screen.

While it's easy enough to learn that Richard Petty and Dale Earnhardt share the record of seven Winston Cup titles, it has been virtually impossible to find something as simple as a list of each season's leading driver in victories.

This book attempts to examine the history, records, and heroes of stock-car racing's premier series as never before.

All records were compiled from data obtained from the actual race reports of the 1,888 *points* races held during the circuit's first 51 years.

Dale Earnhardt celebrated a record-tying seventh Winston Cup championship in 1994.

A Guided Tour
Of Terms
And Definitions

Before we delve into the history and records that follow, *please* read this explanation of terms. Many may appear familiar, but in order to understand, value, and enjoy this reference material, you will need to know precisely *what* these terms mean and *how* their definitions factor in the context of this book.

The Best Way to Rate Drivers: The Performance Index

This book attempts to rank the drivers throughout Winston Cup history—not just in terms of victories, poles, or championships, but in many other categories of on-track performance. It endeavors to provide fans the necessary information to make knowledgeable judgments about the greatest stockcar drivers in history—and those who fall far short of that status.

While this book tries to provide fans more significant information than ever has been available, it also offers a short cut to determine the most successful drivers in history, in any given year, and in how they rank in relation to each other: the Performance Index.

For a generation, Leonard Wood (foreground) and his brother, Glen, headed the fastest pit crew in motorsports. Their lightening-quick pit stops helped 16 drivers capture a total of 96 victories in Wood brothers-owned Fords and Mercurys through 1999.

For those who are seeking a simple method to determine, for example, what Richard Petty's best season was, the Performance Index is the way, the truth, and the light.

No list of the all-time Winston Cup point standings exists, partially because there have been a number of different methods employed over the years to determine those standings.

Anyone who simply wants to compute the all-time point standings based on the current system should nix that idea for one glaring reason: Shorter schedules would place drivers whose principal achievements have come since 1972 at a distinct disadvantage. How, for example, could the 28-race 1985 season be compared to the 62-race 1964 campaign?

How NASCAR Adopted a System That Triggers So Many Complaints

NASCAR's current point system awards 175 points to the race winner, 170 to the second-place car, etc., with a five-point differential through sixth place. The differential becomes four points through 11th place and three points for each place from 12th through 43rd. It also awards a five-point bonus to any driver who leads a lap and an additional five-point bonus to the driver who leads the most laps.

When the current system was introduced in 1975, it marked the fifth time in nine years the system had been changed—a strong indication that NASCAR never had been particularly happy with its point system.

It also marked the first system in which all races were worth an equal number of points and the first time that bonus points were awarded to drivers for leading laps. The system was designed with at least two factors in mind:

- Three drivers had won 27 of the 30 races held in 1974—Richard Petty (10), Cale Yarborough (10), and David Pearson (7). And since Pearson achieved his seven victories despite skipping all 10 short-track races because the purses simply weren't lucrative enough to entice his car owners, the Wood brothers, to compete, it was hoped that perhaps a point system that treated all races equally would.

- While Yarborough was a classic charger who tried to lead every lap, Petty and Pearson were far more conservative drivers who simply endeavored to stay on the lead lap until what they figured to be the final caution flag. So the bonus points for lap leaders were an effort to try to get Petty and Pearson to challenge Yarborough for the lead from the outset instead of waiting for the late stages of a race in an era in which there were seldom more than a couple of cars that finished on the lead lap.

Despite the current system's flaws, it was certainly better than the one it replaced. In the 1974 Southern 500, for example, Darrell Waltrip finished second and received 95 points, while Petty finished 35th and received 160.

So none of the point systems NASCAR has employed is the best way to rank the accomplishments of the more than 2,700 drivers who strapped themselves into Winston Cup cars during the circuit's first 51 years.

And money, which is rarely mentioned in this book, was not an option.

"You used to be able to measure an athlete's accomplishments by the money he made," Petty said in the late '80s. "You can't now because of the inflation rate. What you've got to do is compare apples to apples."

Petty became the first Winston Cup driver to reach $1 million in career earnings when he captured the 1971 Dixie 500 at Atlanta for his 134th career victory.

By comparison, Jeff Gordon earned $9,306,584— in 1998 *alone*.

"What I'd really like to see is no points for qualifying or leading a lap or stuff like that," Petty said a few days before his retirement in 1992. "Just because there are 40 cars starting, all of them getting points is not right. We should do it like Formula One (in which only the top six finishers earn points), but they should modify it, like 20 or 25 positions. Then, at the end of the year, that would really determine who is best. The winner should get more than anybody else—points and money. Where it stands now, I can run second and get as many points as the guy who finishes first. That's not right."

Added Waltrip, a three-time Winston Cup champion: "There's just not too much incentive for winning. We really need some sort of bonus system for guys who win races."

How the Performance Index Is Very Clearly Structured

The Performance Index rewards a driver's accomplishments and takes into consideration an important fact that fans and competitors long have realized and that NASCAR's current point system doesn't: All events are *not* created equal. There is absolutely no logical reason, for example, why a 50-mile race on the one-third-mile Greensboro Fairgrounds dirt track should be worth the same as the Daytona 500. After all, it certainly isn't worth the same in money, media attention, attendance, tradition, or any other factor that enhances a race's stature.

The Performance Index also corrects the disparity of the illogical gaps between sixth and seventh place and between 11th and 12th. There is only one significant gap that matters, or should matter, in terms of purse, prestige, or points: the difference between first and second place. So the Performance Index replaces those gaps with only one gap: a significant difference between the rewards for first and second place. The Performance Index further eliminates giving points to drivers simply for starting a race, an oversight particularly offensive under the current rules, in which seven provisional starting spots are available to cars that aren't fast enough to qualify for the field, effectively reducing the number of potential challengers. That scenario guarantees, among other things, the most recent past champion a spot in every field the next season, which in 2000, is worth a minimum of 1,156 points—even if the champion should unexplainably be 40 mph slower than any other driver who attempts to qualify.

The Performance Index divides races throughout Winston Cup history into six categories: (1) classics, (2) 500-mile races, (3) 400-mile races, (4) other superspeedway or road races, (5) short-track races of 250 miles or more, and

Darrell Waltrip, a three-time Winston Cup champion who won 84 times during the Winston Cup Series' inaugural 51 seasons, is a critic of the point system that has been in place during most of his career. "We really need some sort of bonus system for guys who win races," he said.

(6) other short-track and dirt races. (Most fans are probably familiar with those terms, but their meanings both in context of the Performance Index and elsewhere in this book are explained later in this section).

The Performance Index also has two other significant features:

- It's very simple;
- And it's much easier to compare a season with a rating of 800 or better, a season with a 375 rating, etc., than under the current system, when the top driver may have 4,488 points, the fifth-place driver 3,858, and the 10th-place driver 3,621 (as was the case in 1988) or the system in effect in 1973, when Winston Cup champion Benny Parsons had 7,173.8 points, the fifth-place driver 6,877.95, and the 10th-place finisher 5,743.9.

How the Performance Index Is Calculated

Only the top 20 finishers earn points in the Performance Index, which awards achievement and not merely attendance, and they are distributed on this basis:

- Classics: 50 points to the winner, 43 to the runner-up, 42 to the third-place finisher, 41 for fourth, etc.
- 500-Mile Races: 45 points to the winner, 38 to the runner-up, 37 to the third-place finisher, 36 for fourth, etc.
- 400-Mile Races: 40 points to the winner, 33 to the runner-up, 32 to the third-place finisher, 31 for fourth, etc.
- Other Superspeedway and Road Races: 35 points to the winner, 28 to the runner-up, 27 to the third-place finisher, 26 for fourth, etc.
- Short-Track Races of 250 Miles or More: 30 points to the winner, 23 to the runner-up, 22 to the third-place finisher, 21 for fourth, etc.
- Short-Track Races of Less Than 250 Miles and Dirt Races: 25 points to the winner, 19 to the runner-up, 18 to the third-place finisher, 17 for fourth, etc.

When Hut Stricklin's Quaker State Ford (26) spun during the 1995 NAPA 500 at Atlanta, both Brett Bodine (11) and Bill Elliott (94) successfully dodged the accident. The ability to avoid calamities on the track has proven a key ingredient to numerous major victories throughout Winston Cup history.

The Performance Index awards points to the top 20 finishers in any given race, not just the top 20 who were *eligible* to receive points because they were full-time Winston Cup competitors—as has often been the case. In the case of the many lesser events that attracted fewer than 20 entrants, each finish was worth the same as it would have been with a larger field. Further, the Performance Index does not subtract points for competing in a non-sanctioned event, which cost Lee Petty the 1950 Winston Cup title, or penalize a driver points *if* he is allowed to keep a victory, which well may have cost Mark Martin the 1990 crown. In the rare case of a dead heat, the driver who started closer to the front is credited with the better finish.

Because the Performance Index is being introduced in this book, no driver in history previously has been aware of its existence. But based on the logical assumption that in every race a driver enters, he'd like to finish as high as possible and that far more emphasis has been placed on winning, say, the Southern 500, than a 25-miler at Bowman Gray Stadium, it's reasonable to assume that drivers throughout history have been trying to improve their Performance Index ratings every time they competed. There is, however, one glaring exception: Drivers who led the Winston Cup standings late in the season under the current system—or past methods—often tried to protect their leads in a system that allowed them to earn points, and perhaps ensure their titles, by finishing 28th, 33rd, or wherever.

As stated earlier, by rating every race equally, the 28-race 1985 season obviously wouldn't be worth as much as the 62-event 1964 campaign. The Performance Index, which emphasizes the quality of events as well as the quantity, doesn't completely correct that problem. The highest possible rating that could be attained in any season, which would have required winning every race, was 1,745 in 1969. The lowest possible perfect rating was 210 for the eight-race campaign in 1949. The average

perfect rating for the Winston Cup Series' first 51 years was 1,222, and the average perfect rating for each era indeed has fluctuated somewhat:

- 1951-55: 1,017;
- 1956-60: 1,353;
- 1961-71: 1,608;
- 1972-99: 1,149.

The highest percentage of the available total ever earned by the leading driver in the Performance Index was the 79.77 percent attained by Gordon in 1998, while the lowest percentage was the 45.71 earned by Red Byron in 1949. Both the average and the median for annual leaders in Winston Cup racing's first 51 years was 66.5.

While the differences in Performance Index ratings for each era may seem inequitable on the surface, further examination reveals that certain seasons *should* be worth more than others. In 1973, the second season in the modern era, a driver who won every race could earn a 1,110 rating. Just two years earlier, in 1971, the last season before the modern era began, a driver could achieve a 1,670 rating—third-highest in history—if he managed to win every race. The 1973 schedule featured 28 races: 16 on superspeedways, including one of 600 miles, 13 500-mile events, and two 400-mile races. It also had two road races, one at 500 miles and the other a 400-miler, and 10 short-track races, all at 250 miles or more.

The 48-race 1971 campaign included 21 superspeedway races: one a 600-miler, nine at 500 miles, eight at 400 miles, and three at fewer than 400 miles. It had the same two road races, also included 10 short-track races of 250 miles or more, and an additional 15 short-track events of less than 250 miles, so it was obviously more demanding.

The Shrinking Ranks of Winston Cup Competitors

A total of 1,968 drivers have posted a top-20 finish in Winston Cup racing and are therefore listed in the Performance Index. Modern drivers, for the most part, dominate the career Performance Index for two reasons: amazing longevity when compared to their predecessors and the steadily decreasing number of Winston Cup drivers.

An average of 108 drivers per season earned top-20 finishes and Performance Index ratings during the first 51 years of Winston Cup racing, but the numbers have dramatically decreased, primarily because of the increasing costs of fielding a car and provisional starting spots that reward loyal campaigners and make it tougher for newcomers to enter the sport.

From 1950-61, an average of 190 drivers per season posted top-20 finishes, including a record 256 in 1951. The average was 119 from 1962-72, 82 from 1973-87, and 50 from 1988-99, including just 44, the fewest ever, in 1993. So a key reason that modern drivers dominate the Performance Index is because the available points are being split by significantly fewer drivers.

Applying the Performance Index retroactively, of course, doesn't mean that the Winston Cup champion was necessarily the leader each year. In fact, on 14 occasions, another driver posted a higher Performance Index rating than the Winston Cup champion. For example, Rex White had an 873 rating in 1961, while the champion, Ned Jarrett, had the second-highest rating, 811. White finished ahead of Jarrett in victories (7-1), top-five finishes (29-23), and top-10 finishes (38-34). The Performance Index rating is not meant to suggest, however, that Jarrett didn't deserve the 1961 Winston Cup title—or that any of the other 13 who failed to lead the Performance Index didn't, either. Even subtle changes in any system could result in different champions, and every Winston Cup champion in history *won his title under the point system that was then in use* and well may have employed a different strategy and been just as successful had the Performance Index been the system to determine the champion. And in the 14 seasons in which the Winston Cup champion failed to lead the Performance Index, more often than not he was merely protecting his lead under the existing system, which doesn't reward achievement as much as it does consistency—and even attendance and past accomplishments (provisional starts that guarantee points).

The Championship Hasn't Always Been The No. 1 Goal

A further note: In the history of Winston Cup racing, the emphasis on the championship is a relatively recent development. Winning races, particularly in the order in which they're rewarded in the Performance Index, instead of competing for points was a much greater goal for many years.

Some notable examples:

- In 1963, Fred Lorenzen finished third in the Winston Cup standings despite skipping 26 of 55 races.
- In 1966, Pearson missed six races, yet won the title.
- In 1970, Bobby Allison skipped a race at Richmond, Va., and lost the title to Bobby Isaac by just 51 points.

"The championship wasn't worth that much back then," Richard Petty said. "We didn't try to work on the car and get back in races. If we had, we probably would have won a couple of more championships."

King Richard, in fact, said after clinching the 1971 championship with a victory at Richmond that winning the race meant more than earning what was then a record-tying third Winston Cup title.

Beyond this introduction, only in the Driver Resumes section is the word "points" used in reference to the Performance Index. The word "points" otherwise is utilized only in mentions of the Winston Cup standings actually in effect at the time. The Performance Index is expressed in terms of ratings of 100 or better, 200 or more, etc., and all references to season positions—number of top-10 seasons, etc.—refer to the Performance Index ratings.

As stated earlier, any change in a point system is going to produce alterations in the finishing order. But most of those are subtle. The top seven drivers in the 1998 Winston Cup standings—Gordon, Martin, Dale Jarrett, Rusty Wallace, Jeff Burton, Bobby Labonte, and Jeremy Mayfield—finished in the same order in the Performance Index. Dale Earnhardt and Terry Labonte were eighth and ninth, respectively, in the Winston Cup standings, but swapped those positions in the Performance Index. Bobby Hamilton was 10th in the 1998 Winston Cup standings, but John Andretti finished 10th and Hamilton 11th in the Performance Index. In 1999, the top 10 drivers in the Performance Index finished in the same order as they did in the Winston Cup standings.

While career Performance Index ratings, which are listed in the Miscellaneous Records section, are objective, judging them is subjective. But it's instructive to note that 150 drivers have won Winston Cup races and 146 have earned career Performance Index ratings of 1,000 or better. Ninety-five drivers have won two or more races, and 90 have a career Performance Index of 2,000 or higher. And 14 drivers have 40 or more victories—while 15 have a career Performance Index rating of 9,000 or higher.

And the Performance Index is certainly the most accurate reflection of career "point" totals in existence—the way, the truth, and the light when comparing drivers of different eras.

Many of the 1,888 Winston Cup races held during the circuit's first 51 years were won and lost in the pits. Mark Martin's Valvoline Ford captured two races in 1994. One reason for those victories was that Martin's crew, under the direction of owner Jack Roush and crew chief Steve Hmiel, was able change four tires and fill the gas tank in roughly the same length of time that it takes to read this caption.

Why the Name Winston Cup Is Used for All 51 Years

Although NASCAR's first season was 1948, the first season for what is now the Winston Cup Series was 1949. The circuit was known as the Strictly Stock Division during that eight-race 1949 campaign, and its name was changed to the NASCAR Grand National circuit in 1950. When the R.J. Reynolds Tobacco Company came on board as the circuit's sponsor in 1971, the name was changed to the NASCAR Winston Cup Grand National Series. Grand National was dropped from the title before the 1986 season, and the circuit has been known as the NASCAR Winston Cup Series ever since. In order to provide consistency, rather than confusion, this book refers to stock-car racing's premier series as the Winston Cup Series throughout the book, even before 1971.

References to the Winston Cup Series as simply NASCAR are incorrect because the sanctioning body operates or has operated some 20 different circuits in its history. Ned Jarrett, who won NASCAR's premier title in 1961 and '65, often is referred to as a two-time Winston Cup champion, although his career predated Winston's involvement. It is incorrect, however, to call Jarrett a two-time NASCAR champion. He won two titles in the Late Model Sportsman division (forerunner of what is now the NASCAR Busch Series Grand National Division) and, therefore, is actually a four-time NASCAR titlist and a two-time Winston Cup champion.

Figuring Out the Name Game

NASCAR's race reports, particularly in the early years, contain numerous inconsistencies. For example, the all-time leader in victories sometimes was listed as "Dick" Petty early in his career, but is referred to only as Richard Petty in this book in order to avoid confusion. Bill Stammer might have been listed under his correct spelling one week, under the name Billy Stamner the next, and as Bill Stamer the following race. By also utilizing the car number, car owner, and manufacturer, however, it's logical to conclude that all were one and the same Bill Stammer. While Paul Dean Holt also raced under the name Paul Dean, Holt and the many drivers

Who has been more successful, Dale Earnhardt (3) or Darrell Waltrip (17)? While Earnhardt led in Winston Cup titles (7–3) during the circuit's first 51 years, Waltrip held the edge in victories (84–74). The Performance Index—and countless other "hidden" records—will offer fans of both drivers opportunities to argue their favorite's case.

who competed under more than one name at various points in their careers are referred to only by the name they used the most. While every effort has been made to verify the correct names of drivers, in the case of many whose careers were early and brief, it is virtually impossible to state with complete certainty that their names are spelled correctly. Finally, many drivers have the designation "II" after their names simply because more than one of the more than 2,700 drivers who have competed in Winston Cup racing had the same name. Jack Smith, one of the most successful drivers in history, is not the same person—nor necessarily related to—Jack Smith II.

Why 1972 Marks the Start Of the Modern Era

Winston's sponsorship involvement began in 1971, but it didn't sponsor every race that season. The "modern era," as is recognized by NASCAR and other historians, began in 1972, when Winston's sponsorship encompassed every race and the schedule was reduced dramatically, from 48 races in 1971 to 31 in 1972.

Counting Victories Isn't As Easy as You'd Think

As noted earlier, only the 1,888 Winston Cup races in which drivers received championship points were used in the totals in this book. Such races as The Winston and the Busch Clash are exhibitions rather than championship events and are therefore not included, just as NASCAR does not include those events in career victory totals. Qualifying races are included for the 1961 World 600 at Charlotte and for the Daytona 500 from 1959-71, with the exception of 1968, when they were canceled because of inclement weather. Those races

were points races and are included in NASCAR's victory totals. But no qualifying races from 1972-99 are included because NASCAR did not award championship points in those events.

In several instances, the victory totals listed in this book differ from those in the *NASCAR Winston Cup Series Media Guide.* Two races were held at Lakewood Speedway in Atlanta after the conclusion of the 1949 season, one on October 23 and the other on November 20. Those races were won by Tim Flock and June Cleveland, respectively, who are credited by the *NASCAR Winston Cup Series Media Guide* with 40 victories and one triumph, respectively. This book credits Flock with 39 victories and Cleveland with none. Those races weren't even sanctioned by NASCAR, but, as *The Atlanta Journal* clearly states in its coverage of those events, by the National Stock Car Racing Association—a *competing* organization.

Two exhibition races were held in 1950, the first on September 30 at Buffalo's Civic Stadium and the second on November 5 in Newark, N.J. Neither of these races, won by Bobby Courtwright and Lee Petty, respectively, awarded championship points or are included in this book. While NASCAR lists Courtwright with one victory, this book credits him with zero. Lee Petty is credited with 54 victories in this book, the same number listed in every *NASCAR Winston Cup Series Media Guide* through 1997. The 1998 *NASCAR Winston Cup Series Media Guide* increased Lee Petty's total, incorrectly this book contends, to 55 victories.

This book also differs with the *NASCAR Winston Cup Series Media Guide* concerning the victory totals of Bobby Allison and Tiny Lund, whom NASCAR lists with 84 and three triumphs, respectively. Six races were held during the 1971 season in which both Winston Cup cars and machines from the defunct Grand American series competed. Lund won two of those races, the Buddy Shuman 276 at Hickory, N.C., on August 28 and the Wilkes 400 at North Wilkesboro, N.C., on November 22, in a Chevrolet Camaro. Allison won the August 6 race in Winston-Salem, N.C., in a Ford Mustang and "has the trophy to prove it."

Side-by-side, bumper-to-bumper action is a key reason that attendance at Winston Cup races grew 65.5 percent from 1990-96.

NASCAR recognizes the victories earned by Richard Petty in a Winston Cup Plymouth in two of those six races, the West Virginia 500 on August 8 at International Raceway Park and the Sandlapper 200 on August 27 at Columbia, S.C., and Allison's triumph in a Winston Cup Ford in the Georgia 500 on November 7 at Macon.

But it lists neither of Lund's victories nor Allison's at Winston-Salem, although it allowed their cars to enter. Incredibly, NASCAR also does not credit the runners-up in Allison's victory (Petty) or in Lund's Buddy Shuman 276 win (Elmo Langley) or Wilkes 400 triumph (Charlie Glotzbach) with victories. NASCAR merely recognizes the results of the three races in which Winston Cup cars won and ignores the others, a gross inconsistency that this book corrects by recognizing Allison with 85 victories and Lund with five.

Determining Poles Is Even Trickier

While there have been 1,888 races, this book credits only 1,827 pole winners—one for each qualifying session in which the fastest driver was awarded the No. 1 starting spot—with one exception.

Once again, there are differences in some of the totals recognized in this book and in the *NASCAR Winston Cup Series Media Guide*. Richard Petty is credited in the latter with a record 126 poles, while this book lists him with 123. And when Pepsi issued a series of bottles honoring the King's achievements during his 1992 farewell tour, Petty was recognized on those bottles as having won 127 poles.

That disputed pole was probably for the 1970 Virginia 500 at Martinsville. Petty captured the No. 1 starting spot in April, but the race was postponed until May 31 because of rain. In the interim, Petty was injured, withdrew the car, skipped the event, and was stripped of the pole by NASCAR.

The other three are poles that were awarded for Daytona qualifying races from 1960-71—with the exception of 1968, when both qualifying races were canceled because of rain. During all of those years, one qualifying session was held to determine the pole winner for the Daytona 500. That pole winner also started on the inside of the front row for the first qualifying race—thus capturing two poles in one try. Further, the *second-fastest*

qualifier in each of those sessions was awarded the pole for the second qualifying race. This book eliminates the inconsistencies of awarding two poles for a single qualifying run or awarding the second-fastest qualifier in pole-position qualifying with a pole. It rewards the fastest qualifier in those sessions with winning the pole only for the Daytona 500 and thus strips Petty of three poles. For that same reason, this book also recognizes three fewer poles for Fireball Roberts; two each for Bobby Isaac, Buddy Baker, and Darel Dieringer, and one apiece for Cotton Owens, Jack Smith, Fred Lorenzen, Dick Hutcherson, Joe Weatherly, Curtis Turner, Paul Goldsmith, Cale Yarborough, Junior Johnson, and A.J. Foyt.

A somewhat similar situation existed at Charlotte Motor Speedway in 1961, when two qualifying races were held for the World 600. Only one qualifying session was staged to determine the starting lineups for both of those races, with Johnson and Lorenzen getting the inside front-row spots. But Richard Petty was awarded the pole for the World 600 based on his victory in the first 100-mile qualifying race, so only Petty's World 600 pole is recognized from that qualifying session—the aforementioned exception to this book's determination of poles.

Further differences between this book and the *NASCAR Winston Cup Series Media Guide* include the total poles listed for Herb Thomas, Fonty Flock, and Courtwright. Both this book and the *1998 NASCAR Winston Cup Series Media Guide* credit Thomas for 39 poles—one more than he had been listed with winning in 1997 and earlier by the *NASCAR Winston Cup Series Media Guide*. Flock is credited in this book with 33 poles and 34 in the *1998 NASCAR Winston Cup Series Media Guide*—four more than he was listed for winning in 1997 and earlier. While this book does not credit Courtwright with a pole, the *1998 NASCAR Winston Cup Series Media Guide* does credit him with a pole, the first time it ever had listed one for Courtwright, whose career ended in 1954.

Fonty Flock won the pole for the November 20, 1949, NSCRA race held at Atlanta's Lakewood Speedway, while the qualifying session for the October 23, 1949, event at Lakewood was rained out. Thomas captured the pole for the 1950 exhibition race at Buffalo and Courtwright for the 1950 exhibition at Newark, helping account for the discrepancies. But none of those was a championship points race, so those poles are not included in this book.

Pole winners had never been listed in the *NASCAR Winston Cup Series Media Guide* before 1988. Listed with one pole apiece were Bill Benson, Bill Jarrick, Paul Parks, Don Porter, Lyle Tadlock, and Joie Ray. A year later, the only driver credited with a pole from that group was Ray, who became the first African-American driver to compete in a Winston Cup event when he started 25th in his only race, on February 10, 1952, at Daytona's Beach & Road Course.

In the 1990 edition, however, Benson, Jarrick, Parks, Porter, and Tadlock all returned to the list of pole winners. But in 1998, the names of Jarrick, Parks, and Ray once again disappeared, although Courtwright was listed for the first time.

According to NASCAR's race reports, none of these drivers ever won a pole and are not credited for having done so in this book.

Understanding The Importance of Track Classifications

NASCAR long has had two distinct classifications of tracks: superspeedways and short tracks. A superspeedway has been defined as any track that measures one mile or longer and a short track any racing surface that is less than a mile in length.

In order to offer a more accurate presentation of special achievements, such as Winston Cup racing's premier road racers or dirt drivers, this book divides tracks into four classifications:

Superspeedways: Superspeedways not only must be a mile or more in length, but they must be *paved*, usually with asphalt or concrete, and must be *an enclosed course* with turns in only one direction—left in the case of every American track. They can be true ovals, like Dover Downs International Speedway in Delaware. They can be tri-ovals, featuring a dogleg on the frontstretch, like Daytona International Speedway in Florida. They can be quad-ovals, with two doglegs in the frontstretch, like Lowe's Motor Speedway in North Carolina. They can be egg-shaped, like Darlington Raceway in South Carolina. They can be virtually square, like Indianapolis Motor Speedway. They can be triangular, like Pocono Raceway in Pennsylvania. But they must have no more than four distinct turns and be an enclosed course.

Short Tracks: These are *paved* tracks that are enclosed, share the same characteristics as superspeedways, but are less than one mile in length.

Dirt Tracks: Depending on the size, dirt tracks either share the characteristics of a superspeedway or a short track, but they are *not* paved. Most dirt tracks were small. But Pennsylvania's Langhorne Speedway was a one-mile circle, and the 1.5-mile Memphis-Arkansas Speedway in LeHi, Ark., was NASCAR's largest closed course when it opened in 1954. But, like the shorter dirt tracks, these are classified as dirt tracks, not superspeedways, because the skills it took to negotiate them had more in common with the shorter dirt tracks that dominated the '50s than the superspeedways that ruled the '90s.

Road Courses: It always has seemed incomprehensible that NASCAR has grouped road courses with the big, oval-type tracks that constitute its superspeedways. Superspeedways and short tracks feature no more than four distinct turns, with additional subtle twists in the case of doglegs, and are somewhat uniform in shape. Road courses, however, usually include 10 or more turns and, unlike superspeedways or short tracks, require both left and right turns. They frequently feature dramatic elevation changes and sharp contrasts in speeds, with hairpin turns that, for example, may force a driver to make a U-turn into a long straightaway, a gradual left turn into a shorter straightaway, and then a very sharp right turn. An aerial view of a road course might resemble a couple of strands of spaghetti thrown against a refrigerator more than a similar view of a superspeedway or short track, which wouldn't look significantly different than a football stadium.

No one in Winston Cup history has had so many reasons to sip champagne at such a young age as Jeff Gordon, who earned his first championship in 1995.

Of the 169 tracks that have played host to Winston Cup races, only one didn't easily fit into one of the four classifications—Daytona's Beach & Road Course. Although it measured more than four miles, it wasn't a superspeedway because just one straightaway was paved, while the other straightaway and both turns were sand. And it certainly wasn't enclosed, since many a spinning car had to be fished out of the Atlantic Ocean on the backstretch. And, at more than four miles in length, it was by no means a short track. For the purposes of this book, the Beach & Road Course is classified as a road course, which is sure to be controversial, but more correct than any of the other three definitions.

All Events Are Not Created Equal

Any races referred to as superspeedway, short track, road course, or dirt events in this book fit the classifications listed above. But there are several other terms used in this book to help define the careers and achievements of the drivers that require explanation:

Grand Slam: While such promotions as the Winston Million and the Winston No Bull 5 have obscured the Grand Slam, the latter achievement was among the primary goals for most top drivers for many years. The four Grand Slam tracks are Darlington Raceway, Daytona International Speedway, Lowe's Motor Speedway, and Atlanta Motor Speedway—the four superspeedways that have been on the Winston Cup schedule longer than any other. Winning races on all four Grand Slam tracks in a career—or better yet, in a single season—long was considered one of stock-car racing's premier achievements. And it's an accomplishment worth recognition.

Classic: While this term is often thrown around loosely in such sports as golf or tennis when promoters are seeking a classy name for their event, for the purposes of this book the term is being lifted from horse racing, which recognizes three American races as classics—the Kentucky Derby, Preakness, and Belmont Stakes.

Golf long has had four recognized major championships—the U.S. Open, British Open, Professional Golfers' Association Championship, and the Masters. Tennis has its four Grand Slam events—the U.S. Open, French Open, Australian Open, and Wimbledon.

And, let's face it, just like golf tournaments, tennis tournaments, or horse races, all stock-car races are *not* created equal. Whether through tradition, larger purses, media attention, demand for tickets, or television ratings, certain events have come to define a driver's career more than others. For example, Derrike Cope has two Winston Cup victories to his credit, both in 1990. Yet he's probably referred to as a former winner of the Daytona 500 at least 1,000 times for every time he's introduced as a former Budweiser 500 victor.

For many years, three events were known as the Triple Crown of stock-car racing: the Southern 500 at Darlington, the World 600, and the Daytona 500. When the Winston Million began in 1985, it combined those three prestigious events with the Winston 500 at Talladega, Ala. The events were billed as the oldest (Southern 500), longest (World 600), richest (Daytona 500), and fastest (Winston 500). With all apologies to R.J. Reynolds—the best sponsor in the history of sports—the Winston 500 was:

- No faster than the Talladega (now Diehard) 500 at the same track;
- Frequently one of the most exciting races of the year and certainly a feather in any winner's cap, but historically lacking the same prestige as the other three events;
- Chosen—and understandably so—because it shared the same sponsor as the Winston Million.

For the purposes of this book, four races are recognized as classics:

- The (now Pepsi) Southern 500: The first edition in 1950 was the first superspeedway event in Winston Cup history, and until 1958 the Labor Day weekend classic was the circuit's only 500-mile race.
- The World (now Coca-Cola) 600: Since its inception in 1960, the race has been the longest annual event on the Winston Cup circuit with the exception of 1969, when it shared that billing with the Yankee 600 at Brooklyn, Mich. For roughly 35 years,

it also was the second-richest event on the circuit. Three other factors have helped keep the race among the elite: its Memorial Day weekend date; that the second quarter-century of Winston Cup racing saw Charlotte become the hub of stock-car racing with virtually every team based in that area, and Lowe's Motor Speedway's massive expansion and improvement project that made it the first luxury palace in motorsports.

- Daytona 500: Since before the green flag fell to start the inaugural running in 1959—or the checkered flag was unfurled on a photo finish that took 61 hours to determine the winner—the centerpiece of SpeedWeeks at the "Birthplace of Speed" has been the most prestigious and, generally, richest event in stock-car racing.
- Brickyard 400: While the event, which began in 1994, certainly lacks the rich tradition of the other classics, its venue, the Indianapolis Motor Speedway, is the oldest superspeedway in the world and has by far the largest seating capacity. The Brickyard 400 has featured the largest or second-largest purse in Winston Cup racing in each year of its existence and annually attracts the largest crowd in stock-car racing. When tickets went on sale for the inaugural edition, the more than one million orders received on the first day made the most anticipated race in Winston Cup history an instant classic.

Distances: The distances of races listed in this book are the distances for which each race was scheduled, not necessarily the distance that actually was completed. Hundreds of races have been shortened because of inclement weather or darkness. A significant portion were reduced because of scoring mishaps, and a number were extended by a lap or two for the same reason.

All race distances are rounded off to the nearest mile with the exception of 400- and 500-mile races that may have been contested at say, 401 or 499 miles, because of track configurations. For example, when NASCAR instituted a uniform method of measuring tracks, Atlanta International Raceway was measured at 1.522 miles instead of 1.5. Its 328-lap races from 1970 until the track was reconfigured to 1.54 miles for the 1997 NAPA 500 were actually 499.216 miles. Running 329 laps would have made the races 500.738 miles long. So races at the track now known as Atlanta Motor Speedway are listed at 500 miles.

This book recognizes victories in 500-mile races as one of auto racing's landmark achievements. Included in those totals are two road races that are too close to that magical figure to ignore: Roberts's victory in a 510-mile race at Augusta (Ga.) International Speedway in 1964 and Foyt's triumph in the 506-mile Motor Trend 500 at Riverside, Calif., in 1970.

Although the names of the races didn't change—the season's first superspeedway race was still the Daytona 500—the distances for the second through the 15th races of the 1974 season did. Because of an energy crisis that often involved a two-hour wait to fill the gas tank in the family car, NASCAR responded by reducing the length of the aforementioned 14 races by 10 percent. Since the Daytona 500, for example, was scheduled for 450 miles, not 500, that race and the others during that period are recognized at the scheduled, rather than the traditional, distances, and are not included in the 500-mile totals.

Streaks: Among the countless records and singular achievements this book offers are numerous examples of streaks, both in terms of seasons and races. When a driver is credited with say, four consecutive superspeedway victories, that means he won four races in succession that were contested on superspeedways. His four consecutive victories on superspeedways may have come in a span of 10 races, for example—if the other six events were held on other types of tracks. And even if a driver won, for example, four consecutive superspeedway races in a span of eight races on big tracks—but skipped the other four—he is not credited with a four-race winning streak on superspeedways. The same is true with poles, with one exception: A driver may be credited with, say, four consecutive poles in a five-race span if inclement weather forced the cancellation of qualifying.

Your Chapter-By-Chapter Owner's Manual

This book contains hundreds—perhaps thousands—of records, many of which previously had not been unearthed. Many of the more obvious records are listed in the Miscellaneous Records section, while many others can be found in the book's 51 chapters. For example, if you want to know who captured the most short-track races from the pole (Richard Petty with 36), a complete listing appears in that section. A less obvious record, such as the only driver to win six races on dirt four years in a row, would be found only in the 1954 chapter on Thomas. And other chapters are devoted to the records of manufacturers, car owners, the oldest and youngest drivers to accomplish certain feats, etc.

Each chapter also includes that season's most memorable race, most significant wreck, most important off-track development, and records & milestones for that season that are not listed elsewhere in the book. The most memorable race and most important off-track developments are, of course, matters of opinion. So are the most significant wrecks, many of which were fatal. In certain cases, however, an accident that did more to change the course of history was chosen instead of a fatal wreck, not to diminish the importance of human life, but simply because of that particular crash's role in the history of the sport. Each season's complete Performance Index is also listed in each chapter, as are the complete list of race winners, pole winners, and manufacturers' victories and poles. Also listed are that season's race-by-race results. For example, here is the first race of the 1998 season:

Daytona 500; Daytona International Speedway/2.5-mile/500 miles
Dale Earnhardt (Chevrolet)/Bobby Labonte (Pontiac)

For each event, the name of the race is listed first—if it has a name. In the early years, many didn't. The name of the track *at that point in history* is listed next, followed by the measurement of the track at that point in history, and the scheduled distance of the race. The next line has the race winner listed first, with the brand of car he drove in parenthesis followed by a slash and the pole winner's name and the make of car he drove. When only one name was listed, there was no qualifying session. A complete list of every track to stage a Winston Cup race, along with its history of name changes, distance changes, location, and other pertinent information, appears in the Miscellaneous Records section.

Resumes for Drivers With the Proper Credentials

Of the more than 2,700 drivers who have competed in Winston Cup racing, 415 have met the minimum achievements to be listed in the Driver Resumes section, which begins on page 293. To be listed, a driver must accomplish one of the following:

- Win a race;
- Win a pole;
- Post a Performance Index rating of 100 or better in a season;
- Finish in the top 25 in the Performance Index in a season.

And only those seasons in which a driver managed one of those accomplishments are listed.

Let's look at Eddie Pagan's resume and how to read it:

EDDIE PAGAN

1956   (109)

Victories
* Bay Meadows Speedway (1-mile dirt; 250 miles) (Ford)

Poles
California State Fairgrounds (1-mile dirt) (Ford)
* Bay Meadows Speedway (1-mile dirt) (Ford)

1957 (13th) (284)

Victories
Portland Speedway (.5-mile; 75 miles) (Ford)
* Los Angeles Fairgrounds (.5-mile dirt; 100 miles) (Ford)
Portland Speedway (.5-mile; 100 miles) (Ford)

Poles
* Los Angeles Fairgrounds (.5-mile dirt) (Ford)
Old Dominion 500; Martinsville Speedway (.5-mile) (Ford)

1958 (8th) (357)

Poles
Old Dominion Speedway (.375-mile) (Ford)
Southern 500; Darlington Raceway (1.375-mile) (Ford)

Although he failed to finish among the top 25 in the Performance Index in 1956, Pagan earned a 109 rating. He also captured a 250-mile race at Bay Meadows Speedway, a one-mile dirt track, in a Ford. He won that race from the pole, as the asterisk indicates, and also won the pole on another one-mile dirt track, the California State Fairgrounds.

A year later, Pagan's 284 rating ranked 13th in the Performance Index, and he captured three races and two poles. Included in those victories was a 100-mile race at the Los Angeles Fairgrounds, a half-mile dirt track, that he won from the pole.

Although Pagan failed to win a race in 1958, he did earn two poles and finished eighth in the Performance Index with a 357 rating.

Pagan made his first Winston Cup start in 1954 and his last in 1963, but only his 1956, 1957, and 1958 campaigns merited sufficient achievements for inclusion in his resume.

Where does Pagan rank among the all-time greats? Or does he belong in their company? That's for the reader to decide. This book will help you make a more informed decision than ever has been possible before.

Winston Cup Racing From 1949–99

At a Glance

Races:	1,888
Dirt:	490
Road:	97
Short-Track:	575
Superspeedway:	726
500-Mile :	470
Grand Slam:	359
Classic:	137

Poles:	1,827
Dirt:	470
Road:	96
Short-Track:	569
Superspeedway:	692
Grand Slam:	331
Classic:	137

Won From Pole:	445
Dirt:	136
Road:	29
Short-Track:	160
Superspeedway:	120
500-Mile:	82
Grand Slam:	54
Classic:	25

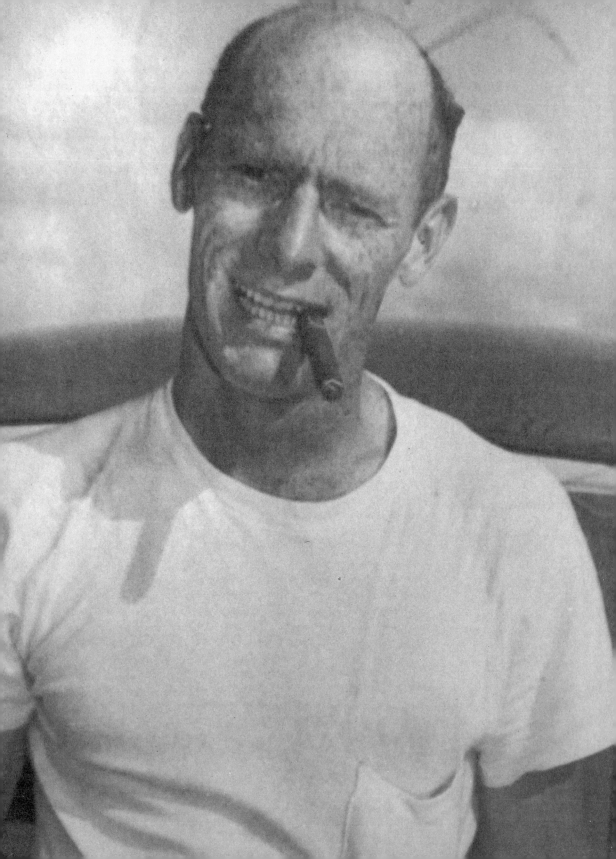

1949
Roots

Perhaps the most significant blight that afflicted auto racing during the sport's infancy was unscrupulous promoters.

The sport's pioneer days, before the inaugural Winston Cup campaign in 1949, featured drivers who had honed their considerable skills by transporting trunkloads of illegal liquor from such outposts in the Appalachian foothills as Dawsonville, Ga., or North Wilkesboro, N.C., and the mechanics who finely tuned those machines to outrun the automobiles the authorities were driving.

Those trailblazing drivers and mechanics often were lured to makeshift dirt bullrings, little more than cow pastures, with the promise of lining their pockets for entertaining the fans on a Sunday afternoon. Long before many a checkered flag was waved, however, the promoter who had lured competitors to the race had pocketed the receipts and fled.

Bill France had been promoting races on the Beach & Road Course in Daytona Beach, Fla., for more than a decade when he invited some 30 of the sport's most influential movers and shakers to meet in the Ebony Bar in Daytona's Streamline Hotel shortly before Christmas in 1947. The meetings, which lasted for four days, resulted in the formation of the National Association for Stock Car Auto Racing.

Mechanic Red Vogt, whom legendary wrench turner Smokey Yunick calls "the godfather of everybody in this garage," is credited with coining the name, which adapted easily to the acronym "NASCAR."

Victories at the Beach & Road Course in Daytona Beach, Fla., and on the half-mile dirt track at Martinsville, Va., helped Red Byron earn the Winston Cup title in 1949, the series' inaugural season.

The organization's primary purposes were to establish:

- A sanctioning body that would guarantee purses, therefore eliminating the dishonest promoters;
- A uniform set of rules;
- A schedule that would produce recognized national champions in each of its divisions.

Red Byron, driving a 1939 Ford owned by Raymond Parks of Atlanta, captured the first event, a modified race held on February 15, 1948, on the Beach & Road Course. Cars had been racing on the sands of Daytona since 1902, and the legendary Sir Malcolm Campbell was credited with a 276 mph run in the famed Bluebird on the beach in 1935. The Beach & Road Course, on which competitors drove north on the beach beside the Atlantic Ocean, made a sharp left turn, then traveled south on a 22-foot-wide strip of Highway A1A—then the principal route for snowbirds bound for Miami—wasn't employed until 1936.

NASCAR was incorporated six days after Byron's victory. France, a high school dropout and part-time race driver who was born in the nation's capital on September 26, 1909, and had been operating a service station since moving to Daytona Beach in 1934 in addition to promoting races on the shores of the Atlantic, was installed as the organization's president.

When France had said in 1947 that he believed stock-car racing could become "a nationally recognized sport," few others shared his vision. While today it is not unusual to see crowds in excess of 100,000 on hand to watch NASCAR Winston Cup racing—not to mention the accompanying soaring TV ratings and booming souvenir sales—it is instructive to recall just how far the sport has come: A newsreel from an early race on the Beach & Road Course refers to "hundreds" of fans converging on Daytona Beach for SpeedWeeks.

Perhaps the most significant brainstorm France had in launching NASCAR into the mainstream of America's sporting culture came in 1949: the formation of the Strictly Stock division. Although the idea seemed revolutionary at the time, racing the same type of family sedans that fans could purchase in their local showrooms evolved into the most prestigious and popular form of motorsports in the world, the NASCAR Winston Cup Series.

France ran the sport as a benevolent dictator until turning over the reins to his namesake early in 1972, 20 years before he and his wife, Anne, who was the long-time secretary and treasurer of the France-owned International Speedway Corporation, passed away within six months of each other.

Although NASCAR's founder and longtime czar was a dictator, as the sport's stature today indicates, that wasn't necessarily a negative.

"Everything he did, he did right," said Richard Childress, the car owner for six of Dale Earnhardt's seven Winston Cup championships. "And he took care of everybody. He didn't just look out for himself."

1949 in Review

Byron garnered the first Winston Cup title, driving an Oldsmobile owned by Parks and tuned by Vogt, whose Atlanta garage long had been Georgia's principal destination for both moonshine runners and government officials who wanted their cars to run faster. Byron and Bob Flock each won a season-high two races, making the '49 campaign one of only two that produced just two multiple winners. Flock was the only two-time pole winner, marking the only time in history that only one driver captured multiple No. 1 starting spots. Byron barely edged Lee Petty and Bill Blair for the Performance Index leadership, garnering a rating of 96, three higher than Petty and four more than Blair. Byron's Performance Index was the lowest for a leader in history, which is to be expected for the eight-race season, by far the shortest in history. But Byron earned only 45.71 percent of the available Performance Index, also the lowest such mark by the leader in history. He had two third-place finishes in addition to his two victories, but in none of the other four races did he finish higher than 13th.

Most Memorable Race

In the first event for France's brainchild, the Strictly Stock division, held on June 19 at the three-quarter-mile Charlotte Speedway, 33 drivers fired their engines, all with designs on winning the then-outrageous sum of $2,000 of the $5,000 purse France had posted. Glenn Dunnaway of Gastonia, N.C., roared through the haze of dust to take checkered flag after 150 miles. When Dunnaway's 1947 Ford was inspected after the race, however, it was found that pieces of steel had been welded illegally from the springs to the chassis, a common practice among bootleggers. Jim Roper of Halstead, Kan., who had crossed the finish line second in a Lincoln, was awarded the victory.

Most Significant Wreck

The only crash in that June 19 race was the season's biggest because history subsequently proved it to be anything but the norm. Petty, the first three-time Winston Cup champion and patriarch of stock-car racing's first family, was the only driver to crash during Winston Cup racing's first event.

Most Important Off-Track Development

Dunnaway's car owner, Hubert Westmoreland, sued NASCAR. When the presiding judge threw the case out of court, the decision empowered France to make and enforce NASCAR's rules.

Records & Milestones

Byron's July 10 victory at the Beach & Road Course was the first for Oldsmobile. . . . Petty's victory at Heidelberg Speedway in Pittsburgh on October 2 was the first for Plymouth. . . . The 1949 season was the only one in history without a superspeedway race and one of only three without a short-track event. . . . The Winston Cup Series visited the fewest tracks (8) and states (5) of any season in its history.

1949 at a Glance

Races:	8
Dirt:	7
Road	1
Winners:	6
Pole Winners:	7
Tracks:	8
States:	5

1949 Performance Index Rankings

1. Red Byron (96)
2. Lee Petty (93)
3. Bill Blair (92)
4. Fonty Flock (77)
5. Bob Flock (76)
6. Curtis Turner (62)
7. Tim Flock (60)
8. Sara Christian (59)
9. Ray Erickson (57)
10. Bill Snowden (54)
11. Glenn Dunnaway (47)
12. Slick Smith (46)
13. Frank Mundy (44)
14. Gober Sosebee (43)
15. Bill Rexford (41)
16. Clyde Minter; Sam Rice; Herb Thomas (34)
19. Jimmy Thompson (32)
20. Jim Roper (31)
21. Jack Russell (27)
22. Joe Littlejohn; Archie Smith; Jack White (26)
25. Bob Apperson; Frank Christian (24)
27. Ken Wagner (21)
28. Jack Etheridge; Dick Linder; Otis Martin (20)
31. Ethel Mobley (19)
32. Ted Chamberlain; Billy Rafter (18)
34. Mike Eagan (17)
35. Marshall Teague (16)
36. Billy Carden; Roy Hall; Lloyd Moore; Frankie Schneider; Louise Smith (15)
41. Bobby Greene; Sterling Long; John Wright (14)
44. Howard Elder; Al Keller; Raymond Lewis; Charles Muscatel; Al Wagoner (13)
49. Al Bonnell; George Lewis (12)
51. Buddy Helms; Ellis Pearce; Don Rogala; Lou Volk; Woodie Wilson (11)
56. Buck Baker; Bill Bennett; Clarence Burris (10)
59. J.D. Edwards; Joe Merola; Budd Olsen; Sam Rider (9)
63. Frank Matthews; Jack Smith; Dick Zimmerman (8)
66. Bob Cameron; Nick Garin; Frank Smith; H.F. Stickleather (7)
70. John Barker; Erwin Blatt (6)
72. Bill Harrison; Jimmie Lewallen; Chuck Mahoney (5)
75. Don Cecchini; Jack O'Brien; B.E. Renfro (4)
78. Jim Carrusso; Bill Greever; Skimp Hersey; Lee Schmidt; Garland Smith (3)
83. Curt Foss; Bob Smith (2)
85. Ken Marriott (1)

1949 Events

Charlotte Speedway/.75-mile dirt/150 miles
Jim Roper (Lincoln)/Bob Flock (Hudson)

Beach & Road Course/4.15-mile road/166 miles
Red Byron (Oldsmobile)/Gober Sosebee (Oldsmobile)

Occoneechee Speedway/1-mile dirt/200 miles
Bob Flock (Oldsmobile)/Bob Flock (Oldsmobile)

Langhorne Speedway/1-mile dirt/200 miles
Curtis Turner (Oldsmobile)/Red Byron (Oldsmobile)

Hamburg Fairgrounds/.5-mile dirt/100 miles
Jack White (Lincoln)/Glenn Dunnaway (Oldsmobile)

Martinsville Speedway/.5-mile dirt/100 miles
Red Byron (Oldsmobile)/Curtis Turner (Oldsmobile)

Heidelberg Speedway/.5-mile dirt/100 miles
Lee Petty (Plymouth)/Al Bonnell (Oldsmobile)

Wilkes 200; North Wilkesboro Speedway/.5-mile dirt/100 miles
Bob Flock (Oldsmobile)/Ken Wagner (Lincoln)

Victories

1. Red Byron; Bob Flock (2)
3. Lee Petty; Jim Roper; Curtis Turner; Jack White (1)

Poles

1. Bob Flock (2)
2. Al Bonnell; Red Byron; Glenn Dunnaway; Gober Sosebee; Curtis Turner; Ken Wagner (1)

Victories

1. Oldsmobile (5)
2. Lincoln (2)
3. Plymouth (1)

Poles

1. Oldsmobile (6)
2. Hudson; Lincoln (1)

1950
First Glimpse
Of the Future

Thanks to a ruling that stripped Lee Petty of 809 points, Bill Rexford captured the 1950 NASCAR Winston Cup championship.

Most Memorable Race

No event in NASCAR history ever gave a clearer picture of the future of Winston Cup racing than the inaugural Southern 500 on September 4, 1950.

When Harold Brasington built Darlington Raceway in the backwoods of South Carolina, the only other superspeedway in the world was the Indianapolis Motor Speedway, which was more than four decades away from welcoming stock cars to its hallowed grounds.

Darlington originally was measured at 1.25 miles, more than twice the size of any other paved facility the Winston Cup drivers had challenged. Further, the track was hardly a model of modern engineering. Its egg-shaped configuration made the first and second turns different from the third and fourth. Add to that oddity a very narrow racing groove in which it was an adventure for the leader to work his way past lap traffic, and the track quickly earned the reputation as "Too Tough to Tame."

Curtis Turner averaged 82.034 mph in a 10-mile qualifying run to win the pole, and the race itself was hardly an artistic success.

Johnny Mantz, the slowest qualifier in the 75-car field, used truck tires to stay on the track while others, such as Tim Flock—who claimed he blew 22 tires—spent most of the day in the pits. Six hours, 38 minutes, and 40 seconds after he took the green flag in a Plymouth owned by a consortium that included NASCAR President Bill France and Turner, Mantz crossed the finish line nine laps ahead of Fireball Roberts, his nearest competitor, for the only victory of his career.

Crowd estimates ranged between 18,000 and 35,000, pitiful by today's standards. When compared to the estimated 5,000 that had witnessed the previous race held in Hamburg, N.Y., however, the Darlington crowd planted the seed for other superspeedways to come. Although Darlington stood alone among superspeedways until the defunct Raleigh Speedway joined the circuit in 1953, NASCAR's original superspeedway set the stage for a series that in 1999 conducted 26 of its 34 races on superspeedways.

1950 in Review

Although he won only one race, Bill Rexford became the youngest champion in Winston Cup history—23 years, seven months, and 15 days old—when he captured the 1950 title. Turner's four victories and Dick Linder's three marked the second year in a row—but the last time in history—that only two drivers posted multiple-victory campaigns.

Most Important Off-Track Development

On July 6, *The Atlanta Journal* reported the series points leaders as Lloyd Moore, Lee Petty, Jimmy Florian, Flock, and Turner. Had it not been for a decision made later that month by France, Rexford would not have captured that crown. France stripped Petty of 809 points—his entire season total to date—for competing in at least one race that wasn't sanctioned by NASCAR. Petty, who lost the Winston Cup title by fewer than 400 points, easily led the Performance Index with a rating of 270, comfortably ahead of the 215 posted by Rexford, the runner-up.

Most Significant Wreck

Moore, who tied for third in the Performance Index with a 197 rating, was injured on August 13 while qualifying at Occoneechee Speedway in Hillsboro, N.C., and missed that race.

Records & Milestones

Bill Blair's victory on June 18 in Vernon, N.Y., was the first for Mercury. . . . Florian became the first driver to put a Ford in victory lane when he won in Dayton, O., on June 25.

1950 at a Glance

Races:	19
Dirt:	15
Road:	1
Short Track:	2
Superspeedway:	1
Winners:	14
Pole Winners:	11
Tracks:	13
States:	8

1950 Performance Index Rankings

1. Lee Petty (270)
2. Bill Rexford (215)
3. Dick Linder; Lloyd Moore (197)
5. Curtis Turner (185)
6. Tim Flock (170)
7. Bill Blair (145)
8. Herb Thomas (132)
9. Fireball Roberts (131)
10. Chuck Mahoney (128)
11. Jimmy Florian (104)
12. Buck Baker (99)
13. George Hartley (91)
14. Red Byron (89)
15. Weldon Adams (79)
16. Johnny Mantz (70)
17. Fonty Flock (66)
18. Johnny Grubb (64)
19. Clyde Minter (63)
20. Glenn Dunnaway (60)
21. Cotton Owens (59)
22. Bob Flock (54)
23. Frank Mundy (52)
24. Dick Burns (50)
25. Art Lamey; Elmer Wilson (46)
27. Harold Kite (44)
28. Gayle Warren; Pap White (42)
30. Jimmy Thompson; Jack White (40)
32. Pappy Hough (39)
33. Dick Clothier; Bob Dickson (38)
35. Hershel McGriff (36)
36. Paul Parks; Bill Snowder (35)
38. Ted Chamberlain (34)
39. Ewell Weddle (33)
40. Jim Paschal (32)
41. John DuBoise; Dick Jerrett (31)
43. Ray Duhigg (30)
44. Buck Barr; Al Gross; Barney Smith (29)
47. Lyle Scott; Gober Sosebee; Donald Thomas (28)
50. Bob Apperson; Art Gill (27)
52. Pepper Cunningham; Joe Eubanks (26)
54. Jack Holloway; Leon Sales; J.C. Van Landingham; Shorty York (25)
58. Herbert Burns; Carl Renner (23)
60. Otis Martin (22)
61. Jim Delaney (20)
62. Gene Austin; June Cleveland; Neil Cole; Red Harvey; Bucky Sager; Jack Smith; Ted Swaim (19)
69. Jim Rathmann; Paul Smith (18)
71. Chuck James; Jimmie Lewallen; Roscoe Thompson (17)
74. Jack Reynolds; Donald White (16)
76. Herschel Buchanan; Bill Long; Ken Wagner (15)
79. John Borden; Len Brown; Duane Carter; Jack Kabat (14)
83. Chuck Garrett; Al Keller; Mike Klapak; Fred Johnson; Bobby Courtwright; Ken Warmington; Jerry Wimbish (13)
90. Bud Boone; Harland Holmes; Frank Luptow; Joe Nagle (12)
94. Will Albright; Huey Dunn (11)
96. Frankie Schneider; Tommy Thompson (10)
98. Leo Caldwell; Bob Collins; Hugh Darragh; Pee Wee Martin; Robert Sprague; Baldy Wilson (9)
104. Russell Bennett; Frank Boylan; Billy Carden; Ralph Dyer; Joe Jernigan; Frank Keller; Tommy Melvin; Harry Sents (8)
112. Sara Christian; Tommy Coates; F.L. Denney; Bill Joslin; Slick Smith (7)
117. Bill Bonner; Ed Jackson; John Manning (6)
120. Jack Russell; Bob Wilson (5)
122. Herb Craig; Frank Dagavar; Bill Greever; Louise Smith; Marshall Teague; Fred Weichman; Jim Wesley (4)
129. Nix Beard; Ann Bunselmeyer; Ray Erickson; Lewis Hawkins; Red Ryder (3)
134. Bill Burton; Curt Foss; Art Hammond; Runt Harris; Ralph Lyden; Macon Powers (2)
140. Bill Harrison; Morris Lamb; Bob Scott; Ace Shearer (1)

1950 Events

Beach & Road Course/4.167-mile road/200 miles
Harold Kite (Lincoln)/Joe Littlejohn (Oldsmobile)

Charlotte Speedway/.75-mile dirt/150 miles
Tim Flock (Lincoln)/Red Byron (Oldsmobile)

Langhorne Speedway/1-mile dirt/150 miles
Curtis Turner (Oldsmobile)/Tim Flock (Lincoln)

Martinsville Speedway/.5-mile dirt/75 miles
Curtis Turner (Oldsmobile)/Buck Baker (Ford)

Poor Man's 500; Canfield Speedway/.5-mile dirt/100 miles
Bill Rexford (Oldsmobile)/Jimmy Florian (Ford)

Vernon Fairgrounds/.5-mile dirt/100 miles
Bill Blair (Mercury)/Chuck Mahoney (Mercury)

Dayton Speedway/.5-mile/100 miles
Jimmy Florian (Ford)/Dick Linder (Oldsmobile)

Monroe County Fairgrounds/.5-mile dirt/100 miles
Curtis Turner (Oldsmobile)/Curtis Turner (Oldsmobile)

Charlotte Speedway/.75-mile dirt/150 miles
Curtis Turner (Oldsmobile)/Curtis Turner (Oldsmobile)

Occoneechee Speedway/1-mile dirt/100 miles
Fireball Roberts (Oldsmobile)/Dick Linder (Oldsmobile)

Dayton Speedway/.5-mile/100 miles
Dick Linder (Oldsmobile)/Curtis Turner (Oldsmobile)

Hamburg Fairgrounds/.5-mile dirt/100 miles
Dick Linder (Oldsmobile)/Dick Linder (Oldsmobile)

Southern 500; Darlington Raceway/1.25-mile/500 miles
Johnny Mantz (Plymouth)/Curtis Turner (Oldsmobile)

Langhorne Speedway/1-mile dirt/200 miles
Fonty Flock (Oldsmobile)/Wally Campbell (Oldsmobile)

Wilkes 200; North Wilkesboro Speedway/.625-m dirt/125 miles
Leon Sales (Plymouth)/Fireball Roberts (Oldsmobile)

Vernon Fairgrounds/.5-mile dirt/100 miles
Dick Linder (Oldsmobile)/Dick Linder (Oldsmobile)

Martinsville Speedway/.5-mile dirt/100 miles
Herb Thomas (Plymouth)/Fonty Flock (Oldsmobile)

Funk's Speedway/.5-mile dirt/100 miles
Lloyd Moore (Mercury)/Dick Linder (Oldsmobile)

Occoneechee Speedway/1-mile dirt/200 miles
Lee Petty (Plymouth)/Fonty Flock (Oldsmobile)

Victories

1. Curtis Turner (4)
2. Dick Linder (3)
3. Bill Blair; Fonty Flock; Tim Flock; Jimmy Florian; Harold Kite; Johnny Mantz; Lloyd Moore; Lee Petty; Bill Rexford; Fireball Roberts; Leon Sales; Herb Thomas (1)

Poles

1. Dick Linder (5)
2. Curtis Turner (4)
3. Fonty Flock (2)
4. Buck Baker; Red Byron; Wally Campbell; Tim Flock; Jimmy Florian; Joe Littlejohn; Chuck Mahoney; Fireball Roberts (1)

Victories

1. Oldsmobile (10)
2. Plymouth (4)
3. Lincoln; Mercury (2)
5. Ford (1)

Poles

1. Oldsmobile (15)
2. Ford (2)
3. Lincoln; Mercury (1)

1951
All in the Family

The more than 2,700 drivers who have competed in Winston Cup races seemingly have more family connections than a Mario Puzo novel.

Seven sets of brothers have won Winston Cup races, led by the Flocks, the only trio of siblings with Winston Cup victories. Two-time Winston Cup champion Tim won 39 races, Fonty 19, and Bob four. And the entire flock of racing Flock brothers visited victory lane in the same season twice: in 1951 and in 1952.

The trio of Bodine brothers has come closest to matching the Flocks. Geoff has won 18 races and Brett one, while Todd has won a pole, but no races. Ironically, the Bodines are one of only two sets of brothers who have won races without either claiming a Winston Cup title. They are joined by Jeff Burton, who has 11 victories, and Ward, who has one.

The victory totals for the other brothers who have captured Winston Cup races, with the Winston Cup champion listed first:

- Bobby Allison (85), Donnie Allison (10);
- Herb Thomas (48), Donald Thomas (1);
- Terry Labonte (21), Bobby Labonte (12);
- Benny Parsons (21), Phil Parsons (1).

Two other Winston Cup champions, three-time titlist Darrell Waltrip and 1989 king Rusty Wallace, won 84 and 49 races, respectively, in Winston Cup racing's first 51 years. Darrell's younger brother, Michael, and Rusty's younger brother, Kenny, each won two poles during that span. But neither captured a race.

Only five father-son combinations have captured Winston Cup victories. Surprisingly, in all five of those cases, the father was a Winston Cup champion.

Three-time Winston Cup champion Lee Petty captured 54 races, and his son, seven-time Winston Cup titlist Richard, earned 200 victories. Kyle, Richard's son, has won eight races. Ned Jarrett, a two-time Winston Cup champion, won 50 races, and his son, Dale, has won

22 and the 1999 title. Buck Baker, also a two-time Winston Cup champion, captured 46 victories, and his son, Buddy, earned 19. And Bobby Allison, the 1983 series champion, won 85 races, while his son, Davey, captured 19.

There have been other drivers who have reached victory lane whose fathers also competed in Winston Cup races, but failed to win. For example, six-time winner Sterling Marlin's father, Coo Coo, was never victorious.

Another father-son combination each won at least one pole in Winston Cup competition. Ironically, the son in that case was a Winston Cup champion: seven-time series king Dale Earnhardt (74 victories and 22 poles), whose father, Ralph, won one pole.

Two uncle-nephew combinations have won Winston Cup races: Donnie Allison and his nephew, Davey, and Mario Andretti and his nephew, John. Donnie is the lone driver to win a Winston Cup race who has a brother and a nephew who also can make that claim. Further, his son-in-law, Hut Stricklin, has captured a pole.

The only grandfather-grandson combination to capture Winston Cup races is, of course, Lee and Kyle Petty.

1951 in Review

Four drivers—Fonty Flock (8), Tim Flock (7), Herb Thomas (7), and Marshall Teague (5)—combined to win 27 of the 41 races. Herb Thomas won his first Winston Cup title and became the first driver to capture three consecutive victories, all on dirt, also enabling him to become the first to win three in a row on that discipline. But Fonty Flock, who established a new record of 13 poles and became the first driver to earn three consecutive poles and three consecutive dirt poles, led the Performance Index with a 514 rating. Neither Thomas nor Fonty could claim particular dominance, however. Flock's rating was only 48.49 percent of the available total, and only Red Byron in 1949 ever led the Performance Index rankings with a lower percentage of the available total. Thomas's 461 rating also trailed Tim Flock's 495.

Most Memorable Race

Teague, a Burt Lancaster look-alike, passed pole winner Tim Flock, who had led the first 27 laps, to take the lead with 12 laps remaining at the Beach & Road Course in Daytona Beach, Fla. Teague's February 11 victory, in which a dozen cars finished on the lead lap, was the first for the "Fabulous Hudson Hornet," a moniker Teague is credited with coining.

Most Significant Wreck

On November 25 in Mobile, Ala., Bob Flock suffered a broken neck when his Oldsmobile was turned upside down in a crash. The oldest of the three racing Flock brothers was sidelined until August 17, 1952, when he returned to action in dramatic fashion by winning at North Carolina's Asheville-Weaverville Speedway—the last triumph of his career.

Most Important Off-Track Development

NASCAR President Bill France decided to stage the Motor City 250 at the Michigan State Fairgrounds in Detroit on August 12. The track had played host to Indy-car races in the past, and in the heart of the U.S. automobile industry, 15 American makes competed: Buick, Cadillac, Chevrolet, Chrysler, Ford, Henry J, Hudson, Lincoln, Mercury, Nash, Oldsmobile, Packard, Plymouth, Pontiac, and Studebaker. For the record, Tommy Thompson won the "Battle of the Brands," becoming the first driver to win in a Chrysler. The primary significance, however, was that showcasing Winston Cup racing in front of the manufacturers led, just as France had planned, to nearly half a century's involvement, although sometimes shaky, by the American automobile industry.

Records & Milestones

Turner's April 1 victory at Charlotte Speedway was the only one in history for Nash.... Seven manufacturers saw their products reach victory lane: Oldsmobile, Hudson, Studebaker, Mercury, Plymouth, Chrysler, and Nash. That record was tied four years later, but never broken.... Frank Mundy became the first driver to win in a Studebaker on June 16 at Columbia, S.C., which was also the first Winston Cup race held at night.... Herb Thomas's victory in the Southern 500 on Labor Day was achieved in an 82-car field, the largest in Winston Cup history.

1951 at a Glance

Races:	41
Dirt:	36
Road:	1
Short Track:	3
Superspeedway:	1
Winners:	14
Pole Winners:	14
Tracks:	32
States:	14

1951 Performance Index Rankings

1. Fonty Flock (514)
2. Tim Flock (495)
3. Herb Thomas (461)
4. Lee Petty (373)
5. Frank Mundy (266)
6. Marshall Teague (201)
7. Bill Snowden (175)
8. Bob Flock (159)
9. Lloyd Moore (158)
10. Jimmie Lewallen (156)
11. Bill Blair (154)
12. Donald Thomas (150)
13. Jim Paschal; Curtis Turner (132)
15. Buddy Shuman (125)
16. Dick Rathmann (124)
17. Gober Sosebee (122)
18. Billy Carden (111)
19. Jim Fiebelkorn (108)
20. Buck Baker (107)
21. Lou Figaro (105)
22. Erick Erickson (101)
23. Joe Eubanks; Jesse James Taylor (86)
25. George Seeger (83)
26. Fireball Roberts (81)
27. Jimmy Florian (78)
28. Don Bailey; Billy Myers (77)
30. Dick Meyer (76)
31. Dell Pearson (75)
32. Johnny Mantz (71)
33. Bud Farrell; Tommy Thompson (67)
35. Lloyd Dane; Pappy Hough; Leon Sales (65)
38. Neil Cole (64)
39. Bill Rexford; Danny Weinberg (61)
41. Ronnie Kohler (60)
42. Cotton Owens (59)
43. Oda Greene (57)
44. Bill Norton (56)
45. Jimmy Ayers; Fred Steinbroner (55)
47. Leonard Tippett (53)

Bobby Allison (right) is the only driver who has captured a Winston Cup race who also has a brother, Donnie (left), and a son, the late Davey Allison, who can make the same claim.

48. Red Byron; Hershel McGriff (51)
50. Weldon Adams (50)
51. Don Eggert; Bill Miller (48)
53. Jack Goodwin; Slick Smith (47)
55. John McGinley; Jack Smith (45)
57. Fred Bince; Dick Linder (44)
59. Charles Gattalia (43)
60. Glenn Dunnaway (41)
61. Jim Delaney; Augie Walackas (40)
63. Harold Kite; Coleman Lawrence (39)
65. Marvin Panch; Walt Sprague; Ewell Weddle; Bill Widenhouse (38)
69. Bill Holland; Bub King; Bud Riley (37)
72. Woody Brown; Pap White (35)
74. Quinton Daniels; Dick Moffitt (34)
76. Jim Reed (33)
77. Chuck Meekins (32)
78. Ed Benedict; Dick Eagan (31)
80. Red Duvall; Wimpy Ervin (30)
82. Bill Stammer; Speedy Thompson (29)
84. Danny Letner; Ed Samples (28)
86. Sonny Black; Bob Dietrich; Don Oldenberg (27)
89. Frank Luptow; Jerry Morese (26)
91. Marvin Burke; Cal Johnson; Barney Smith; Jesse White (25)
95. Les Snow (24)
96. John DuBoise; Ray Chase (23)
98. Walt Davis; Jack Reynolds (22)
100. Robert Caswell; Ted Chamberlain (21)
102. Leland Colvin; Bill Joslin (20)
104. Jack Holloway; Al Jacobs; Joe Merola; Clyde Minter; Lyle Scott; Shorty York (19)
110. Dick Stone (18)
111. Nelson Applegate; Sam Hawks; Ed Massey; Bill Osborne; Jim Romine (17)
116. Jack Flynn; Tom Jerris; Paul Newkirk; Reino Tulonen (16)
120. Les Bomar; Jim Byrd; Lamar Crabtree; Tommie Elliott; Charles Gillman; Hap Jones; Iggy Katona; Bill Ledbetter; Tommy Moon; Earl Moss; Claude Wallington (15)
131. Pug Blalock; Ed Camrud; Hal Cole; Frank Gise; Burt Jackson; Furman Lancaster; Norm McCarthy; Bill Stickler; Chuck Stimus (14)
140. Jerry Carver; C.H. Dingler; Freddie Farmer; Alton Haddock; Mike Klapak; Fred Russell; Joe Sommers; Nook Walters; Jerry Wimbish (13)
149. Dick Bailey; Leo Beiethaupt; Bill Champion; Bill Cheesbourg; Bill Cintia; Jerry Groh; Russ Hepler; Jim Little; Chuck Mahoney; Harry Scott; John Soares; Herb Trimble; Dale Williams; Ernie Yorton (12)
163. Bill Braun; Bud Erb; Len Fanelli; Jim Harris; Red Harvey; Allen Heath; Tommy Lane; Bobby Myers (11)
171. Hully Bunn; Carson Dyer; Wade Fields; Bill Lillenthal; Bill Majot; Harold Mays; Eddie Sheeler; Roscoe Thompson (10)
179. John Barker; James Ellis; Dudley Froy; Ben Gregory; Bill Harrison; Owen Jones; Dawson Lechlider; Ray Throckmorton; Jack White (9)
188. Fuzzy Anderson; George Cavana; Gene Comstock; Oliver Dial; Ray Duhigg; Herb Gott; Buddy Helms; Jim Mayes; Stan Noble; Neil Roberts; James Shields; Gene Tapia; Johnny Thompson; Gayle Warren (8)
202. Bobby Booth; Steve Dabb; Hank Lee; Don McLeish; Paul Pettit; Doug Wimpy; Whitey Worton (7)
209. Maudis Brissette; Willard Brooks; Bob Carpenter; Ray Erickson; V.E. Miller; Art Plas; Red Ryder; Ted Tedrow; Billy Tibbett; Marshall Weatherly (6)
219. Victor Brenzelli; Wally Campbell; George Clark; Bob Greer; Johnny Grubb; Jim Hart; Charles Kleber; Sandy Lynch; Otis Martin; Bill Schade; Ruel Smith; Paul Stanley; Bob Walters (5)
232. Joe Carver; Walt Hartman; Gus Linder; Jim Ross; Rod Therrian; Lou Volk (4)

238. Joe Bellinato; O.A. Dean; Bob Jeffries; Louis Luther; Jack McClure; Andy Pierce; Dan Rush (3)
245. Pepper Cunningham; Jimmy Ingram; Fran Jischke; Al King; Tommy Melvin; Rusty Rushton; Jack Wade (2)
252. Roy Forsythe; Coleman Grant; Richard Hancock; Irving Leitch; Ed Lenz (1)

1951 Events

Beach & Road Course/4.1-mile road/160 miles
Marshall Teague (Hudson)/Tim Flock (Lincoln)

Charlotte Speedway/.75-mile dirt/113 miles
Curtis Turner (Nash)/Fonty Flock (Oldsmobile)

Lakeview Speedway/.75-mile dirt/113 miles
Tim Flock (Oldsmobile)

Carrell Speedway/.5-mile dirt/100 miles
Marshall Teague (Hudson)/Andy Pierce (Buick)

Occoneechee Speedway/1-mile dirt/150 miles
Fonty Flock (Oldsmobile)/Fonty Flock (Oldsmobile)

Arizona State Fairgrounds/1-mile dirt/150 miles
Marshall Teague (Hudson)/Fonty Flock (Oldsmobile)

Wilkes County 150; North Wilkesboro Speedway/.625-m dirt/94m
Fonty Flock (Oldsmobile)/Fonty Flock (Oldsmobile)

Martinsville Speedway/.5-mile dirt/100 miles
Curtis Turner (Oldsmobile)/Tim Flock (Oldsmobile)

Poor Man's 500; Canfield Speedway/.5-mile dirt/100 miles
Marshall Teague (Hudson)/Bill Rexford (Oldsmobile)

Columbus Speedway/.5-mile dirt/100 miles
Tim Flock (Oldsmobile)/Gober Sosebee (Cadillac)

Columbia Speedway/.5-mile dirt/100 miles
Frank Mundy (Studebaker)/Joe Eubanks (Oldsmobile)

Dayton Speedway/.5-mile dirt/100 miles
Curtis Turner (Oldsmobile)/Tim Flock (Oldsmobile)

Carrell Speedway/.5-mile dirt/100 miles
Lou Figaro (Hudson)/Lou Figaro (Hudson)

Grand River Speedrome/.5-mile dirt/100 miles
Marshall Teague (Hudson)/Marshall Teague (Hudson)

Bainbridge Speedway/1-mile dirt/100 miles
Fonty Flock (Oldsmobile)/Fonty Flock (Oldsmobile)

Heidelberg Speedway/.5-mile dirt/100 miles
Herb Thomas (Oldsmobile)/Fonty Flock (Oldsmobile)

Asheville-Weaverville Speedway/.5-mile dirt/100 miles
Fonty Flock (Oldsmobile)/Billy Carden (Oldsmobile)

Monroe County Fairgrounds/.5-mile dirt/100 miles
Lee Petty (Plymouth)/Fonty Flock (Oldsmobile)

Altamont Speedway/.5-mile dirt/100 miles
Fonty Flock (Oldsmobile)/Fonty Flock (Oldsmobile)

Motor City 250; Michigan State Fairgrounds/1-mile dirt/250 m
Tommy Thompson (Chrysler)/Marshall Teague (Hudson)

Fort Miami Speedway/.5-mile dirt/100 miles
Tim Flock (Oldsmobile)/Fonty Flock (Oldsmobile)

Morristown Speedway/.5-mile dirt/100 miles
Tim Flock (Oldsmobile)/Tim Flock (Oldsmobile)

Greenville-Pickens Speedway/.5-mile dirt/100 miles
Bob Flock (Oldsmobile)/Tim Flock (Oldsmobile)

Southern 500; Darlington Raceway/1.25-mile/500 miles
Herb Thomas (Hudson)/Frank Mundy (Studebaker)

Columbia Speedway/.5-mile dirt/100 miles
Tim Flock (Oldsmobile)/Tim Flock (Oldsmobile)

Central City Speedway/.5-mile dirt/100 miles
Herb Thomas (Plymouth)/Bob Flock (Oldsmobile)

Langhorne Speedway/1-mile dirt/150 miles
Herb Thomas (Hudson)/Fonty Flock (Oldsmobile)

Charlotte Speedway/.75-mile dirt/150 miles
Herb Thomas (Hudson)/Billy Carden (Oldsmobile)

Dayton Speedway/.5-mile/100 miles
Fonty Flock (Oldsmobile)/Fonty Flock (Oldsmobile)

Wilson Speedway/.5-mile dirt/100 miles
Fonty Flock (Oldsmobile)/Fonty Flock (Oldsmobile)

Occoneechee Speedway/1-mile dirt/150 miles
Herb Thomas (Hudson)/Herb Thomas (Hudson)

Thompson Speedway/.5-mile/100 miles
Neil Cole (Oldsmobile)/Neil Cole (Oldsmobile)

Pine Grove Speedway/.5-mile dirt/100 miles
Tim Flock (Oldsmobile)

Martinsville Speedway/.5-mile dirt/100 miles
Frank Mundy (Oldsmobile)/Herb Thomas (Hudson)

Oakland Stadium/.625-mile dirt/250 miles
Marvin Burke (Mercury)/Dick Rathmann (Hudson)

Wilkes 200; North Wilkesboro Speedway/.625-m dirt/125 miles
Fonty Flock (Oldsmobile)/Herb Thomas (Hudson)

Hanford Motor Speedway/.5-mile dirt/100 miles
Danny Weinberg (Studebaker)/Dick Rathmann (Hudson)

Speedway Park/.5-mile dirt/100 miles
Herb Thomas (Hudson)/Herb Thomas (Hudson)

Lakewood Speedway/1-mile dirt/100 miles
Tim Flock (Hudson)/Frank Mundy (Studebaker)

Carrell Speedway/.5-mile dirt/100 miles
Bill Norton (Mercury)/Fonty Flock (Oldsmobile)

Lakeview Speedway/.75-mile dirt/113 miles
Frank Mundy (Studebaker)/Frank Mundy (Studebaker)

Victories

1. Fonty Flock (8)
2. Tim Flock; Herb Thomas (7)
4. Marshall Teague (5)
5. Frank Mundy; Curtis Turner (3)
7. Marvin Burke; Neil Cole; Lou Figaro; Bob Flock; Bill Norton; Lee Petty; Tommy Thompson; Danny Weinberg (1)

Poles

1. Fonty Flock (13)
2. Tim Flock (6)
3. Herb Thomas (4)
4. Frank Mundy (3)
5. Billy Carden; Dick Rathmann; Marshall Teague (2)
8. Neil Cole; Lou Figaro; Bob Flock; Andy Pierce; Bill Rexford; Gober Sosebee; Joe Eubanks (1)

Victories

1. Oldsmobile (20)
2. Hudson (12)
3. Studebaker (3)
4. Mercury; Plymouth (2)
6. Chrysler; Nash (1)

Poles

1. Oldsmobile (24)
2. Hudson (9)
3. Studebaker (3)
4. Buick; Cadillac; Lincoln (1)

1952
Thomas Reached His Lone Milestone Early; Gant Aged Like a Fine Wine

Many fans probably are aware of Harry Gant's prowess behind the wheel of a Winston Cup car at an age when most drivers have forsaken racing for the golf course.

Gant, whose four-race winning streak in the fall of 1991 inspired campaign buttons in stock-car racing's grandstands that read, "Life Begins at 51," is indeed the oldest driver to capture a Winston Cup race. The Taylorsville, N.C., driver was 52 years, seven months, and six days old when he won the Champion Spark Plug 400 on August 16, 1992, at Brooklyn, Mich.

In fact, Gant accomplished eight of the 20 "oldest" feats compiled for this chapter and can claim that he is the most accomplished driver in Winston Cup history who was eligible for membership in the American Association of Retired Persons.

Lee Petty and Geoff Bodine, with three "oldest" achievements apiece, qualify as Gant's nearest challengers for success in stock cars at an age when many longtime opponents were relaxing in rocking chairs.

Donald Thomas, who on November 16, 1952, at the age of 20 years, four months, and six days, became the youngest driver to win a Winston Cup race, can't make a similar claim.

Jeff Gordon owns nine of the 20 "youngest" achievements, and Thomas's victory at Atlanta's Lakewood Speedway was the only one of his career. Further, Thomas wasn't the youngest driver to take the checkered flag in a Winston Cup race, because he was relieved by his brother and car owner, the legendary Herb Thomas, who actually drove the Hudson across the finish line. The youngest driver who actually took the check-

ered flag in a Winston Cup race was Fireball Roberts, who was 21 years, six months, and 24 days old when he won at Occoneechee Speedway in Hillsboro, N.C., on August 13, 1950.

Oldest Winners

Dirt
*Lee Petty—Speedway Park
11/20/60 (age: 46/8/6)

Short Track
Harry Gant—Goody's 500; Martinsville Speedway
9/22/91 (age: 51/8/12)

Superspeedway
**Harry Gant—Champion Spark Plug 400; Michigan Int. Speedway
8/16/92 (age: 52/7/6)

Road Course
Geoff Bodine—The Bud at the Glen; Watkins Glen International
8/11/96 (age: 47/3/24)

500-Mile
Harry Gant—Heinz Southern 500; Darlington Raceway
9/1/91 (age: 51/7/22)

Grand Slam
Harry Gant—Heinz Southern 500; Darlington Raceway
9/1/91 (age: 51/7/22)

Classic
Harry Gant—Heinz Southern 500; Darlington Raceway
9/1/91 (age: 51/7/22)

1961 season
**Oldest winner*

Oldest to Win From the Pole

Dirt
* Lee Petty—Heidelberg Stadium
7/10/60 (age: 46/3/26)

Short Track
Bobby Allison—Wrangler Sanforset 400; Richmond Fgds. Raceway
9/12/82 (age: 44/9/9)

Superspeedway
Geoff Bodine—GM Goodwrench Dealer 400; Michigan Int. Speedway
8/21/94 (age: 45/4/3)

Road Course
David Pearson—Riverside 400; Riverside International Raceway
6/13/76 (age: 41/5/22)

500-Mile
Geoff Bodine—Miller Genuine Draft 500; Pocono Int. Raceway
7/17/94 (age: 45/2/29)

Grand Slam
Cale Yarborough—Daytona 500; Daytona International Speedway
2/19/84 (age: 44/10/23)

Classic
Cale Yarborough—Daytona 500; Daytona International Speedway
2/19/84 (age: 44/10/23)

* Oldest to win from the pole*

Oldest Pole Winners *

Dirt
** Lee Petty—Charlotte Fairgrounds
  11/6/60 (age: 46/7/23)

Short Track
*** Harry Gant—Goody's 500; Bristol International Raceway
  8/27/94 (age: 54/7/17)

Superspeedway
Harry Gant—Hooters 500; Atlanta Motor Speedway
  11/14/93 (age: 53/10/4)

Road Course
Morgan Shepherd—Budweiser at the Glen; Watkins Glen Int.
  8/13/89 (age: 47/9/23)

Grand Slam
Harry Gant—Hooters 500; Atlanta Motor Speedway
  11/14/93 (age: 53/10/4)

Classic
David Pearson—Southern 500; Darlington International Raceway
  9/26/82 (age: 47/8/15)

All dates are date of race
**1961 season*
***Oldest pole winner*

Youngest Winners

Dirt
* Donald Thomas—Lakewood Speedway
  11/16/52 (age: 20/4/6)

Short Track
Richard Petty—Virginia 500; Martinsville Speedway
  4/10/60 (age: 22/9/8)

Superspeedway
Bobby Hillin Jr.—Talladega 500; Alabama Int. Motor Speedway
  7/27/86 (age: 22/1/22)

Road Course
Parnelli Jones—Kitsap County Airport
  8/4/57 (age: 23/11/23)

500-Mile
Bobby Hillin Jr.—Talladega 500; Alabama Int. Motor Speedway
  7/27/86 (age: 22/1/22)

Grand Slam
Jeff Gordon—Coca-Cola 600; Charlotte Motor Speedway
  5/29/94 (age: 22/9/25)

Classic:
Jeff Gordon—Coca-Cola 600; Charlotte Motor Speedway
  5/29/94 (age: 22/9/25)

Donald Thomas, the youngest winner, was relieved by Herb Thomas. The youngest to take the checkered flag was Fireball Roberts at Occoneechee Speedway in Hillsboro, N.C., on 8/13/50 (21/6/24).

Youngest to Win From the Pole

Dirt
* Donald Thomas—Lakewood Speedway
  11/16/52 (age: 20/4/6)

Short Track
Richard Petty—Huntsville Speedway
  8/8/62 (age: 25/1/6)

Superspeedway
** Jeff Gordon—Coca-Cola 600; Charlotte Motor Speedway
  5/29/94 (age: 22/9/25)

Road Course
Richard Petty—Bridgehampton Raceway
  7/21/63 (age: 26/0/19)

500-Mile
Jeff Gordon—Goodwrench 500; North Carolina Motor Speedway
  2/26/95 (age: 23/6/22)

Grand Slam
** Jeff Gordon—Coca-Cola 600; Charlotte Motor Speedway
  5/29/94 (age: 22/9/25)

Classic
** Jeff Gordon—Coca-Cola 600; Charlotte Motor Speedway
  5/29/94 (age: 22/9/25)

Donald Thomas, the youngest to win from the pole, was relieved by Herb Thomas. The youngest to take the checkered flag on dirt when starting from the pole was Richard Petty at Orange Speedway in Hillsboro, N.C., on 9/18/60 (23/2/16).
**Youngest to take the checkered flag from the pole*

Youngest Pole Winners *

Dirt
** Donald Thomas—Lakewood Speedway
  11/16/52 (age: 20/4/6)

Short Track
Mark Martin—Busch Nashville 420; Nashville Int. Raceway
  7/11/81 (age: 22/6/2)

Superspeedway
Jeff Gordon—Mello Yello 500; Charlotte Motor Speedway
  10/10/93 (age: 22/2/6)

Road Course
*** Banjo Matthews—Beach & Road Course
  2/17/57 (age: 25/0/3)

Grand Slam
Jeff Gordon—Mello Yello 500; Charlotte Motor Speedway
  10/10/93 (age: 22/2/6)

Classic
Jeff Gordon—Coca-Cola 600; Charlotte Motor Speedway
  5/29/94 (age: 22/9/25)

All dates are dates of races
**Youngest pole winner*
***The youngest pole winner on a road course other than the Beach & Road Course in Daytona Beach, Fla., was Terry Labonte, who won the pole for the Budweiser 400 at Riverside International Raceway in Riverside, Calif, on 6/13/82 (25/6/28).*

1952 in Review

Tim Flock earned his first Winston Cup title and shared the season lead in victories (8) with Herb Thomas, whose 10 poles led the circuit. Flock barely edged Lee Petty for the Performance Index leadership, 536-533.

Most Memorable Race

Fonty Flock's victory in the Southern 500 at Darlington, S.C., in which he led 341 of the 400 laps and beat Johnny Patterson to the finish line by more than a lap, wasn't exactly spine-tingling. But the race earned its niche in stock-car racing lore when Fonty, who competed, as he frequently did, clad in Bermuda shorts, led the estimated Labor Day gathering of 30,000 in a stirring rendition of "Dixie" after his victory.

Most Significant Wreck

Rookie Larry Mann became the first driver to die of injuries suffered in a Winston Cup race on September 14 at Langhorne, Pa. Mann suffered massive head injuries and died later that day in a hospital.

Most Important Off-Track Development

NASCAR announced that any driver convicted of a reckless driving charge that occurred while away from the track would be punished by the sanctioning body.

Records & Milestones

Buddy Shuman's July 1 win at Stamford Park in Niagara Falls, Ont., was the first of two Winston Cup points races ever held outside the United States. . . . When Dick Rathmann won three consecutive races (Langhorne on May 4; Darlington on May 10, and Dayton, O., on May 18), he became the first driver to win three in a row on a three different disciplines: dirt (Langhorne), superspeedway (Darlington), and short track (Dayton).

When Harry Gant (left), the oldest driver ever to win a Winston Cup race, competed for the final time in the Hooters 500 on November 13, 1994, at Atlanta Motor Speedway, his former car owner, Burt Reynolds, served as the race's Grand Marshal.

1952 at a Glance

Races:	34
Dirt:	28
Road:	1
Short Track:	3
Superspeedway:	2
Winners:	12
Pole Winners:	12
Tracks:	25
States:	11*

* plus Canada

1952 Performance Index Rankings

1. Tim Flock (536)
2. Lee Petty (533)
3. Herb Thomas (514)
4. Fonty Flock (407)
5. Dick Rathmann (339)
6. Donald Thomas (252)
7. Bill Blair (248)
8. Joe Eubanks (206)
9. Ray Duhigg (191)
10. Buddy Shuman (170)
11. Perk Brown (152)
12. Jimmie Lewallen (151)
13. Buck Baker (148)
14. Ted Chamberlain (138)
15. Jim Paschal (134)
16. Gober Sosebee (129)
17. Neil Cole (118)
18. Bub King (115)
19. Lloyd Moore (105)
20. Herschel Buchanan (104)
21. Frankie Schneider (86)
22. Ralph Liguori (85)
23. Jack Reynolds (83)
24. Jack Smith (82)
25. Johnny Patterson (77)
26. Charles Gattalia (76)
27. Pat Kirkwood; Bucky Sager (70)
29. Gene Comstock (67)
30. Ed Samples; Marshall Teague (65)
32. Coleman Lawrence (62)
33. Fred Dove (58)
34. Weldon Adams; Tommy Moon (57)
36. Dick Passwater (53)
37. Banjo Matthews; Frank Mundy (51)
39. Clyde Minter; Bob Moore (49)
41. Dave Terrell (47)
42. Jim Reed (45)

43. Speedy Thompson (42)
44. Slick Smith (41)
45. Bobby Courtwright; Otis Martin (40)
47. Bud Farrell; Jimmy Florian; Iggy Katona; E.C. Ramsey (39)
51. June Cleveland (37)
52. Ed Benedict; George Bush; Leonard Tippett (36)
55. Barney Smith (35)
56. Clyde Pittinger; Curtis Turner (34)
58. Rollin Smith (33)
59. Jimmy Thompson (32)
60. Elton Hildreth; Pappy Hough (31)
62. Fireball Roberts; Tommy Thompson (30)
64. Bill Snowden; Joe Weatherly (29)
66. Red Duvall; Al Keller (28)
68. Keith Hamner (27)
69. Bruce Atchley; Bob Flock (25)
71. Cotton Owens; Ewell Weddle (23)
73. Allan Clarke (22)
74. Roscoe Thompson (21)
75. Ernie Boost; Hershel McGriff; Joe Staton (20)
78. Larry Shurter (19)
79. David Ezell; Bill Rexford; Jerry Wimbish (18)
82. Charles Barry; Leo Caldwell; Billy Carden (17)
85. Marion Edwards; J.E. Hardie; Ronnie Kohler; Larry Mann; Eddie Van Horn; Bill Widenhouse (16)
91. Fred Bethune; Rags Carter; Dick Eagan; Coleman Grant (15)
95. Nelson Applegate; Tom Dawson; Bob Dugan; Carson Dyer; George Gallup; Glen Larsen; Pop McGinnis; Jim Millard; Julian Petty (14)
104. Bill Davis; Stuart Joyce; Dick Meyer (13)
107. Walt Carver; Al Funderburk; Albert Lemieux; Herschel White (11)
111. Jim Clark; Joe Deloach; Earl Moss; Gibb Orr; Bob Welborn; J.C. White (10)
117. Red Harrelson; Dutch Hoag; Paul Magee; Harold Morese; Nelson Stacy; Paul Wensink (9)
123. Eddie Adams; Erwin Blatt; Shorty Gibbs; Jack Harrison; Harvey Henderson; Marion Leech; Jack Mulrain; Hank Tillman; Nook Walters; Harold Wright (8)
133. Olin Allen; Bill Hammersley; Russ Hepler; Zane Howell; Fran Jischke; Ed Lenz; Dub Livingston; Bill Miller; Billy Myers; Robbie Robinson (7)
143. Bill Barker; Gordon Bishop; Zeke DeRose; Mike Ernest; Oda Greene; Stew Hayes; Charlie Hill; Bill James; Dick Martin; Paul Pettit; Leo Richards (6)
154. Stan Parnell; Don Price; Rod Turcott; Charles Weidler (5)
158. Jack Hauher; Walt Regan; Bob Schwingle; Pete Toth; Dick Turcott (4)
163. Jimmy Ayers; Hank Carruthers; Bill Deakin; Joe Kusler; Herb Legg; Johnny Thompson; Red Tomlinson; Smokey Yunick (3)
171. Ray Atkinson; Bill Brown; Lamar Crabtree; Gene Darragh; Hank Pollard; Ken Rauch; Lucky Sawyer; Charles Stark (2)
179. Buck Clardy; C.H. Dingler; Don Kent; Pete Vail (1)

1952 Events

Palm Beach Speedway/.5-mile dirt/100 miles
Tim Flock (Hudson)/Tim Flock (Hudson)

Beach & Road Course/4.1-mile road/200 miles
Marshall Teague (Hudson)/Pat Kirkwood (Chrysler)

Speedway Park/.5-mile dirt/100 miles
Marshall Teague (Hudson)/Marshall Teague (Hudson)

Wilkes County 200; N. Wilkesboro Speedway/.625-m dirt/125m
Herb Thomas (Hudson)/Herb Thomas (Hudson)

Martinsville Speedway/.5-mile dirt/100 miles
Dick Rathmann (Hudson)/Buck Baker (Hudson)

Columbia Speedway/.5-mile dirt/100 miles
Buck Baker (Hudson)/Buck Baker (Hudson)

Lakewood Speedway/1-mile dirt/100 miles
Bill Blair (Oldsmobile)/Tim Flock (Hudson)

Central City Speedway/.5-mile dirt/150 miles
Herb Thomas (Hudson)/Jack Smith (Studebaker)

Langhorne Speedway/1-mile dirt/150 miles
Dick Rathmann (Hudson)/Herb Thomas (Hudson)

Darlington Raceway/1.25-mile/100 miles
Dick Rathmann (Hudson)

Dayton Speedway/.5-mile/100 miles
Dick Rathmann (Hudson)/Fonty Flock (Oldsmobile)

Poor Man's 500; Canfield Speedway/.5-mile dirt/100 miles
Herb Thomas (Hudson)/Dick Rathmann (Ford)

Hayloft Speedway/.5-mile dirt/100 miles
Gober Sosebee (Chrysler)/Tommy Moon (Hudson)

Fort Miami Speedway/.5-mile dirt/100 miles
Tim Flock (Hudson)/Fonty Flock (Oldsmobile)

Occoneechee Speedway/1-mile dirt/100 miles
Tim Flock (Hudson)/Fonty Flock (Oldsmobile)

Charlotte Speedway/.75-mile dirt/113 miles
Herb Thomas (Hudson)/Fonty Flock (Oldsmobile)

Motor City 250; Michigan State Fairgrounds/1-mile dirt/250 m
Tim Flock (Hudson)/Dick Rathmann (Hudson)

Stamford Park/.5-mile dirt/100 miles
Buddy Shuman (Hudson)/Herb Thomas (Hudson)

Wine Creek Race Track/.5-mile dirt/100 miles
Tim Flock (Hudson)/Tim Flock (Hudson)

Monroe Speedway/.5-mile dirt/100 miles
Tim Flock (Hudson)/Tim Flock (Hudson)

Morristown Speedway/.5-mile dirt/100 miles
Lee Petty (Plymouth)/Herb Thomas (Hudson)

Playland Park Speedway/.5-mile dirt/100 miles
Tim Flock (Hudson)/Herb Thomas (Hudson)

Monroe County Fairgrounds/.5-mile dirt/100 miles
Tim Flock (Hudson)

Asheville-Weaverville Speedway/.5-mile dirt/100 miles
Bob Flock (Hudson)/Herb Thomas (Hudson)

Southern 500; Darlington Raceway/1.25-mile/500 miles
Fonty Flock (Oldsmobile)/Fonty Flock (Oldsmobile)

Central City Speedway/.5-mile dirt/150 miles
Lee Petty (Plymouth)/Fonty Flock (Oldsmobile)

Langhorne Speedway/1-mile dirt/250 miles
Lee Petty (Plymouth)/Herb Thomas (Hudson)

Dayton Speedway/.5-mile/150 miles
Dick Rathmann (Hudson)/Fonty Flock (Oldsmobile)

Wilson Speedway/.5-mile dirt/100 miles
Herb Thomas (Hudson)/Herb Thomas (Hudson)

Occoneechee Speedway/1-mile dirt/150 miles
Fonty Flock (Oldsmobile)/Bill Blair (Oldsmobile)

Martinsville Speedway/.5-mile dirt/100 miles
Herb Thomas (Hudson)/Perk Brown (Hudson)

Wilkes 200; North Wilkesboro Speedway/.625-m dirt/125 miles
Herb Thomas (Hudson)/Herb Thomas (Hudson)

Lakewood Speedway/1-mile dirt/100 miles
Donald Thomas (Hudson)/Donald Thomas (Hudson)

Palm Beach Speedway/.5-mile dirt/100 miles
Herb Thomas (Hudson)/Herb Thomas (Hudson)

Victories
1. Tim Flock; Herb Thomas (8)
3. Dick Rathmann (5)
4. Lee Petty (3)
5. Fonty Flock; Marshall Teague (2)
7. Buck Baker; Bill Blair; Bob Flock; Buddy Shuman; Gober Sosebee; Donald Thomas (1)

Poles
1. Herb Thomas (10)
2. Fonty Flock (7)
3. Tim Flock (4)
4. Buck Baker; Dick Rathmann (2)
6. Bill Blair; Perk Brown; Pat Kirkwood; Tommy Moon; Jack Smith; Marshall Teague; Donald Thomas (1)

Victories
1. Hudson (27)
2. Oldsmobile; Plymouth (3)
4. Chrysler (1)

Poles
1. Hudson (21)
2. Oldsmobile (8)
3. Chrysler; Ford; Studebaker (1)

1953
A Rare Feat
For the King
And Silver Fox

Drivers Who Won on All Four Disciplines

Driver	Dirt	Short Track	Road Course	Superspeedway
Bobby Allison	1	31	6	47
Buck Baker	40	2	1	3
Darel Dieringer	1	3	1	2
Paul Goldsmith	4	1	1	3
Marvin Panch	5	6	2	4
David Pearson	23	27	4	51
Lee Petty	42	10	1	1
Richard Petty	31	107	6	56
Fireball Roberts	12	5	2	14
Jack Smith	14	4	1	2
Cale Yarborough	1	31	3	48

Drivers Who Won Poles on All Four Disciplines

Driver	Dirt	Short Track	Road Course	Superspeedway
Bobby Allison	1	34	5	18
Buck Baker	38	3	3	1
Tim Flock	31	3	3	1
Paul Goldsmith	2	1	3	2
Dick Hutcherson	15	4	1	1
Junior Johnson	18	21	1	5
Marvin Panch	6	8	1	6
David Pearson	19	28	8	58
Lee Petty	12	4	1	1
Richard Petty	26	68	6	23
Jack Smith	12	9	1	1

No fewer than 150 drivers have won Winston Cup races, but only 11 have one of the most amazing feats of versatility on their resumes: victories on superspeedways, short tracks, road courses, and dirt.

Dick Rathmann entered the 1953 season as the first driver with a shot at that elusive goal—needing only a victory on a road course. But his best showings in four races on road courses during the next three seasons were two fourth-place finishes, leaving him short of the target.

The special achievement of winning on all four disciplines is, of course, impossible for those whose careers began after September 30, 1970, when a Winston Cup race was contested on dirt for the last time. And drivers in the '50s—and even the '60s—had far fewer opportunities on superspeedways than drivers during the modern era.

So it is unfair to criticize the achievements of the Darrell Waltrips, Dale Earnhardts, and Jeff Gordons, who never raced on dirt in Winston Cup competition, for failing to have this notable distinction on their resumes.

But the 11 drivers who did win races on superspeedways, short tracks, road courses, and dirt—or the 11 of the 175 pole winners who earned the No. 1 starting spot on all four disciplines—should be recognized in any discussion of history's most versatile stock-car pilots.

Note that eight drivers appear on both lists: Bobby Allison, Buck Baker, Paul Goldsmith, Marvin Panch, David Pearson, Lee Petty, Richard Petty, and Jack Smith, who, remarkably, wasn't chosen as one of NASCAR's 50 greatest drivers during its 50th anniversary celebration.

Each of the 11 drivers who won on all four disciplines also has a Grand Slam victory on his resume, and only Goldsmith and Smith failed to capture a classic. Smith was the only driver among the 11 who never won a 500-mile race.

Eight of the 11 drivers who won poles on all four disciplines earned at least one Grand Slam pole, with Tim Flock, Dick Hutcherson, and Lee Petty the exceptions. And, although both Panch and Smith won Grand Slam poles, neither captured a classic pole.

Although 73 drivers have won races from the pole, one of the most exclusive clubs in stock-car racing includes drivers who won races from the pole on all four disciplines. This distinction is so rare that it is limited to two drivers who, not coincidentally, rank first and second on the all-time lists in victories, poles, and victories from the pole: Richard Petty and Pearson.

Drivers Who Won From the Pole on All Four Disciplines

Driver	Dirt	Short Track	Road Course	Superspeedway
David Pearson	6	10	2	19
Richard Petty	16	36	2	7

Further, both King Richard and the Silver Fox earned Grand Slam, classic, and 500-mile victories from the pole.

1953 in Review

Few drivers in history have dominated a season like Herb Thomas did in 1953. He led the series with a dozen victories and as many poles and in each category posted more than twice as many as his nearest competitor. Thomas also earned his second Winston Cup title and held a 691-640 edge over Lee Petty in the Performance Index rankings. That marked the first time a champion held sole possession of the season title in both victories and poles and also posted the highest Performance Index, a feat repeated only eight times since. Thomas also earned 71.24 percent of the available Performance Index, the highest percentage any driver gained during Winston Cup racing's first 16 seasons.

Most Memorable Race

Bill Blair captured the February 15 shootout at Daytona Beach, Fla., when Fonty Flock's Oldsmobile ran out of gas on the final 4.1-mile lap around the Beach & Road Course. Flock, who led by one minute and nine seconds before his gas tank emptied, was pushed for three miles by fellow Atlanta driver Slick Smith's car. But it wasn't enough, and Blair finished 26 seconds in front.

Most Significant Wreck

Frank Arford died June 20 as a result of injuries received when he crashed in qualifying for the next day's International 200 at Langhorne, Pa.

David Pearson is one of only two drivers who captured victories from the pole on superspeedways, short tracks, dirt tracks, and road courses.

Most Important Off-Track Development

Raleigh Speedway, the second superspeedway to stage a NASCAR race, made its debut in dramatic fashion. Driving an Oldsmobile owned by Frank Christian, Fonty Flock rallied from the 41st starting position in a field of 49 on the one-mile North Carolina oval to beat Speedy Thompson by more than three laps in the Raleigh 300 on May 30.

Records & Milestones

Lee Petty's victory at West Palm Beach, Fla., on February 1 was the first for Dodge.

1953 at a Glance

Races:	37
Dirt:	34
Road:	1
Superspeedway:	2
Winners:	11
Pole Winners:	11
Tracks:	29
States:	13

1953 Performance Index Rankings

1. Herb Thomas (691)
2. Lee Petty (640)
3. Dick Rathmann (523)
4. Buck Baker (515)
5. Fonty Flock (453)
6. Tim Flock (344)
7. Joe Eubanks (256)
8. Jimmie Lewallan (237)
9. Jim Paschal (236)
10. Dick Passwater (233)
11. Gober Sosebee (194)
12. Slick Smith (181)
13. Curtis Turner (180)
14. Bill Blair (176)
15. Speedy Thompson (168)
16. Elton Hildreth (157)
17. Fred Dove; Ray Duhigg (139)
19. Donald Thomas (138)
20. Herschel Buchanan (112)
21. Bob Welborn (109)
22. Gene Comstock (103)
23. Bub King (94)
24. Pop McGinnis (82)
25. Ralph Liguori (75)
26. Otis Martin (68)
27. Ralph Dyer (67)
28. Andy Winfree (59)
29. John Meggers (57)
30. Ted Chamberlain (56)
31. C.H. Dingler (52)
32. Johnny Patterson (49)
33. Don Oldenberg (48)

34. Bill Harrison (45)
35. Clyde Minter (44)
36. Neil Roberts (43)
37. Elbert Allen; Dick Meyer (41)
39. Ronnie Kohler; Bob Walden (40)
41. Jimmy Ayers (37)
42. Bobby Myers (36)
43. Arden Mounts; George Osborne (33)
45. Coleman Lawrence; Buddy Shuman (31)
47. Bill O'Dell; Tommy Thompson (30)
49. Dub Livingston; Ewell Weddle (29)
51. Lloyd Hulette; Mike Klapak (28)
53. Bill Adams; Mel Krueger; Bill Rexford (27)
56. Johnny Beauchamp; Carl Burris (26)
58. Buck Smith (25)
59. Tubby Harrison; Ralph Rose; Eddie Skinner (24)
62. Dick Allwine (23)
63. Gordon Bracken (22)
64. Tom Cherry; Virgil Livengood (21)
66. Jim Reed (19)
67. Hershel McGriff (18)
68. Marvin Copple; Red Duvall; Jerry Wimbish (16)
71. Bob Cameron; Ed DeWolff; Emory Lewis; Eddie Riker (15)
75. Ed Benedict; Byron Clouse; Fred Moore (14)
78. Frank Arford; Charles Barry; Jerry Earl; Nick Fornoro; Joe Guide Jr.;
    Chuck Housley; Frank Price; Leo Ray; Ermon Rush (13)
87. Obie Chupp; Wimpy Ervin; Dick Fellows; Bill Jennings; Ed Massey;
    Bill Morgan; Billy Oswald; Russ Truelove (12)
95. Bill Cleveland; Sam DiRusso; George Gallup; Keith Hamner; Ted Lee;
    Keith Lucas; Mike Magill; Lyle Scott; Sandy Slack; Gifford Wood (11)
105. Lamar Crabtree; Ernie Derr; Ned Jarrett; Dick Linder; Bill Mann;
    Neil McDonald; Charlie Miller; Ed Paskovich; Cotton Priddy; Mickey
    Rorer; John Ross; Ray Springer; Nero Steptoe; Glen Wood (10)
119. Jerry Draper; Ralph Dutton; Curtis Estes; J.W. Gentry; Lou Johnson;
    Red Knuter; Frank Katucka; Leon Lundy; Steve McGrath; Wayne
    Niedecken; Frankie Schneider; Ralph Sheeler; Jack Smith II; Parks
    Surrat; Hildrey Thomas (9)
134. Jim Baker; Roxy Dancy; Marion Edwards; Al Kent; Buddy Krebs; Paul
    Newkirk; Bob Sampson; Roscoe Thompson; John Torrese; Don Vershure (8)
144. Leo Bergeron; Robert Caswell; Billy Fritts; Don Glass; Jim Lacy;
    Jack Lawrence; Snuffy Smith; Red Untiedt (7)
152. Jack Culpepper; Charlie Hoff; Leonard Lawrence; Buck Mason;
    Elmer Musclow; Don Ostendorf; Bud Rinaldo; Lucky Sawyer; Virgil
    Stockton (6)
161. Charles Causey; Phil Demola; Jim Fox; Bud Harless; Max King; Gene
    Tapia; Herb Tillman (5)
168. Russell Armentrout; Geoffrey Dessault; Dick Girvin; Wimpy Sipple;
    Eddie Van Horn; Chet Williams (4)
174. Allan Clarke; Pepper Cunningham; Red Dowdy; Marvin Panch; Tony
    Polito; Billy Rafter; Gwyn Staley; Ernie Weidler (3)
182. Dick Hagey; Frank Kapack; Al Keller; Harold Nash (2)
186. John McGorrien; Nick Nicolette; Don Price; Hank Ribet; Ed Spencer (1)

1953 Events

Palm Beach Speedway/.5-mile dirt/100 miles
Lee Petty (Dodge)/Dick Rathmann (Hudson)

Beach & Road Course/4.1-mile road/160 miles
Bill Blair (Oldsmobile)/Bob Pronger (Oldsmobile)

Harnett Speedway/.5-mile dirt/100 miles
Herb Thomas (Hudson)/Herb Thomas (Hudson)

Wilkes County 200; N. Wilkesboro Speedway/.625-m dirt/125m
Herb Thomas (Hudson)/Herb Thomas (Hudson)

Charlotte Speedway/.75-mile dirt/113 miles
Dick Passwater (Oldsmobile)/Tim Flock (Hudson)

Richmond 200; Atlantic Rural Fairgrounds/.5-m dirt/100 m
Lee Petty (Dodge)/Buck Baker (Oldsmobile)

Central City Speedway/.5-mile dirt/100 miles
Dick Rathmann (Hudson)

Langhorne Speedway/1-mile dirt/150 miles
Buck Baker (Oldsmobile)

Columbia Speedway/.5-mile dirt/100 mile
Buck Baker (Oldsmobile)/Herb Thomas (Hudson)

Hickory Speedway/.5-mile dirt/100 miles
Tim Flock (Hudson)/Herb Thomas (Hudson)

Martinsville Speedway/.5-mile dirt/100 miles
Lee Petty (Dodge)/Joe Eubanks (Hudson)

Powell Motor Speedway/.5-mile dirt/100 miles
Herb Thomas (Hudson)/Fonty Flock (Oldsmobile)

Raleigh 300; Raleigh Speedway/1-mile/300 miles
Fonty Flock (Hudson)/Slick Smith (Oldsmobile)

Louisiana Fairgrounds/.5-mile dirt/100 miles
Lee Petty (Dodge)/Herb Thomas (Hudson)

Five Flags Speedway/.5-mile dirt/100 miles
Herb Thomas (Hudson)/Dick Rathmann (Hudson)

International 200; Langhorne Speedway/1-m dirt/200 miles
Dick Rathmann (Hudson)/Lloyd Shaw (Jaguar)

Tri-City Speedway/.5-mile dirt/100 miles
Herb Thomas (Hudson)/Herb Thomas (Hudson)

Wilson Speedway/.5-mile dirt/100 miles
Fonty Flock (Hudson)/Buck Baker (Oldsmobile)

Monroe County Fairgrounds/.5-mile dirt/100 miles
Herb Thomas (Hudson)

Piedmont Interstate Fairgrounds/.5-mile dirt/100 miles
Lee Petty (Dodge)/Buck Baker (Oldsmobile)

Morristown Speedway/.5-mile dirt/100 miles
Dick Rathmann (Hudson)/Herb Thomas (Hudson)

Lakewood Speedway/1-mile dirt/100 miles
Herb Thomas (Hudson)/Herb Thomas (Hudson)

Rapid Valley Speedway/.5-mile dirt/100 miles
Herb Thomas (Hudson)/Herb Thomas (Hudson)

Lincoln City Fairgrounds/.5-mile dirt/100 miles
Dick Rathmann (Hudson)/Herb Thomas (Hudson)

Davenport Speedway/.5-mile dirt/100 miles
Herb Thomas (Hudson)/Buck Baker (Oldsmobile)

Occoneechee Speedway/1-mile dirt/100 miles
Curtis Turner (Oldsmobile)/Curtis Turner (Oldsmobile)

Asheville-Weaverville Speedway/.5-mile dirt/100 miles
Fonty Flock (Hudson)/Curtis Turner (Oldsmobile)

Princess Anne Speedway/.5-mile dirt/100 miles
Herb Thomas (Hudson)/Curtis Turner (Oldsmobile)

Hickory Speedway/.5-mile dirt/100 miles
Fonty Flock (Hudson)/Tim Flock (Hudson)

Southern 500; Darlington Raceway/1.375-mile/500 miles
Buck Baker (Oldsmobile)/Fonty Flock (Hudson)

Central City Speedway/.5-mile dirt/100 miles
Speedy Thompson (Oldsmobile)/Joe Eubanks (Hudson)

Langhorne Speedway/1-mile dirt/250 miles
Dick Rathmann (Hudson)/Herb Thomas (Hudson)

Bloomsburg Fairgrounds/.5-mile dirt/100 miles
Herb Thomas (Hudson)/Jim Paschal (Dodge)

Wilson Speedway/.5-mile dirt/100 miles
Herb Thomas (Hudson)/Herb Thomas (Hudson)

Wilkes 160; North Wilkesboro Speedway/.625-mile dirt/100 m
Speedy Thompson (Oldsmobile)/Buck Baker (Oldsmobile)

Martinsville Speedway/.5-mile dirt/100 miles
Jim Paschal (Dodge)/Fonty Flock (Oldsmobile)

Lakewood Speedway/1-mile dirt/100 miles
Buck Baker (Oldsmobile)/Tim Flock (Hudson)

Victories
1. Herb Thomas (12)
2. Lee Petty; Dick Rathmann (5)
4. Buck Baker; Fonty Flock (4)
6. Speedy Thompson (2)
7. Bill Blair; Tim Flock; Jim Paschal; Dick Passwater; Curtis Turner (1)

Poles
1. Herb Thomas (12)
2. Buck Baker (5)
3. Fonty Flock; Tim Flock; Curtis Turner (3)
6. Dick Rathmann; Joe Eubanks (2)
8. Jim Paschal; Bob Pronger; Lloyd Shaw; Slick Smith (1)

Victories
1. Hudson (22)
2. Oldsmobile (9)
3. Dodge (6)

Poles
1. Hudson (20)
2. Oldsmobile (12)
3. Dodge; Jaguar (1)

1954
No One Ever Dominated On Dirt Like Tobacco Farmer Herb Thomas

No driver in history compiled as dominating a record on dirt tracks as Herb Thomas, but his prowess on the prevailing surface of the '50s overshadows one of his most significant achievements: He was the first driver ever to capture four consecutive superspeedway races.

Like so many drivers of his era, Herb Thomas's career was a short one, particularly by today's standards.

Thomas, for example, posted just seven seasons with a Performance Index of 100 or more and only eight seasons in the top 25. But he recorded five seasons in the top three, including four in a row from 1951-54.

An examination beyond his 48 victories and 39 poles—which rank among the top dozen in both categories—reveals that few drivers have made a more lasting impact on the record books than the Olivia, N.C., truck driver and tobacco farmer.

Thomas's run from 1951-54 was one of the greatest four-year success stories in Winston Cup history.

Thomas posted at least 12 victories in both 1953 and '54. Back-to-back 12-victory seasons is a feat later equaled twice by Richard Petty and once each by Ned Jarrett and Darrell Waltrip—but never bettered.

Thomas recorded at least eight victories three years in a row (1952-54), a streak exceeded only by Petty. And only Petty and Jeff Gordon have bettered Thomas's four consecutive seasons (1951-54) of at least seven victories.

Forty-one of Thomas's victories came on dirt, the dominant discipline of his era. Those 41 wins are one fewer than the dirt victories recorded by Lee Petty, the all-time leader in that category, and Thomas's 37 poles on dirt rank in a first-place tie with Buck Baker.

But even the eldest member of the Petty clan had to take a back seat to Thomas when it came to dominating performances on dirt. In 1953 and 1954, Thomas re-

corded the only back-to-back seasons of at least 10 victories on that surface, and he won eight dirt races in 1952. No other driver ever managed to capture as many as seven dirt victories three years in a row, and only Thomas, who won at least six dirt races a year from 1951-54, and Jarrett had four consecutive seasons of at least *four* dirt triumphs.

Thomas's feat of winning at least eight poles in three consecutive seasons (1952-54) has been matched only by Richard Petty, and only Richard Petty and David Pearson managed more than three straight years with at least six poles. In 1952 and '53, Thomas became the only driver to capture 10 or more dirt poles in consecutive years, and he won another five in '54. No other driver managed three consecutive seasons with at least five poles on dirt.

Thomas, in fact, won at least four dirt poles four years in a row (1951-54), while no other driver achieved a four-season streak of even three dirt poles, and only Baker had a longer run of seasons in which he won multiple dirt poles than Thomas's six in a row from 1951-56.

Thomas won at least four victories from the pole from 1952-54, and only Richard Petty can claim he also accomplished that feat in three consecutive seasons. In fact, Thomas won at least two races from the pole four years in a row beginning in 1951, and only Richard Petty and Waltrip have longer streaks of seasons with multiple victories from the pole.

Thomas won at least five dirt races from the pole in both 1953 and '54, at least four dirt races from the pole three years in a row (1952-54), and at least two dirt races from the pole four years in a row (1951-54). No other driver posted as many as three consecutive seasons of multiple dirt victories from the pole. In fact, only Baker and Richard Petty ever managed to string together five consecutive seasons with at least one dirt victory from the pole.

Thomas held at least a share of the season leadership in victories three years in a row (1952-54), a feat bettered only by Waltrip and Gordon. Thomas also held sole posession of the Winston Cup circuit lead in poles three years in a row (1952-54), a feat exceeded only by Pearson and matched by Waltrip.

Thomas also was the first driver to win three consecutive races, earn four poles in a row, and capture four straight dirt poles, a record he shares with Tim Flock. Thomas also posted the first three three-race winning streaks on dirt.

Perhaps the most remarkable nugget on Thomas's resume, however, is that he was the first driver to win four consecutive superspeedway races, sweeping the two on the schedule in 1954 and again in '55. That record of four consecutive superspeedway victories was never bettered until 1998, when Gordon captured five in succession. In an era of few superspeedway races and only one classic, Thomas became the first to post back-to-back classic and 500-mile victories when he won the Southern 500 at Darlington, S.C., in both 1954 and '55.

At age 33, Thomas already had won two Winston Cup titles and held an 8,514-8,268 lead over Baker in the 1956 points chase with four races remaining. But slightly past the midway point of the 53rd event on the 56-race schedule, a 100-miler at the Cleveland County Fairgrounds in Shelby, N.C., on October 23, Thomas suffered serious head injuries and left the track unconscious and in critical condition.

Thomas returned to action in the Raleigh 250 in North Carolina's capital city on Independence Day in 1957. But he drove in only one more race during that 1957 season and another in 1962 and never finished better than 14th after that wreck in Shelby.

1954 in Review

Thomas led the circuit in victories (12) and poles (8), but Lee Petty won seven times on his way to his first Winston Cup crown. Lee Petty also held a 613-595 edge over Thomas in the Performance Index.

Most Memorable Race

Thomas started from the pole in his Hudson and led the final 52 laps of the 100-mile race at Atlanta's one-mile Lakewood Speedway on March 21. But Thomas had to fight off the challenges of Baker, the runner-up, and third-place finisher Dick Rathmann, who each finished less than a car length behind.

Most Significant Wreck

Lou Figaro flipped the Ray Erickson-owned Hudson he was driving in the Wilkes 160 at North Wilkesboro, N.C., on October 24. Figaro died a day later to become the first driver who had won a Winston Cup race to die as a result of injuries suffered in a Winston Cup race.

Most Important Off-Track Development

Fireproof driving suits were introduced.

Records & Milestones

Al Keller's victory on a two-mile road course at Linden Airport in Linden, N.J., on June 13 was the first road race in Winston Cup history other than on the Beach & Road Course in Daytona Beach, Fla. More significantly, Keller's victory came behind the wheel of a Jaguar, marking the only triumph in Winston Cup history by a foreign automobile.... For the second year in a row and the third and final time in the first 51 years of the Winston Cup Series, no races were held on short tracks.

1954 at a Glance

Races:	37
Dirt:	33
Road:	2
Superspeedway:	2
Winners:	11
Pole Winners:	13
Tracks:	31
States:	13

1954 Performance Index Rankings

1. Lee Petty (613)
2. Herb Thomas (595)
3. Buck Baker (555)
4. Dick Rathmann (534)
5. Joe Eubanks (441)
6. Hershel McGriff (379)
7 Jim Paschal (235)
8. Ralph Liguori (221)
9. Jimmie Lewallen (207)
10. Bill Blair (191)
11. Al Keller (189)
12. Curtis Turner (184)
13. Dave Terrell (180)
14. Blackie Pitt (173)
15. Laird Bruner (156)
16. Gober Sosebee (151)
17. Marvin Panch (142)
18. John Soares (107)
19. Clyde Minter (97)
20. Elton Hildreth (93)
21. Eddie Skinner (90)
22. Arden Mounts (86)
23. Ray Duhigg (82)
24. Donald Thomas; Bob Welborn (80)
26. Fireball Roberts (78)
27. Speedy Thompson (77)
28. Jim Reed (70)
29. Joel Million (65)
30. Lloyd Dane (64)
31. Slick Smith (59)
32. Fred Dove; Walt Flinchum; Danny Letner (57)
35. Fonty Flock (54)
36. Erick Erickson (50)
37. Don Oldenberg (49)
38. Charlie Cregar (48)
39. Ben Gregory (47)
40. Jim Clark; Johnny Patterson (45)
42. Tim Flock; Emory Lewis; Bill Widenhouse (44)
45. Eddie Riker (41)
46. Russ Hepler (39)
47. Ted Chamberlain (38)
48. Tommie Elliott; Bill Irvin; Gwyn Staley (37)
51. Allen Adkins (35)
52. Harvey Eakin; Lou Figaro; Elmo Langley (33)
55. Gene Comstock; Ken Fisher (32)
57. Dink Widenhouse (31)
58. Jack Smith (30)
59. Tony Nelson; Clyde Palmer (29)
61. Parks Surrat (28)
62. Bob Grossman; Joe Valente (26)
64. Jack Clarke; Jim Graham; Harry LaVois (25)
67. Bill Claren (24)
68. Bill Amick; Bob Havenmann; Virgil Stockton (23)
71. Whitey Brainerd; Junior Johnson; Chuck Meekins; Bill Smith; Andy Winfree (22)
76. John McGinley; Ted Rambo (21)
78. George Clark; Stan Kross (20)
80. Robert Caswell; Charles Pemberton; Don White (19)
83. Earl Beer; Jim Cook; C.H. Dingler; Otis Martin (18)
87. Elbert Allen; Phillips Bell; Woody Brown; Floyd Curtis; Bud Harless (17)
92. Herschel Buchanan; Byron King; Paul Pettit; Tom Rivers; George Seeger (16)
97. Jack Conley; Chuck Hansen; Sam Hawks; Pop McGinnis; Cotton Owens; Bill West (15)
103. Perk Brown; Chuck Garrett; Joe Kilgore; Joe Weatherly (14)
107. John Dodd Jr.; Ed Samples (13)
109. John Dodd; Jim Heath; Charlie Mincey; Van Van Wey (12)
113. Bill Bade; Fred Cole; Ronnie Kohler; Gary Mathieson; Billy Minter; Tommy Moon; Bill Moore; Dean Pelton (11)
121. Tex Brooks; Bobby Courtwright; Clare Lawicki; Al Metz; John W. Smith; Bill Tuten; Art Watts (10)
128. Bob Flock; Chuck Neale; Eddie Pagan; Hal Ruyle; Dick Sanford; Bill Stammer; Fred Starr; Buster Whaley (9)
136. Jack Cumiford; Wimpy Ervin; Rick Henderson; Mel Krueger; Roland LaRue; Cliff Roberts; Sam Smith; Frank Stutts; Don Welch (8)
145. Bud Bennett; Mike Brown; Charles Hardiman; Hooker Hood; Ken Reeder; Hassell Reid; Bob Tyrell; Dick Vermillion; Jerry Wimbish (7)
154. Allan Clarke; Art Dugan; Bill Galdarisi; Elmer Musclow; Ed Normi; Hank Russ; Ken Taylor; Eddie Van Horn; Al Watkins (6)
163. Andy Biddle; Mason Bright; Bud Diamond; Tom Drake; Gene Roberts; Frank Ropp; Frank Smith II; Billy Vee (5)
171. Jimmy Ayers; Al Bolinger; Matt Gowan; Dick Jennette; Reds Kagle; H.R. Kahl; Sam Pearson; Bob Schwingle; Eli Vukovich (4)
180. Bill Barker; Dick Carter; Ralph Dutton; Jim Ewing; Ned Jarrett; Bub King; Ken Kiser; Marian Pagan; Ted Wright (3)
189. Fred Bince; Joe Bossard; Richard Brownlee; Bill Chevalier; Danny Curley; John Erickson; Al Neves; Bill O'Dell; George Parrish; Paul Phipps; Wallace Simpson (2)
200. George Cole; Bo Fields; Marshall Harless; John Kieper; Ken Pace; Peck Peckham; Johnny Roberts; Bucky Sager; Gifford Wood (1)

1954 Events

Palm Beach Speedway/.5-mile dirt/100 miles
Herb Thomas (Hudson)/Dick Rathmann (Hudson)

Beach & Road Course/4.1-mile road/160 miles
Lee Petty (Chrysler)/Lee Petty (Chrysler)

Speedway Park/.5-mile dirt/100 miles
Herb Thomas (Hudson)/Curtis Turner (Oldsmobile)

Lakewood Speedway/1-mile dirt/100 miles
Herb Thomas (Hudson)/Herb Thomas (Hudson)

Oglethorpe Speedway/.5-mile dirt/100 miles
Al Keller (Hudson)/Herb Thomas (Hudson)

Oakland Stadium/.5-mile dirt/125 miles
Dick Rathmann (Hudson)/Hershel McGriff (Oldsmobile)

Wilkes County 160; N. Wilkesboro Speedway/.625-m dirt/100 m
Dick Rathmann (Hudson)/Gober Sosebee (Oldsmobile)

Orange Speedway/1-mile dirt/100 miles
Herb Thomas (Hudson)/Buck Baker (Oldsmobile)

Central City Speedway/.5-mile dirt/100 miles
Gober Sosebee (Oldsmobile)/Dick Rathmann (Hudson)

Langhorne Speedway/1-mile dirt/150 miles
Herb Thomas (Hudson)/Lee Petty (Chrysler)

Wilson Speedway/.5-mile dirt/100 miles
Buck Baker (Oldsmobile)/Jim Paschal (Oldsmobile)

Martinsville Speedway/.5-mile dirt/100 miles
Jim Paschal (Oldsmobile)

Sharon Speedway/.5-mile dirt/100 miles
Lee Petty (Chrysler)/Dick Rathmann (Hudson)

Raleigh 250; Raleigh Speedway/1-mile/250 miles
Herb Thomas (Hudson)/Herb Thomas (Hudson)

Charlotte Speedway/.75-mile dirt/100 miles
Buck Baker (Oldsmobile)/Al Keller (Hudson)

Carrell Speedway/.5-mile dirt/250 miles
John Soares (Dodge)/Danny Letner (Hudson)

Columbia Speedway/.5-mile dirt/100 miles
Curtis Turner (Oldsmobile)/Buck Baker (Oldsmobile)

Linden Airport/2-mile road/100 miles
Al Keller (Jaguar)/Buck Baker (Oldsmobile)

Hickory Speedway/.4-mile dirt/80 miles
Herb Thomas (Hudson)/Herb Thomas (Hudson)

Monroe County Fairgrounds/.5-mile dirt/100 miles
Lee Petty (Chrysler)/Herb Thomas (Hudson)

Williams Grove Speedway/.5-mile dirt/100 miles
Herb Thomas (Hudson)/Dick Rathmann (Hudson)

Piedmont Interstate Fairgrounds/.5-mile dirt/100 miles
Herb Thomas (Hudson)/Hershel McGriff (Oldsmobile)

Asheville-Weaverville Speedway/.5-mile dirt/100 miles
Herb Thomas (Hudson)/Herb Thomas (Hudson)

Santa Fe Speedway/.5-mile dirt/100 miles
Dick Rathmann (Hudson)/Buck Baker (Oldsmobile)

Grand River Speedrome/.5-mile dirt/100 miles
Lee Petty (Chrysler)/Herb Thomas (Hudson)

Morristown Speedway/.5-mile dirt/100 miles
Buck Baker (Oldsmobile)/Buck Baker (Oldsmobile)

Oakland Stadium/.5-mile dirt/150 miles
Danny Letner (Hudson)/Marvin Panch (Dodge)

Southern States Fairgrounds/.5-mile dirt/100 miles
Lee Petty (Chrysler)/Buck Baker (Oldsmobile)

Bay Meadows Speedway/1-mile dirt/250 miles
Hershel McGriff (Oldsmobile)/Hershel McGriff (Oldsmobile)

Corbin Speedway/.5-mile dirt/100 miles
Lee Petty (Chrysler)/Jim Paschal (Oldsmobile)

Southern 500; Darlington Raceway/1.375-mile/500 miles
Herb Thomas (Hudson)/Buck Baker (Oldsmobile)

Central City Speedway/.5-mile dirt/100 miles
Hershel McGriff (Oldsmobile)/Tim Flock (Oldsmobile)

Southern States Fairgrounds/.5-mile dirt/100 miles
Hershel McGriff (Oldsmobile)/Hershel McGriff (Oldsmobile)

Langhorne Speedway/1-mile dirt/250 miles
Herb Thomas (Hudson)/Herb Thomas (Hudson)

Mid-South 250; Memphis-Arkansas Speedway/1.5-mile dirt/250m
Buck Baker (Oldsmobile)/Junior Johnson (Cadillac)

Martinsville Speedway/.5-mile dirt/100 miles
Lee Petty (Chrysler)/Lee Petty (Chrysler)

Wilkes 160; North Wilkesboro Speedway/.625-m dirt/100 miles
Hershel McGriff (Oldsmobile)/Hershel McGriff (Oldsmobile)

Victories
1. Herb Thomas (12)
2. Lee Petty (7)
3. Buck Baker; Hershel McGriff (4)
5. Dick Rathmann (3)
6. Al Keller (2)
7. Danny Letner; Jim Paschal; John Soares; Gober Sosebee; Curtis Turner (1)

Poles
1. Herb Thomas (8)
2. Buck Baker (7)
3. Hershel McGriff (5)
4. Dick Rathmann (4)
5. Lee Petty (3)
6. Jim Paschal (2)
7. Tim Flock; Junior Johnson; Al Keller; Danny Letner; Marvin Panch; Gober Sosebee; Curtis Turner (1)

Victories
1. Hudson (17)
2. Oldsmobile (11)
3. Chrysler (7)
4. Dodge; Jaguar (1)

Poles
1. Oldsmobile (17)
2. Hudson (14)
3. Chrysler (3)
4. Cadillac; Dodge (1)

1955
The 'Fabulous Flock Family'

If someone merely glanced at the results of the first eight years of Winston Cup competition, he or she quickly would conclude that the dominant driver of the era was the fellow who posted 62 victories and earned 74 poles.

A closer look at the name connected with those spectacular statistics, however, would reveal that the Flock who performed those feats was actually a three-headed brother combination rightfully known as the "Fabulous Flock Family."

Tim, youngest of the 10 Flock children, captured 39 races and 38 poles, including 18 of each in 1955. Fonty earned 19 victories and 33 poles, while Bob contributed four victories and three poles. The brothers weren't the only members of the family who raced, however. Ethel Mobley, their sister, didn't share her brothers' success. She earned a very modest Performance Index rating of 19 for her career, but only two women in history have recorded a higher rating.

The Flocks honed their driving skills by hauling moonshine around the Georgia mountains for their uncle, Peachtree Williams of Atlanta, one of the city's most prominent bootleggers.

Tim contended that the family's competitive spirit and athletic ability was genetic. "Our father, Carl Lee, was a daredevil," Tim recalled not long before his death in 1998, "and I'm sure we inherited being adventuresome from him. He was great at doing tricks on bicycles, and he walked tightropes. He had an incredible sense of balance. I think we got those genes from him, and they helped make us good race drivers."

The Flock brothers made an immediate impact on NASCAR. Fonty won a season-high 15 races and barely lost the 1948 modified title—and the accompanying $1,250 bonus—to Red Byron. Fonty did capture the modified crown in 1949, as well as managing a fourth-place finish in the Winston Cup Performance Index. All three brothers finished in the top seven in the Performance Index in 1949, and Bob led the circuit in poles and tied Byron for the lead in victories.

Bob, the oldest of the racing Flock brothers, didn't post the impressive victory totals of his younger brothers, perhaps because of a broken neck suffered in the 1951 season finale at Mobile, Ala. That injury sidelined him until August 17, 1952, when he returned in storybook fashion by winning a 100-mile race at Asheville-Weaverville Speedway in the North Carolina mountains. Despite that stirring comeback, he never won again and rarely competed thereafter.

Fonty, who usually wore Bermuda shorts in competition, finished among the top five in the Performance Index four times in the first five years of Winston Cup racing. He led the circuit in victories (8) and poles (13) in 1951 and had the highest Performance Index, although he lost the championship to Herb Thomas. Fonty's career ended at age 36 in the 1957 Southern 500 at Darlington, S.C. Paul Goldsmith's car ran into Flock's machine, which had stalled on the track. When Billy Myers's car also slammed into Fonty's stalled vehicle, Myers was killed and Fonty suffered career-ending injuries.

Tim posted seven victories in 1951 and finished second to Fonty in the Performance Index. He then won eight races on his way to the Winston Cup title in 1952, a season in which a monkey named Jocko Flocko accompanied him during eight races. Tim's back-to-back seasons with at least seven victories on dirt are bettered only by Thomas.

Only Richard Petty ever won more races in a season than Tim's 18 in 1955, and Tim's record of 18 poles that season endured for 14 years. The youngest Flock captured 10 races from the pole that season, a remarkable record that lasted until 1967. Tim's 16 victories and 15 poles on dirt in 1955 are single-season records.

At one point during the 1955 season, the Flocks combined to win nine consecutive poles, seven by Tim and two by Fonty, with Tim winning four races and Fonty one during that stretch.

Tim began the 1956 campaign in the same magnificent fashion. He won the season opener at Hickory, N.C., then added a second consecutive victory from the pole at the Beach & Road Course in Daytona Beach, Fla., the same venue in which he'd quit the sport in 1954 when he was disqualified after an apparent victory. But Tim abruptly decided to quit driving a Chrysler for Carl Kiekhaefer, then the sport's premier owner, after winning the Wilkes County 160 at North Wilkesboro, N.C. He later won at Road America in Elkhart Lake, Wis., to become the first driver to win on road courses twice in one year. Tim finished in the top seven in the Performance Index for the seventh time in eight years, but that triumph at Road America was his final victory.

Tim competed sporadically until his career ended in 1961 at age 37, when he was banned from NASCAR for life for his role in attempting to help Curtis Turner organize the drivers as the Federation of Professional Athletes.

1955 in Review

Few drivers have been more dominant than Tim Flock was in 1955, when he joined Thomas as a two-time Winston Cup champion. Tim also joined Thomas as the second champion to lead the circuit in victories, poles, and Performance Index rating. His 18 victories were three times as many as his nearest competitor, Lee Petty, and his 18 poles were triple those of the runner-up in that category, his brother Fonty. Tim's Performance Index rating of 771—the highest ever posted at that point—easily outdistanced Buck Baker, who finished second with a 656 rating.

Most Significant Wreck

Thomas suffered a broken leg and a concussion, among other injuries, in a wreck at Charlotte Speedway on May 1.

Most Memorable Race

In his third race back behind the wheel of his Buick, Thomas returned to victory lane on August 20 in a 100-miler at Raleigh, capturing the first superspeedway event ever held at night.

Most Important Off-Track Development

The American Automobile Association—now more famous for the emergency towing services and hotel discounts it offers its members—had sanctioned Indy-car racing, including the Indianapolis 500, since 1909. When AAA withdrew its involvement in auto racing in August, NASCAR's visibility and clout as a sanctioning body was enhanced. "There is serious question that racing contributes in a material way to better cars or better parts of cars," said Andrew J. Sordoni, president of AAA.

Records & Milestones

Although Chryslers dominated the season, setting new records of 27 victories and 27 poles, the 1955 campaign was one of only two in history (along with 1951) in which seven makes of automobiles visited victory lane. In addition to Chrysler, the victorious manufacturers were Oldsmobile, Buick, Chevrolet, Ford, Dodge, and Hudson. . . . Chevrolet got its first victory when Fonty Flock won at Columbia, S.C., on March 26. . . . Baker's victory in the Wilkes County 160 at North Wilkesboro on April 3 was the first for Buick.

1955 at a Glance

Races:	45
Dirt:	39
Road:	1
Short Track:	2
Superspeedway:	3
Winners:	10
Pole Winners:	14
Tracks:	35
States:	13

Following page: Tim Flock, the youngest brother among the three Flocks who captured Winston Cup victories, counted 16 wins and 15 poles on dirt tracks—both single-season records—among the 18 triumphs and 18 poles he earned in 1955. Although the race cars of Flock's era weren't as aerodynamically advanced as those of today, applying a layer or two of tape to the front helped its resistance to the wind.

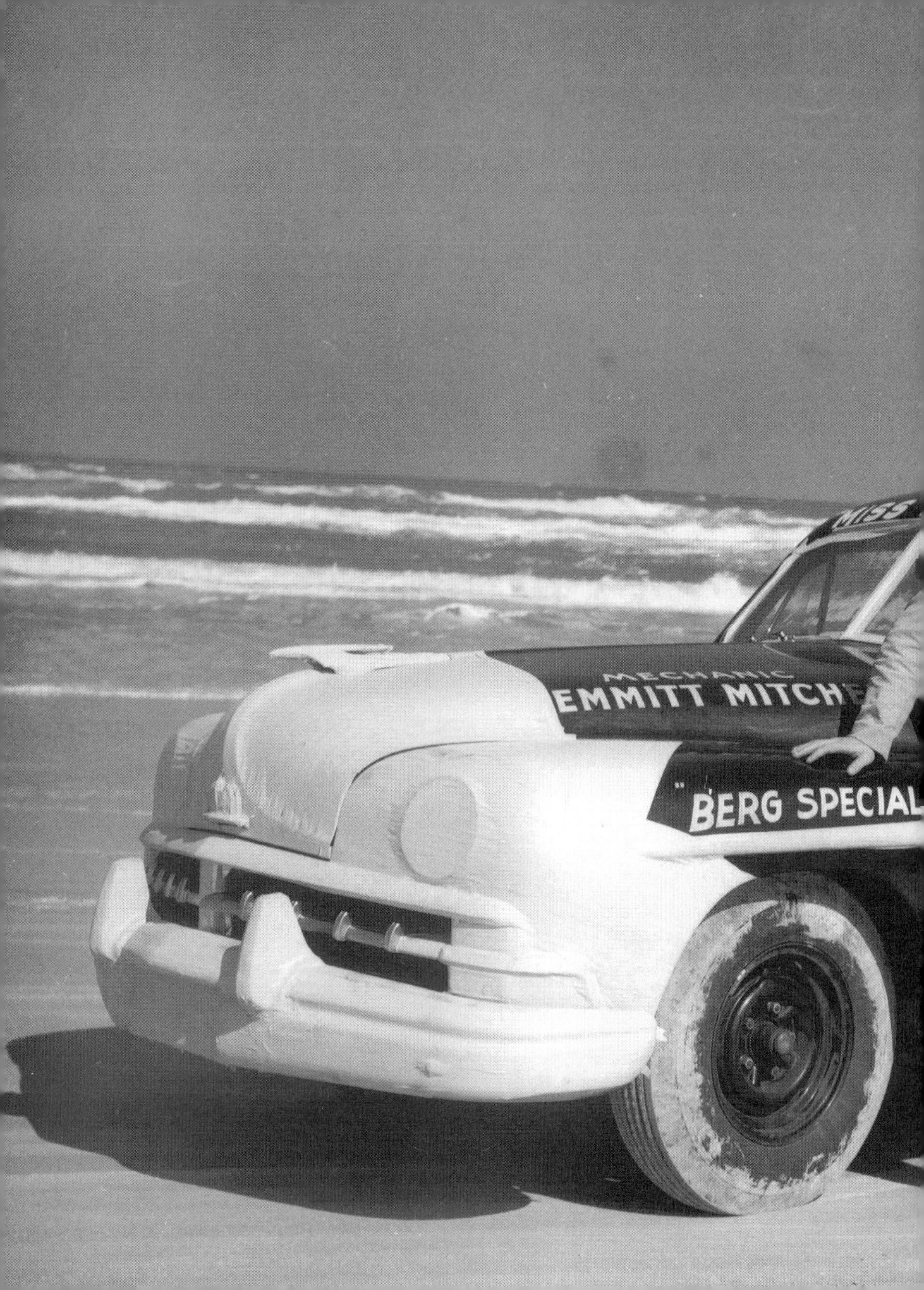
MISS
MECHANIC
EMMITT MITCHE
"BERG SPECIAL

1955 Performance Index Rankings

1. Tim Flock (771)
2. Buck Baker (656)
3. Lee Petty (581)
4. Bob Welborn (401)
5. Junior Johnson (385)
6. Jim Paschal (366)
7. Eddie Skinner (329)
8. Herb Thomas (324)
9. Jimmie Lewallen (311)
10. Fonty Flock (306)
11. Gwyn Staley (266)
12. Dave Terrell (228)
13. Dick Rathmann (183)
14. Gene Simpson (164)
15. Jimmy Massey (149)
16. Speedy Thompson (148)
17. Blackie Pitt (144)
18. Harvey Henderson (134)
19. Dink Widenhouse (132)
20. Marvin Panch (129)
21. Ralph Liguori (123)
22. John Dodd Jr. (119)
23. Jim Reed (117)
24. Joe Eubanks (112)
25. Joel Million (93)
26. Curtis Turner (91)
27. Arden Mounts (85)
28. Donald Thomas (76)
29. Gordon Smith (73)
30. Bill Widenhouse (72)
31. Billy Carden (71)
32. John Lindsay (70)
33. Banks Simpson (61)
34. Joe Weatherly (60)
35. Danny Letner (59)
36. Banjo Matthews (58)
37. Ed Cole; Don White (56)
39. Nace Mattingly (55)
40. Cotton Owens (54)
41. Jack Choquette; Mack Hanbury (53)
43. Carl Krueger (52)
44. Allen Adkins; Fred Dove; John McVitty (49)
47. Lou Spears (48)
48. George Parrish (45)
49. Gober Sosebee (43)
50. Lloyd Dane (41)
51. Larry Flynn (40)
52. Russ Truelove (39)
53. Richard Brownlee (36)
54. Ed Brown; Bud Graham; Bobby Waddell (35)
57. Bill Blair; Charles Dyer (34)
59. Bill Amick; Chuck Hansen (33)
61. Ted Cannady; Bill West (32)
63. Bob Havenmann; Bill Tanner (29)
65. Norm Nelson; Volney Schulze; Jack Smith (28)
68. Bill Bowman; Ray Duhigg; Buddy Shuman; Slick Smith; Jimmy Thompson (27)
73. Johnny Roberts (26)
74. Bill Champion; Don Oldenberg (25)
76. Ken Johns; Bill Stammer (24)
78. John Gouveia; Pappy Hough; Dick Joslin; John Kieper (23)
82. Henry Ford; Chuck Meekins (22)

84. Bob Dawson; Jim Ord; Tommy Ringstaff; Ernie Young (21)
88. Ken Fisher; Jack Radtke (20)
90. Herb Crawford; John Dodd; Fred Harb; Bud Harless; Bill Hyde; Bud Kutina; Al Watkins (19)
97. Bill Harrison; Elmo Langley; Clyde Palmer (18)
100. Lloyd Chick; Sherman Clark; Dutch Hoag; Ed Paskovich (17)
104. Marvin Copple; Bob Flock; Jim Murray; Ted Pitcher; Al Weber (16)
109. Axel Anderson; Emory Mahon; Bob Ruppert (15)
112. Ray Clark; Ben Gregory; Bill Gross; Johnny Mantz; Billy Myers; Cliff Richmond (14)
118. Jimmy Ayers; Perk Brown; Bo Fields; Willard Holt; Mel Larson; Dutch Munsinger; Julian Petty (13)
125. Dick Hallock; Clyde Minter; Johnny Mock; Ed Negre; Mario Rossi; Millard Wright (12)
131. Jim Roland; Bob Stanclift; Jim Wilson (11)
134. Bob Beck; Max Berrier; Ray Chaike; Marion Edwards; Tom Francis; Owen Loggins; Ed Normi; Ken Pace (10)
142. Bill Brown; Allan Clarke; Clarence DeZalia; Lloyd Moore; Willard Starney; Fred Steinbroner; Dick Zimmerman (9)
149. Sonny Black; George Combs; Jim Cramblitt; Joe Guide Jr.; Hooker Hood; Pee Wee Jones; Mike McGreevey; Bunk Moore; Bill Morton; FiFi Scott (8)
159. Jim Bossic; Doug Cox; Clayton Danello; Al Hager; Elton Hildreth; Gene Holcomb; Ron Hornaday; Pop McGinnis; Paul Pettit; Frank Powell (7)
169. Rick DeLewis; Frank Douglas; Bob Gould; Royce Haggerty; Morris Hill; John Lansaw; Chick Norris; Leland Sewell (6)
177. Art McBurney (5)
178. Johnny Allen; Tony DeStafano; Harvey Eakin; Eddie Pagan; Jack Richardson; Dick Walters (4)
184. Herk Moak; Walt Regan; Woody Richmond (3)
187. John Capps; Bud Geiselman; Ken Goudermoat; Junie Gough; Boyce Hildreth; Herb Hill; Gene Rose; Jim Thompson (2)
195. Bob Coleman; Virgil Martin; Jim McLain; Roscoe Rann; Joe Roletto; Walt Schubert; John Soares (1)

1955 Events

Tri-City Speedway/.5-mile dirt/100 miles
Lee Petty (Chrysler)/Herb Thomas (Hudson)

Palm Beach Speedway/.5-mile dirt/100 miles
Herb Thomas (Hudson)/Dick Rathmann (Hudson)

Speedway Park/.5-mile dirt/100 miles
Lee Petty (Chrysler)/Dick Rathmann (Hudson)

Beach & Road Course/4.1-mile road/160 miles
Tim Flock (Chrysler)/Tim Flock (Chrysler)

Oglethorpe Speedway/.5-mile dirt/100 miles
Lee Petty (Chrysler)/Dick Rathmann (Hudson)

Columbia Speedway/.5-mile dirt/100 miles
Fonty Flock (Chevrolet)/Tim Flock (Chrysler)

Orange Speedway/1-mile dirt/100 miles
Jim Paschal (Oldsmobile)/Tim Flock (Chrysler)

Wilkes County 160; N. Wilkesboro Speedway/.625-m dirt/100 m
Buck Baker (Oldsmobile)/Dink Widenhouse (Oldsmobile)

Chisholm Speedway/.5-mile dirt/100 miles
Tim Flock (Chrysler)/Jim Paschal (Oldsmobile)

Langhorne Speedway/1-mile dirt/150 miles
Tim Flock (Chrysler)/Tim Flock (Chrysler)

Charlotte Speedway/.75-mile dirt/100 miles
Buck Baker (Buick)/Herb Thomas (Buick)

Hickory Speedway/.4-mile dirt/80 miles
Junior Johnson (Oldsmobile)/Tim Flock (Chrysler)

Arizona State Fairgrounds/1-mile dirt/100 miles
Tim Flock (Chrysler)/Bill Amick (Dodge)

Tucson Rodeo Grounds/.5-mile dirt/100 miles
Danny Letner (Oldsmobile)/Bill Amick (Dodge)

Martinsville Speedway/.5-mile dirt/100 miles
Tim Flock (Chrysler)/Jim Paschal (Oldsmobile)

Richmond 200; Atlantic Rural Fairgrounds/.5-mile dirt/100 m
Tim Flock (Chrysler)

State Fairgrounds/.5-mile dirt/100 miles
Junior Johnson (Oldsmobile)/Tim Flock (Chrysler)

Forsyth County Fairgrounds/.5-mile dirt/100 miles
Lee Petty (Chrysler); Fonty Flock (Chrysler)

Lincoln Speedway/.5-mile dirt/100 miles
Junior Johnson (Oldsmobile)/Junior Johnson (Oldsmobile)

Monroe County Fairgrounds/.5-mile dirt/100 miles
Tim Flock (Chrysler)/Buck Baker (Chrysler)

Fonda Speedway/.5-mile dirt/100 miles
Junior Johnson (Oldsmobile)/Fonty Flock (Chrysler)

Airborne Speedway/.5-mile dirt/100 miles
Lee Petty (Chrysler)/Lee Petty (Chrysler)

Southern States Fairgrounds/.5-mile dirt/100 miles
Tim Flock (Chrysler)/Tim Flock (Chrysler)

Piedmont Interstate Fairgrounds/.5-mile dirt/100 miles
Tim Flock (Chrysler)/Tim Flock (Chrysler)

Columbia Speedway/.5-mile dirt/100 miles
Jim Paschal (Oldsmobile)/Jimmie Lewellan (Oldsmobile)

Asheville-Weaverville Speedway/.5-mile dirt/100 miles
Tim Flock (Chrysler)/Tim Flock (Chrysler)

Morristown Speedway/.5-mile dirt/100 miles
Tim Flock (Chrysler)/Tim Flock (Chrysler)

Altamont-Schnectady Fairgrounds/.5-mile dirt/100 miles
Junior Johnson (Oldsmobile)/Tim Flock (Chrysler)

New York State Fairgrounds./1-mile dirt/100 miles
Tim Flock (Chrysler)/Tim Flock (Chrysler)

Bay Meadows Speedway/1-mile dirt/250 miles
Tim Flock (Chrysler)/Fonty Flock (Chrysler)

Southern States Fairgrounds/.5-mile dirt/100 miles
Jim Paschal (Oldsmobile)/Tim Flock (Chrysler)

Forsyth County Fairgrounds/.5-mile dirt/100 miles
Lee Petty (Dodge)/Tim Flock (Chrysler)

Mid-South 250; Memphis-Arkansas Speedway/1.5-mile dirt/250m
Fonty Flock (Chrysler)/Fonty Flock (Chrysler)

Raleigh Speedway/1-mile/100 miles
Herb Thomas (Buick)/Tim Flock (Chrysler)

Southern 500; Darlington Raceway/1.375-mile/500 miles
Herb Thomas (Chevrolet)/Fireball Roberts (Buick)

Montgomery Speedway/.5-mile/100 miles
Tim Flock (Chrysler)/Tim Flock (Chrysler)

Langhorne Speedway/1-mile dirt/250 miles
Tim Flock (Chrysler)/Tim Flock (Chrysler)

Raleigh Speedway/1-mile/100 miles
Fonty Flock (Chrysler)/Fonty Flock (Chrysler)

Greenville-Pickens Speedway/.5-mile dirt/100 miles
Tim Flock (Chrysler)/Bob Welborn (Chevrolet)

Memphis-Arkansas Speedway/1.5-mile dirt/300 miles
Speedy Thompson (Ford)/Fonty Flock (Chrysler)

Columbia Speedway/.5-mile dirt/100 miles
Tim Flock (Chrysler)/Junior Johnson (Oldsmobile)

Martinsville Speedway/.5-mile/100 miles
Speedy Thompson (Chrysler)

Las Vegas Park Speedway/1-mile dirt/150 miles
Norm Nelson (Chrysler)/Norm Nelson (Chrysler)

Wilkes 160; North Wilkesboro Speedway/.625-m dirt/100 miles
Buck Baker (Ford)/Buck Baker (Ford)

Orange Speedway/1-mile dirt/100 miles
Tim Flock (Chrysler)/Tim Flock (Chrysler)

Victories

1. Tim Flock (18)
2. Lee Petty (6)
3. Junior Johnson (5)
4. Buck Baker; Fonty Flock; Jim Paschal; Herb Thomas (3)
8. Speedy Thompson (2)
9. Danny Letner; Norm Nelson (1)

Poles

1. Tim Flock (18)
2. Fonty Flock (6)
3. Dick Rathmann (3)
4. Bill Amick; Buck Baker; Junior Johnson; Jim Paschal; Herb Thomas (2)
9. Jimmie Lewallen; Norm Nelson; Lee Petty; Fireball Roberts; Bob Welborn; Dink Widenhouse (1)

Victories

1. Chrysler (27)
2. Oldsmobile (10)
3. Buick; Chevrolet; Ford (2)
6. Dodge; Hudson (1)

Poles

1. Chrysler (27)
2. Oldsmobile (6)
3. Hudson (4)
4. Buick; Dodge (2)
6. Chevrolet; Ford (1)

1956
Eight Car Owners Have Held Keys To Success

Although the principal subject of this treatise is the achievements of stock-car drivers, let's face it: They couldn't accomplish much without a car owner who could build and refine an automobile—or hire a crew to prepare a machine—better than the competition.

Eight such owners dominated Winston Cup racing in its first 51 years, beginning with Carl Kiekhaefer's magnificent two-year reign in 1955 and 1956. Kiekhaefer and those other seven car owners—Petty Enterprises, Bud Moore, Holman-Moody, the Wood brothers, Junior Johnson, Richard Childress, and Rick Hendrick—have combined to win 874 races (46.29 percent) and 32 of 51 championships. The only other car owner to win more than one championship was Herb Thomas, who captured the 1951 and '53 crowns in his Hudson Hornets.

There have been periods in Winston Cup history when a handful of those eight teams were virtually unbeatable. "At one time, if something happened to No. 11 (owned by Johnson) and No. 43 (Petty Enterprises), we knew we were home free," Leonard Wood recalled more than a decade after the No. 21 car he and his brother, Glen, fielded was no longer one of the dominant entries.

Further magnifying the importance of those eight car owners is that during the first 51 years of Winston Cup racing, 30 of the 41 drivers who won 13 or more races claimed at least one victory as an employee of one of those eight.

After his retirement, Cale Yarborough was quick to note the importance of earning a job with one of those eight. "The Wood brothers set my career on fire," he said.

The first of those eight to make a lasting impact did so in a mere two seasons. Despite his brief time on stock-car racing's biggest stage, Kiekhaefer's automobiles captured 52 races—out of 101 contested in 1955 and 1956—and both Winston Cup championships.

Tim Flock was the most successful driver behind the wheel of Kiekhaefer's automobiles, winning 18 races and the 1955 Winston Cup title and garnering three more victories before he quit the team in 1956. Buck Baker captured 14 races and the 1956 Winston Cup title for Kiekhaefer, and Speedy Thompson, Fonty Flock, Jack Smith, Norm Nelson, and Thomas also won races in Kiekhaefer's white Chryslers.

Kiekhaefer, a Mercury Outboard motors dealer in Wisconsin, entered the sport as an advertising vehicle. Obviously, he figured the best way to advertise his product was to have his cars toasted in victory lane.

Kiekhaefer hired meteorologists, had studies done of soil samples from the dirt tracks that were so prevalent in that era, and cloistered his drivers and crew members in the same motel, along with their wives—who were segregated to a different wing or floor—once they had arrived at the sites of races.

Baker's victory at Lakewood Speedway in Atlanta on March 25, 1956, began the most incredible streak by one team the sport has known. Seven more triumphs by Baker, four by Thompson, one by Tim Flock, and three by Thomas, culminating with the latter's victory at Merced, Calif., on June 3, gave Kiekhaefer cars a record 16 consecutive victories.

Ford and Chevrolet established factory teams to compete with Kiekhaefer's Chryslers, but that wasn't the impetus for his decision to leave the sport after two years. When his drivers began entering victory lane accompanied by a chorus of boos, Kiekhaefer decided that perhaps sales of his outboard motors would suffer, so he said goodbye to the sport forever.

The most successful car owner in history is unquestionably Petty Enterprises, with 270 victories and 10 championships. Patriarch Lee Petty earned 54 of those victories and three titles, and his son, Richard, captured 198 wins and seven championships for the family operation. Jim Paschal, Buddy Baker, Pete Hamilton, Bobby Hamilton, Marvin Panch, and John Andretti also won races for Petty Enterprises.

Fred Lorenzen (right) captured 25 of his 26 Winston Cup victories in the employ of Holman-Moody. Ralph Moody (left) had a brief but successful stint as a driver—five victories and five poles during the 1956 and '57 seasons—before teaming with John Holman to form the legendary Ford team.

Cars owned by Junior Johnson, who for several years shared the ownership of his team with former Charlotte Motor Speedway General Manager Richard Howard, captured 140 races and six titles, three each by Yarborough and Darrell Waltrip, who won 55 and 43 races, respectively, behind the wheel of Johnson's cars. Lee Roy Yarbrough, Bobby Allison, Bill Elliott, Terry Labonte, Geoff Bodine, Neil Bonnett, Jimmy Spencer, Darel Dieringer, Charlie Glotzbach, and Earl Ross also won for Johnson.

The partnership of John Holman and Ralph Moody posted 93 victories and two Winston Cup titles, both captured by David Pearson, whose 30 victories were the most for that Charlotte-based Ford outfit. Fred Lorenzen earned superstar status by winning 25 races for Holman-Moody, while Dick Hutcherson, Fireball Roberts, Joe Weatherly, Nelson Stacy, Curtis Turner, Dan Gurney, Mario Andretti, and Allison also won for Holman-Moody.

Moore's cars won 63 races, led by Joe Weatherly's 20. Weatherly won his first Winston Cup title driving for Moore in 1962 and, although he was employed by a variety of car owners in winning his second a year later, he drove in more races for Moore than any other. Ricky Rudd, Buddy Baker, Billy Wade, Dale Earnhardt, Benny Parsons, Morgan Shepherd, Allison, Bodine, and Dieringer also drove Moore-owned Fords and Mercurys into victory lane.

Hendrick Motorsports captured a record four consecutive titles from 1995-98, three by Jeff Gordon and one by Labonte. Although Gordon's 49 victories have led the way for Hendrick's Chevrolets, Tim Richmond, Ken Schrader, Labonte, Waltrip, Bodine, and Rudd have contributed 44 more.

Childress's Chevrolets have won six titles, all by Earnhardt, who also has 65 of the team's 67 victories, with Rudd garnering the other two.

Only the Wood brothers of Stuart, Va., rank among the top eight car owners in victories without a Winston Cup title to their credit. During the glory years—from the mid-'60s through the '70s—the Woods skipped numerous races and didn't focus on that goal. Pearson claimed 43 of the 96 triumphs for the Wood brothers, making him the only driver with the most victories for two of the eight most successful car owners in the

sport's history. No other team in history had more different drivers capture races than the Wood brothers, a "Who's Who" that includes Glen Wood himself, Tiny Lund, A.J. Foyt, Parnelli Jones, Donnie Allison, Kyle Petty, Dale Jarrett, Gurney, Turner, Thompson, Panch, Yarborough, Bonnett, Shepherd, and Buddy Baker, who, along with Bobby Allison and Rudd, won races for three of the "Big Eight."

"I'll tell you why the Wood brothers win," Pearson once said during his glory days behind the wheel of their Purolator-sponsored Mercury. "They put their heart in it. When it comes five o'clock, they're not thinking about going to get a beer. They think racing 24 hours a day."

1956 in Review

The season clearly belonged to Winston Cup champion Buck Baker, who led the circuit with 14 victories and 12 poles and held a comfortable 822-703 margin over Thomas in the Performance Index.

Most Memorable Race

Buck Baker outdueled Thompson by less than three feet, with Lee Petty just a couple of car lengths in arrears, on May 13 at Orange Speedway in Hillsboro, N.C.

Most Significant Wreck

Thomas's career all but ended when he hit the wall at the Cleveland County Fairgrounds in Shelby, N.C., on October 23 and left the track unconscious and in critical condition with a variety of injuries.

Most Important Off-Track Development

Tim Flock decided to leave Kiekhaefer's team after earning his 21st victory in 15 months on the job on April 8 at North Wilkesboro, N.C. Flock, who was just shy of his 32nd birthday, earned only one of his 39 victories afterward.

Records & Milestones

The Winston Cup Series visited 17 states, a record that was not equaled until 1998. . . . Forty races were held on dirt, the most in one season. . . . Races were held on 40 tracks, equaling the most ever. Forty tracks also played host to Winston Cup races in 1958 and 1964. . . . Nineteen different drivers won races, setting a record later tied in

1958 and 1961. . . . Tim Flock's August 12 victory at Road America in Elkhart Lake, Wis., was the only race in Winston Cup history ever contested in a rainstorm.

Roberts's July 21 victory at Soldier Field in Chicago marked the only time in Winston Cup history that a race was held at the home of an active National Football League team. . . . Portland Speedway, a half-mile short track in Oregon, became the first facility to play host to four Winston Cup races in one year.

1956 at a Glance

Races:	56
Dirt:	40
Road:	3
Short Track:	11
Superspeedway:	2
Winners:	19
Pole Winners:	21
Tracks:	40
States:	17

1956 Performance Index Rankings

1. Buck Baker (822)
2. Herb Thomas (703)
3. Speedy Thompson (642)
4. Lee Petty (582)
5. Jim Paschal (529)
6. Billy Myers (470)
7. Fireball Roberts (443)
8. Ralph Moody (434)
9. Tim Flock (342)
10. Marvin Panch (284)
11. Rex White (282)
12. Gwyn Staley (274)
13. Johnny Allen (249)
14. Joe Eubanks (244)
15. Joe Weatherly (227)
16. Bill Amick (188)
17. Tiny Lund (179)
18. Lloyd Dane (167)
19. Paul Goldsmith (159)
20. Billy Carden (138)
21. Curtis Turner (134)
22. Jim Reed (132)
23. Jack Smith (128)
24. John Kieper (127)
25. Harold Hardesty (126)
26. Al Watkins (116)
27. Chuck Meekins (112)
28. Frank Mundy (110)
29. Eddie Pagan (109)
30. Clyde Palmer (103)
31. Blackie Pitt (100)
32. Harvey Henderson (98)
33. Bobby Keck (94)
34. Bill Champion; Bobby Johns (92)
36. Johnny Dodson (91)
37. Ed Cole (84)
38. Jimmy Massey (83)
39. Fonty Flock (74)
40. Bob Keefe (73)
41. Allen Adkins; Brownie King (72)
43. Gordon Haines (71)
44. Junior Johnson (67)
45. Cotton Owens (66)
46. Scotty Cain; Ed Negre (65)
48. Curley Barker; Dick Beaty; Bill Blair; Jim Blomgren (64)
52. Pat Kirkwood (63)
53. Royce Haggerty (59)
54. Pete Yow (58)
55. Ralph Liguori (51)
56. Dink Widenhouse (47)
57. Harold Beal (46)
58. Johnny Patterson (45)
59. Bill Hyde; Billy Rafter (44)
61. Al Keller (43)
62. Bob Welborn (42)
63. Erick Erickson; George Green; Jimmie Lewallen; Lou Sherman (41)
67. Art Watts (40)
68. Ken Milligan; Bunk Moore (39)
70. Bobby Myers (37)
71. Sherman Clark; Joe Bill McGraw (35)
73. Darvin Randahl (34)
74. Bob Ross (33)
75. Roz Howard; Charles Jackson; Mel Larson; Emanuel Zervakis (32)
79. Ray Chaike; Jim Cook; Bill Walker (31)
82. John Lindsay; Chuck Stevenson (30)
84. Jim Graham (28)
85. Doug Cox; Bob Flock; Parnelli Jones; Johnny Mantz; Bill Moore; George Seeger (27)
91. Elmo Langley (26)
92. Russ Truelove; Shorty York (25)
94. Bob Havenmann; Donald Thomas (24)
96. Danny Letner; Walt Schubert; Bill Widenhouse (23)
99. Ted Cannady; Bob Korf (22)
101. Fred Johnson; Bobby Waddell (21)
103. Wayne Fielden; Fred Frazier (20)
105. Guy Cork; Ralph Earnhardt; Jim Sills; Pete Stewart (19)
109. Sherman Utsman (18)
110. Carl Hammill; Nace Mattingly; Jack Radtke; Bob Ruppert; Jim Watkins (17)
115. Chester Barron; Bob Duell; Frank Jamison; Jim Pardue; Johnny Roberts; Bill West (16)
121. Rat Garner; Jack Goodwin II; John McVitty; Lennie Page; Gene Simpson; Ted Sweeney; Al White (15)
128. Carl Anderson; Chuck Blewitt; C.H. Dingler; Pete Diviney; Joe Prismo (14)
133. Gordon Campbell; Jim Donovan; Augie Howerton; Jim Rhoades; Jesse James Taylor; Dave Terrell; Ernie Young (13)
140. Bill Bowman; Jack Choquette; Joy Fair; Curley Hatfield; Benny Rakestraw; Eddie Skinner; Sam Speers; Bill Sullivan; Nolan Swift (12)
149. Roy Bentley; Reitzel Darner; John Dodd Jr.; Ansel Rakestraw; Richard Riley; Whitey Norman; Charlie Scott (11)
156. Dick Allwine; Bob Esposito; Herb Estes; Red Farmer; John Fite; Larry Flynn; Jake Hatcher; Hoss Kagle; Harold Kite; Charlie Mincey; Jerry Morese; Bill Stammer; Len Sutton; Bill Thurber (10)
170. Chuck Akerblade; Dick Blackwell; Vince Cougineri; Frank Edwards; Bud Graham; Ned Jarrett; Reds Kagle; Chuck Mahoney; Banjo Matthews; Ken Seibel; Bob Slensby; Joe Sykes; Ken Wagner; Jack Zink (9)
184. Benny DeRosier; Bill Massey; Peck Peckham; Chet Thompson; Hank Trice; Jack Tykarski; Chub Williams; Jim Wilson (8)

192. Sonny Black; Dick Burns; Freddy Fryar; Ken Johnson; Pee Wee Jones; Lucky Long; Chuck Mesler; Earl Moss (7)
200. Joe Guide Jr.; Don Hildreth; Fred Hunt; James Jones; Cecil Lassiter; Jess Nelson; Howard Phillippi; Don Porter (6)
208. Don Carr; Gene Goodman; Bob Anderson; Larry Marx; Don Oldenberg; Wilbur Rakestraw; Sal Tovella; Buzz Woodward; Millard Wright (5)
217. Bud Emra; Wally Gervais; Dick Getty; Fred Harb; Lyle Matlock; Bill Osborne; Bill Poor; Cy Spencer; Jack Williams; Doug Yates (4)
227. Bob Carroll; Bun Emery; Nick Lari; Fred Lorenzen; Joel Million (3)
232. Ray Baxter; Dick Denise; Clyde Mitchell; Jim Mundy; Larry Odo; Bill Parks; Andy Wilson (2)
239. Spook Crawford; Bud Geiselman; Jack D. McCoy; John Montgangelo; Al Pombo (1)

1956 Events

Hickory Speedway/.4-mile dirt/80 miles
Tim Flock (Chrysler)/Tim Flock (Chrysler)

Charlotte Speedway/.75-mile dirt/100 miles
Fonty Flock (Chrysler)/Fonty Flock (Chrysler)

Willow Springs Speedway/2.5-mile dirt road/200 miles
Chuck Stevenson (Ford)/Jim Reed (Chevrolet)

Palm Beach Speedway/.5-mile/100 miles
Herb Thomas (Chevrolet)/Fonty Flock (Chrysler)

Arizona State Fairgrounds/1-mile dirt/150 miles
Buck Baker (Chrysler)/Joe Weatherly (Ford)

Beach & Road Course/4.1-mile road/160 miles
Tim Flock (Chrysler)/Tim Flock (Chrysler)

Palm Beach Speedway/.5-mile/100 miles
Billy Myers (Mercury)/Buck Baker (Dodge)

Wilson Speedway/.5-mile dirt/100 miles
Herb Thomas (Chevrolet)/Herb Thomas (Chevrolet)

Lakewood Speedway/1-mile dirt/100 miles
Buck Baker (Chrysler)/Tim Flock (Chrysler)

Wilkes County 160; N. Wilkesboro Speedway/.625-m dirt/100 m
Tim Flock (Chrysler)/Junior Johnson (Pontiac)

Langhorne Speedway/1-mile dirt/150 miles
Buck Baker (Chrysler)/Buck Baker (Chrysler)

Richmond 200; Atlantic Rural Fairgrounds/.5-m dirt/100 miles
Buck Baker (Dodge)/Buck Baker (Dodge)

Columbia Speedway/.5-mile dirt/100 miles
Speedy Thompson (Dodge)/Buck Baker (Dodge)

Concord Speedway/.5-mile dirt/100 miles
Speedy Thompson (Chrysler)/Speedy Thompson (Chrysler)

Greenville-Pickens Speedway/.5-mile dirt/100 miles
Buck Baker (Dodge)/Rex White (Chevrolet)

Hickory Speedway/.4-mile dirt/80 miles
Speedy Thompson (Chrysler)/Speedy Thompson (Chrysler)

Orange Speedway/.9-mile dirt/90 miles
Buck Baker (Chrysler)/Buck Baker (Chrysler)

Virginia 500; Martinsville Speedway/.5-mile/250 miles
Buck Baker (Dodge)/Buck Baker (Dodge)

Lincoln Speedway/.5-mile dirt/100 miles
Buck Baker (Dodge)/Speedy Thompson (Dodge)

Charlotte Speedway/.75-mile dirt/100 miles
Speedy Thompson (Chrysler)/Speedy Thompson (Chrysler)

Portland Speedway/.5-mile/100 miles
Herb Thomas (Chrysler)/John Kieper (Oldsmobile)

New York State Fairgrounds/1-mile dirt/150 miles
Buck Baker (Chrysler)/Buck Baker (Chrysler)

Eureka Speedway/.625-mile dirt/125 miles
Herb Thomas (Chrysler)/John Kieper (Oldsmobile)

Merced Fairgrounds/.5-mile dirt/100 miles
Herb Thomas (Chrysler)/Herb Thomas (Chrysler)

Memphis-Arkansas Speedway/1.5-mile dirt/250 miles
Ralph Moody (Ford)/Buck Baker (Chrysler)

Southern States Fairgrounds/.5-mile dirt/100 miles
Speedy Thompson (Chrysler)/Fireball Roberts (Ford)

Monroe County Fairgrounds/.5-mile dirt/100 miles
Speedy Thompson (Chrysler)/Jim Paschal (Mercury)

Portland Speedway/.5-mile/100 miles
John Kieper (Oldsmobile)/Herb Thomas (Chrysler)

Asheville-Weaverville Speedway/.5-mile dirt/100 miles
Lee Petty (Dodge)/Fireball Roberts (Ford)

Raleigh 250; Raleigh Speedway/1-mile/250 miles
Fireball Roberts (Ford)/Lee Petty (Dodge)

Piedmont Interstate Fairgrounds/.5-mile dirt/100 miles
Lee Petty (Dodge)/Fireball Roberts (Ford)

California State Fairgrounds/1-mile dirt/100 miles
Lloyd Dane (Mercury)/Eddie Pagan (Ford)

Soldier Field/.5-mile/100 miles
Fireball Roberts (Ford)/Billy Myers (Mercury)

Cleveland County Fairgrounds/.5-mile dirt/100 miles
Speedy Thompson (Dodge)/Ralph Moody (Ford)

Montgomery Speedway/.5-mile/100 miles
Marvin Panch (Ford)/Marvin Panch (Ford)

Oklahoma State Fairgrounds/.5-mile dirt/100 miles
Jim Paschal (Mercury)/Speedy Thompson (Dodge)

Road America/4-mile road/252 miles
Tim Flock (Mercury)/Buck Baker (Dodge)

Old Bridge Stadium/.5-mile/100 miles
Ralph Moody (Ford)/Jim Reed (Chevrolet)

Bay Meadows Speedway/1-mile dirt/250 miles
Eddie Pagan (Ford)/Eddie Pagan (Ford)

Norfolk Speedway/.4-mile dirt/100 miles
Billy Myers (Mercury)/Ralph Moody (Ford)

Piedmont Interstate Fairgrounds/.5-mile dirt/100 miles
Ralph Moody (Ford)/Ralph Moody (Ford)

Coastal Speedway/.5-mile dirt/100 miles
Fireball Roberts (Ford)/Ralph Moody (Ford)

Portland Speedway/.5-mile/125 miles
Royce Haggerty (Dodge)/John Kieper (Oldsmobile)

Southern 500; Darlington Raceway/1.375-mile/500 miles
Curtis Turner (Ford)/Speedy Thompson (Chrysler)

Chisholm Speedway/.5-mile dirt/100 miles
Buck Baker (Chrysler)/Tim Flock (Ford)

Southern States Fairgrounds/.5-mile dirt/100 miles
Ralph Moody (Ford)/Joe Eubanks (Ford)

Langhorne Speedway/1-mile dirt/300 miles
Paul Goldsmith (Chevrolet)/Buck Baker (Chrysler)

Portland Speedway/.5-mile/125 miles
Lloyd Dane (Ford)/Royce Haggerty (Dodge)

Columbia Speedway/.5-mile dirt/100 miles
Buck Baker (Dodge)/Tim Flock (Ford)

Orange Speedway/.9-mile dirt/99 miles
Fireball Roberts (Ford)/Speedy Thompson (Chrysler)

Newport Speedway/.5-mile dirt/100 miles
Fireball Roberts (Ford)/Joe Eubanks (Ford)

Charlotte Speedway/.75-mile dirt/100 miles
Buck Baker (Chrysler)/Ralph Moody (Ford)

Cleveland County Fairgrounds/.5-mile dirt/100 miles
Buck Baker (Chrysler)/Doug Cox (Ford)

Old Dominion 400; Martinsville Speedway/.5-mile/200 miles
Jack Smith (Dodge)/Buck Baker (Chrysler)

Buddy Shuman 250; Hickory Speedway/.4-mile dirt/100 miles
Speedy Thompson (Chrysler)/Ralph Earnhardt (Ford)

Wilson Speedway/.5-mile dirt/100 miles
Buck Baker (Chrysler)/Buck Baker (Chrysler)

Victories

1. Buck Baker (14)
2. Speedy Thompson (8)
3. Fireball Roberts; Herb Thomas (5)
5. Tim Flock; Ralph Moody (4)
7. Lloyd Dane; Billy Myers; Lee Petty (2)
10. Fonty Flock; Paul Goldsmith; Royce Haggerty; John Kieper; Eddie Pagan; Marvin Panch; Jim Paschal; Jack Smith; Chuck Stevenson; Curtis Turner (1)

Poles

1. Buck Baker (12)
2. Speedy Thompson (7)
3. Tim Flock; Ralph Moody (5)
5. John Kieper; Fireball Roberts; Herb Thomas (3)
8. Joe Eubanks; Fonty Flock; Eddie Pagan; Jim Reed (2)
12. Doug Cox; Ralph Earnhardt; Royce Haggerty; Junior Johnson; Billy Myers; Marvin Panch; Jim Paschal; Lee Petty; Joe Weatherly; Rex White (1)

Victories

1. Chrysler (22)
2. Ford (14)
3. Dodge (11)
4. Mercury (5)
5. Chevrolet (3)
6. Oldsmobile (1)

Poles

1. Chrysler (19)
2. Ford (18)
3. Dodge (9)
4. Chevrolet (4)
5. Oldsmobile (3)
6. Mercury (2)
7. Pontiac (1)

1957
There's No Bucking Baker's Place in History

Buck Baker's 46 victories, 45 poles, and Winston Cup championships in 1956 and 1957 establish his place among Winston Cup racing's elite.

But perhaps Baker's greatest legacy is that he was the first driver to enjoy a lengthy career of sustained excellence.

Because Baker was 30 years old when he finished 11th in the first Winston Cup race ever held, on June 19, 1949, in Charlotte, where he had been employed as a city bus driver, it wasn't reasonable to expect that he'd become the first driver to record:

- 18 consecutive seasons with a Performance Index rating of 100 or better (1951-68);
- 15 consecutive seasons with a Performance Index rating of 200 or better (1953-67);
- 12 consecutive seasons with a Performance Index rating of 300 or better (1953-64);
- Six consecutive seasons with a Performance Index rating of 500 or better (1953-58);
- Four consecutive seasons with a Performance Index rating of 600 or better (1955-58);
- 18 consecutive seasons in the top 24 in the Performance Index (1950-67);
- 17 consecutive seasons in the top 21 in the Performance Index (1950-66);
- 15 consecutive seasons in the top 20 in the Performance Index (1950-64);

- 13 consecutive seasons in the top 13 in the Performance Index (1952-64);
- 10 consecutive years with at least one pole (1952-61);
- Nine consecutive years with multiple poles (1952-60);
- 10 consecutive years with at least one dirt pole (1952-61);
- A record nine consecutive years with multiple dirt poles (1952-60).

Despite those accomplishments, it would be a mistake to dismiss Baker's career merely as the first of extended consistency.

In 1956 and '57, Baker became the first driver to post back-to-back seasons of 700 or better in the Performance Index and the first to capture back-to-back Winston Cup championships. During those two seasons, he became one of only two champions in history to hold sole possession of the season titles in victories and poles and post the highest Performance Index in consecutive campaigns.

In both the 1956 and '57 campaigns, Baker captured at least eight victories on dirt, a string bettered only by Herb Thomas. And just four times in history were back-to-back seasons of at least five dirt poles recorded, with Baker earning half of those, once in 1953 and '54 and again in 1956 and '57. In 1956 and '57, Baker also became the second driver to post back-to-back double-figure victory campaigns.

Further, Baker finished in the top two in the Performance Index a record four consecutive seasons (1955-58), and his six consecutive seasons in the top three (1954-59) is equaled only by Richard Petty and Dale Earnhardt. In fact, Baker finished in the top five in the Performance Index eight seasons in a row (1953-60), a string surpassed only by Richard and Lee Petty.

Forty of Baker's victories came on dirt, which ranks him third in that category, and his 37 poles on that surface share the record. He also posted at least three dirt victories six years in a row (1953-58), a record. Baker also shares another record with Richard Petty: capturing at least one dirt victory from the pole in five consecutive seasons (1954-58).

Although most of Baker's crowning achievements came on dirt, he won the fabled Southern 500 at Darlington, S.C., on three occasions, in 1953, 1960, and 1964, when he earned the final victory of his Winston Cup career at age 45.

Buck Baker, the first driver to win back-to-back Winston Cup titles, finished in the top two in the Performance Index a record four consecutive seasons from 1955-58.

1957 in Review

After Carl Kiekhaefer, Baker's car owner when he captured the 1956 title in a Chrysler, left the sport, Baker began the 1957 campaign driving a Chevrolet for Hugh Babb. By the season's 23rd race, Baker was driving his own Chevrolet. But that didn't deter him from capturing his second straight Winston Cup title, rolling to a 767-644 margin over Marvin Panch for the Performance Index leadership, and leading the circuit in both victories (10) and poles (6). That marked the second year in a row that Baker had held sole possession of the lead in all four categories, an accomplishment achieved only once since.

Most Memorable Race

Speedy Thompson and Curtis Turner were both fined by NASCAR for their duel in the Buddy Shuman 250 at Hickory, N.C., on July 20. Thompson ran into Turner and suffered a damaged front end that forced him to the pits, but returned in time to retaliate, leaving Jack Smith to pick up the spoils with a 4.5-second victory over Lee Petty.

Most Significant Wreck

When Billy Myers drove a Bill Stroppe-owned Mercury through an 18-inch retaining wall and crashed into a board fence during the Virginia 500 at Martinsville on May 19, an eight-year-old boy who was standing in an area marked "off limits" to spectators died as a result of injuries he suffered.

Most Important Off-Track Development

The Automobile Manufacturers Association decided in June to withdraw factory support from the sport, largely as a result of Myers's wreck. The AMA stated that its mission was to "encourage owners and drivers to evaluate passenger cars in terms of useful power and ability to provide safe, reliable, and comfortable transportation, rather than in terms of capacity for speed."

Records & Milestones

For the first time in history, six drivers—Baker (10), Fireball Roberts (8), Panch (6), Paul Goldsmith (4), Lee Petty (4), and Smith (4)—captured four or more victories. The record was tied five times in the next eight years, but never broken. . . . A record eight drivers won at least three poles: Baker (6), Art Watts (5), Goldsmith (4), Panch (4), Roberts (4), Thompson (4), Tiny Lund (3), and Lee Petty

(3). . . . In addition to the aforementioned eight drivers with three or more poles, Bill Amick, Eddie Pagan, Gwyn Staley, and Smith won two apiece, making 1957 the only campaign with 12 multiple pole winners. . . . Five races were held on road courses, the most in one season. . . . Cotton Owens's victory on the Beach & Road Course at Daytona Beach, Fla., on February 17 was the first for Pontiac.

1957 At a Glance

Races:	53
Dirt:	38
Road:	5
Short Track:	8
Superspeedway:	2
Winners:	18
Pole Winners:	23
Tracks:	37
States:	12

1957 Performance Index Rankings

1. Buck Baker (767)
2. Marvin Panch (644)
3. Fireball Roberts (619)
4. Lee Petty (612)
5. Jack Smith (549)
6. Speedy Thompson (488)
7. Johnny Allen (437)
8. L.D. Austin (368)
9. Jim Paschal (342)
10. Paul Goldsmith (340)
11. Tiny Lund (339)
12. Brownie King (319)
13. Eddie Pagan (284)
14. Billy Myers (249)
15. Bill Amick (226)
16. Dick Beaty (219)
17. Lloyd Dane; Gwyn Staley (195)
19. Clarence DeZalia (188)
20. Joe Weatherly (169)
21. Cotton Owens (165)
22. Dick Getty (148)
23. Scotty Cain (145)
24. Curtis Turner (138)
25. George Green (125)
26. Frankie Schneider (120)
27. Ralph Moody (115)
28. Rex White (112)
29. George Seeger (106)
30. Whitey Norman (101)
31. Ken Rush (100)
32. Mel Larson (97)
33. Jim Reed (92)
34. Danny Graves (91)
35. Possum Jones (87)
36. Ralph Earnhardt (81)
37. Bob Welborn (80)

38. Huck Spaulding (79)
39. Don Porter (77)
40. Bobby Keck; Chuck Meekins (75)
42. Art Watts (74)
43. Glen Wood (73)
44. Marvin Porter (69)
45. Parnelli Jones (67)
46. Jimmie Lewallen (63)
47. Ed Negre (61)
48. Darel Dieringer; T.A. Toomes (59)
50. Bill Benson; Bud Emra; Eddie Gray; Bill Morton (58)
54. Billy Carden; Roy Tyner (57)
56. Johnny Mackison (53)
57. Bob Ross; Bill Walker (50)
59. Charlie Cregar (46)
60. Harold Beal; Jimmy Thompson (44)
62. Marshall Sargent (42)
63. Nace Mattingly; Norman McGriff (39)
65. Jim Blomgren; Larry Frank; Bob Rauscher (36)
68. Doug Cox; Jack D. McCoy (35)
70. Johnny Dodson; Jim Linke; Jimmy Massey (34)
73. Danny Letner; Peck Peckham (33)
75. Bill Champion; Lennie Page; Clyde Palmer (32)
78. Bill Bowman; Bob Keefe; Tom Pistone (30)
81. Chuck Hansen; Bobby Johns (29)
83. Johnny Beauchamp; Banjo Matthews; Mike McGreevey (28)
86. Jim Cook; Fonty Flock (27)
88. Lamoine Frey; Dick Walters (26)
90. John Findlay; Bill Lutz; Billy Rafter (24)
93. Allen Adkins; Fred Harb (23)
95. Dick Klank; Jack Marsh; Jack Oldenhage (22)
98. Al White (21)
99. Dick Joslin (20)
100. Bill Hidden; Jim Hurtubise (19)
102. Sherman Clark; Spook Crawford; Tim Flock; Howard Phillippi; Chuck Thompson (18)
107. Gene Blair; Dean Layfield; Phil Orr; Cliff Yiskis; Ernie Young (17)
112. Billy Cantrell; Don Oldenberg (16)
114. Ted Chamberlain; Duke DeBrizzi; Gene Long; Rod Perry; Bob Rose; Dave Terrell (15)
120. Royce Haggerty; Fred Knapp; Walt Mortz; Bob Osborne (14)
124. Ed Brown; Don Johns; Ken Marriott; George Norton; Ansel Rakestraw; Volney Schulze; Buzz Woodward (13)
131. Tommie Elliott; Joe Eubanks (12)
133. John Dodd; Harold Hardesty; Claude Holliday; Bill Jarlick; Lou Spears (11)
138. Reggie Ausmus; Ray Campbell; Jim Delaney; Harvey Eakin; George Fleming; Ron Hornaday; Elmo Langley; Clyde Mitchell; Bill Poor; Bud Vaughn (10)
148. R.L. Combs; Bob Duell; Ed Fiola; Bob Havenmann (9)
152. E.J. Brewer; Ed Cole; Wally Gore; Ed Jackson (8)
156. Harvey Henderson; Jake Jacobs; Barney Oldfield (7)
159. Bill Bade; Chuck Blewitt; Frank Jamison; Pee Wee Jones; Bill Lone; George Parrish; Rick Simon; Al Stearn; Bob Whitmire (6)
168. Roger Baldwin; Don Gray; Ted Hauser; Lee Humphers; Carl Joiner; John Kieper; Jim Russell; Buzz Wilson; Emanuel Zervakis (5)
177. Bob Perry; Bob Wood (4)
179. Neil Castles; Johnny Frank; Gene Glover; Russ Hepler; Bill Massey; Keith Olson; John Smith; Gus Wilson (3)
187. Herb Gibson; Ned Jarrett; Earl Mosbach; Bobby Myers (2)
191. Don Bailey; Herman Beam; Ray Davis; Bill Hazel; Junior Johnson (1)

1957 Events

Willow Springs Speedway/2.5-mile dirt road/150 miles
Marvin Panch (Ford)/Marvin Panch (Ford)

Concord Speedway/.5-mile dirt/100 miles
Marvin Panch (Ford)/Curtis Turner (Ford)

Indian River Gold Cup 100; Titusville-Cocoa Sp./1.6-m rd/90m
Fireball Roberts (Ford)/Paul Goldsmith (Chevrolet)

Beach & Road Course/4.1-mile road/160 miles
Cotton Owens (Pontiac)/Banjo Matthews (Pontiac)

Concord Speedway/.5-mile dirt/100 miles
Jack Smith (Chevrolet)/Mel Larson (Ford)

Wilson Speedway/.5-mile dirt/100 miles
Ralph Moody (Ford)/Fireball Roberts (Ford)

Orange Speedway/.9-mile dirt/99 miles
Buck Baker (Chevrolet)/Fireball Roberts (Ford)

Asheville-Weaverville Speedway/.5-mile dirt/100 miles
Buck Baker (Chevrolet)/Marvin Panch (Ford)

Wilkes County 160; N. Wilkesboro Speedway/.625-m dirt/100 m
Fireball Roberts (Ford)/Fireball Roberts (Ford)

Langhorne Speedway/1-mile dirt/150 miles
Fireball Roberts (Ford)/Paul Goldsmith (Ford)

Southern States Fairgrounds/.5-mile dirt/100 miles
Fireball Roberts (Ford)/Marvin Panch (Ford)

Piedmont Interstate Fairgrounds/.5-mile dirt/100 miles
Marvin Panch (Ford)/Speedy Thompson (Chevrolet)

Greensboro Fairgrounds/.333-mile dirt/83 miles
Paul Goldsmith (Ford)/Buck Baker (Chevrolet)

Portland Speedway/.5-mile dirt/50 miles
Art Watts (Ford)/Art Watts (Ford)

Cleveland County Fairgrounds/.5-mile dirt/100 miles
Fireball Roberts (Ford)/Tiny Lund (Pontiac)

Richmond 200; Atlantic Rural Fairgrounds/.5-m dirt/100 miles
Paul Goldsmith (Ford)/Russ Hepler (Pontiac)

Virginia 500; Martinsville Speedway/.5-mile dirt/250 miles
Buck Baker (Chevrolet)/Paul Goldsmith (Ford)

Portland Speedway/.5-mile dirt/75 miles
Eddie Pagan (Ford)/Art Watts (Ford)

Eureka Speedway/.625-mile dirt/125 miles
Lloyd Dane (Ford)/Parnelli Jones (Ford)

Lincoln Speedway/.5-mile dirt/100 miles
Buck Baker (Chevrolet)/Marvin Panch (Ford)

Lancaster Speedway/.5-mile dirt/100 miles
Paul Goldsmith (Ford)/Buck Baker (Chevrolet)

Los Angeles Fairgrounds/.5-mile dirt/100 miles
Eddie Pagan (Ford)/Eddie Pagan (Ford)

Newport Speedway/.5-mile dirt/100 miles
Fireball Roberts (Ford)/Speedy Thompson (Chevrolet)

Columbia Speedway/.5-mile dirt/100 miles
Jack Smith (Chevrolet)/Buck Baker (Chevrolet)

Capitol Speedway/.5-mile dirt/100 miles
Bill Amick (Ford)/Art Watts (Ford)

Piedmont Interstate Fairgrounds/.5-mile dirt/100 miles
Lee Petty (Oldsmobile)/Lee Petty (Oldsmobile)

Jacksonville Speedway/.5-mile dirt/100 miles
Buck Baker (Chevrolet)/Lee Petty (Oldsmobile)

Raleigh 250; Raleigh Speedway/1-mile/250 miles
Paul Goldsmith (Ford)/Frankie Schneider (Chevrolet)

Southern States Fairgrounds/.5-mile dirt/100 miles
Marvin Panch (Ford)/Tiny Lund (Pontiac)

Memphis-Arkansas Speedway/1.5-mile dirt/201 miles
Marvin Panch (Pontiac)/Speedy Thompson (Chevrolet)

Portland Speedway/.5-mile/100 miles
Eddie Pagan (Ford)/Art Watts (Ford)

Buddy Shuman 250; Hickory Speedway/.4-mile dirt/100 miles
Jack Smith (Chevrolet)/Gwyn Staley (Chevrolet)

Norfolk Speedway/.4-mile dirt/100 miles
Buck Baker (Chevrolet)/Bill Amick (Ford)

Lancaster Speedway/.5-mile dirt/100 miles
Speedy Thompson (Chevrolet)/Speedy Thompson (Chevrolet)

The Glen 101.2; Watkins Glen International/2.3-m road/101 m
Buck Baker (Chevrolet)/Buck Baker (Chevrolet)

Kitsap County Airport/.9-mile road/72 miles
Parnelli Jones (Ford)/Art Watts (Ford)

Lincoln Speedway/.5-mile dirt/100 miles
Marvin Panch (Ford)/Tiny Lund (Pontiac)

Old Bridge Stadium/.5-mile/100 miles
Lee Petty (Oldsmobile)/Rex White (Chevrolet)

Coastal Speedway/.5-mile dirt/100 miles
Gwyn Staley (Chevrolet)/Johnny Allen (Plymouth)

Southern 500; Darlington Raceway/1.375-mile/500 miles
Speedy Thompson (Chevrolet)/Cotton Owens (Pontiac)

New York State Fairgrounds/1-mile dirt/100 miles
Gwyn Staley (Chevrolet)/Gwyn Staley (Chevrolet)

Asheville-Weaverville Speedway/.5-mile/100 miles
Lee Petty (Oldsmobile)/Bill Amick (Ford)

California State Fairgrounds/1-mile dirt/100 miles
Danny Graves (Chevrolet)/Danny Graves (Chevrolet)

Santa Clara Fairgrounds/.5-mile dirt/100 miles
Marvin Porter (Ford)

Langhorne Speedway/1-mile dirt/300 miles
Gwyn Staley (Chevrolet)/Paul Goldsmith (Ford)

Columbia Speedway/.5-mile dirt/100 miles
Buck Baker (Chevrolet)/Buck Baker (Chevrolet)

Cleveland County Fairgrounds/.5-mile dirt/100 miles
Buck Baker (Chevrolet)/Buck Baker (Chevrolet)

Southern States Fairgrounds/.5-mile dirt/100 miles
Lee Petty (Oldsmobile)/Lee Petty (Oldsmobile)

Old Dominion 500; Martinsville Speedway/.5-mile/250 miles
Bob Welborn (Chevrolet)/Eddie Pagan (Ford)

Newberry Speedway/.5-mile dirt/100 miles
Fireball Roberts (Ford)/Jack Smith (Chevrolet)

Concord Speedway/.5-mile dirt/100 miles
Fireball Roberts (Ford)/Jack Smith (Chevrolet)

Wilkes 160; North Wilkesboro Speedway/.625-mile/100 miles
Jack Smith (Chevrolet)/Fireball Roberts (Ford)

Greensboro Fairgrounds/.333-mile dirt/83 miles
Buck Baker (Chevrolet)/Ken Rush (Ford)

Victories
1. Buck Baker (10)
2. Fireball Roberts (8)
3. Marvin Panch (6)
4. Paul Goldsmith; Lee Petty; Jack Smith (4)
7. Eddie Pagan; Gwyn Staley (3)
9. Speedy Thompson (2)
10. Bill Amick; Lloyd Dane; Danny Graves; Parnelli Jones; Ralph Moody; Cotton Owens; Marvin Porter; Art Watts; Bob Welborn (1)

Poles
1. Buck Baker (6)
2. Art Watts (5)
3. Paul Goldsmith; Marvin Panch; Fireball Roberts; Speedy Thompson (4)
7. Tiny Lund; Lee Petty (3)
9. Bill Amick; Eddie Pagan; Jack Smith; Gwyn Staley (2)
13. Johnny Allen; Danny Graves; Russ Hepler; Parnelli Jones; Mel Larson; Banjo Matthews; Cotton Owens; Ken Rush; Frankie Schneider; Curtis Turner; Rex White (1)

Victories
1. Ford (26)
2. Chevrolet (21)
3. Oldsmobile (4)
4. Pontiac (2)

Poles
1. Ford (24)
2. Chevrolet (18)
3. Pontiac (6)
4. Oldsmobile (3)
5. Plymouth (1)

1958
Was Turner
The Best?
Record Says No

Curtis Turner usually is listed among the greatest drivers of all time; some observers even rank him No. 1.

Allow Bruton Smith, chairman of the board of Speedway Motorsports, Inc., and one of NASCAR's pioneer promoters, to speak on Turner's behalf: "You had to see Curtis Turner. He could move anybody out of the way without ever changing the line he was driving his car. He was the best."

Turner, of course, was included in NASCAR's 50th anniversary listing of its 50 greatest drivers. Considering that more than 2,700 drivers have started Winston Cup races, that's no small accomplishment.

But Turner's record, which includes 17 victories and 16 poles, leaves him far short of qualifying as a serious candidate to rank as the most successful ever. Turner never enjoyed what might be called a "blockbuster" season, earning a career high-four victories in 1950 and enjoying three-win seasons in 1951 and 1958.

In fact, Turner ranks among the top 20 only in the following: dirt poles (11), classic poles (2), dirt wins from the pole (5), three consecutive years (1949-51) with a dirt victory, two seasons in a row (1958-59) with multiple dirt victories, two years in a row (1958-59) with a dirt victory from the pole, and seasons in which he led the series in victories (1).

Turner's best year was 1950, when he led the circuit with four victories. He had the fifth-highest Performance Index rating that season despite skipping three races. In fact, he never competed for a full season with designs on the championship.

And, if the colorful Virginian, who reportedly made and lost fortunes in the lumber business and other ventures, didn't invent parties, certainly no other driver in the history of stock-car racing has been as famous for his off-the-track revelry.

In 1961, a year after Charlotte Motor Speedway, which Smith and Turner founded, went bankrupt, Turner solicited help from the Teamsters Union in an effort to save the track by agreeing to unionize the drivers as the Federation of Professional Athletes. NASCAR President Bill France quickly ended that endeavor by banning any FPA member for life. Turner and Tim Flock were the only drivers who didn't resign within days, and they became the only longtime recipients of the ban.

Turner was reinstated in 1965, and his greatest triumph came on Halloween, when the 41-year-old legend ended a six-year victory drought by winning the American 500, the first race held at the North Carolina Motor Speedway, despite hitting the wall twice in the Wood brothers' Ford.

By the time Turner was reinstated, fireproof driving suits had become standard equipment. Turner didn't quickly embrace the safety apparel, however. He finally agreed to wear a suit while driving and finished third in the Sandlapper 200 in a Junior Johnson-owned Ford on August 18, 1966, at Columbia, S.C. Turner's attire, however, was a three-piece business suit. "Holly Farms told me that I was going to have to wear a suit," Turner said. "They didn't specify what kind of suit, so I wore my best."

In 1968, Turner became the first NASCAR driver to grace the cover of *Sports Illustrated*, still a rare achievement, with a headline that read: King of the Wild Road.

Turner, perhaps the first driver to own and regularly fly his own plane, and a man Smith once accused of having "suicidal tendencies," was killed when he crashed his plane on October 4, 1970, near Du Bois, Pa.

1958 in Review

Lee Petty earned his second Winston Cup championship and led the Performance Index for the third time with a sound 853-687 margin over Buck Baker. Petty's seven victories also led the circuit, while Speedy Thompson and Rex White shared the lead with seven poles apiece.

Most Memorable Race

There have been few happier homecomings in Winston Cup history than Junior Johnson's six-second triumph over Jack Smith in the Wilkes County 160 at North Wilkesboro on May 18. Johnson hadn't won a race since 1955 and had spent 11 months in an Ohio correctional facility after being caught by federal agents at the family's still in Ronda, N.C., just a few laps across North Carolina Highway 268 from North Wilkesboro.

Most Significant Wreck

On July 18 at the Canadian National Exposition Stadium in Toronto, Richard Petty clipped the fence and finished 17th in his Winston Cup debut. Petty later contended that he was hit by the eventual winner, his father, Lee.

Most Important Off-Track Development

Riverside International Raceway, the California road course that played host to more Winston Cup races than all other road courses combined in the circuit's first 51 years, on June 1 held its first Winston Cup race, the Crown America 500 won by Eddie Gray.

Records & Milestones

Nineteen drivers won races, tying a record set in 1956 and equaled in 1961. . . . A total of 24 drivers captured poles, the most in one season. . . . The 40 tracks that played host to races in 1958 equaled the record set in 1956. . . . Lee Petty's victory at Toronto on July 18 marked the last time a Winston Cup points race was held outside the United States. . . . White became the first driver in three years to capture four consecutive poles, and when he won the pole for the August 10 Nashville 200 at Fairgrounds Speedway he became the first driver to win the pole for four consecutive short-track races.

1958 at a Glance

Races:	51
Dirt:	26
Road:	3
Short Track:	19
Superspeedway:	3
Winners:	19
Pole Winners:	24
Tracks:	40
States:	11 *

* plus Canada

1958 Performance Index Rankings

1. Lee Petty (853)
2. Buck Baker (687)
3. Speedy Thompson (532)
4. Jack Smith (439)
5. Shorty Rollins (415)
6. Junior Johnson (403)
7. Rex White (358)
8. Eddie Pagan (357)
9. Bob Welborn (348)
10. Cotton Owens (320)
11. L.D. Austin (291)
12. Jim Reed (283)
13. Fireball Roberts (273)
14. Curtis Turner (253)
15. Bobby Keck (189)
16. Fred Harb (188)
17. Brownie King (187)
18. Clarence DeZalia; Billy Rafter (183)
20. Doug Cox (173)
21. Bill Poor (171)
22. Tiny Lund (165)
23. Joe Weatherly (163)
24. Johnny Allen (150)
25. Roy Tyner (144)
26. Marvin Panch (136)
27. Bob Duell (130)
28. Glen Wood (128)
29. Bob Walden (125)
30. Herb Estes (119)
31. Wilbur Rakestraw (111)
32. Reds Kagle (106)
33. George Dunn (101)
34. Buzz Woodward (99)
35. Frankie Schneider; Gene White (95)
37. Jimmy Thompson (89)
38. Johnny Mackison (86)
39. Jim Paschal (85)
40. Larry Frank (82)
41. Gwyn Staley (78)
42. Shep Langdon; Jim Parsley (75)
44. Jimmy Massey (74)
45. Lloyd Dane; Joe Eubanks (71)
47. Harvey Hege; Elmo Langley (70)
49. Barney Shore (67)
50. Peck Peckham (65)
51. Ken Rush (63)
52. Joe Lee Johnson; Whitey Norman (61)
54. Tommy Irwin (58)
55. Billy Carden; Lennie Page (53)
57. Parnelli Jones (52)
58. Chuck Hansen; Bill Morton (49)
60. Gober Sosebee (48)
61. Al White (47)
62. Ted Chamberlain; Paul Goldsmith (46)
64. Eddie Gray; Bobby Johns (40)
66. John Findlay; Bob Keefe (39)
68. R.L. Combs; Dean Layfield (38)

Curtis Turner was the first stock-car driver ever featured on the cover of *Sports Illustrated*.

70. Marvin Porter (37)
71. George Green; Volney Schulze (35)
73. John Lindsay (34)
74. Tiny Benson; Dave James (33)
76. E.J. Brewer; Johnny Gardner; Richard Petty (32)
79. G.C. Spencer; Carl Tyler (29)
81. Jim Cook (27)
82. Mike Batinick; Pete Frazee; Lloyd Ragon (26)
85. Ben Benz (25)
86. Bill Benson; Jack D. McCoy (24)
88. Mario Rossi; Otis Skinner; Dave White (23)
91. Axel Anderson; Scotty Cain (22)
93. Jerry Draper; Nace Mattingly; Howard Phillippi (21)
96. Paul Aars; Lucky Long (20)
98. Bob Ross (19)
99. Ken Johnson; Jack Rounds; Eddie Skinner; Danny Weinberg (18)
103. Erwin Blatt; Carl Burris; Emory Mahon; George Norton (17)
107. Harold Hardesty; Charlie Mincey; Blackie Pitt; John Seeley; Dick Walters; Art Watts (16)
113. J.V. Hamby; Charles Sanchez; Charlie Stone; Ernie Young (15)
117. Roz Howard; Bill Olson; Ward Towers (14)
120. Bill Jarlick; Benny Rakestraw (13)
122. Bob Finale; Bill Jones; Jack Lawrence; Buzz Wilson; Cecil Wray (12)
127. Bill Boldt; Neil Castles; Ray Fanning; Dick Foley; Mel Larson; Ralph Roberts; John Walker (11)
134. Dick Bailey; Bill Blair; Sam Colvin; Jerry Johnson; Bob Seharns; Paul Walton (10)
140. Thomas Aiken; Barney Hatchell; Bobby Lee; Gus Wilson; Bailey Wynkoop (9)
145. Don Angel; Bud Gardner; Charley Griffith; Neil Haight; Bob Havenmann; John McDaniel; Frank Thompson (8)
152. Spook Crawford; Darel Dieringer; Squirt Johns; Banjo Matthews; Ruben Thrash; Bill Walker (7)
158. George Alsobrook; Buck Brigance; Ray Campbell; Elgin Holmes; Jim Linke; Bunk Moore; Johnny Nave; Bill Wimble (6)
166. Clyde Goons; Don Gray (5)
168. Harry Leake; Ken Love; Dave Terrell; Marv Thorpe (4)
172. Cannonball Brown; Dick Carter; Tim Flock; Harvey Henderson; Vernon West; Paul Wilson (3)
178. Dick Beaty; Chauncey Christ; Eddie McDonald; Jug Pierce; Buddy Ragsdale (2)
183. Tom Nundy; Richard Spittle (1)

1958 Events

Champion Speedway/.333-mile/50 miles
Rex White (Chevrolet)/Jack Smith (Chevrolet)

Beach & Road Course/4.1-mile road/160 miles
Paul Goldsmith (Pontiac)/Paul Goldsmith (Pontiac)

Concord Speedway/.5-mile dirt/100 miles
Lee Petty (Oldsmobile)/Speedy Thompson (Chevrolet)

Champion Speedway/.333-mile/50 miles
Curtis Turner (Ford)/Lee Petty (Oldsmobile)

Wilson Speedway/.5-mile dirt/100 miles
Lee Petty (Oldsmobile)/Marvin Panch (Ford)

Orange Speedway/.9-mile dirt/99 miles
Buck Baker (Chevrolet)/Buck Baker (Chevrolet)

Champion Speedway/.333-mile/50 miles
Bob Welborn (Chevrolet)/Lee Petty (Oldsmobile)

Columbia Speedway/.5-mile dirt/100 miles
Speedy Thompson (Chevrolet)/Possum Jones (Chevrolet)

Piedmont Interstate Fairgrounds/.5-mile dirt/100 miles
Speedy Thompson (Chevrolet)/Speedy Thompson (Chevrolet)

Lakewood Speedway/1-mile dirt/100 miles
Curtis Turner (Ford)/Joe Weatherly (Ford)

Southern States Fairgrounds/.5-mile dirt/100 miles
Curtis Turner (Ford)/Curtis Turner (Ford)

Virginia 500; Martinsville Speedway/.5-mile dirt/250 miles
Bob Welborn (Chevrolet)/Buck Baker (Chevrolet)

Old Dominion Speedway/.375-mile/56 miles
Frankie Schneider (Chevrolet)/Eddie Pagan (Ford)

Old Bridge Stadium/.5-mile/100 miles
Jim Reed (Ford)/Jim Reed (Ford)

Greenville-Pickens Speedway/.5-mile dirt/100 miles
Jack Smith (Chevrolet)/Jack Smith (Chevrolet)

Greensboro Fairgrounds/.333-mile dirt/50 miles
Bob Welborn (Chevrolet)/Bob Welborn (Chevrolet)

Starkey Speedway/.25-mile/38 miles
Jim Reed (Ford)/Jim Reed (Ford)

Wilkes County 160; North Wilkesboro Speedway/.625-mile/100 m
Junior Johnson (Ford)/Jack Smith (Chevrolet)

Bowman Gray Stadium/.25-mile/38 miles
Bob Welborn (Chevrolet)/Rex White (Chevrolet)

Northern 500; Trenton Speedway/1-mile/500 miles
Fireball Roberts (Chevrolet)/Marvin Panch (Ford)

Crown America 500; Riverside Int. Raceway/2.631-m road/500 m
Eddie Gray (Ford)/Danny Graves (Chevrolet)

Columbia Speedway/.5-mile dirt/100 miles
Junior Johnson (Ford)/Buck Baker (Chevrolet)

New Bradford Speedway/.333-mile dirt/50 miles
Junior Johnson (Ford)/Bob Duell (Ford)

Reading Fairgrounds/.5-mile dirt/100 miles
Junior Johnson (Ford)/Speedy Thompson (Chevrolet)

Lincoln Speedway/.5-mile dirt/100 miles
Lee Petty (Oldsmobile)/Ken Rush (Chevrolet)

Buddy Shuman 250; Hickory Speedway/.4-mile dirt/100 miles
Lee Petty (Oldsmobile)/Speedy Thompson (Chevrolet)

Asheville-Weaverville Speedway/.5-mile dirt/100 miles
Rex White (Chevrolet)/Rex White (Chevrolet)

Raleigh 250; Raleigh Speedway/1-mile/250 miles
Fireball Roberts (Chevrolet)/Cotton Owens (Pontiac)

McCormick Field/.25-mile/38 miles
Jim Paschal (Chevrolet)/Jim Paschal (Chevrolet)

State Line Speedway/.333-mile dirt/50 miles
Shorty Rollins (Ford)/Lee Petty (Oldsmobile)

Canadian National Exposition Stadium/.333-mile/33 miles
Lee Petty (Oldsmobile)/Rex White (Chevrolet)

Civic Stadium/.25-mile/25 miles
Jim Reed (Ford)/Rex White (Chevrolet)

Monroe County Fairgrounds/.5-mile dirt/100 miles
Cotton Owens (Pontiac)/Rex White (Chevrolet)

Wall Stadium/.333-mile/100 miles
Jim Reed (Ford)/Rex White (Chevrolet)

Bridgehampton Raceway/2.85-mile road/100 miles
Jack Smith (Chevrolet)/Jack Smith (Chevrolet)

Columbia Speedway/.5-mile dirt/100 miles
Speedy Thompson (Chevrolet)/Speedy Thompson (Chevrolet)

Nashville 200; Fairgrounds Speedway/.5-mile/100 miles
Joe Weatherly (Ford)/Rex White (Chevrolet)

Western N.C. 500; Asheville-Weaverville Speedway/.5-m/250 m
Fireball Roberts (Chevrolet)/Jimmy Massey (Pontiac)

Bowman Gray Stadium/.25-mile/50 miles
Lee Petty (Oldsmobile)/George Dunn (Mercury)

Rambi Raceway/.5-mile dirt/100 miles
Bob Welborn (Chevrolet)/Speedy Thompson (Chevrolet)

Southern 500; Darlington Raceway/1.375-mile/500 miles
Fireball Roberts (Chevrolet)/Eddie Pagan (Ford)

Southern States Fairgrounds/.5-mile dirt/100 miles
Buck Baker (Chevrolet)/Lee Petty (Oldsmobile)

Alabama State Fairgrounds/.5-mile dirt/100 miles
Fireball Roberts (Chevrolet)/Cotton Owens (Pontiac)

California State Fairgrounds/1-mile dirt/100 miles
Parnelli Jones (Ford)/Parnelli Jones (Ford)

Gastonia Fairgrounds/.333-mile dirt/67 miles
Buck Baker (Chevrolet)/Tiny Lund (Chevrolet)

Richmond 200; Atlantic Rural Fairgrounds/.5-mile dirt/100 m
Speedy Thompson (Chevrolet)/Speedy Thompson (Chevrolet)

Orange Speedway/.9-mile dirt/99 miles
Joe Eubanks (Pontiac)/Tiny Lund (Chevrolet)

Salisbury Speedway/.625-mile dirt/100 miles
Lee Petty (Oldsmobile)/Gober Sosebee (Chevrolet)

Old Dominion 500; Martinsville Speedway/.5-mile/250 miles
Fireball Roberts (Chevrolet)/Glen Wood (Ford)

Wilkes 160; North Wilkesboro Speedway/.625-mile/100 miles
Junior Johnson (Ford)/Glen Wood (Ford)

Lakewood Speedway/1-mile dirt/150 miles
Junior Johnson (Ford)/Glen Wood (Ford)

Victories

1. Lee Petty (7)
2. Junior Johnson; Fireball Roberts (6)
4. Bob Welborn (5)
5. Jim Reed; Speedy Thompson (4)
7. Buck Baker; Curtis Turner (3)
9. Jack Smith; Rex White (2)
11. Joe Eubanks; Paul Goldsmith; Eddie Gray; Parnelli Jones; Cotton Owens; Jim Paschal; Shorty Rollins; Frankie Schneider; Joe Weatherly (1)

Poles

1. Speedy Thompson; Rex White (7)
3. Lee Petty; Jack Smith (4)
5. Buck Baker; Glen Wood (3)
7. Tiny Lund; Cotton Owens; Eddie Pagan; Marvin Panch; Jim Reed (2)
12. Bob Duell; George Dunn; Paul Goldsmith; Danny Graves; Parnelli Jones; Possum Jones; Jimmy Massey; Jim Paschal; Ken Rush; Gober Sosebee; Curtis Turner; Joe Weatherly; Bob Welborn (1)

Victories

1. Chevrolet (24)
2. Ford (17)
3. Oldsmobile (7)
4. Pontiac (3)

Poles

1. Chevrolet (29)
2. Ford (13)
3. Oldsmobile; Pontiac (4)
5. Mercury (1)

Lee Petty, the first three-time Winston Cup champion, retired with 54 victories, a record until it was eclipsed by his son, Richard.

1959
The Patriarch
Of Petty
Enterprises

Richard Petty and Dale Earnhardt have demonstrated by winning seven Winston Cup championships apiece that few drivers have had their knowledge of what it takes to win titles.

If anyone did, however, it was Lee Petty, who in 1959 became the first three-time Winston Cup champion and led the Performance Index four times despite being 35 years old during the circuit's inaugural season.

The patriarch of Petty Enterprises posted top-two seasons in the Performance Index in each of the first two seasons. He then became the first driver to manage that feat three years in a row (1952-54). Although Lee managed only 12 top-25 seasons in his career, they were all top-four campaigns, and *all 12 were in a row* (1949-60). Only Richard also managed 12 consecutive top-four finishes, and no other driver has had more than eight straight top-*five* campaigns.

To put Lee's amazing 12-year run in the Performance Index in perspective, his 12 top-four seasons trail only Richard and are tied for second with Earnhardt, and his nine top-three seasons and seven top-two seasons trail only the two seven-time champions.

Considering that Lee captured 54 races—still seventh on the all-time list and the record at the time of his retirement—and one-third that many poles, he was among the first to realize in the days when winning a pole or leading laps paid but a few pennies that the only lap it truly mattered to lead was the last one.

"We had more determination because we were racing for a living," Petty said a quarter-century after his retirement.

That was never more evident than on June 14, 1959, at Atlanta's Lakewood Speedway. Richard, driving a 1957 Oldsmobile, took the checkered flag for the first time in his career. Lee, who finished second in a 1959 Plymouth, protested. NASCAR President Bill France had instituted a $400 bonus for any driver who won in a current-model automobile, and Lee knew Petty Enterprises could use the extra cash.

"I remembered passing (Richard) twice, so I knew he was a lap down," Lee recalled. "I was running a current automobile, and he was running one that was older. Back then you got extra money if you won with a current automobile. So I was thinking of the monetary value."

Richard wasn't about to argue.

"I'd never run second before, so I was tickled to death to run second," he recalled more than 30 years after Lee's protest was upheld. "And, at that time, we needed the extra money more than I needed the win."

Keeping one eye focused on eluding trouble on the track and another out for the bottom line on the company balance sheet didn't keep Lee out of victory lane. For example, he posted a career-high 11 victories in 1959, but none of them were from the pole, a record later tied but never broken.

The eldest Petty's contribution to the record books are further examples of his amazing consistency:

- 13 consecutive seasons with at least one dirt victory (1949-61);
- Eight straight multiple-victory seasons on dirt (1953-60);
- 42 dirt victories.

Lee also was the first driver to win a race in 13 consecutive years (1949-61), a streak bettered by only six drivers, and the first to post nine straight multiple-victory seasons (1952-60), a streak bettered by only four drivers. He not only became the first driver to win on short tracks four consecutive years (1957-60), but for good measure, all four included multiple victories on that discipline.

Lee was still going strong at age 46, when he pocketed $800 of the $3,985 purse for winning a 100-mile race on the dirt at Jacksonville on November 20, 1960, the second race of the 1961 season. In his next outing, however, he suffered season-ending injuries in a 100-mile race on the 2.5-mile tri-oval at Daytona Beach, Fla. Essentially, the injury ended Lee's illustrious career. Although he drove in six races during the next three years, he never won again, except in most of his matches on the fabled golf courses of Pinehurst, located just across the county line from his home in Randleman, N.C.

Lee's son overtook him as the all-time Winston Cup victory leader just three years after he drove in his final race. But Lee, who died on April 5, 2000—just three days after his great grandson, Adam Petty, made his Winston Cup debut—wasn't the type to worry about his legacy.

"Earnhardt and (Rusty) Wallace would have been good back in my day," Lee said in the late '80s. "Bobby Allison was a good one, too. They're more knowledgeable about how to set a car up now. We had to manhandle them. It's hard to compare different times when the question arises about who is the best or who was the best. How are you going to compare? Who's the best basketball player? It might be Michael Jordan. But did you ever see Bill Russell? A few years ago, it was ol' Larry Bird. I don't care how good you are; somebody comes along and outdoes you."

1959 in Review

Lee Petty romped to his second consecutive Winston Cup title and the third of his career, and his 772-511 margin over Cotton Owens easily enabled him to lead the Performance Index for the fourth time. Lee Petty also posted a season-high 11 victories, and Bob Welborn and Rex White shared the lead in poles with five apiece.

Most Important Off-Track Development

Only the opening of Darlington Raceway on South Carolina farmland in 1950 compared to the first impressions drivers had of Daytona International Speedway.

"There have been other tracks that separated the men from the boys. This is the track that will separate the brave from the weak after the boys are gone," said Jimmy Thompson.

"There wasn't a man there who wasn't scared to death of the place," Lee Petty added. "We never had raced on a track like that before. Darlington was big, but it wasn't banked like Daytona. What it amounted to was that we were all rookies going 30 to 40 mph faster than we had ever gone before. There were some scared cats out there."

Most Memorable Race

Welborn won the pole for the inaugural Daytona 500 on the 31-degree banked, 2.5-mile tri-oval, a track Richard Petty called "super humongous." But Owens was the fastest qualifier with a speed of 143.198 mph in a Pontiac. When the white flag fell in the accident-free race, only two drivers were still on the lead lap, Lee Petty in an Oldsmobile and Johnny Beauchamp in a Ford. By the time they reached the finish line, Petty's car was in the middle of a three-car photo finish, with fifth-place finisher Joe Weatherly on the outside in a Chevrolet. Beauchamp was flagged the winner. "I was there by two feet," Beauchamp said in victory lane. "I beat him."

Lee Petty didn't agree. "If they let that decision stand, it will really be the worst under-the-table blow ever delivered in stock-car racing," he told *The Atlanta Journal*. "When I crossed the finish line, I saw Beauchamp behind me. I just hope somebody got an accurate photograph of that finish."

France confiscated nearly every roll of film he could find, as well as TV footage. Sixty-one hours later, on February 27, Lee Petty was awarded the victory, by roughly the same two feet Beauchamp thought he'd beaten Petty.

Most Significant Wreck

Weatherly, whose victory in the 1958 Nashville 200 at Fairgrounds Speedway had hinted of future stardom, was injured in a wreck on June 18 at Columbia, S.C. Weatherly finished 16th and 23rd in two of the next four races and missed the other two on his way to a winless season.

Records & Milestones

The 1959 campaign marked the first year—and one of only three in history—that no race was held on a road course. . . . Bob Burdick, driving a Ford owned by his father, Roy, captured the pole for the May 17 race at Trenton, N.J., his first Winston Cup start. After qualifying ninth in his next start and seeing qualifying rained out in his third, Burdick won the pole for his fourth career start—and third qualifying session—for the June 18 race at Columbia. Those were the only two poles of the 22-year-old Burdick's career.

1959 at a Glance

Races:	44
Dirt:	26
Short Track:	13
Superspeedway:	5
Winners:	16
Pole Winners:	16
Tracks:	24
States:	9

1959 Performance Index Rankings

1. Lee Petty (772)
2. Cotton Owens (511)
3. Buck Baker (420)
4. Tom Pistone (366)
5. Junior Johnson (345)
6. Rex White (330)
7. Tommy Irwin (311)
8. Speedy Thompson (297)
9. Jack Smith (293)
10. Roy Tyner (292)
11. Bob Welborn (289)
12. L.D. Austin (284)
13. Herman Beam (276)
14. Tiny Lund (273)
15. Jim Reed (256)
16. Glen Wood (254)
17. Richard Petty (222)
18. Joe Weatherly (217)
19. Larry Frank (201)
20. G.C. Spencer (190)
21. Shep Langdon (172)
22. Ned Jarrett (165)
23. Joe Lee Johnson (148)
24. Curtis Turner (133)
25. George Green (126)
26. Johnny Beauchamp (117)
27. Fred Harb (116)
28. Bob Burdick (109)
29. Fireball Roberts (101)
30. Joe Eubanks (100)
31. Brownie King (98)
32. Ken Rush (96)
33. Buddy Baker (95)
34. Jim Paschal (93)
35. Shorty Rollins (82)
36. Gene White (81)
37. Charley Griffith (78)
38. Bobby Keck; Marvin Porter (77)
40. Bobby Johns (73)
41. Johnny Allen (71)
42. Harvey Hege; Jimmy Thompson (69)
44. Richard Riley (65)
45. Buck Brigance (59)
46. Dick Freeman (58)
47. Harlan Richardson (55)
48. Elmo Langley (54)
49. Eduardo Dibos (50)
50. Charlie Cregar (47)
51. Benny Rakestraw (45)
52. Raul Cilloniz; Jerry Draper (44)
54. R.L. Combs (43)
55. George Alsobrook; Al White; Dave White (41)
58. Reds Kagle (40)
59. Fritz Wilson (39)
60. Ben Benz; Tim Flock; Parnelli Jones (35)
63. Tiny Benson; Jim Pardue; Bob Ross (34)
66. Bill Champion; Lloyd Dane (33)
68. Joe Caspolich (32)
69. Lucky Long (31)
70. Ken Johnson (30)
71. Dominic Persicketti (29)
72. John Dodd; Marvin Panch; John Potter; Barney Shore (28)
76. Curtis Crider (27)
77. Joe Halton; J.C. Hendrix; Doug Cox (26)
80. Eddie Gray; Tommy Thompson (25)
82. Pedro Rodriguez; Bill Scott; Bobby Waddell (24)
85. Mel Larson; Bunk Moore (23)
87. Jim Austin (22)
88. Scotty Cain; Neil Castles; Ernie Gesell (21)
91. Chester Barron; Aubrey Boles; Billy Carden; Jimmie Lewallen (19)
95. Bernie Hentges; Danny Weinberg (18)
97. Runt Harris; Dick Joslin; Bob Keefe; Bob Perry; Buzz Woodward (16)
102. Don Dahle; Dave James; Ralph Moody (15)
105. Bill Brown; Bob Duell (14)
107. Jim Cook; Jim Parsley; Wilbur Rakestraw (13)
110. Fuzzy Clifton; Earl Moss; Bob Reuther; Don Strain (12)
114. Bud Crothers; Eddie Pagan; Lennie Page; Bill Taylor (11)
118. George Dunn; Jim McGuirk; Bob Price; John Seeley; Jerry Smith; Don Taylor (10)
124. Jim Lamport; Sam Massey; Bill Poor; Shorty York (9)
128. Don Angel; Bob Hogle; Bob Hundley; Bill Morton; Ermon Rush; August Sand; Roscoe Thompson; Chuck Webb (8)
136. Max Berrier; Fred Boles; Russ Gemberling; Owen Loggins; Dick Santee (7)
141. Jack Austin; Whitey Norman; Bob Tyrell; Bill Woolkin (6)
145. Dick Blackwell; Jim Blomgren; Ray Fanning; Larry Lyndstrom; Paul Walton (5)
150. Gerald Duke; John Findlay; Jack D. McCoy (4)
153. Ted Chamberlain; Clarence DeZalia; Ronny Myers; E.J. Trivette; Gus Wilson (3)
158. Dick Bailey; Dick Carter; Pee Wee Jones; Pete Kelly (2)
162. Herb Lewis; Layman Utsman; Russ Whitman (1)

1959 Events

Champion Speedway/.333-mile/50 miles
Bob Welborn (Chevrolet)/Bob Welborn (Chevrolet)

Daytona International Speedway/2.5-mile/100 miles
Bob Welborn (Chevrolet)/Fireball Roberts (Pontiac)

Daytona 500; Daytona International Speedway/2.5-m/500 miles
Lee Petty (Oldsmobile)/Bob Welborn (Chevrolet)

Orange Speedway/.9-mile dirt/99 miles
Curtis Turner (Ford)/Curtis Turner (Ford)

Concord Speedway/.5-mile dirt/100 miles
Curtis Turner (Ford)/Buck Baker (Chevrolet)

Lakewood Speedway/1-mile dirt/100 miles
Johnny Beauchamp (Ford)/Buck Baker (Chevrolet)

Wilson Speedway/.5-mile dirt/100 miles
Junior Johnson (Ford)

Bowman Gray Stadium/.25-mile/50 miles
Jim Reed (Ford)/Rex White (Chevrolet)

Columbia Speedway/.5-mile dirt/100 miles
Jack Smith (Chevrolet)/Jack Smith (Chevrolet)

Gwyn Staley 160; North Wilkesboro Speedway/.625-m/100 miles
Lee Petty (Oldsmobile)/Speedy Thompson (Chevrolet)

Reading Speedway/.5-mile dirt/100 miles
Junior Johnson (Ford)

Hickory 250; Hickory Speedway/.4-mile dirt/100 miles
Junior Johnson (Ford)/Junior Johnson (Ford)

Virginia 500; Martinsville Speedway/.5-mile/250 miles
Lee Petty (Oldsmobile)/Bobby Johns (Chevrolet)

Trenton Speedway/1-mile/150 miles
Tom Pistone (Ford)/Bob Burdick (Ford)

Charlotte Fairgrounds/.5-mile dirt/100 miles
Lee Petty (Oldsmobile)/Bob Welborn (Chevrolet)

Music City 200; Fairgrounds Speedway/.5-mile/100 miles
Rex White (Chevrolet)/Rex White (Chevrolet)

Ascot Stadium/.4-mile dirt/200 miles
Parnelli Jones (Ford)/Jim Reed (Chevrolet)

Piedmont Interstate Fairgrounds/.5-mile dirt/100 miles
Jack Smith (Chevrolet)/Cotton Owens (Pontiac)

Greenville-Pickens Speedway/.5-mile dirt/100 miles
Junior Johnson (Ford)/Jack Smith (Chevrolet)

Lakewood Speedway/1-mile dirt/150 miles
Lee Petty (Plymouth)

Columbia Speedway/.5-mile dirt/100 miles
Lee Petty (Plymouth)/Bob Burdick (Ford)

Wilson Speedway/.5-mile dirt/100 miles
Junior Johnson (Ford)

Richmond 200; Atlantic Rural Fairgrounds/.5-m dirt/100 miles
Tom Pistone (Ford)/Buck Baker (Chevrolet)

Bowman Gray Stadium/.25-mile/50 miles
Rex White (Chevrolet)/Lee Petty (Plymouth)

Asheville-Weaverville Speedway/.5-mile/100 miles
Rex White (Chevrolet)/Glen Wood (Ford)

Firecracker 250; Daytona International Speedway/2.5-m/250 m
Fireball Roberts (Pontiac)/Fireball Roberts (Pontiac)

Heidelberg Raceway/.25-mile dirt/50 miles
Jim Reed (Chevrolet)/Dick Bailey (Plymouth)

Charlotte Fairgrounds/.5-mile dirt/100 miles
Jack Smith (Chevrolet)/Buck Baker (Chevrolet)

Rambi Raceway/.5-mile dirt/100 miles
Ned Jarrett (Ford)/Bob Welborn (Chevrolet)

Charlotte Fairgrounds/.5-mile dirt/100 miles
Ned Jarrett (Ford)/Bob Welborn (Chevrolet)

Nashville 300; Fairgrounds Speedway/.5-mile/150 miles
Joe Lee Johnson (Chevrolet)/Rex White (Chevrolet)

Western N.C. 500; Asheville-Weaverville Speedway/.5-m/250 m
Bob Welborn (Chevrolet)/Rex White (Chevrolet)

Bowman Gray Stadium/.25-mile/50 miles
Rex White (Chevrolet)/Rex White (Chevrolet)

Greenville-Pickens Speedway/.5-mile dirt/100 miles
Buck Baker (Chevrolet)/Lee Petty (Plymouth)

Columbia Speedway/.5-mile dirt/100 miles
Lee Petty (Plymouth)

Southern 500; Darlington Raceway/1.375-mile/500 miles
Jim Reed (Chevrolet)/Fireball Roberts (Pontiac)

Buddy Shuman 250; Hickory Speedway/.4-mile dirt/100 miles
Lee Petty (Plymouth)

Capital City 200; Atlantic Rural Fairgrounds/.5-m dirt/100 m
Cotton Owens (Ford)/Cotton Owens (Ford)

California State Fairgrounds/1-mile dirt/100 miles
Eddie Gray (Ford)

Orange Speedway/.9-mile dirt/99 miles
Lee Petty (Plymouth)/Jack Smith (Chevrolet)

Old Dominion 500; Martinsville Speedway/.5-mile/250 miles
Rex White (Chevrolet)/Glen Wood (Ford)

Asheville-Weaverville Speedway/.5-mile/100 miles
Lee Petty (Plymouth)/Tommy Irwin (Ford)

Wilkes 160; North Wilkesboro Speedway/.625-mile/100 miles
Lee Petty (Plymouth)/Glen Wood (Ford)

Lee Kirby 300; Concord Speedway/.5-mile dirt/150 miles
Jack Smith (Chevrolet)

Victories

1. Lee Petty (11)
2. Junior Johnson; Rex White (5)
4. Jack Smith (4)
5. Jim Reed; Bob Welborn (3)
7. Ned Jarrett; Tom Pistone; Curtis Turner (2)
10. Buck Baker; Johnny Beauchamp; Eddie Gray; Joe Lee Johnson; Parnelli Jones; Cotton Owens; Fireball Roberts (1)

Poles

1. Bob Welborn; Rex White (5)
3. Buck Baker (4)
4. Fireball Roberts; Jack Smith; Glen Wood (3)
7. Bob Burdick; Cotton Owens; Lee Petty (2)
10. Dick Bailey; Tommy Irwin; Bobby Johns; Junior Johnson; Jim Reed; Speedy Thompson; Curtis Turner (1)

Victories

1. Chevrolet; Ford (16)
3. Plymouth (7)
4. Oldsmobile (4)
5. Pontiac (1)

Poles

1. Chevrolet (20)
2. Ford (9)
3. Pontiac (4)
4. Plymouth (3)

1960
Grand Slam:
A Grand
Achievement

Most Important Off-Track Development

A new era was launched in 1960, when Charlotte Motor Speedway, Atlanta International Raceway, and the 1.4-mile Marchbanks Speedway in Hanford, Calif., opened just one year after the debut of Daytona International Speedway.

South Carolina's Darlington Raceway was NASCAR's original superspeedway, opening with the inaugural Southern 500 in 1950. From 1953-57, the Winston Cup Series competed on two superspeedways, Darlington and the one-mile Raleigh Speedway. New Jersey's Trenton Speedway, then a one-mile track, joined the circuit in 1958, Raleigh Speedway's last season, and was still around in 1959, when the 2.5-mile tri-oval in Daytona Beach, Fla., opened.

The opening of the big tracks in Hampton, Ga.; Concord, N.C., and Hanford, Calif., in 1960 doubled the number of superspeedways. And, although Trenton would not play host to another Winston Cup race until 1967, it was obvious that NASCAR was seeking bigger and faster paved speedways on which its elite division could compete. For example, NASCAR sanctioned the Empire State 200 on July 17, 1960, on a two-mile track constructed at New York's Montgomery Air Base.

In the process, perhaps the most subtle and significant change in the manner drivers would rise to the top was made. Winston Cup racing began to test drivers and their machines at much higher speeds over far greater distances. Although vision and strength are certainly important physical attributes for a race driver, no quality is more significant than world-class reflexes. Thousands of drivers have dominated at short tracks across the country, yet have been unable to excel at stock-car racing's highest levels. Those drivers either lack the nearly superhuman reflexes required by higher speeds or simply haven't had the opportunity.

Marchbanks, located about 25 miles south of Fresno, didn't hold a Winston Cup race after 1961, leaving the superspeedway ranks to Darlington, Daytona, Charlotte, and Atlanta until the North Carolina Motor Speedway at Rockingham opened in 1965.

Those four tracks, which are frequently called—quite incorrectly—NASCAR's four original superspeedways, quickly assumed a special aura and became known as the "Grand Slam" tracks.

Races at those four venues became far more significant than races at their counterparts, particularly in the '60s and perhaps until the Winston Million was inaugurated in 1985.

"To become the first to win four big ones in a single season and to do it at home . . . well, there's just nothing like it," Cale Yarborough of Timmonsville, S.C., said after he captured the 1968 Southern 500.

Although Yarborough had won the Virginia 500 at Martinsville, the other three triumphs to which he referred were victories in the Daytona 500, the Atlanta 500, and Daytona's Firecracker 400.

Sadly and inexplicably, the concept of the Grand Slam—drivers who can win on all four of those tracks in a single season or during their careers—has been all but forgotten.

Yet it remains a significant milestone in the career of virtually any driver and one that has been open to all since 1960. With the exception of 1968, when the qualifying races for the Daytona 500 were canceled because of rain, Daytona staged four points races per year from 1960-71 and three in 1959. Charlotte staged four and Atlanta three in 1961. For the most part, the two annual visits to Darlington, Daytona, the track now known as Atlanta Motor Speedway, and Charlotte, which changed its name to Lowe's Motor Speedway in 1999, remain among the highlights on the Winston Cup calendar.

Just how difficult is winning on all four of those tracks in the same season?

It has been accomplished only three times. Lee Roy Yarborough captured the Daytona 500 and Firecracker 400 at Daytona, the Rebel 400 and the Southern 500 at Darlington, the Dixie 500 at Atlanta, and the World 600 at Charlotte in 1969. Seven years later, David Pearson won the Daytona 500, the Atlanta 500, the World 600, and both Darlington races. Finally, in 1998, Jeff Gordon captured the Coca-Cola 600 at Charlotte, the Pepsi Southern 500 at Darlington, the Pepsi 400 at Daytona, and the NAPA 500 at Atlanta.

Winning poles on all four Grand Slam venues in a single season has been equally difficult, likewise accomplished on three occasions.

Fireball Roberts accomplished the feat in 1962, sweeping both Charlotte poles. Richard Petty joined him in 1966 and Yarborough in 1969, when he won both Darlington poles.

As the following charts show, only a select group of drivers have won races and poles at all four Grand Slam tracks during their careers.

Drivers Who Have Won at All Four Grand Slam Tracks

Driver	Atlanta	Charlotte	Darlington	Daytona	Total
David Pearson	4	4	10	8	26
Dale Earnhardt	8	5	9	3	25
Richard Petty	6	5	3	10	24
Cale Yarborough	7	3	5	9	24
Bobby Allison	5	6	5	6	22
Bill Elliott	5	2	5	4	16
Jeff Gordon	3	4	5	4	16
Darrell Waltrip	3	6	5	1	15
Fred Lorenzen	4	4	2	2	12
Buddy Baker	2	4	2	2	10
Lee Roy Yarbrough	2	3	2	3	10
Dale Jarrett	1	3	2	3	9
Junior Johnson	1	2	1	4	8
Neil Bonnett	3	2	1	1	7
Benny Parsons	1	2	1	1	5

Drivers Who Have Won Poles at All Four Grand Slam Tracks

Driver	Atlanta	Charlotte	Darlington	Daytona	Total
David Pearson	3	14	12	2	31
Cale Yarborough	6	4	2	12	24
Fireball Roberts	5	4	6	6	21
Bill Elliott	4	4	5	4	17
Buddy Baker	7	3	1	5	16
Richard Petty	4	3	4	1	12
Bobby Allison	2	2	4	2	10
Geoff Bodine	3	2	4	1	10
Bobby Labonte	2	3	1	2	8
Neil Bonnett	1	3	1	1	6
Mark Martin	1	2	2	1	6
Junior Johnson	2	1	1	1	5
Darrell Waltrip	1	2	1	1	5

With 46 condominiums and 141 luxury suites overlooking the track, Atlanta Motor Speedway, along with the sport of Winston Cup racing, has experienced dramatic growth since it helped usher in a new era when it opened in 1960 as one of NASCAR's four "Grand Slam" tracks.

Although winning at all four Grand Slam tracks has proved to be a rare feat, even more exclusive is the club of nine drivers who have won both races and poles at Atlanta, Charlotte, Darlington, and Daytona: Bobby Allison, Buddy Baker, Neil Bonnett, Bill Elliott, Junior Johnson, Darrell Waltrip, Yarborough, Pearson, and Petty. Of course, the most exclusive club is for those drivers who have won races from the pole at all four Grand Slam tracks: No one has joined yet.

1960 in Review

Chevrolet pilot Rex White captured a season-high seven races and three poles on his way to the Winston Cup title and a comfortable 848-696 margin over Petty in the Performance Index ratings. Roberts led the circuit with six poles, but finished a distant 36th in the Performance Index.

Most Memorable Race

White took the checkered flag in the Southern 500 on September 5, but he wasn't the winner. Buck Baker, driving Bud Moore's Pontiac, had led the final 50 laps, but he spun on the penultimate lap and continued on a flat tire. Scoring later determined that Baker actually had nursed his car across the finish line seconds ahead of White. Paul McDuffie, who had been the crew chief for Roberts's 1958 Southern 500 victory, Charles Sweatland, and NASCAR official Joe Taylor were killed during the race. McDuffie and Sweatland, both members of Joe Lee Johnson's crew, and Taylor were killed when Bobby Johns and Roy Tyner wrecked on the 96th lap. Johns's car flipped four times before it landed 100 yards away and threw McDuffie and Taylor onto the track.

Most Significant Wreck

Johns held a seven-second lead with 28 laps to go in the Daytona 500 on Valentine's Day when the rear window flew out of his car, and he almost swerved into Lake Lloyd on the 2.5-mile track's backstretch. Johns lost about 30 seconds and finished second, 23 seconds behind Junior Johnson. "I heard something pop. It was my back window flying out, all in one piece," Johns said. "The air current came through the car and lifted me off the ground and spun me around. I landed all right and continued, but the time cost me the victory."

Records & Milestones

The 1960 season was the second in a row, and one of only three in history, in which no race was held on a road course. . . . Glen Wood became the first driver to capture three victories on the same track in one year, earning three trips to victory lane at Bowman Gray Stadium in Winston-Salem, N.C. Ironically, those three victories comprised 75 percent of Wood's career total. . . . *Thunder in Carolina*, the first feature-length film about stock-car racing, opened in May. When the Oscars were presented, however, *West Side Story* was accorded best picture, and neither *Thunder in Carolina*, nor its star, Rory Calhoun, got so much as a nomination.

1960 at a Glance

Races:	44
Dirt:	21
Short Track:	11
Superspeedway:	12
Winners:	18
Pole Winners:	19
Tracks:	26
States:	11

1960 Performance Index Rankings

1. Rex White (848)
2. Richard Petty (696)
3. Lee Petty (643)
4. Ned Jarrett (628)
5. Buck Baker (568)
6. Junior Johnson (427)
7. Bobby Johns (307)
8. Herman Beam (294)
9. Joe Weatherly (282)
10. L.D. Austin (265)
11. Jim Pardue (264)
12. Bob Welborn (254)
13. Emanuel Zervakis (238)
14. Doug Yates (208)
15. Joe Lee Johnson; G.C. Spencer (207)
17. Jack Smith (205)
18. David Pearson (198)
19. Jim Paschal (195)
20. Curtis Crider (192)
21. Tommy Irwin (191)
22. Tom Pistone (190)
23. Banjo Matthews (180)
24. Paul Lewis; Cotton Owens (171)
26. Fred Harb (167)
27. Johnny Beauchamp; Fred Lorenzen (166)
29. Speedy Thompson (156)
30. Glen Wood (151)
31. Gerald Duke (150)
32. Johnny Allen (141)
33. Possum Jones (134)
34. Bunkie Blackburn (133)
35. Neil Castles (132)
36. Fireball Roberts (116)
37. Marvin Panch (111)
38. Roy Tyner (104)
39. Buddy Baker (101)
40. Larry Frank (97)
41. Herb Tillman (89)
42. Jimmy Massey (88)
43. Shorty Rollins (80)
44. Bob Burdick (78)
45. Tiny Lund; Jim Reed; John Rostek (75)
48. Bob Potter (63)
49. Elmo Henderson (61)
50. Shep Langdon; Wilbur Rakestraw (60)
52. Curtis Turner (58)
53. Jim Cook (55)
54. Joe Eubanks (54)
55. Darrell Dake (53)
56. Mel Larson (52)
57. Lennie Page (46)
58. Lloyd Dane (45)
59. Fritz Wilson (44)
60. Bruce Worrell (43)
61. Whitey Gerkin (42)
62. Jimmy Thompson (41)
63. Scotty Cain; Marvin Porter; Jim Whitman (40)
66. James Norton (39)
67. Elmo Langley; Dick Smith (38)
69. Gene Marmor (36)
70. Joe Caspolich; Roz Howard (35)
72. Charley Griffith (34)
73. Don Noel (33)
74. Clem Proctor; Bill Slater (32)
76. Bob Duell; Ken Johnson; E.J. Trivette (31)
79. Eddie Gray; Bob Perry (30)
81. Al White (29)
82. Dick Joslin; Bob Price; Al Self (28)
85. Spook Crawford (27)
86. Jim Blomgren; Ron Hornaday; Brownie King; Danny Weinberg (26)
90. Maurice Petty (25)
91. Roscoe Thompson (24)
92. Nace Mattingly; Art Watts (23)
94. Tim Flock; Dick Getty; Bill Parnell (21)
97. Wes Morgan (19)
98. Buck Brigance; Charlie Chapman; Dick Foley (18)
101. Richard Riley; Johnny Sudderth; Nook Walters (17)
104. Ed Andrews (16)
105. Parnelli Jones; Kuzie Kuzmanich; Clyde Mitchell (15)
108. Sal Tovella (14)
109. Eddie Riker (13)
110. Bill Cook; Pappy Crane; Bob Kosiski; Bob Ross (12)
114. Jimmie Lewallen; Bill Morgan; Burrhead Nantz (11)
117. Red Farmer; Ernie Gahan; Owen Loggins; Shorty York (10)
121. Jim Austin; George Green; Al Tasnady (9)
124. Jack Hart; Bunk Moore; Jack Norton; Lee Parris; Bob Reuther; Cale Yarborough (7)
130. Bill Massey; Frank Secrist (6)
132. Runt Harris; Al Pombo; Lyle Stelter; Bill Whitley (5)
136. John Potter; Chuck Tombs; Bobby Waddell (4)
139. Smokey Cook; Hubert Johnson; Paul Parks; Bob Roberts (3)
143. John Dodd Jr. (2)
144. Barney Shore (1)

1960 Events

Charlotte Fairgrounds/.5-mile dirt/100 miles
Jack Smith (Chevrolet)/Buck Baker (Chevrolet)

Columbia Speedway/.5-mile dirt/100 miles
Ned Jarrett (Ford)/Junior Johnson (Dodge)

Daytona International Speedway/2.5-mile/100 miles
Fireball Roberts (Pontiac)

Daytona International Speedway/2.5-mile/100 miles
Jack Smith (Pontiac)

Daytona 500; Daytona International Speedway/2.5-m/500 miles
Junior Johnson (Chevrolet)/Cotton Owens (Pontiac)

Charlotte Fairgrounds/.5-mile dirt/100 miles
Richard Petty (Plymouth)/Lee Petty (Plymouth)

Gwyn Staley 160; North Wilkesboro Speedway/.625-m/100 miles
Lee Petty (Plymouth)/Junior Johnson (Chevrolet)

Copper Cup 100; Arizona State Fairgrounds/1-m dirt/100 miles
John Rostek (Ford)/Mel Larson (Pontiac)

Columbia Speedway/.5-mile dirt/100 miles
Rex White (Chevrolet)/Doug Yates (Plymouth)

Virginia 500; Martinsville Speedway/.5-mile/250 miles
Richard Petty (Plymouth)/Glen Wood (Ford)

Hickory 250; Hickory Speedway/.4-mile dirt/100 miles
Joe Weatherly (Ford)/Rex White (Chevrolet)

Wilson Speedway/.5-mile dirt/100 miles
Joe Weatherly (Ford)/Emanuel Zervakis (Chevrolet)

Bowman Gray Stadium/.25-mile/50 miles
Glen Wood (Ford)/Glen Wood (Ford)

Greenville 200; Greenville-Pickens Speedway/.5-m dirt/100 m
Ned Jarrett (Ford)/Curtis Turner (Ford)

Asheville-Weaverville Speedway/.5-mile/100 miles
Lee Petty (Plymouth)/Junior Johnson (Ford)

Rebel 300; Darlington Raceway/1.375-mile/300 miles
Joe Weatherly (Ford)/Fireball Roberts (Pontiac)

Piedmont Interstate Fairgrounds/.5-mile dirt/100 miles
Ned Jarrett (Ford)/Jack Smith (Pontiac)

Orange Speedway/.9-mile dirt/99 miles
Lee Petty (Plymouth)/Richard Petty (Plymouth)

Richmond 200; Atlantic Rural Faigrounds/.5-m dirt/100 miles
Lee Petty (Plymouth)/Ned Jarrett (Ford)

California 250; Marchbanks Speedway/1.4-mile/250 miles
Marvin Porter (Ford)/Frank Secrist (Ford)

World 600; Charlotte Motor Speedway/1.5-mile/600 miles
Joe Lee Johnson (Chevrolet)/Fireball Roberts (Pontiac)

International 200; Bowman Gray Stadium/.25-mile/50 miles
Glen Wood (Ford)/Lee Petty (Plymouth)

Firecracker 250; Daytona International Speedway/2.5-m/250 m
Jack Smith (Pontiac)/Jack Smith (Pontiac)

Heidelberg Stadium/.5-mile dirt/100 miles
Lee Petty (Plymouth)/Lee Petty (Plymouth)

Empire State 200; Montgomery Air Base/2-mile/200 miles
Rex White (Chevrolet)/John Rostek (Ford)

Rambi Raceway/.5-mile dirt/100 miles
Buck Baker (Chevrolet)/Ned Jarrett (Ford)

Dixie 300; Atlanta International Raceway/1.5-mile/300 miles
Fireball Roberts (Pontiac)/Fireball Roberts (Pontiac)

Dixie Speedway/.25-mile/50 miles
Ned Jarrett (Ford)/Ned Jarrett (Ford)

Nashville 400; Fairgrounds Speedway/.5-mile/200 miles
Johnny Beauchamp (Chevrolet)/Rex White (Chevrolet)

Western N.C. 500; Asheville-Weaverville Speedway/.5-m/250 m
Rex White (Chevrolet)/Jack Smith (Pontiac)

Piedmont Interstate Fairgrounds/.5-mile dirt/100 miles
Cotton Owens (Pontiac)/Cotton Owens (Pontiac)

Columbia Speedway/.5-mile dirt/150 miles
Rex White (Chevrolet)/Tommy Irwin (Ford)

South Boston Speedway/.25-mile dirt/38 miles
Junior Johnson (Chevrolet)/Ned Jarrett (Ford)

Bowman Gray Stadium/.25-mile/50 miles
Glen Wood (Ford)/Glen Wood (Ford)

Southern 500; Darlington Raceway/1.375-mile/500 miles
Buck Baker (Pontiac)/Fireball Roberts (Pontiac)

Buddy Shuman 250; Hickory Speedway/.4-mile dirt/100 miles
Junior Johnson (Chevrolet)/Buck Baker (Chevrolet)

California State Fairgrounds/1-mile dirt/100 miles
Jim Cook (Dodge)/Jim Cook (Dodge)

Gamecock Speedway/.25-mile dirt/50 miles
Ned Jarrett (Ford)/David Pearson (Chevrolet)

Orange Speedway/.9-mile dirt/99 miles
Richard Petty (Plymouth)/Richard Petty (Plymouth)

Old Dominion 500; Martinsville Speedway/.5-mile/250 miles
Rex White (Chevrolet)/Glen Wood (Ford)

Wilkes 320; North Wilkesboro Speedway/.625-mile/200 miles
Rex White (Chevrolet)/Rex White (Chevrolet)

National 400; Charlotte Motor Speedway/1.5-mile/400 miles
Speedy Thompson (Ford)/Fireball Roberts (Pontiac)

Capital City 200; Atlantic Rural Fairgrounds/.5-m dirt/100 m
Speedy Thompson (Ford)/Ned Jarrett (Ford)

Atlanta 500; Atlanta International Raceway/1.5-m/500 miles
Bobby Johns (Pontiac)/Fireball Roberts (Pontiac)

Victories

1. Rex White (6)
2. Ned Jarrett; Lee Petty (5)
4. Junior Johnson; Richard Petty; Jack Smith; Joe Weatherly; Glen Wood (3)
9. Buck Baker; Fireball Roberts; Speedy Thompson (2)
12. Johnny Beauchamp; Jim Cook; Bobby Johns; Joe Lee Johnson; Cotton Owens; Marvin Porter; John Rostek (1)

Poles

1. Fireball Roberts (6)
2. Ned Jarrett (5)
3. Glen Wood (4)
4. Junior Johnson; Lee Petty; Jack Smith; Rex White (3)
8. Buck Baker; Cotton Owens; Richard Petty (2)
11. Jim Cook; Tommy Irwin; Mel Larson; David Pearson; John Rostek; Frank Secrist; Curtis Turner; Doug Yates; Emanuel Zervakis (1)

Victories

1. Ford (15)
2. Chevrolet (13)
3. Plymouth (8)
4. Pontiac (7)
5. Dodge (1)

Poles

1. Ford (14)
2. Pontiac (12)
3. Chevrolet (8)
4. Plymouth (6)
5. Dodge (2)

1961
Marty Robbins
Was the Only
Genuine Article

Of the more than 2,700 drivers who competed in Winston Cup races during the sport's inaugural 51 seasons, legendary country singer Marty Robbins was the only one who was more famous for his exploits outside of motorsports.

The most successful Winston Cup driver whose fame stemmed from something other than auto racing was unquestionably Marty Robbins.

The legendary country singer competed sporadically in Winston Cup racing from the mid-'6os through the early '8os. Robbins's Performance Index rating of 365 ranks 238th on the all-time list, one spot ahead of 1950 Winston Cup champion Bill Rexford. But Robbins's legacy is the tune "El Paso," not the career-best fifth-place finish he logged in the 1974 Motor State 400 at Michigan International Speedway.

Perusing the results of the 1,888 races contested in Winston Cup racing's first 51 seasons might lead to the conclusion that Robbins was not the only famous person from another walk of life to try his luck in major-league stock-car racing. Rest assured, these other famous names are merely namesakes.

Woodie Wilson, the 1961 Rookie of the Year, shared his name with Woodrow, the 28th President of the United States. Men named John Kennedy, George Bush, and Bill Clinton also have taken the green flag in Winston Cup cars. So have men who shared names with such presidential hopefuls as Ted Kennedy, longtime New York Mayor John Lindsay, and two Bob Kennedys. Remaining true to stock-car racing's Southern roots, so has Jeff Davis.

Don't forget the notorious: Ben Arnold, no relation to Revolutionary War traitor Benedict; Bobby Baker, the central figure in a scandal during Lyndon Johnson's presidency, and Jim Jones, who convinced a legion of his followers to commit suicide.

All-Americans Larry Miller, Charlie Scott, and Walt(er) Davis of North Carolina; Jimmy Walker of Providence, and Al(bert) King of Maryland would be a powerful basketball team, with Tennessee's Jerry Green coaching. If Green isn't available, Bill Foster might be. There are two from which to choose. One's resume included coaching at Rutgers, Utah, Duke, South Carolina, and Northwestern, and the other made stops at UNC Charlotte, Clemson, Miami, and Virginia Tech. The team could play in the Big Ten, under Commissioner Jim Delaney, a teammate of Miller and Scott at North Carolina.

Former National Football League quarterbacks Ken Anderson and Jim Hart or 49ers legend Steve Young could throw to Gary Collins (not the talk-show host) and Bob Carpenter, Army's lonesome end. Jack (Hacksaw) Reynolds would anchor the defense.

Hall of Fame pitcher Dizzy Dean could call on Randy Myers for relief and hope that Bob Allison, who hit 256 big-league homers, could provide the power.

Former U.S. and British Open champion Johnny Miller would be in demand as a partner at charity golf tournaments, while Robert Vaughn and Don Johnson would be the headliners for skits at charity auctions.

Ironically, George Gallup never won a pole, and Henry Ford drove a Chrysler in his five 1955 starts.

Truly confined to the press box and not behind the wheel would be Jim Murray and Dave Anderson, two of the four sportswriters to win the Pulitzer Prize for commentary; Bill James, author of *Historical Baseball Abstract*; legendary Washington columnist Jack Anderson, and Bob Prince, voice of the Pittsburgh Pirates for generations. They'd be joined in the press box by Bob Myers and both drivers named Bob Moore, who share names with two of the most distinguished motorsports journalists in history.

Although all of the aforementioned people indeed competed in Winston Cup racing, only Robbins was the genuine article.

1961 in Review

Despite capturing only one victory—in a 100-miler on a half-mile dirt track in Birmingham, Ala.—Ned Jarrett earned his first Winston Cup championship. Rex White, who captured seven victories and seven poles, led the Performance Index for the second consecutive season, holding an 873-811 edge over Jarrett. Joe Weatherly's nine victories and Junior Johnson's nine poles led the circuit in those categories.

Most Memorable Race

The Dixie 400 at Atlanta International Raceway on September 17 ranks as one of the most bizarre events in the sport's history. Nelson Stacy had led 43 consecutive laps until his engine expired with 24 laps remaining. Banjo Matthews inherited the lead, but the engine in his Ford blew with five laps left. Pole sitter Fireball Roberts then took the lead, but ran out of gas with two laps to go. Bunkie Blackburn, relief driver for Junior Johnson, then seized the lead and took the white flag. That was the only lap Blackburn led before he ran out

of gas. He took the checkered flag, however, driving the Pontiac across the finish line at about 50 mph. But on the final turn of the race, David Pearson had taken the lead in Ray Fox's Pontiac and protested that he was actually the winner. Indeed he was. Joe Epton, NASCAR's chief scorer, told *The Atlanta Journal* that he had relayed the message to flag Blackburn the winner, but said that no one had told the flagman when Pearson passed Blackburn in the final 200 yards. "My crew told me to get Johnson's car (driven by Blackburn)," said Pearson, who led only the final lap. "I saw it, and I got it. I knew then that I had won the race."

Most Significant Wreck

Lee Petty suffered multiple injuries, including a broken thigh and collarbone, when his car flew over a guardrail in a 100-mile race at Daytona Beach, Fla., on February 24. "That wreck in '61 took the desire out of me," he said nearly three decades later. Petty, who then held the career record of 54 victories, didn't race again until 1962 and never won again. Ironically, he was bumped by Johnny Beauchamp, who had lost a controversial photo finish to Petty in the 1959 Daytona 500.

Most Important Off-Track Development

Curtis Turner, in an effort to rejuvenate the sagging fortunes of Charlotte Motor Speedway, which he had founded along with Bruton Smith, attempted to organize the drivers as the Federation of Professional Athletes. Turner involved the Teamsters Union, and NASCAR President Bill France was unyielding. "If I had the union stuffed down my throat, I would plow up my Daytona Beach track and the other tracks I'm part owner of," France was quoted in *The Atlanta Journal* on August 10. "I won't be dictated to by the union."

France also threatened any union member with a lifetime ban from NASCAR. Those who resigned from the union were reinstated, but Turner and Tim Flock were banned for "life."

Records & Milestones

Nineteen different drivers reached victory lane, tying a record set in 1956 and equaled in 1958. . . . A record 12 drivers earned multiple victories: Weatherly, Johnson (7), White (7), Cotton Owens (4), Fred Lorenzen (3),

Pearson (3), Eddie Gray (2), Jim Paschal (2), Richard Petty (2), Jack Smith (2), Emanuel Zervakis (2), and Roberts (2). . . . Beginning with the Virginia 500 at Martinsville on April 30 and extending through a 50-mile race at Hartsville, S.C., on June 23, 13 different drivers won in a span of as many races, the longest such streak in the sport's history. The winners, in order: Johnson, Lorenzen, Richard Petty, Weatherly, Lloyd Dane, Gray, Pearson, Paschal, Jarrett, Smith, White, Zervakis, and Buck Baker.

When White won the first two short-track events of the season, at Asheville-Weaverville Speedway and Bowman Gray Stadium in North Carolina, he became the first driver to capture four consecutive races on short tracks. . . . The 1961 season was the first campaign in which the majority of races were staged on paved tracks.

1961 at a Glance

Races:	52
Dirt:	21
Road:	1
Short Track:	16
Superspeedway:	14
Winners:	19
Pole Winners:	21
Tracks:	29
States:	9

1961 Performance Index Rankings

1. Rex White (873)
2. Ned Jarrett (811)
3. Emanuel Zervakis (701)
4. Junior Johnson (575)
5. Richard Petty; Joe Weatherly (526)
7. Jim Pardue (472)
8. Buck Baker (467)
9. Herman Beam (441)
10. Fireball Roberts (432)
11. Jim Paschal (401)
12. Jack Smith (383)
13. G.C. Spencer (337)
14. Johnny Allen (333)
15. Cotton Owens (301)
16. Bob Welborn (274)
17. David Pearson (266)
18. Tommy Irwin (259)
19. Curtis Crider (258)
20. Nelson Stacy (245)
21. L.D. Austin (233)
22. Doug Yates (217)
23. Fred Lorenzen (216)
24. Bob Barron (202)
25. Ralph Earnhardt (197)
26. Bobby Johns (193)
27. Marvin Panch (187)
28. Fred Harb (178)
29. Elmo Langley (172)
30. Wendell Scott (155)
31. Paul Lewis (149)
32. Tiny Lund (148)
33. Jim Reed (136)
34. Harry Leake; Lee Reitzel (126)
36. Banjo Matthews (120)
37. Darel Dieringer (119)
38. Buddy Baker (111)
39. Larry Thomas (109)
40. Bob Burdick (93)
41. Eddie Gray (92)
42. Curtis Turner (89)
43. Joe Lee Johnson (88)
44. Maurice Petty; Tom Pistone (87)
46. Don Noel (81)
47. Roscoe Thompson (76)
48. Larry Frank; Woodie Wilson (74)
50. Eddie Pagan (71)
51. George Green; Marvin Porter (67)
53. Lloyd Dane; Glen Wood (64)
55. Paul Goldsmith (62)
56. Danny Weinberg (60)
57. Lee Petty (58)
58. Bill Morgan; Bob Perry (57)
60. Charlie Glotzbach; Ken Rush; Roy Tyner (55)
63. Tim Flock (54)
64. Jim Cook; Joe Eubanks (51)
66. Friday Hassler (50)
67. T.C. Hunt (49)
68. E.J. Trivette (48)
69. Jack Norton; Bruce Worrell (46)
71. Bobby Waddell (45)
72. Bill Morton (43)
73. Scotty Cain (41)
74. Jim Blomgren; Tom Dill (40)
76. Charlie Chapman; Joe Jones (39)
78. Dick Cook; Speedy Thompson (37)
80. Dick Smith (35)
81. Reds Kagle; Frank Secrist (33)
83. George Alsobrook (32)
84. Sal Tovella (31)
85. Ernie Gahan; Jimmy Mairs (30)
87. Dick Getty; Danny Letner; Reb Wickersham (27)
90. Tubby Gonzales; Ron Hornaday; Joe Kelly; Ed Livingston (26)
94. J.C. Hendrix; Herb Tillman (25)
96. Elmo Henderson (24)
97. Buck Fulp; Tommy Wells (23)
99. Al Brand; Carl Joiner; Bob Price; Marshall Sargent (22)
103. Doug Cox; Dick Miller (21)
105. Don O'Dell (20)
106. Jim Bennett; Wilbur Rakestraw; Bob Ross; Dick Santee (19)
110. Bob Presnell (18)
111. Art Malone; Robert Roeber (17)
113. Gus Newman; Sherman Utsman (16)
115. Clem Proctor; Bob Pronger (15)
117. Johnny Beauchamp; Dave Mader; Ed Negre; Chuck Webb; Buzz Woodward (14)
122. Dick Bown; Jim Hendrickson; Kuzie Kuzmanich; Dominic Persicketti (13)

126. Crash Bond; Bill Ferrier; Marvin Heinis; Cliff Hill; Bobby Isaac; Sammy Packard (12)
132. Larry Flynn; Wes Morgan; Mike Saathoff; Gene Stokes (11)
136. Bobby Allison; Bill Clinton; Mark Hurley (10)
139. Pete Boland; Ed Flemke; Homer Galloway; J.V. Hamby; Jim Stewart (9)
144. Robert Berrier; Al Disney; Ronnie Fones; Harvey Hege; Budd Olsen (8)
149. Brownie King; Harold Wilcox (7)
151. Bob Devine; Bill Latham; Doc Lee (6)
154. Ed Brown; Hoss Kagle; T.R. Miller; Jimmy Thompson (4)
158. David Ezell; Jack Hart; Bryant Wallace; Keith Wilkinson (3)
162. Bunk Moore; Oren Prosser; Charles Williamson (2)
165. Bunkie Blackburn; Gerald Duke; Harvey Henderson; Bill Whitley (1)

1961 Events

Charlotte Fairgrounds/.5-mile dirt/100 miles
Joe Weatherly (Ford)/Lee Petty (Plymouth)

Speedway Park/.5-mile dirt/100 miles
Lee Petty (Plymouth)/Junior Johnson (Pontiac)

Daytona International Speedway/2.5-mile/100 miles
Fireball Roberts (Pontiac)

Daytona International Speedway/2.5-mile/100 miles
Joe Weatherly (Pontiac)

Daytona 500; Daytona International Speedway/2.5-m/500 miles
Marvin Panch (Pontiac)/Fireball Roberts (Pontiac)

Piedmont Interstate Fairgrounds/.5-mile dirt/100 miles
Cotton Owens (Pontiac)/Ned Jarrett (Ford)

Asheville-Weaverville Speedway/.5-mile/100 miles
Rex White (Chevrolet)/Rex White (Chevrolet)

Marchbanks Speedway/1.4-mile/250 miles
Fireball Roberts (Pontiac)/Bob Ross (Ford)

Atlanta 500; Atlanta International Raceway/1.5-m/500 miles
Bob Burdick (Pontiac)/Marvin Panch (Pontiac)

Greenville 200; Greenville-Pickens Speedway/.5-m dirt/100 m
Emanuel Zervakis (Chevrolet)/Junior Johnson (Pontiac)

Orange Speedway/.9-mile dirt/99 miles
Cotton Owens (Pontiac)/Ned Jarrett (Chevrolet)

Bowman Gray Stadium/.25-mile/38 miles
Rex White (Chevrolet)/Glen Wood (Ford)

Grand National 200; Martinsville Speedway/.5-mile/100 miles
Fred Lorenzen (Ford)/Rex White (Chevrolet)

Gwyn Staley 400; North Wilkesboro Speedway/.625-m/250 miles
Rex White (Chevrolet)/Junior Johnson (Pontiac)

Columbia Speedway/.5-mile dirt/100 miles
Cotton Owens (Pontiac)/Ned Jarrett (Chevrolet)

Hickory 250; Hickory Speedway/.4-mile dirt/100 miles
Junior Johnson (Pontiac)/Junior Johnson (Pontiac)

Richmond 200; Atlantic Rural Fairgrounds/.5-mile dirt/100 m
Richard Petty (Plymouth)/Richard Petty (Plymouth)

Virginia 500; Martinsville Speedway/.5-mile/250 miles
Junior Johnson (Pontiac)/Rex White (Chevrolet)

Rebel 300; Darlington Raceway/1.375-mile/300 miles
Fred Lorenzen (Ford)/Fred Lorenzen (Ford)

Charlotte Motor Speedway/1.5-mile/100 miles
Richard Petty (Plymouth)

Charlotte Motor Speedway/1.5-mile/100 miles
Joe Weatherly (Pontiac)

Riverside International Raceway/2.58-mile road/100 miles
Lloyd Dane (Chevrolet)/Eddie Gray (Ford)

Ascot Speedway/.5-mile dirt/100 miles
Eddie Gray (Ford)/Danny Weinberg (Ford)

World 600; Charlotte Motor Speedway/1.5-mile/600 miles
David Pearson (Pontiac)/Richard Petty (Plymouth)

Piedmont Interstate Fairgrounds/.5-mile dirt/100 miles
Jim Paschal (Pontiac)/Joe Weatherly (Pontiac)

Alabama State Fairgrounds/.5-mile dirt/100 miles
Ned Jarrett (Chevrolet)/Johnny Allen (Chevrolet)

Pickens 200; Greenville-Pickens Speedway/.5-m dirt/100 miles
Jack Smith (Pontiac)/Ned Jarrett (Chevrolet)

Myers Brothers 200; Bowman Gray Stadium/.25-mile/50 miles
Rex White (Chevrolet)/Junior Johnson (Pontiac)

Yankee 500; Norwood Arena/.25-mile/125 miles
Emanuel Zervakis (Chevrolet)/Rex White (Chevrolet)

Hartsville Speedway/.333-mile dirt/50 miles
Buck Baker (Chrysler)/Emanuel Zervakis (Chevrolet)

Starkey Speedway/.25-mile/38 miles
Junior Johnson (Pontiac)/Rex White (Chevrolet)

Firecracker 250; Daytona International Speedway/2.5-m/250 m
David Pearson (Pontiac)/Fireball Roberts (Pontiac)

Festival 250; Atlanta International Raceway/1.5-m/250 miles
Fred Lorenzen (Ford)/Fireball Roberts (Pontiac)

Columbia Speedway/.5-mile dirt/100 miles
Cotton Owens (Pontiac)/Cotton Owens (Pontiac)

Rambi Raceway/.5-mile dirt/100 miles
Joe Weatherly (Pontiac)/Joe Weatherly (Pontiac)

Volunteer 500; Bristol International Speedway/.5-m/250 miles
Jack Smith (Pontiac)/Fred Lorenzen (Ford)

Nashville 500; Fairgrounds Speedway/.5-mile/250 miles
Jim Paschal (Pontiac)/Rex White (Chevrolet)

Bowman Gray Stadium/.25-mile/38 miles
Rex White (Chevrolet)/Junior Johnson (Pontiac)

Western N.C. 500; Asheville-Weaverville Speedway/.5-m/250 m
Junior Johnson (Pontiac)/Jim Paschal (Pontiac)

Southside Speedway/.25-mile/38 miles
Junior Johnson (Pontiac)/Junior Johnson (Pontiac)

South Boston Speedway/.25-mile dirt/50 miles
Junior Johnson (Pontiac)/Cotton Owens (Pontiac)

Southern 500; Darlington Raceway/1.375-mile/500 miles
Nelson Stacy (Ford)/Fireball Roberts (Pontiac)

Buddy Shuman 250; Hickory Speedway/.4-mile dirt/100 miles
Rex White (Chevrolet)/Rex White (Chevrolet)

Capital City 250; Atlantic Rural Fairgrounds/.5-m dirt/125 m
Joe Weatherly (Pontiac)/Junior Johnson (Pontiac)

California State Fairgrounds/1-mile dirt/100 miles
Eddie Gray (Ford)/Bill Amick (Pontiac)

Dixie 400; Atlanta International Raceway/1.5-mile/400 miles
David Pearson (Pontiac)/Fireball Roberts (Pontiac)

Old Dominion 500; Martinsville Speedway/.5-mile/250 miles
Joe Weatherly (Pontiac)/Fred Lorenzen (Ford)

Wilkes 320; North Wilkesboro Speedway/.625-mile/200 miles
Rex White (Chevrolet)/Junior Johnson (Pontiac)

National 400; Charlotte Motor Speedway/1.5-mile/400 miles
Joe Weatherly (Pontiac)/David Pearson (Pontiac)

Southeastern 500; Bristol Int. Speedway/.5-mile/250 miles
Joe Weatherly (Pontiac)/Bobby Johns (Pontiac)

Greenville-Pickens Speedway/.5-mile dirt/100 miles
Junior Johnson (Pontiac)/Buck Baker (Chrysler)

Orange Speedway/.9-mile dirt/149 miles
Joe Weatherly (Pontiac)/Joe Weatherly (Pontiac)

Victories

1. Joe Weatherly (9)
2. Junior Johnson; Rex White (7)
4. Cotton Owens (4)
5. Fred Lorenzen; David Pearson (3)
7. Eddie Gray; Jim Paschal; Richard Petty; Fireball Roberts; Jack Smith; Emanuel Zervakis (2)
13. Buck Baker; Bob Burdick; Lloyd Dane; Ned Jarrett; Marvin Panch; Lee Petty; Nelson Stacy (1)

Poles

1. Junior Johnson (9)
2. Rex White (7)
3. Fireball Roberts (5)
4. Ned Jarrett (4)
5. Fred Lorenzen; Joe Weatherly (3)
7. Cotton Owens; Richard Petty (2)
9. Johnny Allen; Bill Amick; Buck Baker; Eddie Gray; Bobby Johns; Marvin Panch; Jim Paschal; David Pearson; Lee Petty; Bob Ross; Danny Weinberg; Glen Wood; Emanuel Zervakis (1)

Victories

1. Pontiac (30)
2. Chevrolet (11)
3. Ford (7)
4. Plymouth (3)
5. Chrysler (1)

Poles

1. Pontiac (24)
2. Chevrolet (12)
3. Ford (8)
4. Plymouth (3)
5. Chrysler (1)

1962
Great Scott, Other Minorities

NASCAR opened for business six years before *Brown v. Board of Education* shook not only Topeka, Kan., but an entire nation, and the Winston Cup Series had been around for 15 years when the Civil Rights Act became the law of the land in 1964.

Yet few members of minority groups have made a significant impact in Winston Cup racing. Members of two minorities, Wendell Scott and Louise Smith, were selected to the International Motorsports Hall of Fame in Talladega, Ala., in 1998, however.

Scott unquestionably ranks as the most successful minority driver in stock-car racing history. In fact, no other minority member can begin to match the accomplishments of the African-American driver from Danville, Va., whose career was immortalized in the Richard Pryor film *Greased Lightening*. Scott is the only minority driver to win a Winston Cup pole, accomplished in 1962 on a half-mile dirt track in Savannah, Ga., and a race, which he managed in a 100-mile dirt race at Jacksonville in 1964. Scott finished in the top 12 in the Performance Index eight consecutive years (1962-69), with a sixth-place finish in 1965. His 4,863 career Performance Index rating ranks 37th on the all-time list.

At least five other African-American drivers have taken the green flag in Winston Cup races. The first was Joie Ray, who finished 51st in a 62-car field on the Beach & Road Course at Daytona Beach, Fla., on February 10, 1952. George Wiltshire, Randy Bethea, Willy T. Ribbs, and Charlie Scott also made Winston Cup starts, but the latter was the only one to earn a top-20 finish.

Thirty-five drivers from six foreign countries are among the 1,968 listed on the Performance Index, led by Trevor Boys of Canada with an 829 rating. Only four other foreign drivers have career Performance Index ratings above 100, and all are Canadian: 1974 Rookie of the Year Earl Ross (541), Don Biederman (211), Vic Parsons (185), and Roy Smith (144). Ross, who captured the 1974 Old Dominion 500 at Martinsville, Va., is the only foreign driver to win a race, and Canada's Lloyd Shaw is the only foreign pole winner.

The other five countries represented by a driver who has finished in the top 20 in a Winston Cup race and the highest Performance Index by a driver from each of those locales:

Driver	Country	Career PI Rating
Terry Byers	Australia	21
Vic Elford	England	98
Joe Schlesser	France	53
Pedro Rodriguez	Mexico	64
Eduardo Dibas	Peru	44

While Ross is the only driver to reach victory lane in Winston Cup competition who is not a U.S. citizen, another foreign-born driver also won a race. Mario Andretti, the 1967 Daytona 500 winner whose career Performance Index is 205, was born in Italy in 1940. But he moved to Nazareth, Pa., in 1955 and was a U.S. citizen when he won stock-car racing's premier event.

The ranks of Winston Cup drivers have been populated by at least 14 females—Christine Beckers, Ann Bunselmeyer, Ann Chester, Sara Christian, Janet Guthrie, Lella Lombardi, Sandy Lynch, Robin McCall, Ethel Mobley, Patty Moise, Marian Pagan, Goldie Parsons, FiFi Scott, and Smith.

Mamie Reynolds, the 19-year-old daughter of U.S. Senator Robert J. Reynolds of Asheville, N.C., became the first woman to field a winning car in a Winston Cup race when Fred Lorenzen piloted a Ford she had purchased from Holman-Moody to victory on September 13, 1962, at Augusta, Ga.

Guthrie has the highest career Performance Index rating (473) among women and finished 20th in 1977. Christian ranks second in that group with a career Performance Index rating of 66. That rating was achieved in six starts in 1949—when she finished with the eighth-highest rating—and one in 1950. Mobley and Smith each have Performance Index ratings of 19, followed by Scott (8), Parsons (7), Lynch (5), Bunselmeyer (3), and Pagan (3). None of the others ever finished in the top 20 in a race.

The 1977 Firecracker 400 at Daytona featured three women: Beckers, Lombardi, and Guthrie. The latter is the only woman to lead a lap in Winston Cup competition, when she paced the 43rd through 47th circuits—all under caution—around the 2.5-mile Ontario Motor Speedway in the Los Angeles Times 500 on November 20, 1977.

Although Guthrie wasn't the first woman to compete in Winston Cup racing, or even among the first five, certainly no female driver's Winston Cup debut ever was accorded more attention.

Guthrie had spent most of the month of May in 1976 at the Indianapolis Motor Speedway in an unsuccessful effort to become the first female to qualify for the Indianapolis 500, which she accomplished a year later. When her first attempt failed, Charlotte Motor Speedway President and General Manager Humpy Wheeler arranged a ride for her in the World 600 behind the wheel of a Chevrolet purchased for the occasion by Lynda Ferreri, a vice president of First Union National Bank in Charlotte. The car was prepared by legendary car builder Ralph Moody, and Guthrie's first visit to the track produced the first large media contingent to attend a testing session.

After her first shakedown run, Guthrie, an accomplished pilot, drove down pit road and asked Moody: "What's the slip angle in the first turn?"

Replied Moody, apparently unfamiliar with that aviation term: "I don't know. I don't speak `injun.' "

"In our pre-race publicity for the World 600, we were getting shot down by her," Wheeler recalled a couple of years later. "Every time she breathed at Indianapolis, it would be on the front of the sports page. I had the urge to make her an offer she couldn't refuse, but I waited until she didn't qualify. I gave her a hell of an offer. She was the hottest thing in racing—maybe the hottest thing that will ever be in racing—but I knew it only would be good for the first time. The biggest ticket day in the history of Charlotte Motor Speedway was the day Janet Guthrie ran here."

Wheeler and track owner Bruton Smith later spent countless millions turning Charlotte Motor Speedway into a motorsports palace. Smith said years later that it was no secret that the grandstands were filled with men and that the additions and improvements were simply to "try to get the ladies to come out."

NASCAR research indicates that 38 percent of its fans today are women, and the attention that surrounded Guthrie's 15th-place finish in the 1976 World 600 was probably the launching pad.

1962 in Review

Joe Weatherly, who won nine races in a Bud Moore-owned Pontiac and captured the Winston Cup championship, became the first driver to record a rating of 1,000 or more in a single season, rolling to a 1,049-933 margin over Richard Petty in the Performance Index ratings. Rex White captured eight victories and a season-high nine poles, and Petty's eight triumphs gave Weatherly, White, and Petty 25 victories in the season's 53 events.

Most Memorable Race

Pole winner Fireball Roberts ran out of gas twice, but still managed to beat Richard Petty by 27 seconds to win the Daytona 500 on February 18. Lee Petty, Richard's car owner, protested that Roberts's crew, led by the legendary Smokey Yunick, had seven men over the wall instead of the allowed six to service the Jim Stephens-owned Pontiac. Roberts, a hometown hero, wasn't concerned about the protest. "You don't think they'll disqualify ol' Fireball in Daytona, do you?" he asked columnist Furman Bisher of *The Atlanta Journal.*

Most Significant Wreck

Johnny Allen's Pontiac sailed over the wall at Bowman Gray Stadium in Winston-Salem, N.C., on June 16. But Allen managed to edge White by less than a foot to win the Myers Brothers 200 seconds *before* he lost control of his car.

Most Important Off-Track Development

Ford resumed factory involvement in June after a five-year absence.

Janet Guthrie has the highest career Performance Index of any woman to compete in Winston Cup racing and also holds the distinction of being the only member of her sex ever to lead a lap in stock-car racing's premier series.

Records & Milestones

The 1962 season marked the fourth time in six years that eight drivers posted three or more victories. The 1957, 1958, and 1960 seasons were the only other such campaigns.... White captured at least four short-track victories for the fourth consecutive year, setting a record that would last a decade and be eclipsed only by Richard Petty and tied by Darrell Waltrip.... White became the second driver, joining Herb Thomas, to win five or more races four years in a row.

Nelson Stacy, the 1961 Southern 500 winner, added three more victories in '62. His four career victories make him the only driver in history with at least three wins who never captured a pole.... The 1962 season was the third time in four years, one of only three seasons in the 20th Century, and the last time that the circuit did not visit a road course.

1962 at a Glance

Races:	53
Dirt:	23
Short Track:	20
Superspeedway:	10
Winners:	14
Pole Winners:	12
Tracks:	28
States:	7

1962 Performance Index Rankings

1. Joe Weatherly (1,049)
2. Richard Petty (933)
3. Ned Jarrett (816)
4. Jack Smith (795)
5. Rex White (609)
6. Jim Paschal (606)
7. Herman Beam (470)
8. Curtis Crider (445)
9. Tom Cox (422)
10. Bob Welborn (406)
11. Wendell Scott (402)
12. Buck Baker (399)
13. Larry Thomas (373)
14. George Green; Jim Pardue (369)
16. Fireball Roberts (364)
17. Fred Lorenzen (347)
18. G.C. Spencer (316)
19. Buddy Baker (312)
20. Marvin Panch (292)
21. Junior Johnson (249)
22. David Pearson (245)
23. Larry Frank (243)
24. Johnny Allen (236)
25. Nelson Stacy (222)
26. Cotton Owens (178)
27. Ralph Earnhardt (165)
28. Bunkie Blackburn (162)
29. Tommy Irwin (157)
30. Sherman Utsman (152)
31. Emanuel Zervakis (130)
32. Tiny Lund (119)
33. Fred Harb (115)
34. Bobby Johns (109)
35. Darel Dieringer (97)
36. Stick Elliott (95)
37. Banjo Matthews (90)
38. Ed Livingston (88)
39. Lee Roy Yarbrough (83)
40. Bob Cooper (63)
41. Jim Cushman; Elmo Langley (62)
43. Billy Wade (61)
44. Ernie Gahan (56)
45. Bill Morton (55)
46. Maurice Petty; Speedy Thompson (54)
48. Red Foote (53)
49. Ray Hughes (48)
50. H.G. Rosier; Jimmy Thompson; Bill Wimble (47)
53. Mel Bradley; Cale Yarborough (45)
55. Jim Bennett; Earl Brooks (44)
57. Dick Getty (40)
58. Harry Leake (39)
59. Paul Barrow (38)
60. Paul Lewis (36)
61. Troy Ruttman (35)
62. Paul Goldsmith (34)
63. George Alsobrook (30)
64. Neil Castles; Doug Yates (27)
66. Dan Gurney; Roscoe Thompson (26)
68. Bill Foster; T.C. Hunt; Worth McMillion (25)
71. Wally Dallenbach (24)
72. Bob Burdick; Woodie Wilson (23)
74. Art Malone; Lee Petty; Jim Reed (20)
77. Red Farmer (19)
78. Bob Devine; Charley Griffith (18)
80. George Dunn (17)
81. Jim McGuirk; Lee Reitzel (16)
83. Harold Carmac (15)
84. Joe Penland (14)
85. Jim Bray; Ronnie Fones; Frank Graham; Roy Hallquist; J.V. Hamby; Frank Sessoms (13)
91. J.C. Hendrix (12)
92. Tubby Gonzales; Ralph Smith; Nero Steptoe; Herb Thomas; Sal Tovella (11)
97. Ray Hendrick; Eddie Pagan; John Rogers (10)
100. Bill McDonald; Sam McQuagg; Gary Sain; Bill Whitley (9)
104. Freddy Fryar; Sammy Packard; Floyd Powell (8)
107. Runt Harris; Ken Rush (7)
109. Weldon Adams; Robert Berrier; Frank Brantley; Bill Dennis (6)
113. Gene Blackburn; Jerry Burnett; Bubba Farr (5)
116. Mark Hurley; Joe Lee Johnson; Joe Jones; Herbert Scott (4)
120. Bill Delaney; Doug Duvall; Jerry Smith (3)
123. Bill Faulkner; Bobby Waddell (2)
125. Steve Garrett; Friday Hassler; Lester Hicks; Al White (1)

1962 Events

Concord Speedway/.5-mile dirt/100 miles
Jack Smith (Pontiac)/Joe Weatherly (Pontiac)

Asheville-Weaverville Speedway/.5-mile/100 miles
Rex White (Chevrolet)/Joe Weatherly (Pontiac)

Daytona International Speedway/2.5-mile/100 miles
Fireball Roberts (Pontiac)

Daytona International Speedway/2.5-mile/100 miles
Joe Weatherly (Pontiac)

Daytona 500; Daytona International Speedway/2.5-m/500 miles
Fireball Roberts (Pontiac)/Fireball Roberts (Pontiac)

Concord Speedway/.5-mile dirt/100 miles
Joe Weatherly (Pontiac)/Joe Weatherly (Pontiac)

Asheville-Weaverville Speedway/.5-mile/100 miles
Joe Weatherly (Pontiac)/Rex White (Chevrolet)

St. Patrick's Day 200; Savannah Speedway/.5-m dirt/100 miles
Jack Smith (Pontiac)/Rex White (Chevrolet)

Orange Speedway/.9-mile dirt/99 miles
Rex White (Chevrolet)/Joe Weatherly (Pontiac)

Richmond 250; Atlantic Rural Fairgrounds/.5-m dirt/125 miles
Rex White (Chevrolet)

Arclite 200; Columbia Speedway/.5-mile dirt/100 miles
Ned Jarrett (Chevrolet)/Joe Weatherly (Pontiac)

Gwyn Staley 400; North Wilkesboro Speedway/.625-m/250 miles
Richard Petty (Plymouth)/Junior Johnson (Pontiac)

Greenville 200; Greenville-Pickens Speedway/.5-m dirt/100 m
Ned Jarrett (Chevrolet)/Ned Jarrett (Chevrolet)

Rambi Raceway/.5-mile dirt/100 miles
Jack Smith (Pontiac)/Ned Jarrett (Chevrolet)

Virginia 500; Martinsville Speedway/.5-mile/250 miles
Richard Petty (Plymouth)/Fred Lorenzen (Ford)

Bowman Gray Stadium/.25-mile/50 miles
Rex White (Chevrolet)/Rex White (Chevrolet)

Volunteer 500; Bristol International Speedway/.5-m/250 miles
Bobby Johns (Pontiac)/Fireball Roberts (Pontiac)

Southside Speedway/.333-mile/67 miles
Jim Pardue (Pontiac)/Rex White (Chevrolet)

Hickory 250; Hickory Speedway/.4-mile dirt/100 miles
Jack Smith (Pontiac)/Jack Smith (Pontiac)

Concord Speedway/.5-mile dirt/100 miles
Joe Weatherly (Pontiac)

Rebel 300; Darlington Raceway/1.375-mile/300 miles
Nelson Stacy (Ford)/Fred Lorenzen (Ford)

Piedmont Interstate Fairgrounds/.5-mile dirt/100 miles
Ned Jarrett (Chevrolet)/Cotton Owens (Pontiac)

World 600; Charlotte Motor Speedway/1.5-mile/600 miles
Nelson Stacy (Ford)/Fireball Roberts (Pontiac)

Atlanta 500; Atlanta International Raceway/1.5-m/500 miles
Fred Lorenzen (Ford)/Banjo Matthews (Pontiac)

Myers Brothers 200; Bowman Gray Stadium/.25-mile/50 miles
Johnny Allen (Pontiac)/Rex White (Chevrolet)

Augusta Speedway/.5-mile dirt/100 miles
Joe Weatherly (Pontiac)/Joe Weatherly (Pontiac)

Southside Speedway/.333-mile/100 miles
Jim Paschal (Pontiac)/Rex White (Chevrolet)

South Boston Speedway/.375-mile/100 miles
Rex White (Chevrolet)/Jack Smith (Pontiac)

Firecracker 250; Daytona International Speedway/2.5-m/250 m
Fireball Roberts (Pontiac)/Banjo Matthews (Pontiac)

Sandlapper 200; Columbia Speedway/.5-mile dirt/100 miles
Rex White (Chevrolet)/Jack Smith (Pontiac)

Asheville Speedway/.4-mile/100 miles
Jack Smith (Pontiac)/Rex White (Chevrolet)

Pickens 200; Greenville-Pickens Speedway/.5-m dirt/100 miles
Richard Petty (Plymouth)/Rex White (Chevrolet)

Augusta Speedway/.5-mile dirt/100 miles
Joe Weatherly (Pontiac)/Jack Smith (Pontiac)

Savannah Speedway/.5-mile dirt/100 miles
Joe Weatherly (Pontiac)/Wendell Scott (Chevrolet)

Rambi Raceway/.5-mile dirt/100 miles
Ned Jarrett (Chevrolet)/Ned Jarrett (Chevrolet)

Southeastern 500; Bristol International Speedway/.5-m/250 m
Jim Paschal (Plymouth)/Fireball Roberts (Pontiac)

Confederate 200; Boyd Speedway/.333-mile/67 miles
Joe Weatherly (Pontiac)/Richard Petty (Plymouth)

Nashville 500; Fairgrounds Speedway/.5-mile/250 miles
Jim Paschal (Plymouth)/Johnny Allen (Pontiac)

Huntsville Speedway/.25-mile/50 miles
Richard Petty (Plymouth)/Richard Petty (Plymouth)

Western N.C. 500; Asheville-Weaverville Speedway/.5-m/250 m
Jim Paschal (Plymouth)/Jack Smith (Pontiac)

Starkey Speedway/.25-mile/50 miles
Richard Petty (Plymouth)/Jack Smith (Pontiac)

International 200; Bowman Gray Stadium/.25-mile/50 miles
Richard Petty (Plymouth)/Jack Smith (Pontiac)

Piedmont Interstate Fairgrounds/.5-mile dirt/100 miles
Richard Petty (Plymouth)/Richard Petty (Plymouth)

Valdosta Speedway/.5-mile dirt/100 miles
Ned Jarrett (Chevrolet)/Richard Petty (Plymouth)

Southern 500; Darlington Raceway/1.375-mile/500 miles
Larry Frank (Ford)/Fireball Roberts (Pontiac)

Buddy Shuman 250; Hickory Speedway/.4-mile dirt/100 miles
Rex White (Chevrolet)/Junior Johnson (Pontiac)

Capital City 300; Atlantic Rural Fairgrounds/.5-m dirt/150 m
Joe Weatherly (Pontiac)/Rex White (Chevrolet)

Dog Track Speedway/.25-mile dirt/63 miles
Ned Jarrett (Chevrolet)/Ned Jarrett (Chevrolet)

Augusta Speedway/.5-mile dirt/100 miles
Fred Lorenzen (Ford)/Joe Weatherly (Pontiac)

Old Dominion 500; Martinsville Speedway/.5-mile/250 miles
Nelson Stacy (Ford)/Fireball Roberts (Pontiac)

Wilkes 320; North Wilkesboro Speedway/.625-mile/200 miles
Richard Petty (Plymouth)/Fred Lorenzen (Ford)

National 400; Charlotte Motor Speedway/1.5-mile/400 miles
Junior Johnson (Pontiac)/Fireball Roberts (Pontiac)

Dixie 400; Atlanta International Raceway/1.5-mile/400 miles
Rex White (Chevrolet)/Fireball Roberts (Pontiac)

Victories

1. Joe Weatherly (9)
2. Richard Petty; Rex White (8)
4. Ned Jarrett (6)
5. Jack Smith (5)
6. Jim Paschal (4)
7. Fireball Roberts; Nelson Stacy (3)
9. Fred Lorenzen (2)
10. Johnny Allen; Larry Frank; Bobby Johns; Junior Johnson; Jim Pardue (1)

Poles

1. Rex White (9)
2. Fireball Roberts (8)
3. Jack Smith; Joe Weatherly (7)
5. Ned Jarrett; Richard Petty (4)
7. Fred Lorenzen (3)
8. Junior Johnson; Banjo Matthews (2)
10. Johnny Allen; Cotton Owens; Wendell Scott (1)

Victories

1. Pontiac (22)
2. Chevrolet (14)
3. Plymouth (11)
4. Ford (6)

Poles

1. Pontiac (28)
2. Chevrolet (14)
3. Plymouth (4)
4. Ford (3)

1963
Was Championship
'Stroke' of Luck?

recalled asking Weatherly about his desire to win stock-car racing's premier championship at any cost. "I'm going to go flat-out, belly-to-the-track whenever I run, championship or no championship," Minter recalled Weatherly saying during a 1960 testing session at Atlanta. "I'm not going to stroke. To win the title, you have to stroke. You have to play it cool. You have to finish every race. I like my way more than I'd like a championship."

Joe Weatherly had only four victories on his resume when the 1961 season opened.

That season, during which he turned 39, Weatherly recorded the first of back-to-back nine-victory campaigns. Only Richard Petty, Cale Yarborough, and Jeff Gordon have had longer streaks of seasons with at least nine triumphs.

Coincidentally or not, Little Joe's best seasons came after his partner in off-track revelry, Curtis Turner, had been banned by NASCAR. Weatherly posted 25 victories and 18 poles, with his most notable achievements on dirt. His 15 dirt victories rank in a 10th-place tie, and his 16 poles on dirt rank 10th on that surface. He won at least three dirt poles three years in a row (1961-63) and at least five dirt poles in consecutive years (1962-63). Only Herb Thomas had longer such streaks.

Weatherly, a stubby and enormously popular Virginian who bore an uncanny resemblance to Uga, the Georgia Bulldogs' mascot, also won at least one superspeedway race each season from 1960-63, a streak exceeded at that time only by Fireball Roberts.

Weatherly captured his first Winston Cup title in 1962 and his second a year later in what ranks as the most improbable campaign a champion ever had.

Weatherly had won the 1962 title behind the wheel of Bud Moore's Pontiac, but Moore declined to field a car in many of the 1963 races. Weatherly competed in 28 races in Moore's Pontiac, another eight in Moore's Mercury, and the others for a variety of owners.

Weatherly, who generally competed in saddle oxfords, golf gloves, and bright sport shirts, frequently was accused of stroking his way to the 1963 title.

In a column written by Jim Minter that appeared in *The Atlanta Journal* after Weatherly was killed on January 19, 1964, in a crash at Riverside, Calif., Minter

1963 in Review

Weatherly finished with 33,398 points to runner-up Richard Petty's 31,170. A closer examination of their seasons reveals that if any driver knew exactly how to milk the point system then in effect for all it was worth, it was Weatherly. Petty not only captured a season-high 14 victories to Weatherly's three, but he bettered Weatherly in top-two finishes (23-8), top-three finishes (25-13), top-four finishes (29-18), top-five finishes (30-20), top-six finishes (35-23), top-10 finishes (39-35), top-15 finishes (49-43), and top-20 finishes (50-47). Petty also competed in 54 races, one more than Weatherly, who missed the May 19 race at Southside Speedway in Richmond, Va., in which Petty finished second.

In the 52 times they competed against each other, Petty finished ahead of his rival 30 times. They competed in separate 100-mile qualifying races at Daytona Beach, Fla., with Petty finishing 12th and Weatherly 13th. Petty's average finish for 54 starts was 7.5, while Weatherly's for 53 was 9.08. To his credit, Weatherly never finished worse than a pair of 24th-place showings. Petty, on the other hand, had four races in which he finished worse than 16th: a 41st-place finish, two 36th-place showings, and a 26th-place effort. Yet Petty finished with a 1,012 rating on the Performance Index, Ned Jarrett won eight races and finished second with an 875 rating, and Weatherly was third with an 844 rating. In no other season did the Winston Cup champion finish so far behind in the Performance Index. Junior Johnson led the circuit with nine poles and finished third with seven victories, but ranked only 10th in the Performance Index.

Most Important Off-Track Development

Weatherly's ability to hustle rides for the races Moore skipped was paramount to his title bid. He drove a Pontiac in eight races for Cliff Stewart; in two for Fred Harb, and in one each for Pete Stewart, Allen McMillion, and Possum Jones. Weatherly also drove a Dodge twice for Wade Younts, a Chevrolet once for Major Melton, and a Plymouth once for Petty Enterprises.

Most Memorable Race

Fred Lorenzen took the white flag in the Firecracker 400 at Daytona on Independence Day. Lorenzen gradually slowed down after passing Roberts on the 158th of 160 laps, trying to get Roberts or Marvin Panch, also locked in the three-car Ford duel, to pass him and allow Lorenzen to use the draft to slingshot around his foes. But neither Roberts nor Panch wanted take the bait. Finally, Roberts overtook Lorenzen in the final turn and beat him to the checkered flag by less than a car length, with Panch right behind. "I got to thinking that all three of us were going mighty slow, maybe 20 or 30 miles an hour slower than we should be," Roberts said. "So I just stepped on it and was lucky enough that Freddie, who tried to use the slingshot, was a little too late. It's just like Russian roulette. My dice rolled lucky."

Most Significant Wreck

Tiny Lund's Ford plowed through a guardrail in the Nashville 400 on August 4. When Lund's car caromed back on the track, it landed on Rex White's Mercury, punching a hole in the roof and destroying the roll bar. White, who had won 28 races and 36 poles since the beginning of the 1956 season, never won another race or pole.

Records & Milestones

When Herman "The Turtle" Beam logged a ninth-place finish at Orange Speedway in Hillsboro, N.C.—located in the same county as the University of North Carolina, from which he earned a degree in chemistry—it marked the 84th consecutive race in which Beam was running at the finish, a record.

1963 at a Glance

Races:	55
Dirt:	17
Road:	3
Short Track:	25
Superspeedway:	10
Winners:	15
Pole Winners:	16
Tracks:	31
States:	11

1963 Performance Index Rankings

1. Richard Petty (1,012)
2. Ned Jarrett (875)
3. Joe Weatherly (844)
4. Fred Lorenzen (636)
5. Buck Baker (607)
6. David Pearson (552)
7. Jim Pardue (539)
8. Jim Paschal; Wendell Scott (464)
10. Junior Johnson (450)
11. Curtis Crider (437)
12. Fireball Roberts (432)
13. Rex White (425)
14. Darel Dieringer (412)
15. Billy Wade (375)
16. Tiny Lund (369)
17. Marvin Panch (337)
18. Larry Thomas (333)
19. G.C. Spencer (315)
20. Bobby Isaac (307)
21. Nelson Stacy (257)
22. Stick Elliott (254)
23. Cale Yarborough (231)
24. Jack Smith (224)
25. Larry Manning (219)
26. Neil Castles (208)
27. Bobby Johns (193)
28. Herman Beam (191)
29. Lee Roy Yarbrough (165)
30. Jimmy Massey (153)
31. Larry Frank (151)
32. Roy Mayne (146)
33. Worth McMillion (136)
34. Fred Harb (133)
35. Troy Ruttman (122)
36. Tommy Irwin (118)
37. Elmo Langley (116)
38. Reb Wickersham (113)
39. Dan Gurney (110)
40. Bob Welborn (106)

Mystery still surrounds the fatal 1964 crash at Riverside, Calif., that took the life of Joe Weatherly, who had won the previous two Winston Cup titles, including a 1963 crown that was the most improbable championship ever.

41. Ed Livingston (101)
42. J.D. McDuffie (89)
43. A.J. Foyt (88)
44. Bob Cooper (85)
45. Major Melton (76)
46. Bill Foster (72)
47. Johnny Rutherford (71)
48. Bob James (66)
49. Bud Harless; E.J. Trivette (63)
51. Dave MacDonald (61)
52. Paul Goldsmith (57)
53. Bunkie Blackburn; Ron Hornaday (54)
55. Buddy Baker (53)
56. Parnelli Jones; Bob Ross (52)
58. Glen Wood (49)
59. Sal Tovella (45)
60. Lee Petty (44)
61. Floyd Powell (40)
62. H.B. Bailey; Maurice Petty; Sherman Utsman (39)
65. Gary Sain (36)
66. Bill Widenhouse (35)
67. Bob Perry (34)
68. Sonny Fogle (33)
69. Johnny Allen; Bobby Keck (32)
71. Frank Waite (31)
72. Ray Hendrick; Danny Letner (30)
74. George Green; Emanuel Zervakis (29)
76. T.C. Hunt; Banjo Matthews (28)
78. Bill Amick (27)
79. Ken Miles; John Rostek (24)
81. Jim McGuirk; Clem Proctor; Art Watts (23)
84. Ralph Earnhardt (22)
85. Richard Brown; Bill Clinton; Mark Hurley (21)
88. Harold Beal; Dick Goode; Marvin Porter; Frank Warren (20)
92. Pete Brock; Roy Hallquist (19)
94. Doug Cooper; Ted Hairfield; Don Noel (18)
97. Jim Cook; H.G. Rosier (17)
99. Bruce Brantley; Earl Brooks; Lloyd Dane (16)
102. Joel Davis; Eddie Gray; Nace Mattingly (15)
105. Jack Anderson; Red Foote; Possum Jones (14)
108. Chuck Huckabee; Jim Hurtubise; Cotton Owens; Fred Thompson (13)
112. Perk Brown; Pete Stewart (12)
114. Buzzy Reutimann; John Rogers (11)
116. Chuck Daigh; Joe Jones (10)
118. Mal Delometer; Jack Deniston; Jimmy Griggs; Roy Tyner (9)
122. Jim Bray; Ray Hughes; Lyle Stelter; Hank Thomas (8)
126. Johnny Clements; Lee Reitzel (7)
128. Joe Kelly (6)
129. Paul Clark; Bob Hurt (5)
131. Smokey Cook; Henry Montgomery (4)
133. Ronnie Bristow; Charley Griffith; Billy Oswald; Jerome Warren (3)
137. Jim Reed; Bill Whitley (2)
139. Dominic Persicketti (1)

1963 Events

Birmingham Raceway/.5-mile/100 miles
Jim Paschal (Plymouth)/Jim Paschal (Plymouth)

Golden Gate Speedway/.333-mile/67 miles
Richard Petty (Plymouth)/Rex White (Chevrolet)

Turkey Day 200; Tar Heel Speedway/.25-mile/50 miles
Jim Paschal (Plymouth)/Glen Wood (Ford)

Riverside 500; Riverside Int. Raceway/2.7-m road/500 miles
Dan Gurney (Ford)/Paul Goldsmith (Pontiac)

Daytona International Speedway/2.5-mile/100 miles
Junior Johnson (Chevrolet)

Daytona International Speedway/2.5-mile/100 miles
Johnny Rutherford (Chevrolet)

Daytona 500; Daytona International Speedway/2.5-m/500 miles
Tiny Lund (Ford)/Fireball Roberts (Pontiac)

Piedmont Interstate Fairgrounds/.5-mile dirt/100 miles
Richard Petty (Plymouth)/Junior Johnson (Chevrolet)

Asheville-Weaverville Speedway/.5-mile/100 miles
Richard Petty (Plymouth)/Junior Johnson (Chevrolet)

Orange Speedway/.9-mile dirt/149 miles
Junior Johnson (Chevrolet)/Joe Weatherly (Pontiac)

Atlanta 500; Atlanta International Raceway/1.5-m/500 miles
Fred Lorenzen (Ford)/Junior Johnson (Chevrolet)

Hickory 250; Hickory Speedway/.4-mile dirt/100 miles
Junior Johnson (Chevrolet)/Junior Johnson (Chevrolet)

Southeastern 500; Bristol International Speedway/.5-m/250 m
Fireball Roberts (Ford)/Fred Lorenzen (Ford)

Augusta Speedway/.5-mile dirt/100 miles
Ned Jarrett (Ford)/Lee Roy Yarbrough (Mercury)

Richmond 250; Atlantic Rural Fairgrounds/.5-m dirt/125 miles
Joe Weatherly (Pontiac)/Rex White (Chevrolet)

Greenville 200; Greenville-Pickens Speedway/.5-m dirt/100 m
Buck Baker (Pontiac)/Jim Pardue (Ford)

South Boston 400; South Boston Speedway/.375-mile/150 miles
Richard Petty (Plymouth)/Ned Jarrett (Ford)

Bowman Gray Stadium/.25-mile/50 miles
Jim Paschal (Plymouth)/Richard Petty (Plymouth)

Virginia 500; Martinsville Speedway/.5-mile/250 miles
Richard Petty (Plymouth)/Rex White (Chevrolet)

Gwyn Staley 400; North Wilkesboro Speedway/.625-m/250 miles
Richard Petty (Plymouth)/Fred Lorenzen (Ford)

Columbia 200; Columbia Speedway/.5-mile dirt/100 miles
Richard Petty (Plymouth)/Richard Petty (Plymouth)

Tar Heel Speedway/.25-mile/50 miles
Jim Paschal (Plymouth)/Ned Jarrett (Ford)

Rebel 300; Darlington Raceway/1.375-mile/300 miles
Joe Weatherly (Pontiac)/Fred Lorenzen (Ford)

Old Dominion Speedway/.375-mile/113 miles
Richard Petty (Plymouth)/Richard Petty (Plymouth)

Southside Speedway/.333-mile/100 miles
Ned Jarrett (Ford)/Ned Jarrett (Ford)

World 600; Charlotte Motor Speedway/1.5-mile/600 miles
Fred Lorenzen (Ford)/Junior Johnson (Chevrolet)

Birmingham Raceway/.5-mile/100 miles
Richard Petty (Plymouth)/Jack Smith (Plymouth)

Dixie 400; Atlanta International Raceway/1.5-mile/400 miles
Junior Johnson (Chevrolet)/Marvin Panch (Ford)

Firecracker 400; Daytona International Speedway/2.5-m/400 m
Fireball Roberts (Ford)/Junior Johnson (Chevrolet)

Speedorama 200; Rambi Raceway/.5-mile dirt/100 miles
Ned Jarrett (Ford)/Richard Petty (Plymouth)

Savannah Speedway/.5-mile dirt/100 miles
Ned Jarrett (Ford)/Richard Petty (Plymouth)

Dog Track Speedway/.25-mile dirt/63 miles
Jim Pardue (Ford)/Junior Johnson (Chevrolet)

Bowman Gray Stadium/.25-mile/50 miles
Glen Wood (Ford)/Glen Wood (Ford)

Asheville Speedway/.333-mile/100 miles
Ned Jarrett (Ford)/David Pearson (Dodge)

Old Bridge Stadium/.5-mile/100 miles
Fireball Roberts (Ford)/Joe Weatherly (Pontiac)

Bridgehampton Raceway/2.85-mile road/100 miles
Richard Petty (Plymouth)/Richard Petty (Plymouth)

Volunteer 500; Bristol International Speedway/.5-m/250 miles
Fred Lorenzen (Ford)/Fred Lorenzen (Ford)

Pickens 200; Greenville-Pickens Speedway/.5-mile dirt/100 miles
Richard Petty (Plymouth)/Ned Jarrett (Ford)

Nashville 400; Fairgrounds Speedway/.5-mile/200 miles
Jim Paschal (Plymouth)/Richard Petty (Plymouth)

Sandlapper 200; Columbia Speedway/.5-mile dirt/100 miles
Richard Petty (Plymouth)/Richard Petty (Plymouth)

Western N.C. 500; Asheville-Weaverville Speedway/.5-m/250 m
Fred Lorenzen (Ford)

Piedmont Interstate Fairgrounds/.5-mile dirt/100 miles
Ned Jarrett (Ford)/Joe Weatherly (Pontiac)

International 200; Bowman Gray Stadium/.25-mile/50 miles
Junior Johnson (Chevrolet)/Junior Johnson (Chevrolet)

Mountaineer 300; West Virginia Int. Speedway/.375-mile/113 m
Fred Lorenzen (Ford)/Fred Lorenzen (Ford)

Southern 500; Darlington Raceway/1.375-mile/500 miles
Fireball Roberts (Ford)/Fred Lorenzen (Ford)

Buddy Shuman 250; Hickory Speedway/.4-mile dirt/100 miles
Junior Johnson (Chevrolet)/David Pearson (Dodge)

Capital City 300; Atlantic Rural Fairgrounds/.5-m dirt/150 m
Ned Jarrett (Ford)/Joe Weatherly (Mercury)

Old Dominion 500; Martinsville Speedway/.5-mile/250 miles
Fred Lorenzen (Ford)/Junior Johnson (Chevrolet)

Dog Track Speedway; Moyock, N.C./.25-mile dirt/75 miles
Ned Jarrett (Ford)/Joe Weatherly (Mercury)

Wilkes 400; North Wilkesboro Speedway/.625-mile/250 miles
Marvin Panch (Ford)/Fred Lorenzen (Ford)

Tar Heel Speedway/.25-mile/50 miles
Richard Petty (Plymouth)/Fred Lorenzen (Ford)

National 400; Charlotte Motor Speedway/1.5-mile/400 miles
Junior Johnson (Chevrolet)/Marvin Panch (Ford)

South Boston 400; South Boston Speedway/.375-mile/150 miles
Richard Petty (Plymouth)/Jack Smith (Plymouth)

Orange Speedway/.9-mile dirt/150 miles
Joe Weatherly (Pontiac)/Joe Weatherly (Pontiac)

Golden State 400; Riverside Int. Raceway/2.7-mile road/400 m
Darel Dieringer (Mercury)/Dan Gurney (Ford)

Victories

1. Richard Petty (14)
2. Ned Jarrett (8)
3. Junior Johnson (7)
4. Fred Lorenzen (6)
5. Jim Paschal (5)
6. Fireball Roberts (4)
7. Joe Weatherly (3)
8. Buck Baker; Darel Dieringer; Dan Gurney; Tiny Lund; Marvin Panch; Jim Pardue; Johnny Rutherford; Glen Wood (1)

Poles

1. Junior Johnson (9)
2. Fred Lorenzen; Richard Petty (8)
4. Joe Weatherly (6)
5. Ned Jarrett (4)
6. Rex White (3)
7. Marvin Panch; David Pearson; Jack Smith; Glen Wood (2)
11. Paul Goldsmith; Dan Gurney; Jim Pardue; Jim Paschal; Fireball Roberts; Lee Roy Yarbrough (1)

Victories

1. Ford (23)
2. Plymouth (19)
3. Chevrolet (8)
4. Pontiac (4)
5. Mercury (1)

Poles

1. Ford (18)
2. Chevrolet (12)
3. Plymouth (11)
4. Pontiac (6)
5. Mercury (3)
6. Dodge (2)

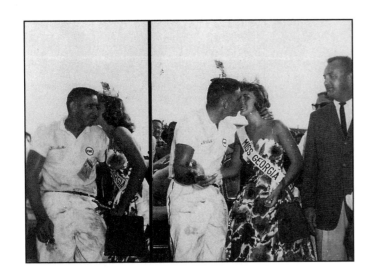

1964
Fireball: Fastest On the Big Tracks

To call Fireball Roberts NASCAR's first superstar would be an insult to Herb Thomas, Lee Petty, the Flocks, and other heroes of yesteryear.

Although it would be much later before Winston Cup racing produced a star who transcended the sport, it's accurate to say that Roberts, a former University of Florida pitcher, was NASCAR's most famous driver when he died in 1964.

Roberts had just turned 19 when he competed in the first sanctioned NASCAR race, a modified event on the Beach & Road Course in Daytona Beach, Fla., on February 15, 1948. Roberts captured his first Winston Cup victory in 1950 at Hillsboro, N.C., but it was six years before he won another. Considering that Roberts finished in the top 10 in the Performance Index ratings only four times in his career, it isn't surprising that he was treated like an overnight success in 1958, when he won the Northern 500 at Trenton, N.J., and the Southern 500 at Darlington, S.C., to become the first driver to capture two 500-mile races in one year.

Roberts was 31, ready to burst into his prime, in 1960, when superspeedways obviously crafted to his skills at Charlotte, Atlanta, and Hanford, Calif., joined the year-old Daytona International Speedway and Darlington Raceway on the Winston Cup Series.

Roberts's pedal-to-the-metal style wasn't conducive to winning championships, and, in fact, he never drove in enough races to be a serious contender. But he was nearly invincible in qualifying on the big tracks. The 1960 season saw Fireball—who detested his moniker and told everyone to call him Glenn—capture six Grand Slam poles, an unmatched feat.

His 33 Winston Cup triumphs made Fireball Roberts a familiar figure in victory lane.

Roberts's extraordinary qualifying feats during that era included:

- Winning at least five Grand Slam poles three years in a row (1960-62), a feat no other driver has managed in consecutive seasons;
- Becoming the only driver in history to lead every lap of a superspeedway race, when he set the pace for all 178 laps of a 250-mile race at California's Marchbanks Speedway on March 12, 1961;
- Earning the pole in five consecutive Grand Slam races, culminating with the 1961 Daytona 500, a feat that has been bettered only once;
- Completing a record string of five consecutive classic poles by starting first in the 1963 Daytona 500;
- Becoming the first driver to win poles on all four Grand Slam tracks in the same season (1962), a feat accomplished only twice since;
- Capturing five straight superspeedway poles in 1960 and '61, a record that would be tied 13 years later but would take 24 years to break;
- Becoming the only driver to win the pole for three classics in one season (1962);
- Winning at least five superspeedway poles three consecutive seasons (1960-62), the second-longest such streak in history;
- Winning at least one classic pole five years in a row (1959-63), a streak bettered only by David Pearson and Jeff Gordon;
- Becoming the first driver to win at least one superspeedway pole in five consecutive seasons (1959-63) and the first to win multiple superspeedway poles in four consecutive seasons (1959-62).

Roberts also was the first driver to capture at least one Grand Slam pole in five consecutive years (1959-63) and had another string of three consecutive classic poles, a streak exceeded only by Bill Elliott's four and equaled by Pearson. Roberts also posted two other streaks of four consecutive Grand Slam poles. Only four other drivers have managed to accomplish that feat once. And streaks of four or more superspeedway poles have been accomplished five times—three of them by Roberts.

More than 35 years after his untimely death, Roberts still ranks second in classic poles (10), third in Grand Slam poles (21), tied for seventh in Grand Slam wins from the pole (3), tied for eighth in superspeedway poles (21), tied for 11th in superspeedway victories from the pole (3), and 18th in poles (32).

Considering his relative lack of opportunities on superspeedways, it would not be inappropriate to call Roberts the best qualifier in the history of NASCAR's big tracks.

That doesn't mean he wasn't capable of finding victory lane, however.

Roberts was the first driver to post four consecutive seasons of multiple superspeedway victories (1960-63), the first to win on Grand Slam tracks six consecutive years (1958-63), and the first to win Grand Slam races from the pole in consecutive seasons (1959-60). His five 500-mile victories were a record at the time of his death, and he still ranks in the top 20 in victories (33), superspeedway wins (14), Grand Slam triumphs (10), dirt victories (12), and road wins (2).

In addition to Roberts, the litany of champions and classic winners who have driven for Hall of Fame mechanic Smokey Yunick includes Tim Flock, Buck Baker, Bobby Isaac, Bobby Allison, Curtis Turner, Mario Andretti, A.J. Foyt, Johnny Rutherford, and Thomas.

"I'm telling you," Yunick said, "that Fireball was the best driver I ever had."

1964 in Review

Four drivers combined to win 40 races and 36 poles, and all four drivers won at least eight races, the only time in history that has happened. Ned Jarrett captured 15 races and nine poles, Richard Petty nine races and eight poles, Pearson eight races and 12 poles, and Fred Lorenzen eight races and seven poles. Three drivers posted Performance Index ratings in excess of 1,000, the only time in history that has happened. Petty, who won his first Winston Cup championship, had a 1,097 rating, Jarrett a 1,091, and Pearson a 1,033.

Most Memorable Race

Jim Paschal called his four-lap victory over Richard Petty, both driving Plymouths for Petty Enterprises, the "easiest race I've ever run." But the World 600 at Charlotte Motor Speedway on May 24 wasn't necessarily memorable because of Paschal's victory.

Junior Johnson's Ford spun into Jarrett's on the eighth lap, and the latter's Ford caught fire. Roberts swerved abruptly to avoid their cars, then bounced into the rear of Jarrett's machine. Roberts's Holman-Moody Ford tagged the wall and landed upside down in a sea of flames.

Jarrett, who had leaped from his burning car, ran to Roberts's car and heard his rival scream: "Oh, my God. Ned, help me. I'm on fire." By the time Jarrett pulled Roberts out of the charred machine, initial reports were that 75 percent of Roberts's body had received third-degree burns. Roberts, whose condition was worsened by asthma, fought for his life at Charlotte Memorial Hospital. He underwent surgery on June 30 and came out of the operation in a coma. Two days later, the most popular driver the sport had known to that point was dead at age 35.

Most Significant Wreck

Joe Weatherly led the Winston Cup point standings in his bid for an unprecedented third consecutive title when he hit the wall in Bud Moore's Mercury on his 87th lap of the Motor Trend 500 on January 19 at Riverside, Calif. Weatherly didn't appear to hit the wall hard, more of a glancing blow, but he careened across the track, came to a stop on the dirt, and was dead on arrival at Riverside Hospital. It was no secret that Little Joe disdained his shoulder harness and preferred to wear only his lap belt. He told The Associated Press one day before he died that he'd "rather flap around in there. I move around so much. I'd rather have the freedom of a seat belt." It has been speculated that Weatherly, unencumbered by a shoulder harness, was killed when his head hit the dashboard or steering wheel.

Most Important Off-Track Development

After Jim Pardue, who had won two races and three poles since the beginning of the 1962 season, was killed in a tire test at Charlotte Motor Speedway in September, Goodyear introduced the inner-liner tire.

Records & Milestones

Billy Wade, who replaced Weatherly behind the wheel of Moore's Mercury, became the first driver to record four consecutive victories. Those were the only four triumphs of his career. . . . A record seven drivers won at least five poles, with Marvin Panch, Johnson, and Wade winning five each to join Pearson, Jarrett, Richard Petty, and Lorenzen. In no other season did seven drivers win as many as four poles. . . . A single-season record 62 races were held. . . . Forty tracks played host to Winston Cup races, tying the record set in 1956 and '58. . . . Twenty races were won from the pole, a record later tied but never broken.

For the first time, more short-track races (25) were held than dirt events (23). . . . Five races were named in honor of deceased drivers: the Joe Weatherly 150 at Orange Speedway; the Gwyn Staley 400 at North Wilkesboro, N.C.; the Fireball Roberts 200 at Old Bridge, N.J.; the Myers Brothers 250 at Winston-Salem, N.C., and the Buddy Shuman 250 at Hickory, N.C. All five races were won from the pole, with Pearson winning the races named for Weatherly and Shuman. Lorenzen (Staley), Wade (Roberts), and Johnson (Myers Brothers) won the others.

1964 at a Glance

Races:	62
Dirt:	23
Road:	4
Short Track:	25
Superspeedway:	10
Winners:	17
Pole Winners:	14
Tracks:	40
States:	12

1964 Performance Index Rankings

1. Richard Petty (1,097)
2. Ned Jarrett (1,091)
3. David Pearson (1,033)
4. Curtis Crider (705)
5. Billy Wade (657)
6. Jim Pardue (654)
7. Wendell Scott (614)
8. Larry Thomas (613)
9. Buck Baker (563)
10. Marvin Panch (561)
11. Neil Castles (464)
12. Lee Roy Yarbrough (447)
13. Roy Tyner (427)
14. Jim Paschal (426)
15. Junior Johnson (401)
16. Darel Dieringer (395)
17. Fred Lorenzen (370)
18. Doug Cooper (330)
19. Cale Yarborough (296)
20. Bobby Isaac; Tiny Lund (280)
22. Buddy Arrington; G.C. Spencer (217)
24. Jack Anderson (215)
25. J.T. Putney (214)
26. Worth McMillion (203)
27. Fireball Roberts (198)
28. Paul Goldsmith (194)
29. Buddy Baker (185)
30. Earl Brooks (184)
31. Doug Moore (171)
32. Bob Derrington (159)
33. Doug Yates (150)
34. Bill McMahan (147)
35. Larry Frank (140)
36. Gene Hobby; Bobby Keck (138)
38. Bunkie Blackburn; Elmo Langley (124)
40. Dave MacDonald (120)
41. Earl Balmer; E.J. Trivette (118)
43. Bobby Johns (116)
44. Rex White (110)
45. Dan Gurney (106)
46. A.J. Foyt (95)
47. Roy Mayne (93)
48. Ralph Earnhardt (88)
49. Ken Spikes (79)
50. Maurice Petty (76)
51. Joe Weatherly (73)
52. John Sears (58)
53. Elmo Henderson (55)
54. Bob Cooper; Walt Hansgen; Sam McQuagg (54)
57. Joe Schlesser; Pete Stewart; Louis Weathersbee (53)
60. Al White (52)
61. Ken Rush; Bob Welborn (51)
63. Johnny Allen; Dick Hutcherson (49)
65. Larry Manning (48)
66. Cotton Owens (44)
67. Jim McElreath; Major Melton (42)
69. Nathan Boutwell (41)
70. Johnny Rutherford (40)
71. Jimmy Helms (39)
72. Jack Smith (37)
73. Bill Amick (36)
74. Frank Warren; Steve Young (35)
76. Fred Harb; Bud Harless; Mark Hurley (34)
79. Chuck Huckabee; Marvin Porter (33)
81. Jim Cook; Skip Hudson (32)
83. Troy Ruttman (30)
84. Graham Shaw; Don White (29)
86. Eddie Gray (28)
87. Bay Darnell (27)
88. Bert Robbins (25)
89. Parnelli Jones; Bruce Worrell (24)
91. J.V. Hamby; James Hylton (23)
93. Jim Bray; Bobby Marshman; Junior Spencer (22)
96. Lloyd Dane; Jim Dimeo (21)
98. Possum Jones; Dick Mitchell; Doug Wilson; Glen Wood (20)
102. Bernard Alvarez (19)
103. Sal Tovella (18)
104. Ken Anderson; Ronnie Chumley; Ed Livingston (17)
107. Darrell Bryant (16)
108. Frank Brantley; Roy Gemberling; Frank Graham (14)
111. Andy Buffington (13)
112. Marshall Sargent (12)

113. Don Branson (11)
114. Gene Lovelace; Mitch Walker; Reb Wickersham (10)
117. Joe Clark (9)
118. Wally Dallenbach; Bill Whitley (8)
120. Ray Carter; Leland Colvin Jr. (7)
122. Don Tilley; Dennis Zimmerman (6)
124. Rene Charland; Frank Tanner; Bill Widenhouse (5)
127. Stick Elliott; Al Farmer; Lee Petty (4)
130. Jimmy Lee Capps; Bobby Schuyler (2)
132. Pete Boland; Joe Cote; Henley Gray; Bud Moore (1)

1964 Events

Textile 250; Concord Speedway/.5-mile dirt/125 miles
Ned Jarrett (Ford)/David Pearson (Dodge)

Augusta International Speedway/3-mile road/510 miles
Fireball Roberts (Ford)/Fred Lorenzen (Ford)

Speedway Park; Jacksonville/.5-mile dirt/100 miles
Wendell Scott (Chevrolet)/Jack Smith (Plymouth)

Sunshine 200; Savannah Speedway/.5-mile dirt/100 miles
Richard Petty (Plymouth)/Ned Jarrett (Ford)

Motor Trend 500; Riverside Int. Raceway/2.7-mile road/500 m
Dan Gurney (Ford)/Fred Lorenzen (Ford)

Daytona International Speedway/2.5-mile/100 miles
Junior Johnson (Dodge)

Daytona International Speedway/2.5-mile/100 miles
Bobby Isaac (Dodge)

Daytona 500; Daytona International Speedway/2.5-m/500 miles
Richard Petty (Plymouth)/Paul Goldsmith (Plymouth)

Richmond 250; Atlantic Rural Fairgrounds/.5-m dirt/125 miles
David Pearson (Dodge)/Ned Jarrett (Ford)

Southeastern 500; Bristol International Speedway/.5-m/250 m
Fred Lorenzen (Ford)/Marvin Panch (Ford)

Greenville 200; Greenville-Pickens Speedway/.5-m dirt/100 m
David Pearson (Dodge)/Dick Hutcherson (Ford)

Bowman Gray Stadium/.25-mile/50 miles
Marvin Panch (Ford)/Marvin Panch (Ford)

Atlanta 500; Atlanta International Raceway/1.5-m/500 miles
Fred Lorenzen (Ford)/Fred Lorenzen (Ford)

Asheville-Weaverville Speedway/.5-mile/100 miles
Marvin Panch (Ford)/Marvin Panch (Ford)

Joe Weatherly 150; Orange Speedway/.9-mile dirt/150 miles
David Pearson (Dodge)/David Pearson (Dodge)

Piedmont Interstate Fairgrounds/.5-mile dirt/100 miles
Ned Jarrett (Ford)/Dick Hutcherson (Ford)

Columbia 200; Columbia Speedway/.5-mile dirt/100 miles
Ned Jarrett (Ford)/David Pearson (Dodge)

Gwyn Staley 400; North Wilkesboro Speedway/.625-m/250 miles
Fred Lorenzen (Ford)/Fred Lorenzen (Ford)

Virginia 500; Martinsville Speedway/.5-mile/250 miles
Fred Lorenzen (Ford)/Fred Lorenzen (Ford)

Savannah 200; Savannah Speedway/.5-mile dirt/100 miles
Lee Roy Yarbrough (Plymouth)/Jim Pardue (Plymouth)

Rebel 300; Darlington Raceway/1.375-mile/300 miles
Fred Lorenzen (Ford)/Fred Lorenzen (Ford)

Tidewater 250; Langley Field Speedway/.4-mile dirt/100 miles
Ned Jarrett (Ford)/David Pearson (Dodge)

Hickory 250; Hickory Speedway/.4-mile dirt/100 miles
Ned Jarrett (Ford)/Junior Johnson (Ford)

South Boston Speedway/.375-mile/100 miles
Richard Petty (Plymouth)/Marvin Panch (Ford)

World 600; Charlotte Motor Speedway/1.5-mile/600 miles
Jim Paschal (Plymouth)/Jim Pardue (Plymouth)

Pickens 200; Greenville-Pickens Speedway/.5-m dirt/100 miles
Lee Roy Yarbrough (Plymouth)/Marvin Panch (Ford)

Asheville Speedway/.333-mile/100 miles
Ned Jarrett (Ford)/Richard Petty (Plymouth)

Dixie 400; Atlanta International Raceway/1.5-mile/400 miles
Ned Jarrett (Ford)/Junior Johnson (Ford)

Concord Speedway/.5-mile dirt/100 miles
Richard Petty (Plymouth)/Richard Petty (Plymouth)

Music City 200; Fairgrounds Speedway/.5-mile/100 miles
Richard Petty (Plymouth)/David Pearson (Dodge)

Confederate 300/.333-mile/100 miles
David Pearson (Dodge)/Richard Petty (Plymouth)

Birmingham Raceway/.5-mile/100 miles
Ned Jarrett (Ford)/David Pearson (Dodge)

Valdosta Speedway/.5-mile dirt/100 miles
Buck Baker (Dodge)/Ned Jarrett (Ford)

Piedmont Interstate Fairgrounds/.5-mile dirt/100 miles
Richard Petty (Plymouth)/David Pearson (Dodge)

Firecracker 400; Daytona International Speedway/2.5-m/400 m
A.J. Foyt (Dodge)/Darel Dieringer (Mercury)

Old Dominion 400; Old Dominion Speedway/.375-mile/150 miles
Ned Jarrett (Ford)/Ned Jarrett (Ford)

Fireball Roberts 200; Old Bridge Stadium/.5-mile/100 miles
Billy Wade (Mercury)/Billy Wade (Mercury)

Bridgehampton Raceway/2.85-mile road/143 miles
Billy Wade (Mercury)/Richard Petty (Plymouth)

Islip Speedway/.2-mile/60 miles
Billy Wade (Mercury)/Billy Wade (Mercury)

The Glen 151.8; Watkins Glen International/2.3-m road/152 m
Billy Wade (Mercury)/Billy Wade (Mercury)

Pennsylvania 200; Lincoln Speedway/.5-mile dirt/100 miles
David Pearson (Dodge)/David Pearson (Dodge)

Volunteer 500; Bristol International Speedway/.5-m/250 miles
Fred Lorenzen (Ford)/Richard Petty (Plymouth)

Nashville 400; Fairgrounds Speedway/.5-mile/200 miles
Richard Petty (Plymouth)/Richard Petty (Plymouth)

Rambi Raceway/.5-mile dirt/100 miles
David Pearson (Dodge)/David Pearson (Dodge)

Western N.C. 500; Asheville–Weaverville Speedway/.5-m/250 m
Ned Jarrett (Ford)/Junior Johnson (Ford)

Moyock 300; Dog Track Speedway/.333-mile/100 miles
Ned Jarrett (Ford)/Ned Jarrett (Ford)

Mountaineer 500; West Virginia Int. Speedway/.4375-m/219 m
Richard Petty (Plymouth)/Billy Wade (Mercury)

Sandlapper 200; Columbia Speedway/.5-mile dirt/100 miles
David Pearson (Dodge)/Ned Jarrett (Ford)

Myers Brothers 250; Bowman Gray Stadium/.25-mile/63 miles
Junior Johnson (Ford)/Junior Johnson (Ford)

Starkey Speedway/.25-mile/50 miles
Junior Johnson (Ford)/Glen Wood (Ford)

Southern 500; Darlington Raceway/1.375-mile/500 miles
Buck Baker (Dodge)/Richard Petty (Plymouth)

Buddy Shuman 250; Hickory Speedway/.4-mile dirt/100 miles
David Pearson (Dodge)/David Pearson (Dodge)

Capital City 300; Virginia State Fairgrounds/.5-m dirt/150 m
Cotton Owens (Dodge)/Ned Jarrett (Ford)

Old Dominion Speedway/.375-mile/188 miles
Ned Jarrett (Ford)/David Pearson (Dodge)

Orange Speedway/.9-mile dirt/150 miles
Ned Jarrett (Ford)/David Pearson (Dodge)

Old Dominion 500; Martinsville Speedway/.5-mile/250 miles
Fred Lorenzen (Ford)/Fred Lorenzen (Ford)

Savannah Speedway/.5-mile dirt/100 miles
Ned Jarrett (Ford)/Ned Jarrett (Ford)

Wilkes 400; North Wilkesboro Speedway/.625-mile/250 miles
Marvin Panch (Ford)/Junior Johnson (Ford)

National 400; Charlotte Motor Speedway/1.5-mile/400 miles
Fred Lorenzen (Ford)/Richard Petty (Plymouth)

Harris Speedway/.3-mile/100 miles
Richard Petty (Plymouth)/Billy Wade (Mercury)

Jaycee 300; Augusta Speedway/.5-mile/150 miles
Darel Dieringer (Mercury)/Ned Jarrett (Ford)

Jacksonville Speedway/.5-mile dirt/100 miles
Ned Jarrett (Ford)/Doug Yates (Plymouth)

Victories

1. Ned Jarrett (15)
2. Richard Petty (9)
3. Fred Lorenzen; David Pearson (8)
5. Billy Wade (4)
6. Junior Johnson; Marvin Panch (3)
8. Buck Baker; Lee Roy Yarbrough (2)
10. Darel Dieringer; A.J. Foyt; Dan Gurney; Bobby Isaac; Cotton Owens; Jim Paschal; Fireball Roberts; Wendell Scott (1)

Poles

1. David Pearson (12)
2. Ned Jarrett (9)
3. Richard Petty (8)
4. Fred Lorenzen (7)
5. Junior Johnson; Marvin Panch; Billy Wade (5)
8. Dick Hutcherson; Jim Pardue (2)
10. Darel Dieringer; Paul Goldsmith; Jack Smith; Glen Wood; Doug Yates (1)

Victories

1. Ford (30)
2. Dodge (14)
3. Plymouth (12)
4. Mercury (5)
5. Chevrolet (1)

Poles

1. Ford (29)
2. Plymouth (13)
3. Dodge (12)
4. Mercury (6)

1965
Few Careers Can Equal Gentleman Ned's Six Years In the Spotlight

When people ask Ned Jarrett how to break into Winston Cup racing, he can't say, "You write somebody a bad check and win two races." But that strategy launched a career in which he captured 50 victories and two Winston Cup titles.

Ned Jarrett was just 20 years old when he made his Winston Cup debut on August 29, 1953, at Hickory Speedway, just a few laps from his home in Newton, N.C. Jarrett finished 11th—in a 12-car field—and retreated to lesser competition.

Jarrett captured two championships in NASCAR's Late Model Sportsman Division, forerunner of the Busch Series, wondering if he'd ever get the break that would propel him into the big time. In August of 1959, Jarrett decided to make his own breaks, which eventually resulted in Winston Cup championships in 1961 and 1965.

"I had been racing in the sportsman division, and I really wanted to try Grand National. I found out that Junior Johnson had a car for sale for $2,000, and that was a lot of money back then," Jarrett recalled many years later. "I knew it was a good car because he had been winning races with it. I told some people I was going to buy that car, and they asked me how I was going to pay for it. There was a race that week at Myrtle Beach, so I told them, `I'll go to Myrtle Beach, and I'll win that race. That pays $950, and I'll go to Charlotte on Sunday and win that race. That pays $950, too. That leaves another $100, and if I get the $1,900, I'll come up with the $100.'

"I got to Myrtle Beach, and I didn't have a chance to practice. I qualified eighth, and I was running with Lee Petty and Bob Welborn. The last 50 miles, something happened to Petty, and it was me and Welborn. I managed to get around him and win. I wasn't accustomed to long-distance races, and my arm was so torn up I swore I could see the bone through it. But I had a job to do, and I was only half through. I won those two races, and I had me a car.

"I look back, and I think, `I must have been crazy to think I could have won those races against all those drivers.' How I could be that foolish, I don't know. People ask me how you can get started in racing. I can't very well say, `You write somebody a bad check and win two races.' "

Jarrett's two victories helped him post the 22nd-highest Performance Index during that 1959 season. His next six campaigns, however, were among the best the sport has known, during which he:

- Never finished worse than fourth in the Performance Index;
- Became one of only three drivers to post back-to-back seasons (1964-65) with a rating of 1,000 or more and logged five consecutive seasons (1961-65) with

a rating of 800 or better, a streak surpassed only by Richard Petty;

- Captured 48 more victories and 35 poles;
- Tied Herb Thomas's record of winning at least six dirt races in four consecutive seasons (1962-65);
- Tied a record then held by Thomas and Rex White by winning at least five races in four consecutive seasons (1962-65);
- Tied a record then held by Thomas and Richard Petty by posting three consecutive seasons of at least eight victories (1963-65);
- Tied David Pearson's record, set in 1964, of four consecutive victories on dirt;
- Became the first driver to post back-to-back seasons of at least 13 victories (1964-65).

Driving the Bondy Long Ford, Jarrett frequently obliterated his competition on the way to the 1965 title. He finished a record 22 laps ahead of his nearest competitor on February 27 at the Piedmont Interstate Fairgrounds in Spartanburg, S.C., then duplicated that feat on May 27 at the Cleveland County Fairgrounds in Shelby, N.C. Jarrett then beat Buck Baker to the checkered flag by 14 laps to win the Southern 500 at Darlington Raceway. At that time, the storied South Carolina track was measured at 1.375 miles, making Jarrett's 19.25-mile margin of victory the greatest in the sport's history.

Jarrett had driven a Chevrolet to the 1961 crown and remains the only driver to win the Winston Cup championship for the top two manufacturers in all-time victories. When "Gentleman Ned," one of the most cooperative and affable champions in history, was asked to make an off-season speech after he won his first title, he readily agreed. When he reached the microphone, Jarrett could think of nothing to say. Embarrassed, he enrolled in a Dale Carnegie course.

"Once you've gone through that course," said Jarrett, who bailed out at least one former publicist on a number of occasions when asked to deliver a last-minute invocation, "you want to tell the world what you know."

Perhaps that's why his lopsided victory in the 1965 Southern 500 was the penultimate triumph of Jarrett's career. When Ford withdrew factory support during the 1966 season, Jarrett stumbled through a winless campaign and finished 17th in the Performance Index ratings. At age 34, Jarrett retired after that '66 campaign to put his Carnegie knowledge to work, first as a promoter and later as one of the most distinguished television and radio commentators in motorsports.

Perhaps the most compelling description of the closing laps of a Winston Cup race in history was Jarrett's call of the 1993 Daytona 500. Dale Earnhardt, then the sport's reigning superstar, was dueling with a rival who had only one victory to his credit. Encouraged by CBS, Jarrett openly coached and encouraged Earnhardt's rival, Ned's son, across the finish line with the cry: "Dale Jarrett has won the Daytona 500."

1965 in Review

Three drivers dominated the 1965 campaign. Ned Jarrett and Johnson each won 13 races and Dick Hutcherson nine, and each of those three drivers captured nine poles—the only year that three drivers have won nine or more poles. Jarrett sailed to his second Winston Cup title and held a 1,162-982 margin over Hutcherson in the Performance Index rankings.

Most Memorable Race.

Curtis Turner, driving the Wood brothers' Ford, nicked the wall twice before he passed Cale Yarborough on the 474th of 500 laps to win the American 500 on Halloween—the first superspeedway race in a year to match Ford and Chrysler factory teams. The first event held at the North Carolina Motor Speedway in Rockingham was Turner's first victory in six years and the 17th and last of his career. "I guess I'm the happiest I've ever been. It's good to be a winner again," said Turner, who was banned for "life" in 1961 by NASCAR President Bill France for his role in organizing a drivers' union and had been reinstated in August.

Most Significant Wreck

Billy Wade, who captured four victories and five poles in 1964, was killed on January 5, when he crashed into the wall in the first turn at Daytona Beach, Fla., while driving Bud Moore's Mercury during a tire test. Less than a month earlier, the guardrail at Daytona International Speedway had been replaced by the concrete wall Wade hit.

Most Important Off-Track Development

Firestone introduced the fuel cell, which replaced the more conventional gas tank.

Records & Milestones

Buoyed by Chrysler's boycott because of a rules dispute about its hemi engine, Ford captured 48 victories and 42 poles, both records. . . . Beginning with Johnson's victory in the second 100-mile qualifying race at Daytona on February 12, Ford reeled off a record 32 victories in a row. Although one manufacturer dominated that stretch, eight different drivers won races: Johnson (10), Ned Jarrett (8), Hutcherson (4), Marvin Panch (4), Fred Lorenzen (3), Tiny Lund (1), Yarborough (1), and A.J. Foyt (1). The streak finally ended when Richard Petty captured the Nashville 400 on July 31 in a Plymouth. . . . The 1965 season marked the third year in a row that three drivers won at least eight poles—the only three seasons in history that happened. . . . The 1965 campaign was the only season in which five drivers won six or more poles, with Petty capturing seven and Lorenzen six to join Jarrett, Johnson, and Hutcherson. . . . For the third time in four years, four drivers won seven or more poles. Those are the only three campaigns that has happened.

1965 at a Glance

Races:	55
Dirt:	19
Road:	2
Short Track:	23
Superspeedway:	11
Winners:	13
Pole Winners:	14
Tracks:	34
States:	12

1965 Performance Index Rankings

1. Ned Jarrett (1,162)
2. Dick Hutcherson (982)
3. Bob Derrington (610)
4. G.C. Spencer (606)
5. Neil Castles (596)
6. Wendell Scott (572)
7. Junior Johnson (564)
8. J.T. Putney (553)
9. Cale Yarborough (516)
10. Darel Dieringer (487)
11. Buddy Baker (477)
12. Marvin Panch (448)
13. Tiny Lund (376)
14. Paul Lewis (371)
15. E.J. Trivette (358)
16. Doug Cooper (304)
17. Elmo Langley (289)
18. Jimmy Helms (286)
19. Fred Lorenzen (285)
20. Buddy Arrington (282)
21. Buck Baker (280)
22. Henley Gray (258)
23. Richard Petty (231)
24. Bobby Johns (216)
25. David Pearson (213)
26. Sam McQuagg (202)
27. Tom Pistone (198)
28. Larry Hess (185)
29. Clyde Lynn (180)
30. Roy Mayne (177)
31. Wayne Smith (172)
32. Junior Spencer (170)
33. Roy Tyner (152)
34. Gene Black (148)
35. Earl Balmer (134)
36. Lee Roy Yarbrough (126)
37. H.B. Bailey (124)
38. Bud Moore (123)
39. Dick Dixon (120)
40. Bub Strickler (117)
41. Donald Tucker (112)
42. Stick Elliott (109)
43. Jim Paschal (106)
44. Worth McMillion (105)
45. Bobby Allison (104)
46. A.J. Foyt (99)
47. Gene Hobby; Larry Manning (98)
49. Curtis Turner (97)
50. Reb Wickersham (80)
51. Jerry Grant; Ned Setzer (79)
53. Lionel Johnson (75)
54. Frank Warren (57)
55. Buren Skeen (55)
56. Jabe Thomas (53)
57. Sonny Hutchins (49)
58. Ray Carter; Dan Gurney; Fred Harb (45)
61. Pedro Rodriguez (40)
62. Curtis Crider; Bill DeCoster; Larry Frank (38)
65. G.T. Nolan (37)
66. Robert Vaughn (36)
67. Gene Davis (35)
68. Eddie Gray (34)

69. Scotty Cain; Al White (33)
71. Sam Stanley (32)
72. Bert Robbins (29)
73. Don Hume; Nat Reeder; Johnny Rutherford (27)
76. Ed Brown; Bill Morton (26)
78. Bob Cooper; Dick Gulstrand; Iggy Katona (25)
81. Bunkie Blackburn; Bob Connor; Walt Hansgen; Frank Weathers (24)
85. Danny Byrd; Pee Wee Ellwanger (23)
87. Bill Amick; Barry Brooks; T.C. Hunt (22)
90. Doug Moore (21)
91. Skip Hudson (20)
92. Bobby Isaac (19)
93. Jack Anderson (18)
94. Jim Hunter; Jimmy Vaughn (17)
96. Possum Jones (16)
97. Johnny Allen; Jim Bray; Jeff Hawkins; Doug Yates (15)
101. Rod Eulenfeld; Bob Grossman; Dan Warlick (14)
104. Don Tilley (12)
105. Bill McMahan; John Sears (11)
107. Elmo Henderson; Harold Painter (10)
109. Joe Penland (9)
110. Allen McMillion; Samuel Smith (8)
112. Bud Harless; Goldie Parsons (7)
114. Darrell Bryant; Hop Holmes (6)
116. David Warren (5)
117. Gil Hearne; Arthur Page (4)
119. Bill Champion (3)
120. Fred Goad; Jim Tatum (2)
122. Walson Gardner; Joe Holder (1)

1965 Events

Motor Trend 500; Riverside Int. Raceway/2.7-m road/500 miles
Dan Gurney (Ford)/Junior Johnson (Ford)

Daytona International Speedway/2.5-mile/100 miles
Darel Dieringer (Mercury)

Daytona International Speedway/2.5-mile/100 miles
Junior Johnson (Ford)

Daytona 500; Daytona International Speedway/2.5-m/500 miles
Fred Lorenzen (Ford)/Darel Dieringer (Mercury)

Piedmont Interstate Fairgrounds/.5-mile dirt/100 miles
Ned Jarrett (Ford)/Dick Hutcherson (Ford)

Fireball 200; Asheville-Weaverville Speedway/.5-m/100 miles
Ned Jarrett (Ford)/Ned Jarrett (Ford)

Richmond 250; Virginia State Fairgrounds/.5-m dirt/125 miles
Junior Johnson (Ford)/Junior Johnson (Ford)

Orange Speedway/.9-mile dirt/150 miles
Ned Jarrett (Ford)/Junior Johnson (Ford)

Atlanta 500; Atlanta International Raceway/1.5-m/500 miles
Marvin Panch (Ford)/Marvin Panch (Ford)

Greenville 200; Greenville-Pickens Speedway/.5-m dirt/100 m
Dick Hutcherson (Ford)/Bud Moore (Plymouth)

Gwyn Staley 400; North Wilkesboro Speedway/.625-m/250 miles
Junior Johnson (Ford)/Junior Johnson (Ford)

Virginia 500; Martinsville Speedway/.5-mile/250 miles
Fred Lorenzen (Ford)/Junior Johnson (Ford)

Columbia 200; Columbia Speedway/.5-mile dirt/100 miles
Tiny Lund (Ford)/Ned Jarrett (Ford)

Southeastern 500; Bristol International Speedway/.5-m/250 m
Junior Johnson (Ford)/Marvin Panch (Ford)

Rebel 300; Darlington Raceway/1.375-mile/300 miles
Junior Johnson (Ford)/Fred Lorenzen (Ford)

Tidewater 250; Langley Field Speedway/.4-mile dirt/100 miles
Ned Jarrett (Ford)/Dick Hutcherson (Ford)

Bowman Gray Stadium/.25-mile/50 miles
Junior Johnson (Ford)/Junior Johnson (Ford)

Hickory 250; Hickory Speedway/.4-mile dirt/100 miles
Junior Johnson (Ford)/G.C. Spencer (Ford)

World 600; Charlotte Motor Speedway/1.5-mile/600 miles
Fred Lorenzen (Ford)/Fred Lorenzen (Ford)

Cleveland County Fairgrounds/.5-mile dirt/100 miles
Ned Jarrett (Ford)/Dick Hutcherson (Ford)

Asheville Speedway/.333-mile/100 miles
Junior Johnson (Ford)/Junior Johnson (Ford)

Harris Speedway/.3-mile/100 miles
Ned Jarrett (Ford)/Paul Lewis (Ford)

Music City 200; Fairgrounds Speedway/.5-mile/100 miles
Dick Hutcherson (Ford)/Tom Pistone (Ford)

Birmingham 200; Birmingham Raceway/.5-mile/100 miles
Ned Jarrett (Ford)/Ned Jarrett (Ford)

Dixie 400; Atlanta International Raceway/1.5-mile/400 miles
Marvin Panch (Ford)/Fred Lorenzen (Ford)

Pickens 200; Greenville-Pickens Speedway/.5-m dirt/100 miles
Dick Hutcherson (Ford)/Ned Jarrett (Ford)

Rambi Raceway/.5-mile dirt/100 miles
Dick Hutcherson (Ford)/Dick Hutcherson (Ford)

Valdosta Speedway/.5-mile dirt/100 miles
Cale Yarborough (Ford)/Dick Hutcherson (Ford)

Firecracker 400; Daytona International Speedway/2.5-m/400 m
A.J. Foyt (Ford)/Marvin Panch (Ford)

Old Dominion Speedway/.375-mile/150 miles
Junior Johnson (Ford)/Ned Jarrett (Ford)

Old Bridge 200; Old Bridge Stadium/.5-mile/100 miles
Junior Johnson (Ford)/Marvin Panch (Ford)

Islip Speedway/.2-mile/50 miles
Marvin Panch (Ford)/Marvin Panch (Ford)

The Glen 151.8/Watkins Glen International/2.3-m road/152 m
Marvin Panch (Ford)

Volunteer 500; Bristol International Speedway/.5-m/250 miles
Ned Jarrett (Ford)/Fred Lorenzen (Ford)

Nashville 400; Fairgrounds Speedway/.5-mile/200 miles
Richard Petty (Plymouth)/Richard Petty (Plymouth)

Cleveland County Fairgrounds/.5-mile dirt/100 miles
Ned Jarrett (Ford)/David Pearson (Dodge)

Western N.C. 500; Asheville-Weaverville Speedway/.5-m/250 m
Richard Petty (Plymouth)/Richard Petty (Plymouth)

Smoky Mountain Raceway/.5-mile dirt/100 miles
Dick Hutcherson (Ford)/Ned Jarrett (Ford)

Piedmont Interstate Fairgrounds/.5-mile dirt/100 miles
Ned Jarrett (Ford)/Dick Hutcherson (Ford)

Augusta Speedway/.5-mile/100 miles
Dick Hutcherson (Ford)/Ned Jarrett (Ford)

Sandlapper 200; Columbia Speedway/.5-mile dirt/100 miles
David Pearson (Dodge)/Dick Hutcherson (Ford)

Moyock 300; Dog Track Speedway/.333-mile/100 miles
Dick Hutcherson (Ford)/Richard Petty (Plymouth)

Beltsville Speedway/.5-mile/100 miles
Ned Jarrett (Ford)/Ned Jarrett (Ford)

Myers Brothers 250; Bowman Gray Stadium/.25-mile/63 miles
Junior Johnson (Ford)/Richard Petty (Plymouth)

Southern 500; Darlington Raceway/1.375-mile/500 miles
Ned Jarrett (Ford)/Junior Johnson (Ford)

Buddy Shuman 250; Hickory Speedway/.4-mile dirt/100 miles
Richard Petty (Plymouth)/Junior Johnson (Ford)

Pennsylvania 200; Lincoln Speedway/.5-mile dirt/100 miles
Dick Hutcherson (Ford)/Richard Petty (Plymouth)

Old Dominion Speedway/.375-mile/150 miles
Richard Petty (Plymouth)/Ned Jarrett (Ford)

Capital City 300; Virginia State Fairgrounds/.5-m dirt/150 m
David Pearson (Dodge)/Dick Hutcherson (Ford)

Old Dominion 500; Martinsville Speedway/.5-mile/250 miles
Junior Johnson (Ford)/Richard Petty (Plymouth)

Wilkes 400; North Wilkesboro Speedway/.625-mile/250 miles
Junior Johnson (Ford)/Fred Lorenzen (Ford)

National 400; Charlotte Motor Speedway/1.5-mile/400 miles
Fred Lorenzen (Ford)/Fred Lorenzen (Ford)

Orange Speedway/.9-mile dirt/101 miles
Dick Hutcherson (Ford)/Dick Hutcherson (Ford)

American 500; North Carolina Motor Speedway/1-mile/500 miles
Curtis Turner (Ford)/Richard Petty (Plymouth)

Tidewater 300; Dog Track Speedway/.333-mile/100 miles
Ned Jarrett (Ford)/Bobby Isaac (Ford)

Victories
1. Ned Jarrett; Junior Johnson (13)
3. Dick Hutcherson (9)
4. Fred Lorenzen; Marvin Panch; Richard Petty (4)
7. David Pearson (2)
8. Darel Dieringer; A.J. Foyt; Dan Gurney; Tiny Lund; Curtis Turner; Cale Yarborough (1)

Poles
1. Dick Hutcherson; Ned Jarrett; Junior Johnson (9)
4. Richard Petty (7)
5. Fred Lorenzen (6)
6. Marvin Panch (5)
7. Darel Dieringer; Bobby Isaac; Paul Lewis; Bud Moore; David Pearson; Tom Pistone; G.C. Spencer (1)

Victories
1. Ford (48)
2. Plymouth (4)
3. Dodge (2)
4. Mercury (1)

Poles
1. Ford (42)
2. Plymouth (8)
3. Dodge; Mercury (1)

1966
'The Last American Hero'

Junior Johnson wasn't the first Winston Cup driver to hone his talents hauling loads of moonshine across winding mountain roads, just the most famous.

"We had all the knowledge of what it took," Johnson said. "It was a training ground for many of the guys who came along and did well in the sport."

For Johnson, raised in North Carolina's Wilkes County, known as the "Moonshine Capital of the World," driving fast cars with trunkloads of illegal liquor was simply joining the family business. Johnson's brother, Fred, preceded Junior into racing and talked Junior into giving it a try.

"I was out plowing and sweating behind an old, stubborn mule," Johnson recalled nearly 25 years after his career ended in 1966. "It seemed like more fun than plowing. I just went right to the race track. There wasn't much problem with transition."

Johnson, whose moonshine-to-glory days were immortalized by Tom Wolfe in "The Last American Hero," won five races and ranked fifth in the Performance Index in 1955. But his career was derailed when he was sent to a federal penitentiary in Ohio for 11 months after being caught at the family still. Thirty years later, he received a full pardon from President Reagan.

Johnson returned with a vengeance; he posted six victories in 1958 and finished in the top six in the Performance Index for the first of four consecutive seasons. By the time Johnson retired in 1966 at age 35, he had won 50 races and 45 poles. He remains tied for eighth on the all-time list in both categories. Johnson still ranks among the top 10 in dirt victories (24), short-track wins (18), dirt poles (18), and short-track poles (21).

Despite his prowess on dirt and short tracks, Johnson's eight superspeedway victories trailed only Fireball Roberts at the time he decided to forsake driving to become a car owner.

Like the adage that great players don't necessarily make great football coaches or baseball managers, the same has pretty much been true for stock-car racing's driving stars who became car owners.

Johnson, however, was a glaring exception. He posted all 50 of his victories behind the wheel of someone else's machine, then, as a car owner, saw his drivers capture 140 victories and six Winston Cup titles. Along the way, Johnson, whom Darrell Waltrip once called "the smartest man in NASCAR," gained a reputation as one of history's craftiest mechanics in terms of stretching the rule book to its limits. For example, Johnson's cars were penalized more than once because of oversized engines and gas tanks.

"I knew when I got in his car that I was going to win a lot of races and a lot of championships," said Waltrip, whose six-year tenure behind the wheel of Johnson's cars produced 43 victories and three Winston Cup titles.

"I have never let anyone drive my car who couldn't run for the front and get all there is out of the car," said Johnson, describing his own driving style. "I've had the pick of the crop. A driver's best years are when he's in his 30s. There comes a time when they're unbeatable, and I had them all when they were unbeatable."

That doesn't mean, however, that Johnson thought his drivers could have beaten him in his prime.

"The Curtis Turners, the Flock boys, Buck Baker—I think the old drivers were far better than today's drivers," said Johnson, who was chosen in 1998 by *Sports Illustrated* as the greatest driver in NASCAR's first half-century. "Very few of them now could drive on dirt. The cars are a lot more sophisticated now than they were 30 years ago. The technology that the guys have today—the equipment that we have compared to the equipment that we used to have—I think we've got the best of the two."

After his cars had reached victory lane only three times in as many years, including a winless 1995 season, Johnson said goodbye to the sport, sold his team, and returned to his farm in Yadkin County, N.C., to raise cattle and, perhaps, even resume his plowing.

1966 in Review

The 1966 season was the first campaign that Richard Petty and David Pearson, who rank first and second in career victories and poles, ranked 1-2 in those categories for the season. Petty, who in 1966 became the first driver to win three consecutive races from the pole, won eight races and 15 poles. Pearson tied the record of four consecutive victories set two years earlier by Billy Wade and earned 15 wins, seven poles, and the Winston Cup title in Cotton Owens's Dodge. Pearson also easily led the Performance Index with a 947-756 margin over James Hylton.

Most Memorable Race

In June of 1964, Jim Hurtubise suffered burns on 45 percent of his body during an Indy-car race in Milwaukee. He spent months in rehabilitation in a San Antonio hospital. After he pleaded with doctors, his immobile hands were sculpted during surgery to allow him to clutch a steering wheel. On March 27, Hurtubise beat Fred Lorenzen by more than a lap in the Atlanta 500 for the biggest victory of his career. After he took the checkered flag, Hurtubise allegedly tossed a wrench into the infield. Hurtubise supposedly had used the wrench unfairly during the race to lower the Norm Nelson-owned Plymouth—an allegation he denied some 15 years later.

Most Significant Wreck

In the Southern 500 on September 5, Earl Balmer's car flipped end over end, destroyed 150 feet of guardrail, and hurled steel debris and gas into the old press box at Darlington, S.C. Veteran motorsports journalist Bob Myers called the wreck "scary."

Most Important Off-Track Development

Ford, which had captured 48 races a year earlier, withdrew its factory teams in April because of restrictions on weight limits and its overhead cam engine. "It seems rather ridiculous that the Ford would have to weigh about 450 pounds more than its competitors," Ford executive Leo Beebe told Bill Robinson of *The Atlanta Journal*.

Records & Milestones

Pearson captured three consecutive dirt victories on three occasions in 1966, the only time a driver has recorded three three-race winning streaks in one discipline in the same season.

1966 at a Glance

Races:	49
Dirt:	15
Road:	2
Short Track:	20
Superspeedway:	12
Winners:	17
Pole Winners:	15
Tracks:	31
States:	10

1966 Performance Index Rankings

1. David Pearson (947)
2. James Hylton (756)
3. John Sears (598)
4. Richard Petty (591)
5. Elmo Langley (552)
6. Henley Gray (551)
7. Wendell Scott (504)
8. Neil Castles (493)
9. J.T. Putney (458)
10. Bobby Allison (446)
11. Paul Goldsmith (414)
12. Clyde Lynn (388)
13. Buck Baker (364)
14. Paul Lewis (351)
15. Jim Paschal (346)
16. Darel Dieringer (340)
17. Ned Jarrett (292)
18. Buddy Baker (270)
19. J.D. McDuffie (264)
20. Marvin Panch (263)
21. G.C. Spencer (262)
22. Dick Hutcherson (259)
23. Cale Yarborough (253)
24. Sam McQuagg (249)
25. Curtis Turner (243)
26. Tiny Lund/Roy Mayne (222)
28. Fred Lorenzen (219)
29. Blackie Watt (210)
30. Jim Hurtubise (201)
31. Don White (194)
32. Tom Pistone (160)

Before he sold his team after the 1995 season, it's no surprise that Junior Johnson's autograph was in demand in NASCAR's garage areas: He earned 50 Winston Cup victories as a driver and 140 more as a car owner.

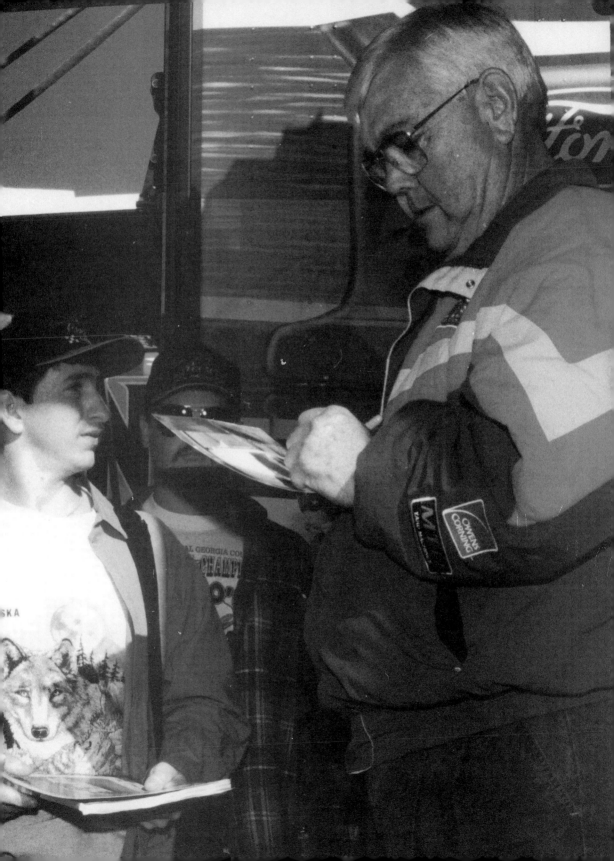

33. Lee Roy Yarbrough (145)
34. Johnny Wynn (144)
35. Hank Thomas (140)
36. Buddy Arrington (136)
37. Frank Warren (134)
38. Stick Elliott (121)
39. Wayne Smith (120)
40. Roy Tyner (118)
41. Jimmy Helms (116)
42. Bill Seifert (110)
43. Doug Cooper; Joel Davis (102)
45. Earl Balmer (100)
46. Larry Manning (94)
47. Worth McMillion (92)
48. Bob Derrington (81)
49. Gordon Johncock (80)
50. Ray Hill II (74)
51. Junior Johnson (69)
52. Larry Hess (63)
53. Paul Connors; Friday Hassler (61)
55. Bobby Isaac (60)
56. Jerry Grant (59)
57. Jabe Thomas (58)
58. Larry Frank (56)
59. Gene Cline; Harold Smith (55)
61. Gene Black; Jack Bowsher (54)
63. Roy Hallquist (50)
64. H.B. Bailey; Ernest Eury (46)
66. Dan Gurney (45)
67. Jeff Hawkins; Max Ledbetter; Eddie MacDonald (44)
70. Earl Brooks (41)
71. Bill Champion (40)
72. Bobby Johns (38)
73. Don Biederman; Wayne Woodward (36)
75. Mario Andretti (34)
76. Billy Foster (33)
77. Donnie Allison; Bunkie Blackburn; Norm Nelson (31)
80. Ron Hornaday (30)
81. Sonny Lanphear (28)
82. Johnny Steele (27)
83. Lefty Bolton; Butch Hartman (26)
85. Don Walker (25)
86. Rene Charland (24)
87. Walt Price (23)
88. Bob Cooper; George England; Edgar Wallen (21)
91. Jerry Oliver (20)
92. A.J. Foyt; G.T. Nolan (19)
94. Nick Rampling; Al White (17)
96. Walter Ballard; Ned Setzer; E.J. Trivette (15)
99. Jim Tatum (14)
100. Coo Coo Marlin (13)
101. Johnny Allen; Don Israel (12)
103. Eddie Yarboro (11)
104. Darrell Bryant (10)
105. Walter Wallace (9)
106. Ed Jordan (8)
107. Buzz Gregory; Mack Hanbury; Bunk Moore; Buster Sexton (7)
111. Paul Dean Holt; Lionel Johnson; Mike Page; Bryant Wallace (6)
115. Paul Bumhaver; Mario Caruso; Bud Moore (5)
118. Charles Triplett (4)
119. Ernie Gahan; Jack Ingram (2)
121. Gil Hearne (1)

1966 Events

Georgia Cracker 300; Augusta Speedway/.5-mile/150 miles
Richard Petty (Plymouth)/Richard Petty (Plymouth)

Motor Trend 500; Riverside Int. Raceway/2.7-mile road/500 m
Dan Gurney (Ford)/David Pearson (Dodge)

Daytona International Speedway/2.5-mile/100 miles
Paul Goldsmith (Plymouth)

Daytona International Speedway/2.5-mile/100 miles
Earl Balmer (Dodge)

Daytona 500; Daytona International Speedway/2.5-m/500 miles
Richard Petty (Plymouth)/Richard Petty (Plymouth)

Peach Blossom 500; North Carolina Motor Speedway/1-m/500 m
Paul Goldsmith (Plymouth)/Paul Goldsmith (Plymouth)

Southeastern 500; Bristol International Speedway/.5-m/250 m
Dick Hutcherson (Ford)/David Pearson (Dodge)

Atlanta 500; Atlanta International Raceway/1.5-m/500 miles
Jim Hurtubise (Plymouth)/Richard Petty (Plymouth)

Hickory 250; Hickory Speedway/.4-mile dirt/100 miles
David Pearson (Dodge)/Elmo Langley (Ford)

Columbia 200; Columbia Speedway/.5-mile dirt/100 miles
David Pearson (Dodge)/Tom Pistone (Ford)

Greenville 200; Greenville-Pickens Speedway/.5-m dirt/100 m
David Pearson (Dodge)/Tiny Lund (Ford)

Bowman Gray Stadium/.25-mile/50 miles
David Pearson (Dodge)/David Pearson (Dodge)

Gwyn Staley 400; North Wilkesboro Speedway/.625-m/250 miles
Jim Paschal (Plymouth)/Jim Paschal (Plymouth)

Virginia 500; Martinsville Speedway/.5-mile/250 miles
Jim Paschal (Plymouth)/Jim Paschal (Plymouth)

Rebel 400; Darlington Raceway/1.375-mile/400 miles
Richard Petty (Plymouth)/Richard Petty (Plymouth)

Tidewater 250; Langley Field Speedway/.4-mile dirt/100 miles
Richard Petty (Plymouth)/Richard Petty (Plymouth)

Speedy Morelock 200; Middle Georgia Raceway/.5-mile/100 miles
Richard Petty (Plymouth)/Richard Petty (Plymouth)

Independent 250; Starlite Speedway/.4-mile dirt/100 miles
Darel Dieringer (Ford)/James Hylton (Dodge)

Richmond 250; Virginia State Fairgrounds/.5-m dirt/125 miles
David Pearson (Dodge)/Tom Pistone (Ford)

World 600; Charlotte Motor Speedway/1.5-mile/600 miles
Marvin Panch (Plymouth)/Richard Petty (Plymouth)

Dog Track Speedway/.333-mile/100 miles
David Pearson (Dodge)/Richard Petty (Plymouth)

Asheville 300; Asheville Speedway/.333-mile/100 miles
David Pearson (Dodge)/Richard Petty (Plymouth)

Piedmont Interstate Fairgrounds/.5-mile dirt/100 miles
Elmo Langley (Ford)/David Pearson (Dodge)

East Tennessee 200; Smoky Mountain Raceway/.5-mile dirt/100 m
David Pearson (Dodge)/Tom Pistone (Ford)

Fireball 300; Asheville-Weaverville Speedway/.5-m/150 miles
Richard Petty (Plymouth)/Richard Petty (Plymouth)

Beltsville 200; Beltsville Speedway/.5-mile/100 miles
Tiny Lund (Ford)/Richard Petty (Plymouth)

Pickens 200; Greenville-Pickens Speedway/.5-m dirt/100 miles
David Pearson (Dodge)/David Pearson (Dodge)

Firecracker 400; Daytona International Speedway/2.5-m/400 m
Sam McQuagg (Dodge)/Lee Roy Yarbrough (Dodge)

Old Dominion Speedway/.375-mile/150 miles
Elmo Langley (Ford)/Bobby Allison (Chevrolet)

Bridgehampton Raceway/2.85-mile road/148 miles
David Pearson (Dodge)/David Pearson (Dodge)

Oxford Plains Speedway/.333-mile/100 miles
Bobby Allison (Chevrolet)/Bobby Allison (Chevrolet)

Fonda Speedway/.5-mile dirt/100 miles
David Pearson (Dodge)/Richard Petty (Plymouth)

Islip Speedway/.2-mile/60 miles
Bobby Allison (Chevrolet)/Tom Pistone (Ford)

Volunteer 500; Bristol International Speedway/.5-m/250 miles
Paul Goldsmith (Plymouth)/Curtis Turner (Chevrolet)

Smoky Mountain 200; Smoky Mountain Raceway/.5-m dirt/100 m
Paul Lewis (Plymouth)/Buddy Baker (Dodge)

Nashville 400; Fairgrounds Speedway/.5-mile/200 miles
Richard Petty (Plymouth)/Richard Petty (Plymouth)

Dixie 400; Atlanta International Raceway/1.5-mile/400 miles
Richard Petty (Plymouth)/Curtis Turner (Chevrolet)

Sandlapper 200; Columbia Speedway/.5-mile dirt/100 miles
David Pearson (Dodge)/Bobby Allison (Chevrolet)

Western N.C. 500; Asheville-Weaverville Speedway/.5-m/250 m
Darel Dieringer (Mercury)/Junior Johnson (Ford)

Maryland 200; Beltsville Speedway/.5-mile/100 miles
Bobby Allison (Chevrolet)/Bobby Allison (Chevrolet)

Myers Brothers 250; Bowman Gray Stadium/.25-mile/63 miles
David Pearson (Dodge)/Richard Petty (Plymouth)

Southern 500; Darlington Raceway/1.375-mile/500 miles
Darel Dieringer (Mercury)/Lee Roy Yarbrough (Dodge)

Buddy Shuman 250; Hickory Speedway/.4-mile dirt/100 miles
David Pearson (Dodge)/Richard Petty (Plymouth)

Capital City 300; Virginia State Fairgrounds/.5-m dirt/150 m
David Pearson (Dodge)/David Pearson (Dodge)

Joe Weatherly 150; Orange Speedway/.9-mile dirt/150 miles
Dick Hutcherson (Ford)/Dick Hutcherson (Ford)

Old Dominion 500; Martinsville Speedway/.5-mile/250 miles
Fred Lorenzen (Ford)/Junior Johnson (Ford)

Wilkes 400; North Wilkesboro Speedway/.625-mile/250 miles
Dick Hutcherson (Ford)/Junior Johnson (Ford)

National 500; Charlotte Motor Speedway/1.5-mile/500 miles
Lee Roy Yarbrough (Dodge)/Fred Lorenzen (Ford)

American 500; North Carolina Motor Speedway/1-mile/500 miles
Fred Lorenzen (Ford)/Fred Lorenzen (Ford)

Victories
1. David Pearson (15)
2. Richard Petty (8)
3. Bobby Allison; Darel Dieringer; Paul Goldsmith; Dick Hutcherson (3)
7. Elmo Langley; Fred Lorenzen; Jim Paschal (2)
10. Earl Balmer; Dan Gurney; Jim Hurtubise; Paul Lewis; Tiny Lund; Sam McQuagg; Marvin Panch; Lee Roy Yarbrough (1)

Poles
1. Richard Petty (15)
2. David Pearson (7)
3. Bobby Allison; Tom Pistone (4)
5. Junior Johnson (3)
6. Fred Lorenzen; Jim Paschal; Curtis Turner; Lee Roy Yarbrough (2)
10. Buddy Baker; Paul Goldsmith; Dick Hutcherson; James Hylton; Elmo Langley; Tiny Lund (1)

Victories
1. Dodge (18)
2. Plymouth (16)
3. Ford (10)
4. Chevrolet (3)
5. Mercury (2)

Poles
1. Plymouth (18)
2. Ford (12)
3. Dodge (11)
4. Chevrolet (6)

1967
The Golden Boy

He wasn't Janet Gaynor or Barbra Streisand. But if ever a star was born in one race, it was the day Fred Lorenzen beat Curtis Turner in a memorable bump-and-run duel in the 1961 Rebel 300 at Darlington, S.C., his "proudest moment in racing."

"I passed Turner with one lap to go for my first big victory. He and I started on the front row, and we went back and forth all day," Lorenzen recalled years later. "I tried to go around Turner on the outside with two laps to go. He pushed me into the wall, and the cement flew. Coming down from the white flag, into turn four, I backed off the gas and then got back on it. I had a lot of momentum built up on him coming off turn four, so I decided to fake him on the outside and go underneath him. I got the white flag, and down the backstretch he tried to put me in the wall. But I held on and took the checkered flag. It was the biggest win of my life.

"Three Atlanta 500 wins and a Daytona 500 win were big," said Lorenzen, who stunned stock-car racing by retiring early in the 1967 season, "but nothing like the first one."

Lorenzen, who had won a short-track race earlier in the 1961 campaign at Martinsville, Va., quickly became NASCAR's Golden Boy. Not only was the blond Midwestern driver a natural on the South's new superspeedways, but he was stock-car racing's first sex symbol.

Like so many drivers of Lorenzen's era, his focus was on Grand Slam events, not the Winston Cup championship. The closest he ever came to the championship was in 1963, when he finished third in the point standings and fourth in the Performance In-

dex—his only finish higher than 17th. Fearless Freddie pocketed $122,588 that year, becoming the first driver to reach the six-figure mark in a single season, but the championship was such a low priority that he started only 29 of 55 races.

During a short career so characteristic of his era, Lorenzen became the first driver to capture:
- A superspeedway race in seven consecutive seasons (1961-67);
- Multiple Grand Slam victories three years in a row (1963-65);
- A 500-mile race five consecutive years (1962-66);
- A Grand Slam race five years in succession (1961-65);
- A superspeedway race from the pole in three consecutive seasons (1964-66);
- A Grand Slam pole six years in a row (1961-66);
- A superspeedway pole six years in a row (1961-66).

And in 1964 and '65, Lorenzen became:
- The only driver to capture at least two Grand Slam victories from the pole in back-to-back seasons;
- The first of only four drivers to win at least two superspeedway races from the pole in back-to-back seasons, a record he shares with Richard Petty, Bobby Allison, and David Pearson;
- The first driver to capture at least three Grand Slam events in consecutive seasons, a string exceeded only by Jeff Gordon.

Although the likes of Petty and Pearson were encroaching on his territory, Lorenzen was arguably the sport's brightest star when the Golden Boy retired after wrecking the Holman-Moody Ford in the Atlanta 500 on April 2, 1967.

Why did Lorenzen quit at age 32? Three decades and a fortune in real estate later, the Elmhurst, Ill., native still didn't have a plausible answer.

"I just woke up one day, and that was it," he said. "Looking back, it was a stupid thing to do, the worst mistake of my career. I got out of it too soon."

After an absence of a little more than four years, Lorenzen returned to racing. In his fourth race back, he won the pole for the Dixie 500 at Atlanta, site of one of his greatest achievements: three consecutive Atlanta 500 victories (1962-64). He captured another pole a year later at Rockingham, N.C., but the sabbatical had removed the Golden Boy's glitter.

Fearless Fred Lorenzen had become the first driver ever to earn at least one superspeedway victory in seven consecutive seasons when he "retired" at age 32 in 1967.

Despite his relatively brief career, Lorenzen still ranks in the top 10 in Grand Slam victories (12), Grand Slam poles (12), short-track poles (15), superspeedway wins from the pole (6), short-track triumphs from the pole (5), and Grand Slam wins from the pole (5). He is also among the top 20 in victories (26), superspeedway wins (13), short-track victories (12), poles (31), superspeedway poles (14), and victories from the pole (11).

1967 in Review

Petty enjoyed a record-shattering season that included 10 victories in a row—twice as long as any other winning streak in history. Petty also rolled to 27 victories, nine more than Tim Flock's previous record and more than four times as many as runner-up Bobby Allison's six triumphs. Petty's 18 poles doubled the number recorded by runner-up Dick Hutcherson as the King cruised to his second Winston Cup title and a resounding 1,130-826 advantage over James Hylton in the Performance Index ratings. Petty gained 74.59 percent of the available Performance Index, the highest rating achieved during the circuit's first 22 years.

Most Memorable Race

Petty's Plymouth and Allison's Ford took turns pushing each other into the wall before Allison passed his rival with just seven laps remaining in the Western North Carolina 500 at Asheville-Weaverville Speedway on November 5. Allison finished half a second in front of Petty to improve Lorenzen's record as his crew chief to two victories in as many starts. Only seven of the 30 cars that started the rough-and-tumble race were around at the finish, when the crews for Petty and Allison nearly squared off.

Most Significant Wreck

Paul Goldsmith achieved in a Plymouth what Ford Motor Company had spent millions trying to do: stop Petty's 10-race winning streak. When the engine in Goldsmith's car expired during the National 500 on October 15 at Charlotte, his car slid sideways into Petty's. The King's car suffered significant damage and eventually was retired with a lame engine. Petty finished 66 laps behind winner Buddy Baker.

Most Important Off-Track Development

When competitors reported for inspection for the July 4 Firecracker 400 at Daytona Beach, Fla., they learned that NASCAR had decided to enforce its rule that required Winston Cup cars to conform with the bodies of standard automobiles. Only Lee Roy Yarbrough, in Bud Moore's Mercury Comet, passed the initial round of inspections.

Records & Milestones

Petty captured the first four races of his 10-race winning streak from the pole. That marked the first time in history—and a record matched only once since—that a driver has won four races in a row from the pole. . . . Twenty of 49 races were won from the pole to tie the record set in the 62-race 1964 campaign.

1967 at a Glance

Races:	49
Dirt:	14
Road:	1
Short Track:	21
Superspeedway:	13
Winners:	12
Pole Winners:	11
Tracks:	30
States:	12

1967 Performance Index Rankings

1. Richard Petty (1,130)
2. James Hylton (826)
3. Bobby Allison (719)
4. Jim Paschal (675)
5. Dick Hutcherson (661)
6. John Sears (654)
7. Elmo Langley (539)
8. Clyde Lynn (474)
9. Neil Castles (447)
10. Wendell Scott (445)
11. David Pearson (404)
12. Bill Seifert (386)
13. Henley Gray (364)
14. Paul Goldsmith (324)
15. Darel Dieringer (298)
16. J.T. Putney (294)
17. Cale Yarborough (284)
18. Donnie Allison (282)
19. Buddy Baker (275)
20. Bobby Isaac (272)
21. G.C. Spencer (267)
22. Earl Brooks (254)
23. Tiny Lund (236)
24. Buck Baker (232)

25. Paul Lewis (207)
26. Friday Hassler (195)
27. Buddy Arrington (185)
28. Lee Roy Yarbrough (181)
29. Charlie Glotzbach (168)
30. George Davis (166)
31. Wayne Smith (148)
32. Frank Warren (142)
33. Paul Dean Holt (138)
34. Mario Andretti; Don Biederman (126)
36. Bobby Wawak (119)
37. Fred Lorenzen; Roy Mayne (113)
39. Bud Moore (112)
40. Doug Cooper (109)
41. Sonny Hutchins (106)
42. Sam McQuagg (105)
43. Dick M. Johnson; George Poulos (96)
45. Jack Harden; Don White (93)
47. Tom Pistone (81)
48. Max Ledbetter (79)
49. Bill Dennis (71)
50. Larry Miller; Ed Negre; Roy Tyner (70)
53. E.J. Trivette (66)
54. A.J. Foyt; Jabe Thomas (64)
56. Bill Champion; Eddie Yarboro (59)
58. Bill Ervin (57)
59. Ramo Stott (55)
60. Gordon Johncock (54)
61. Joel Davis (53)
62. Bob Cooper (49)
63. Dorus Wisecraver (47)
64. Bobby Johns (46)
65. Red Farmer; Parnelli Jones (45)
67. H.B. Bailey (42)
68. Swede Savage (41)
69. Jerry Grant (40)
70. Norm Nelson (37)
71. Jim Hurtubise (36)
72. Bruce Worrell (34)
73. Scotty Cain (33)
74. Stick Elliott (31)
75. Charles Prickett (30)
76. Worth McMillion; Jerry Oliver; Harold Stockton (29)
79. Jack Ingram; Curley Mills; Bo Reeder (28)
82. Jim Hunter (27)
83. Dan Gurney; Armond Holley (26)
85. Whitey Gerkin; Jimmy Helms; Blackie Watt (25)
88. George England (24)
89. Don Noel (23)
90. John Martin (22)
91. Coo Coo Marlin (21)
92. Gary Bettenhausen; Innes Ireland; Clyde Prickett (20)
95. Mel Bradley (19)
96. Bosco Lowe; Joe Edd Neubert; Gary Sain (15)
99. Bob Pickell (14)
100. Jack Etheridge; Don Stives (13)
102. Bobby Mausgrover (12)
103. Don Schissler; Ken Spikes (11)
105. Larry Manning; G.T. Nolan; Johnny Steele; Don Tarr (9)
109. Tom Raley (8)
110. Jim Conway; Harold Fagan; Paul Radford (7)
113. Herb Estes; J.D. McDuffie; Bill Vanderhoff (3)
116. Ken Rice (2)

1967 Events

Augusta 300; Augusta Speedway/.5-mile/150 miles
Richard Petty (Plymouth)/Dick Hutcherson (Ford)

Motor Trend 500; Riverside Int. Raceway/2.7-mile road/500 m
Parnelli Jones (Ford)/Dick Hutcherson (Ford)

Daytona International Speedway/2.5-mile/100 miles
Lee Roy Yarbrough (Dodge)

Daytona International Speedway/2.5-mile/100 miles
Fred Lorenzen (Ford)

Daytona 500; Daytona International Speedway/2.5-m/500 miles
Mario Andretti (Ford)/Curtis Turner (Chevrolet)

Fireball 300; Asheville-Weaverville Speedway/.5-m/150 miles
Richard Petty (Plymouth)/Darel Dieringer (Ford)

Southeastern 500; Bristol International Speedway/.5-m/250 m
David Pearson (Dodge)/Darel Dieringer (Ford)

Greenville 200; Greenville-Pickens Speedway/.5-m dirt/100 m
David Pearson (Dodge)/Dick Hutcherson (Ford)

Bowman Gray Stadium/.25-mile/50 miles
Bobby Allison (Chevrolet)/Bobby Allison (Chevrolet)

Atlanta 500; Atlanta International Raceway/1.5-m/500 miles
Cale Yarborough (Ford)/Cale Yarborough (Ford)

Columbia 200; Columbia Speedway/.5-mile dirt/100 miles
Richard Petty (Plymouth)/Dick Hutcherson (Ford)

Hickory 250; Hickory Speedway/.4-mile dirt/100 miles
Richard Petty (Plymouth)/Richard Petty (Plymouth)

Gwyn Staley 400; North Wilkesboro Speedway/.625-m/250 miles
Darel Dieringer (Ford)/Darel Dieringer (Ford)

Virginia 500; Martinsville Speedway/.5-mile/250 miles
Richard Petty (Plymouth)/Darel Dieringer (Ford)

Savannah Speedway/.5-mile dirt/100 miles
Bobby Allison (Chevrolet)/John Sears (Ford)

Richmond 250; Virginia State Fairgrounds/.5-m dirt/125 miles
Richard Petty (Plymouth)/Richard Petty (Plymouth)

Rebel 400; Darlington Raceway/1.375-mile/400 miles
Richard Petty (Plymouth)/David Pearson (Ford)

Beltsville 200; Beltsville Speedway/.5-mile/100 miles
Jim Paschal (Plymouth)/Richard Petty (Plymouth)

Tidewater 250; Langley Field Speedway/.4-mile dirt/100 miles
Richard Petty (Plymouth)/Richard Petty (Plymouth)

World 600; Charlotte Motor Speedway/1.5-mile/600 miles
Jim Paschal (Plymouth)/Cale Yarborough (Ford)

Asheville 300; Asheville Speedway/.333-mile/100 miles
Jim Paschal (Plymouth)/Richard Petty (Plymouth)

Macon 300; Middle Georgia Raceway/.5-mile/150 miles
Richard Petty (Plymouth)/Richard Petty (Plymouth)

East Tennessee 200; Smoky Mountain Raceway/.5-m dirt/100 m
Richard Petty (Plymouth)/Jim Hunter (Chevrolet)

Birmingham Speedway/.625-mile/100 miles
Bobby Allison (Dodge)/Jim Paschal (Plymouth)

Carolina 500; North Carolina Motor Speedway/1-mile/500 miles
Richard Petty (Plymouth)/Dick Hutcherson (Ford)

Pickens 200; Greenville-Pickens Speedway/.5-m dirt/100 miles
Richard Petty (Plymouth)/Richard Petty (Plymouth)

Montgomery Speedway/.5-mile/100 miles
Jim Paschal (Plymouth)/Richard Petty (Plymouth)

Firecracker 400; Daytona International Speedway/2.5-m/400 m
Cale Yarborough (Ford)/Darel Dieringer (Ford)

Northern 300; Trenton Speedway/1-mile/300 miles
Richard Petty (Plymouth)/Richard Petty (Plymouth)

Maine 300; Oxford Plains Speedway/.333-mile/100 miles
Bobby Allison (Chevrolet)/James Hylton (Dodge)

Fonda Speedway/.5-mile dirt/100 miles
Richard Petty (Plymouth)/Richard Petty (Plymouth)

Islip 300; Islip Speedway/.2-mile/60 miles
Richard Petty (Plymouth)/Richard Petty (Plymouth)

Volunteer 500; Bristol International Speedway/.5-m/250 miles
Richard Petty (Plymouth)/Richard Petty (Plymouth)

Smoky Mountain 200; Smoky Mountain Raceway/.5-m dirt/100 m
Dick Hutcherson (Ford)/Dick Hutcherson (Ford)

Nashville 400; Fairgrounds Speedway/.5-mile/200 miles
Richard Petty (Plymouth)/Dick Hutcherson (Ford)

Dixie 500; Atlanta International Raceway/1.5-mile/500 miles
Dick Hutcherson (Ford)/Darel Dieringer (Ford)

Myers Brothers 250; Bowman Gray Stadium/.25-mile/63 miles
Richard Petty (Plymouth)/Richard Petty (Plymouth)

Sandlapper 200; Columbia Speedway/.5-mile dirt/100 miles
Richard Petty (Plymouth)/Richard Petty (Plymouth)

Savannah Speedway/.5-mile dirt/100 miles
Richard Petty (Plymouth)/Richard Petty (Plymouth)

Southern 500; Darlington Raceway/1.375-mile/500 miles
Richard Petty (Plymouth)/Richard Petty (Plymouth)

Buddy Shuman 250; Hickory Speedway/.4-mile/100 miles
Richard Petty (Plymouth)/Dick Hutcherson (Ford)

Capital City 300; Virginia State Fairgrounds/.5-m dirt/150 m
Richard Petty (Plymouth)

Maryland 300; Beltsville Speedway/.5-mile/150 miles
Richard Petty (Plymouth)/Richard Petty (Plymouth)

Hillsborough 150; Orange Speedway/.9-mile dirt/150 miles
Richard Petty (Plymouth)/Richard Petty (Plymouth)

Old Dominion 500; Martinsville Speedway/.5-mile/250 miles
Richard Petty (Plymouth)/Cale Yarborough (Ford)

Wilkes 400; North Wilkesboro Speedway/.625-mile/250 miles
Richard Petty (Plymouth)/Dick Hutcherson (Ford)

National 500; Charlotte Motor Speedway/1.5-mile/500 miles
Buddy Baker (Dodge)/Cale Yarborough (Ford)

American 500; North Carolina Motor Speedway/1-mile/500 miles
Bobby Allison (Ford)/David Pearson (Ford)

Western N.C. 500; Asheville-Weaverville Speedway/.5-m/250 m
Bobby Allison (Ford)/Bobby Allison (Ford)

Victories
1. Richard Petty (27)
2. Bobby Allison (6)
3. Jim Paschal (4)
4. Dick Hutcherson; David Pearson; Cale Yarborough (2)
7. Mario Andretti; Buddy Baker; Darel Dieringer; Parnelli Jones; Fred Lorenzen; Lee Roy Yarbrough (1)

Poles
1. Richard Petty (18)
2. Dick Hutcherson (9)
3. Darel Dieringer (6)
4. Cale Yarborough (4)
5. Bobby Allison; David Pearson (2)
7. Jim Hunter; James Hylton; Jim Paschal; John Sears; Curtis Turner (1)

Victories
1. Plymouth (31)
2. Ford (10)
3. Dodge (5)
4. Chevrolet (3)

Poles
1. Ford (23)
2. Plymouth (19)
3. Chevrolet (3)
4. Dodge (1)

1968 Stock-Car Racing's Greatest Rivalry

Like Duke vs. North Carolina in college basketball, Ohio State vs. Michigan in college football, or the Giants vs. Dodgers in baseball, stock-car racing has been blessed with its share of intense, sometimes even bitter, rivalries.

Cale Yarborough vs. Darrell Waltrip or Dale Earnhardt vs. any of the following—Waltrip, Ricky Rudd, Geoff Bodine, Bill Elliott, or Jeff Gordon—come to mind. Bobby Allison vs. Waltrip and Richard Petty vs. David Pearson certainly were among the greatest rivalries the sport has known.

But no rivalry in stock-car racing ever fueled such intensity among fans, the media, or the drivers themselves as the wars waged by Allison and Petty during the late '60s and early '70s. Allison points to his victory in Islip, N.Y., on July 7, 1968, as the beginning of the rivalry. Allison took the checkered flag, driving, as he recalls, a Chevrolet inferior to Petty's Plymouth.

"Richard was leading the race, and I was running second," Allison recalled. "He was coming to lap me. He was already a big star, and I guess he didn't like this new guy challenging him. I was in heavy traffic. When I didn't get out of the way as fast as he would have liked, he thumped me, trying to get by me, and bent his fender a little bit.

"Or I hit the nose of his car with my rear bumper," he added with a smile. "That helped me to go on and win the race."

Maurice Petty, Richard's brother and engine builder, and Dale Inman, Richard's cousin, crew chief, and lifelong best friend, had to be restrained when they pursued Allison after the race.

Indeed, Petty was stock-car racing's premier gate attraction. He already had 82 of his 200 career victories under his belt, while the Islip 300 triumph was only the 11th for Allison, who was just five months Petty's junior. But Allison was on his way to 85 victories, which trails only Petty and Pearson on the career list, and a career Performance Index that through 1999 trailed only Petty and Earnhardt.

During the next few years, both drivers became painfully aware that the other was the primary roadblock to victory lane. The rivalry became so heated that, at one point, Donnie Allison, Bobby's brother and the winner of 10 Winston Cup races, approached Inman and told him that they had to do something to stop the bad blood.

"I remember when Donnie came to me and told me that," Inman recalled years later. "You know what I told him? I said, 'Donnie, if I look up on the track and the entire field is going in one direction and Richard is going in the other and he gets hit, I'm going to blame Bobby.'

"Donnie just looked at me, threw up his hands, and walked away," Inman said, laughing.

Bobby thought the rivalry's intensity helped the sport.

"Richard and I ran into each other an awful lot, way more than two individuals ran into each other in those days. Instead of just riding around out there, there were two guys who were friendly with the fans who were going against each other hard enough that nobody thought it was a fake," Bobby recalled. "There were Richard Petty fans who couldn't wait until the next race to see if Richard was going to hit the kid from Alabama. Richard and I could rub on each other on the 10th lap of a 500-lapper, and that gave the fans 490 laps of edge-of-their-seat excitement. Maybe nothing would happen, but they knew we'd go after each other."

Among the more notable examples:

- Petty appeared to be in command in the Alabama 200 at Montgomery on December 8, 1968, until a late caution allowed Allison to catch up, pass Petty on the last lap, and win by the length of a fender.
- Petty edged Allison by a mere two car lengths to capture the 1971 Dixie 500 at Atlanta, with their nearest competitor nine laps behind.
- One race later, in the West Virginia 500 at International Raceway Park, the duo bumped and banged

throughout the race until Petty prevailed by two laps.

- A week later in the Yankee 400 at Michigan, Allison passed Petty with three laps left. Petty tried to regain the lead until the final turn, when he backed off and then claimed Allison was toying with him.

- Just seven days later, Allison took the white flag in the Talladega 500 at Alabama International Motor Speedway, with Petty and Pete Hamilton right behind him. Petty and Hamilton bumped on the backstretch, Hamilton wrecked, and Allison cruised home 2.1 seconds in front of Petty, who blamed Allison for the wreck.

- In the 1972 Old Dominion 500 at Martinsville, Va., Petty and Allison combined to lead all but four of the 500 laps. Allison repeatedly ignored the black flag, and Petty repeatedly refused to move over when signaled to do so by the flagman. Petty eventually beat Allison by six seconds.

- Perhaps the most intense race in the rivalry came just one week later in the Wilkes 400 at North Wilkesboro, N.C. Allison took the lead from pole winner Buddy Baker on the second lap, and he and Petty swapped the lead on a dozen occasions—never allowing another driver to lead—until Petty gained the advantage on the 389th of 400 laps. Allison regained the lead with less than three laps to go, but when Petty passed Allison on the final lap, Petty's Dodge and Allison's Chevrolet crunched into each other. As Petty's car sailed toward the fence, Allison cruised toward the finish line, only to be passed by Petty, who beat his archrival by two car lengths.

"I mean, he was in the fence and came back and beat me," Allison said. "That might be the most unbelievable race I ever lost."

An inebriated fan attacked Petty in victory lane, and Maurice retaliated with a right hook to the head.

Ironically, that race pretty much ended the fender-to-fender bumping and banging between those two superstars. Allison earned 11 victories driving for Holman-Moody in 1971 and 10 behind the wheel of Junior Johnson's Chevrolet the next season. After that season, Allison left to drive his own Chevrolet. He was no longer the man Petty had to beat, and the rivalry's intensity gradually fizzled.

Both drivers now consider those fierce exchanges among the highlights of their careers.

"We had a little trouble to begin with. For two or three years there, when it came down to the end of the race, it seemed like it always came down to me and Bobby," Petty recalled. "But we never intentionally knocked each other out of the race. It was great. It was good for Bobby and good for me in the long run. It was good for the sport. It stimulated a lot of racing fans and added a lot of spice. There's not many people I have more respect for than Bobby Allison."

Allison, as fierce a competitor as stock-car racing has ever known, reluctantly agrees.

"It was always tough for me to compliment a competitor. It was a lot easier for me to find their faults," he said. "I always took pride in the fact that I honored the rules I competed under—the car rules and the race rules. I raced against a lot of guys who did not. But you look back at a guy like Richard Petty, and I have to say, 'Hey, he performed.' "

1968 in Review

The 1968 season once again belonged to Pearson and Petty, who each won 16 races and 12 poles. Pearson parlayed a four-race winning streak in the Holman-Moody Ford into his second Winston Cup title and held a 1,052-905 advantage over Petty in the Performance Index ratings.

Most Memorable Race

Yarborough and Pearson were dueling for the lead in the Southern 500 at Darlington, S.C., on September 2 when they collided with 44 laps remaining. Pearson's Ford spun into the infield, and Yarborough's Wood brothers' Ford bounced off the guardrail. When they recovered, Yarborough led by 25 seconds. With 10 laps remaining, however, Pearson had trimmed his deficit to two seconds. Pearson reduced the gap even further, but Yarborough prevailed by four car lengths. "This is the greatest day of my life," said Yarborough, whose pre-

Bobby Allison recalls stock-car racing's greatest rivalry beginning with a race at Islip, N.Y., in which he may have hit the "nose of (Richard Petty's) car with my rear bumper."

vious victories in the Daytona 500 and Atlanta 500 enabled him to become the first driver to win three 500-mile races in one year.

Most Significant Wreck

John Sears escaped injury when his L.G. DeWitt-owned Ford split a guardrail and bounced end over end in the Sandlapper 200 at Columbia, S.C., on August 8.

Most Important Off-Track Development

Sears probably was aided by Ford Motor Company's introduction of the window safety net.

Records & Milestones

The 16 victories apiece by Petty and Pearson marked the only time two drivers won that many races in a season. . . . Thirty races were held on short tracks, a record equaled only in 1969.

1968 at a Glance

Races:	49
Dirt:	7
Road:	1
Short Track:	30
Superspeedway:	11
Winners:	10
Pole Winners:	11
Tracks:	31
States:	12

1968 Performance Index Rankings

1. David Pearson (1,052)
2. Richard Petty (905)
3. Bobby Isaac (868)
4. James Hylton (627)
5. John Sears (609)
6. Elmo Langley (608)
7. Clyde Lynn (598)
8. Bobby Allison (572)
9. Lee Roy Yarbrough (472)
10. Buddy Baker (448)
11. Cale Yarborough (439)
12. Wendell Scott (429)
13. Jabe Thomas (423)
14. Roy Tyner (382)
15. Neil Castles (364)
16. Bill Seifert (358)
17. Charlie Glotzbach (351)
18. Friday Hassler (298)
19. Tiny Lund (295)
20. Donnie Allison (294)
21. Darel Dieringer (263)
22. Henley Gray (250)
23. J.D. McDuffie (234)
24. Bud Moore (215)
25. Earl Brooks (213)
26. Paul Dean Holt (159)
27. G.C. Spencer (156)
28. Paul Goldsmith (154)
29. Pete Hamilton (146)
30. Dave Marcis (142)
31. Butch Hartman (137)
32. Curtis Turner (135)
33. Don Tarr (125)
34. Richard Brickhouse (119)
35. Bill Champion (118)
36. Buck Baker (109)
37. E.J. Trivette (107)
38. Stan Meserve (104)
39. Walson Gardner (100)
40. Larry Manning (90)
41. Ed Negre (86)
42. Sam McQuagg (76)
43. Jerry Grant; Tom Pistone; Al Unser (75)
46. Wayne Smith (71)
47. A.J. Foyt; Ray Hendrick (63)
49. Ben Arnold; Jim Hurtubise (56)
51. Don White (55)
52. Eddie Yarboro (53)
53. Bob Cooper (50)
54. Swede Savage (49)
55. Paul Lewis; Bob Moore II (48)
57. Bobby Johns (47)
58. Harold Fagan; Dan Gurney; Frank Warren (45)
61. Dick M. Johnson (44)
62. Lennie Waldo (43)
63. Parnelli Jones (37)
64. Andy Hampton (35)
65. Bob Pronger; Ervin Pruitt (34)
67. Jack Ingram; Dave James; Bob Senneker (32)
70. Scotty Cain (31)
71. Harold Smith (30)

72. Jim Cook (29)
73. Gene Black; Hoss Ellington; Marty Robbins (28)
76. Blaine Kauffman; Clyde Prickett (26)
78. Willie Crane; Jack McCoy (25)
80. Guy Jones (24)
81. Mario Andretti; Frank Burnett; Bill Vanderhoff (23)
84. Sam Rose (22)
85. Red Farmer (21)
86. Norm Nelson; Dub Simpson (20)
88. Cecil Gordon; Worth McMillion (19)
90. George Davis; Bill Ervin (18)
92. Roy Trantham (15)
93. George England; Jack Marlin (11)
95. Bobby Mausgrover; Dave Mote; Sam Waldrop (10)
98. John Winger (9)
99. Niles Gage (8)
100. Ken Meisenhelder; Bryant Wallace (7)
102. Bob Burcham; Jeff Hawkins; Bosco Lowe; Don Tomberlin; Phil Wendt (6)
107. Jim Paschal (5)
108. Max Ledbetter; Glenn Luce (4)
110. Don Biederman; G.T. Nolan (2)

1968 Events

Middle Georgia 500; Middle Georgia Raceway/.5625-mile/281 m
Bobby Allison (Ford)/Lee Roy Yarbrough (Ford)

Montgomery Speedway/.5-mile/100 miles
Richard Petty (Plymouth)/Richard Petty (Plymouth)

Motor Trend 500; Riverside Int. Raceway/2.7-mile road/500 m
Dan Gurney (Ford)/Dan Gurney (Ford)

Daytona 500; Daytona International Speedway/2.5-m/500 miles
Cale Yarborough (Mercury)/Cale Yarborough (Mercury)

Southeastern 500; Bristol International Speedway/.5-m/250 m
David Pearson (Ford)/Richard Petty (Plymouth)

Richmond 250; Virginia State Fairgrounds/.5-m dirt/125 miles
David Pearson (Ford)/Bobby Isaac (Dodge)

Atlanta 500; Atlanta International Raceway/1.5-m/500 miles
Cale Yarborough (Mercury)/Lee Roy Yarbrough (Mercury)

Hickory 250; Hickory Speedway/.4-mile/100 miles
Richard Petty (Plymouth)/David Pearson (Ford)

Greenville 200; Greenville-Pickens Speedway/.5-m dirt/100 m
Richard Petty (Plymouth)/David Pearson (Ford)

Columbia 200; Columbia Speedway/.5-mile dirt/100 miles
Bobby Isaac (Dodge)/Richard Petty (Plymouth)

Gwyn Staley 400; North Wilkesboro Speedway/.625-m/250 miles
David Pearson (Ford)/David Pearson (Ford)

Virginia 500; Martinsville Speedway/.5-mile/250 miles
Cale Yarborough (Mercury)/David Pearson (Ford)

Dixie 250; Augusta Speedway/.5-mile/125 miles
Bobby Isaac (Dodge)/Bobby Isaac (Dodge)

Fireball 300; Asheville-Weaverville Speedway/.5-m/150 miles
David Pearson (Ford)/David Pearson (Ford)

Rebel 400; Darlington Raceway/1.375-mile/400 miles
David Pearson (Ford)/Lee Roy Yarbrough (Ford)

Beltsville 300; Beltsville Speedway/.5-mile/150 miles
David Pearson (Ford)/Richard Petty (Plymouth)

Tidewater 250; Langley Field Speedway/.4-mile/100 miles
David Pearson (Ford)/Richard Petty (Plymouth)

World 600; Charlotte Motor Speedway/1.5-mile/600 miles
Buddy Baker (Dodge)/Donnie Allison (Ford)

Asheville 300; Asheville Speedway/.333-mile/100 miles
Richard Petty (Plymouth)/Richard Petty (Plymouth)

Macon 300; Middle Georgia Raceway/.5-mile/150 miles
David Pearson (Ford)/David Pearson (Ford)

Smoky Mountain Raceway/.5-mile/100 miles
Richard Petty (Plymouth)/David Pearson (Ford)

Birmingham Speedway/.625-mile/100 miles
Richard Petty (Plymouth)/David Pearson (Ford)

Carolina 500; North Carolina Motor Speedway/1-mile/500 miles
Donnie Allison (Ford)/Lee Roy Yarbrough (Ford)

Pickens 200; Greenville-Pickens Speedway/.5-m dirt/100 miles
Richard Petty (Plymouth)/David Pearson (Ford)

Firecracker 400; Daytona International Speedway/2.5-m/400 m
Cale Yarborough (Mercury)/Charlie Glotzbach (Dodge)

Islip 300; Islip Speedway/.2-mile/60 miles
Bobby Allison (Chevrolet)/Buddy Baker (Dodge)

Maine 300; Oxford Plains Speedway/.333-mile/100 miles
Richard Petty (Plymouth)/Buddy Baker (Dodge)

Fonda 200; Fonda Speedway/.5-mile dirt/100 miles
Richard Petty (Plymouth)/David Pearson (Ford)

Northern 300; Trenton Speedway/1-mile/300 miles
Lee Roy Yarbrough (Ford)/Lee Roy Yarbrough (Ford)

Volunteer 500; Bristol International Speedway/.5-m/250 miles
David Pearson (Ford)/Lee Roy Yarbrough (Ford)

Smoky Mountain 200; Smoky Mountain Raceway/.5-m/100 miles
Richard Petty (Plymouth)/Bobby Isaac (Dodge)

Nashville 400; Fairgrounds Speedway/.5-mile/200 miles
David Pearson (Ford)/Richard Petty (Plymouth)

Dixie 500; Atlanta International Raceway/1.5-mile/500 miles
Lee Roy Yarbrough (Mercury)/Buddy Baker (Dodge)

Sandlapper 200; Columbia Speedway/.5-mile dirt/100 miles
David Pearson (Ford)/Buddy Baker (Dodge)

Myers Brothers 250; Bowman Gray Stadium/.25-mile/63 miles
David Pearson (Ford)/Richard Petty (Plymouth)

Western N.C. 500; Asheville-Weaverville Speedway/.5-m/250 m
David Pearson (Ford)/Darel Dieringer (Plymouth)

South Boston Speedway/.375-mile/100 miles
Richard Petty (Plymouth)/Richard Petty (Plymouth)

Crabber 250; Langley Field Speedway/.4-mile/100 miles
David Pearson (Ford)/David Pearson (Ford)

Southern 500; Darlington Raceway/1.375-mile/500 miles
Cale Yarborough (Mercury)/Charlie Glotzbach (Dodge)

Buddy Shuman 250; Hickory Speedway/.4-mile/100 miles
David Pearson (Ford)/Richard Petty (Plymouth)

Capital City 300; Virginia State Fairgrounds/.625-mile/188 m
Richard Petty (Plymouth)/Richard Petty (Plymouth)

Maryland 300; Beltsville Speedway/.5-mile/150 miles
Bobby Isaac (Dodge)/Cale Yarborough (Mercury)

Hillsborough 150; Orange Speedway/.9-mile dirt/150 miles
Richard Petty (Plymouth)/Richard Petty (Plymouth)

Old Dominion 500; Martinsville Speedway/.5-mile/250 miles
Richard Petty (Plymouth)/Cale Yarborough (Mercury)

Wilkes 400; North Wilkesboro Speedway/.625-mile/250 miles
Richard Petty (Plymouth)/Bobby Allison (Plymouth)

Augusta 200; Augusta Speedway/.5-mile/100 miles
David Pearson (Ford)/Bobby Allison (Plymouth)

National 500; Charlotte Motor Speedway/1.5-mile/500 miles
Charlie Glotzbach (Dodge)/Charlie Glotzbach (Dodge)

American 500; North Carolina Motor Speedway/1-mile/500 miles
Richard Petty (Plymouth)/Cale Yarborough (Mercury)

Peach State 200; Jeffco Speedway/.5-mile/100 miles
Cale Yarborough (Mercury)/David Pearson (Ford)

Victories

1. David Pearson; Richard Petty (16)
3. Cale Yarborough (6)
4. Bobby Isaac (3)
5. Bobby Allison; Lee Roy Yarbrough (2)
7. Donnie Allison; Buddy Baker; Charlie Glotzbach; Dan Gurney (1)

Poles

1. David Pearson; Richard Petty (12)
3. Lee Roy Yarbrough (6)
4. Buddy Baker; Cale Yarborough (4)
6. Charlie Glotzbach; Bobby Isaac (3)
8. Bobby Allison (2)
9. Donnie Allison; Darel Dieringer; Dan Gurney (1)

Victories

1. Ford (20)
2. Plymouth (16)
3. Mercury (7)
4. Dodge (5)
5. Chevrolet (1)

Poles

1. Ford (19)
2. Plymouth (15)
3. Dodge (10)
4. Mercury (5)

1969
Yarbrough: 'It Might Have Been'

If John Greenleaf Whittier had chronicled the history of stock-car racing, only Tim Richmond would have been as likely a recipient of his most famous line, "It might have been," than Lee Roy Yarbrough.

In the glare of the spotlight—in classic events and on Grand Slam tracks—few, if any, drivers enjoyed a more dazzling season than Yarbrough's 1969 campaign behind the wheel of Junior Johnson's Fords and Mercurys.

If Yarbrough had a dominant car, he did an excellent job of disguising it. For example, he became the only driver to win as many as seven races in one year without capturing a pole.

Three drivers posted double-figure victory seasons in 1969. But none matched the quality of Yarbrough's seven superspeedway triumphs, three more than the record set a year earlier.

Yarbrough's first victory of the season came in stock-car racing's premier event, when he passed Charlie Glotzbach on the last lap to win the Daytona 500 by three car lengths. He won the Rebel 400 at Darlington, S.C., after he overcame a late wreck in the final five laps that also involved Bobby Allison and Cale Yarborough. He later won the World 600 at Charlotte, the Firecracker 400 at Daytona, and the Dixie 500 at Atlanta. Yarbrough added a record fifth consecutive Grand Slam victory when he passed David Pearson on the final lap and beat him to the checkered flag by a car length in the Southern 500 at Darlington.

Yarbrough's Southern 500 victory enabled him to become the first driver to win three classics in a season—the Daytona 500, the World 600, and the Southern 500, then known as stock-car racing's Triple Crown. Yarbrough celebrated his 31st birthday, then added a victory in the American 500 at Rockingham, N.C., that gave him an unprecedented four 500-mile victories in one season. Pearson and Jeff Gordon are the only other drivers to win on all four Grand Slam tracks in one season, and no one has matched Yarbrough's six victories on Grand Slam venues in the same campaign.

A victory in the National 500 at Charlotte a year later gave Yarbrough at least one Grand Slam triumph for the fifth consecutive year, a streak bettered only by Yarborough, Pearson, Gordon, and Fireball Roberts. But that was to be the last of his 14 victories.

Yarbrough, who posted his only top-10 seasons in the Performance Index in 1968 and '69, suffered a concussion in a tire test at Texas World Speedway late in the 1970 season and had amnesia for several days. And he was lucky to survive a horrifying, season-ending crash the next May in the Indianapolis 500.

Or was he?

Yarbrough drove in 18 races in 1972, most of them in Bill Seifert's Ford, and managed a 20th-place season in the Performance Index, only the fifth time he'd finished that high. He drifted out of the sport, and during the '70s, there were frequent rumors of drug addiction and dramatic weight loss. In 1980, Yarbrough tried to strangle his mother at her Jacksonville home and was placed in a mental institution, where he died at age 46 from a brain hemorrhage suffered in a fall.

Yarbrough still ranks among the top 10 in Grand Slam triumphs (10) and among the top 20 in superspeedway victories (12) and 500-mile wins (7). But that magical 1969 season at age 30 gives an indication of what "might have been."

"He had the most confidence of anybody I ever had," Johnson said a quarter-century after that '69 campaign. "He was fearless."

1969 in Review

The 1969 campaign was the only season in which three drivers reached double figures in victories. Bobby Isaac, who also won a record 19 poles, led the way with 17 triumphs. Pearson posted 11 victories and Richard Petty 10. Yarbrough's seven victories and Allison's five gave five drivers 50 wins in the season's 54 races. Pearson joined Lee Petty as a three-time Winston Cup champion and held a 1,182-1,004 advantage over Richard Petty in the Performance Index.

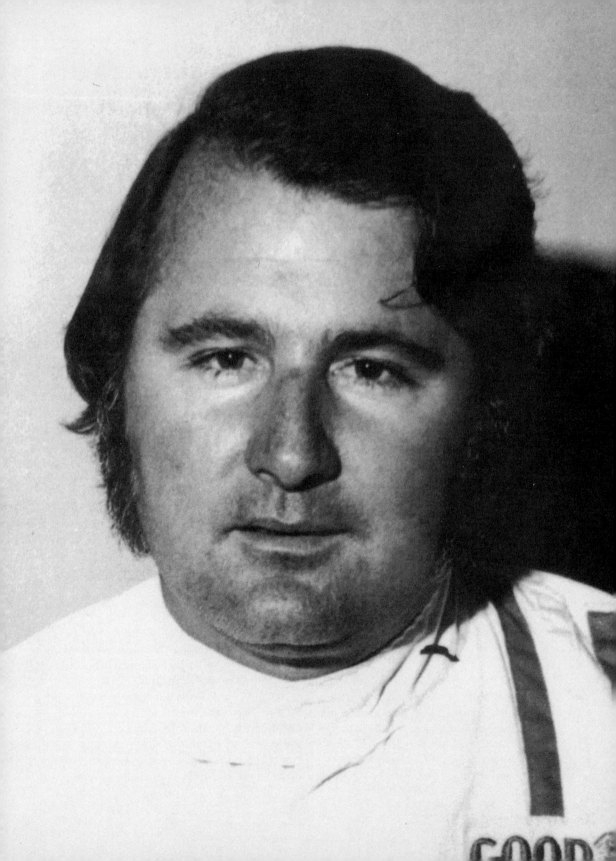

Most Memorable Race

That Richard Brickhouse captured his only Winston Cup victory is a mere footnote to the inaugural Talladega 500 on September 14. NASCAR President Bill France's new Alabama International Motor Speedway was the largest closed course ever built: 2.66 miles. It also featured turns with 33-degree banking, two degrees steeper than Daytona International Speedway, and was 12 feet wider than Daytona. The fastest track ever built—and the ability of the tires to withstand the speeds—definitely concerned the drivers. The Professional Drivers Association, led by President Richard Petty, had been formed earlier in the year, and rumors about a boycott of France's new facility had been rampant for weeks. "The track is simply not ready. The surface is tearing up, and the tire people can't find us anything to race on," Petty said less than 24 hours before the green flag was scheduled to fall. "We think the track's unsafe and that we ought to come back in 30 days and race when the place is ready." The PDA members indeed packed up and left, including Glotzbach, who had qualified Ray Nichels's Dodge at a record 199.466 mph. France, however, was determined that the show would go on. Thirty-six cars started, 24 of them from NASCAR's Grand Touring division. Isaac, who inherited the pole with a speed of 196.386 mph, was the only marquee driver from the Winston Cup ranks to participate. France relayed word to the crowd of 45,000 before the race that their ticket stubs would be good for a future race at Daytona or Talladega, and Brickhouse drove the car vacated by Glotzbach to a seven-second victory over Jim Vandiver as Dodges swept the first four spots.

Most Significant Wreck

Richard Petty suffered chest injuries when a tire exploded and his Plymouth crashed into the wall at North Carolina's Asheville-Weaverville Speedway on May 4. Although Petty certainly had more famous accidents, shortly before his retirement in 1992 he called the crash at Asheville-Weaverville "the worst lick I ever took. I never felt worse."

Lee Roy Yarbrough's storybook 1969 season saw him become the first driver to capture three classic races in a season—the Daytona 500, the World 600, and the Southern 500—the highlight of a tragic life.

Most Important Off-Track Development

NASCAR introduced a standard method of measuring speedways, finally legitimizing the reported speeds for races and time trials.

Records & Milestones

The 1969 season was the only campaign in which two drivers, Isaac and Pearson (14), captured at least 14 poles.... Thirty short-track events were held, tying the record set a year earlier.... Four superspeedways staged their first Winston Cup races: Michigan International Speedway, Dover Downs International Speedway in Delaware, Texas International Speedway, and Alabama International Motor Speedway.

1969 at a Glance

Races:	54
Dirt:	5
Road:	1
Short Track:	30
Superspeedway:	18
Winners:	8
Pole Winners:	9
Tracks:	33
States:	14

1969 Performance Index Rankings

1. David Pearson (1,182)
2. Richard Petty (1,004)
3. James Hylton (919)
4. Bobby Isaac (900)
5. Neil Castles (811)
6. Lee Roy Yarbrough (724)
7. Elmo Langley (667)
8. John Sears (662)
9. Jabe Thomas (618)
10. E.J. Trivette (536)
11. Wendell Scott (527)
12. Bobby Allison (498)
13. Cecil Gordon (495)
14. J.D. McDuffie (428)
15. Bill Seifert (423)
16. Ben Arnold (420)
17. Bill Champion (399)
18. Dave Marcis (386)
19. Buddy Baker (383)
20. Donnie Allison (379)
21. Dick Brooks (366)
22. Henley Gray (364)
23. Richard Brickhouse (295)
24. Friday Hassler (291)
25. Cale Yarborough (286)
26. Earl Brooks (254)
27. Charlie Glotzbach (249)

28. G.C. Spencer (242)
29. Hoss Ellington (238)
30. Ed Hessert (216)
31. Buddy Young (209)
32. Paul Goldsmith (166)
33. Ed Negre (161)
34. Don Tarr (153)
35. Buddy Arrington (150)
36. Dick M. Johnson (137)
37. Wayne Smith (136)
38. Roy Mayne (135)
39. Frank Warren (132)
40. Ray Elder (124)
41. Roy Tyner (115)
42. A.J. Foyt (105)
43. Benny Parsons (100)
44. Sonny Hutchins (90)
45. Pete Hazelwood (75)
46. Dub Simpson (72)
47. Coo Coo Marlin (71)
48. Johnny Halford (69)
49. Swede Savage (64)
50. H.B. Bailey (63)
51. Ken Meisenhelder (62)
52. Ramo Stott (58)
53. Pete Hamilton (57)
54. Vic Elford; Paul Dean Holt; Jim Vandiver (53)
57. Dick Poling (52)
58. John Kennedy (51)
59. Don Biederman (47)
60. Andy Hampton; Al Unser (36)
62. Jack McCoy; Jimmy Vaughn (33)
64. Scotty Cain; Walson Gardner; Billy Hagan; Bobby Mausgrover; Sam McQuagg; Ervin Pruitt (32)
70. Tiny Lund (31)
71. Harold Hardesty (30)
72. Ray Johnstone; Bill Ward (29)
74. Larry Baumel; Dick Bown; Ernie Shaw (28)
77. Amos Johnson (27)
78. Bobby Fleming; Bobby Unser (26)
80. Gerald Chamberlain (25)
81. Randy Dodd (24)
82. Bob Ashbrook; Ron Grana; Frank Sessoms; Marvin Sjolin (23)
86. Mario Andretti; Buck Baker (22)
88. Dick Lawrence (21)
89. Paul Dorrity; Wilbur Pickett (20)
91. Tommy Gale; Clyde Lynn (18)
93. George Ashbrook (17)
94. Billy Taylor; Eldon Yarbrough (16)
96. Bobby Johns (14)
97. James Cox; Don Patton (13)
99. Ray Hendrick (12)
100. Worth McMillion (11)
101. Roy Hallquist (10)
102. Bill Shirey (8)
103. Wayne Gillette (7)
104. Bill Ervin (6)
105. Lee Gordon (5)
106. Dick Watson (4)
107. Red Farmer; J.C. Yarborough (1)

1969 Events

Georgia 500; Middle Georgia Raceway/.5-mile/250 miles
Richard Petty (Plymouth)/David Pearson (Ford)

Alabama 200; Montgomery Speedway/.5-mile/100 miles
Bobby Allison (Plymouth)/Richard Petty (Plymouth)

Motor Trend 500; Riverside Int. Raceway/2.7-mile road/500 m
Richard Petty (Ford)/A.J. Foyt (Ford)

Daytona International Speedway/2.5-mile/125 miles
David Pearson (Ford)

Daytona International Speedway/2.5-mile/125 miles
Bobby Isaac (Dodge)

Daytona 500; Daytona International Speedway/2.5-m/500 miles
Lee Roy Yarbrough (Ford)/Buddy Baker (Dodge)

Carolina 500; North Carolina Motor Speedway/1-mile/500 miles
David Pearson (Ford)/David Pearson (Ford)

Cracker 200; Augusta Speedway/.5-mile/100 miles
David Pearson (Ford)/Bobby Isaac (Dodge)

Southeastern 500; Bristol International Speedway/.5-m/250 m
Bobby Allison (Dodge)/Bobby Isaac (Dodge)

Atlanta 500; Atlanta International Raceway/1.5-m/500 miles
Cale Yarborough (Mercury)/David Pearson (Ford)

Columbia 200; Columbia Speedway/.5-mile dirt/100 miles
Bobby Isaac (Dodge)/Bobby Isaac (Dodge)

Hickory 250; Hickory Speedway/.4-mile/100 miles
Bobby Isaac (Dodge)/Bobby Isaac (Dodge)

Greenville 200; Greenville-Pickens Speedway/.5-m dirt/100 m
Bobby Isaac (Dodge)/David Pearson (Ford)

Richmond 500; Virginia State Fairgrounds/.5-mile/250 miles
David Pearson (Ford)/David Pearson (Ford)

Gwyn Staley 400; North Wilkesboro Speedway/.625-m/250 miles
Bobby Allison (Dodge)/Bobby Isaac (Dodge)

Virginia 500; Martinsville Speedway/.5-mile/250 miles
Richard Petty (Ford)/Bobby Allison (Dodge)

Fireball 300; Asheville-Weaverville Speedway/.5-m/150 miles
Bobby Isaac (Dodge)/Bobby Isaac (Dodge)

Rebel 400; Darlington Raceway/1.375-mile/400 miles
Lee Roy Yarbrough (Mercury)/Cale Yarborough (Mercury)

Beltsville 300; Beltsville Speedway/.5-mile/150 miles
Bobby Isaac (Dodge)/Bobby Isaac (Dodge)

Tidewater 375; Langley Field Speedway/.4-mile/150 miles
David Pearson (Ford)/David Pearson (Ford)

World 600; Charlotte Motor Speedway/1.5-mile/600 miles
Lee Roy Yarbrough (Mercury)/Donnie Allison (Ford)

Macon 300; Middle Georgia Raceway/.5-mile/150 miles
Bobby Isaac (Dodge)/David Pearson (Ford)

Maryville 300; Smoky Mountain Raceway/.5-mile/150 miles
Bobby Isaac (Dodge)/David Pearson (Ford)

Motor State 500; Michigan International Speedway/2-m/500 m
Cale Yarborough (Mercury)/Donnie Allison (Ford)

Kingsport 250; Kingsport Speedway/.4-mile/100 miles
Richard Petty (Ford)/Bobby Isaac (Dodge)

Pickens 200; Greenville-Pickens Speedway/.5-m dirt/100 miles
Bobby Isaac (Dodge)/Bobby Isaac (Dodge)

North State 200; State Fairgrounds/.5-mile dirt/100 miles
David Pearson (Ford)/Bobby Isaac (Dodge)

Firecracker 400; Daytona International Speedway/2.5-m/400 m
Lee Roy Yarbrough (Ford)/Cale Yarborough (Mercury)

Mason-Dixon 300; Dover Downs Int. Speedway/1-mile/300 miles
Richard Petty (Ford)/David Pearson (Ford)

Thompson 200; Thompson Speedway/.625-mile/125 miles
David Pearson (Ford)/David Pearson (Ford)

Northern 300; Trenton Speedway/1.5-mile/300 miles
David Pearson (Ford)/Bobby Isaac (Dodge)

Maryland 300; Beltsville Speedawy/.5-mile/150 miles
Richard Petty (Ford)/Richard Petty (Ford)

Volunteer 500; Bristol International Speedway/.533-m/267 m
David Pearson (Ford)/Cale Yarborough (Mercury)

Nashville 400; Fairgrounds Speedway/.5-mile/200 miles
Richard Petty (Ford)/Richard Petty (Ford)

Smoky Mountain 200; Smoky Mountain Raceway/.5-m/100 miles
Richard Petty (Ford)/David Pearson (Ford)

Dixie 500; Atlanta International Raceway/1.5-mile/500 miles
Lee Roy Yarbrough (Ford)/Cale Yarborough (Mercury)

Yankee 600; Michigan International Speedway/2-mile/600 miles
David Pearson (Ford)/David Pearson (Ford)

South Boston 100; South Boston Speedway/.375-mile/100 miles
Bobby Isaac (Dodge)/Bobby Isaac (Dodge)

Myers Brothers 250; Bowman Gray Stadium/.25-mile/63 miles
Richard Petty (Ford)/Richard Petty (Ford)

Western N.C. 500; Asheville-Weaverville Speedway/.5-m/250 m
Bobby Isaac (Dodge)/Bobby Isaac (Dodge)

Southern 500; Darlington Raceway/1.375-mile/500 miles
Lee Roy Yarbrough (Ford)/Cale Yarborough (Mercury)

Buddy Shuman 250; Hickory Speedway/.4-mile/100 miles
Bobby Isaac (Dodge)/Bobby Isaac (Dodge)

Capital City 250; Virginia State Fairgrounds/.5625-m/260 m
Bobby Allison (Dodge)/Richard Petty (Ford)

Talladega 500; Alabama Int. Motor Speedway/2.66-m/500 miles
Richard Brickhouse (Dodge)/Bobby Isaac (Dodge)

Sandlapper 200; Columbia Speedway/.5-mile dirt/100 miles
Bobby Isaac (Dodge)/Richard Petty (Ford)

Old Dominion 500; Martinsville Speedway/.5-mile/250 miles
Richard Petty (Ford)/David Pearson (Ford)

Wilkes 400; North Wilkesboro Speedway/.625-mile/250 miles
David Pearson (Ford)/Bobby Isaac (Dodge)

National 500; Charlotte Motor Speedway/1.5-mile/500 miles
Donnie Allison (Ford)/Cale Yarborough (Mercury)

Savannah Speedway/.5-mile/100 miles
Bobby Isaac (Dodge)/Bobby Isaac (Dodge)

Augusta Speedway/.5-mile/100 miles
Bobby Isaac (Dodge)/Bobby Isaac (Dodge)

American 500; North Carolina Motor Speedway/1.017-mile/500 m
Lee Roy Yarbrough (Ford)/Charlie Glotzbach (Dodge)

Jeffco 200; Jeffco Speedway/.5-mile/100 miles
Bobby Isaac (Dodge)/David Pearson (Ford)

Georgia 500; Middle Georgia Raceway/.548-mile/274 miles
Bobby Allison (Dodge)/Bobby Isaac (Dodge)

Texas 500; Texas International Speedway/2-mile/500 miles
Bobby Isaac (Dodge)/Buddy Baker (Dodge)

Victories

1. Bobby Isaac (17)
2. David Pearson (11)
3. Richard Petty (10)
4. Lee Roy Yarbrough (7)
5. Bobby Allison (5)
6. Cale Yarborough (2)
7. Donnie Allison; Richard Brickhouse (1)

Poles

1. Bobby Isaac (19)
2. David Pearson (14)
3. Richard Petty; Cale Yarborough (6)
5. Donnie Allison; Buddy Baker (2)
7. Bobby Allison; A.J. Foyt; Charlie Glotzbach (1)

Victories

1. Ford (26)
2. Dodge (22)
3. Mercury (4)
4. Plymouth (2)

Poles

1. Dodge (23)
2. Ford (22)
3. Mercury (6)
4. Plymouth (1)

1970
A 'Voice' Ended Isaac's Time Among the Elite

Bobby Isaac's 37 victories and 49 poles certainly rank him among stock-car racing's elite. But one aspect of his resume is even more remarkable: Thirty-five of those victories and 39 of those poles came during a four-year stretch from 1968-71.

Even more amazing is that Isaac earned 28 victories and 32 poles in 1969 and 1970, when he produced one of the finest two-year runs in Winston Cup history, particularly on the short tracks.

Driving a Dodge owned by Nord Krauskopf and engineered by Harry Hyde, Isaac captured 19 poles, 14 short-track poles, and eight short-track races from the pole in 1969, all single-season records. He set a single-season record with 10 victories from the pole in 1969, the same year he became the last driver to win three consecutive dirt races.

Isaac ranked third in the Performance Index in 1968 and fourth in '69. He captured the Winston Cup title in 1970, when he became one of only seven drivers to earn a Performance Index rating of 1,000 or higher in a season and one of only four drivers to win five or more short-track events in a row.

During that fabulous two-year stretch in 1969 and '70, Isaac became:

- One of only two drivers in history with 13 or more poles in back-to-back seasons;
- The only driver to win at least six short-track races from the pole in consecutive years;
- One of only two drivers to record consecutive seasons of double-figure short-track victories;
- One of only two drivers to win at least six races from the pole in consecutive seasons;

- One of only three drivers to win at least eight short-track poles two years in a row.

And Isaac's back-to-back seasons with at least 11 victories has been equaled, but never beaten.

Isaac posted a Performance Index rating of at least 800 from 1968-70, and only Richard Petty and Ned Jarrett had more consecutive seasons with a rating of 800 or better. Isaac's 1971 campaign featured four victories, four poles, and a fourth consecutive season of seventh or better in the Performance Index—the only four seasons he finished higher than 15th. In 1972, Isaac captured nine poles, including a then-record eight on superspeedways, but only one race. He split with Krauskopf and Hyde late that season, at age 40.

The next season, Isaac was behind the wheel of Bud Moore's Ford during the Talladega 500 at Alabama International Motor Speedway when he heard a "voice" tell him to park the car. "Something told me to quit," he said.

Isaac heeded the advice and, not surprisingly, lost his ride.

Isaac, known as a loner, was the only standout driver who didn't join the Professional Drivers Association and therefore didn't boycott the inaugural Talladega 500 in 1969. While preparing for the 1975 National 500 at Charlotte, Isaac was asked if he thought he'd ever recapture his past glory. "No, I don't. You've got to have good equipment," he said. "I had that. I don't now, and I don't think I ever will again."

Indeed, after he heard that voice, Isaac never won another race or pole, and in 1977 he suffered a fatal heart attack in a late-model race at Hickory, N.C., in his home county. He still ranks in the top 10 in poles, short-track victories (26), short-track poles (30), victories from the pole (20), and short-track wins from the pole (17) and in the top 20 in victories, dirt wins (6), and superspeedway poles (15).

1970 in Review

Although Petty led the circuit with 18 victories and finished second with nine poles, Isaac parlayed 11 triumphs and a season-high 13 poles into the Winston Cup championship. Isaac also led the Performance Index ratings, beating Bobby Allison, 1,060-1,011, with Petty third with a 958 rating.

Driving the K & K Insurance Dodge owned by Nord Krauskopf and tuned by Harry Hyde, Bobby Isaac won 19 poles, 14 short-track poles, and eight short-track races from the pole—all single-season records—in 1969, then captured the Winston Cup title a year later.

Most Memorable Race

Pete Hamilton, whose father was the dean of Northeastern University's business school in Boston, hardly fit the mold of the typical stock-car driver of his era. But he managed to pass David Pearson with nine laps to go and beat him by a half a second to win the Daytona 500 on February 22.

Most Significant Wreck

In the Rebel 400 on May 9 at Darlington, S.C., Petty's Plymouth hit the outside wall, then slammed into the pit wall at 125 mph. His car then flipped four times and came to rest on its top. "I remember thinking, 'What are we going to do without Richard Petty?'" said Dick Thompson, a longtime executive at Virginia's Martinsville Speedway. Petty was unconscious when he left the track, but escaped with only a separated shoulder, a chipped bone in his arm, and a cut behind his left ear. Petty, who entered the Rebel 400 in first place in the Winston Cup standings, missed the next five races.

Most Important Off-Track Development

Upon the completion of the 1970 campaign, Ford announced that it was withdrawing support of its four factory teams: the Wood brothers (Cale Yarborough), Junior Johnson (Lee Roy Yarbrough), Banjo Matthews (Donnie Allison), and Holman-Moody (Pearson). Chrysler responded by reducing its support to only two Petty Enterprises cars, driven by Buddy Baker and Petty.

Records & Milestones

Petty's victory in the Home State 200 at the State Fairgrounds in Raleigh on September 30 was the last Winston Cup race held on dirt.

1970 at a Glance

Races:	48
Dirt:	3
Road:	2
Short Track:	25
Superspeedway:	18
Winners:	12
Pole Winners:	14
Tracks:	30
States:	15

1970 Performance Index Rankings

1. Bobby Isaac (1,060)
2. Bobby Allison (1,011)
3. Richard Petty (958)
4. James Hylton (937)
5. Benny Parsons (649)
6. Neil Castles (639)
7. Jabe Thomas (603)
8. Elmo Langley (598)
9. Cale Yarborough (492)
10. Dick Brooks (488)
11. Pete Hamilton (472)
12. Dave Marcis (451)
13. John Sears (435)
14. Donnie Allison (425)
15. David Pearson (421)
16. Friday Hassler (404)
17. Bill Champion (363)
18. Buddy Baker (361)
19. Wendell Scott (354)
20. Lee Roy Yarbrough (340)
21. Cecil Gordon (335)
22. J.D. McDuffie (322)
23. Charlie Glotzbach (313)
24. Frank Warren (302)
25. Joe Frasson (299)
26. Ben Arnold (292)
27. Bill Seifert (275)
28. G.C. Spencer (238)
29. Roy Mayne (212)
30. Coo Coo Marlin; Don Tarr (192)
32. Buddy Arrington (186)
33. Henley Gray; Jim Vandiver (184)
35. Bill Dennis (175)
36. Raymond Williams (150)
37. Johnny Halford (140)
38. Bill Shirey (116)
39. Tiny Lund (99)
40. Ramo Stott (91)
41. Ray Elder; Ed Negre (74)
43. Ken Meisenhelder (73)
44. Earl Brooks (71)
45. Richard Brickhouse (64)
46. A.J. Foyt; Ron Keselowski (61)
48. Dick Gulstrand (60)
49. Larry Baumel (57)
50. Joe Phipps (56)
51. Roy Tyner (50)
52. John Kenney (49)
53. James Sears (44)
54. Bugs Stevens (39)
55. Jim Hurtubise; Roger McCluskey (38)
57. Fred Lorenzen (37)
58. Dick Bown (36)
59. Tommy Gale (35)
60. Freddy Fryar; Dan Gurney (34)
62. Hoss Ellington; Dub Simpson (32)
64. Jerry Oliver; John Soares Jr. (31)
66. Dick May; Buddy Young (30)
68. Jack McCoy; Parnelli Jones (29)
70. Kevin Terris (28)
71. Joe Clark (27)
72. Mel Larson (26)

73. Jim Paschal; Sam Rose (25)
75. Dave Alonzo; Butch Hirst; Bill Hollar (24)
78. Don Simkins (23)
79. Bob England; Lee Gordon; Dick Kranzler (22)
82. Paul Dorrity; Ron Grana; Bob Hale (21)
85. Paul Feldner; Sonny Hutchins; Frank James (20)
88. Clyde Lynn (17)
89. Eddie Yarboro (16)
90. Glenn Francis (15)
91. Ed Hessert; Morgan Shepherd (14)
93. Buck Baker; Joe Hines Jr.; John Jennings; Dick Trickle (13)
97. Pop McGinnis; E.J. Trivette (12)
99. Wayne Smith; Jimmy Watson (11)
101. Bob Ashbrook; Bill Kimmel; Tom Usry (10)
104. Lee Roy Carrigg (9)
105. Bub Strickler (6)
106. Rodney Bruce (4)
107. Cliff Tyler (3)
108. Pete Hazelwood (2)

1970 Events

Motor Trend 500; Riverside Int. Raceway/2.62-mile road/506 m
A.J. Foyt (Ford)/Parnelli Jones (Mercury)

Daytona International Speedway/2.5-mile/125 miles
Cale Yarborough (Mercury)

Daytona International Speedway/2.5-mile/125 miles
Charlie Glotzbach (Dodge)

Daytona 500; Daytona International Speedway/2.5-m/500 miles
Pete Hamilton (Plymouth)/Cale Yarborough (Mercury)

Richmond 500; Virginia State Fairgrounds/.542-mile/271 miles
James Hylton (Ford)/Richard Petty (Plymouth)

Carolina 500; North Carolina Motor Speedway/1.017-mile/500 m
Richard Petty (Plymouth)/Bobby Allison (Dodge)

Savannah 200; Savannah Speedway/.5-mile/100 miles
Richard Petty (Plymouth)/Richard Petty (Plymouth)

Atlanta 500; Atlanta International Raceway/1.522-m/500 miles
Bobby Allison (Dodge)/Cale Yarborough (Mercury)

Southeastern 500; Bristol Int. Speedway/.533-mile/267 miles
Donnie Allison (Ford)/David Pearson (Ford)

Alabama 500; Alabama Int. Motor Speedway/2.66-mile/500 miles
Pete Hamilton (Plymouth)/Bobby Isaac (Dodge)

Gwyn Staley 400; North Wilkesboro Speedway/.625-m/250 miles
Richard Petty (Plymouth)/Bobby Isaac (Dodge)

Columbia 200; Columbia Speedway/.5-mile dirt/100 miles
Richard Petty (Plymouth)/Larry Baumel (Ford)

Rebel 400; Darlington Raceway/1.375-mile/400 miles
David Pearson (Ford)/Charlie Glotzbach (Dodge)

Beltsville 300; Beltsville Speedway/.5-mile/150 miles
Bobby Isaac (Dodge)/James Hylton (Ford)

Tidewater 300; Langley Field Speedway/.4-mile/120 miles
Bobby Isaac (Dodge)/Bobby Isaac (Dodge)

World 600; Charlotte Motor Speedway/1.5-mile/600 miles
Donnie Allison (Ford)/Bobby Isaac (Dodge)

Maryville 200; Smoky Mountain Raceway/.52-mile/104 miles
Bobby Isaac (Dodge)/Bobby Allison (Dodge)

Virginia 500; Martinsville Speedway/.525-mile/263 miles
Bobby Isaac (Dodge)/Lee Roy Yarbrough (Ford)

Motor State 400; Michigan Int. Speedway/2-mile/400 miles
Cale Yarborough (Mercury)/Pete Hamilton (Plymouth)

Falstaff 400; Riverside Int. Raceway/2.62-m road/400 miles
Richard Petty (Plymouth)/Bobby Allison (Dodge)

Hickory 276; Hickory Speedway/.363-mile/100 miles
Bobby Isaac (Dodge)/Bobby Isaac (Dodge)

Kingsport 100; Kingsport Speedway/.337-mile/100 miles
Richard Petty (Plymouth)/Richard Petty (Plymouth)

Greenville 200; Greenville-Pickens Speedway/.5-m/100 miles
Bobby Isaac (Dodge)/Bobby Isaac (Dodge)

Firecracker 400; Daytona International Speedway/2.5-m/400 m
Donnie Allison (Ford)/Cale Yarborough (Mercury)

Albany-Saratoga 250; Albany-Saratoga Speedway/.362-mile/91 m
Richard Petty (Plymouth)/Bobby Isaac (Dodge)

Thompson 200; Thompson Speedway/.542-mile/108 miles
Bobby Isaac (Dodge)/Bobby Isaac (Dodge)

Schaefer 300; Trenton Speedway/1.5-mile/300 miles
Richard Petty (Plymouth)/Bobby Isaac (Dodge)

Volunteer 500; Bristol International Speedway/.533-m/267 m
Bobby Allison (Dodge)/Cale Yarborough (Mercury)

East Tennessee 200; Smoky Mountain Raceway/.52-m/104 miles
Richard Petty (Plymouth)/Richard Petty (Plymouth)

Nashville 420; Fairgrounds Speedway/.596-mile/250 miles
Bobby Isaac (Dodge)/Lee Roy Yarbrough (Ford)

Dixie 500; Atlanta International Raceway/1.522-m/500 miles
Richard Petty (Plymouth)/Fred Lorenzen (Dodge)

Sandlapper 200; Columbia Speedway/.5-mile dirt/100 miles
Bobby Isaac (Dodge)/Richard Petty (Plymouth)

West Virginia 300; International Raceway Park/.4375-m/131 m
Richard Petty (Plymouth)/Bobby Allison (Dodge)

Yankee 400; Michigan International Speedway/2.04-m/400 miles
Charlie Glotzbach (Dodge)/Charlie Glotzbach (Dodge)

Talladega 500; Alabama Int. Motor Speedway/2.66-m/500 miles
Pete Hamilton (Plymouth)/Bobby Isaac (Dodge)

Myers Brothers 250; Bowman Gray Stadium/.25-mile/63 miles
Richard Petty (Plymouth)/Richard Petty (Plymouth)

Halifax County 100; South Boston Speedway/.357-m/100 miles
Richard Petty (Plymouth)/Richard Petty (Plymouth)

Southern 500; Darlington Raceway/1.366-mile/500 miles
Buddy Baker (Dodge)/David Pearson (Ford)

Buddy Shuman 276; Hickory Speedway/.363-mile/100 miles
Bobby Isaac (Dodge)/Bobby Isaac (Dodge)

Capital City 500; Virginia State Fairgrounds/.542-mile/271 m
Richard Petty (Plymouth)/Richard Petty (Plymouth)

Mason-Dixon 300; Dover Downs Int. Speedway/1-mile/300 miles
Richard Petty (Plymouth)/Bobby Isaac (Dodge)

Home State 200; State Fairgrounds/.5-mile dirt/100 miles
Richard Petty (Plymouth)/John Sears (Dodge)

Wilkes 400; North Wilkesboro Speedway/.625-mile/250 miles
Bobby Isaac (Dodge)/Bobby Isaac (Dodge)

National 500; Charlotte Motor Speedway/1.5-mile/500 miles
Lee Roy Yarbrough (Mercury)/Charlie Glotzbach (Dodge)

Old Dominion 500; Martinsville Speedway/.525-mile/263 miles
Richard Petty (Plymouth)/Bobby Allison (Dodge)

Georgia 500; Middle Georgia Raceway/.548-mile/274 miles
Richard Petty (Plymouth)/Richard Petty (Plymouth)

American 500; North Carolina Motor Speedway/1.017-mile/500 m
Cale Yarborough (Mercury)/Charlie Glotzbach (Dodge)

Tidewater 300; Langley Field Speedway/.395-mile/119 miles
Bobby Allison (Dodge)/Benny Parsons (Ford)

Victories

1. Richard Petty (18)
2. Bobby Isaac (11)
3. Bobby Allison; Donnie Allison; Pete Hamilton; Cale Yarborough (3)
7. Charlie Glotzbach (2)
8. Buddy Baker; A.J. Foyt; James Hylton; David Pearson; Lee Roy Yarbrough (1)

Poles

1. Bobby Isaac (13)
2. Richard Petty (9)
3. Bobby Allison (5)
4. Charlie Glotzbach; Cale Yarborough (4)
6. David Pearson; Lee Roy Yarbrough (2)
8. Larry Baumel; Pete Hamilton; James Hylton; Parnelli Jones; Fred Lorenzen; Benny Parsons; John Sears (1)

Victories

1. Plymouth (21)
2. Dodge (17)
3. Ford (6)
4. Mercury (4)

Poles

1. Dodge (24)
2. Plymouth (10)
3. Ford (7)
4. Mercury (5)

1971
'Like a Marriage Made in Heaven'

Most Important Off-Track Development

Watch the scoreboard during a big-league baseball game or a National Basketball Association contest. You're virtually guaranteed to see the Cleveland Indians, Houston Rockets, or whatever team is playing host to the event thank participating sponsors several times during the course of the game.

Until baseball's ultimate showdown is known as the Al's Junkyard World Series or the Pete's Plumbing Bulls capture the NBA title, however, baseball and basketball, like virtually every other sport, will continue to trail NASCAR in terms of sponsor identification.

Quite simply, NASCAR wrote the book on using Corporate America's money to finance and promote its sport. "It's the only sport that's completely sponsor driven," said two-time Winston Cup champion and Kellogg's Corn Flakes salesman Terry Labonte.

The introduction in 1971 of the most significant sponsor in NASCAR history, perhaps in the history of sports, marked a huge turning point for the sport.

Junior Johnson was seeking sponsorship for his team in the wake of Ford's withdrawal of factory support and approached Ralph Seagraves, an executive with R.J. Reynolds Tobacco Company, whose company recently had been banned from TV advertising by the federal government. Johnson was seeking roughly $800,000 per season. Seagraves, however, was looking for ways to spend an advertising budget 50 times that size.

As a result, Winston initiated a $100,000 point fund for the 1971 season and became the title sponsor for the Grand National Division's races of 250 miles or longer. A year later, the schedule was streamlined, and the Winston Cup Series encompassed the entire season. Under the leadership of first Seagraves and later T. Wayne

Robertson, both of whom died in 1998, Winston's sponsorship of NASCAR's premier series has been not only the longest in the history of sports, but unquestionably the best partnership of sports and Corporate America.

"The merging of NASCAR and Winston was like a marriage made in heaven," said Benny Parsons, whose 1973 series title earned an $18,000 bonus from Winston, less than one percent of Jeff Gordon's bounty for winning the 1998 crown.

"RJR/Nabisco really developed this sport," said Bruton Smith, chairman of the board of Speedway Motorsports, Inc., which owns six Winston Cup facilities. "They promoted; they spent money at the speedways. They also taught us something about marketing. They gave us tremendous lessons on what to do.

"The change, the growth, came when RJR/Nabisco came into the sport. They knew marketing. Nobody in the sport knew marketing."

Winston not only sold a lot of cigarettes, but the company encouraged other non-automotive entities to advertise their products via NASCAR. Sponsorship of a Winston Cup car now puts between $4 million and $11 million a year in a team's pockets, and the cost of sponsoring a typical race is in the $1 million range.

The first company to climb aboard NASCAR's sponsorship bandwagon was Pure Oil Company. Through various mergers and name changes, that now familiar "76" ball has signified the company's role as NASCAR's official fuel supplier since 1951.

Perhaps the first to recognize the value of Winston Cup racing as an advertising vehicle was Carl Kiekhaefer. His cars were sponsored by the Mercury Outboard motors he was selling when they won 52 races and two Winston Cup titles during the 1955 and '56 seasons.

An example of just how extensive the sponsorship of NASCAR races and cars has become:

In 1996, Atlanta Motor Speedway President and General Manager Ed Clark was asked to give a speech to the Atlanta Sports Council, the group responsible for bringing the Olympics, Super Bowl, NCAA Final Four, and numerous other events to the city. To illustrate his speech, Clark decided to visit a grocery store and procure every product that sponsored a car or a race in either the Winston Cup or Busch Series. Two shopping carts were overflowing and a third was necessary to

hold all the Tide, Coca-Cola, Kodak film, Goody's Headache Powders, Holly Farms chicken, and other products that sponsored NASCAR races and cars.

"I went into Kroger the other day," Clark said two years later, "and I saw cereal boxes, crackers, and snack foods with pictures of Winston Cup drivers, Ricky Rudd and Dale Earnhardt on Coke bottles—you name it. Then, when I saw a NASCAR 50th anniversary package of Kleenex, I knew we had arrived."

Considering that a 1997 Performance Research Study revealed that 71 percent of Winston Cup fans say they'll intentionally buy a sponsor's product because of its involvement in the sport—some 75 percent higher than any other sport—it's a safe bet that NASCAR will remain the premier advertising vehicle in sports for years to come.

1971 in Review

Richard Petty and Bobby Allison combined to win two-thirds of the 48 races held in 1971, with Petty capturing 21 and Allison 11. Petty and Allison shared the lead with nine poles apiece, and each fashioned a five-race winning streak. Petty's record of 10 consecutive victories in 1967 was the only other time that a driver won more than four races in a row. Petty also became the first driver to win four consecutive 500-mile races, the first to win seven 500-mile races in a season, and recorded a Performance Index of 1,313. That Performance Index rating is the highest in history, and his 78.62 percent of the available total was the highest recorded until 1998. While Petty joined his father, Lee, and David Pearson as a three-time Winston Cup champion, James Hylton edged Allison for the second-highest Performance Index, 999-993.

Executives of R.J. Reynolds Tobacco Company no doubt were enthused to see the Ford driven by Jimmy Spencer and sponsored by their Camel brand at the head of the pack. But most observers credit the company's entry into Winston Cup racing in 1971 as the impetus that led to the involvement of so many others. Those 200 mph billboards include Budweiser, McDonald's, Kmart, Remington, Kodak, Kellogg's Corn Flakes, Tide, and DuPont, as well as many traditional automotive sponsors.

Most Memorable Race

When pole sitter Fred Lorenzen, Bobby Wawak, and Elmo Langley crashed with three laps to go in the Carolina 500 at Rockingham, N.C., on March 14, Petty drove through the wreckage to beat Bobby Isaac to the finish line.

Most Significant Wreck

Charlie Glotzbach captured the pole for the May 30 World 600—the first pole for Chevrolet in four years—and was running second shortly past the halfway point in his bid to become the first Chevy driver to win a race in three years. But Glotzbach's dream ended when he and Speedy Thompson—who was ending a nine-year retirement—tangled and Glotzbach's Chevy hit the Charlotte Motor Speedway wall. "All of a sudden, Speedy pulled over in front me," Glotzbach said.

Records & Milestones

A total of 21 superspeedway races were held, the most in a season until 1997. . . . Petty and Allison each won seven superspeedway races to tie the existing record set by Lee Roy Yarbrough in 1969. . . . Ontario Motor Speedway, a 2.5-mile track in California, held its first Winston Cup race. . . . Bobby Isaac's victory in the Greenville 200 at South Carolina's Greenville-Pickens Speedway on April 10 was televised by ABC—the first Winston Cup race to be televised live in its entirety. . . . Glotzbach, with relief help from Friday Hassler, ended Chevrolet's three-year victory drought by winning the Volunteer 500 at Bristol, Tenn., on July 11.

1971 at a Glance

Races:	48
Road:	2
Short Track:	25
Superspeedway:	21
Winners:	12
Pole Winners:	14
Tracks:	30
States:	14

1971 Performance Index Rankings

1. Richard Petty (1,313)
2. James Hylton (999)
3. Bobby Allison (993)
4. Cecil Gordon (831)
5. Elmo Langley (664)
6. Jabe Thomas (608)
7. Bobby Isaac (604)
8. Buddy Baker (560)

9. Bill Champion (503)
10. Benny Parsons (500)
11. Friday Hassler (424)
12. Walter Ballard (418)
13. Pete Hamilton (402)
14. Bill Dennis (398)
15. Dave Marcis (393)
16. Frank Warren (392)
17. J.D. McDuffie (378)
18. Dick Brooks (364)
19. Fred Lorenzen (328)
20. Ed Negre (323)
21. Henley Gray (312)
22. Donnie Allison (305)
23. Bill Seifert (286)
24. Joe Frasson (285)
25. Neil Castles (284)
26. Wendell Scott (280)
27. Ben Arnold (278)
28. Charlie Glotzbach (269)
29. Tiny Lund (258)
30. David Pearson (253)
31. John Sears (227)
32. Ron Keselowski (221)
33. Earl Brooks (198)
34. Jim Vandiver (182)
35. A.J. Foyt (160)
36. Raymond Williams (159)
37. Richard D. Brown (148)
38. Roy Mayne (132)
39. G.C. Spencer (123)
40. Dean Dalton (118)
41. Maynard Troyer (116)
42. Ray Elder (111)
43. Marv Acton; Larry Baumel (104)
45. David Ray Boggs (96)
46. Marty Robbins (95)
47. Lee Roy Yarbrough (94)
48. Charlie Roberts (93)
49. Jim Paschal (90)
50. Tommy Gale (88)
51. Ramo Stott (87)
52. Bill Hollar (85)
53. Coo Coo Marlin (77)
54. Jack McCoy (73)
55. Bill Shirey (72)
56. Ken Meisenhelder (62)
57. Kevin Terris (61)
58. Buck Baker (60)
59. Wayne Andrews; Carl Joiner; Eddie Yarboro (57)
62. Jim Hurtubise (55)
63. Dick May; Paul Tyler (54)
65. John Soares Jr. (52)
66. Bob England (50)
67. Bobby Brack (47)
68. Don Tarr (42)
69. Jimmy Insolo; Bobby Wawak (41)
71. George Althiede; David Sisco (40)
73. D.K. Ulrich (38)
74. Bobby Mausgrover (37)
75. Frank Sessoms (33)
76. Randy Hutchison (32)
77. Freddy Fryar; Jerry Oliver; Larry Smith (30)
80. G.T. Tallas; Speedy Thompson (29)

82. Hershel McGriff (28)
83. Scotty Cain; Richard Childress (27)
85. Pat Fay; Joe Dean Huss; Dick Kranzler (26)
88. Frank James (25)
89. Dick Bown (24)
90. Bill Ward; Cale Yarborough (23)
92. Doc Faustina (22)
93. Jerry Churchill; Ron Gautsche; Ron Grana (21)
96. Bill Chevalier; Stick Elliott; Red Farmer; Don Noel (20)
100. Ivan Baldwin (19)
101. Ernie Shaw (17)
102. Ray Johnstone (15)
103. Leonard Blanchard; Clyde Lynn; Gary Myers; Dub Simpson (14)
107. James Cox; Al Grinnan (12)
109. Buddy Arrington (11)
110. Vic Elford; E.J. Trivette (10)
112. Ronnie Chumley (9)
113. Tommy Andrews; Fred Hill (8)
115. Pete Arnold; H.B. Bailey; Robert Brown; Ken Rush (7)
119. Jimmy Vaughn; Bob Williams (5)

1971 Events

Motor Trend 500; Riverside Int. Raceway/2.62-mile road/500 m
Ray Elder (Dodge)/Richard Petty (Plymouth)

Daytona International Speedway/2.5-mile/125 miles
Pete Hamilton (Plymouth)

Daytona International Speedway/2.5-mile/125 miles
David Pearson (Mercury)

Daytona 500; Daytona International Speedway/2.5-m/500 miles
Richard Petty (Plymouth)/A.J. Foyt (Mercury)

Miller High Life 500; Ontario Motor Speedway/2.5-m/500 miles
A.J. Foyt (Mercury)/A.J. Foyt (Mercury)

Richmond 500; Richmond Fairgrounds Raceway/.542-m/271 miles
Richard Petty (Plymouth)/Dave Marcis (Dodge)

Carolina 500; North Carolina Motor Speedway/1.017-mile/500 m
Richard Petty (Plymouth)/Fred Lorenzen (Plymouth)

Hickory 276; Hickory Speedway/.363-mile/100 miles
Richard Petty (Plymouth)/Bobby Allison (Dodge)

Southeastern 500; Bristol International Speedway/.533-m/267m
David Pearson (Ford)/David Pearson (Ford)

Atlanta 500; Atlanta International Raceway/1.522-m/500 miles
A.J. Foyt (Mercury)/A.J. Foyt (Mercury)

Columbia 200; Columbia Speedway/.5-mile/100 miles
Richard Petty (Plymouth)/James Hylton (Ford)

Greenville 200; Greenville-Pickens Speedway/.5-m/100 miles
Bobby Isaac (Dodge)/David Pearson (Ford)

Maryville 200; Smoky Mountain Raceway/.52-mile/104 miles
Richard Petty (Plymouth)/Friday Hassler (Chevrolet)

Gwyn Staley 400; North Wilkesboro Speedway/.625-m/250 miles
Richard Petty (Plymouth)/Bobby Isaac (Dodge)

Virginia 500; Martinsville Speedway/.525-mile/263 miles
Richard Petty (Plymouth)/Donnie Allison (Mercury)

Rebel 400; Darlington Raceway/1.366-mile/400 miles
Buddy Baker (Dodge)/Donnie Allison (Mercury)

Halifax County 100; South Boston Speedway/.357-m/100 miles
Benny Parsons (Ford)/Bobby Isaac (Dodge)

Winston 500; Alabama Int. Motor Speedway/2.66-mile/500 miles
Donnie Allison (Mercury)/Donnie Allison (Mercury)

Asheville 300; Asheville Speedway/.333-mile/100 miles
Richard Petty (Plymouth)/Richard Petty (Plymouth)

Kingsport 300; Kingsport Speedway/.337-mile/101 miles
Bobby Isaac (Dodge)/Bobby Isaac (Dodge)

World 600; Charlotte Motor Speedway/1.5-mile/600 miles
Bobby Allison (Mercury)/Charlie Glotzbach (Chevrolet)

Mason-Dixon 500; Dover Downs Int. Speedway/1-mile/500 miles
Bobby Allison (Ford)/Richard Petty (Plymouth)

Motor State 400; Michigan Int. Speedway/2.04-mile/400 miles
Bobby Allison (Mercury)/Bobby Allison (Mercury)

Winston Golden St. 400; Riverside Int. Race./2.62-m rd./400m
Bobby Allison (Mercury)/Bobby Allison (Mercury)

Space City 300; Meyer Speedway/.5-mile/150 miles
Bobby Allison (Dodge)/Bobby Allison (Dodge)

Pickens 200; Greenville-Pickens Speedway/.5-mile/100 miles
Richard Petty (Plymouth)/Bobby Allison (Ford)

Firecracker 400; Daytona International Speedway/2.5-m/400 m
Bobby Isaac (Dodge)/Donnie Allison (Mercury)

Volunteer 500; Bristol International Speedway/.533-m/267 m
Charlie Glotzbach (Chevrolet)/Richard Petty (Plymouth)

Albany-Saratoga 250; Albany-Saratoga Speedway/.362-m/91 m
Richard Petty (Plymouth)/Richard Petty (Plymouth)

Islip 250; Islip Speedway/.2-mile/50 miles
Richard Petty (Plymouth)/Richard Petty (Plymouth)

Northern 300; Trenton Speedway/1.5-mile/300 miles
Richard Petty (Plymouth)/Friday Hassler (Chevrolet)

Nashville 420; Fairgrounds Speedway/.596-mile/250 miles
Richard Petty (Plymouth)/Richard Petty (Plymouth)

Dixie 500; Atlanta International Raceway/1.522-m/500 miles
Richard Petty (Plymouth)/Buddy Baker (Dodge)

Myers Brothers 250; Bowman Gray Stadium/.25-mile/63 miles
Bobby Allison (Ford)/Richard Petty (Plymouth)

West Virginia 500; International Raceway Park/.4375-m/219 m
Richard Petty (Plymouth)/Bobby Allison (Ford)

Yankee 400; Michigan International Speedway/2.04-m/400 miles
Bobby Allison (Mercury)/Pete Hamilton (Plymouth)

Talladega 500; Alabama Int. Motor Speedway/2.66-m/500 miles
Bobby Allison (Mercury)/Donnie Allison (Mercury)

Sandlapper 200; Columbia Speedway/.51-mile/102 miles
Richard Petty (Plymouth)/Richard Petty (Plymouth)

Buddy Shuman 276; Hickory Speedway/.363-mile/100 miles
Tiny Lund (Chevrolet)/Dave Marcis (Dodge)

Southern 500; Darlington Raceway/1.366-mile/500 miles
Bobby Allison (Mercury)/Bobby Allison (Mercury)

Old Dominion 500; Martinsville Speedway/.525-mile/263 miles
Bobby Isaac (Dodge)/Bobby Isaac (Dodge)

National 500; Charlotte Motor Speedway/1.5-mile/500 miles
Bobby Allison (Mercury)/Charlie Glotzbach (Chevrolet)

Delaware 500; Dover Downs Int. Speedway/1-mile/500 miles
Richard Petty (Plymouth)/Bobby Allison (Mercury)

American 500; North Carolina Motor Speedway/1.017-mile/500 m
Richard Petty (Plymouth)/Charlie Glotzbach (Chevrolet)

Georgia 500; Middle Georgia Raceway/.548-mile/274 miles
Bobby Allison (Ford)/Bobby Allison (Ford)

Capital City 500; Richmond Fairgrounds Raceway/.542-m/271 m
Richard Petty (Plymouth)/Bill Dennis (Mercury)

Wilkes 400; North Wilkesboro Speedway/.625-mile/250 miles
Tiny Lund (Chevrolet)/Charlie Glotzbach (Chevrolet)

Texas 500; Texas World Speedway/2-mile/500 miles
Richard Petty (Plymouth)/Pete Hamilton (Plymouth)

Victories
1. Richard Petty (21)
2. Bobby Allison (11)
3. Bobby Isaac (4)
4. A.J. Foyt; Tiny Lund; David Pearson (2)
7. Donnie Allison; Buddy Baker; Ray Elder; Charlie Glotzbach; Pete Hamilton; Benny Parsons (1)

Poles
1. Bobby Allison; Richard Petty (9)
3. Donnie Allison (5)
4. Charlie Glotzbach; Bobby Isaac (4)
6. A.J. Foyt (3)
7. Pete Hamilton; Friday Hassler; Dave Marcis; David Pearson (2)
11. Buddy Baker; Bill Dennis; James Hylton; Fred Lorenzen (1)

Victories
1. Plymouth (22)
2. Mercury (11)
3. Dodge (7)
4. Ford (5)
5. Chevrolet (3)

Poles
1. Mercury (13)
2. Plymouth (12)
3. Dodge (9)
4. Chevrolet; Ford (6)

1972
Foyt Leads Parade of 10 Indy-Car Winners Who Also Earned Winston Cup Glory

The Winston Cup Series concluded its 51st season as the most popular and prestigious racing circuit in America.

That was by no means the case throughout its history, however. For many years, the Winston Cup Series played second fiddle—or at least was rivaled in prestige and popularity—to Indy-car racing, which was first sanctioned by the American Automobile Association, then the United States Auto Club, and is now plagued by a war between Championship Auto Racing Teams and the Indy Racing League.

During the first three decades of Winston Cup racing, it was far more common to find Indy-car drivers in Winston Cup fields—and vice versa—than it was at the conclusion of Winston Cup racing's fifth decade.

Ten drivers have captured both Indy-car and Winston Cup races, and all 10 spent more time behind the wheel of Indy-cars than Winston Cup machines. A number of Winston Cup drivers—most notably Donnie and Bobby Allison, Cale Yarborough, and Lee Roy Yarbrough—have dabbled at Indy-car racing, but none has ever won. More recently, Tim Richmond and John Andretti got their starts in Indy-car racing before winning on the Winston Cup circuit, but neither ever won in an Indy-car.

The Indy-car driver who enjoyed the most success in Winston Cup racing was A.J. Foyt, a seven-time Indy-car champion and a four-time winner of the Indianapolis 500.

Foyt captured seven Winston Cup victories, including the 1972 Daytona 500, five other superspeedway triumphs, five 500-mile wins, and nine poles. Stock-car racing's Hall of Fame has drivers with fewer victories and lower career Performance Index ratings than Foyt's 1,658—the only Performance Index higher than 859 for an Indy-car driver.

Dan Gurney captured five Winston Cup victories and four poles, all on the road course at Riverside, Calif., and only Rusty Wallace has equaled his streak of four consecutive seasons (1963-66) with at least one victory on a road course. And Gurney's five victories on road courses trail only Richard Petty, Bobby Allison, and Wallace, each with six, on the career list.

Mario Andretti captured the 1967 Daytona 500 and is the only driver other than Foyt who has won both stock-car racing's premier event and the Indianapolis 500.

Three other Indy 500 winners also captured Winston Cup victories: Parnelli Jones with four and Mark Donohue and Johnny Rutherford with one each. Rutherford is one of six drivers to win his Winston Cup debut, joining Jim Roper and Jack White in 1949, Harold Kite and Leon Sales in 1950, and Marvin Burke in 1951. Rutherford's victory in a 100-mile race at Daytona Beach, Fla., in 1963 is the only time a driver captured his Winston Cup debut on a superspeedway.

Tony Stewart, the 1997 IRL champion, won three Winston Cup races as the 1999 Rookie of the Year. Three other drivers also won on both circuits: 1952 Indy-car champion Chuck Stevenson, Jim Hurtubise, and Johnny Mantz, winner of NASCAR's first superspeedway race, the 1950 Southern 500 at Darlington, S.C.

Although Indy-car drivers have enjoyed more success in Winston Cup racing than the other way around, Foyt declined to say near the end of his illustrious career which drivers were better.

"I've always enjoyed coming down South and racing with Richard, Cale, David (Pearson), and the boys," he

Although he's more famous for his four Indianapolis 500 victories and seven Indy-car championships, A.J. Foyt captured seven triumphs and nine poles in Winston Cup racing, and the 1972 Daytona 500 winner had a better record in stock-car racing's premier series than some members of the sport's Hall of Fame.

said. "They're the best at what they do. And I've always enjoyed Indianapolis-type racing with guys like Rutherford, the Unsers (Al and Bobby), and (Gordon) Johncock.

"Racing doesn't take the talent it used to," Foyt said. "The cars are very fast, but with the old cars, you had to manhandle 'em. The reason you're seeing older drivers than you used to is because of the cars. With the old cars, you didn't have the protection, so you actually just got killed in them."

1972 in Review

Bobby Allison earned a season-high 10 victories and 11 poles, and he tied the existing record of seven superspeedway victories in a season. But Petty captured eight races and became the first four-time Winston Cup champion. Bobby, however, edged Petty in the Performance Index ratings, 962-957, and both his 962 rating and 77.58 percent of the available total were the highest in the modern era until Jeff Gordon rewrote the record books in 1998.

Most Memorable Race

After Foyt was sidelined with an injury, the Wood brothers enlisted Pearson's services for the Firecracker 400 on Independence Day at Daytona International Speedway. Frank Warren's blown engine with 19 laps to go brought out a caution flag that set up a three-car dash to the finish. Pearson, Petty, and Bobby Allison raced nose to tail and side by side until Pearson beat Petty by four feet, with Allison less than a car length behind in third. "I can't remember a closer finish," said Pearson, who had canceled a vacation to Hawaii.

Most Significant Wreck

Friday Hassler, who enjoyed his best season in 1971—winning two poles and finishing with the 11th-highest Performance Index rating—suffered fatal head and neck injuries when David Boggs cut a tire in the second turn and triggered a 13-car accident in a 125-mile qualifying race for the Daytona 500 on February 17. "It was absolutely the worst wreck I've ever seen," G.C. Spencer, who also was involved in the accident, told Jim Hunter of *The Atlanta Journal.*

Most Important Off-Track Development

William Henry Getty France, NASCAR's founder and president, retired in January. He was replaced by 38-year-old William Clifton "Billy" France, who frequently is incorrectly referred to as Bill Jr.

Records & Milestones

NASCAR's modern era began, with the schedule trimmed from 48 races in 1971 to 31 in '72. . . . The 1972 campaign is the only one in the modern era in which two drivers won at least nine poles—Bobby Allison and Bobby Isaac (9). . . . The 1972 season was the first in which the majority of races were held on superspeedways.

1972 at a Glance

Races:	31
Road:	2
Short Track:	9
Superspeedway:	20
Winners:	8
Pole Winners:	6
Tracks:	17
States:	12

1972 Performance Index Rankings

1. Bobby Allison (962)
2. Richard Petty (957)
3. James Hylton (786)
4. Cecil Gordon (598)
5. Benny Parsons (583)
6. David Pearson (478)
7. Walter Ballard (475)
8. Ben Arnold (454)
9. Elmo Langley (449)
10. John Sears (402)
11. Dave Marcis (393)
12. Buddy Arrington (383)
13. Buddy Baker (371)
14. Jabe Thomas (364)
15. Bobby Isaac (358)
16. Dean Dalton (344)
17. Raymond Williams (336)
18. Bill Champion (320)
19. Charlie Roberts (298)
20. Lee Roy Yarbrough (288)
21. Larry Smith (283)
22. J.D. McDuffie (233)
23. Frank Warren (224)
24. Coo Coo Marlin (221)
25. A.J. Foyt (207)
26. Ron Keselowski (197)
27. Henley Gray (193)
28. Ed Negre (188)
29. Fred Lorenzen (184)
30. David Ray Boggs (173)
31. Joe Frasson (155)
32. Jim Vandiver (143)
33. David Sisco (142)
34. Cale Yarborough (134)
35. Ramo Stott (132)
36. Hershel McGriff (127)
37. Richard D. Brown (122)
38. Ray Elder (111)
39. Neil Castles (102)
40. Donnie Allison (94)
41. Darrell Waltrip (88)
42. Dick Bown (71)
43. Clarence Lovell (70)
44. H.B. Bailey (69)
45. Johnny Halford; Marty Robbins; G.C. Spencer (68)
48. George Althiede (67)
49. Bill Dennis (66)
50. Tommy Gale; Wendell Scott (63)
52. Dick May (62)
53. Carl Joiner (58)
54. Paul Tyler (57)
55. Pete Hamilton; John Soares Jr. (56)
57. Dick Brooks (55)
58. Paul Jett; Kevin Terris (52)
60. D.K. Ulrich (51)
61. Johnny Anderson; Richard Childress (44)
63. Charlie Glotzbach (43)
64. Bill Butts (40)
65. Mel Larson (38)
66. Red Farmer; Jackie Oliver (36)
68. Vic Elford; Butch Hartman (35)
70. Bill Seifert (33)
71. Friday Hassler (31)
72. Jimmy Finger; Jim Paschal; Eddie Yarboro (29)
75. Carl Adams; Tiny Lund; Jack McCoy (28)
78. Bill Shirey (27)
79. Frank James; Wayne Smith (26)
81. Earle Canavan; Mark Donohue; Ed Hessert (25)
84. Jimmy Crawford; Cliff Garner; Don Noel (24)
87. Ronnie Daniel (22)
88. Chuck Bown; Jim Danielson; Bobby Mausgrover; Jim Whitt (21)
92. Ivan Baldwin; Jimmy Hensley (20)
94. Dick Kranzler (19)
95. Paul Dorrity; Bob Greeley (17)
97. Jimmy Insolo; Vic Parsons (16)
99. Doc Faustina (15)
100. Dub Simpson (14)
101. Earl Brooks (12)
102. Phil Finney (9)
103. Max Berrier (7)

1972 Events

Winston Western 500; Riverside Int. Raceway/2.62-m rd./500 m
Richard Petty (Plymouth)/A.J. Foyt (Mercury)

Daytona 500; Daytona International Speedway/2.5-m/500 miles
A.J. Foyt (Mercury)/Bobby Isaac (Dodge)

Richmond 500; Richmond Fairgrounds Raceway/.542-m/271 miles
Richard Petty (Plymouth)/Bobby Allison (Chevrolet)

Miller High Life 500; Ontario Motor Speedway/2.5-m/500 miles
A.J. Foyt (Mercury)/A.J. Foyt (Mercury)

Carolina 500; North Carolina Motor Speedway/1.017-mile/500 m
Bobby Isaac (Dodge)/Bobby Isaac (Dodge)

Atlanta 500; Atlanta International Raceway/1.522-m/500 miles
Bobby Allison (Chevrolet)/Bobby Allison (Chevrolet)

Southeastern 500; Bristol International Speedway/.533-m/267m
Bobby Allison (Chevrolet)/Bobby Allison (Chevrolet)

Rebel 400; Darlington Raceway/1.366-mile/400 miles
David Pearson (Mercury)/David Pearson (Mercury)

Gwyn Staley 400; North Wilkesboro Speedway/.625-m/250 miles
Richard Petty (Plymouth)/Bobby Isaac (Dodge)

Virginia 500; Martinsville Speedway/.525-mile/263 miles
Richard Petty (Plymouth)/Bobby Allison (Chevrolet)

Winston 500; Alabama Int. Motor Speedway/2.66-mile/500 miles
David Pearson (Mercury)/Bobby Isaac (Dodge)

World 600; Charlotte Motor Speedway/1.5-mile/600 miles
Buddy Baker (Dodge)/Bobby Allison (Chevrolet)

Mason-Dixon 500; Dover Downs Int. Speedway/1-mile/500 miles
Bobby Allison (Chevrolet)/Bobby Isaac (Dodge)

Motor State 400; Michigan International Speedway/2-m/400 m
David Pearson (Mercury)/Bobby Isaac (Dodge)

Golden State 400; Riverside Int. Raceway/2.62-m road/400 m
Ray Elder (Dodge)/Richard Petty (Plymouth)

Lone Star 500; Texas World Speedway/2-mile/500 miles
Richard Petty (Plymouth)/Richard Petty (Plymouth)

Firecracker 400; Daytona International Speedway/2.5-m/400 m
David Pearson (Mercury)/Bobby Isaac (Dodge)

Volunteer 500; Bristol International Speedway/.533-m/267 m
Bobby Allison (Chevrolet)/Bobby Allison (Chevrolet)

Northern 300; Trenton Speedway/1.5-mile/300 miles
Bobby Allison (Chevrolet)/Bobby Isaac (Dodge)

Dixie 500; Atlanta International Raceway/1.522-m/500 miles
Bobby Allison (Chevrolet)/David Pearson (Mercury)

Talladega 500; Alabama Int. Motor Speedway/2.66-m/500 miles
James Hylton (Mercury)/Bobby Isaac (Dodge)

Yankee 400; Michigan International Speedway/2-mile/400 miles
David Pearson (Mercury)/Richard Petty (Dodge)

Nashville 420; Fairgrounds Speedway/.596-mile/250 miles
Bobby Allison (Chevrolet)/Bobby Allison (Chevrolet)

Southern 500; Darlington Raceway/1.366-mile/500 miles
Bobby Allison (Chevrolet)/Bobby Allison (Chevrolet)

Capital City 500; Richmond Fairgrounds Raceway/.542-m/271 m
Richard Petty (Plymouth)/Bobby Allison (Chevrolet)

Delaware 500; Dover Downs Int. Speedway/1-mile/500 miles
David Pearson (Mercury)/Bobby Allison (Chevrolet)

Old Dominion 500; Martinsville Speedway/.525-mile/263 miles
Richard Petty (Plymouth)/Bobby Allison (Chevrolet)

Wilkes 400; North Wilkesboro Speedway/.625-mile/250 miles
Richard Petty (Plymouth)/Buddy Baker (Dodge)

National 500; Charlotte Motor Speedway/1.5-mile/500 miles
Bobby Allison (Chevrolet)/David Pearson (Mercury)

American 500; North Carolina Motor Speedway/1.017-mile/500 m
Bobby Allison (Chevrolet)/David Pearson (Mercury)

Texas 500; Texas World Speedway/2-mile/500 miles
Buddy Baker (Dodge)/A.J. Foyt (Mercury)

Victories
1. Bobby Allison (10)
2. Richard Petty (8)
3. David Pearson (6)
4. Buddy Baker; A.J. Foyt (2)
6. Ray Elder; James Hylton; Bobby Isaac (1)

Poles
1. Bobby Allison (11)
2. Bobby Isaac (9)
3. David Pearson (4)
4. A.J. Foyt; Richard Petty (3)
6. Buddy Baker (1)

Victories
1. Chevrolet (10)
2. Mercury (9)
3. Plymouth (8)
4. Dodge (4)

Poles
1. Chevrolet; Dodge (11)
3. Mercury (7)
4. Plymouth (2)

1973
Parsons Was NASCAR's Most Popular Driver Among His Rivals In the Garage

Benny Parsons spent most of his career competing in the long shadows cast by the Pettys, Pearsons, Allisons, Yarboroughs, and Waltrips.

Parsons never enjoyed a truly blockbuster year. His only four-victory season came in 1977, and the Volunteer 500 at Bristol, Tenn., was his only triumph during his 1973 Winston Cup championship campaign.

Yet, usually driving cars that were a cut or two below those of his aforementioned rivals, Parsons won the Winston Cup championship, the 1975 Daytona 500, and overcame those long shadows to record a stellar career of long-term consistency.

For example, Parsons:

• Finished in the top 12 in the Performance Index ratings 13 consecutive seasons (1970-82); only Richard Petty and Ricky Rudd enjoyed longer streaks.

• Posted 11 consecutive years (1970-80) in the top 10 of the Performance Index, a feat bettered only by Richard and Lee Petty and Darrell Waltrip.

• Ranks among the top 10 in numerous other Performance Index categories that measure consistent achievement over an extended period, including five consecutive seasons with a rating of 600 or better (1976-80) and top-five seasons (8).

Parsons also ranks among the top 10 with seven years in a row with a superspeedway triumph (1975-81), six consecutive seasons (1976-81) with multiple wins, six straight seasons (1975-80) with a victory in a 500-mile race, five consecutive seasons with a short-track pole (1975-79), and four straight years with multiple short-track poles (1975-78).

Look beyond Parsons's 21 victories, including nine in 500-mile races, and 20 poles, and the most distinguishing phenomenon about his career is the incredible popularity of his two greatest triumphs.

In 1973, Parsons entered the season finale, the American 500 at Rockingham's North Carolina Motor Speedway, with a healthy lead over Cale Yarborough in the Winston Cup point standings. But Parsons's Chevrolet, owned by L.G. DeWitt, who also owned the track, was involved in an early crash with the Mercury being driven by Johnny Barnes. When Parsons's crumpled Chevrolet was hauled into the garage for extensive repairs, crew members from practically every team in the sport rushed to help repair the battered machine.

"This crowd in racing—everybody helps everybody," said Maurice Petty, Richard's brother and engine builder. "Benny needed help, so everybody pitched in and helped him. Benny's just a good, all-around guy. The man doesn't cause any waves. He handles himself well."

Parsons returned to the race more than an hour after the accident and finished 28th, 184 laps behind the victorious David Pearson, but that enabled him to beat Yarborough, 7,173.8-7,106.65, for the Winston Cup title. The reception he received upon the race's conclusion was unprecedented, much like the handshakes Dale Earnhardt received from practically everyone on pit road after he captured the 1998 Daytona 500. And Parsons, who during much of his racing career served as president of the Parent Teachers Association in Ellerbe, N.C., just a few laps from Rockingham, was wildly applauded by the hometown crowd of 30,000.

"It was fantastic. All the crews cheered when I went down pit road and, as I went around the track, I could see people waving me on," Parsons recalled shortly after his retirement. "That's the first time anything like that ever happened, and I'll never forget it."

Before he earned Winston Cup glory by winning the 1973 title, the 1975 Daytona 500, and a host of other achievements in his Hall of Fame career, Benny Parsons called the 1963 Daytona 500 his "biggest thrill" because H.B. Bailey's wife gave him a pit pass that allowed him to "go over and watch 'em pump gas."

Perhaps the greatest irony of Parsons's career is that he was never selected NASCAR's Most Popular Driver. Had the vote been conducted by those who knew the drivers best—their rivals in the garage—he might have won every year of his career.

So it was little surprise that the reception from his rivals was nearly as dramatic two years later, when Pearson's spin in the third turn with a little more than three laps remaining enabled Parsons to pass him and win the Daytona 500.

"I came in '63 as a spectator. I came down to the infield and hung on that fence like a monkey, just trying to look at the cars in the garage," Parsons recalled of his first visit to Daytona International Speedway. "The biggest thrill of my life was H.B. Bailey's wife giving me a pit pass, so I got to go over and watch 'em pump gas.

"That's why 1975 was such a dramatic moment for me. All it meant was a dream come true. I came off the corner, and I saw David spinning. When I saw David spin, I knew I had the race won. The funny thing is, he'd had so much success in the past few years that you never saw that No. 21 car in trouble."

Parsons scored other subsequent dramatic victories—officially trading the lead with Waltrip six times in the final 26 laps to win the 1980 World 600 at Charlotte by half a car length and edging Earnhardt and Yarborough by half a second to capture the 1984 Coca-Cola 500 at Atlanta.

"But nothing will ever compare to Daytona," he said. "That was *the* highlight."

Parsons's unpretentious style has served him well as an Emmy Award-winning motorsports commentator for ESPN and a popular radio host. No other star athlete, perhaps, in fact, no other human, has excelled at remembering the names of so many people as the former Detroit cab driver.

"Am I good with names? I didn't even realize it," Parsons said a couple of years ago.

Perhaps in a previous life, before he became the only Automobile Racing Club of America champion to add the Winston Cup crown, Parsons was an elephant.

Parsons's guest on his radio program one Monday evening in the mid-'90s was a speedway general manager, whose appearance was primarily a gesture of goodwill by Parsons to help promote an upcoming race.

Embarrassingly, the general manager couldn't remember the phone number of his track's ticket office, a number he either called or recited 100 times a day. Parsons, who rarely has had reason to use that number during his 30 years in the sport, quickly recited it.

1973 in Review

Although Parsons captured the Winston Cup championship, Yarborough led the Performance Index ratings. Parsons held a 641-633 lead over Richard Petty entering the season finale, but neither driver posted a top-20 finish. Yarborough's third-place finish enabled him to edge Buddy Baker, who finished second in the American 500, 652-649, in the Performance Index ratings. Pearson was fifth in the Performance Index ratings despite making only 18 starts in the Wood brothers' Mercury. But he won a season-high 11 of those races, set new records of 10 superspeedway triumphs and eight 500-mile victories, and led the circuit with eight poles.

Most Memorable Race

When Yarborough's Junior Johnson-owned Chevrolet beat Richard Petty's Dodge by 1.4 seconds to win the National 500 at Charlotte on October 7, the fun was just beginning. Bobby Allison, who finished three laps behind in third, quickly paid a fee of $100 per car to protest the legality of the top two cars. Officials dismantled Allison's Chevrolet and quickly declared it legal. More than six hours after the checkered flag fell, NASCAR finally said a decision would be made the next day at Daytona Beach, Fla. NASCAR allowed the results to stand because of inadequate inspection procedures, although a NASCAR official who refused to be identified told a novice reporter, "Cale had about an engine and a half, and Petty's was nearly that big."

Allison later met with NASCAR President Billy France and was ordered to keep quiet about the proceedings. "Basically, he told me it wouldn't happen again," Allison said more than 20 years later.

Most Significant Wreck

Larry Smith, the 1972 Rookie of the Year, died of massive head injuries when he crashed into the wall moments after he completed his 13th lap in the Talladega 500 on August 12 at Alabama International Motor Speedway. "Things happen to me (at Talladega) that just don't happen anywhere else," Smith had told The Associated Press a month earlier.

Most Important Off-Track Development

The rules were changed at midseason to reduce the cubic-inch displacement of engines. Larger engines were penalized, and the new rule rendered obsolete Chrysler's famous hemi engine, which Richard Petty said had been "a thorn in (NASCAR's) side ever since it was built."

Records & Milestones

Four drivers —Pearson (8), Allison (6), Baker (5), and Yarborough (5)—captured at least five poles, a modern record. . . . Only five drivers captured a pole, the fewest in a season. . . . The 28-race season and the 28-race 1985 season were the shortest in the modern era. . . . Mark Donohue's victory in the Winston Western 500 on January 21 at Riverside, Calif., was the first for a Matador.

1973 at a Glance

Races:	28
Road:	2
Short Track:	10
Superspeedway:	16
Winners:	8
Pole Winners:	5
Tracks:	15
States:	11

1973 Performance Index Rankings

1. Cale Yarborough (652)
2. Buddy Baker (649)
3. Benny Parsons (641)
4. Richard Petty (633)
5. David Pearson (593)
6. Cecil Gordon (558)
7. James Hylton (550)
8. Bobby Allison (521)
9. J.D. McDuffie (393)
10. Walter Ballard (364)
11. Elmo Langley (360)
12. Buddy Arrington; Jabe Thomas (354)
14. Dick Brooks (332)
15. Coo Coo Marlin (314)
16. David Sisco (307)
17. Richard Childress (301)
18. Henley Gray (295)
19. Lennie Pond (286)
20. Dave Marcis (253)
21. Ed Negre (240)
22. Darrell Waltrip (233)
23. Frank Warren (227)
24. Charlie Roberts (225)
25. Bobby Isaac (220)
26. Dean Dalton (185)
27. Donnie Allison (181)
28. Larry Smith (176)
29. Bill Champion (170)
30. Vic Parsons (169)
31. Joe Frasson (162)
32. Jim Vandiver (157)
33. Raymond Williams (141)
34. Rick Newsom (114)
35. Jack McCoy (80)
36. G.C. Spencer (78)
37. Randy Tissot (74)
38. John Sears (70)
39. Ramo Stott (69)
40. Johnny Barnes; Hershel McGriff (68)
42. Clarence Lovell (67)
43. Jimmy Insolo (66)
44. Ray Elder (64)
45. Richard White (61)
46. Gordon Johncock (60)
47. Bill Dennis (57)
48. Ron Keselowski (55)
49. Wendell Scott (54)
50. L.D. Ottinger (53)
51. Charles Barrett (52)
52. Earle Canavan; Roy Mayne (51)
54. Eddie Bond; Jimmy Crawford (48)
56. Mel Larson (46)
57. Mark Donohue (45)
58. A.J. Foyt (41)
59. Alton Jones (37)
60. Bobby Unser (36)
61. Jody Ridley; Dick Trickle (35)
63. Earl Brooks (34)
64. Dick Simon (33)
65. Charlie Glotzbach (32)
66. Jim Danielson (31)
67. Eddie Pettyjohn (30)
68. H.B. Bailey; Harry Gant (29)
70. Carl Adams; Tommy Gale; Marty Robbins; Johnny Rutherford; D.K. Ulrich (27)
75. Earl Ross (26)
76. Charlie Blanton; Chuck Bown; Bill Hollar; Gerald Thompson (25)
80. Tony Bettenhausen Jr. (24)
81. Dick Bown; Richie Panch (23)
83. Bobby Mausgrover; Bill Ward; Jim Whitt (22)
86. Leon Fox (21)
87. Ed Sczech (20)
88. George Behlman (19)
89. Jimmy Hensley (18)
90. Glenn Francis (17)
91. Yvon DuHamel; Mike James; John Utsman (15)
94. Richard D. Brown; Ray Hendrick (14)
96. Ronnie Daniel (9)
97. Robert Brown (6)

1973 Events

Winston Western 500; Riverside Int. Raceway/2.62-m road/500m
Mark Donohue (Matador)/David Pearson (Mercury)

Daytona 500; Daytona International Speedway/2.5-m/500 miles
Richard Petty (Dodge)/Buddy Baker (Dodge)

Richmond 500; Richmond Fairgrounds Raceway/.542-m/271 miles
Richard Petty (Dodge)/Bobby Allison (Chevrolet)

Carolina 500; North Carolina Motor Speedway/1.017-mile/500 m
David Pearson (Mercury)/David Pearson (Mercury)

Southeastern 500; Bristol International Speedway/.533-m/267m
Cale Yarborough (Chevrolet)/Cale Yarborough (Chevrolet)

Atlanta 500; Atlanta International Raceway/1.522-m/500 miles
David Pearson (Mercury)

Gwyn Staley 400; North Wilkesboro Speedway/.625-m/250 miles
Richard Petty (Dodge)/Bobby Allison (Chevrolet)

Rebel 500; Darlington Raceway/1.366-mile/500 miles
David Pearson (Mercury)/David Pearson (Mercury)

Virginia 500; Martinsville Speedway/.525-mile/263 miles
David Pearson (Mercury)/David Pearson (Mercury)

Winston 500; Alabama Int. Motor Speedway/2.66-mile/500 miles
David Pearson (Mercury)/Buddy Baker (Dodge)

Music City 420; Fairgrounds Speedway/.596-mile/250 miles
Cale Yarborough (Chevrolet)/Cale Yarborough (Chevrolet)

World 600; Charlotte Motor Speedway/1.5-mile/600 miles
Buddy Baker (Dodge)/Buddy Baker (Dodge)

Mason-Dixon 500; Dover Downs Int. Speedway/1-mile/500 miles
David Pearson (Mercury)/David Pearson (Mercury)

Alamo 500; Texas World Speedway/2-mile/500 miles
Richard Petty (Dodge)/Buddy Baker (Dodge)

Tuborg 400; Riverside Int. Raceway/2.62-mile road/400 miles
Bobby Allison (Chevrolet)/Richard Petty (Dodge)

Motor State 400; Michigan International Speedway/2-m/400 m
David Pearson (Mercury)/Buddy Baker (Dodge)

Firecracker 400; Daytona International Speedway/2.5-m/400 m
David Pearson (Mercury)/Bobby Allison (Chevrolet)

Volunteer 500; Bristol International Speedway/.533-m/267 m
Benny Parsons (Chevrolet)/Cale Yarborough (Chevrolet)

Dixie 500; Atlanta International Raceway/1.522-m/500 miles
David Pearson (Mercury)/Richard Petty (Dodge)

Talladega 500; Alabama Int. Motor Speedway/2.66-m/500 miles
Dick Brooks (Plymouth)/Bobby Allison (Chevrolet)

Nashville 420; Fairgrounds Speedway/.596-mile/250 miles
Buddy Baker (Dodge)/Cale Yarborough (Chevrolet)

Southern 500; Darlington Raceway/1.366-mile/500 miles
Cale Yarborough (Chevrolet)/David Pearson (Mercury)

Capital City 500; Richmond Fairgrounds Raceway/.542-m/271 m
Richard Petty (Dodge)/Bobby Allison (Chevrolet)

Delaware 500; Dover Downs Int. Speedway/1-mile/500 miles
David Pearson (Mercury)/David Pearson (Mercury)

Wilkes 400; North Wilkesboro Speedway/.625-mile/250 miles
Bobby Allison (Chevrolet)/Bobby Allison (Chevrolet)

Old Dominion 500; Martinsville Speedway/.525-mile/263 miles
Richard Petty (Dodge)/Cale Yarborough (Chevrolet)

National 500; Charlotte Motor Speedway/1.5-mile/500 miles
Cale Yarborough (Chevrolet)/David Pearson (Mercury)

American 500; North Carolina Motor Speedway/1.017-mile/500 m
David Pearson (Mercury)/Richard Petty (Dodge)

Victories

1. David Pearson (11)
2. Richard Petty (6)
3. Cale Yarborough (4)
4. Bobby Allison; Buddy Baker (2)
6. Dick Brooks; Mark Donohue; Benny Parsons (1)

Poles

1. David Pearson (8)
2. Bobby Allison (6)
3. Buddy Baker; Cale Yarborough (5)
5. Richard Petty (3)

Victories

1. Mercury (11)
2. Dodge (8)
3. Chevrolet (7)
4. Matador; Plymouth (1)

Poles

1. Chevrolet (11)
2. Dodge; Mercury (8)

1974
The Silver Fox

"Racing is a thinking game," David Pearson said in 1996. "I guess I played it pretty well."

In many ways, no one played it better than the Silver Fox. Perhaps the coolest customer ever to drive a race car, Pearson's many memorable feats included 1973 and 1974 campaigns in which he became the only driver to post consecutive seasons with at least four superspeedway victories from the pole or back-to-back seasons of four or more Grand Slam victories.

Although he earned Rookie of the Year honors and captured a pole at Gamecock Speedway, a quarter-mile South Carolina dirt bullring, in 1960 at age 25, Pearson truly established himself the next season. Pearson, who had been working in a cotton mill in his native Spartanburg, S.C., was hardly among the favorites in the 1961 World 600 at Charlotte.

"I was still one of those guys who are running around trying to figure out what to do," Pearson recalled. "Even after I won that race, I didn't even know if I'd still have the ride the next week."

Perhaps more significant was another memory Pearson has about that race. "I knew I'd be racing Fireball (Roberts), Ned (Jarrett), and all them," he said. "But I didn't think it was any different from any other race."

It wasn't in one respect: Pearson never lost his cool, even after he suffered a punctured tire with two laps to go. He kept his John Masoni-owned Pontiac on the track and beat Roberts to the checkered flag by more than two laps. Subsequent victories in two of the season's other premier events, the Firecracker 250 at Daytona Beach, Fla., and the Dixie 400 at Atlanta, perpetuated Pearson's nickname, "David the Giant Killer." The moniker would not endure, however, simply because Pearson himself became one of the true giants in stock-car racing history.

In 1964, Pearson became the first driver to capture four consecutive dirt victories, and he put together three different three-race winning streaks on dirt in 1966, when he also tied the existing record of four consecutive victories and captured his first Winston Cup title behind the wheel of Cotton Owens's Dodge.

In 1968 and '69, driving the Holman-Moody Ford, Pearson snared back-to-back Winston Cup championships and became:

- The only driver to win at least nine short-track poles in back-to-back seasons;
- One of only three drivers to win 12 or more poles in consecutive seasons;
- One of only three drivers to record back-to-back seasons with a Performance Index of at least 1,000;
- One of only six drivers with back-to-back seasons of at least 11 victories.

"Back then, I just tried to lead every lap and run wide open," Pearson recalled. "I found out that's not the way to win a race."

Pearson earned only three additional victories before he left Holman-Moody after a 31st-place finish in the 1971 Rebel 400 at Darlington, S.C. Perhaps betrayed by Pearson's prematurely silver hair, most observers figured the Silver Fox's halcyon days were behind him.

But Pearson's true glory days hadn't even started. Glen Wood, who had taken a swing at Pearson after a 1965 wreck involving Marvin Panch, then the Wood brothers' driver, was seeking someone to drive the Woods' Mercury when A.J. Foyt was unavailable. He called on the "washed up" Pearson, who won the 1972 Rebel 400 in his debut for the Wood brothers and captured three subsequent races for the Woods that season.

When Pearson became the full-time driver behind the wheel of the Wood brothers' candy-apple-red-and-cream Mercury in 1973, he posted the best single-season winning percentage in history (61.11 percent) by capturing 11 of 18 starts. Pearson also tied the existing record held by Herb Thomas by capturing four consecutive superspeedway events, became the first driver to win 10 superspeedway races in a season, and the first to win eight 500-mile races in a year. Further sticking it to the critics who had declared him washed up just two years earlier, Pearson won four 500-mile races from the pole. At that point, no one had won more than three in a *career*. Pearson's 1976 campaign was nearly as magical: He became the second driver to win what was then known as stock-car racing's Triple Crown—the Daytona 500, World 600, and Southern 500 at Darlington—and added five other superspeedway victories and a record-tying two wins in a season on road courses.

During his tenure with Glen and Leonard Wood, Pearson became the only driver to record seven consecutive years (1972-78) with multiple Grand Slam poles, post five consecutive seasons (1974-78) with multiple classic poles, and earn a 500-mile victory from the pole four years in a row (1973-76). Pearson also won at least three Grand Slam poles seven consecutive years (1972-78), and Jeff Gordon is the only other driver who has managed a string of seven successive seasons with at least one Grand Slam pole. Further, Pearson won at least one classic pole six years in a row (1973-78), three or more superspeedway races five consecutive seasons (1972-76), and a Grand Slam victory from the pole three seasons in a row (1972-74)—all records that were tied by Gordon in 1999.

"When I was in the Woods' car, I went into every race confident that I had a chance," Pearson said.

For good measure, Pearson won five superspeedway races from the pole in 1974 and again in '76, and he earned three Grand Slam victories from the pole in each of those seasons, feats no other driver has managed even once. The Silver Fox also recorded six consecutive years (1973-78) with at least five superspeedway poles, four years in a row with at least six superspeedway poles (1973-76), and three consecutive years (1974-76) with at least seven superspeedway poles. No one else has put together more than three consecutive years with at least five superspeedway poles, and no other driver has won as many as six superspeedway poles two years in a row.

Among other records Pearson still shares that he set during those glory days in the Wood brothers' Mercury are four consecutive seasons as the Winston Cup Series leader in poles (1973-76), consecutive seasons (1973-74) with seven or more superspeedway victories, consecutive seasons (1973-74) with multiple superspeedway victories from the pole, two classic victories from the pole in one season (1976), and three consecutive poles on road courses.

"David is the best driver we've ever had—one of the all-time greats," Glen Wood said more than 15 years after their reign of terror over their foes had ended.

Pearson was unceremoniously fired by the Wood brothers after he lost two tires while exiting pit road in a communications mishap during the 1979 Rebel 400.

"The only thing that would have been as big a shock would have been if I'd have fired myself (from Petty Enterprises)," Richard Petty said a few days later.

Pearson rebounded to capture the 1979 Southern 500 in Rod Osterlund's Chevrolet, then won, ironically, the 1980 CRC Chemicals Rebel 500. Appropriately, that victory, in a race and on the Darlington track that had been such a defining point in Pearson's career, was his last.

Although Pearson made his final start in 1986, it was several years later before the Silver Fox finally admitted, albeit because of a bad back, that his career was over. "That's the hardest thing in the world to do, to say you've retired," he said. "It kills you."

The records the Silver Fox still holds include Grand Slam victories (26), superspeedway poles (58), Grand Slam poles (31), classic poles (13), superspeedway victories from the pole (19), Grand Slam wins from the pole (8), most seasons leading the Winston Cup Series in poles (6), and a streak of 20 consecutive seasons with at least one pole (1963-82). Pearson also earned at least one superspeedway victory in 13 consecutive seasons (1968-80), a record he shares with Cale Yarborough.

Among the host of categories in which Pearson ranks second are victories (105), superspeedway wins (51), consecutive seasons with a victory (17), consecutive Grand Slam victories (4), consecutive seasons with six or more superspeedway victories (3), consecutive seasons with a Grand Slam triumph (7), and consecutive years with multiple 500-mile wins (5). The Silver Fox also ranks no worse than second in poles (113), road-course poles (8), consecutive seasons with multiple poles (14), consecutive Grand Slam poles (4), consecutive seasons with a superspeedway pole (11), victories from the pole (37), and 500-mile wins from the pole (10). His career Performance Index of 11,528 ranks seventh on the all-time list, and he ranks among the top 10 in virtually every Performance Index category, including three seasons with a rating of 1,000 or better (second) and four campaigns with a rating of 900 or higher (second).

"You want to win," Pearson said after beating Petty to the checkered flag to complete the 1976 Triple Crown with a Southern 500 victory. "I really want to win any race I run. It

Many thought three-time Winston Cup champion David Pearson's best days were behind him when he became the pilot of the Wood brothers' Purolator Mercury in 1972, but he proved the skeptics wrong with a record-setting tenure that included 43 victories.

doesn't matter if you're racing on a cornfield, a dirt track, or here. I want to win. I really don't know what the secret is. If I did, I wouldn't tell. Part of it is not letting things bother you. You try to forget the races you had bad luck in. If you take all the good luck and the bad luck, it balances out."

Some 20 years later, with the same ageless good looks that stirred the hearts of more Southern women than Brad Pitt, Pearson summarized the quiet confidence and incomparable temperament he displayed as the idol of thousands of fans a generation or two ago. "I always felt I was as good as anyone out there," he said. "Every driver feels that way, or he wouldn't be out there."

Maybe they all feel that way, but Pearson's record proves that, in a "thinking game," his thinking was justified.

1974 in Review

Petty and Yarborough each won 10 races and Pearson seven, giving them victories in 90 percent of the season's 30 races. Petty extended his record to five Winston Cup championships and claimed an 835-801 advantage over Yarborough in the Performance Index, and Pearson's 11 poles paced the circuit.

Most Memorable Race

After Pearson, driving the Wood brothers' Mercury, led the penultimate lap in the Firecracker 400 at Daytona on July 4, he slowed down dramatically. Petty, running directly behind him in second, quickly pushed his Dodge ahead of the apparently troubled Pearson. The Silver Fox then followed Petty and was in perfect position to use the draft to slingshot his rival less than a quarter-mile from the finish line and win by a car length. Yarborough and Buddy Baker finished in a dead heat for third. "That was a stupid move on David's part," Petty said. "David usually drives a safer, saner race than that. He's lucky I didn't crash both of us."

Most Significant Wreck

Donnie Allison led the Daytona 500 on February 17 by nearly 30 seconds until Bob Burcham suffered a blown engine with 12 laps to go. Allison punctured a tire in Burcham's debris, skidded into the infield, lost a lap, and finished sixth behind the victorious Petty.

Most Important Off-Track Development

When the drivers arrived for the Talladega 500 on August 11 at Alabama International Motor Speedway, more than 15 found that their cars had been sabotaged. Oil lines and water lines were cut, bolts loosened, tires slashed, gas tanks filled with a foreign substance, and front-end alignments damaged. "Whoever it was had to be some kind of nut," Baker told *The Atlanta Journal.* "What he did is what I would call attempted murder." Talladega Sheriff Gene Mitchell said he had four deputies on duty throughout the night, but that none reported seeing anything suspicious. To this day, the culprits remain at large.

Records & Milestones

Pearson captured five consecutive superspeedway poles to tie the record then held by Roberts. . . . The 10 victories apiece by Petty and Yarborough marked the only time in the modern era that two drivers reached double figures in wins. . . . The 1974 campaign marked the only time in the modern era that three drivers earned seven or more victories. . . . Only five drivers won races in 1974, the fewest in one season. . . . Only Petty, Yarborough, Pearson, and Bobby Allison (2) captured multiple victories, setting a record, tied in 1993, for the fewest drivers to post multiple victories in the modern era. . . . A new superspeedway, Pocono International Raceway in Long Pond, Pa., joined the Winston Cup Series.

1974 at a Glance

Races:	30
Road:	2
Short Track:	10
Superspeedway:	18
Winners:	5
Pole Winners:	8
Tracks:	16
States:	11

1974 Performance Index Rankings

1. Richard Petty (835)
2. Cale Yarborough (801)
3. Dave Marcis (585)
4. David Pearson (578)
5. Bobby Allison (532)
6. Earl Ross (483)
7. David Sisco (454)
8. Cecil Gordon (434)
9. Benny Parsons (432)
10. J.D. McDuffie (419)
11. James Hylton (409)
12. Lennie Pond (380)
13. Buddy Baker (377)
14. Darrell Waltrip (373)
15. Frank Warren (364)
16. Walter Ballard (354)
17. Bob Burcham (291)
18. Donnie Allison; Jackie Rogers (289)
20. Richie Panch (288)
21. Coo Coo Marlin (268)
22. Richard Childress (259)
23. Elmo Langley (230)
24. Tony Bettenhausen Jr. (215)
25. Buddy Arrington (213)
26. Charlie Glotzbach (188)
27. George Follmer (168)
28. Ed Negre (158)
29. Ramo Stott (155)
30. Dick Brooks (144)
31. Joe Frasson (142)
32. Bobby Isaac (136)
33. Gary Bettenhausen (118)
34. Dick Trickle (103)
35. D.K. Ulrich (96)
36. Roy Mayne (95)
37. Earle Canavan; Jerry Schild (88)
39. Jim Vandiver (86)
40. A.J. Foyt; Marty Robbins (76)
42. Dean Dalton (68)
43. Kenny Brightbill (62)
44. Joe Mihalic (56)
45. Sam McQuagg (55)
46. Hershel McGriff (53)
47. Sonny Easley (51)
48. Henley Gray (50)
49. Dick May (48)
50. Travis Tiller (46)
51. Carl Adams (44)
52. Harry Gant (43)
53. Don Reynolds; Chuck Wahl (42)
55. Bill Dennis (41)
56. Neil Castles (40)
57. Grant Adcox; G.C. Spencer (39)
59. Pee Wee Wentz (35)
60. Bill Champion; Harry Jefferson (33)
62. Alton Jones; Jan Opperman (32)
64. Dan Daughtry (30)
65. Jim Danielson (29)
66. Bruce Hill; Dick Skillen (27)
68. Jimmy Crawford; Rick Newsom (26)
70. Ron Keselowski; Charlie Roberts (24)
72. Joe Millikan; Jabe Thomas (23)
74. Eddie Bradshaw; Jimmy Hensley; Jimmy Insolo; Richard White (21)
78. Johnny Anderson (20)
79. Buck Peralta (19)
80. Ross Surgenor (18)
81. Clyde Dagit; Glenn Francis (17)
83. Leon Fox; Ernie Shaw; Bob Whitlow; Satch Worley (16)
87. Iggy Katona (15)
88. Jack Simpson (14)
89. Joey Arrington (13)
90. Mike James (12)
91. Hugh Pearson (11)
92. Chuck Bown (10)
93. Bobby Ore (8)
94. Jimmy Hailey; Ray Hendrick (7)
96. Bobby Fleming; Dub Simpson (6)
98. Jack Donohue (2)

1974 Events

Winston Western 500; Riverside Int. Raceway/2.62-m road/500m
Cale Yarborough (Chevrolet)/David Pearson (Mercury)

Daytona 500; Daytona International Speedway/2.5-m/450 miles
Richard Petty (Dodge)/David Pearson (Mercury)

Richmond 500; Richmond Fairgrounds Raceway/.542-m/244 miles
Bobby Allison (Chevrolet)/Bobby Allison (Chevrolet)

Carolina 500; North Carolina Motor Speedway/1.017-mile/451 m
Richard Petty (Dodge)/Cale Yarborough (Chevrolet)

Southeastern 500; Bristol International Speedway/.533-m/240m
Cale Yarborough (Chevrolet)/Donnie Allison (Chevrolet)

Atlanta 500; Atlanta International Raceway/1.522-m/451 miles
Cale Yarborough (Chevrolet)/David Pearson (Mercury)

Rebel 500; Darlington Raceway/1.366-mile/450 miles
David Pearson (Mercury)/Donnie Allison (Chevrolet)

Gwyn Staley 400; North Wilkesboro Speedway/.625-m/225 miles
Richard Petty (Dodge)/Bobby Allison (Chevrolet)

Virginia 500; Martinsville Speedway/.525-mile/237 miles
Cale Yarborough (Chevrolet)/Cale Yarborough (Chevrolet)

Winston 500; Alabama Int. Motor Speedway/2.66-mile/450 miles
David Pearson (Mercury)/David Pearson (Mercury)

Music City USA 420; Fairgrounds Speedway/.596-mile/238 miles
Richard Petty (Dodge)/Bobby Allison (Chevrolet)

Mason-Dixon 500; Dover Downs Int. Speedway/1-mile/450 miles
Cale Yarborough (Chevrolet)/David Pearson (Mercury)

World 600; Charlotte Motor Speedway/1.5-mile/540 miles
David Pearson (Mercury)/David Pearson (Mercury)

Tuborg 400; Riverside Int. Raceway/2.62-mile road/362 miles
Cale Yarborough (Chevrolet)/George Follmer (Matador)

Motor State 400; Michigan Int. Speedway/2-mile/360 miles
Richard Petty (Dodge)/David Pearson (Mercury)

Firecracker 400; Daytona International Speedway/2.5-m/400 m
David Pearson (Mercury)/David Pearson (Mercury)

Volunteer 500; Bristol International Speedway/.533-m/267 m
Cale Yarborough (Chevrolet)/Richard Petty (Dodge)

Nashville 420; Fairgrounds Speedway/.596-mile/250 miles
Cale Yarborough (Chevrolet)/Darrell Waltrip (Chevrolet)

Dixie 500; Atlanta International Raceway/1.522-m/500 miles
Richard Petty (Dodge)/Cale Yarborough (Chevrolet)

Purolator 500; Pocono International Raceway/2.5-m/500 miles
Richard Petty (Dodge)/Buddy Baker (Ford)

Talladega 500; Alabama Int. Motor Speedway/2.66-m/500 miles
Richard Petty (Dodge)/David Pearson (Mercury)

Yankee 400; Michigan International Speedway/2-mile/400 miles
David Pearson (Mercury)/David Pearson (Mercury)

Southern 500; Darlington Raceway/1.366-mile/500 miles
Cale Yarborough (Chevrolet)/Richard Petty (Dodge)

Capital City 500; Richmond Fairgrounds Raceway/.542-m/271 m
Richard Petty (Dodge)/Richard Petty (Dodge)

Delaware 500; Dover Downs Int. Speedway/1-mile/500 miles
Richard Petty (Dodge)/Buddy Baker (Ford)

Wilkes 400; North Wilkesboro Speedway/.625-mile/250 miles
Cale Yarborough (Chevrolet)/Richard Petty (Dodge)

Old Dominion 500; Martinsville Speedway/.525-mile/263 miles
Earl Ross (Chevrolet)/Richard Petty (Dodge)

National 500; Charlotte Motor Speedway/1.5-mile/500 miles
David Pearson (Mercury)/David Pearson (Mercury)

American 500; North Carolina Motor Speedway/1.017-mile/500 m
David Pearson (Mercury)/Richard Petty (Dodge)

Los Angeles Times 500; Ontario Motor Speedway/2.5-mile/500 m
Bobby Allison (Matador)/Richard Petty (Dodge)

Victories

1. Richard Petty; Cale Yarborough (10)
3. David Pearson (7)
4. Bobby Allison (2)
5. Earl Ross (1)

Poles

1. David Pearson (11)
2. Richard Petty (7)
3. Bobby Allison; Cale Yarborough (3)
5. Donnie Allison; Buddy Baker (2)
7. George Follmer; Darrell Waltrip (1)

Victories

1. Chevrolet (12)
2. Dodge (10)
3. Mercury (7)
4. Matador (1)

Poles

1. Mercury (11)
2. Chevrolet (9)
3. Dodge (7)
4. Ford (2)
5. Matador (1)

1975
NASCAR's King

"The only comparable person to contribute as much as Richard Petty to a sport is Arnold Palmer," longtime Lowe's Motor Speedway President Humpy Wheeler said in 1992. "There's just no measuring the impact that Richard's magnetism has meant."

Perhaps no king in history has had such complete rule over his subjects as Petty, who in 1975 recorded his 10th consecutive season with at least six victories. Like Palmer, he brought legions of new fans to the sport. And, like golf's King, Petty's popularity was as much because of his incredible willingness to sign autographs for hours, his uncanny patience in suffering fools gladly, and the ever-present smile that seemed to set a world record for the most pearly whites in a single mouth.

"Richard has that charisma that everyone is looking for in a star," said 1973 Winston Cup champion Benny Parsons. "Whether Richard Petty had a good day or a bad day, he always flashed that grin at you. That told the people a car race is not life or death. It's just another sporting event."

But comparing him to Palmer grossly understates Petty's accomplishments.

Although King Richard is the Babe Ruth of his sport, his hold on stock-car racing's record books is such that there will never be room for a Hank Aaron, a Roger Maris, or a Mark McGwire to erase his mightiest achievements.

The debate over the identity of the greatest driver—or the best baseball player, running back, or golfer—can rage until Jeff Gordon sips Geritol from his rocking chair.

But there can be little argument: Richard Petty was, by virtually any standard, the most *successful* driver in the first 51 years of Winston Cup racing. As Gordon, the latest challenger to the King's place in history, said: "He's the dynasty that we all want to be."

Petty's domination of the record books and his incredible list of singular achievements is so complete that they must be examined by categories:

Victories

Not only are the King's 200 victories nearly double the total of his nearest rival, but his 27 wins in one season are 50 percent more than any other driver has managed. In an era of shorter seasons, those records should endure longer than the lives of anyone who can remember Petty's driving career.

Petty also holds the records for most consecutive seasons with a victory—18 from 1960-77—and in each of those seasons he posted multiple victories. He won at least three races 16 years in a row (1962-77) and at least four 14 years in a row (1962-75), both records. And his 10 years in a row (1966-75) with six or more victories is twice as long a string as that of any other driver.

Petty also won at least eight races seven years in a row (1966-72). No other driver has managed to win as many as eight more than three consecutive seasons. Likewise, Petty's five consecutive seasons with at least 10 triumphs (1967-71) and back-to-back campaigns of at least 18 victories (1970-71) are unchallenged. Petty followed his 27-victory 1967 season with 16 more trips to victory lane in 1968. Ned Jarrett is the only other driver who has put together back-to-back seasons of at least 13 victories.

One record Petty doesn't hold is the longest streak of seasons with at least one short-track victory. Darrell Waltrip had a string of 15 such seasons, while Petty had a 14-year streak that extended through 1975. But move over, Darrell. In each of those 14 seasons, Petty posted at least three short-track victories; no other driver ever had such a string beyond four years. The King also holds these records: seven consecutive years (1966-72) with at least four short-track wins, six consecutive years (1967-72) with five or more short-track victories, and five years in a row (1967-71) with eight or more short-track triumphs. For good measure, Petty won at least a dozen short-track events in both 1967 and '68 and set a single-season record of 14 short-track victories in 1971. And Petty's 107 victories on short tracks exceed the career totals of any other driver on all disciplines combined.

Petty's trips to victory lane were just as frequent on other venues. He holds the records for superspeedway victories (56), 500-mile wins (38), seasons leading the Winston Cup Series in victories (7), and eight consecutive years (1970-77) with multiple 500-mile victories. He is one of three drivers with a record six victories on road courses and one of three with at least 10 classic victories, including a record seven in the Daytona 500.

In 1967, Petty captured a record 10 consecutive victories, a record five in a row on dirt, and eight consecutive short-track victories, a record later tied by Cale Yarborough. In his 21-victory season of 1971, Petty added a five-race winning streak that has been exceeded only by his record of 10 in a row. He also captured that season's last three 500-mile races and became the first driver to win four consecutive 500-mile events when he won the 1972 season opener at Riverside, Calif. In fact, Petty posted 10 other three-race winning streaks from 1962-75, and only 12 other drivers have more *total* victories than Petty's 45 achieved in winning streaks of three or more races.

Victories From the Pole

Only five other drivers have posted more *total* victories than the King's 61 wins from the pole, and only six other drivers have won more races from the pole in a career than the 15 Petty claimed in 1967, when he also set a record with eight dirt triumphs from the pole. That same season, Petty became the first driver to win four consecutive races from the pole, a feat matched only once since. His 13 consecutive years (1960-72) of winning at least one race from the pole is a record, and his 10 years in a row (1962-71) with multiple victories from the pole are twice as many as any other driver. So is his record of six consecutive years (1966-71) with three or more victories from the pole. The King also is the only driver to win seven or more races from the pole in consecutive seasons (1966-67), and his five years in a row (1960-64) with at least one dirt victory from the pole ties another record. He holds the records of 10 consecu-

tive seasons (1962-71) with at least one short-track win from the pole and seven years in a row (1965-71) with multiple short-track triumphs from the pole. His six consecutive years (1966-71) with three or more short-track victories from the pole are twice the total of his nearest rival, and his three consecutive seasons (1966-68) with at least four short-track victories from the pole is another unchallenged mark.

Petty's 36 short-track victories from the pole are double the total of his nearest challenger, and he is the only driver to capture three consecutive dirt races from the pole (1967) or three straight short-track events from the pole (1971). The King also shares the record of two consecutive seasons with multiple superspeedway victories from the pole, and only five times in history has a driver captured three or more races in a row from the pole. On three of those occasions, that driver was Petty.

Poles

Petty's 123 poles, 68 short-track poles, and 16 consecutive seasons (1960-75) with multiple poles are records. He also won at least three poles in 14 consecutive seasons (1962-75), twice as long a string as any other driver. In fact, the King won at least four poles 10 years in a row (1962-71), at least six in nine consecutive years (1963-71), and at least seven six years in succession (1963-68), all records. Winning five consecutive poles on short tracks has been accomplished six times, but Petty is the only driver to manage it twice, in 1966 and in 1971. He won at least 12 poles three years in a row (1966-68), while no other driver has managed to win more than eight poles in three consecutive seasons. Petty's back-to-back campaigns (1966-67) with at least 15 poles is another record.

Petty also holds the records of 11 consecutive seasons (1960-70) with at least one dirt pole and 10 seasons in a row (1962-71) with multiple short-track poles. In fact, he won at least four short-track poles eight years in a row (1964-71), a string twice as long as any other driver's, and captured at least five short-track poles in seven consecutive seasons (1965-71). No one else has managed to do that even three years in a row.

Richard Petty's records include 200 victories and 123 poles, but they don't begin to measure the reasons he is NASCAR royalty: the King.

Performance Index

Petty led the season Performance Index on seven occasions, a record he shares with Dale Earnhardt, who in 1994 joined the King as a seven-time Winston Cup champion. But the King's 22,321 career rating is more than 50 percent higher than any other driver's, and he holds all records for most seasons with a rating of 100 or better, 200 or higher, etc., through the single-season mark of 1,313 set in 1971.

The most impressive of Petty's many Performance Index records include:

- Half of the four seasons with a rating of 1,100 or better;
- 10 seasons with a rating of 900 or better, six more than any other driver;
- 12 seasons with a rating of 800 or better, seven more than any rival.

Petty also holds or shares the records for most consecutive seasons in each of the rating categories: from 34 consecutive seasons (1959-92) with a rating of 100 or better through six consecutive campaigns (1967-72) with a rating of 900 or higher.

Although he shares the record of No. 1 seasons with Earnhardt, the King does not share his throne with anyone for most top-two seasons (13), top-three seasons (15), top-25 seasons (31)—or anything in between.

He also holds or shares the records for consecutive top-three seasons (six from 1967-72), top-25 seasons (29 from 1959-87), and in 16 other categories in between. Perhaps the most impressive of those records are his 18 consecutive top-nine seasons (1966-83) and the record of 12 top-four seasons in a row (1966-77) he shares with his father, Lee.

Petty, who passed his father as the sport's all-time victory leader when he won the 1967 Rebel 400 at Darlington, S.C., 50 days before his 30th birthday, was the first stock-car driver whose fame transcended the sport.

Although his 1967 season is more celebrated, Petty's finest year may have been 1971, when his 1,313 Performance Index rating was a record 314 higher than his nearest rival. Although he won "only" 21 races in '71, six were 500-mile events, including the Daytona 500.

In 1975, Petty set a modern record of 13 victories, then captured eight more wins during the next two seasons. But the greatest dynasty in stock-car racing history began showing signs of wear and tear during a winless 1978 season, and Petty's imminent retirement was a frequent rumor.

"Nobody is going to quit when they're on top, and nobody's going to quit when they're down because they don't want to quit a loser," he said. "All the top Indy drivers and the top Grand National drivers are older men. It takes a certain amount of maturity to be a top race driver. When me and David (Pearson) and Bobby (Allison) and Cale and all those other cats first came up, there was a big changeover. Until three or four years from now, when all us cats leave, them other cats aren't going to be able to get in. There are just so many winning mechanics and just so many winning cars. The number of those just about balances out with the number of winning drivers. You can't win without a good car. A bad driver can win with a good car, but for a good driver to win with a bad car, it has to be a freak deal."

That winless 1978 season saw Petty Enterprises abandon the Chrysler products in which the King had earned 178 of his 185 victories in favor of a Chevrolet, the team's primary car when Petty won his final Winston Cup title in 1979 after having 40 percent of his stomach surgically removed during the off-season. Then, after the King captured his seventh Daytona 500 in 1981, Dale Inman—Richard's cousin, crew chief, and best friend—left Petty Enterprises. Two years later, the King followed suit, leaving the family business—and taking the Day-Glo red and Petty blue, No. 43, STP-sponsored cars with him. Petty won two races in 1984 for Mike Curb, including a stirring duel with Yarborough in the Firecracker 400. The King spent another year and a half with Curb and then another seven behind the wheel after he returned to Petty Enterprises in Level Cross, N.C. But that 1984 Independence Day triumph was the last of his 200 victories.

Considering his incredible legacy, it's obviously difficult for Petty to pinpoint his greatest achievement. "The big thrill at Daytona was the 200th win, and finally winning at Charlotte (in the 1975 World 600) was huge," he said late in his career. "The 10 in a row we won in '67 might be the most impressive. Winning 10 in a row is a huge deal even if it's 10 10-lap heat races. But what happens is that all that stuff gets lost because you do something that gets bigger and overshadows what you've already done."

And no one has done more than Petty, who was asked in the final days before his 1992 retirement how he had coped with the eight winless seasons that had followed his quarter-century of glory. "There's no one—and I mean no one—who got more fun from his success," he said. "I've had a love affair driving that race car like nobody else ever."

The debate will rage forever over the identity of history's best stock-car driver. Petty declines to participate in the discussion.

"Personally," he said, "I'd rather be remembered as a winning driver than a good driver."

In that case, his legacy is safe forever.

1975 in Review

Petty's 13 victories established a modern record that would not be equaled for 23 years and were more than three times as many as his nearest competitor, Buddy Baker, who won four times. Petty also claimed his sixth Winston Cup title and held a 910-652 advantage over James Hylton in the Performance Index—the highest differential any leader has claimed during the modern era. Pearson led the circuit with seven poles, and Pearson, Allison, and Yarborough each won three times to give five drivers 26 victories in the 30-race campaign.

Most Memorable Race

Allison lost two laps when he was black flagged early in the Rebel 500 at Darlington on April 13, and he said NASCAR officials never told him why he was penalized. Allison regained a lap when he chose to keep his Roger Penske-owned Matador on the track instead of joining the leaders in the pits after Bruce Hill suffered a blown engine with 32 laps remaining. When Benny Parsons and Pearson wrecked while dueling for the lead 15 laps later, Allison managed to get back in the lead lap. Allison then beat Darrell Waltrip—who was seeking his first Winston Cup victory—and Donnie Allison, his younger brother, to the checkered flag in a three-way photo finish. "It sure wasn't a good finish for me and Benny, but the spectators must have thought it was a good one," Pearson said.

Most Significant Wreck

Tiny Lund, a five-time winner on the Winston Cup circuit, was killed in a six-car crash on the eighth lap of the Talladega 500 on August 17 at Alabama International Motor Speedway. Baker, who enjoyed fishing with Lund—a world-record holder as an angler—didn't learn that his 6-foot-4, 260-pound pal had been killed until he was asked about him in his post-race news conference. "I think everybody on the race track loved him," the victorious Baker said as tears rolled down his cheeks.

Most Important Off-Track Development

The 40-car field for the World 600 on May 25 at Charlotte included Chevrolets, Fords, Mercurys, Dodges, and Plymouths. Joe Frasson, however, failed to earn a spot on the grid in his Pontiac. In front of an amazed crowd of perhaps 100, Frasson produced a large sledgehammer and literally destroyed his race car. As Frasson rapidly exited the garage area hauling the battered remains of his Pontiac, Petty said, "Ol' Joe never drove a race car that fast."

Records & Milestones

The 1975 season was the first of only two years in the modern era in which seven drivers captured three or more poles. Trailing Pearson were Dave Marcis with four and Allison, Baker, Parsons, Petty, and Yarborough with three apiece.

1975 at a Glance

Races:	30
Road:	2
Short Track:	10
Superspeedway:	18
Winners:	8
Pole Winners:	9
Tracks:	16
States:	11

1975 Performance Index Rankings

1. Richard Petty (910)
2. James Hylton (652)
3. Richard Childress (605)
4. Dave Marcis (596)
5. David Pearson (562)
6. Buddy Baker (547)
7. Cecil Gordon (545)
8. Benny Parsons (533)
9. Cale Yarborough (517)
10. Elmo Langley (461)
11. Dick Brooks (457)
12. Frank Warren (449)
13. Bruce Hill (424)
14. Darrell Waltrip (421)
15. Coo Coo Marlin (387)
16. Walter Ballard (375)
17. Bobby Allison (368)
18. David Sisco (364)
19. J.D. McDuffie (346)
20. Buddy Arrington (345)
21. Ed Negre (330)
22. Bruce Jacobi (299)
23. Lennie Pond (289)
24. Carl Adams; Jabe Thomas (248)
26. Donnie Allison (205)
27. Dean Dalton (198)
28. Ferrel Harris (177)
29. Jim Vandiver (157)
30. D.K. Ulrich (142)
31. Richie Panch (131)
32. Grant Adcox (110)
33. Joe Frasson (107)
34. Skip Manning (105)
35. Dick May (104)
36. A.J. Foyt (95)
37. Darel Dieringer (91)
38. Henley Gray (82)
39. Rick Newsom (81)
40. Hershel McGriff (80)
41. Joe Mihalic; Jackie Rogers (78)
43. Bill Champion; Randy Tissot (74)
45. Earle Canavan (66)
46. Harry Jefferson (65)
47. Ray Elder (63)
48. Gary Matthews; Chuck Wahl (57)
50. Bob Burcham; Bill Schmitt (54)
52. Ricky Rudd (44)
53. Ramo Stott (40)
54. Charlie Glotzbach (39)
55. G.C. Spencer (36)
56. Kenny Brightbill; Jimmy Insolo; Bobby Isaac (33)
59. Alton Jones; Earl Ross (32)
61. Gene Riniker (30)
62. Glenn Francis; Don Hall; Jody Ridley (29)
65. Chuck Bown; Don Puskarich (28)
67. Baxter Price (27)
68. Terry Bivins; Jim Boyd (26)
70. Clyde Dagit; Larry Esau; Don Hoffman (25)
73. Bill Osborne II; Travis Tiller; Pete Torres (24)
76. Hugh Pearson; Warren Tope (22)
78. Billy Hagan; Glenn McDuffie; Richard White (21)
81. Jeff Handy; John Kieper; Don Reynolds; Tom Williams (20)
85. Jimmy Hensley; Salt Walther (18)
87. Tommy Gale (17)
88. John Banks (15)
89. Neil Bonnett (11)
90. Bill Hollar (9)
91. Earl Brooks; Richard D. Brown (8)
93. Neil Castles (7)

1975 Events

Winston Western 500; Riverside Int. Raceway/2.62-m road/500m
Bobby Allison (Matador)/Bobby Allison (Matador)

Daytona 500; Daytona International Speedway/2.5-m/500 miles
Benny Parsons (Chevrolet)/Donnie Allison (Chevrolet)

Richmond 500; Richmond Fairgrounds Raceway/.542-m/271 miles
Richard Petty (Dodge)/Richard Petty (Dodge)

Carolina 500; North Carolina Motor Speedway/1.017-mile/500 m
Cale Yarborough (Chevrolet)/Buddy Baker (Ford)

Southeastern 500; Bristol International Speedway/.533-m/267m
Richard Petty (Dodge)/Buddy Baker (Ford)

Atlanta 500; Atlanta International Raceway/1.522-m/500 miles
Richard Petty (Dodge)/Richard Petty (Dodge)

Gwyn Staley 400; North Wilkesboro Speedway/.625-m/250 miles
Richard Petty (Dodge)/Darrell Waltrip (Chevrolet)

Rebel 500; Darlington Raceway/1.366-mile/500 miles
Bobby Allison (Matador)/David Pearson (Mercury)

Virginia 500; Martinsville Speedway/.525-mile/263 miles
Richard Petty (Dodge)/Benny Parsons (Chevrolet)

Winston 500; Alabama Int. Motor Speedway/2.66-mile/500 miles
Buddy Baker (Ford)/Buddy Baker (Ford)

Music City 420; Nashville Speedway/.596-mile/250 miles
Darrell Waltrip (Chevrolet)/Darrell Waltrip (Chevrolet)

Mason-Dixon 500; Dover Downs Int. Speedway/1-mile/500 miles
David Pearson (Mercury)/David Pearson (Mercury)

World 600; Charlotte Motor Speedway/1.5-mile/600 miles
Richard Petty (Dodge)/David Pearson (Mercury)

Tuborg 400; Riverside Int. Raceway/2.62-mile road/400 miles
Richard Petty (Dodge)/Bobby Allison (Matador)

Motor State 400; Michigan Int. Speedway/2-mile/400 miles
David Pearson (Mercury)/Cale Yarborough (Chevrolet)

Firecracker 400; Daytona International Speedway/2.5-m/400 m
Richard Petty (Dodge)/Donnie Allison (Chevrolet)

Nashville 420; Nashville Speedway/.596-mile/250 miles
Cale Yarborough (Chevrolet)/Benny Parsons (Chevrolet)

Purolator 500; Pocono International Raceway/2.5-mile/500 miles
David Pearson (Mercury)/Bobby Allison (Matador)

Talladega 500; Alabama Int. Motor Speedway/2.66-m/500 miles
Buddy Baker (Ford)/Dave Marcis (Dodge)

Champion Spark Plug 400; Michigan Int. Speedway/2-mile/400 m
Richard Petty (Dodge)/David Pearson (Mercury)

Southern 500; Darlington Int. Raceway/1.366-mile/500 miles
Bobby Allison (Matador)/David Pearson (Mercury)

Delaware 500; Dover Downs Int. Speedway/1-mile/500 miles
Richard Petty (Dodge)/Dave Marcis (Dodge)

Wilkes 400; North Wilkesboro Speedway/.625-mile/250 miles
Richard Petty (Dodge)/Richard Petty (Dodge)

Old Dominion 500; Martinsville Speedway/.525-mile/263 miles
Dave Marcis (Dodge)/Cale Yarborough (Chevrolet)

National 500; Charlotte Motor Speedway/1.5-mile/500 miles
Richard Petty (Dodge)/David Pearson (Mercury)

Capital City 500; Richmond Fairgrounds Raceway/.542-m/271 m
Darrell Waltrip (Chevrolet)/Benny Parsons (Chevrolet)

American 500; North Carolina Motor Speedway/1.017-mile/500 m
Cale Yarborough (Chevrolet)/Dave Marcis (Dodge)

Volunteer 500; Bristol International Speedway/.533-mile/267m
Richard Petty (Dodge)/Cale Yarborough (Chevrolet)

Dixie 500; Atlanta International Raceway/1.522-m/500 miles
Buddy Baker (Ford)/Dave Marcis (Dodge)

Los Angeles Times 500; Ontario Motor Speedway/2.5-mile/500 m
Buddy Baker (Ford)/David Pearson (Mercury)

Victories

1. Richard Petty (13)
2. Buddy Baker (4)
3. Bobby Allison; David Pearson; Cale Yarborough (3)
6. Darrell Waltrip (2)
7. Dave Marcis; Benny Parsons (1)

Poles

1. David Pearson (7)
2. Dave Marcis (4)
3. Bobby Allison; Buddy Baker; Benny Parsons; Richard Petty; Cale Yarborough (3)
8. Donnie Allison; Darrell Waltrip (2)

Victories

1. Dodge (14)
2. Chevrolet (6)
3. Ford (4)
4. Matador; Mercury (3)

Poles

1. Chevrolet (10)
2. Dodge; Mercury (7)
4. Ford; Matador (3)

1976
The Greatest
Race in NASCAR
History

Most Memorable Race

"The 1976 Daytona 500 had to be the race of races," Richard Petty recalled more than 15 years later. "Circumstances made it like that—one of those Hollywood script deals."

Or maybe it was just too good to be true for the silver screen.

"If it had been one of those Hollywood deals," Petty said, "nobody would have believed it."

Indeed, the 1976 Daytona 500 was the greatest of the 1,888 races in the first 51 years of Winston Cup racing. As Petty said, Hollywood couldn't have scripted it any better than he and David Pearson did on that sun-kissed Florida afternoon of February 15.

Since its inception in 1959, the Daytona 500 has been NASCAR's premier showcase, its equivalent of the Super Bowl, World Series, or Kentucky Derby. As long-time motorsports broadcaster Ken Squier so aptly nicknamed it, the Daytona 500 has become the "Great American Race."

And its principals in the most memorable race—and by far the most dramatic lap—in Winston Cup annals were none other than Petty and Pearson, who rank first and second in countless categories in the record books, most notably victories.

When the 42-car field fired its engines, King Richard was seeking the 178th victory of his career and the Silver Fox his 89th.

Pearson had ruled the superspeedways since teaming with the Wood brothers. In 1973 and 1974, he captured 17 of the 34 races on NASCAR's big tracks. The King countered that challenge to his throne by earning a modern-record 13 victories in 1975, a mark that stood unequaled for 23 years. Pearson accepted that counter punch by capturing the season-opening Winston Western 500 on the road course at Riverside, Calif.

"Both of us would just as soon outrun the other as any other car out there," Pearson said.

Despite their stature in the sport, however, Petty and Pearson had been in the shadows during SpeedWeeks.

When the world turned its attention to the Birthplace of Speed for qualifying, A.J. Foyt drew the headlines with a lap of 187.477 mph in Hoss Ellington's Chevrolet. Upstart Darrell Waltrip was right behind at 186.617 mph in the DiGard Chevrolet, with Dave Marcis third with a 186.548 mph clocking in the Nord Krauskopf-owned, Harry Hyde-prepared Dodge. That trio, and rookie Bruce Hill, the ninth-fastest qualifier, got even bigger headlines when they were disqualified by NASCAR officials, Foyt and Waltrip for illegal "fuel pressure assist" systems and Marcis for a radiator block that flopped down from its normal position when his car reached a certain speed.

Their disqualifications left an unlikely front row of Iowa-bred Chevrolet drivers: Ramo Stott, whose 183.456 mph clocking gave him the only pole of his career, and Terry Ryan, who was making his Winston Cup debut. Petty's STP Dodge was sixth on the starting grid and Pearson's Wood brothers' Purolator Mercury seventh.

Thirty-three official lead changes had been recorded before Pearson overtook defending champion Benny Parsons on the 177th of 200 laps around the 2.5-mile tri-oval. Petty took command 11 laps later and led Pearson under the white flag to set the stage for the most exciting lap in the history of stock-car racing.

Pearson moved toward the inside lane on the backstretch exiting the second turn. When Petty drifted high, Pearson used the middle of the track to grab a lead of a little more than a car length as they entered the third turn. But Pearson entered the turn too fast and drifted high, allowing Petty to duck inside. When the drivers exited the last of 800 turns, Petty's Dodge was perhaps three feet in front.

At that point, Petty apparently angled his steering wheel toward the outside retaining wall, with Pearson's car angled slightly toward the grass on the frontstretch.

"My car was loose, pushing, and I tried to pass him back on the inside and messed him up. I touched him first. It was my fault, and I told him that," Petty said.

"I don't think he meant to do it," Pearson said. "I drafted him down the backstretch. I guess his car got to pushing, and he just pushed right on into me. He hit me and spun me around."

Petty then tapped the wall and saw his car spin to a 45-degree angle, yet move six feet ahead of his rival. Pearson then spun into the outside wall, and Petty managed to get his Dodge straightened out and headed toward the finish line.

The nose of Pearson's Mercury then clipped Petty's right rear quarter-panel, sending the King spinning head-on into the wall. Petty bounced off the wall and spun across the tri-oval. The King appeared poised to spin his car all the way across the finish line before the infield grass stopped his badly damaged Dodge's inertia some 75 yards short of the line. While the Petty Enterprises crew sprinted across the grass to their driver's aid, the Silver Fox guided his equally disfigured Mercury across the grass, returned to the pavement less than 10 yards from the finish line, and captured the only Daytona 500 victory of his career, taking the checkered flag at perhaps 15 mph.

"That was as tough a race as I ever lost," said Petty, who would finish his career with a record 200 victories.

"He was trying to win the race, just like I was," said Pearson, who would close his career with 105 triumphs, second only to the King. "I got my clutch in after I hit the wall and was able to get across the line."

Someone asked Pearson if his victory was tainted.

"If I'd *backed* across that finish line, it wouldn't have made any difference—as long as I was first," he said.

Surprisingly enough, despite the high stakes and circumstances, neither driver was particularly upset with the other. But Petty, who already had five Daytona 500 victories under his belt and would claim two more, wasn't happy with himself.

"I wasn't exactly hollering, 'Hurray for me,' " the King said.

1976 in Review

Pearson led the circuit with 10 victories and nine poles, but Cale Yarborough parlayed his nine victories in Junior Johnson's Chevrolet into his first Winston Cup championship. Yarborough edged Parsons, 735-733, in the Performance Index ratings—the closest such finish in history. Pearson, who competed in only 22 of the season's 30 races, and Petty weren't far behind, posting ratings of 728 and 702, respectively.

Most Significant Wreck

Bobby Allison escaped with minor chest injuries when he flipped the Roger Penske-owned Mercury 13 times down the backstretch of the North Carolina Motor Speedway at Rockingham during the Carolina 500 on February 29. Allison's airborne car finally landed on the hood of Richard Childress's Chevrolet in the resulting eight-car crash. "All of a sudden, I saw Bobby Allison's Mercury flying through the air, coming right at me," Childress said.

Most Important Off-Track Development

Goodyear's annual attendance survey reported that the Winston Cup Series led all motorsports circuits in season attendance for the first time.

Records & Milestones

Neil Bonnett captured the first pole of his career, qualifying first for the July 17 Nashville 420 at 103.049 mph in Penske's Mercury. But Bonnett, who was substituting for Allison, didn't get to start the race.

1976 at a Glance

Races:	30
Road:	2
Short Track:	10
Superspeedway:	18
Winners:	8
Pole Winners:	11
Tracks:	16
States:	11

1976 Performance Index Rankings

1. Cale Yarborough (735)
2. Benny Parsons (733)
3. David Pearson (728)
4. Richard Petty (702)
5. Lennie Pond (599)
6. Bobby Allison (581)
7. Dave Marcis (508)
8. Dick Brooks (505)
9. Buddy Baker (477)
10. Richard Childress (464)
11. D.K. Ulrich (425)
12. James Hylton (421)
13. Darrell Waltrip (414)
14. Skip Manning (396)
15. Cecil Gordon (391)
16. Frank Warren (382)
17. J.D. McDuffie (379)
18. David Sisco (357)
19. Bobby Wawak (311)
20. Grant Adcox (276)
21. Buddy Arrington; Terry Bivins (267)
23. Ed Negre (252)
24. Coo Coo Marlin (229)
25. Jackie Rogers (222)
26. Donnie Allison (187)
27. Bruce Hill (182)
28. Dick May (180)
29. Neil Bonnett (144)
30. Joe Mihalic (135)
31. Henley Gray; Jimmy Means (120)
33. Sonny Easley (111)
34. Walter Ballard (110)
35. Darrell Bryant (106)
36. Terry Ryan (105)
37. John Utsman (100)
38. Buck Baker (95)
39. Dean Dalton (88)
40. Tighe Scott (77)
41. Tommy Gale; Janet Guthrie (70)
43. Joe Frasson; Harold Miller (63)
45. Ray Elder (62)
46. Jimmy Insolo (59)
47. Elmo Langley (57)
48. Chuck Bown (56)
49. Rick Newsom; Ricky Rudd (49)
51. Jabe Thomas (45)
52. Earl Brooks (41)
53. Eddie Bradshaw (37)
54. Harry Gant (36)
55. Bobby Isaac (34)
56. Salt Walther (33)
57. A.J. Foyt; Sam Sommers (31)
59. Jimmy Lee Capps; Bill Schmitt (30)
61. Jim Hurtubise; Travis Tiller (29)
63. Earle Canavan (28)
64. Bill Elliott; Larry Esau; Gary B. Myers; Larry Phillips; Jim Vandiver (27)
69. Bob Burcham; Ron Esau (26)
71. Don Puskarich; Roy Smith (25)
73. Gene Felton (24)
74. David Hobbs; Gary Matthews; G.C. Spencer (23)
77. Jack Donohue; Dale Earnhardt; Budd Hagelin; Junior Miller (21)
81. Carl Joiner (20)
82. Jimmy Hensley; Dick Skillen (18)
84. Chuck Wahl (17)
85. Johnny Rutherford (15)
86. Bill Polich (13)
87. Don Reynolds (12)
88. Bruce Blodgett; Jerry Sisco (10)
90. Bill Champion; Larry LeMay (9)
92. Walter Wallace (7)
93. Baxter Price; Ernie Shaw (5)

1976 Events

Winston Western 500; Riverside Int. Raceway/2.62-m road/500m
David Pearson (Mercury)/Bobby Allison (Matador)

Daytona 500; Daytona International Speedway/2.5-m/500 miles
David Pearson (Mercury)/Ramo Stott (Chevrolet)

Carolina 500; North Carolina Motor Speedway/1.017-mile/500 m
Richard Petty (Dodge)/Dave Marcis (Dodge)

Richmond 400; Richmond Fairgrounds Raceway/.542-m/217 miles
Dave Marcis (Dodge)/Bobby Allison (Mercury)

Southeastern 400; Bristol International Speedway/.533-m/213m
Cale Yarborough (Chevrolet)/Buddy Baker (Ford)

Atlanta 500; Atlanta International Raceway/1.522-m/500 miles
David Pearson (Mercury)/Dave Marcis (Dodge)

Gwyn Staley 400; North Wilkesboro Speedway/.625-m/250 miles
Cale Yarborough (Chevrolet)/Dave Marcis (Dodge)

Rebel 500; Darlington International Raceway./1.366-mile/500m
David Pearson (Mercury)/David Pearson (Mercury)

Virginia 500; Martinsville Speedway/.525-mile/263 miles
Darrell Waltrip (Chevrolet)/Dave Marcis (Dodge)

Winston 500; Alabama Int. Motor Speedway/2.66-mile/500 miles
Buddy Baker (Ford)/Dave Marcis (Dodge)

Music City USA 420; Nashville Speedway/.596-mile/250 miles
Cale Yarborough (Chevrolet)/Benny Parsons (Chevrolet)

Mason-Dixon 500; Dover Downs Int. Speedway/1-mile/500 miles
Benny Parsons (Chevrolet)/Dave Marcis (Dodge)

World 600; Charlotte Motor Speedway/1.5-mile/600 miles
David Pearson (Mercury)/David Pearson (Mercury)

Riverside 400; Riverside Int. Raceway/2.62-m road/248 miles
David Pearson (Mercury)/David Pearson (Mercury)

Cam2 Motor Oil 400; Michigan Int. Speedway/2-mile/400 miles
David Pearson (Mercury)/Richard Petty (Dodge)

Firecracker 400; Daytona International Speedway/2.5-m/400 m
Cale Yarborough (Chevrolet)/A.J. Foyt (Chevrolet)

Nashville 420; Nashville Speedway/.596-mile/250 miles
Benny Parsons (Chevrolet)/Neil Bonnett (Mercury)

Purolator 500; Pocono International Raceway/2.5-m/500 miles
Richard Petty (Dodge)/Cale Yarborough (Chevrolet)

Talladega 500; Alabama Int. Motor Speedway/2.66-m/500 miles
Dave Marcis (Dodge)/Dave Marcis (Dodge)

Champion Spark Plug 400; Michigan Int. Speedway/2-mile/400 m
David Pearson (Mercury)/David Pearson (Mercury)

Volunteer 400; Bristol International Speedway/.533-mile/213m
Cale Yarborough (Chevrolet)/Darrell Waltrip (Chevrolet)

Southern 500; Darlington Int. Raceway/1.366-mile/500 miles
David Pearson (Mercury)/David Pearson (Mercury)

Capital City 400; Richmond Fairgrounds Raceway/.542-m/217 m
Cale Yarborough (Chevrolet)/Benny Parsons (Chevrolet)

Delaware 500; Dover Downs Int. Speedway/1-mile/500 miles
Cale Yarborough (Chevrolet)/Cale Yarborough (Chevrolet)

Old Dominion 500; Martinsville Speedway/.525-mile/263 miles
Cale Yarborough (Chevrolet)/Darrell Waltrip (Chevrolet)

Wilkes 400; North Wilkesboro Speedway/.625-mile/250 miles
Cale Yarborough (Chevrolet)/Darrell Waltrip (Chevrolet)

National 500; Charlotte Motor Speedway/1.5-mile/500 miles
Donnie Allison (Chevrolet)/David Pearson (Mercury)

American 500; North Carolina Motor Speedway/1.017-mile/500 m
Richard Petty (Dodge)/David Pearson (Mercury)

Dixie 500; Atlanta International Raceway/1.522-m/500 miles
Dave Marcis (Dodge)/Buddy Baker (Ford)

Los Angeles Times 500; Ontario Motor Speedway/2.5-mile/500 m
David Pearson (Mercury)/David Pearson (Mercury)

Victories

1. David Pearson (10)
2. Cale Yarborough (9)
3. Dave Marcis; Richard Petty (3)
5. Benny Parsons (2)
6. Donnie Allison; Buddy Baker; Darrell Waltrip (1)

Poles

1. David Pearson (8)
2. Dave Marcis (7)
3. Darrell Waltrip (3)
4. Bobby Allison; Buddy Baker; Benny Parsons; Cale Yarborough (2)
8. Neil Bonnett; A.J. Foyt; Richard Petty; Ramo Stott (1)

Victories

1. Chevrolet (13)
2. Mercury (10)
3. Dodge (6)
4. Ford (1)

Poles

1. Mercury (10)
2. Chevrolet (9)
3. Dodge (8)
4. Ford (2)
5. Matador (1)

1977
Some Drivers' Considerable Achievements Have Been Unfairly Overlooked

Success in stock-car racing, like any other endeavor, is relative.

Buddy Arrington never won a race, and James Hylton captured just two. But they finished eighth and ninth, respectively, in the Performance Index in 1977—just one of many years in which their amazing consistency helped them compile career records that, while short on victories, were long on respectable finishes.

Hylton has the 11th-highest career Performance Index in history, a 9,858 rating. Further, he finished second in the Performance Index on four occasions, third twice, and fourth twice. Only two drivers have posted more seasons with a rating of 900 or better than Hylton's three, and he ranks fourth in seasons with a rating of 800 or better (4) and fifth in seasons with a rating of 700 or higher (6).

Yet Hylton won only twice in his career and, like so many other drivers who consistently drove their machines back to the garage in one piece ahead of most of the field—but rarely, if ever, into victory lane—his accomplishments are generally forgotten.

These drivers frequently have been unfairly labeled as "strokers." Although no one is suggesting that their accomplishments are comparable to those of Richard Petty, their abilities often were compromised by a lack of competitive equipment—or the funds or sponsorship to upgrade their outfits.

"My only regret is that I don't have the money to run the way I'd like to, but I'm tickled to death to have what I've got," Arrington said in 1988, his last season in a career than spanned a quarter of a century.

Arrington not only never won a race, but he never even finished second or captured a pole. Yet his career Performance Index of 7,100 ranks 22nd on the all-time list.

"I eat good. I take a bath like everybody else does—twice a day most times. If I had it to do over, I'd do it again. No regrets," he added. "I've done my thing. I'm satisfied."

J.D. McDuffie's hands were badly burned in a wreck in a 125-mile qualifying race at Daytona Beach, Fla., in 1988, and he lost his life in a crash at Watkins Glen, N.Y., three years later. His one moment of glory in 25 years in Winston Cup racing was winning the pole for the 1978 Delaware 500 at Dover, but he never quit trying to earn that elusive victory.

"I was lucky to get out of it," he said not long after the crash at Daytona. "My hands got burned pretty bad.

"I'm not going to let this get me down," he added. "All I've ever done is race. It makes it all worthwhile when you run good. You find out the drive is still there. The love of the sport—that's all I know."

The following charts identify the drivers fans may have forgotten, but certainly shouldn't:

Highest Career Performance Index Ratings Among Drivers Who Never Won a Race or a Pole

Driver	Rank	Rating	Special Achievement
Buddy Arrington	22nd	7,100	22 seasons at 100 or better
Cecil Gordon	30th	5,601	Five top-eight seasons
Neil Castles	39th	4,649	Five top-nine seasons
Richard Childress	44th	3,951	Six top-11 seasons
Frank Warren	50th	3,724	13 seasons at 100 or better
Jabe Thomas	55th	3,461	Three seasons at 600 or better
Jimmy Means	T-56th	3,434	12 seasons at 100 or better
Henley Gray	66th	3,076	Seven top-22 seasons
D.K. Ulrich	72nd	2,728	Eight seasons at 100 or better
Ed Negre	80th	2,356	Eight seasons at 100 or better

Buddy Arrington never won a Winston Cup race or a pole, but he posted 22 seasons with a Performance Index of 100 or better and has a career rating of 7,100—22nd on the all-time list at the conclusion of the Winston Cup circuit's 51st season.

Highest Career Performance Index Ratings Among Drivers Who Won at Least One Pole But Not a Race

Driver	Rank	Rating	Special Achievement
J.D. McDuffie	28th	5,882	16 top-25 seasons
Michael Waltrip	33rd	5,371	13 top-23 seasons
G.C. Spencer	46th	3,849	14 seasons at 100 or better
John Sears	49th	3,726	Three seasons at 600 or better
Ted Musgrave	T-56th	3,434	Five seasons at 400 or better
Joe Ruttman	71st	2,770	Three seasons at 400 or better
Rick Mast	73rd	2,703	Seven seasons at 200 or better
Dick Trickle	78th	2,455	10 seasons at 100 or better
Hut Stricklin	81st	2,349	Eight seasons at 200 or better
Rick Wilson	96th	1,970	Seven seasons at 100 or better

Highest Career Performance Index Ratings Among Drivers Who Won Only One Race

Driver	Rank	Rating	Special Achievement
Dick Brooks	32nd	5,375	11 seasons at 300 or better
Wendell Scott	37th	4,863	Eight top-12 seasons
Lake Speed	38th	4,660	16 seasons at 100 or better
Bobby Hillin Jr.	42nd	4,033	Seven seasons at 300 or better
Brett Bodine	48th	3,784	Nine seasons at 200 or better

Highest Career Performance Index Ratings For Drivers at Each Number of Victories Between Two and Nine

Driver	Wins	Rank	Rating	Special Achievement
James Hylton	2	11th	9,858	Eight top-four seasons
Bobby Hamilton	3	61st	3,284	Five seasons at 400 or better
Morgan Shepherd	4	21st	7,088	13 seasons at 300 or better
Dave Marcis	5	13th	9,612	25 seasons at 100 or better
Sterling Marlin	6	21st	7,374	12 seasons at 400 or better
Darel Dieringer	7	76th	2,568	Six top-21 seasons in a row
Kyle Petty	8	17th	8,206	19 seasons at 200 or better
Bob Welborn	9	79th	2,450	Five top-12 seasons

Because 10 drivers listed on those charts drove in Winston Cup races during the series' 51st season, the careers of Michael Waltrip, Ted Musgrave, Rick Mast, Dick Trickle, Hut Stricklin, Brett Bodine, Bobby Hamilton, Dave Marcis, Sterling Marlin, and Kyle Petty still may be a work in progress.

1977 in Review

Cale Yarborough earned a season-high nine victories and easily outdistanced Richard Petty in the Performance Index, 902-778, on his way to his second consecutive Winston Cup championship.

Most Memorable Race

Darrell Waltrip outdueled Yarborough, Benny Parsons, and Donnie Allison in one of the wildest four-car shootouts in Winston Cup history to capture the Winston 500 at Talladega, Ala., on May 1. Waltrip broke the draft down the backstretch by taking the lower groove on the track, but the other three drivers worked together to catch him. By the time the quartet exited the final turn, Yarborough had drawn even with Waltrip. With Yarborough and Parsons waging a fierce bumping duel, Waltrip won by three-tenths of a second, with Yarborough edging Parsons for second by a foot and Allison right behind in fourth. "Maybe it was superior driving," Yarborough said of Waltrip's daring move down the backstretch.

Most Significant Wreck

David Pearson's 2.5-second victory over Allison in the Southern 500 at Darlington, S.C., on September 5 might not have been possible had it not been for the accident that involved not only D.K. Ulrich and Terry Bivins, but Waltrip and Yarborough, who were battling for the lead when they crashed with 140 laps remaining.

Most Important Off-Track Development

Yarborough was fined twice, first for $200 and then for $500, during August when NASCAR officials discovered an oversized gas tank in his Junior Johnson-owned Chevrolet.

Records & Milestones

The 1977 season was one of only two in the modern era in which seven drivers won at least three poles. Leading the way was Neil Bonnett (6), followed by Richard Petty (5), Pearson (5), Allison (3), Parsons (3), Waltrip (3), and Yarborough (3).

1977 at a Glance

Races:	30
Road:	2
Short Track:	10
Superspeedway:	18
Winners:	7
Pole Winners:	9
Tracks:	16
States:	11

1977 Performance Index Rankings

1. Cale Yarborough (902)
2. Richard Petty (778)
3. Darrell Waltrip (769)
4. Benny Parsons (747)
5. Buddy Baker (625)
6. Dick Brooks (575)
7. David Pearson (552)
8. Buddy Arrington (508)
9. James Hylton (493)
10. Bobby Allison (454)
11. Richard Childress (451)
12. J.D. McDuffie (391)
13. Cecil Gordon (390)
14. Donnie Allison (381)
15. Skip Manning (379)
16. Neil Bonnett (340)
17. Sam Sommers (331)
18. Ricky Rudd (326)
19. Jimmy Means (293)
20. Janet Guthrie (288)
21. Tighe Scott (259)
22. D.K. Ulrich (253)
23. Coo Coo Marlin (249)
24. Dave Marcis (242)
25. Frank Warren (236)
26. Lennie Pond (177)
27. Ed Negre (163)
28. Bruce Hill (161)
29. Bill Elliott (144)
30. Dick May (138)
31. A.J. Foyt; Butch Hartman (131)
33. Tommy Gale (125)
34. Gary B. Myers (111)
35. G.C. Spencer (100)
36. Ferrel Harris; Ron Hutcherson (97)
38. Terry Ryan (94)
39. Bobby Wawak (78)
40. Morgan Shepherd (62)
41. Terry Bivins (60)
42. Ramo Stott (54)
43. Henley Gray (52)
44. Harold Miller (50)
45. Sonny Easley; Peter Knab (48)
47. Jimmy Lee Capps; Joe Mihalic (44)
49. Baxter Price (40)
50. Bob Burcham (36)
51. Walter Ballard (35)
52. Kenny Brightbill (28)
53. Joe Ruttman (27)
54. Jimmy Insolo; Billy McGinnis; Jody Ridley (26)
57. Grant Adcox; Mike Kempton; Jim Vandiver; Roland Wlodyka (25)
61. Norm Palmer (24)
62. Hershel McGriff; Bill Seifert (23)
64. Harry Jefferson; Hugh Pearson; Marty Robbins (22)
67. Dean Dalton; Steve Moore (21)
69. Eddie Bradshaw; Elliott Forbes-Robinson; Jim Hurtubise; Randy Myers (20)
73. Jimmy Hensley; Elmo Langley (19)
75. Chuck Bown; John Dineen (17)
77. Bill Baker; Jim Thirkettle (14)
79. David Sisco; Chuck Wahl (12)
81. Junior Miller; Bill Schmitt (11)
83. Gary Johnson; Robin Schildnecht; Ernie Stierly (10)
86. Ralph Jones; Rick Newsom (9)
88. Earl Brooks (8)
89. Roger Hamby; Ronnie Thomas (6)

1977 Events

Winston Western 500; Riverside Int. Raceway/2.62-m road/312m
David Pearson (Mercury)/Cale Yarborough (Chevrolet)

Daytona 500; Daytona International Speedway/2.5-m/500 miles
Cale Yarborough (Chevrolet)/Donnie Allison (Chevrolet)

Richmond 400; Richmond Fairgrounds Raceway/.542-m/217 miles
Cale Yarborough (Chevrolet)/Neil Bonnett (Dodge)

Carolina 500; North Carolina Motor Speedway/1.017-mile/500 m
Richard Petty (Dodge)/Donnie Allison (Chevrolet)

Atlanta 500; Atlanta International Raceway/1.522-m/500 miles
Richard Petty (Dodge)/Richard Petty (Dodge)

Gwyn Staley 400; North Wilkesboro Speedway/.625-m/250 miles
Cale Yarborough (Chevrolet)/Neil Bonnett (Dodge)

Rebel 500; Darlington International Raceway/1.366-mile/500 m
Darrell Waltrip (Chevrolet)/David Pearson (Mercury)

Southeastern 500; Bristol International Speedway/.533-m/267m
Cale Yarborough (Chevrolet)/Cale Yarborough (Chevrolet)

Virginia 500; Martinsville Speedway/.525-mile/263 miles
Cale Yarborough (Chevrolet)/Neil Bonnett (Dodge)

Winston 500; Alabama Int. Motor Speedway/2.66-mile/500 miles
Darrell Waltrip (Chevrolet)/A.J. Foyt (Chevrolet)

Music City USA 420; Nashville Speedway/.596-mile/250 miles
Benny Parsons (Chevrolet)/Darrell Waltrip (Chevrolet)

Mason-Dixon 500; Dover Downs Int. Speedway/1-mile/500 miles
Cale Yarborough (Chevrolet)/Richard Petty (Dodge)

World 600; Charlotte Motor Speedway/1.5-mile/600 miles
Richard Petty (Dodge)/David Pearson (Mercury)

NAPA Riverside 400; Riverside Int. Raceway/2.62-m road/249 m
Richard Petty (Dodge)/Richard Petty (Dodge)

Cam2 Motor Oil 400; Michigan Int. Speedway/2-mile/400 miles
Cale Yarborough (Chevrolet)/David Pearson (Mercury)

Firecracker 400; Daytona International Speedway/2.5-m/400 m
Richard Petty (Dodge)/Neil Bonnett (Dodge)

Nashville 420; Nashville Speedway/.596-mile/250 miles
Darrell Waltrip (Chevrolet)/Benny Parsons (Chevrolet)

Coca-Cola 500; Pocono International Raceway/2.5-m/500 miles
Benny Parsons (Chevrolet)/Darrell Waltrip (Chevrolet)

Talladega 500; Alabama Int. Motor Speedway/2.66-m/500 miles
Donnie Allison (Chevrolet)/Benny Parsons (Chevrolet)

Champion Spark Plug 400; Michigan Int. Speedway/2-mile/400 m
Darrell Waltrip (Chevrolet)/David Pearson (Mercury)

Volunteer 400; Bristol International Speedway/.533-mile/213m
Cale Yarborough (Chevrolet)/Cale Yarborough (Chevrolet)

Southern 500; Darlington Int. Raceway/1.366-mile/500 miles
David Pearson (Mercury)/Darrell Waltrip (Chevrolet)

Capital City 400; Richmond Fairgrounds Raceway/.542-m/217 m
Neil Bonnett (Dodge)/Benny Parsons (Chevrolet)

Delaware 500; Dover Downs Int. Speedway/1-mile/500 miles
Benny Parsons (Chevrolet)/Neil Bonnett (Dodge)

Old Dominion 500; Martinsville Speedway/.525-mile/263 miles
Cale Yarborough (Chevrolet)/Neil Bonnett (Dodge)

Wilkes 400; North Wilkesboro Speedway/.625-mile/250 miles
Darrell Waltrip (Chevrolet)/Richard Petty (Dodge)

NAPA National 500; Charlotte Motor Speedway/1.5-m/500 miles
Benny Parsons (Chevrolet)/David Pearson (Mercury)

American 500; North Carolina Motor Speedway/1.017-mile/500 m
Donnie Allison (Chevrolet)/Donnie Allison (Chevrolet)

Dixie 500; Atlanta International Raceway/1.522-m/500 miles
Darrell Waltrip (Chevrolet)/Sam Sommers (Chevrolet)

Los Angeles Times 500; Ontario Motor Speedway/2.5-mile/500 m
Neil Bonnett (Dodge)/Richard Petty (Dodge)

Victories

1. Cale Yarborough (9)
2. Darrell Waltrip (6)
3. Richard Petty (5)
4. Benny Parsons (4)
5. Donnie Allison; Neil Bonnett; David Pearson (2)

Poles

1. Neil Bonnett (6)
2. David Pearson; Richard Petty (5)
4. Donnie Allison; Benny Parsons; Darrell Waltrip; Cale Yarborough (3)
8. A.J. Foyt; Sam Sommers (1)

Victories

1. Chevrolet (21)
2. Dodge (7)
3. Mercury (2)

Poles

1. Chevrolet (14)
2. Dodge (11)
3. Mercury (5)

1978
Was Yarborough The Best Driver Ever?

If Cale Yarborough ever thought there was a way to drive a race car other than mashing the gas pedal to the floor and trying to lead every lap—especially the last one—he never demonstrated it.

Although countless others with the same philosophy often saw their victory hopes evaporate because they pushed their machine beyond its capabilities or their aggression resulted in a careless mistake, Yarborough managed to end 83 Winston Cup races with a celebration in victory lane and is the only driver to earn three consecutive Winston Cup titles (1976-78).

"Cale's probably the best race driver in the world right now," Maurice Petty, Richard's brother and engine builder, said in the late '70s. "I don't think there is anybody else who can drive as hard as he does every lap and still be around at the end—and win."

A year after Dale Earnhardt tied Richard Petty's record of seven Winston Cup championships by winning the 1994 title, he was being questioned about his achievements and his chances of capturing an eighth crown during a post-race news conference. Between questions, he leaned over and told the moderator: "These questions are fun, but everybody knows Cale was the best ever."

Yarborough may or may not have been the best stock-car driver of all-time, but certainly any serious debate should include his name. And Yarborough wouldn't participate in the debate unless it's serious. When he teamed with David Pearson, Bobby Allison, Buddy Baker, Darrell Waltrip, and Richard Petty in the '70s to record an album, NASCAR Goes Country, the recordings became the talk of the sport for months. And it wasn't because people were suggesting that Baker and Pearson, for example, should quit their day jobs.

Yarborough, however, didn't find the album humorous. "I took it seriously," he said. "I take *everything* I do seriously."

Yarborough led the Performance Index in each of his three championship seasons. During the eight years (1973-80) he drove for Junior Johnson, primarily in Chevrolets, he never finished worse than ninth in the Performance Index, including five consecutive seasons (1976-80) in the top three. Yarborough's Performance Index of 11,358 ranks ninth on the all-time list. And only four drivers posted more top-25 seasons (22), while just three posted more top-two campaigns (6).

Yarborough captured multiple victories 13 years in a row (1973-85), the second-longest such streak in history, and his eight consecutive years behind the wheel of Johnson's cars each produced at least three victories, a string only two others have bettered. In each of his championship campaigns, Yarborough won at least nine races, a record matched in the modern era only by Jeff Gordon. Yarborough ranks in the top five in victories, poles (69), and consecutive seasons with at least one pole (12 from 1973-84). He also captured a record-tying five consecutive poles in 1980, when he won a modern-record 14 poles in a season, including a record-tying five in a row on short tracks.

Yarborough, who led the Winston Cup Series in victories four times and in poles on three occasions, was equally feared on superspeedways and short tracks. From 1973-85, Yarborough captured at least one superspeedway victory, a 13-year string equaled only by Richard Petty. In each of those 13 seasons, however, Yarborough posted multiple superspeedway victories. No other driver has had more than seven such campaigns in succession. He also captured at least one 500-mile triumph in each of those seasons, another record, and posted at least one Grand Slam victory a record 10 years in a row (1976-85). Yarborough is also the only driver to record two separate strings of four consecutive years of multiple 500-mile victories, accomplishing that feat from 1977-80 and again from 1982-85.

Yarborough captured six consecutive Grand Slam poles in 1969 and 1970, and he ranks in the top five in superspeedway victories (48), 500-mile wins (34), Grand Slam victories (24), superspeedway poles (46), Grand Slam poles (24), classic poles (7), superspeedway victories from the pole (9), Grand Slam triumphs from the pole

(4), classic wins from the pole (2), superspeedway victories from the pole (9), and 500-mile wins from the pole (7). Yarborough's streak of five consecutive seasons (1980-84) with multiple superspeedway poles ranks him in a second-place tie on the all-time list, and he also ranks fourth with nine classic victories—a record five in the Southern 500 at Darlington, S.C., and four more in the Daytona 500.

Yarborough not only is tied for third in short-track victories (31), but during his three consecutive championship seasons, he captured 18 of the 30 short-track races, including a record-tying eight in a row—the last four in 1976 and the first four in 1977. Yarborough was also an accomplished road racer, winning a record-tying two road races in one year (1974) and ranking in a 10th-place tie on the all-time list with three road victories.

Although Yarborough didn't make his first official start until the 1959 Southern 500, legend has it that he sneaked behind the wheel of a car during a race at fabled Darlington Raceway, just a few miles from his home in Timmonsville, only to be removed by NASCAR officials because of his age. That's certainly possible, because he made a brief relief appearance for Bob Weatherly in the 1957 Southern 500 at age 18.

Yarborough earned his first victory in a 100-mile dirt race at Valdosta, Ga., eight years later, then became one of the circuit's dominant drivers from 1967-70 while piloting the Wood brothers' Fords and Mercurys. After he spent the next two years primarily driving poorly financed, power-starved Indy-cars, Yarborough returned to the Winston Cup Series in 1973 for an eight-year stint driving for Johnson that became one of the most successful driver-owner combinations in history.

Yarborough left Johnson after the 1980 season, saying he wanted to run a limited schedule in order to spend more time with his family. He won 14 times during the next five seasons, all on superspeedways, includ-

ing a daring last-lap slingshot of Waltrip to capture the 1984 Daytona 500 and a last-lap pass of Harry Gant to win the Winston 500 at Talladega, Ala., that same season. Yarborough was 46 when he won the latter event, which featured a Winston Cup-record 75 lead changes among 13 drivers.

After three winless seasons, Yarborough retired after the 1988 campaign to form his own team. "I had no regrets whatsoever," he said. "I wouldn't change a thing. I'm happy I had a good career."

That he did.

1978 in Review

Yarborough became the first Winston Cup champion since Richard Petty in 1967 who also held the undisputed season lead in both victories (10) and poles (8). He also led the Performance Index by a healthy 870-738 margin over Allison.

Most Memorable Race

Yarborough passed Baker in the tri-oval on the final lap to win the Winston 500 on May 14 at Talladega. "If I'd tried him down the backstretch, he might have had time to pass me back," Yarborough said.

Most Significant Wreck

Yarborough's ability to avoid a crash on September 4 enabled him to edge Waltrip and become the first driver to win the Southern 500 four times. Grant Adcox, Coo Coo Marlin, D.K. Ulrich, and Pearson were involved in the wreck with 200 laps remaining. "I just did miss it," Yarborough said. "After Coo Coo hit Adcox, I just barely squeezed under them."

Most Important Off-Track Development

After driving Chrysler products for all but nine of his 185 victories, Richard Petty switched from a Dodge Magnum he called "hopeless" to a Chevrolet in August.

Records & Milestones

Lennie Pond won half of the season's 10 short-track poles, including four in a row—one shy of the record. Ironically, those were the only five poles of Pond's career. . . . Yarborough's victory in the season-opening Winston Western 500 at Riverside, Calif., was the first

Cale Yarborough, the only driver to win three consecutive Winston Cup championships during the circuit's first 51 years, was equally successful on superspeedways and short tracks. He earned multiple superspeedway victories a record 13 years in a row and claimed 18 of 30 short-track events held during his championship string.

for Oldsmobile since Lee Petty captured a 100-mile dirt race at the Charlotte Fairgrounds on May 22, 1959.

President Carter and his wife, Rosalynn, played host to the NASCAR drivers, crews, officials, and media at the White House during the week before the September 17 Delaware 500 at Dover Downs International Speedway. President Carter, who worked at Atlanta International Raceway during race weekends in the '60s before he was elected Georgia's governor, was unable to attend because he was at Camp David to negotiate peace in the Middle East.

1978 at a Glance

Races:	30
Road:	2
Short Track:	10
Superspeedway:	18
Winners:	7
Pole Winners:	9
Tracks:	16
States:	11

1978 Performance Index Rankings

1. Cale Yarborough (870)
2. Bobby Allison (738)
3. Dave Marcis (725)
4. Benny Parsons (701)
5. Darrell Waltrip (656)
6. Dick Brooks (582)
7. Buddy Arrington (580)
8. Lennie Pond (575)
9. Richard Petty (568)
10. Richard Childress (468)
11. David Pearson (414)
12. J.D. McDuffie (382)
13. Dick May (354)
14. Tighe Scott (336)
15. Donnie Allison (307)
16. D.K. Ulrich (297)
17. Neil Bonnett (292)
18. Buddy Baker (283)
19. Jimmy Means (280)
20. James Hylton (275)
21. Tommy Gale; Roger Hamby (271)
23. Frank Warren (251)
24. Bill Elliott (248)
25. Ferrel Harris (239)
26. Cecil Gordon (238)
27. Ronnie Thomas (234)
28. Skip Manning (215)
29. Gary B. Myers (173)
30. Grant Adcox (166)
31. Baxter Price (163)
32. Dale Earnhardt (149)
33. Bruce Hill (148)
34. Al Holbert (140)
35. Ricky Rudd (121)
36. Terry Labonte (98)
37. Ed Negre; Satch Worley (85)
39. Janet Guthrie (81)
40. Joe Frasson (73)
41. Jim Thirkettle (64)
42. Coo Coo Marlin (63)
43. Jimmy Insolo; Connie Saylor (56)
45. Harry Gant (54)
46. Bill Schmitt; Roland Wlodyka (48)
48. Ralph Jones (47)
49. Blackie Wangerin (46)
50. Earle Canavan (44)
51. Ron Hutcherson (41)
52. A.J. Foyt; Hershel McGriff (37)
54. Sterling Marlin (36)
55. Rick McCray (35)
56. Morgan Shepherd (33)
57. Richard White (32)
58. John Utsman (29)
59. Sam Sommers (28)
60. Jerry Jolly; Bobby Wawak (25)
62. Ray Elder (24)
63. Dave Watson (23)
64. Claude Ballot-Lena; Marty Robbins (22)
66. Joe Mihalic; Nestor Peles; Roy Smith (21)
69. Woody Fisher; Glenn Jarrett; Rocky Moran (20)
72. Norm Palmer (16)
73. Lynn Carroll; Harry Goularte; Ernie Stierly (11)
76. Junior Miller (10)
77. Joe Booher; Elmo Langley (9)
79. Nelson Oswald (7)
80. Joey Arrington; Jimmy Lee Capps (2)

1978 Events

Winston Western 500; Riverside Int. Raceway/2.62-m road/312m
Cale Yarborough (Oldsmobile)/David Pearson (Mercury)

Daytona 500; Daytona International Speedway/2.5-m/500 miles
Bobby Allison (Ford)/Cale Yarborough (Oldsmobile)

Richmond 400; Richmond Fairgrounds Raceway/.542-m/217 miles
Benny Parsons (Chevrolet)/Neil Bonnett (Dodge)

Carolina 500; North Carolina Motor Speedway/1.017-mile/500 m
David Pearson (Mercury)/Neil Bonnett (Dodge)

Atlanta 500; Atlanta International Raceway/1.522-m/500 miles
Bobby Allison (Ford)/Cale Yarborough (Oldsmobile)

Southeastern 500; Bristol International Raceway/.533-m/267 m
Darrell Waltrip (Chevrolet)/Neil Bonnett (Dodge)

Rebel 500; Darlington International Raceway/1.366-mile/500 m
Benny Parsons (Chevrolet)/Bobby Allison (Ford)

Gwyn Staley 400; North Wilkesboro Speedway/.625-m/250 miles
Darrell Waltrip (Chevrolet)/Benny Parsons (Chevrolet)

Virginia 500; Martinsville Speedway/.525-mile/263 miles
Darrell Waltrip (Chevrolet)/Lennie Pond (Chevrolet)

Winston 500; Alabama Int. Motor Speedway/2.66-mile/500 miles
Cale Yarborough (Oldsmobile)/Cale Yarborough (Oldsmobile)

Mason-Dixon 500; Dover Downs Int. Speedway/1-mile/500 miles
David Pearson (Mercury)/Buddy Baker (Chevrolet)

World 600; Charlotte Motor Speedway/1.5-mile/600 miles
Darrell Waltrip (Chevrolet)/David Pearson (Mercury)

Music City USA 420; Nashville Speedway/.596-mile/250 miles
Cale Yarborough (Oldsmobile)/Lennie Pond (Chevrolet)

NAPA Riverside 400; Riverside Int. Raceway/2.62-m road/249 m
Benny Parsons (Chevrolet)/David Pearson (Mercury)

Gabriel 400; Michigan International Speedway/2-m/400 miles
Cale Yarborough (Oldsmobile)/David Pearson (Mercury)

Firecracker 400; Daytona International Speedway/2.5-m/400 m
David Pearson (Mercury)/Cale Yarborough (Oldsmobile)

Nashville 420; Nashville Speedway/.596-mile/250 miles
Cale Yarborough (Oldsmobile)/Lennie Pond (Chevrolet)

Coca-Cola 500; Pocono International Raceway/2.5-m/500 miles
Darrell Waltrip (Chevrolet)/Benny Parsons (Chevrolet)

Talladega 500; Alabama Int. Motor Speedway/2.66-m/500 miles
Lennie Pond (Oldsmobile)/Cale Yarborough (Oldsmobile)

Champion Spark Plug 400; Michigan Int. Speedway/2-mile/400 m
David Pearson (Mercury)/David Pearson (Mercury)

Volunteer 500; Bristol International Raceway/.533-mile/267 m
Cale Yarborough (Oldsmobile)/Lennie Pond (Oldsmobile)

Southern 500; Darlington International Raceway/1.366-m/500 m
Cale Yarborough (Oldsmobile)/David Pearson (Mercury)

Capital City 400; Richmond Fairgrounds Raceway/.542-m/217 m
Darrell Waltrip (Chevrolet)/Darrell Waltrip (Chevrolet)

Delaware 500; Dover Downs Int. Speedway/1-mile/500 miles
Bobby Allison (Ford)/J.D. McDuffie (Chevrolet)

Old Dominion 500; Martinsville Speedway/.525-mile/263 miles
Cale Yarborough (Oldsmobile)/Lennie Pond (Chevrolet)

Wilkes 400; North Wilkesboro Speedway/.625-mile/250 miles
Cale Yarborough (Oldsmobile)/Darrell Waltrip (Chevrolet)

NAPA National 500; Charlotte Motor Speedway/1.5-m/500 miles
Bobby Allison (Ford)/David Pearson (Mercury)

American 500; North Carolina Motor Speedway/1.017-mile/500 m
Cale Yarborough (Oldsmobile)/Cale Yarborough (Oldsmobile)

Dixie 500; Atlanta International Raceway/1.522-m/500 miles
Donnie Allison (Chevrolet)/Cale Yarborough (Oldsmobile)

Los Angeles Times 500; Ontario Motor Speedway/2.5-mile/500 m
Bobby Allison (Ford)/Cale Yarborough (Oldsmobile)

Victories

1. Cale Yarborough (10)
2. Darrell Waltrip (6)
3. Bobby Allison (5)
4. David Pearson (4)
5. Benny Parsons (3)
6. Donnie Allison; Lennie Pond (1)

Poles

1. Cale Yarborough (8)
2. David Pearson (7)
3. Lennie Pond (5)
4. Neil Bonnett (3)
5. Benny Parsons; Darrell Waltrip (2)
7. Bobby Allison; Buddy Baker; J.D. McDuffie (1)

Victories

1. Oldsmobile (11)
2. Chevrolet (10)
3. Ford (5)
4. Mercury (4)

Poles

1. Chevrolet (10)
2. Oldsmobile (9)
3. Mercury (7)
4. Dodge (3)
5. Ford (1)

1979
There's No Easy Definition For Rookies

Six Winston Cup champions—Richard Petty, David Pearson, Dale Earnhardt, Rusty Wallace, Alan Kulwicki, and Jeff Gordon—first demonstrated their future promise by earning Rookie of the Year acclaim.

Or did they? Earnhardt had a Performance Index rating of 149—spectacular considering that he made only four starts—in 1978, a year *before* his 1979 Rookie of the Year campaign.

The rules governing the Rookie of the Year award during the Winston Cup Series' 51st season stated that a driver who has competed in no more than five Winston Cup races in a single season is eligible for Rookie of the Year acclaim. That hasn't always been the case, however. Petty, for example, competed in nine races in 1958, yet was the 1959 Rookie of the Year.

To determine its Winston Cup Rookie of the Year, NASCAR uses only a rookie's 15 best race finishes and awards:

- One point to any rookie who earns a berth in the starting lineup;
- 10 points to the highest-finishing rookie, nine to the second-highest rookie finisher, etc.;
- 10 points for a victory, nine points for a runner-up finish, etc., through 10th place;
- 10 points to the highest rookie in the Winston Cup standings after the 10th, 20th, and final races; nine points to the second-highest rookie in the Winston Cup standings at those three points in the season, etc., through the top 10 rookies;
- "Discretionary" points—whatever those are.

And while Jimmy Hensley and Dick Trickle certainly met the existing eligibility requirements during their Rookie of the Year campaigns, they competed in their first Winston Cup races 20 and 19 years, respectively, before they earned Rookie of the Year honors.

There are, of course, countless ways a driver's eligibility for Rookie of the Year honors could be determined and certainly simpler, if not as necessarily as equitable, methods to determine the winner. The Rookie Performance Index recognizes drivers only in the first year they post a top-20 finish and, subsequently, are listed in the Performance Index. Therefore, those drivers who, like Earnhardt in 1978, made four or fewer starts in order to preserve their Rookie of the Year eligibility, are at an obvious disadvantage. The Rookie Performance Index leader is simply the highest-finishing driver in the Performance Index ratings who doesn't have a previous top-20 finish. As a bonus, determining the Rookie Performance Index leader doesn't require a doctorate in math or even a working knowledge of calculus or logarithms.

Considering the vast differences in eligibility requirements, it shouldn't be surprising that only 11 NASCAR Rookie of the Year award winners—Pearson, Tom Cox, Pete Hamilton, Dick Brooks, Lennie Pond, Ron Bouchard, Ken Bouchard, Bobby Hamilton, Ricky Craven, Johnny Benson Jr., and Tony Stewart—also were the Rookie Performance Index leaders.

The highest Rookie Performance Index rating—almost double that of his nearest challenger—was the 859 Stewart posted during his three-victory campaign to rank fourth in the 1999 Performance Index. The second-best rating came during Gordon's 1993 Rookie of the Year campaign. Ironically, however, that 441 rating belonged to Bobby Labonte, who was 15th in the Performance

Using a criteria that defines a driver as a rookie in the first season in which he earns a top-20 finish, the second-best season for a first-year Winston Cup driver came in 1993, when Jeff Gordon earned Rookie of the Year acclaim. Ironically, however, Gordon's Performance Index of 420 was only the fourth-highest rating for a driver in the first year he recorded a top-20 finish. That same season, Bobby Labonte (pictured) posted a 441 rating, the best for a driver in the first year he earned a top-20 finish until it was eclipsed by teammate Tony Stewart in 1999.

Index, two spots higher than Gordon, who had a 420 rating. Labonte had driven in two Winston Cup races and Gordon one prior to 1993, but neither had logged a top-20 finish. The only other driver who ever posted a higher Rookie Performance Index rating than Gordon was Ralph Moody, who, like Stewart, had not driven in a Winston Cup race before his rookie campaign, which produced a 434 Performance Index rating—and a rookie-record four victories—in 1956. Although he didn't meet the Performance Index's definition of a rookie, the highest finish by a Rookie of the Year was the second-place effort in the 1966 Performance Index logged by James Hylton's 756 rating.

Note that Darrell Waltrip, who in 1973 lost to Pond in one of the most celebrated Rookie of the Year battles ever staged, was the Rookie Performance Index leader—*a year earlier.* Although six NASCAR Rookie of the Year award winners became Winston Cup champions, only three Rookie Performance Index leaders have done so—Pearson, Waltrip, and Red Byron, who, like everyone in 1949, Winston Cup racing's inaugural season, was a rookie.

Rookie Performance Index Leaders

1949—Red Byron	1966—Blackie Watt	1983—Trevor Boys
1950—Fireball Roberts	1967—George Davis	1984—Doug Heveron
1951—Buddy Shuman	1968—Pete Hamilton	1985—Eddie Bierschwale
1952—Perk Brown	1969—Dick Brooks	1986—Chet Fillip
1953—Andy Winfree	1970—Joe Frasson	1987—Steve Christman
1954—Blackie Pitt	1971—Richard D. Brown	1988—Ken Bouchard
1955—Gene Simpson	1972—Darrell Waltrip	1989—Jimmy Spencer
1956—Ralph Moody	1973—Lennie Pond	1990—Jack Pennington
1957—L.D. Austin	1974—Jackie Rogers	1991—Bobby Hamilton
1958—Shorty Rollins	1975—Bruce Jacobi	1992—Mike Wallace
1959—Bob Burdick	1976—Jimmy Means	1993—Bobby Labonte
1960—David Pearson	1977—Ron Hutcherson	1994—Todd Bodine
1961—Bob Barron	1978—Al Holbert	1995—Ricky Craven
1962—Tom Cox	1979—Kyle Petty	1996—Johnny Benson Jr.
1963—Larry Manning	1980—Lake Speed	1997—David Green
1964—Buddy Arrington	1981—Ron Bouchard	1998—Buckshot Jones
1965—Larry Hess	1982—Philip Duffie	1999—Tony Stewart

1979 in Review

The 1979 season was the first, and one of only two seasons in history, in which the driver who led the Winston Cup standings entering the season finale failed to capture the title. Waltrip carried a two-point lead over Petty into the last race of the season, the Los Angeles Times 500 at Ontario, Calif. Petty finished fifth and Waltrip eighth, giving Petty his seventh Winston Cup title by a 4,830-4,819 margin. Petty held an equally slim edge over Waltrip in the Performance Index, 873-867. Waltrip's seven victories and Buddy Baker's seven poles paced the Winston Cup Series in those categories.

Most Memorable Race

With less than half a lap remaining in the Daytona 500 on February 18, Donnie Allison led Cale Yarborough by inches, with their nearest challengers more than a mile behind. As the leaders entered the third turn, Yarborough's Junior Johnson-owned Oldsmobile appeared to drift high into Allison. Then, Allison's Hoss Ellington-owned Chevrolet appeared to drift low into Yarborough. The cars then bumped a second time, much harder, and Yarborough's machine shoved Allison's into the outside wall. While they slid down the banking toward the infield grass, Petty made up his deficit to nip Waltrip by a car length, with A.J. Foyt another five car lengths behind. During the cool-down lap, Bobby Allison—who had been involved in a wreck with his brother and Yarborough while battling for the lead on the 30th of 200 laps—stopped to examine the damage to the two wrecked cars. Within seconds, a national TV audience was treated to a fistfight between the Allisons and Yarborough. Here is each participant's version of the events:

Donnie: "When (Yarborough) tried to pass me low, he went off the track. He spun and hit me. When Bobby came up to find out if we were all right, Cale went over and punched Bobby right through the netting in his window."

Yarborough: "My left wheels were over the dirt, and Donnie knocked me over on the dirt further. I started spinning, and Donnie started spinning. It was the worst thing I've ever seen in racing. It just felt like I was being double teamed."

Bobby: "I felt like it was bad all the way around. It was a spontaneous thing. Certainly, it was a malicious act, but it was not the big deal that some people made of it."

Petty: "I figured I was racing for third place. I sure lucked out on this one."

Most Significant Wreck

Dave Watson had led six consecutive laps in the Atlanta 500 on March 18 when he drove his Chevrolet down pit road on the 123rd lap. "I was out of gas when I came into the pits," Watson said. "I pushed the clutch in to try and restart it. When I did, something locked up on the rear end. The car just took off like it was on a piece of ice." Watson's attempt to reach his pit safely failed, and his car skidded into 18-year-old crew member Dennis Wade, who was killed when he tumbled nearly 100 feet down pit road. Watson not only parked his car, but he never competed in Winston Cup racing again.

Most Important Off-Track Development

As Pearson neared the exit to pit road in the Rebel 500 at Darlington, S.C., on April 8, both left wheels fell off of the Wood brothers' Mercury. Pearson had thought his crew was changing only right-side tires and left his pit without lug nuts on the left-side tires. It was announced the next morning that the Wood brothers had fired Pearson after seven years and 43 victories.

Records & Milestones

The 1979 campaign was the first in the modern era in which six drivers won three or more races: Waltrip, Bobby Allison (5), Petty (5), Yarborough (4), Neil Bonnett (3), and Baker (3). The only other seasons in the modern era in which six drivers won at least three races were 1995 and 1999.

1979 at a Glance

Races:	31
Road:	2
Short Track:	10
Superspeedway:	19
Winners:	9
Pole Winners:	12
Tracks:	17
States:	12

1979 Performance Index Rankings

1. Richard Petty (873)
2. Darrell Waltrip (867)
3. Cale Yarborough (790)
4. Bobby Allison (753)
5. Benny Parsons (654)
6. Joe Millikan (603)
7. Ricky Rudd (594)
8. Dale Earnhardt (593)
9. Richard Childress (554)
10. Buddy Arrington (505)
11. Buddy Baker (482)
12. Terry Labonte (455)
13. D.K. Ulrich (452)
14. James Hylton (443)
15. J.D. McDuffie (403)
16. Donnie Allison (375)
17. Dick Brooks (359)
18. Tighe Scott (311)
19. Dave Marcis (295)
20. Harry Gant (290)
21. Neil Bonnett (284)
22. Frank Warren (273)
23. Bill Elliott (267)
24. Tommy Gale (260)
25. Cecil Gordon (233)
26. Jimmy Means (216)
27. David Pearson; Ronnie Thomas (187)
29. Baxter Price (145)
30. Lennie Pond (127)
31. Bruce Hill (122)
32. Chuck Bown (119)
33. Kyle Petty (101)
34. Dick May (92)
35. Ed Negre (74)
36. John Anderson (73)
37. Roger Hamby (71)
38. A.J. Foyt (67)
39. Coo Coo Marlin (66)
40. Jody Ridley (65)
41. Slick Johnson (57)
42. Grant Adcox; Blackie Wangerin (55)
44. Bill Schmitt (48)
45. Al Holbert (47)
46. Freddy Smith (46)
47. H.B. Bailey (39)
48. Bill Elswick; John Kennedy (37)
50. Dave Watson (35)
51. Bill Dennis (31)
52. Ralph Jones (30)
53. Bob Burcham; Butch Hartman; Buck Simmons; Jim Vandiver (26)
57. Rick Newsom (25)
58. Kevin Housby; John Rezek (24)
60. Steve Moore (23)
61. Norm Palmer; Connie Saylor; Jim Thirkettle (22)
64. Jimmy Finger; Nestor Peles; Tim Williamson (21)
67. Steve Peles (20)
68. Gary Balough (19)
69. Hal Callentine; Billy Hagan; Steve Spencer (18)
72. Earle Canavan; Vince Giamformaggio (17)
74. Sandy Satullo (16)
75. Ed Hale (15)
76. Jimmy Insolo; Richard White (14)

78. Wayne Watercutter (13)
79. Bobby Wawak; Dick Whalen (11)
81. John Borneman; Al Elmore; Sterling Marlin (10)
84. Mike Potter; Ernie Shaw (9)
86. Mike Kempton (7)
87. Dave Dion (2)
88. Joe Fields (1)

1979 Events

Winston Western 500; Riverside Int. Raceway/2.62-m road/312m
Darrell Waltrip (Chevrolet)/David Pearson (Mercury)

Daytona 500; Daytona International Speedway/2.5-m/500 miles
Richard Petty (Oldsmobile)/Buddy Baker (Oldsmobile)

Carolina 500; North Carolina Motor Speedway/1.017-mile/500 m
Bobby Allison (Ford)/Bobby Allison (Ford)

Richmond 400; Richmond Fairgrounds Raceway/.542-m/217 miles
Cale Yarborough (Oldsmobile)/Bobby Allison (Ford)

Atlanta 500; Atlanta International Raceway/1.522-m/500 miles
Buddy Baker (Oldsmobile)/Buddy Baker (Oldsmobile)

Northwestern Bank 400; No. Wilkesboro Speedway/.625-m/250 m
Bobby Allison (Ford)/Benny Parsons (Chevrolet)

Southeastern 500; Bristol International Raceway/.533-m/267 m
Dale Earnhardt (Chevrolet)/Buddy Baker (Chevrolet)

CRC Chem. Rebel 500; Darlington Int. Raceway/1.366-m/500 m
Darrell Waltrip (Chevrolet)/Donnie Allison (Chevrolet)

Virginia 500; Martinsville Speedway/.525-mile/263 miles
Richard Petty (Chevrolet)/Darrell Waltrip (Chevrolet)

Winston 500; Alabama Int. Motor Speedway/2.66-mile/500 miles
Bobby Allison (Ford)/Darrell Waltrip (Oldsmobile)

Sun-Drop Music City USA 420; Nash. Int. Race./.596-mile/250m
Cale Yarborough (Oldsmobile)/Joe Millikan (Chevrolet)

Mason-Dixon 500; Dover Downs Int. Speedway/1-mile/500 miles
Neil Bonnett (Mercury)/Darrell Waltrip (Chevrolet)

World 600; Charlotte Motor Speedway/1.5-mile/600 miles
Darrell Waltrip (Chevrolet)/Neil Bonnett (Mercury)

Texas 400; Texas World Speedway/2-mile/400 miles
Darrell Waltrip (Chevrolet)/Buddy Baker (Chevrolet)

NAPA Riverside 400; Riverside Int. Raceway/2.62-m road/249 m
Bobby Allison (Ford)/Dale Earnhardt (Chevrolet)

Gabriel 400; Michigan International Speedway/2-m/400 miles
Buddy Baker (Chevrolet)/Neil Bonnett (Mercury)

Firecracker 400; Daytona International Speedway/2.5-m/400 m
Neil Bonnett (Mercury)/Buddy Baker (Oldsmobile)

Busch Nashville 420; Nashville Int. Raceway/.596-m/250 miles
Darrell Waltrip (Chevrolet)/Darrell Waltrip (Chevrolet)

Coca-Cola 500; Pocono International Raceway/2.5-m/500 miles
Cale Yarborough (Chevrolet)/Harry Gant (Chevrolet)

Talladega 500; Alabama Int. Motor Speedway/2.66-m/500 miles
Darrell Waltrip (Oldsmobile)/Neil Bonnett (Mercury)

Champion Spark Plug 400; Michigan Int. Speedway/2-mile/400 m
Richard Petty (Chevrolet)/David Pearson (Chevrolet)

Volunteer 500; Bristol International Raceway/.533-mile/267 m
Darrell Waltrip (Chevrolet)/Richard Petty (Chevrolet)

Southern 500; Darlington Int. Raceway/1.366-mile/500 miles
David Pearson (Chevrolet)/Bobby Allison (Ford)

Capital City 400; Richmond Fairgrounds Raceway/.542-m/217 m
Bobby Allison (Ford)/Dale Earnhardt (Chevrolet)

CRC Chemicals 500; Dover Downs Int. Speedway/1-m/500 miles
Richard Petty (Chevrolet)/Dale Earnhardt (Chevrolet)

Old Dominion 500; Martinsville Speedway/.525-mile/263 miles
Buddy Baker (Chevrolet)/Darrell Waltrip (Chevrolet)

NAPA National 500; Charlotte Motor Speedway/1.5-m/500 miles
Cale Yarborough (Chevrolet)/Neil Bonnett (Mercury)

Holly Farms 400; North Wilkesboro Speedway/.625-m/250 miles
Benny Parsons (Chevrolet)/Dale Earnhardt (Chevrolet)

American 500; North Carolina Motor Speedway/1.017-mile/500 m
Richard Petty (Chevrolet)/Buddy Baker (Chevrolet)

Dixie 500; Atlanta International Raceway/1.522-m/500 miles
Neil Bonnett (Mercury)/Buddy Baker (Chevrolet)

Los Angeles Times 500; Ontario Motor Speedway/2.5-mile/500 m
Benny Parsons (Chevrolet)/Cale Yarborough (Oldsmobile)

Victories

1. Darrell Waltrip (7)
2. Bobby Allison; Richard Petty (5)
4. Cale Yarborough (4)
5. Buddy Baker; Neil Bonnett (3)
7. Benny Parsons (2)
8. Dale Earnhardt; David Pearson (1)

Poles

1. Buddy Baker (7)
2. Darrell Waltrip (5)
3. Neil Bonnett; Dale Earnhardt (4)
5. Bobby Allison (3)
6. David Pearson (2)
7. Donnie Allison; Harry Gant; Joe Millikan; Benny Parsons; Richard Petty; Cale Yarborough (1)

Victories

1. Chevrolet (18)
2. Ford; Oldsmobile (5)
4. Mercury (3)

Poles

1. Chevrolet (18)
2. Mercury; Oldsmobile (5)
4. Ford (3)

1980
Baker's Imposing Size Overshadowed Long Career Of Consistent Productivity

Few drivers in history loomed as large as 6-foot-5 Buddy Baker, the 1980 Daytona 500 winner whose driving style seemingly involved using all of his considerably more than 200 pounds to mash the gas pedal to the floorboard.

Baker's career as a radio and television commentator has allowed the world to enjoy his marvelous sense of humor, often self-deprecating.

Hours before the 1994 Coca-Cola 600 at Charlotte Motor Speedway, Baker was watching the waning laps of the Indianapolis 500 on television. When the leader, Emerson Fittipaldi, wrecked while trying to pass Al Unser Jr., the only other driver in the lead lap, Baker shook his head and yelled at the television: "That's the dumbest thing I've seen . . . "

After a long pause, Baker added with a big grin, "I guess since I hit the pace car at Texas."

Baker led the 1969 Texas 500 at College Station with 21 laps to go until the Cotton Owens-owned Dodge he was driving suffered irreparable damage when he crashed into the back of another car during a caution period. Depending on the source, Baker either was trying to signal his pit crew or light a cigarette.

But Baker's size, modesty, wit, and impressive superspeedway resume often obscure his most significant achievement: Other than Richard Petty, no driver in Winston Cup history enjoyed a longer career of consistent productivity.

Baker finished in the top 10 in the Performance Index only six times, including 1973, when his career-high 649 rating was the season's second-highest. Baker never won the Winston Cup title or led the circuit in victories, so it's easy to overlook his considerable accomplishments: finishing in the top 20 in the Performance Index a record 24 consecutive seasons (1965-88) and posting 24 consecutive seasons with a rating of 200 or better, second only to Petty. Baker's 11,001 career Performance Index rating ranks 10th among the more than 2,700 drivers who have competed in Winston Cup racing.

Baker earned 19 victories and 38 poles, and the faster the speeds and the more prestige involved, the better he performed. He ranks in the top five in superspeedway poles (29) and Grand Slam poles (16), and only David Pearson and Fireball Roberts posted longer streaks of seasons with at least five superspeedway poles than the back-to-back campaigns (1979-80) Baker managed.

Baker ranks in the top 10 in Grand Slam victories (10), classic wins (5), classic poles (6), Grand Slam triumphs from the pole (3), classic victories from the pole (2), and 500-mile wins from the pole (3). His 17 superspeedway and 11 500-mile victories both rank among the top 12 on the all-time list.

Baker was only 18 years old when he made his Winston Cup debut on April 4, 1959, with a 14th-place finish at Columbia, S.C., in a Chevrolet owned by his father, Buck, winner of the 1956 and 1957 Winston Cup titles. After Buddy, a Charlotte native, captured his first victory in the 1967 National 500 at Charlotte in a Dodge owned by Ray Fox, Buck told *The Atlanta Journal:* "That boy of mine is a race driver."

Buddy, the first driver to win the World 600 three times, later called his victory in Owens's Dodge in the 1970 Southern 500 at Darlington, S.C., "a country boy's dream."

But Baker's most emotional victory came a decade later, when he won the Daytona 500 in Harry Ranier's Oldsmobile. "I've just been coming here so long, trying to win this thing, that I can't tell you what it means," he said in victory lane.

Following pages: The 6-foot-5 Buddy Baker cut an imposing figure behind the wheel of a stock car for a long time. In fact, he finished in the top 20 in the Performance Index a record 24 consecutive seasons.

Baker won only twice after that memorable triumph and not at all after 1983. He developed a blood clot in his brain as a result of a crash in the 1988 Coca-Cola 600, but didn't hang up his helmet for good until 1994.

As Winston Cup racing's 50th season came to a conclusion, Baker analyzed for *The Atlanta Constitution* how a driver should know his career is over: "It's not over until you lose that competitive edge. If you get hurt physically, then you start sliding. I really think, as long as you're mentally alert and keep yourself in great shape, you'll be OK. If you get tired in a race car, that's when you know your days are numbered. You start hearing a guy say, 'Well, halfway, I kind of ran out of steam.' "

1980 in Review

Although Cale Yarborough led the Winston Cup Series with six victories and set a modern record by winning 14 poles, Dale Earnhardt parlayed five victories into his first Winston Cup title and held an 816-770 edge over Yarborough in the Performance Index.

Most Memorable Race

Pearson led a tight pack of cars on the penultimate lap of the Southern 500 on September 1 when the engine in Frank Warren's Dodge expired and left a trail of oil and debris on the Darlington oval. Earnhardt slid in the oil in the second turn, nicked Pearson, and hit the wall. Benny Parsons also slid in the oil, and Pearson nicked the wall but continued. "At that moment, I thought, 'Oh, boy. I've got a chance to finish second to Pearson,' " said Terry Labonte, who pulled his Chevrolet around Pearson's damaged machine with 400 yards remaining and beat the Silver Fox to the line by three feet for his first victory.

Most Significant Wreck

Rookie Ricky Knotts was killed when he bumped into another car, hit the outside wall, careened back across the track, and slammed into the inside retaining wall in a 125-mile qualifying race for the Daytona 500 on Valentine's Day. "Every time you buckle yourself into one of these things, you have to accept that possibility," said race winner Donnie Allison. "None of us wants to get hurt or killed. But every one of us accepts the fact that it could happen."

Most Important Off-Track Development

Earnhardt led Petty by a mere 47 points in the Winston Cup standings when Jake Elder quit as crew chief for Earnhardt's Rod Osterlund-owned Chevrolet after the Coca-Cola 600 in May. Earnhardt went on to win the Winston Cup title with 20-year-old Doug Richert as his crew chief.

Records & Milestones

The 1980 campaign marked the fourth consecutive season that four drivers—Yarborough, Earnhardt, Darrell Waltrip (5), and Bobby Allison (4)—captured four or more races. Those four seasons are the only times that happened in the modern era until 1999. . . . Parsons's victory in the Los Angeles Times 500 on November 15 was the last Winston Cup race held at Ontario Motor Speedway, a 2.5-mile California track modeled after the Indianapolis Motor Speedway.

1980 at a Glance

Races:	31
Road:	2
Short Track:	10
Superspeedway:	19
Winners:	10
Pole Winners:	7
Tracks:	17
States:	12

1980 Performance Index Rankings

1. Dale Earnhardt (816)
2. Cale Yarborough (770)
3. Richard Petty (657)
4. Benny Parsons (640)
5. Jody Ridley (627)
6. Darrell Waltrip (593)
7. Bobby Allison (563)
8. Richard Childress (559)
9. Terry Labonte (541)
10. Harry Gant (527)
11. Neil Bonnett (495)
12. Buddy Arrington (467)
13. Dave Marcis (458)
14. Buddy Baker (453)
15. James Hylton (385)
16. Jimmy Means (340)
17. Tommy Gale (288)
18. Lake Speed (287)
19. Cecil Gordon (269)
20. Ronnie Thomas (266)
21. J.D. McDuffie (255)
22. Dick Brooks (243)
23. Kyle Petty (237)

24. Lennie Pond (230)
25. Dick May (224)
26. David Pearson (220)
27. Roger Hamby (214)
28. Donnie Allison (208)
29. Slick Johnson (205)
30. Bill Elliott (197)
31. Ricky Rudd (193)
32. John Anderson (188)
33. Joe Millikan (146)
34. Sterling Marlin (113)
35. Bobby Wawak (91)
36. D.K. Ulrich (87)
37. Stan Barrett (86)
38. Joe Booher (73)
39. Billie Harvey; Bill Schmitt (71)
41. Steve Moore (70)
42. Tim Richmond (69)
43. Baxter Price (68)
44. Rusty Wallace (64)
45. Dave Dion (61)
46. Tighe Scott (60)
47. Frank Warren (59)
48. Connie Saylor (57)
49. Kenny Hemphill; Coo Coo Marlin; Don Whittington (50)
52. Junior Miller (45)
53. Bill Elswick (39)
54. Jim Vandiver (37)
55. Jeff McDuffie (36)
56. Chuck Bown; Janet Guthrie (34)
58. Blackie Wangerin (32)
59. Joel Stowe (31)
60. Harry Dinwiddie; Glenn Jarrett (28)
62. Marty Robbins (27)
63. Ferrel Harris; Jim Ingram (25)
65. Charlie Chamblee; Don Puskarich (24)
67. Kevin Housby (23)
68. Jimmy Finger; Bill Whittington (22)
70. Rick McCray; Clay Young (21)
72. Don Waterman; Rick Wilson (20)
74. Wayne Watercutter (19)
75. Mike Potter; Roy Smith; Don Sprouse (17)
78. Mike Alexander; Phil Finney; Nelson Oswald (15)
81. Tommy Houston (14)
82. Vince Giamformaggio; Jim Robinson (10)
84. Buck Simmons (9)
85. Joey Arrington (8)
86. Rick Newsom; Bub Strickler (7)
88. John Utsman (5)

1980 Events

Winston Western 500; Riverside Int. Raceway/2.62-m road/312m
Darrell Waltrip (Chevrolet)/Darrell Waltrip (Chevrolet)

Daytona 500; Daytona International Speedway/2.5-m/500 miles
Buddy Baker (Oldsmobile)/Buddy Baker (Oldsmobile)

Richmond 400; Richmond Fairgrounds Raceway/.542-m/217 miles
Darrell Waltrip (Chevrolet)/Darrell Waltrip (Chevrolet)

Carolina 500; North Carolina Motor Speedway/1.017-mile/500 m
Cale Yarborough (Oldsmobile)/Darrell Waltrip (Chevrolet)

Atlanta 500; Atlanta International Raceway/1.522-m/500 miles
Dale Earnhardt (Chevrolet)/Buddy Baker (Oldsmobile)

Valleydale Southeastern 500; Bristol Int. Race./.533-m/267 m
Dale Earnhardt (Chevrolet)/Cale Yarborough (Chevrolet)

CRC Chem. Rebel 500; Darlington Int. Raceway/1.366-m/500 m
David Pearson (Chevrolet)/Benny Parsons (Chevrolet)

Northwestern Bank 400; No. Wilkesboro Speedway/.625-m/250 m
Richard Petty (Chevrolet)/Bobby Allison (Ford)

Virginia 500; Martinsville Speedway/.525-mile/263 miles
Darrell Waltrip (Chevrolet)/Darrell Waltrip (Chevrolet)

Winston 500; Alabama Int. Motor Speedway/2.66-mile/500 miles
Buddy Baker (Oldsmobile)/David Pearson (Oldsmobile)

Music City 420; Nashville Int. Raceway/.596-mile/250 miles
Richard Petty (Chevrolet)/Cale Yarborough (Chevrolet)

Mason-Dixon 500; Dover Downs Int. Speedway/1-mile/500 miles
Bobby Allison (Ford)/Cale Yarborough (Chevrolet)

World 600; Charlotte Motor Speedway/1.5-mile/600 miles
Benny Parsons (Chevrolet)/Cale Yarborough (Chevrolet)

NASCAR 400; Texas World Speedway/2-mile/400 miles
Cale Yarborough (Chevrolet)/Cale Yarborough (Chevrolet)

W.W. Hodgdon 400; Riverside Int. Raceway/2.62-m road/249 m
Darrell Waltrip (Chevrolet)/Cale Yarborough (Chevrolet)

Gabriel 400; Michigan International Speedway/2-m/400 miles
Benny Parsons (Chevrolet)/Benny Parsons (Chevrolet)

Firecracker 400; Daytona International Speedway/2.5-m/400 m
Bobby Allison (Mercury)/Cale Yarborough (Oldsmobile)

Busch Nashville 420; Nashville Int. Raceway/.596-m/250 miles
Dale Earnhardt (Chevrolet)/Cale Yarborough (Chevrolet)

Coca-Cola 500; Pocono International Raceway/2.5-m/500 miles
Neil Bonnett (Mercury)/Cale Yarborough (Chevrolet)

Talladega 500; Alabama Int. Motor Speedway/2.66-m/500 miles
Neil Bonnett (Mercury)/Buddy Baker (Oldsmobile)

Champion Spark Plug 400; Michigan Int. Speedway/2-mile/400 m
Cale Yarborough (Chevrolet)/Buddy Baker (Chevrolet)

Busch Volunteer 500; Bristol Int. Raceway/.533-m/267 miles
Cale Yarborough (Chevrolet)/Cale Yarborough (Chevrolet)

Southern 500; Darlington Int. Raceway/1.366-mile/500 miles
Terry Labonte (Chevrolet)/Darrell Waltrip (Chevrolet)

Capital City 400; Richmond Fairgrounds Raceway/.542-m/217 m
Bobby Allison (Ford)/Cale Yarborough (Oldsmobile)

CRC Chemicals 500; Dover Downs Int. Speedway/1-m/500 miles
Darrell Waltrip (Chevrolet)/Cale Yarborough (Chevrolet)

Holly Farms 400; North Wilkesboro Speedway/.625-m/250 miles
Bobby Allison (Ford)/Cale Yarborough (Oldsmobile)

Old Dominion 500; Martinsville Speedway/.525-mile/263 miles
Dale Earnhardt (Chevrolet)/Buddy Baker (Chevrolet)

National 500; Charlotte Motor Speedway/1.5-mile/500 miles
Dale Earnhardt (Chevrolet)/Buddy Baker (Buick)

American 500; North Carolina Motor Speedway/1.017-mile/500 m
Cale Yarborough (Chevrolet)/Donnie Allison (Chevrolet)

Atlanta Journal 500; Atlanta Int. Raceway/1.522-m/500 miles
Cale Yarborough (Chevrolet)/Bobby Allison (Mercury)

Los Angeles Times 500; Ontario Motor Speedway/2.5-mile/500 m
Benny Parsons (Chevrolet)/Cale Yarborough (Chevrolet)

Victories

1. Cale Yarborough (6)
2. Dale Earnhardt; Darrell Waltrip (5)
4. Bobby Allison (4)
5. Benny Parsons (3)
6. Buddy Baker; Neil Bonnett; Richard Petty (2)
9. Terry Labonte; David Pearson (1)

Poles

1. Cale Yarborough (14)
2. Buddy Baker (6)
3. Darrell Waltrip (5)
4. Bobby Allison; Benny Parsons (2)
6. Donnie Allison; David Pearson (1)

Victories

1. Chevrolet (22)
2. Ford; Mercury; Oldsmobile (3)

Poles

1. Chevrolet (21)
2. Oldsmobile (7)
3. Buick; Ford; Mercury (1)

1981
The Drivers Fans
Have Loved
To Hate

Winston Cup racing has evolved from a sport that virtually existed in a vacuum in its infancy to America's fastest-growing spectator sport. As its 51st season ended, NASCAR may not have supplanted the National Football League in popularity, but it could defend its case as a serious rival.

Yet stock-car racing has retained a curious element that remains somewhat of a mystery. The Michael Jordans, Joe Montanas, and Arnold Palmers have been warmly embraced by the public, but NASCAR ticket buyers have exercised their unalienable right to boo.

When he won his first Winston Cup title in 1981, Darrell Waltrip was probably the first champion who spent the season listening to more jeers than cheers.

Among those who have been the recipients of the fans' wrath during pre-race introductions include Dale Earnhardt, the "Intimidator," and Geoff Bodine, who angered Earnhardt's supporters by feuding with their hero. Rusty Wallace became the fans' favorite target when he made the mistake of ramming the nose of his Pontiac into the rear of Waltrip's Chevrolet, sending the latter spinning, on the penultimate green-flag lap of The Winston at Charlotte in 1989—just when Waltrip was gaining the fans' adoration after 15 years as NASCAR's most hated driver. When Wallace drove into victory lane, he wasn't greeted warmly.

"They'll cheer 41 drivers and boo me. A couple of wrecks with Waltrip, and they're on you," Wallace said during his Winston Cup championship season of 1989. "I went into that race with a ton of fans. All I heard was cheers. But one race after that, all I heard was boos. In one race, it all changed. We drive the cars as fast as we can for as long as we can, trying to win races. Sometimes it's inevitable you're going to get into somebody.

"People who know me know me know I'm hyper and that I talk. Sometimes I say things that are taken wrong. A lot of fans like the kind of guy who holds it inside. I'm not like that. I always say what's on my mind. I give straight answers. A lot of people don't like that. Hell, yeah, I care what (the fans) think. They're going to think what they want, but I love them to death. A new, young, cocky kid comes along and starts winning, so they booed him. They booed Waltrip. They booed Earnhardt. Now, they boo me. If you win, you're going to get booed. The only way they'll stop booing me is if I have a lot of bad luck and start wrecking, and I don't plan on that happening."

The fans eventually quit booing Wallace and, in fact, cheered lustily when he tapped Jeff Gordon's Chevrolet and sent his rival spinning into the wall while they were dueling for the lead in the late stages of the 1998 Pontiac Excitement 400 at Richmond, Va.

That's because Gordon had become the driver the fans loved to hate—and for no apparent reason other than the fact he has the highest winning percentage in history. "It doesn't have to make sense," Gordon said. "You've got to understand the fans in our sport are unique."

Compare Gordon's achievements with those of golfer Tiger Woods, who is five years his junior. Woods is well on his way to becoming one of the greatest golfers in history. Gordon already has established himself as one of history's greatest race drivers.

"It's only human nature to prefer cheers over boos," Gordon said. "I'm sure I would rather have them cheering for me, but I really don't think about it that much. As long as I'm pulling into victory lane, I could care less what they're doing. The others, I'm sure, probably added fuel to the fire, but they were still winning three or four times a year to start with."

Waltrip is the first to admit he added fuel to the fire. Like Gordon, he had the looks of a matinee idol, and no driver in Winston Cup history was quicker to needle his rivals, usually in a humorous fashion. Before he'd ever won a race, Waltrip's obvious potential, willingness to talk, and frequently hilarious quips made him a favorite of the media. But it didn't necessarily endear him to the sport's established stars.

Cale Yarborough nicknamed Waltrip "Jaws," fans began booing him, and he long since had established himself as one of history's greatest drivers before the boos finally turned to cheers.

"I've never seen anything quite like the anti-Waltrip booing," Bobby Allison said during the early 1980s, when that duo was battling for the Winston Cup title every year.

"It occurred to me that I might be doing something wrong," Waltrip said not long after he won the 1989 Daytona 500. "I have as much fun as anybody exchanging good-natured quips and cuts, but it had gone beyond that. It's not all that amusing to stay in an uproar all the time. That's what was happening, even to the point that the fans were being swept into the controversies. I said at the time that the boos didn't bother me and rationalized that even Richard Petty, undoubtedly the most popular driver of all time, got booed on occasion. But deep down, I knew I was fibbing to myself. It's human nature to thrive on cheers, not boos. It got to the point where I dreaded race day."

When Waltrip's Daytona 500 victory proved to be a surprisingly popular one, followed three months later by his wreck with Wallace, his days as NASCAR's reigning villain were finally over.

"It was like a bunch of people woke up one morning and said, 'You know, Darrell Waltrip isn't such a bad guy.' I'd go to an autograph session in the past and sit there signing for an hour or two," he said. "Since winning (the 1989 Daytona 500), there've been times when I'd have to sit for four or five hours and have to tell them to come back tomorrow. I've been around a long time, and people have gotten used to me. People used to ask me, 'When will fans quit booing you?' I always answered, 'When hell freezes over and I'm voted Most Popular Driver.' "

Waltrip captured that title in both 1989 and 1990, but for most of the previous 15 years, Adolph Hitler and Attila the Hun surely got more votes.

"It just shows you that people may not forget, but they will forgive," Waltrip said. "I think we've all experienced in our careers and in our lifetimes athletes who are controversial, that the media and the fans kind of abuse at some point in their careers. But, as time goes by, there is acceptance. I can remember how people felt about Muhammad Ali. People couldn't wait for him to fight,

hoping that somebody would beat him. Many people really hated Ali. Now, he's a folk hero, and it's hard to find anything bad about him. Jack Nicklaus is another one like that, whose popularity has gone 180 degrees. I never thought about how unpopular I was or what a burden that was to bear. I never felt that people didn't like me or didn't approve of me except on Sunday. The sales of my souvenirs were high. The functions I spoke at were well attended, and sponsors seemed to approve of me. But it seemed I couldn't get the fans at the driver introductions to approve of me. It was a contradiction.

"I never thought it would change. I thought I'd retire from the sport being one of the most disliked drivers who ever drove a race car. People talk about how a career isn't complete until you win the Daytona 500 or this or that other race. My career could not have been complete without winning the approval of the fans.

"I think the changing of the guard had a lot to do with the (ceasing of boos). I came along in the era when the heroes were Petty, (David) Pearson, Allison, (Buddy) Baker, and Cale, and I intruded a little bit. If you beat all those guys, you beat the fans' heroes. If you told everybody you were going to do it, that was worse. And I had a habit of doing that."

Gordon should take heart from Waltrip, as Wallace did before him.

"A few years back, everybody hated Darrell Waltrip, absolutely hated him," Wallace said when he was the recipient of the lion's share of the fans' ire. "Now, they all love him."

1981 in Review

Waltrip led the Winston Cup Series with 12 victories and 11 poles, but it took one of the greatest rallies in history for him to win his first NASCAR championship. Waltrip trailed Allison by 331 points with 14 races

remaining, but won three of the next five events. Waltrip still trailed Allison with six races to go before he became the second and final driver to win four consecutive races from the pole. Waltrip ended the season with a runner-up effort and a sixth-place finish to beat Allison—who had a victory and three second-place finishes in the final six races—by 53 points. Waltrip also outdistanced Allison in the Performance Index, 879-844.

Most Memorable Race

In a season that perhaps produced more exciting finishes than any other, Allison rallied from seventh place on the final green-flag lap to capture the Gabriel 400 at Michigan International Speedway on June 21. When Kyle Petty suffered a blown engine in his Buick with seven laps remaining, Yarborough slid in the oil from Petty's car and hit the wall. Baker also spun, and Waltrip and Earnhardt collided with each other. Benny Parsons also spun, but didn't hit anything, and Harry Gant slowed to miss the wreck. Allison's Buick passed

Yarborough, Baker, Waltrip, Earnhardt, Gant, and, finally, Parsons for the victory. "That's the first time that I've won one like that," he said.

Most Significant Wreck

Allison's victory in the World 600 on May 24 at Charlotte was bittersweet. His younger brother, Donnie, was unconscious for two hours and suffered a concussion, a broken right knee and shoulder, fractured ribs, and a bruised lung when he hit the outside wall, slid back across the track, then unavoidably was rammed by Dick Brooks's Buick. Donnie, who won 10 races and 17 poles in Winston Cup competition, never added to those totals after that crash. "My heart's been in my throat all afternoon," Bobby said.

Most Important Off-Track Development

After the season opener at Riverside, Calif., Winston Cup cars were downsized, with the wheelbase reduced from 115 to 110 inches.

Records & Milestones

Buick, which had won two races in the first 32 years of Winston Cup racing, captured 22 in 1981.... A modern-record 10 races were captured from the pole.... The 1981 season was the first of three in the modern era to feature three races on road courses.... ESPN televised its first Winston Cup race, the Atlanta Journal 500 on November 8 at Hampton, Ga.... The NASCAR Winston Cup Awards Banquet was moved from Daytona Beach, Fla., to the Waldorf-Astoria Hotel in New York.

1981 at a Glance

Races:	31
Road:	3
Short Track:	10
Superspeedway:	18
Winners:	9
Pole Winners:	13
Tracks:	17
States:	12

1981 Performance Index Rankings

1. Darrell Waltrip (879)
2. Bobby Allison (844)
3. Jody Ridley (658)
4. Harry Gant (620)
5. Terry Labonte (591)
6. Dale Earnhardt (568)
7. Ricky Rudd (552)
8. Richard Petty (521)
9. Buddy Arrington (454)
10. Dave Marcis (435)
11. Cale Yarborough (411)
12. Benny Parsons (396)
13. Kyle Petty (395)
14. Ron Bouchard (392)
15. Morgan Shepherd (384)
16. Joe Millikan (364)
17. Buddy Baker (359)
18. Tim Richmond (353)
19. Tommy Gale (345)
20. Neil Bonnett (299)
21. Jimmy Means (297)
22. J.D. McDuffie (292)
23. Lake Speed (287)
24. Joe Ruttman (279)
25. Bill Elliott (266)
26. James Hylton (226)
27. Richard Childress (219)
28. Mike Alexander (184)
29. Johnny Rutherford (161)
30. Stan Barrett (149)
31. Cecil Gordon (146)
32. D.K. Ulrich (140)
33. Elliott Forbes-Robinson (139)
34. Lennie Pond (131)
35. Ronnie Thomas (130)
36. Connie Saylor (111)
37. Dick May (101)
38. Donnie Allison (97)
39. Gary Balough; Bobby Wawak (90)
41. Dick Brooks (81)
42. Rick Wilson (76)
43. Tommy Houston (71)
44. David Pearson (69)
45. Bill Elswick (61)
46. Mark Martin (51)
47. Don Whittington (47)
48. H.B. Bailey; Jim Robinson (44)
50. Tommy Ellis (36)
51. Don Waterman (35)
52. Rusty Wallace (34)
53. Geoff Bodine; A.J. Foyt (33)
55. Jack Ingram; Don Sprouse (31)
57. Ronnie Sanders (27)
58. Terry Herman; Glenn Jarrett; Bob McElee (26)
61. Chuck Bown (25)
62. John Anderson (24)
63. Delma Cowart; Roy Smith (22)
65. Joe Booher; Rick Newsom (20)
67. Bruce Hill (19)
68. John Borneman; Lowell Cowell; Jimmy Hensley; Gary Kershaw (18)
72. Steve Pfeifer; Bill Schmitt (16)
74. Joe Fields; Rick Knoop; Randy Ogden (15)
77. Rick O'Dell (14)
78. Don Puskarich (13)
79. Bob Bondurant; Steve Spencer (12)
81. Mike Potter (10)
82. Junior Miller (5)
83. Henry Jones (1)

1981 Events

Winston Western 500; Riverside Int. Raceway/2.62-m road/312m
Bobby Allison (Chevrolet)/Darrell Waltrip (Chevrolet)

Daytona 500; Daytona International Speedway/2.5-m/500 miles
Richard Petty (Buick)/Bobby Allison (Pontiac)

Richmond 400; Richmond Fairgrounds Raceway/.542-m/217 miles
Darrell Waltrip (Buick)/Morgan Shepherd (Pontiac)

Carolina 500; North Carolina Motor Speedway/1.017-mile/500 m
Darrell Waltrip (Buick)/Cale Yarborough (Buick)

Coca-Cola 500; Atlanta International Raceway/1.522-mile/500m
Cale Yarborough (Buick)/Terry Labonte (Buick)

Valleydale 500; Bristol International Raceway/.533-m/267 m
Darrell Waltrip (Buick)/Darrell Waltrip (Buick)

Northwestern Bank 400; No. Wilkesboro Speedway/.625-m/250 m
Richard Petty (Buick)/Dave Marcis (Chevrolet)

CRC Chem. Rebel 500; Darlington Int. Raceway/1.366-m/500 m
Darrell Waltrip (Buick)/Bill Elliott (Ford)

Virginia 500; Martinsville Speedway/.525-mile/263 miles
Morgan Shepherd (Pontiac)/Ricky Rudd (Buick)

Winston 500; Alabama Int. Motor Speedway/2.66-m/500 miles
Bobby Allison (Buick)/Bobby Allison (Buick)

Melling Tool 420; Nashville Int. Raceway/.596-mile/250 miles
Benny Parsons (Ford)/Ricky Rudd (Buick)

Mason-Dixon 500; Dover Downs Int. Speedway/1-mile/500 miles
Jody Ridley (Ford)/David Pearson (Oldsmobile)

World 600; Charlotte Motor Speedway/1.5-mile/600 miles
Bobby Allison (Buick)/Neil Bonnett (Ford)

Budweiser NASCAR 400; Texas World Speedway/2-mile/400 miles
Benny Parsons (Ford)/Terry Labonte (Buick)

Warner W. Hodgdon 400; Riverside Int. Race./2.62-m rd./249 m
Darrell Waltrip (Buick)/Darrell Waltrip (Buick)

Gabriel 400; Michigan International Speedway/2-m/400 miles
Bobby Allison (Buick)/Darrell Waltrip (Buick)

Firecracker 400; Daytona International Speedway/2.5-m/400 m
Cale Yarborough (Buick)/Cale Yarborough (Buick)

Busch Nashville 420; Nashville Int. Raceway/.596-m/250 miles
Darrell Waltrip (Buick)/Mark Martin (Pontiac)

Mountain Dew 500; Pocono International Raceway/2.5-m/500 m
Darrell Waltrip (Buick)/Darrell Waltrip (Buick)

Talladega 500; Alabama Int. Motor Speedway/2.66-m/500 miles
Ron Bouchard (Buick)/Harry Gant (Buick)

Champion Spark Plug 400; Michigan Int. Speedway/2-mile/400 m
Richard Petty (Buick)/Ron Bouchard (Buick)

Busch 500; Bristol International Raceway/.533-mile/267 miles
Darrell Waltrip (Buick)/Darrell Waltrip (Buick)

Southern 500; Darlington International Raceway/1.366-m/500 m
Neil Bonnett (Ford)/Harry Gant (Pontiac)

Wrangler Sanforset 400; Richmond Fgds. Raceway/.542-m/217 m
Benny Parsons (Ford)/Mark Martin (Pontiac)

CRC Chemicals 500; Dover Downs Int. Speedway/1-m/500 miles
Neil Bonnett (Ford)/Ricky Rudd (Chevrolet)

Old Dominion 500; Martinsville Speedway/.525-mile/263 miles
Darrell Waltrip (Buick)/Darrell Waltrip (Buick)

Holly Farms 400; North Wilkesboro Speedway/.625-m/250 miles
Darrell Waltrip (Buick)/Darrell Waltrip (Buick)

National 500; Charlotte Motor Speedway/1.5-mile/500 miles
Darrell Waltrip (Buick)/Darrell Waltrip (Buick)

American 500; North Carolina Motor Speedway/1.017-mile/500 m
Darrell Waltrip (Buick)/Darrell Waltrip (Buick)

Atlanta Journal 500; Atlanta Int. Raceway/1.522-m/500 miles
Neil Bonnett (Ford)/Harry Gant (Pontiac)

Winston Western 500; Riverside Int. Raceway/2.62-m road/312m
Bobby Allison (Buick)/Darrell Waltrip (Buick)

Victories

1. Darrell Waltrip (12)
2. Bobby Allison (5)
3. Neil Bonnett; Benny Parsons; Richard Petty (3)
6. Cale Yarborough (2)
7. Ron Bouchard; Jody Ridley; Morgan Shepherd (1)

Poles

1. Darrell Waltrip (11)
2. Harry Gant; Ricky Rudd (3)
4. Bobby Allison; Terry Labonte; Mark Martin; Cale Yarborough (2)
8. Neil Bonnett; Ron Bouchard; Bill Elliott; Dave Marcis; David Pearson; Morgan Shepherd (1)

Victories

1. Buick (22)
2. Ford (7)
3. Chevrolet; Pontiac (1)

Poles

1. Buick (19)
2. Pontiac (6)
3. Chevrolet (3)
4. Ford (2)
5. Oldsmobile (1)

1982
Successful
Transitions

When Winston Cup racing's 51st season ended, Benny Parsons (left) and Ned Jarrett had made the transition from driving champions to popular television and radio commentators. But both had been part of successful transitions before. The retirements of Jarrett, Junior Johnson, and Marvin Panch after the 1966 season ended a three-year period in which eight drivers who won 17 or more races hung up their helmets. And Parsons (21 victories) competed for the final time in 1988, when Bobby Allison (85 victories), Cale Yarborough (83), and Donnie Allison (10) also made their final Winston Cup starts.

In stock-car racing, as in any other sport or historical realm, it's sometimes difficult to pinpoint the beginning or the end of a particular era.

Those who grew up in the wildest decade of the 20th Century, the '60s, for example, might contend that era, as it is remembered today, didn't begin until President Kennedy was assassinated on November 22, 1963, and didn't end until sometime in the '70s, perhaps on August 9, 1974, the day President Nixon resigned.

Stock-car racing officials no doubt wonder if the fans' interest will wane once the Earnhardts, Elliotts, Waltrips, Wallaces, Labontes, and Gordons are no longer around.

But there is little reason to worry. Not only has Winston Cup racing survived two very significant transition periods, it has thrived. In fact, one of the most amazing streaks in Winston Cup history is that for 32 consecutive seasons, from 1951-82, at least one driver who captured a Winston Cup race made his final appearance, some via retirement and others because of career-ending or fatal injuries.

The first great transition began during the 1964 season, when a record 10 drivers who had earned a career Performance Index rating of 1,000 or more made their final Winston Cup appearances: Winston Cup champions Lee Petty, Rex White, and Joe Weatherly and Fireball Roberts, Jack Smith, Bob Welborn, Jim Pardue, Cotton Owens, Larry Thomas, and Billy Wade. That season also marked the only time in history that five drivers with 20 or more victories—Petty (54), Roberts (33), White (28), Weatherly (25), and Smith (21)—made their final appearances, and Owens and Welborn were nine-time winners. The first great transition in stock-car racing was completed two years later when Ned Jarrett and Junior Johnson, who each

won 50 races, and 17-time winner Marvin Panch made their final appearances.

If any year rivaled those for a changing of the guard, it was 1988, when three Winston Cup champions—Bobby Allison (85 victories), Cale Yarborough (83), and Benny Parsons (21)—and 10-time winner Donnie Allison competed for the final time.

That transition continued in 1992 with the retirement of seven-time Winston Cup champion Richard Petty, winner of a record 200 races. Those making their final appearances during the 1993 season included 1992 Winston Cup champion Alan Kulwicki, 19-time winner Davey Allison, and 18-time winner Neil Bonnett. Completing the transition in 1994 were the retirements of Buddy Baker (19 victories) and Harry Gant (18).

The following chart lists the driver who earned the most victories who made his final appearance during each season of that remarkable 32-year streak from 1951-82 and includes all drivers who reached double figures in career victories and said farewell to driving during that period:

Farewells

Year	Drivers	Career Wins
1951	Red Byron	2
1952	Marshall Teague	7
1953	Neil Cole, Bill Norton, Dick Passwater, Bill Rexford	1
1954	Lou Figaro, Jimmy Florian	1
1955	Dick Rathmann	13
1956	Bob Flock	4
1957	Fonty Flock	19
1958	Bill Blair, Gwyn Staley	3
1959	Gober Sosebee	2
1960	Shorty Rollins	1
1961	Tim Flock	39
1962	Herb Thomas	48
1963	Jim Reed	7
1964	Lee Petty	54
	Fireball Roberts	33
	Rex White	28
	Joe Weatherly	25
	Jack Smith	21
1965	Nelson Stacy	4
1966	Ned Jarrett, Junior Johnson	50
	Marvin Panch	17
1967	Dick Hutcherson	14
1968	Curtis Turner	17
1969	Paul Goldsmith	9
1970	Parnelli Jones	4
1971	Speedy Thompson	20
1972	Fred Lorenzen	26
	Jim Paschal	25
	Lee Roy Yarbrough	14
1973	Pete Hamilton	4
1974	Sam McQuagg	1
1975	Darel Dieringer	7
1976	Buck Baker	46
	Bobby Isaac	37
1977	John Kieper	1
1978	Ray Elder	2
1979	Jim Hurtubise	1
1980	Dan Gurney	5
1981	Elmo Langley	2
1982	Richard Brickhouse	1

1982 in Review

For the second year in a row, Darrell Waltrip captured the Winston Cup title and held the series lead in victories (12), poles (7), and Performance Index (a 768-751 advantage over Bobby Allison). Buck Baker is the only other driver to lead the circuit in all four categories twice in a row (1956 and 1957).

Most Memorable Race

When rain began to fall on the 276th lap of the Coca-Cola 500 on March 21 at Atlanta, Richard Petty entered the third turn with a narrow lead over Waltrip. But Waltrip guided the Junior Johnson-owned Buick past Petty and beat him to the finish line by two inches to win the race, which was shortened by rain. "Richard went into the third turn a little too hard," Waltrip said. "His car shoved up a little bit, and I was able to get under him. It's mainly a matter of keeping your head when you know the caution is about to come out, knowing where you need to be, getting into position, remaining calm, then making your move."

Most Significant Wreck

In a crash that also involved Tim Richmond's Buick, Dale Earnhardt's Bud Moore-owned Ford became airborne and ripped a hole in the concrete wall in the first turn during the Mountain Dew 500 at Pocono International Raceway in Long Pond, Pa., on July 25. Earnhardt suffered a broken kneecap in the wreck, which resulted in an hour-long, 23-lap caution flag, and finished 35th and 30th in his next two starts.

Most Important Off-Track Development

Ford Motor Company, which left the sport after the 1969 season, returned to Winston Cup racing.

Records & Milestones

Buick established a modern record with 25 victories. Buicks have visited victory lane 65 times in Winston Cup history. Forty-seven of those wins came in 1981 and 1982.

1982 at a Glance

Races:	30
Road:	2
Short Track:	10
Superspeedway:	18
Winners:	8
Pole Winners:	15
Tracks:	15
States:	11

1982 Performance Index Rankings

1. Darrell Waltrip (768)
2. Bobby Allison (751)
3. Terry Labonte (636)
4. Harry Gant (588)
5. Buddy Arrington (555)
6. Dave Marcis (513)
7. Richard Petty (502)
8. Ron Bouchard (489)
9. Jimmy Means (467)
10. Morgan Shepherd (445)
11. Tim Richmond (441)
12. Benny Parsons (438)
13. Ricky Rudd (419)
14. Geoff Bodine (418)
15. Bill Elliott (407)
16. Joe Ruttman (405)
17. Neil Bonnett (391)
18. Jody Ridley (389)
19. Dale Earnhardt (373)
20. Buddy Baker (357)
21. Mark Martin (338)
22. Cale Yarborough (330)
23. Kyle Petty (324)
24. Tommy Gale (306)
25. J.D. McDuffie (278)
26. D.K. Ulrich (251)
27. Lake Speed (248)
28. Slick Johnson (141)
29. James Hylton (131)
30. Lennie Pond (128)
31. Donnie Allison (126)
32. Bobby Wawak (122)
33. Dick May (113)
34. Joe Millikan (112)
35. Rick Newsom (102)
36. Gary Balough (95)
37. Philip Duffie (92)
38. Rick Wilson (88)
39. Lowell Cowell (75)
40. Cecil Gordon (70)
41. Brad Teague (69)
42. Connie Saylor (68)
43. David Pearson (67)
44. Ronnie Thomas (65)
45. Jim Sauter (63)
46. Roy Smith (59)
47. Bobby Hillin Jr. (55)
48. John Anderson (43)
49. Dean Combs (40)
50. Charlie Baker (38)
51. Jim Bown (33)
52. Rodney Combs; Jim Reich (31)
54. Bosco Lowe (29)
55. Rick Baldwin (28)
56. Tom Sneva (25)
57. Al Loquasto (24)
58. Butch Lindley (23)
59. Steve Moore; Travis Tiller (22)
61. Randy Baker; Tommy Ellis; Mike Potter; Darryl Sage (20)
65. Don Waterman (19)
66. Delma Cowart (18)
67. Joe Booher; Terry Herman; Scott Miller (17)
70. Glenn Francis; Jimmy Hensley; Rick McCray (16)
73. John Krebs (11)
74. Don Puskarich; Jim Robinson (10)
76. Jeff McDuffie (9)
77. Bob Schacht (5)

1982 Events

Daytona 500; Daytona International Speedway/2.5-m/500 miles
Bobby Allison (Buick)/Benny Parsons (Pontiac)

Richmond 400; Richmond Fairgrounds Raceway/.542-m/217 miles
Dave Marcis (Chevrolet)/Darrell Waltrip (Buick)

Valleydale 500; Bristol International Raceway/.533-m/267 m
Darrell Waltrip (Buick)/Darrell Waltrip (Buick)

Coca-Cola 500; Atlanta International Raceway/1.522-m/500 m
Darrell Waltrip (Buick)/Dale Earnhardt (Ford)

W.W. Hodgdon Car. 500; N.C. Motor Speedway/1.017-mile/500m
Cale Yarborough (Buick)/Benny Parsons (Pontiac)

CRC Chem. Rebel 500; Darlington Int. Raceway/1.366-mile/500m
Dale Earnhardt (Ford)/Buddy Baker (Buick)

Northwestern Bank 400; No. Wilkesboro Speedway/.625-m/250 m
Darrell Waltrip (Buick)/Darrell Waltrip (Buick)

Va. National Bank 500; Martinsville Speedway/.525-mile/263 m
Harry Gant (Buick)/Terry Labonte (Chevrolet)

Winston 500; Alabama Int. Motor Speedway/2.66-mile/500 miles
Darrell Waltrip (Buick)/Benny Parsons (Pontiac)

Cracker Barrel 420; Nashville Int. Raceway/.596-m/250 miles
Darrell Waltrip (Buick)/Darrell Waltrip (Buick)

Mason-Dixon 500; Dover Downs Int. Speedway/1-mile/500 miles
Bobby Allison (Chevrolet)/Darrell Waltrip (Buick)

World 600; Charlotte Motor Speedway/1.5-mile/600 miles
Neil Bonnett (Ford)/David Pearson (Buick)

Van Scoy Diamond Mine 500; Pocono Int. Raceway/2.5-m/500 m
Bobby Allison (Buick)

Budweiser 400; Riverside Int. Raceway/2.62-m road/250 miles
Tim Richmond (Buick)/Terry Labonte (Buick)

Gabriel 400; Michigan International Speedway/2-m/400 miles
Cale Yarborough (Buick)/Ron Bouchard (Buick)

Firecracker 400; Daytona International Speedway/2.5-m/400 m
Bobby Allison (Buick)/Geoff Bodine (Pontiac)

Busch Nashville 420; Nashville Int. Raceway/.596-m/250 miles
Darrell Waltrip (Buick)/Morgan Shepherd (Buick)

Mountain Dew 500; Pocono Int. Raceway/2.5-mile/500 miles
Bobby Allison (Buick)/Cale Yarborough (Buick)

Talladega 500; Alabama Int. Motor Speedway/2.66-m/500 miles
Darrell Waltrip (Buick)/Geoff Bodine (Pontiac)

Champion Spark Plug 400; Michigan Int. Speedway/2-mile/400 m
Bobby Allison (Buick)/Bill Elliott (Ford)

Busch 500; Bristol International Raceway/.533-mile/267 miles
Darrell Waltrip (Buick)/Tim Richmond (Buick)

Southern 500; Darlington International Raceway/1.366-m/500 m
Cale Yarborough (Buick)/David Pearson (Buick)

Wrangler Sanforset 400; Richmond Fgds. Raceway/.542-m/217 m
Bobby Allison (Chevrolet)/Bobby Allison (Chevrolet)

CRC Chemicals 500; Dover Downs Int. Speedway/1-m/500 miles
Darrell Waltrip (Buick)/Ricky Rudd (Pontiac)

Holly Farms 400; North Wilkesboro Speedway/.625-m/250 miles
Darrell Waltrip (Buick)/Darrell Waltrip (Buick)

National 500; Charlotte Motor Speedway/1.5-mile/500 miles
Harry Gant (Buick)/Harry Gant (Buick)

Old Dominion 500; Martinsville Speedway/.525-mile/263 miles
Darrell Waltrip (Buick)/Ricky Rudd (Pontiac)

W.W. Hodgdon Amer. 500; N.C. Motor Speed./1.017-m/500 miles
Darrell Waltrip (Buick)/Cale Yarborough (Buick)

Atlanta Journal 500; Atlanta Int. Raceway/1.522-m/500 miles
Bobby Allison (Buick)/Morgan Shepherd (Buick)

Winston Western 500; Riverside Int. Raceway/2.62-m road/312m
Tim Richmond (Buick)/Darrell Waltrip (Buick)

Victories

1. Darrell Waltrip (12)
2. Bobby Allison (8)
3. Cale Yarborough (3)
4. Harry Gant; Tim Richmond (2)
6. Neil Bonnett; Dale Earnhardt; Dave Marcis (1)

Poles

1. Darrell Waltrip (7)
2. Benny Parsons (3)
3. Geoff Bodine; Terry Labonte; David Pearson; Ricky Rudd; Morgan Shepherd; Cale Yarborough (2)
9. Bobby Allison; Buddy Baker; Ron Bouchard; Dale Earnhardt; Bill Elliott; Harry Gant; Tim Richmond (1)

Victories

1. Buick (25)
2. Chevrolet (3)
3. Ford (2)

Poles

1. Buick (18)
2. Pontiac (7)
3. Chevrolet; Ford (2)

1983
Allison's Faith
Was Tested
More than Job's

Richard Petty often called 1983 Winston Cup champion Bobby Allison the toughest driver to pass on the track.

Perhaps that's because stock-car racing has never known a more determined competitor. Regardless of the pursuit—driving a race car, competing in a fishing tournament, you name it—the only thing that bothered Allison more than losing was the suspicion that he had not been beaten according to Hoyle.

"I always took pride in the fact that I honored the rules I competed under—the car rules and the race rules," Allison said. "I raced against a lot of guys who did not."

Perhaps it was fate that Allison, who grew up in Miami but moved to Hueytown, Ala., early in his career, would become a race driver: The first official sale of an American automobile in 1898 was to a man named Bob Allison.

As the leader of the "Alabama Gang," an unofficial regiment of drivers that also included his brother Donnie, short-track legend Red Farmer, Neil Bonnett, and, later, his son Davey, Bobby probably did more favors for more promoters than any driver in history.

Long after he had established himself as one of the greatest drivers in history, Allison continued to barnstorm the nation's short tracks, more in search of competition than purse money—calling it his "golf game." For years, the financial picture of countless local speedways was considerably brightened by an Allison appearance that filled their grandstands.

"I felt like I helped the sport. In 1960, I ran 154 races. I went anywhere that I heard of a race that was in range of that pickup truck pulling that trailer," he said. "In 1987, I ran 90 races."

Allison, who celebrated his 50th birthday in 1987, doesn't know how many races he won—or if he captured as many as short-track legends Ray Hendrick, Dick Trickle, and Farmer. "I never counted the heat races," he said. "If I did, I've won more than 1,500."

Allison had won two NASCAR Modified championships before he earned his first Winston Cup victory in a 100-mile race on a one-third-mile bullring in Oxford, Me., in 1966. Six subsequent victories earned him a ride in the Holman-Moody Ford, in which he won the 1967 American 500 at Rockingham, N.C., in his first start—his initial superspeedway triumph.

"When I won that first race in Oxford, I said, 'Well, I can win.' Then, when I won the American 500 at Rockingham, I said, 'Well, I can win a 500-mile superspeedway race.' I felt I was on my way. I never thought in terms of being the biggest star. I was never concerned with that part of the deal," Allison said. "But I really felt like I could win the race on a given day or trade cars with David Pearson, Richard Petty, or Cale Yarborough and win the race and they would finish second."

Indeed he could. Upon returning to Holman-Moody in 1971, Allison reeled off 11 victories, including five in a row—equaling the second-longest winning streak in history—and became the only driver to record two three-race winning streaks on superspeedways in the same season. He also won nine poles and became one of only three drivers to capture three consecutive races from the pole.

He left Holman-Moody to drive a Chevrolet for Junior Johnson in 1972. Although Chevrolet had not posted a superspeedway victory in nine years, Allison captured 10 more victories and became the first driver to win a record-tying seven superspeedway races in consecutive seasons. He also won 11 poles, including five straight and five in a row in short-track races, records he still shares. In 1971 and 1972, Allison also became one of only four drivers to win at least three Grand Slam races in consecutive seasons, one of only four to earn a classic

Bobby Allison is one of the most successful drivers in Winston Cup history, but one of his proudest feats is an unofficial record he claims to hold: most autographs signed by a stock-car driver.

win from the pole in back-to-back campaigns, and led a record 39 consecutive races. And only one driver has produced more consecutive seasons with at least nine poles and at least five victories from the pole, which Allison managed in both 1971 and 1972.

Allison abruptly left Johnson after the 1972 season. During the next three seasons, he won seven races and became the first driver to win three consecutive poles on road courses, a record he still shares. After Allison was injured in two terrifying wrecks in 1976, one at Rockingham and another on a Minnesota short track, he lost considerable weight and made regular visits to the famed Mayo Clinic in Minnesota. Most observers took a look at Allison's suddenly frail frame and winless seasons in 1976 and 1977 and figured his days as a winner had passed.

"It's funny. The wreck at Rockingham, I thought I was dying. The one in Minnesota, other people thought I was dying, and I didn't. I just crashed, cut my face open, and broke 11 bones," he said. "I'm convinced that all that stuff worked together to make me lose the weight and all. My weight got down to less than 150.

"I still don't know what the problem was. I never did find out. I just got better. The second time I was there, the doctor who treated me weighed about 400 pounds. He was all sweating and probably the worst physical specimen I've ever seen. He sat there for 20 minutes and told me his problems. Then, he told me I ought to quit racing. I told him maybe he ought to quit doctoring."

Allison was far from finished, however. He posted six consecutive seasons (1978-83) of four or more victories, the third-longest such streak in history, and seven consecutive years (1978-84) with multiple superspeedway victories, the second-longest such streak. On two occasions, he won at least four 500-mile races in back-to-back seasons (1971-72 and 1982-83)—the only driver to do so. He also won a classic race in four consecutive seasons (1981-84), a string exceeded only by Jeff Gordon, and recorded three consecutive 500-mile victories in 1982—11 years after he had done that the first time. And, in 1983, he captured the most overdue Winston Cup title in history.

Allison's final victory was one of the most dramatic in Winston Cup history. He beat his oldest son, Davey, by two car lengths to win the 1988 Daytona 500 at age 50. Four months later, Bobby suffered career-ending injuries—a fractured leg, broken ribs, and severe head trauma—when his Miller High Life Buick was involved in a first-lap wreck in the Miller High Life 500 at Pocono International Raceway in Long Pond, Pa.

"I was supposed to die in that wreck at Pocono," he said. "I woke up in the hospital, and I knew nothing. I remember thinking, 'Where am I? What has gone wrong? Why do I hurt so bad?' The return of my ability to apply logic to anything was so slow and painful. When I came back into the world, my memory was so damaged that I couldn't even think in terms of what my career had been, what I'd achieved."

What Allison had achieved was one of the greatest legacies in Winston Cup history. His 85 victories—one more than NASCAR mysteriously credits him for winning—rank third on the all-time list. The more notable categories in which he ranks among the top five include superspeedway victories (47), 500-mile wins (37), Grand Slam victories (22), short-track triumphs (31), poles (58), short-track poles (34), road-course poles (5), victories from the pole (20), 500-mile wins from the pole (6), short-track triumphs from the pole (12), and road-course victories from the pole (2). He shares the record for victories on road courses (6) and is one of only three drivers to win as many as 10 classics: four in the Southern 500 and three each in the Daytona 500 and World 600. He also has the distinction of being the only driver to win at least five races at all four Grand Slam tracks.

Allison's career Performance Index of 14,653 ranks third, and he is in the top five in virtually every Performance Index category. The most impressive nuggets on his resume are his record-tying 22 consecutive seasons with a rating of 300 or better and top-17 seasons (1966-87); 18 top-10 seasons (tied for second), 14 top-seven seasons (third), and six top-two seasons (tied for fourth).

Perhaps the only place where Allison has been a more familiar figure than victory lane is in the more than 2,000 Catholic churches in which he has attended mass. Allison's undying faith served him well during the '90s, when he suffered blows that would have destroyed mere mortals and had his faith tested more than Job.

First came the death of "Pop," father of Bobby and the other 12 children in the Allison clan. Several months later, Allison's youngest son, Clifford, was killed in a practice session at Michigan International Speedway. Less than a year later, Davey, hero to a generation of younger Winston Cup fans, lost his life in a helicopter accident. Then, Bonnett, whose relationship with Bobby was part brother and part son, died while practicing for a comeback at Daytona International Speedway. Finally, Allison's marriage of 36 years ended, largely, he believes, as a result of the deaths of Clifford and Davey, and his race team disbanded for financial reasons.

"From early on, my Catholic education and my perception of the Catholic faith is that none of us have a contract and that we must accept life as it comes," Allison said. "I felt we were so much more fortunate because we'd been able to have the good times. I knew other families that had had the bad times, but hadn't had the good times."

Yet Allison never lost faith, never asked, "Why me?" or "When will it end?"

"Neither one," he said.

Allison still has little, if any, recollection of the events of 1988, including his dramatic victory over Davey in the Daytona 500 or the career-ending accident. He'll frequently preface sentences with the caveat that his memory and mind aren't as sharp as they once were, but few people on the planet have better recollections of past events. Anyone who has the opportunity to meet Allison—who may be the most genuinely congenial and approachable superstar in the history of sports—should tell him that you know someone else who has met him. Refresh his memory only slightly, and he'll recite chapter and verse about his first and most recent encounters with your cousin's neighbor.

Yet, despite his congeniality, the competitive fires still burn brightly in one of the most popular drivers in stock-car racing history. For instance, there's a record Allison insists that he, not his archrival Petty, holds. "Real early on, I got a big kick out of people asking me for an autograph," he said. "I also figured I could write my name a lot faster than Richard with all those curlicues. He has signed a lot of autographs, but I could sign three or four to his one. I've signed more than he has because I can write so much faster than him. Secondly, like Richard, I did develop a really good following."

1983 in Review

Bobby Allison, who had lost the 1981 and 1982 Winston Cup titles to Darrell Waltrip by 53 and 72 points, respectively, edged Waltrip by 47 points to win the 1983 championship. Waltrip won a season-high seven poles, and Waltrip and Allison shared the season lead with six victories. Allison, who edged Waltrip, 821-818, in the Performance Index, had finished as a runner-up for the Winston Cup title on five occasions before snaring the 1983 crown driving DiGard Buicks and Chevrolets with Gary Nelson serving as crew chief and Robert Yates as engine builder.

Most Memorable Race

Bobby Allison and Bill Elliott were dueling for the lead in the World 600 at Charlotte on May 29 until Sterling Marlin's Chevrolet blew a tire with 58 laps remaining. Slick Johnson, Elliott, and Allison wrecked in the resulting debris, but Allison still finished third despite a damaged steering column. Bonnett led the last 53 laps and beat Petty by one second despite countless attempts by the latter to take the lead. "(Petty) was closing on me so much that I was having to go into the corners about 150 feet deeper than I should have," Bonnett said.

Most Significant Wreck

Phil Parsons and Waltrip were racing side by side on May 1 in the Winston 500 at Talladega, Ala., when Parsons's car flipped nearly a dozen times and he suffered a broken collarbone. The accident also eliminated Tim Richmond, David Pearson, A.J. Foyt, Kyle Petty, Jody Ridley, and Yarborough, the pole winner. "It looked like Waltrip got into Parsons going into the first turn, and that got the whole thing started," Yarborough said.

Most Important Off-Track Development

Richard Petty captured the Miller High Life 500 on October 9 at Charlotte, but he was fined $35,000 and penalized 104 points because his Pontiac's engine measured 38.983 cubic inches more than the allowable 350 and because left-side tires had been illegally mounted on the right side of his car during a pit stop with 37 laps remaining. "I just drive the car," Petty said. "I don't know what was going on."

Junior Johnson, who owned the Chevrolet driven by Waltrip, the runner-up, wasn't happy that Petty was allowed to keep his 198th and final victory with Petty Enterprises. "In my opinion, NASCAR is crookeder than Petty," Johnson told *The Atlanta Journal*.

Records & Milestones

When Waltrip won the pole for the November 20 running of the Winston Western 500 at Riverside, Calif., he became the only driver to capture a record-tying three consecutive poles on road courses on more than one occasion.

1983 at a Glance

Races:	30
Road:	2
Short Track:	10
Superspeedway:	18
Winners:	12
Pole Winners:	10
Tracks:	15
States:	11

1983 Performance Index Rankings

1. Bobby Allison (821)
2. Darrell Waltrip (818)
3. Bill Elliott (709)
4. Richard Petty (682)
5. Terry Labonte (615)
6. Neil Bonnett (611)
7. Harry Gant (522)
8. Dale Earnhardt (517)
9. Ricky Rudd (478)
10. Tim Richmond (460)
11. Dave Marcis (445)
12. Joe Ruttman (434)
13. Morgan Shepherd (419)
14. Ron Bouchard (412)
15. Kyle Petty (393)
16. Buddy Baker (391)
17. Dick Brooks (374)
18. Jimmy Means (347)
19. Buddy Arrington (332)
20. Lake Speed (318)
21. Geoff Bodine (317)
22. Cale Yarborough (308)
23. D.K. Ulrich (300)
24. Sterling Marlin (295)
25. Trevor Boys (262)
26. Benny Parsons (245)
27. Mark Martin (190)
28. Bobby Hillin Jr. (164)
29. Jody Ridley (163)
30. Ken Ragan (154)
31. Ronnie Thomas (141)
32. Lennie Pond (135)
33. David Pearson (130)
34. Tommy Gale (121)
35. J.D. McDuffie (107)
36. Bobby Wawak (97)
37. Dean Combs (79)
38. Ronnie Hopkins (75)
39. Bob Senneker (65)
40. Phil Parsons (53)
41. Rick Baldwin; Dean Roper (52)
43. Cecil Gordon (49)
44. Jimmy Ingalls (45)
45. Tom Sneva (38)
46. Al Elmore; Rick Newsom (37)
48. A.J. Foyt (34)
49. Joe Fields (32)
50. Clark Dwyer; Tommy Ellis (30)
52. Laurent Rioux; Jim Sauter (29)
54. Jerry Bowman (27)
55. Sumner McKnight (26)
56. Travis Tiller (25)
57. Hershel McGriff (22)
58. Bill Schmitt (21)
59. John Callis; Slick Johnson; Darryl Sage (20)
62. Jim Robinson (19)
63. Greg Sacks (18)
64. Connie Saylor (17)
65. Donnie Allison; Glenn Francis (16)
67. Randy Becker (15)
68. Doug Wheeler (12)
69. Bob Kennedy II (11)
70. Butch Lindley; Don Waterman (10)
72. Joe Millikan; Mike Potter (7)
74. Don Satterfield (6)

1983 Events

Daytona 500; Daytona International Speedway/2.5-m/500 miles
Cale Yarborough (Pontiac)/Ricky Rudd (Chevrolet)

Richmond 400; Richmond Fairgrounds Raceway/.542-m/217 miles
Bobby Allison (Chevrolet)/Ricky Rudd (Chevrolet)

W.W. Hodgdon Car. 500; N.C. Motor Speedway/1.017-mile/500m
Richard Petty (Pontiac)/Ricky Rudd (Chevrolet)

Coca-Cola 500; Atlanta International Raceway/1.522-m/500 m
Cale Yarborough (Chevrolet)/Geoff Bodine (Pontiac)

TranSouth 500; Darlington International Raceway/1.366-m/500m
Harry Gant (Buick)/Tim Richmond (Pontiac)

Northwestern Bank 400; No. Wilkesboro Speedway/.625-m/250 m
Darrell Waltrip (Chevrolet)/Neil Bonnett (Chevrolet)

Va. National Bank 500; Martinsville Speedway/.525-mile/263 m
Darrell Waltrip (Chevrolet)/Ricky Rudd (Chevrolet)

Winston 500; Alabama Int. Motor Speedway/2.66-mile/500 miles
Richard Petty (Pontiac)/Cale Yarborough (Chevrolet)

Marty Robbins 420; Nashville Int. Raceway/.596-m/250 miles
Darrell Waltrip (Chevrolet)/Darrell Waltrip (Chevrolet)

Mason-Dixon 500; Dover Downs Int. Speedway/1-mile/500 miles
Bobby Allison (Buick)/Joe Ruttman (Buick)

Valleydale 500; Bristol International Raceway/.533-mile/267m
Darrell Waltrip (Chevrolet)/Neil Bonnett (Chevrolet)

World 600; Charlotte Motor Speedway/1.5-mile/600 miles
Neil Bonnett (Chevrolet)/Buddy Baker (Ford)

Budweiser 400; Riverside Int. Raceway/2.62-m road/250 miles
Ricky Rudd (Chevrolet)/Darrell Waltrip (Chevrolet)

Van Scoy Diamond Mine 500; Pocono Int. Raceway/2.5-mile/500m
Bobby Allison (Buick)/Darrell Waltrip (Chevrolet)

Gabriel 400; Michigan International Speedway/2-m/400 miles
Cale Yarborough (Chevrolet)/Terry Labonte (Chevrolet)

Firecracker 400; Daytona International Speedway/2.5-m/400 m
Buddy Baker (Ford)/Cale Yarborough (Chevrolet)

Busch Nashville 420; Nashville Int. Raceway/.596-m/250 miles
Dale Earnhardt (Ford)/Ron Bouchard (Buick)

Like Cola 500; Pocono International Raceway/2.5-m/500 miles
Tim Richmond (Pontiac)/Tim Richmond (Pontiac)

Talladega 500; Alabama Int. Motor Speedway/2.66-m/500 miles
Dale Earnhardt (Ford)/Cale Yarborough (Chevrolet)

Champion Spark Plug 400; Michigan Int. Speedway/2-mile/400 m
Cale Yarborough (Chevrolet)/Terry Labonte (Chevrolet)

Busch 500; Bristol International Raceway/.533-mile/267 miles
Darrell Waltrip (Chevrolet)/Joe Ruttman (Pontiac)

Southern 500; Darlington International Raceway/1.366-m/500 m
Bobby Allison (Buick)/Neil Bonnett (Chevrolet)

Wrangler Sanforset 400; Richmond Fgds. Raceway/.542-m/217 m
Bobby Allison (Buick)/Darrell Waltrip (Chevrolet)

Budweiser 500; Dover Downs International Speedway/1-m/500 m
Bobby Allison (Buick)/Terry Labonte (Chevrolet)

Goody's 500; Martinsville Speedway/.525-mile/263 miles
Ricky Rudd (Chevrolet)/Darrell Waltrip (Chevrolet)

Holly Farms 400; North Wilkesboro Speedway/.625-m/250 miles
Darrell Waltrip (Chevrolet)/Darrell Waltrip (Chevrolet)

Miller High Life 500; Charlotte Motor Speedway/1.5-mile/500m
Richard Petty (Pontiac)/Tim Richmond (Pontiac)

W.W. Hodgdon Amer. 500; N.C. Motor Speedway/1.017-m/500m
Terry Labonte (Chevrolet)/Neil Bonnett (Chevrolet)

Atlanta Journal 500; Atlanta Int. Raceway/1.522-m/500 miles
Neil Bonnett (Chevrolet)/Tim Richmond (Pontiac)

Winston Western 500; Riverside Int. Raceway/2.62-m road/313m
Bill Elliott (Ford)/Darrell Waltrip (Chevrolet)

Victories

1. Bobby Allison; Darrell Waltrip (6)
3. Cale Yarborough (4)
4. Richard Petty (3)
5. Neil Bonnett; Dale Earnhardt; Ricky Rudd (2)
8. Buddy Baker; Bill Elliott; Harry Gant; Terry Labonte; Tim Richmond (1)

Poles

1. Darrell Waltrip (7)
2. Neil Bonnett; Tim Richmond; Ricky Rudd (4)
5. Terry Labonte; Cale Yarborough (3)
7. Joe Ruttman (2)
8. Buddy Baker; Geoff Bodine; Ron Bouchard (1)

Victories

1. Chevrolet (15)
2. Buick (6)
3. Pontiac (5)
4. Ford (4)

Poles

1. Chevrolet (21)
2. Pontiac (6)
3. Buick (2)
4. Ford (1)

1984 Classic Success Stories

Golf has its four major championships—the Masters, U.S. Open, British Open, and Professional Golfers' Association Championship. Thoroughbred racing has its Triple Crown races—the Kentucky Derby, Preakness, and Belmont Stakes—and the Breeders' Cup. Tennis has its Grand Slam events—Wimbledon and the U.S., French, and Australian Opens.

Although the concept of "classic" stock-car races is being introduced in this book, it is merely a refinement. Long before the Winston Million's 13-year run from 1985-97, both fans and media paid considerable attention to the Triple Crown of stock-car racing—the Southern 500 at Darlington, S.C.; the Daytona 500 at Daytona Beach, Fla., and the Coca-Cola (originally World) 600 at Lowe's (originally Charlotte) Motor Speedway.

Like the aforementioned events in golf, horse racing, and tennis, those races and the newest classic—the Brickyard 400 at Indianapolis—draw considerably more media attention than other races and generate interest from fans who don't necessarily follow Winston Cup racing on a weekly basis.

Dominating the classics obviously isn't easy. In fact, only three times—1976, 1984, and 1985—during the first 51 years of Winston Cup racing were even two of those races captured from the pole in the same season *by any drivers*, much less the *same* driver.

Only three times have drivers won the three original classics—the Triple Crown—in a single season: Lee Roy Yarbrough in 1969, David Pearson in 1976, and Jeff Gordon in 1997. The addition of the Brickyard 400 in 1994 has made it easier to capture three classics in a season. Both Dale Jarrett in 1996 and Gordon in 1998 accomplished that feat, aided by a victory in the Brickyard 400.

Only two drivers have managed to win all four classics in a career, Dale Earnhardt and Gordon. In addition to Pearson and Yarbrough, four other drivers won the three original classics during their careers—Bobby Allison, Buddy Baker, Richard Petty, and Darrell Waltrip. Of those six drivers, only Waltrip had the opportunity to drive in Winston Cup competition at Indianapolis.

Gordon passed Allison and Petty to become the all-time leader in classics when he captured his second Daytona 500 victory in 1999. Gordon, who shares the record of two Brickyard 400 victories with Jarrett, also has three wins in the 600-mile classic at Charlotte and earned four consecutive Southern 500 victories from 1995-98—the only time a driver has won the same classic four years in a row. Allison won the Southern 500 four times and the Daytona 500 and World 600 on three occasions, and Petty captured a record seven Daytona 500 victories, two World 600 triumphs and the 1967 Southern 500. Cale Yarborough and Waltrip hold the records for most victories in the Southern 500 and Charlotte's 600, respectively, with five.

Pearson won a record 13 classic poles, including six in the Southern 500 and the World 600, both records. Petty and Baker share the record of four Daytona 500 poles, while Gordon holds the Brickyard mark with three.

No driver in the first 51 years of Winston Cup racing managed to win the pole for all four classics, but nine drivers have won the pole for each of the three Triple Crown races: Fireball Roberts, Bill Elliott, Ken Schrader, Bobby Labonte, Pearson, Petty, Yarborough, and Bobby and Donnie Allison. Gordon has won the pole for three classics, but not the Southern 500.

Elliott and Gordon are the only drivers to capture four classic victories from the pole. Elliott (the 1985 Daytona 500 and Southern 500) and Pearson (the 1976 World 600 and Southern 500) are the only drivers to capture two classics from the pole in the same season. Gordon is the only driver to win the same classic from the pole on three occasions: Charlotte's 600-miler in 1994, 1997, and 1998.

Behind the wheel of the No. 24 DuPont Automotive Finishes Chevrolet, Jeff Gordon had won 11 classic races—four in the Southern 500, three in the 600-miler at Charlotte, two in the Brickyard 400, and two in the Daytona 500—through 1999.

1984 in Review

Terry Labonte won only two races in a Chevrolet owned by Billy Hagan, but he captured his first Winston Cup championship and enabled Dale Inman—crew chief for all seven of Petty's championship seasons—to become the only man to serve as crew chief for eight championship campaigns. Elliott held a narrow edge over Labonte in the Performance Index ratings, 760-739, with Harry Gant (737) and Earnhardt (724) close behind. Waltrip was fifth in the Performance Index ratings despite winning a season-high seven victories and sharing the lead in poles with Ricky Rudd, Yarborough, and Elliott, who earned four apiece.

Most Memorable Race

With President Reagan giving the command to fire the engines from Air Force One and subsequently comfortably shielded from the Florida sunshine in an air-conditioned luxury suite at Daytona International Speedway, Petty and Yarborough treated the leader of the free world to an incredible Firecracker 400 on Independence Day. With less than two laps to go, Yarborough overtook Petty down the backstretch. When Doug Heveron's Chevrolet went airborne in the tri-oval, both Petty and Yarborough realized the race would end under caution and that the leader of that lap would be the winner. Petty dived low in the fourth turn and successfully regained the lead. Petty and Yarborough then repeatedly bumped fenders through the tri-oval before the President saw the King prevail by four inches. Yarborough then absentmindedly pulled into the pits, losing second place to Gant. Petty had a chance to visit with Reagan after the 200th and final victory of his career. "It just blew his mind that we were running at each other at 200 miles an hour, that we were touching at that speed," said Petty, whose victorious Pontiac is still on display at the Smithsonian Institute in Washington.

Most Significant Wreck

Terry Schoonover, making his second Winston Cup start, was killed on November 11 in the Atlanta Journal 500 at Hampton, Ga. Schoonover died of "massive head and internal injuries" after his Chevrolet hit the wall in the second turn, slid down the backstretch, and smashed into a dirt bank in the infield.

Most Important Off-Track Development

Petty left Petty Enterprises, for which he had won 198 races from 1960-83, to spend the 1984 and '85 seasons behind the wheel of a Pontiac owned by Mike Curb.

Records & Milestones

The 1984 season was the first of two in which a modern-record nine drivers posted multiple victories: Waltrip, Geoff Bodine (3), Elliott (3), Gant (3), Yarborough (3), Bobby Allison (2), Earnhardt (2), Labonte (2), and Petty (2).... Only two manufacturers won poles—Ford (20) and Chevrolet (9)—the first time in history and one of only four seasons that only two brands captured poles.

When Neil Bonnett captured the first pole of his career in 1976, he didn't get to start the race because he was substituting for Bobby Allison. Pearson won the 113th—and last—pole of his career for the June 10 Van Scoy Diamond Mine 500 at Long Pond, Pa. But Pearson didn't get to start the race: He was substituting for Bonnett in Junior Johnson's Chevrolet.... Race sponsors who had a difficult time using victory lane photos for commercial purposes included the Sovran Bank 500 at Martinsville, Va. (won by Bodine in the Northwestern Securities Chevrolet); the Coors 420 at Nashville (won by Waltrip in the Budweiser Chevrolet), and the Miller High Life 400 at Michigan International Speedway and the Miller High Life 500 at Charlotte (both won by Elliott in the Coors Ford).

1984 at a Glance

Races:	30
Road:	2
Short Track:	10
Superspeedway:	18
Winners:	12
Pole Winners:	11
Tracks:	15
States:	11

1984 Performance Index Rankings

1. Bill Elliott (760)
2. Terry Labonte (739)
3. Harry Gant (737)
4. Dale Earnhardt (724)
5. Darrell Waltrip (667)
6. Bobby Allison (658)
7. Ricky Rudd (623)
8. Geoff Bodine (549)
9. Ron Bouchard (536)
10. Neil Bonnett (532)
11. Richard Petty (506)
12. Cale Yarborough (478)
13. Tim Richmond (444)
14. Dave Marcis (432)
15. Rusty Wallace (404)
16. Dick Brooks (395)
17. Buddy Baker (379)
18. Trevor Boys (347)
19. Benny Parsons (340)
20. Joe Ruttman (339)
21. Kyle Petty (324)
22. Lake Speed (304)
23. Phil Parsons (283)
24. Jimmy Means (254)
25. Jody Ridley (195)
26. Buddy Arrington (190)
27. Clark Dwyer (189)
28. Tommy Ellis (186)
29. Bobby Hillin Jr. (175)
30. Mike Alexander (147)
31. Greg Sacks (144)
32. Lennie Pond (124)
33. David Pearson (116)
34. Sterling Marlin (113)
35. Morgan Shepherd (111)
36. Ken Ragan (86)
37. Doug Heveron (71)
38. Tommy Gale (62)
39. J.D. McDuffie (61)
40. Dean Combs (53)
41. Jim Sauter (48)
42. Dick May (45)
43. Elliott Forbes-Robinson; D.K. Ulrich (41)
45. Jim Southard (40)
46. Ronnie Thomas (39)
47. Dean Roper (29)
48. Derrike Cope (27)
49. Joe Millikan (23)
50. Jerry Bowman; Gene Coyle; Steve Moore; Mark Stahl (22)

54. Hershel McGriff (21)
55. Laurent Rioux (20)
56. Bill Schmitt (17)
57. Jim Robinson (16)
58. Glenn Francis; Ken Schrader (14)
60. Dale Jarrett; Sumner McKnight (11)
62. Bobby Gerhart (6)
63. Jimmy Hensley; Jeff Hooker (5)

1984 Events

Daytona 500; Daytona International Speedway/2.5-m/500 miles
Cale Yarborough (Chevrolet)/Cale Yarborough (Chevrolet)

Miller High Life 400; Richmond Fgds. Raceway/.542-mile/217 m
Ricky Rudd (Ford)/Darrell Waltrip (Chevrolet)

W.W. Hodgdon Car. 500; N.C. Motor Speedway/1.017-mile/500m
Bobby Allison (Buick)/Harry Gant (Chevrolet)

Coca-Cola 500; Atlanta International Raceway/1.522-mile/500m
Benny Parsons (Chevrolet)/Buddy Baker (Ford)

Valleydale 500; Bristol International Raceway/.533-mile/267m
Darrell Waltrip (Chevrolet)/Ricky Rudd (Ford)

Northwestern Bank 400; No. Wilkesboro Speedway/.625-m/250 m
Tim Richmond (Pontiac)/Ricky Rudd (Ford)

TranSouth 500; Darlington International Raceway/1.366-m/500m
Darrell Waltrip (Chevrolet)/Benny Parsons (Chevrolet)

Sovran Bank 500; Martinsville Speedway/.526-mile/263 miles
Geoff Bodine (Chevrolet)/Joe Ruttman (Chevrolet)

Winston 500; Alabama Int. Motor Speedway/2.66-mile/500 miles
Cale Yarborough (Chevrolet)/Cale Yarborough (Chevrolet)

Coors 420; Nashville International Raceway/.596-m/250 miles
Darrell Waltrip (Chevrolet)/Darrell Waltrip (Chevrolet)

Budweiser 500; Dover Downs International Speedway/1-m/500 m
Richard Petty (Pontiac)/Ricky Rudd (Ford)

World 600; Charlotte Motor Speedway/1.5-mile/600 miles
Bobby Allison (Buick)/Harry Gant (Chevrolet)

Budweiser 400; Riverside Int. Raceway/2.62-m road/250 miles
Terry Labonte (Chevrolet)/Terry Labonte (Chevrolet)

Van Scoy Diamond Mine 500; Pocono Int. Raceway/2.5-mile/500m
Cale Yarborough (Chevrolet)/David Pearson (Chevrolet)

Miller High Life 400; Michigan Int. Speedway/2-m/400 miles
Bill Elliott (Ford)/Bill Elliott (Ford)

Pepsi Firecracker 400; Daytona Int. Speedway/2.5-m/400 miles
Richard Petty (Pontiac)/Cale Yarborough (Chevrolet)

Pepsi 420; Nashville International Raceway/.596-m/250 miles
Geoff Bodine (Chevrolet)/Ricky Rudd (Ford)

Like Cola 500; Pocono International Raceway/2.5-m/500 miles
Harry Gant (Chevrolet)/Bill Elliott (Ford)

Talladega 500; Alabama Int. Motor Speedway/2.66-m/500 miles
Dale Earnhardt (Chevrolet)/Cale Yarborough (Chevrolet)

Champion Spark Plug 400; Michigan Int. Speedway/2-mile/400 m
Darrell Waltrip (Chevrolet)/Bill Elliott (Ford)

Busch 500; Bristol International Raceway/.533-mile/267 miles
Terry Labonte (Chevrolet)/Geoff Bodine (Chevrolet)

Southern 500; Darlington International Raceway/1.366-m/500 m
Harry Gant (Chevrolet)/Harry Gant (Chevrolet)

Wrangler Sanforset 400; Richmond Fgds. Raceway/.542-m/217 m
Darrell Waltrip (Chevrolet)/Darrell Waltrip (Chevrolet)

Delaware 500; Dover Downs International Speedway/1-mile/500m
Harry Gant (Chevrolet)

Goody's 500; Martinsville Speedway/.526-mile/263 miles
Darrell Waltrip (Chevrolet)/Geoff Bodine (Chevrolet)

Miller High Life 500; Charlotte Motor Speedway/1.5-mile/500m
Bill Elliott (Ford)/Benny Parsons (Chevrolet)

Holly Farms 400; North Wilkesboro Speedway/.625-m/250 miles
Darrell Waltrip (Chevrolet)/Darrell Waltrip (Chevrolet)

W.W. Hodgdon Amer. 500; N.C. Motor Speedway/1.017-m/500m
Bill Elliott (Ford)/Geoff Bodine (Chevrolet)

Atlanta Journal 500; Atlanta Int. Raceway/1.522-m/500 miles
Dale Earnhardt (Chevrolet)/Bill Elliott (Ford)

Winston Western 500; Riverside Int. Raceway/2.62-m road/313m
Geoff Bodine (Chevrolet)/Terry Labonte (Chevrolet)

Victories

1. Darrell Waltrip (7)
2. Geoff Bodine; Bill Elliott; Harry Gant; Cale Yarborough (3)
6. Bobby Allison; Dale Earnhardt; Terry Labonte; Richard Petty (2)
10. Benny Parsons; Tim Richmond; Ricky Rudd (1)

Poles

1. Bill Elliott; Ricky Rudd; Darrell Waltrip; Cale Yarborough (4)
5. Geoff Bodine; Harry Gant (3)
7. Terry Labonte; Benny Parsons (2)
9. Buddy Baker; David Pearson; Joe Ruttman (1)

Victories

1. Chevrolet (21)
2. Ford (4)
3. Pontiac (3)
4. Buick (2)

Poles

1. Chevrolet (20)
2. Ford (9)

1985
'Jaws' Took A Very Big Bite Out of NASCAR's Record Book

When Darrell Waltrip joined the Winston Cup Series on a full-time basis in 1973, stock-car racing had never seen anyone quite like him.

The Owensboro, Ky., native was 26 years old, brash, cocky, witty, outspoken—and enormously talented. Before Waltrip, who earned his third Winston Cup title in 1985, had even won a race, he was suggesting that the sport's established stars should consider retirement before they were enveloped in his wake.

Waltrip quickly became a media favorite, although hardly a darling of the fans or his rivals. When Cale Yarborough nicknamed Waltrip "Jaws," because his mouth never seemed to stop moving, Waltrip painted a shark on his race car in reference to the popular adventure movie. Waltrip further upstaged Yarborough, who had a habit of describing his victories as among the toughest races he had ever contested, by rating races' degree of difficulty on the "Cale Scale." And, just as he had predicted, Waltrip was busily carving his niche as one of the greatest stock-car drivers in history.

"I never really wanted to drive for one of the so-called 'big-three' teams. Nobody had come in for a long time and been able to break the domination of the 'big-three' teams in Grand National racing until we managed to do it. We were the first team to start from scratch and beat the big three or big four. I was able to beat the gi-

ants. I've gotten a great deal of satisfaction out of that," Waltrip said before the 1981 season, when he spent $325,000 to buy his way out of his contract with DiGard to join one of the sport's three powerhouse car owners of the day, Junior Johnson.

By the time Waltrip left Johnson six seasons later, he had added 43 victories, three Winston Cup championships, and firmly established himself as one of the "giants" of stock-car racing.

During a rain delay in the final race of the 1998 season, the NAPA 500 at Atlanta, in which the struggling Waltrip would start last in the 43-car field for the 20th time that season, he told ESPN: "We've had so many new fans come into this sport that a lot of them don't remember what I did or what Richard Petty did."

What Waltrip has done is accumulate a brilliant resume that includes more modern records than any other driver.

For example, Waltrip is the only driver in the modern era who has posted:

- Three or more victories 10 years in a row (1977-86) or five or more wins in eight consecutive seasons (1977-84);
- Multiple short-track victories 10 years in a row (1975-84), four consecutive seasons (1981-84) with five or more short-track wins, or three consecutive seasons (1981-83) with six or more short-track triumphs;
- Seven consecutive years (1978-84) with a victory from the pole, five successive campaigns (1980-84) with multiple victories from the pole, or three seasons in a row (1980-82) with three or more triumphs from the pole;
- Seven years in a row (1978-84) with a short-track win from the pole, five consecutive years (1980-84) with multiple short-track wins from the pole, or consecutive campaigns (1981-82) with four or more short-track triumphs from the pole;
- Seven successive years (1979-85) with multiple short-track poles, five consecutive years (1981-85) with three or more short-track poles, or four consecutive years (1981-84) with four or more short-track poles.

Not only are all of the aforementioned feats modern records, but Waltrip ranks second on the all-time list in all of them.

Three-time Winston Cup champion Darrell Waltrip holds more records during NASCAR's modern era than any other driver.

He also is the only driver in the modern era to post back-to-back seasons (1981-82) with 12 or more victories, win a pole 13 seasons in a row (1974-86), or multiple poles 11 years in a row (1975-85). He shares the modern records of seven consecutive years (1979-85) with at least four poles and consecutive campaigns (1981-82) with at least four victories from the pole.

Waltrip's entries in the record books aren't limited to the modern era, however. He is the only driver in history to win nine poles on road courses, earn a short-track victory 15 years in a row (1975-89), win a short-track pole in 12 consecutive seasons (1974-85), win five or more 500-mile races in back-to-back seasons (1981-82), or win three poles on road courses in one year (1981). He also shares the records of winning five consecutive short-track poles (in 1981 and 1982), winning four consecutive races from the pole (1981), and two victories on road courses in a season (1980). Waltrip is also the only driver who has won a record-tying three poles in a row on road courses on more than one occasion.

Every year from 1981-84, Waltrip either won or shared the season lead in both victories and poles. No other driver has led or shared the lead in both categories four years in a row.

Waltrip's career Performance Index of 14,496 ranks fourth on the all-time list and is the second-highest in the modern era. He is the only driver in history to post 20 consecutive seasons with a rating of 400 or better (1975-94) or rank in the top 16 for 21 consecutive years (1974-94), and he's among the top five in virtually every Performance Index category. Among the more impressive are 11 consecutive seasons (1977-87) in the top six and 23 consecutive campaigns (1973-95) in the top 22, both among his host of modern records.

Although Waltrip ranks fourth on the all-time list in both victories (84) and poles (59), both are modern records. Among the more notable categories in which he also ranks among the top five are seasons leading the circuit in victories (6), short-track victories (a modern-record 47), road-course wins (5), victories from the pole (24), short-track victories from the pole (18), road-course triumphs from the pole (3), and short-track poles (35). Waltrip also ranks in the top 10 in, among other things, superspeedway wins (32), Grand Slam victories (15), 500-mile triumphs (24), and

classic victories (7), including a record five in Charlotte's 600-mile race.

By the time he won the 1989 Daytona 500, Waltrip had evolved from cocky kid to elder statesman and his driving style from daring to conservative.

"There are some guys who seem to be thinking lead at all costs. I just want to lead the last lap—or the last three feet," he said. "I'm not willing to take the chances some guys are. If the gain is worth the chance, I'll take it. If it isn't, I won't. I've been able to win without taking those chances.

"My philosophy is: If the reward is not worth the risk, why do it? Racing for the championship does that to you. You become a little more conservative. You start to realize that you don't have to lead every lap, smoking everybody off. That's driver ego. That's part of getting a little bit older, realizing I don't have to take those risks.

"Winning a championship takes patience. Believe me, I've got plenty of patience," he added. "And no matter how many races you win, a national driving title shines brighter than all the wins combined."

Waltrip spent five hours on the operating table after suffering serious leg injuries in a practice crash with Dave Marcis in July of 1990 at Daytona Beach, Fla. He bounced back to capture two victories in 1991 and three more, including the Mountain Dew Southern 500 at Darlington, S.C.—his final triumph—in 1992. But he walked with a severe limp until he underwent surgery again after the 1995 season. In 1998, Waltrip sold his team in midseason and suffered through his sixth consecutive winless campaign. Waltrip, who frequently said in his early days that he'd never race past age 40, turned 53 shortly before the start of the 2000 season—which he says will be his last.

1985 in Review

Waltrip trailed Bill Elliott by 206 points with eight races remaining, but he posted two of his three 1985 victories, two runner-up finishes, a third-place effort, and a fourth-place showing in the last eight races to defeat Elliott, 4,292-4,191, for his third Winston Cup championship. Elliott, who won 11 races and 11 poles—all on superspeedways—to lead the circuit in both categories, outdistanced Waltrip in the Performance Index, 791-764.

Most Memorable Race

A pit stop that took one minute and nine seconds left Elliott within a couple of seconds of being two laps down in the Winston 500 at Talladega, Ala., on May 5. Without benefit of a caution flag, however, Elliott needed only 97 laps to make up that five-mile deficit and push the Harry Melling-owned Ford into the lead. Elliott overtook Yarborough with 20 laps to go and beat Kyle Petty to the checkered flag by two seconds. "To be honest, I didn't think I had a chance of making up that time," said Elliott, whose average speed of 186.288 mph established a new record for a Winston Cup race.

Most Important Off-Track Development

R.J. Reynolds established The Winston, an all-star race won by Waltrip, and the Winston Million, in which a driver who won any three of the Daytona 500, Winston 500, World 600, or Southern 500 would earn a $1 million bonus.

Most Significant Wreck

Elliott already had won the Daytona 500 and the Winston 500, but his chances of adding the September 1 Southern 500 didn't appear particularly good until Dale Earnhardt, who had led 147 laps and was dueling with Yarborough for the lead, hit the wall on the 318th of 367 laps and slid down the backstretch. Earnhardt barely missed Elliott, who subsequently won the race and the Winston Million. "For a while there, I thought I was going to be the guy to keep (Elliott) from winning it," Earnhardt said.

Records & Milestones

The 28-race schedule in 1985 equaled the 1973 season for the fewest races held in the modern era. . . . Only two manufacturers won races, Chevrolet and Ford. The only other seasons in history in which only two makes visited victory lane were 1984, 1994, and 1995. . . . Only 14 tracks played host to Winston Cup races, the fewest in the modern era.

1985 at a Glance

Races:	28
Road:	2
Short Track:	8
Superspeedway:	18
Winners:	9
Pole Winners:	7
Tracks:	14
States:	11

1985 Performance Index Rankings

1. Bill Elliott (791)
2. Darrell Waltrip (764)
3. Neil Bonnett (675)
4. Ricky Rudd (651)
5. Harry Gant (622)
6. Geoff Bodine (613)
7. Lake Speed (573)
8. Terry Labonte (535)
9. Kyle Petty; Tim Richmond (528)
11. Dale Earnhardt (500)
12. Bobby Allison (452)
13. Ron Bouchard (448)
14. Ken Schrader (415)
15. Buddy Baker (404)
16. Bobby Hillin Jr. (396)
17. Richard Petty (382)
18. Buddy Arrington (354)
19. Rusty Wallace (327)
20. Greg Sacks (296)
21. Phil Parsons (289)
22. Cale Yarborough (273)
23. Dave Marcis (265)
24. Benny Parsons (216)
25. Joe Ruttman (212)
26. Jimmy Means (207)
27. Clark Dwyer (198)
28. Eddie Bierschwale (184)
29. Lennie Pond (164)
30. Morgan Shepherd (147)
31. Mike Alexander (99)
32. Slick Johnson (78)
33. Bobby Wawak (69)
34. Tommy Ellis (68)
35. Trevor Boys (61)
36. Sterling Marlin (57)
37. Dick Brooks (55)
38. Davey Allison; J.D. McDuffie (51)
40. Phil Good (49)
41. Jerry Bowman (47)
42. David Pearson; Ken Ragan (43)
44. Glenn Steurer (38)
45. Don Hume; Ronnie Thomas (36)
47. A.J. Foyt; Jim Robinson (35)
49. Alan Kulwicki (29)

50. Dick Trickle (27)
51. Derrike Cope; Randy LaJoie; Bob Riley (26)
54. Tommie Crozier (25)
55. Bosco Lowe; Mike Potter (23)
57. Dick Skillen; Rick Wilson (22)
59. Doug Heveron (21)
60. Michael Waltrip (17)
61. Ruben Garcia; Sumner McKnight (16)
63. Jim Sauter; Bill Schmitt (15)
65. Jim Bown (14)
66. John Soares Jr. (11)
67. Glenn Francis (10)
68. Butch Lindley (2)

1985 Events

Daytona 500; Daytona International Speedway/2.5-m/500 miles
Bill Elliott (Ford)/Bill Elliott (Ford)

Miller High Life 400; Richmond Fgds. Raceway/.542-mile/217 m
Dale Earnhardt (Chevrolet)/Darrell Waltrip (Chevrolet)

Carolina 500; North Carolina Motor Speedway/1.017-mile/500 m
Neil Bonnett (Chevrolet)/Terry Labonte (Chevrolet)

Coca-Cola 500; Atlanta International Raceway/1.522-mile/500m
Bill Elliott (Ford)/Neil Bonnett (Chevrolet)

Valleydale 500; Bristol International Raceway/.533-mile/267m
Dale Earnhardt (Chevrolet)/Harry Gant (Chevrolet)

TranSouth 500; Darlington International Raceway/1.366-m/500m
Bill Elliott (Ford)/Bill Elliott (Ford)

Northwestern Bank 400; No. Wilkesboro Speedway/.625-m/250 m
Neil Bonnett (Chevrolet)/Darrell Waltrip (Chevrolet)

Sovran Bank 500; Martinsville Speedway/.526-mile/263 miles
Harry Gant (Chevrolet)/Darrell Waltrip (Chevrolet)

Winston 500; Alabama Int. Motor Speedway/2.66mile/500 miles
Bill Elliott (Ford)/Bill Elliott (Ford)

Budweiser 500; Dover Downs International Speedway/1-m/500 m
Bill Elliott (Ford)/Terry Labonte (Chevrolet)

World 600; Charlotte Motor Speedway/1.5-mile/600 miles
Darrell Waltrip (Chevrolet)/Bill Elliott (Ford)

Budweiser 400; Riverside Int. Raceway/2.62-m road/249 miles
Terry Labonte (Chevrolet)/Darrell Waltrip (Chevrolet)

Van Scoy Diamond Mine 500; Pocono Int. Raceway/2.5-m/500 m
Bill Elliott (Ford)/Bill Elliott (Ford)

Miller 400; Michigan International Speedway/2-mile/400 miles
Bill Elliott (Ford)

Pepsi Firecracker 400; Daytona Int. Speedway/2.5-m/400 miles
Greg Sacks (Chevrolet)/Bill Elliott (Ford)

Summer 500; Pocono International Raceway/2.5-mile/500 miles
Bill Elliott (Ford)/Bill Elliott (Ford)

Talladega 500; Alabama Int. Motor Speedway/2.66-m/500 miles
Cale Yarborough (Ford)/Bill Elliott (Ford)

Champion Spark Plug 400; Michigan Int. Speedway/2-mile/400 m
Bill Elliott (Ford)/Bill Elliott (Ford)

Busch 500; Bristol International Raceway/.533-mile/267 miles
Dale Earnhardt (Chevrolet)/Dale Earnhardt (Chevrolet)

Southern 500; Darlington International Raceway/1.366-m/500 m
Bill Elliott (Ford)/Bill Elliott (Ford)

Wrangler Sanforset 400; Richmond Fgds. Raceway/.542-m/217 m
Darrell Waltrip (Chevrolet)/Geoff Bodine (Chevrolet)

Delaware 500; Dover Downs International Speedway/1-m/500 m
Harry Gant (Chevrolet)/Bill Elliott (Ford)

Goody's 500; Martinsville Speedway/.526-mile/263 miles
Dale Earnhardt (Chevrolet)/Geoff Bodine (Chevrolet)

Holly Farms 400; North Wilkesboro Speedway/.625-mile/250 miles
Harry Gant (Chevrolet)/Geoff Bodine (Chevrolet)

Miller 500; Charlotte Motor Speedway/1.5-mile/500 miles
Cale Yarborough (Ford)/Harry Gant (Chevrolet)

Nationwise 500; North Carolina Motor Speedway/1.017-m/500 m
Darrell Waltrip (Chevrolet)/Terry Labonte (Chevrolet)

Atlanta Journal 500; Atlanta Int. Raceway/1.522-m/500 miles
Bill Elliott (Ford)/Harry Gant (Chevrolet)

Winston Western 500; Riverside Int. Raceway/2.62-m road/312m
Ricky Rudd (Ford)/Terry Labonte (Chevrolet)

Victories

1. Bill Elliott (11)
2. Dale Earnhardt (4)
3. Harry Gant; Darrell Waltrip (3)
5. Neil Bonnett; Cale Yarborough (2)
7. Terry Labonte; Ricky Rudd; Greg Sacks (1)

Poles

1. Bill Elliott (11)
2. Terry Labonte; Darrell Waltrip (4)
4. Geoff Bodine; Harry Gant (3)
6. Neil Bonnett; Dale Earnhardt (1)

Victories

1. Chevrolet; Ford (14)

Poles

1. Chevrolet (16)
2. Ford (11)

1986
Playboy
Of the Pits

When Dale Earnhardt captured his second Winston Cup title in 1986, few predicted he was on his way to a record-tying seven championships.

That's because many observers thought the next decade would belong to a driver who earned seven victories, eight poles, and finished second to Earnhardt in the Performance Index in 1986.

Tim Richmond first proved to be a force to be reckoned with in 1982, when he won twice on road courses.

In 1986, Richmond became the first driver to win two road races in a season twice and the first to capture two road races from the pole in the same season. Although Richmond's background in road racing had served him well, he also won a short-track race and four superspeedway events in 1986, including the Southern 500 at Darlington, S.C. His daring last-lap pass of Geoff Bodine in the Summer 500 at Pocono International Raceway in Long Pond, Pa., in which Richmond edged Bodine and Ricky Rudd in a photo finish, showed the same flair for the dramatic that Richmond long had demonstrated off the track.

The popular bachelor had been the premier playboy of the pits since his days as the 1980 Indianapolis 500 Rookie of the Year. Perhaps in accordance with his youth, Richmond also was a frequent target of drug rumors.

Richmond suffered what appeared to be a temporary setback on his way to stock-car racing immortality when, before the 1987 season began, he became ill. The illness was first reported as influenza, then pneumonia, then double pneumonia.

Richmond didn't make his first start of the 1987 season until the Miller High Life 500 at Pocono on June 14, when he beat Bill Elliott by one second to earn one of the most emotional victories in history. "I had tears

in my eyes when I came across to take the checkered flag," he said.

A week later, Richmond won at Riverside, Calif., his third consecutive victory on a road course and the 13th triumph of his career. Three races later, Richmond's storybook comeback continued in the Summer 500 at Pocono, where he captured his 14th career pole. But after a 29th-place finish at Michigan International Speedway on August 16, Richmond returned to the sidelines. A month later, he resigned from Hendrick Motorsports.

Richmond wanted to drive in the 1988 Daytona 500, but NASCAR refused to give him permission until he passed a drug test. He failed, reportedly because of a banned masking agent. NASCAR said Richmond would be allowed to compete as soon as it received his medical records from his personal physician. A day before the race, Richmond called a news conference, saying he didn't trust the sanctioning body and that he wanted "to clear the family name." During the race, an airplane flew over Daytona International Speedway with a trailing banner that said: "Fans, I Miss You—Tim Richmond."

Richmond subsequently passed a drug test and sued NASCAR, but the case never went to court. Richmond was 34 years old when he died on August 7, 1989. Several days later, his family revealed the cause of death as Acquired Immune Deficiency Syndrome, which had been rumored, but denied, for many months. Nearly a decade after his untimely death, Richmond remained the most prominent race driver—and perhaps the most famous athlete—to die of AIDS.

1986 in Review

Earnhardt captured five victories, his second Winston Cup title, and held a 778-736 advantage over Richmond in the Performance Index. Richmond's seven victories led the circuit, and his eight poles shared the lead with Bodine.

Most Memorable Race

Kyle Petty became the first third-generation driver to capture a Winston Cup victory in a wild edition of the Miller High Life 400 at Richmond, Va., on February 23. Earnhardt and Darrell Waltrip were

battling for the lead on the 397th of 400 laps when Earnhardt apparently plowed into his rival. When Bobby Allison, Joe Ruttman, and Bodine also wrecked in the resulting debris, Petty overcame a half-lap deficit, passed the four cars ahead of him on what proved to be the final green-flag lap, and guided the Wood brothers' Ford into victory lane. "By the time I got into the third turn, there were fenders, bumpers, oil, and water everywhere. Somehow, I managed to get through," Petty said.

A furious Waltrip probably wasn't soothed by Earnhardt's comment: "You win some, lose some, and wreck some."

Most Significant Wreck

Buddy Baker appeared on his way to victory in Daytona's Pepsi Firecracker 400 on July 4 until he spun into Connie Saylor with eight laps remaining, allowing Richmond to win and relegating Baker to a 14th-place finish. "I've had a lot of disappointments in racing, but this is the most disappointing of all," said Baker, who had earned what proved to be the final victory of his career three years earlier in the same race.

Most Important Off-Track Development

After six years, 43 victories, and three Winston Cup championships, Waltrip left Junior Johnson after the season to drive for Hendrick Motorsports.

Records & Milestones

Bodine's pole for the April 20 First Union 400 at North Wilkesboro, N.C., was his record-tying fifth in a row on a short track. . . . Bodine failed to win any of the eight races for which he won poles. The only other driver to win eight poles in a season without winning any of those races was Bobby Isaac in 1972. . . . Richmond, Bodine, Elliott (4), and Harry Gant (2) were the only four drivers to win multiple poles, the fewest in the modern era. . . . For only the second of three times in the modern era, the 1986 season featured three races on road courses.

When the flamboyant Tim Richmond embarked on a Winston Cup career driving a Chevrolet for D.K. Ulrich (right), many predicted the triumphs—if not the tragedy—that awaited him.

1986 at a Glance

Races:	29
Road:	3
Short Track:	8
Superspeedway:	18
Winners:	13
Pole Winners:	10
Tracks:	15
States:	12

1986 Performance Index Rankings

1. Dale Earnhardt (778)
2. Tim Richmond (736)
3. Darrell Waltrip (723)
4. Bill Elliott (610)
5. Rusty Wallace (603)
6. Ricky Rudd (590)
7. Bobby Allison (578)
8. Kyle Petty (568)
9. Bobby Hillin Jr. (558)
10. Geoff Bodine (509)
11. Terry Labonte (491)
12. Richard Petty (451)
13. Neil Bonnett (438)
14. Harry Gant (429)
15. Joe Ruttman (422)
16. Alan Kulwicki (366)
17. Morgan Shepherd (332)
18. Michael Waltrip (331)
19. Buddy Baker (329)
20. Dave Marcis (301)
21. Ken Schrader (288)
22. Tommy Ellis (286)
23. Buddy Arrington (258)
24. Rick Wilson (220)
25. Phil Parsons (217)
26. Cale Yarborough (194)
27. Jimmy Means (190)
28. Ron Bouchard; Benny Parsons (185)
30. Jody Ridley (151)
31. Sterling Marlin (143)
32. J.D. McDuffie (141)
33. Doug Heveron (106)
34. Jim Sauter (103)
35. Lake Speed (100)
36. D.K. Ulrich (96)
37. Eddie Bierschwale (90)
38. Trevor Boys (72)
39. Chet Fillip (68)
40. Ken Ragan (61)
41. H.B. Bailey (56)
42. Dick Trickle (53)
43. Ronnie Thomas (50)
44. Davey Allison (47)
45. Mark Martin (46)
46. Rodney Combs; Connie Saylor (45)
48. Pancho Carter (40)
49. Jerry Cranmer (36)
50. Glenn Steurer (34)
51. Greg Sacks (32)
52. Larry Pearson; Bill Schmitt (28)
54. Brett Bodine (27)
55. David Pearson (25)
56. Mark Stahl (24)
57. Johnny Coy Jr.; A.J. Foyt (23)
59. Charlie Baker; Joe Booher; Kirk Bryant (22)
62. Delma Cowart; Bobby Wawak (21)
64. Jack Ely; Tommy Riggins (20)
66. George Follmer; Chad Little (17)
68. Derrike Cope (16)
69. Rick Knoop; Jim Robinson (15)
71. Ron Esau (14)
72. Jimmy Hensley (12)
73. Al Unser (10)
74. Butch Miller (9)

1986 Events

Daytona 500; Daytona International Speedway/2.5-m/500 miles
Geoff Bodine (Chevrolet)/Bill Elliott (Ford)

Miller High Life 400; Richmond Fgds. Raceway/.542-mile/217 m
Kyle Petty (Ford)

Goodwrench 500; North Carolina Motor Speedway/1.017-m/500m
Terry Labonte (Oldsmobile)/Terry Labonte (Oldsmobile)

Motorcraft 500; Atlanta International Raceway/1.522-m/500 m
Morgan Shepherd (Buick)/Dale Earnhardt (Chevrolet)

Valleydale 500; Bristol International Raceway/.533-mile/267m
Rusty Wallace (Pontiac)/Geoff Bodine (Chevrolet)

TranSouth 500; Darlington International Raceway/1.366-m/500m
Dale Earnhardt (Chevrolet)/Geoff Bodine (Chevrolet)

First Union 400; North Wilkesboro Speedway/.625-m/250 miles
Dale Earnhardt (Chevrolet)/Geoff Bodine (Chevrolet)

Sovran Bank 500; Martinsville Speedway/.526-mile/263 miles
Ricky Rudd (Ford)/Tim Richmond (Chevrolet)

Winston 500; Alabama Int. Motor Speedway/2.66-mile/500 miles
Bobby Allison (Buick)/Bill Elliott (Ford)

Budweiser 500; Dover Downs International Speedway/1-m/500 m
Geoff Bodine (Chevrolet)/Ricky Rudd (Ford)

Coca-Cola 600; Charlotte Motor Speedway/1.5-mile/600 miles
Dale Earnhardt (Chevrolet)/Geoff Bodine (Chevrolet)

Budweiser 400; Riverside Int. Raceway/2.62-m road/249 miles
Darrell Waltrip (Chevrolet)/Darrell Waltrip (Chevrolet)

Miller High Life 500; Pocono Int. Raceway/2.5-mile/500 miles
Tim Richmond (Chevrolet)/Geoff Bodine (Chevrolet)

Miller American 400; Michigan Int. Speedway/2-mile/400 miles
Bill Elliott (Ford)/Tim Richmond (Chevrolet)

Pepsi Firecracker 400; Daytona Int. Speedway/2.5-m/400 miles
Tim Richmond (Chevrolet)/Cale Yarborough (Ford)

Summer 500; Pocono International Raceway/2.5-mile/500 miles
Tim Richmond (Chevrolet)/Harry Gant (Chevrolet)

Talladega 500; Alabama Int. Motor Speedway/2.66-m/500 miles
Bobby Hillin Jr. (Buick)/Bill Elliott (Ford)

Budweiser at the Glen; Watkins Glen Int./2.428-m road/219 m
Tim Richmond (Chevrolet)/Tim Richmond (Chevrolet)

Champion Spark Plug 400; Michigan Int. Speedway/2-mile/400 m
Bill Elliott (Ford)/Benny Parsons (Oldsmobile)

Busch 500; Bristol International Raceway/.533-mile/267 miles
Darrell Waltrip (Chevrolet)/Geoff Bodine (Chevrolet)

Southern 500; Darlington International Raceway/1.366-m/500 m
Tim Richmond (Chevrolet)/Tim Richmond (Chevrolet)

Wrangler Indigo 400; Richmond Fgds. Raceway/.542-m/217 miles
Tim Richmond (Chevrolet)/Harry Gant (Chevrolet)

Delaware 500; Dover Downs International Speedway/1-m/500 m
Ricky Rudd (Ford)/Geoff Bodine (Chevrolet)

Goody's 500; Martinsville Speedway/.526-mile/263 miles
Rusty Wallace (Pontiac)/Geoff Bodine (Chevrolet)

Holly Farms 400; North Wilkesboro Speedway/.625-m/250 miles
Darrell Waltrip (Chevrolet)/Tim Richmond (Chevrolet)

Oakwood Homes 500; Charlotte Motor Speedway/1.5-m/500 miles
Dale Earnhardt (Chevrolet)/Tim Richmond (Chevrolet)

Nationwise 500; North Carolina Motor Speedway/1.017-m/500 m
Neil Bonnett (Chevrolet)/Tim Richmond (Chevrolet)

Atlanta Journal 500; Atlanta Int. Raceway/1.522-m/500 miles
Dale Earnhardt (Chevrolet)/Bill Elliott (Ford)

Winston Western 500; Riverside Int. Raceway/2.62-m road/312m
Tim Richmond (Chevrolet)/Tim Richmond (Chevrolet)

Victories
1. Tim Richmond (7)
2. Dale Earnhardt (5)
3. Darrell Waltrip (3)
4. Geoff Bodine; Bill Elliott; Ricky Rudd; Rusty Wallace (2)
8. Bobby Allison; Neil Bonnett; Bobby Hillin Jr.; Terry Labonte; Kyle Petty; Morgan Shepherd (1)

Poles
1. Geoff Bodine; Tim Richmond (8)
3. Bill Elliott (4)
4. Harry Gant (2)
5. Dale Earnhardt; Terry Labonte; Benny Parsons; Ricky Rudd; Darrell Waltrip; Cale Yarborough (1)

Victories
1. Chevrolet (18)
2. Ford (5)
3. Buick (3)
4. Pontiac (2)
5. Oldsmobile (1)

Poles
1. Chevrolet (20)
2. Ford (6)
3. Oldsmobile (2)

1987
The Easiest
To Tame?

While Darlington Raceway long has enjoyed a reputation as "Too Tough to Tame," it might be said that certain tracks are the easiest.

The two tracks that have been the sites of more initial victories than any other—Daytona International Speedway (13) and Martinsville Speedway (11)—are the only two tracks that played host to 100 or more Winston Cup races during the series' first 51 seasons.

Of the tracks that have played host to 50 or more races, Talladega Superspeedway has produced the highest percentage (13) of first-time winners, including Davey Allison, the only driver to post his first victory in 1987.

The complete list of where every driver who ever reached victory lane did it first, with the track name listed as it was the last time it played host to a Winston Cup race:

Alabama
Montgomery Speedway: Marvin Panch.
Talladega Superspeedway: Davey Allison; Ron Bouchard; Richard Brickhouse; Dick Brooks; Bobby Hillin Jr.; Phil Parsons; Lennie Pond; Ken Schrader.

Arizona
Arizona State Fairgrounds: John Rostek.
Phoenix International Raceway: Bobby Hamilton; Alan Kulwicki.

Arkansas
Memphis–Arkansas Speedway: Ralph Moody.

California
Bay Meadows Speedway: Hershel McGriff; Eddie Pagan.
California State Fairgrounds: Jim Cook; Lloyd Dane; Danny Graves.
Capitol Speedway: Bill Amick.
Carrell Speedway: Lou Figaro; Bill Norton; John Soares.
Hanford Speedway: Danny Weinberg.
Oakland Stadium: Danny Letner; Marvin Burke.
Willow Springs Speedway: Chuck Stevenson.
Riverside International Raceway: Darel Dieringer; Mark Donohue; Ray Elder; Bill Elliott; Eddie Gray; Dan Gurney; Tim Richmond; Ricky Rudd.
Santa Clara Fairgrounds: Marvin Porter.

Canada
Stamford Park: Buddy Shuman.

Connecticut
Thompson Speedway: Neil Cole.

Delaware
Dover Downs International Speedway: Jody Ridley.

Florida
Beach & Road Course: Red Byron; Harold Kite; Cotton Owens; Marshall Teague.
Daytona International Speedway: John Andretti; Mario Andretti; Earl Balmer; Derrike Cope; A.J. Foyt; Pete Hamilton; Bobby Isaac; Tiny Lund; Sterling Marlin; Sam McQuagg; Johnny Rutherford; Greg Sacks; Jimmy Spencer.
Palm Beach Speedway: Billy Myers.
Speedway Park: Wendell Scott.

Georgia
Atlanta Motor Speedway: Bob Burdick; Jim Hurtubise; Bobby Johns.
Central City Speedway: Speedy Thompson.
Hayloft Speedway: Gober Sosebee.
Lakewood Speedway: Johnny Beauchamp; Donald Thomas.
Oglethorpe Speedway: Al Keller.
Savannah Speedway: Lee Roy Yarbrough.
Valdosta Speedway: Cale Yarborough.

Indiana
Funk's Speedway: Lloyd Moore.

Maine
Oxford Plains Speedway: Bobby Allison.

Michigan
Michigan Speedway: Dale Jarrett.
Michigan State Fairgrounds: Tommy Thompson.

Nevada
Las Vegas Park Speedway: Norm Nelson.

New Hampshire
New Hampshire International Speedway: Joe Nemechek.

New Jersey
Old Bridge Stadium: Jim Reed; Billy Wade.
Trenton Speedway: Tom Pistone.

New York
Hamburg Fairgrounds: Jack White.
State Line Speedway: Shorty Rollins.
Vernon Fairgrounds: Bill Blair.

North Carolina
Bowman Gray Stadium: Johnny Allen; Glen Wood.
Champion Speedway: Rex White.
Charlotte Fairgrounds: Richard Petty.

Charlotte Speedway: Tim Flock; Dick Passwater; Jim Roper.
Hickory Speedway: Junior Johnson.
Lowe's Motor Speedway: Buddy Baker; Charlie Glotzbach; Jeff Gordon; Bobby Labonte; David Pearson.
North Carolina Speedway: Donnie Allison; Ward Burton; Mark Martin.
North Wilkesboro Speedway: Brett Bodine; Leon Sales.
Orange Speedway: Joe Eubanks; Bob Flock; Fireball Roberts.

Ohio
Canfield Speedway: Bill Rexford.
Dayton Speedway: Jimmy Florian; Dick Linder.

Oregon
Portland Speedway: Royce Haggerty; John Kieper; Art Watts.

Pennsylvania
Langhorne Speedway: Fonty Flock; Paul Goldsmith; Curtis Turner.
Heidelberg Raceway: Lee Petty.
Pocono Raceway: Jeremy Mayfield.

South Carolina
Coastal Speedway: Gwyn Staley.
Columbia Speedway: Buck Baker; Frank Mundy.
Darlington Raceway: Larry Frank; Terry Labonte; Johnny Mantz; Lake Speed; Nelson Stacy.
Greenville-Pickens Speedway: Dick Hutcherson; Emanuel Zervakis.
Piedmont Interstate Fairgrounds: Elmo Langley.
Rambi Raceway: Ned Jarrett.

Tennessee
Bristol Motor Speedway: Dale Earnhardt; Ernie Irvan; Rusty Wallace.
Nashville International Raceway: Joe Lee Johnson; Darrell Waltrip; Joe Weatherly.
Smoky Mountain Raceway: Paul Lewis.

Texas
Texas Motor Speedway: Jeff Burton.

Virginia
Martinsville Speedway: Geoff Bodine; Harry Gant; Fred Lorenzen; Dave Marcis; Jim Paschal; Dick Rathmann; Earl Ross; Morgan Shepherd; Jack Smith; Herb Thomas; Bob Welborn.
Old Dominion Speedway: Frankie Schneider.
Richmond Fairgrounds Raceway: Neil Bonnett; James Hylton; Kyle Petty.
Richmond International Raceway: Tony Stewart.
South Boston Speedway: Benny Parsons.
Southside Speedway: Jim Pardue.

Washington
Kitsap County Airport: Parnelli Jones.

1987 in Review

Dale Earnhardt won a season-high 11 races and earned his second consecutive Winston Cup championship and the third of his career. Earnhardt also out-distanced Bill Elliott, who captured six races and a season-high eight poles, in the Performance Index, 885-682.

Most Memorable Race

Geoff Bodine held a 23-second advantage and was on his way to his second consecutive Daytona 500 victory on February 15. But Bodine ran out of gas with three laps to go, allowing Elliott to beat Benny Parsons by three car lengths. "It was a calculated risk," Bodine said. "If we didn't think we could have made it, we wouldn't have tried it."

Most Significant Wreck

Bobby Allison's Stavola brothers' Buick got airborne, and the rear end spun into the fence exiting the fourth turn on the 22nd lap of the Winston 500 on May 3 at Talladega. Allison's car spun eight times after it hit the ground, but no one hit him. "When I looked up and saw him crashing, my heart sank," said winner Davey Allison, Bobby's son. "It was the worst wreck I ever saw in my life." A two-hour, 38-minute red flag was required to repair the damage to the fence. The accident also resulted in a rule that required carburetor restrictor plates to slow the speeds in future races at both Talladega and Daytona International Speedway.

Most Important Off-Track Development

Tim Richmond, who had missed the first 11 races of the season before returning with back-to-back victories, resigned from Hendrick Motorsports in September because of career-ending health problems.

Johnny Rutherford, a three-time Indianapolis 500 winner, captured his only Winston Cup victory at Daytona International Speedway—making him one of a record 13 drivers whose first victory came on the 2.5-mile Florida tri-oval. Rutherford is one of only six drivers to win his Winston Cup debut and the only driver ever to accomplish that feat on a superspeedway.

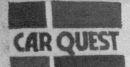

Records & Milestones

The 1987 campaign was the last of three in the modern era in which three races were contested on road courses.

1987 at a Glance

Races:	29
Road:	3
Short Track:	8
Superspeedway:	18
Winners:	10
Pole Winners:	12
Tracks:	15
States:	12

1987 Performance Index Rankings

1. Dale Earnhardt (885)
2. Bill Elliott (682)
3. Darrell Waltrip (671)
4. Terry Labonte (645)
5. Rusty Wallace (634)
6. Kyle Petty (580)
7. Richard Petty (577)
8. Ricky Rudd (553)
9. Neil Bonnett (536)
10. Ken Schrader (497)
11. Davey Allison (487)
12. Sterling Marlin (483)
13. Bobby Allison (466)
14. Geoff Bodine (453)
15. Phil Parsons (433)
16. Buddy Baker (424)
17. Benny Parsons (390)
18. Morgan Shepherd (386)
19. Alan Kulwicki (380)
20. Bobby Hillin Jr. (354)
21. Dave Marcis (345)
22. Michael Waltrip (304)
23. Lake Speed (211)
24. Cale Yarborough (195)
25. Dale Jarrett (185)
26. Harry Gant (181)
27. Buddy Arrington (168)
28. Tim Richmond (160)
29. Jimmy Means (151)
30. Rick Wilson (142)
31. Brett Bodine (127)
32. Rodney Combs (116)
33. Steve Christman (95)
34. Eddie Bierschwale (94)
35. Joe Ruttman (82)
36. Slick Johnson (72)
37. H.B. Bailey (66)
38. Ron Bouchard (60)
39. Ernie Irvan (53)
40. Trevor Boys (51)
41. Brad Teague (50)
42. Randy Baker; Charlie Rudolph (48)

44. Connie Saylor (46)
45. Greg Sacks (41)
46. Jim Sauter (36)
47. Larry Pearson (34)
48. J.D. McDuffie (33)
49. Larry Pollard; D.K. Ulrich (32)
51. Derrike Cope (31)
52. Chad Little (30)
53. Ken Ragan (28)
54. Bobby Wawak (26)
55. Hut Stricklin (24)
56. Tommy Ellis; Mark Stahl (23)
58. Chet Fillip; A.J. Foyt; Rick Knoop (20)
61. Hershel McGriff; Jim Robinson (18)
63. George Follmer (14)
64. Jim Fitzgerald (13)
65. Ruben Garcia (11)
66. Harry Goularte (10)
67. Mike Potter; Tony Spanos (7)
69. Jerry Cranmer (5)

1987 Events

Daytona 500; Daytona International Speedway/2.5-m/500 miles
Bill Elliott (Ford)/Bill Elliott (Ford)

Goodwrench 500; North Carolina Motor Speedway/1.017-m/500m
Dale Earnhardt (Chevrolet)/Davey Allison (Ford)

Miller High Life 400; Richmond Fgds. Raceway/.542-mile/217 m
Dale Earnhardt (Chevrolet)/Alan Kulwicki (Ford)

Motorcraft Qual. Parts 500; Atl. Int. Raceway/1.522-m/500 m
Ricky Rudd (Ford)/Dale Earnhardt (Chevrolet)

TranSouth 500; Darlington International Raceway/1.366-m/500m
Dale Earnhardt (Chevrolet)/Ken Schrader (Ford)

First Union 400; North Wilkesboro Speedway/.625-m/250 miles
Dale Earnhardt (Chevrolet)/Bill Elliott (Ford)

Valleydale 500; Bristol International Raceway/.533-mile/267m
Dale Earnhardt (Chevrolet)/Harry Gant (Chevrolet)

Sovran Bank 500; Martinsville Speedway/.526-mile/263 miles
Dale Earnhardt (Chevrolet)/Morgan Shepherd (Buick)

Winston 500; Alabama Int. Motor Speedway/2.66-mile/500 miles
Davey Allison (Ford)/Bill Elliott (Ford)

Coca-Cola 600; Charlotte Motor Speedway/1.5-mile/600 miles
Kyle Petty (Ford)/Bill Elliott (Ford)

Budweiser 500; Dover Downs International Speedway/1-m/500 m
Davey Allison (Ford)/Bill Elliott (Ford)

Miller High Life 500; Pocono Int. Raceway/2.5-mile/500 miles
Tim Richmond (Chevrolet)/Terry Labonte (Chevrolet)

Budweiser 400; Riverside Int. Raceway/2.62-m road/249 miles
Tim Richmond (Chevrolet)/Terry Labonte (Chevrolet)

Miller American 400; Michigan Int. Speedway/2-mile/400 miles
Dale Earnhardt (Chevrolet)/Rusty Wallace (Pontiac)

Pepsi Firecracker 400; Daytona Int. Speedway/2.5-m/400 miles
Bobby Allison (Buick)/Davey Allison (Ford)

Summer 500; Pocono International Raceway/2.5-mile/500 miles
Dale Earnhardt (Chevrolet)/Tim Richmond (Chevrolet)

Talladega 500; Alabama Int. Motor Speedway/2.66-m/500 miles
Bill Elliott (Ford)/Bill Elliott (Ford)

Budweiser at the Glen; Watkins Glen Int./2.428-m road/219 m
Rusty Wallace (Pontiac)/Terry Labonte (Chevrolet)

Champion Spark Plug 400; Michigan Int. Speedway/2-mile/400 m
Bill Elliott (Ford)/Davey Allison (Ford)

Busch 500; Bristol International Raceway/.533-mile/267 miles
Dale Earnhardt (Chevrolet)/Terry Labonte (Chevrolet)

Southern 500; Darlington International Raceway/1.366-m/500 m
Dale Earnhardt (Chevrolet)/Davey Allison (Ford)

Wrangler Indigo 400; Richmond Fgds. Raceway/.542-m/217 miles
Dale Earnhardt (Chevrolet)/Alan Kulwicki (Ford)

Delaware 500; Dover Downs International Speedway/1-m/500 m
Ricky Rudd (Ford)/Alan Kulwicki (Ford)

Goody's 500; Martinsville Speedway/.526-mile/263 miles
Darrell Waltrip (Chevrolet)/Geoff Bodine (Chevrolet)

Holly Farms 400; North Wilkesboro Speedway/.625-m/250 miles
Terry Labonte (Chevrolet)/Bill Elliott (Ford)

Oakwood Homes 500; Charlotte Motor Speedway/1.5-m/500 miles
Bill Elliott (Ford)/Bobby Allison (Buick)

AC Delco 500; North Carolina Motor Speedway/1.017-mile/500 m
Bill Elliott (Ford)/Davey Allison (Ford)

Winston Western 500; Riverside Int. Raceway/2.62-m road/312m
Rusty Wallace (Pontiac)/Geoff Bodine (Chevrolet)

Atlanta Journal 500; Atlanta Int. Raceway/1.522-m/500 miles
Bill Elliott (Ford)/Bill Elliott (Ford)

Victories

1. Dale Earnhardt (11)
2. Bill Elliott (6)
3. Davey Allison; Tim Richmond; Ricky Rudd; Rusty Wallace (2)
7. Bobby Allison; Terry Labonte; Kyle Petty; Darrell Waltrip (1)

Poles

1. Bill Elliott (8)
2. Davey Allison (5)
3. Terry Labonte (4)
4. Alan Kulwicki (3)
5. Geoff Bodine (2)
6. Bobby Allison; Dale Earnhardt; Harry Gant; Tim Richmond; Ken Schrader; Morgan Shepherd; Rusty Wallace (1)

Victories

1. Chevrolet (15)
2. Ford (11)
3. Pontiac (2)
4. Buick (1)

Poles

1. Ford (17)
2. Chevrolet (9)
3. Buick (2)
4. Pontiac (1)

1988 'Awesome Bill From Dawsonville'

The best season any stock-car driver ever enjoyed on superspeedways during the first 51 years of Winston Cup racing inspired perhaps the two best nicknames in the sport's history: "Awesome Bill From Dawsonville" and "Million Dollar Bill."

By the time he celebrated his 30th birthday late in that 1985 season, Bill Elliott of Dawsonville, Ga., had driven the Harry Melling-owned, Elliott-family-operated Ford to victories in the Daytona 500, the Winston 500 at Talladega, Ala., and the Southern 500 at Darlington, S.C. That netted Elliott, who had to wait until 1988 to earn the Winston Cup title, a $1 million bonus from the R.J. Reynolds Tobacco Company for capturing the Winston Million in its inaugural season.

By the time the 1985 season ended, Elliott had captured 11 victories and 11 poles, all on superspeedways. Both his 11 superspeedway victories and poles are single-season records. His nine 500-mile triumphs, including a record six in a row, and his six 500-mile victories from the pole are also single-season marks. The eight consecutive superspeedway poles Elliott won that season are three more than any other driver has ever strung together. For good measure, Elliott added a record-tying five poles in a row, two classic victories from the pole in the same season, and won four consecutive superspeedway races to tie what was then a record. He also began the second-longest string of classic poles by winning all three in 1985 and the No. 1 starting spot for the 1986 Daytona 500.

Awesome indeed, especially considering that Elliott suffered a broken leg in the season's third race at Rockingham, N.C.

"We let it slip away in '85," Elliott said of the Winston Cup title he lost to Darrell Waltrip. "It was a learning ex-perience. We didn't give away the championship. It was just that Junior (Johnson, Waltrip's car owner) and Darrell had a lot more experience at that time than we did. I had more pressure on me than any of the guys in the garage. I had a lot to deal with—the stardom, the attention from the media. We were under so much pressure."

Three years later, Elliott finally got a Winston Cup title, edging Rusty Wallace for the crown, 4488-4464. Along the way, "Awesome Bill" won two of the year's most exciting races. He came from the 38th starting spot to edge Rick Wilson by three feet in Daytona's Pepsi Firecracker 400 and barely held off Wallace to capture the Southern 500.

Yet Elliott was the target of unjust criticism when Wallace captured the season finale, the Atlanta Journal 500 at Hampton, Ga., because Elliott protected his points lead with a conservative 11th-place finish.

"I feel badly that we didn't try to win the race, especially in front of the hometown fans," Elliott said. "But I hope they understand. I wasn't about to throw it away. We did what we had to do. When we started racing in Winston Cup, we had no idea what we were getting into. We were just a bunch of boys from the mountains of Georgia who had a dream. If it weren't for Harry Melling back in the winter of 1980, we wouldn't have anything. We were about ready to hang it up. We never had a single thought then that we would be able to come this far."

Perhaps Elliott's legacy will be his record-breaking exploits in 1985 or his Winston Cup title in 1988. In many ways, however, those seasons overshadow the consistent excellence of Elliott's efforts. For example, he won at least four superspeedway poles five years in a row (1984-88) and earned at least three superspeedway victories three consecutive seasons (1987-89). In both the 1987 and '88 seasons, he captured at least five

Bill Elliott's 11 victories and 11 poles on superspeedways—both records—in 1985 may have been his finest season. But the warm smile and handshake with which Elliott greeted Bruton Smith (right), Chairman of the Board of Speedway Motorsports, Inc., may have contributed as heavily to his selection as NASCAR's Most Popular Driver a record 14 times through 1999.

superspeedway victories and poles and four or more 500-mile races. All of those streaks rank among the top five in history. So do his 27 500-mile victories, 42 superspeedway poles, 17 Grand Slam poles, eight classic poles, 13 superspeedway victories from the pole, and six Grand Slam wins from the pole.

Elliott has earned 40 victories and 49 poles. He holds the record for 500-mile victories from the pole (11) and shares the record for classic wins from the pole (4). His 12 consecutive seasons with at least one superspeedway pole (1984-95) is a record.

Elliott's career Performance Index rating of 11,921 ranks sixth, and he has led the Performance Index four times. He ranks in the top 10 in virtually every Performance Index category, including a share of the modern record of eight consecutive seasons with a rating of 600 or better (1983-90). Among his most impressive achievements are 13 consecutive seasons with a rating of 500 or better and 13 consecutive top-11 seasons from 1983-95. Both streaks rank among the top three such strings in history. His 11 seasons with a rating of 600 or better, 14 seasons with a rating of 500 or better, eight consecutive top-six seasons (1983-90), and 11 consecutive top-nine campaigns (1983-93) all rank among the top five.

When Elliott left the family operation after the 1991 season to drive Johnson's Ford, he captured four consecutive victories in the first five races of the 1992 season, won the season finale at Atlanta, and lost the closest points battle in Winston Cup history to Alan Kulwicki. But his last two years with Johnson resulted in only one victory, the 1994 Southern 500, and Elliott ended the 1999 season with five consecutive winless seasons as the driver for a team he owned.

1988 in Review

Elliott and Wallace each won a season-high six races. Elliott also led the circuit with six poles and edged Wallace for Winston Cup championship and in the Performance Index, 851-826.

Most Memorable Race

In the history of sports, no other event of such magnitude has produced a 1-2 finish with father beating son to rival the Daytona 500 on Valentine's Day, in which Bobby Allison edged his oldest son, Davey, by two car lengths. "I've got mixed emotions about it. I've had dreams for a long time about battling down to the wire with my dad. The only difference was that I never had dreams of finishing second. The whole race I was trying to put myself in position where I was going to win the race and, hopefully, Dad would finish second. My whole concentration was on winning. If my car could have beaten him, it would have. I didn't think of him as my dad until the checkered flag fell," Davey said.

"It's just a special feeling," Bobby added. "I saw the nose of his car coming out of the corner of my eye, and I thought I had the suds to beat him. He is a fine young man, a tremendous competitor. He drove the wheels off. It's a great feeling to see somebody you think is the best coming up in the sport and know it's your son."

The more Davey thought about it, the less the defeat bothered him. "It's better than if I had won myself," he said. "He's always been my hero."

The Daytona 500 also featured one of the most spectacular wrecks of Richard Petty's career: His car barrel rolled seven times entering the tri-oval. A.J. Foyt, Phil Barkdoll, and Kulwicki also were involved in the horrifying crash. Petty was removed on a stretcher, but escaped with only a badly sprained right ankle and torn ligaments.

Most Significant Wreck

On June 19 at Long Pond, Pa., Bobby Allison's Buick suffered a blown tire on the first lap of the Miller High Life 500 and was broadsided in the driver's door by Jocko Maggiacomo. Allison suffered a severe concussion, abdominal trauma, and a broken left leg. Allison, winner of 85 Winston Cup races, was hospitalized for months and never competed again.

Most Important Off-Track Development

Neil Bonnett's victory in the Pontiac Excitement 400 at Richmond, Va., on February 21 came on Hoosier tires, marking the first time in the modern era that a tire manufacturer other than Goodyear had won a Winston Cup race. Hoosier tires were mounted on eight more victorious cars in 1988.

Records & Milestones

Fourteen drivers won races, setting a modern record later tied in both 1990 and 1991. . . . Riverside International Raceway, the California track that played host to more races than any road course in Winston Cup history, staged its final Winston Cup race: the Budweiser 400 on June 12 won by Wallace.

1988 at a Glance

Races:	29
Road:	2
Short Track:	8
Superspeedway:	19
Winners:	14
Pole Winners:	12
Tracks:	17
States:	13

1988 Performance Index Rankings

1. Bill Elliott (851)
2. Rusty Wallace (826)
3. Dale Earnhardt (755)
4. Terry Labonte (662)
5. Ken Schrader (634)
6. Geoff Bodine (590)
7. Davey Allison (578)
8. Phil Parsons (573)
9. Darrell Waltrip (555)
10. Sterling Marlin (540)
11. Ricky Rudd (495)
12. Bobby Hillin Jr. (469)
13. Kyle Petty (457)
14. Neil Bonnett; Mark Martin (433)
16. Alan Kulwicki (363)
17. Lake Speed (336)
18. Buddy Baker (328)
19. Rick Wilson (297)
20. Michael Waltrip (291)
21. Brett Bodine (289)
22. Ken Bouchard (274)
23. Morgan Shepherd (266)
24. Mike Alexander (261)
25. Bobby Allison (258)
26. Dale Jarrett (241)
27. Dave Marcis (230)
28. Benny Parsons (221)
29. Richard Petty (207)
30. Harry Gant (173)
31. Ernie Irvan (165)
32. Greg Sacks (151)
33. Cale Yarborough (126)
34. Joe Ruttman (112)
35. Brad Noffsinger (98)
36. Jimmy Means (90)
37. Derrike Cope (69)
38. Jim Sauter (66)
39. Jimmy Horton (64)

40. Brad Teague (63)
41. Eddie Bierschwale (49)
42. Trevor Boys; Chad Little (36)
44. Rodney Combs (35)
45. A.J. Foyt (28)
46. Rob Moroso (26)
47. H.B. Bailey (24)
48. Lee Faulk; Ben Hess (20)
50. Bill Schmitt (18)
51. Rick Hendrick (15)
52. Tom Kendall (12)
53. Butch Miller (8)

Daytona 500; Daytona International Speedway/2.5-m/500 miles
Bobby Allison (Buick)/Ken Schrader (Chevrolet)

Pontiac Excitement 400; Richmond Fgds. Raceway/.542-m/217 m
Neil Bonnett (Pontiac)/Morgan Shepherd (Buick)

Goodwrench 500; North Carolina Motor Speedway/1.017-m/500m
Neil Bonnett (Pontiac)/Bill Elliott (Ford)

Motorcraft Qual. Parts 500; Atl. Int. Raceway/1.522-m/500 m
Dale Earnhardt (Chevrolet)/Geoff Bodine (Chevrolet)

TranSouth 500; Darlington International Raceway/1.366-m/500m
Lake Speed (Oldsmobile)/Ken Schrader (Chevrolet)

Valleydale Meats 500; Bristol Int. Raceway/.533-m/267 miles
Bill Elliott (Ford)/Rick Wilson (Oldsmobile)

First Union 400; North Wilkesboro Speedway/.625-m/250 miles
Terry Labonte (Chevrolet)/Terry Labonte (Chevrolet)

Pannill Sweatshirts 500; Martinsville Speedway/.526-m/263 m
Dale Earnhardt (Chevrolet)/Ricky Rudd (Buick)

Winston 500; Alabama Int. Motor Speedway/2.66-mile/500 miles
Phil Parsons (Oldsmobile)/Davey Allison (Ford)

Coca-Cola 600; Charlotte Motor Speedway/1.5-mile/600 miles
Darrell Waltrip (Chevrolet)/Davey Allison (Ford)

Budweiser 500; Dover Downs International Speedway/1-m/500 m
Bill Elliott (Ford)/Alan Kulwicki (Ford)

Budweiser 400; Riverside Int. Raceway/2.62-m road/249 miles
Rusty Wallace (Pontiac)/Ricky Rudd (Buick)

Miller High Life 500; Pocono Int. Raceway/2.5-mile/500 miles
Geoff Bodine (Chevrolet)/Alan Kulwicki (Ford)

Miller High Life 400; Michigan Int. Speedway/2-m/400 miles
Rusty Wallace (Pontiac)/Bill Elliott (Ford)

Pepsi Firecracker 400; Daytona Int. Speedway/2.5-m/400 miles
Bill Elliott (Ford)/Darrell Waltrip (Chevrolet)

AC Spark Plug 500; Pocono International Raceway/2.5-m/500 m
Bill Elliott (Ford)/Morgan Shepherd (Pontiac)

Talladega Diehard 500; Ala. Int. Motor Speedway/2.66-m/500 m
Ken Schrader (Chevrolet)/Darrell Waltrip (Chevrolet)

The Budweiser at the Glen; Watkins Glen Int./2.428-m rd/219m
Ricky Rudd (Buick)/Geoff Bodine (Chevrolet)

Champion Spark Plug 400; Michigan Int. Speedway/2-mile/400 m
Davey Allison (Ford)/Bill Elliott (Ford)

Busch 500; Bristol International Raceway/.533-mile/267 miles
Dale Earnhardt (Chevrolet)/Alan Kulwicki (Ford)

Southern 500; Darlington International Raceway/1.366-m/500 m
Bill Elliott (Ford)/Bill Elliott (Ford)

Miller High Life 400; Richmond Int. Raceway/.75-m/300 miles
Davey Allison (Ford)/Davey Allison (Ford)

Delaware 500; Dover Downs Int. Speedway/1-mile/500 miles
Bill Elliott (Ford)/Mark Martin (Ford)

Goody's 500; Martinsville Speedway/.526-mile/263 miles
Darrell Waltrip (Chevrolet)/Rusty Wallace (Pontiac)

Oakwood Homes 500; Charlotte Motor Speedway/1.5-m/500 miles
Rusty Wallace (Pontiac)/Alan Kulwicki (Ford)

Holly Farms 400; North Wilkesboro Speedway/.625-m/250 miles
Rusty Wallace (Pontiac)/Bill Elliott (Ford)

AC Delco 500; North Carolina Motor Speedway/1.017-mile/500 m
Rusty Wallace (Pontiac)/Bill Elliott (Ford)

Checker 500; Phoenix International Raceway/1-mile/312 miles
Alan Kulwicki (Ford)/Geoff Bodine (Chevrolet)

Atlanta Journal 500; Atlanta Int. Raceway/1.522-m/500 miles
Rusty Wallace (Pontiac)/Rusty Wallace (Pontiac)

Victories
1. Bill Elliott; Rusty Wallace (6)
3. Dale Earnhardt (3)
4. Davey Allison; Neil Bonnett; Darrell Waltrip (2)
7. Bobby Allison; Geoff Bodine; Alan Kulwicki; Terry Labonte; Phil Parsons; Ricky Rudd; Ken Schrader; Lake Speed (1)

Poles
1. Bill Elliott (6)
2. Alan Kulwicki (4)
3. Davey Allison; Geoff Bodine (3)
5. Ricky Rudd; Ken Schrader; Morgan Shepherd; Rusty Wallace; Darrell Waltrip (2)
10. Terry Labonte; Mark Martin; Rick Wilson (1)

Victories
1. Ford (9)
2. Chevrolet; Pontiac (8)
4. Buick; Oldsmobile (2)

Poles
1. Ford (14)
2. Chevrolet (8)
3. Buick; Pontiac (3)
5. Oldsmobile (1)

1989
'Bad to the Bone'

It didn't take long for Rusty Wallace to make his mark in Winston Cup racing. He finished second to Dale Earnhardt in the 1980 Atlanta 500 in his first start—the best debut in the modern era.

But it wasn't until 1986, two years after he joined the circuit on a full-time basis, that the hyperactive Wallace finally visited victory lane, winning short-track events at Bristol, Tenn., and Martinsville, Va. A year later, he tied a record by winning two races on road courses in the same season.

"When you win one, everybody says it's a fluke. When you win two, everybody says, 'That son of a gun is serious.' Then, you win a couple more, and everybody says, 'Hey, maybe this guy is going to stick around,' " Wallace said during a six-victory campaign in 1988, a year before he earned the Winston Cup title.

Indeed, Wallace has stuck around and was still going strong when the 1999 season ended. He had posted victories in each of the last 14 campaigns, the sixth-longest such streak in history. At 43 years of age when the Winston Cup Series' 51st season ended, Wallace obviously can continue to add to his considerable legacy.

Wallace's 49 victories rank in a 10th-place tie on the all-time list. He has been equally adept on superspeedways and short tracks, winning 21 races on big tracks and 22 on the latter to rank in the top 10 in both categories. He also has a record-tying six victories on road courses and a record-tying four consecutive years (1987-90) with at least one victory in a road race.

Rusty Wallace, one of Winston Cup racing's cockiest, yet friendliest, drivers, compiled an admirable record of versatility during the circuit's first 51 years: 21 victories on superspeedways, 22 on short tracks, and a record–tying six triumphs on road courses.

Wallace had an eventful run to the Winston Cup title in 1989 and may have been even better in 1993 and 1994, when he won at least five superspeedway, four 500-mile, and three short-track races each season. Each of those streaks individually rank among the top five in history. In 1994, he captured three consecutive races on superspeedways, and a year earlier he had put together a three-race short-track winning streak—a feat that hadn't been accomplished since Wallace did it in 1988 and 1989 and hasn't been matched since.

Wallace's future didn't look particularly bright in August of 1988, when he suffered life-threatening injuries during a practice crash at Bristol. Dr. Jerry Punch, an emergency physician and ESPN commentator, is credited with rushing to the scene to save Wallace's life.

Wallace reacted angrily in the spring of 1989 to rumors that he was not happy driving Raymond Beadle's Pontiac, but in July he filed suit to get out of his contract with Beadle. Yet the native of St. Louis County's suburban west side still entered the season finale needing only an 18th-place finish in the Atlanta Journal 500 to lock up the season title. While Earnhardt was pulling away to an easy victory, Wallace encountered a host of trouble. But he finished 15th to edge Earnhardt for the Winston Cup crown by 12 points.

"We got caught on a green-flag stop and lost a lap. Then, when I cut a tire and then had loose lug nuts on the left side, I kept seeing the championship slip away," recalled Wallace, who finished three laps in arrears. "I was very worried about it. We didn't run bad. We had bad luck. I knew I was very close to the magic number of 18th place. But I really didn't know how close, and the team couldn't tell me. All they said on the radio was, 'Keep driving as hard as you can.' So I did. I didn't know I'd won the title until the final lap, when I went by the pit and the guys were going crazy.

"It's the completion of a lifelong dream," Wallace added. "Just because I come from Missouri doesn't mean that I didn't have the same dream as a Dale Earnhardt or a Bill Elliott or a Darrell Waltrip or a Cale Yarborough. Our dreams were exactly the same—to win the championship of the biggest stock-car series in the world and beat the best to get it. I've reached the ultimate goal in life."

When Wallace capped a 10-victory 1993 season in Roger Penske's Pontiac by winning the season-ending Hooters 500 at Atlanta, he was still searching for his second Winston Cup crown. "If somebody had told me before the season that we'd win 10 races and still not take the championship," Wallace said, "I would have told them they were crazy. It seems like if you lead all the laps and win all the races, you'd be the champion."

There's still time for Wallace to earn a second title and, based on his record, it's a safe bet he'll be a contender. In each of his 16 full seasons, he has had a Performance Index rating of 300 or better. And in each of the last 14 seasons through 1999, he had posted a rating of 400 or better and finished in the top 14 in the standings.

Wallace has a career Performance Index rating of 9,679, 12th on the all-time list. Among the categories in which he already has earned top-10 status are top-two seasons (4), top-six seasons (9), top-15 seasons (15), seasons with a rating of 600 or better (9), and seasons with a rating of 500 or more (12). He also ranks among the top 10 in 500-mile victories (14), 500-mile wins from the pole (4), and superspeedway triumphs from the pole (4).

And it's a safe bet that Wallace, one of Winston Cup racing's cockiest, yet friendliest, drivers and an unabashed fan of rock 'n roll, would describe his chances at another Winston Cup title—and his already impressive resume—with one of his favorite expressions: "It's bad to the bone."

1989 in Review

Although Wallace earned the Winston Cup title by a narrow 4,176-4,164 margin over Earnhardt, the latter edged Wallace in the Performance Index ratings, 730-707. Waltrip and Wallace each captured six races to share the season lead in victories, and Alan Kulwicki and Mark Martin won six poles apiece to lead the Winston Cup Series in that category.

Most Memorable Race

Waltrip pitted with 53 laps to go, then gambled that he could go the distance in the Daytona 500 on February 19 after he inherited the lead when his rivals made late pit stops. "With five laps to go, I'm feeling good. With four laps, I'm out of gas. With three, I'm feeling

good again. With two, I'm out of gas. Then, when I took the white flag, I didn't know what was going on. Jeff (Hammond, his crew chief) was hollering, 'Shake, baby, shake.' I thought I was home listening to the radio. I mean, the fuel pressure went down to nothing *twice*. But it came back up. Jeff had three heart attacks in the last four laps," Waltrip said after racing an incredible 132.5 miles on one tank of fuel to beat Ken Schrader by six seconds. "I have really anguished over this race for a lot of years. There is no race that I've ever won that meant more than this one. I'd look around and see other turkeys who have won it, and I wondered, 'How come I never won?' I didn't want to end my career without winning the Super Bowl of our sport. Not winning the Daytona 500 bothered me. I didn't know why I'd never won the Daytona 500. Something always seemed to happen. It was just an incredible chain of events that made that win possible. We can run 53 laps at Daytona on one tank of gas. How incredible is it that we had exactly 53 laps to go after our last pit stop? It's just luck. We weren't the fastest, but we beat them with our brains."

Earnhardt had led until he pitted for gas with 10 laps remaining and settled for a third-place finish. "I was hoping Darrell would run out of gas," he said. "I didn't think he'd make it, but he did. But I sure would like to see his gas tank."

An unidentified NASCAR inspector who did see Waltrip's gas tank after the race told The Associated Press: "For $5, I'd drink what's left."

Most Significant Wreck

Earnhardt took the white flag and was battling Ricky Rudd for the lead on the final lap of the Holly Farms 400 on October 15 at North Wilkesboro, N.C., when they collided and finished 10th and ninth, respectively. Earnhardt had to be restrained from attacking Rudd. "(Rudd) just knocked the hell out of me," said Earnhardt, who added that he thought NASCAR should "fine and suspend Rudd for the remainder of the season." Had Earnhardt not been involved in the accident, he likely would have finished first or second, which would have been worth 46 or 41 additional points, respectively, in the Winston Cup standings. Earnhardt lost the title three races later by 12 points.

Most Important Off-Track Development

Goodyear responded to the encroachment on its monopoly by Hoosier by introducing radial racing tires. Hoosier left Winston Cup racing in May.

Records & Milestones

Kulwicki became the first driver in history to capture six poles yet suffer through a winless season. . . . Sears Point International Raceway in Sonoma, Calif., a 2.52-mile road course, joined the Winston Cup circuit on June 11, when Rudd won the Banquet Frozen Foods 300. . . . Wallace's victory in the Goodwrench 500 at Rockingham, N.C., was the only triumph from the pole all season. The only other year with so few victories from the pole was the eight-race campaign in 1949. . . . Jimmy Hensley captured the pole for the September 24 Goody's 500 at Martinsville, but didn't start the race. Hensley was substituting for Earnhardt, whose arrival was delayed by Hurricane Hugo.

1989 at a Glance

Races:	29
Road:	2
Short Track:	8
Superspeedway:	19
Winners:	11
Pole Winners:	9
Tracks:	16
States:	13

1989 Performance Index Rankings

1. Dale Earnhardt (730)
2. Rusty Wallace (707)
3. Mark Martin (670)
4. Darrell Waltrip (664)
5. Ken Schrader (616)
6. Bill Elliott (610)
7. Terry Labonte (570)
8. Harry Gant (522)
9. Ricky Rudd (520)
10. Morgan Shepherd (508)
11. Sterling Marlin (507)
12. Geoff Bodine (497)
13. Davey Allison (464)
14. Bobby Hillin Jr. (441)
15. Neil Bonnett (430)
16. Rick Wilson (400)
17. Brett Bodine (397)
18. Alan Kulwicki (389)
19. Phil Parsons (381)
20. Dick Trickle (379)
21. Michael Waltrip (336)
22. Kyle Petty (314)
23. Hut Stricklin (307)
24. Dave Marcis (294)
25. Lake Speed (276)
26. Larry Pearson (273)
27. Dale Jarrett (268)
28. Ernie Irvan (253)
29. Derrike Cope (238)
30. Richard Petty (172)
31. Jimmy Spencer (168)
32. Jim Sauter (149)
33. Rick Mast (132)
34. Greg Sacks (77)
35. Ben Hess; Joe Ruttman (66)
37. Jimmy Means (51)
38. Eddie Bierschwale (48)
39. A.J. Foyt (46)
40. Phil Barkdoll (45)
41. Tommy Ellis (31)
42. Ken Bouchard (29)
43. Jimmy Horton; Chad Little (27)
45. Grant Adcox (22)
46. Terry Byers (21)
47. Mickey Gibbs (20)
48. Darin Brassfield (18)
49. Hershel McGriff (16)
50. Tracy Leslie (15)
51. Lennie Pond (14)
52. Bill Schmitt (13)
53. Brad Teague (8)

1989 Events

Daytona 500; Daytona International Speedway/2.5-m/500 miles
Darrell Waltrip (Chevrolet)/Ken Schrader (Chevrolet)

Goodwrench 500; North Carolina Motor Speedway/1.017-m/500m
Rusty Wallace (Pontiac)/Rusty Wallace (Pontiac)

Motorcraft Qual. Parts 500; Atlanta Int. Raceway/1.522-m/500m
Darrell Waltrip (Chevrolet)/Alan Kulwicki (Ford)

Pontiac Excitement 400; Richmond Int. Raceway/.75-m/300 miles
Rusty Wallace (Pontiac)/Geoff Bodine (Chevrolet)

TranSouth 500; Darlington Int. Raceway/1.366-mile/500 miles
Harry Gant (Oldsmobile)/Mark Martin (Ford)

Valleydale Meats 500; Bristol Int. Raceway/.533-m/267 miles
Rusty Wallace (Pontiac)/Mark Martin (Ford)

First Union 400; North Wilkesboro Speedway/.625-m/250 miles
Dale Earnhardt (Chevrolet)/Rusty Wallace (Pontiac)

Pannill Sweatshirts 500; Martinsville Speedway/.526-m/263 m
Darrell Waltrip (Chevrolet)/Geoff Bodine (Chevrolet)

Winston 500; Talladega Superspeedway/2.66-mile/500 miles
Davey Allison (Ford)/Mark Martin (Ford)

Coca-Cola 600; Charlotte Motor Speedway/1.5-mile/600 miles
Darrell Waltrip (Chevrolet)/Alan Kulwicki (Ford)

Budweiser 500; Dover Downs International Speedway/1-m/500 m
Dale Earnhardt (Chevrolet)/Mark Martin (Ford)

Banquet Fr. Foods 300; Sears Pt. Int. Raceway/2.52-m rd./187m
Ricky Rudd (Buick)/Rusty Wallace (Pontiac)

Miller High Life 500; Pocono International Raceway/2.5-m/500m
Terry Labonte (Ford)/Rusty Wallace (Pontiac)

Miller High Life 400; Michigan Int. Speedway/2-mile/400 miles
Bill Elliott (Ford)/Ken Schrader (Chevrolet)

Pepsi 400; Daytona International Speedway/2.5-mile/400 miles
Davey Allison (Ford)/Mark Martin (Ford)

AC Spark Plug 500; Pocono International Raceway/2.5-m/500 m
Bill Elliott (Ford)/Ken Schrader (Chevrolet)

Talladega Diehard 500; Talladega Superspeedway/2.66-m/500 m
Terry Labonte (Ford)/Mark Martin (Ford)

Budweiser at the Glen; Watkins Glen Int./2.428-m road/219 m
Rusty Wallace (Pontiac)/Morgan Shepherd (Pontiac)

Champion Spark Plug 400; Michigan Int. Speedway/2-m/400 miles
Rusty Wallace (Pontiac)/Geoff Bodine (Chevrolet)

Busch 500; Bristol International Raceway/.533–mile/267 miles
Darrell Waltrip (Chevrolet)/Alan Kulwicki (Ford)

Heinz Southern 500; Darlington Int. Raceway/1.366-m/500 miles
Dale Earnhardt (Chevrolet)/Alan Kulwicki (Ford)

Miller High Life 400; Richmond Int. Raceway/.75-m/300 miles
Rusty Wallace (Pontiac)/Bill Elliott (Ford)

Peak Performance 500; Dover Downs Int. Speedway/1-m/500 miles
Dale Earnhardt (Chevrolet)/Davey Allison (Ford)

Goody's 500; Martinsville Speedway/.526-mile/263 miles
Darrell Waltrip (Chevrolet)/Jimmy Hensley (Chevrolet)

All Pro Auto Parts 500; Charlotte Motor Speedway/1.5-m/500 m
Ken Schrader (Chevrolet)/Bill Elliott (Ford)

Holly Farms 400; North Wilkesboro Speedway/.625-m/250 miles
Geoff Bodine (Chevrolet)

AC Delco 500; North Carolina Motor Speedway/1.017-m/500 miles
Mark Martin (Ford)/Alan Kulwicki (Ford)

Autoworks 500; Phoenix International Raceway/1-mile/312 miles
Bill Elliott (Ford)/Ken Schrader (Chevrolet)

Atlanta Journal 500; Atlanta Int. Raceway/1.522-m/500 miles
Dale Earnhardt (Chevrolet)/Alan Kulwicki (Ford)

Victories
1. Rusty Wallace; Darrell Waltrip (6)
3. Dale Earnhardt (5)
4. Bill Elliott (3)
5. Davey Allison; Terry Labonte (2)
7. Geoff Bodine; Harry Gant; Mark Martin; Ricky Rudd; Ken Schrader (1)

Poles
1. Alan Kulwicki; Mark Martin (6)
3. Ken Schrader; Rusty Wallace (4)
5. Geoff Bodine (3)
6. Bill Elliott (2)
7. Davey Allison; Jimmy Hensley; Morgan Shepherd (1)

Victories
1. Chevrolet (13)
2. Ford (8)
3. Pontiac (6)
4. Buick; Oldsmobile (1)

Poles
1. Ford (15)
2. Chevrolet (8)
3. Pontiac (5)

1990
Nobody's Come As Close as Often As Mark Martin

In the first 51 seasons of Winston Cup racing, no driver was a more consistent contender for stock-car racing's premier title, yet failed to win it, than Mark Martin.

Martin, who lost the 1990 and 1997 titles by fewer than 30 points, may be one of the few drivers who comprehends just how significant a role luck can play.

"I believe in my heart the championships in today's era are won and lost on luck rather than performance," he said. "You can do everything right and score all the points you want and be ahead by 100 points in Atlanta and have the sky fall in. You could have a meteor fall on your car, and you'd lose. It's like that every year. One flat tire in 1997 (for Jeff Gordon) would have meant different champions. So it's a lot luck."

Martin underwent back surgery after the 1999 season, then turned 41 before he began another pursuit of that elusive championship.

Through the 1999 season, Martin had posted:

- 11 consecutive campaigns with a Performance Index rating of 500 or better, eight seasons in a row with a rating of 600 or higher, five seasons in succession with a rating of 700 or more, and three in a row with a rating of 800 or better;
- Eight consecutive top-six seasons and seven consecutive top-five seasons.
- 10 seasons with a rating of 600 or higher, seven top-three seasons, nine top-five seasons, 10 top-six seasons, and 11 top-seven seasons.

Every driver ranked ahead of him in *any* of those categories had secured a Winston Cup championship. In fact, no other driver ever has finished as high as 10th for nine consecutive years without earning a Winston Cup title.

Martin burst onto the scene in 1981 with a flourish. When he captured the pole for the Busch Nashville 420, he became the youngest driver to win a short-track pole, and the first two top-20 finishes of his career came from the pole.

Martin soon learned, however, that he didn't have the proper financing to sustain that promising start. In 1983, he auctioned his team and drove for J.D. Stacy. Two races after an impressive third-place finish in the 1983 TranSouth 500 at Darlington, S.C., however, Martin was fired by Stacy.

"I waded in over my head, trying to do it with my own team," he recalled. "Then, I was mad because I had failed. I left the series a broken man—mentally, physically, and financially. But didn't I say I'd be back? It makes me feel pretty proud to have come to Winston Cup and come back against some pretty steep odds to do what we have done."

After he lost his ride with Stacy, Martin focused his efforts on the Busch Series, in which he is the all-time victory leader, and the American Speed Association, in which he is a four-time champion. He returned to Winston Cup racing when Jack Roush hired him to drive his Ford before the 1988 season.

During the next 12 years with Roush, Martin won 31 races and 37 more poles—leading the circuit in poles on three occasions and capturing at least one pole every season—to move into the top 20 in both victories and poles. He ranks in the top 10 in superspeedway victories (21), superspeedway poles (22), road-course wins (4), and road-course poles (4). Martin's four road-course victories from the pole are a record, he is the only driver to win a road race from the pole in three consecutive seasons (1993-95), and he compiled a four-race winning streak in 1993.

Despite those accomplishments, Martin has improved with age. For four straight seasons from 1995-98, he won at least three poles, and he earned at least three superspeedway triumphs in both 1997 and 1998. Both streaks are among the top 10 in history, and only two drivers have put together longer strings of 800 seasons in the Performance Index than the three in a row Martin posted from 1997-99. Martin's career Performance Index rating of 9,086 ranks 15th in history, and the best may be yet to come: He posted a Performance Index rating of 866 and earned a career-high seven victories in 1998, then earned a career-high 872 rating in 1999.

"I had thought that I may have seen the best years of my career already prior to 1998," Martin told *The Atlanta Constitution's* Al Levine, "and now I'm pretty sure that I haven't seen my best years yet. That's sort of a relief."

1990 in Review

Dale Earnhardt led the series with nine victories—including eight on superspeedways—and four poles on his way to his fourth Winston Cup title.

Most Important Off-Track Development

After Martin captured the Pontiac Excitement 400 at Richmond, Va., on February 25, a post-race inspection revealed that the spacer between the carburetor and intake manifold on his Roush Racing Ford was a half-inch taller than the two-inch limit. Martin was allowed to keep the victory, but he was fined $40,000—a new record—and 46 points. Earnhardt edged Martin for the Winston Cup title, 4,430-4,404. If Martin—who edged Earnhardt, 800-796, in the Performance Index—had not been assessed the 46-point penalty, he would have captured the title by 20 points.

Most Memorable Race

When Earnhardt took the white flag with a half-lap lead in the Daytona 500 on February 18, he had led 155 of the first 199 laps. But Earnhardt's Richard Childress-owned Chevrolet slowed dramatically exiting the second turn of the last lap because of a flat tire. Derrike Cope beat Terry Labonte to the checkered flag by a little more than a car length for his first Winston Cup victory, and Earnhardt limped home in fifth. "This is the biggest buildup and the biggest letdown I've ever had in racing. You can't kick the car and cry and pout and lay down and squall and bawl, but I can't believe it happened," Earnhardt said.

"Dale's taking it like the real champion he is. He told me that after he throws up a couple of times, he'll feel a lot better," Childress added.

As the 21st Century began, Mark Martin was "pretty sure that I haven't seen my best years yet." Considering that he had finished in the top seven in the Performance Index 11 consecutive seasons and earned 31 victories and 39 poles by the time the 1999 season ended, a long overdue Winston Cup title was still within reach.

"I had no real vision of winning this race," Cope said. "You always dream, but that was a little far-fetched. But I'm going home the winner of the Daytona 500. I've seen other people win races by default. That's one thing that makes this sport so exciting: The obvious doesn't always happen. I'm tickled—my first win, and it's the Daytona 500. I've dreamed about this. If I never win again the rest of my life, I've won the Daytona 500."

Most Significant Wreck

When Ernie Irvan and Ken Schrader spun on the 212th lap of the TranSouth 500 on April 1, it triggered a 13-car crash that also involved Sterling Marlin, Rick Wilson, Jimmy Means, Richard Petty, Rusty Wallace, Rob Moroso, Geoff Bodine, Ricky Rudd, Neil Bonnett, Martin, and Cope. Bonnett suffered a serious head injury that virtually ended his career. Bonnett, who captured 18 victories and 20 poles, didn't race again until he made two starts in 1993 and never again won a race or a pole.

Records & Milestones

Fourteen different drivers captured at least one victory, tying a modern record set in 1988 and equaled a year later.... Five different manufacturers won races—Chevrolet, Ford, Pontiac, Buick, and Oldsmobile—to tie a modern record set in 1973 and equaled in 1975, 1986, 1988, and 1989.

1990 at a Glance

Races:	29
Road:	2
Short Track:	8
Superspeedway:	19
Winners:	14
Pole Winners:	13
Tracks:	16
States:	13

1990 Performance Index Rankings

1. Mark Martin (800)
2. Dale Earnhardt (796)
3. Geoff Bodine (671)
4. Bill Elliott (648)
5. Morgan Shepherd (573)
6. Rusty Wallace (570)
7. Terry Labonte (538)
8. Ken Schrader (537)
9. Kyle Petty (533)
10. Alan Kulwicki (527)
11. Ernie Irvan (523)
12. Ricky Rudd (518)
13. Brett Bodine (515)
14. Sterling Marlin (498)
15. Davey Allison (483)
16. Darrell Waltrip (481)
17. Harry Gant (474)
18. Derrike Cope (451)
19. Michael Waltrip (413)
20. Bobby Hillin Jr. (351)
21. Dale Jarrett (316)
22. Dick Trickle (278)
23. Dave Marcis (266)
24. Butch Miller (258)
25. Rick Wilson (248)
26. Hut Stricklin (239)
27. Jimmy Spencer (221)
28. Greg Sacks (210)
29. Richard Petty (147)
30. Rob Moroso (144)
31. Chad Little (130)
32. Jack Pennington (119)
33. Larry Pearson (101)
34. Rick Mast (80)
35. Phil Parsons (74)
36. Jimmy Horton (65)
37. Mike Alexander (64)
38. Lake Speed (58)
39. Neil Bonnett (56)
40. Mickey Gibbs; Jimmy Means (52)
42. Irv Hoerr (42)
43. Buddy Baker (30)
44. Tom Kendall; Bill Schmitt; Bill Venturini (22)
47. Dave Mader III (20)
48. Terry Fisher (15)
49. Stan Barrett (13)
50. Bill Sedgwick (10)

1990 Events

Daytona 500; Daytona International Speedway/2.5-m/500 miles
Derrike Cope (Chevrolet)/Ken Schrader (Chevrolet)

Pontiac Excitement 400; Richmond Int. Raceway/.75-mile/300 m
Mark Martin (Ford)/Ricky Rudd (Chevrolet)

Goodwrench 500; North Carolina Motor Speedway/1.017-m/500m
Kyle Petty (Pontiac)/Kyle Petty (Pontiac)

Motorcraft Qual. Parts 500; Atl. Int. Raceway/1.522-m/500 m
Dale Earnhardt (Chevrolet)

TranSouth 500; Darlington International Raceway/1.366-m/500m
Dale Earnhardt (Chevrolet)/Geoff Bodine (Ford)

Valleydale Meats 500; Bristol Int. Raceway/.533-m/267 miles
Davey Allison (Ford)/Ernie Irvan (Oldsmobile)

First Union 400; North Wilkesboro Speedway/.625-m/250 miles
Brett Bodine (Buick)/Mark Martin (Ford)

Hanes Activewear 500; Martinsville Speedway/.526-m/263 miles
Geoff Bodine (Ford)/Geoff Bodine (Ford)

Winston 500; Talladega Superspeedway/2.66-mile/500 miles
Dale Earnhardt (Chevrolet)/Bill Elliott (Ford)

Coca-Cola 600; Charlotte Motor Speedway/1.5-mile/600 miles
Rusty Wallace (Pontiac)/Ken Schrader (Chevrolet)

Budweiser 500; Dover Downs International Speedway/1-m/500 m
Derrike Cope (Chevrolet)/Dick Trickle (Pontiac)

Banquet Fr. Foods 300; Sears Pt. Int. Race./2.52-m road/187m
Rusty Wallace (Pontiac)/Ricky Rudd (Chevrolet)

Miller Genuine Draft 500; Pocono Int. Raceway/2.5-mile/500 m
Harry Gant (Oldsmobile)/Ernie Irvan (Oldsmobile)

Miller Genuine Draft 400; Michigan Int. Speedway/2-mile/400m
Dale Earnhardt (Chevrolet)

Pepsi 400; Daytona International Speedway/2.5-mile/400 miles
Dale Earnhardt (Chevrolet)/Greg Sacks (Chevrolet)

AC Spark Plug 500; Pocono International Raceway/2.5-mile/500 m
Geoff Bodine (Ford)/Mark Martin (Ford)

Talladega Diehard 500; Talladega Superspeedway/2.66-m/500 m
Dale Earnhardt (Chevrolet)/Dale Earnhardt (Chevrolet)

Budweiser at the Glen; Watkins Glen Int./2.428-m road/219 m
Ricky Rudd (Chevrolet)/Dale Earnhardt (Chevrolet)

Champion Spark Plug 400; Michigan Int. Speedway/2-mile/400 m
Mark Martin (Ford)/Alan Kulwicki (Ford)

Busch 500; Bristol International Raceway/.533-mile/267 miles
Ernie Irvan (Chevrolet)/Dale Earnhardt (Chevrolet)

Heinz Southern 500; Darlington Int. Raceway/1.366-mile/500 m
Dale Earnhardt (Chevrolet)/Dale Earnhardt (Chevrolet)

Miller Genuine Draft 400; Richmond Int. Raceway/.75-m/300 m
Dale Earnhardt (Chevrolet)/Ernie Irvan (Chevrolet)

Peak Antifreeze 500; Dover Downs Int. Speedway/1-m/500 miles
Bill Elliott (Ford)/Bill Elliott (Ford)

Goody's 500; Martinsville Speedway/.526-mile/263 miles
Geoff Bodine (Ford)/Mark Martin (Ford)

Tyson Holly Farms 400; No. Wilkesboro Speedway/.625-m/250 m
Mark Martin (Ford)/Kyle Petty (Pontiac)

Mello Yello 500; Charlotte Motor Speedway/1.5-mile/500 miles
Davey Allison (Ford)/Brett Bodine (Buick)

AC Delco 500; North Carolina Motor Speedway/1.017-m/500 m
Alan Kulwicki (Ford)/Ken Schrader (Chevrolet)

Checker 500; Phoenix International Raceway/1-mile/312 miles
Dale Earnhardt (Chevrolet)/Rusty Wallace (Pontiac)

Atlanta Journal 500; Atlanta Motor Speedway/1.522-mile/500 m
Morgan Shepherd (Ford)/Rusty Wallace (Pontiac)

Victories

1. Dale Earnhardt (9)
2. Geoff Bodine; Mark Martin (3)
4. Davey Allison; Derrike Cope; Rusty Wallace (2)
7. Brett Bodine; Bill Elliott; Harry Gant; Ernie Irvan; Alan Kulwicki; Kyle Petty; Ricky Rudd; Morgan Shepherd (1)

Poles

1. Dale Earnhardt (4)
2. Ernie Irvan; Mark Martin; Ken Schrader (3)
5. Geoff Bodine; Bill Elliott; Kyle Petty; Ricky Rudd; Rusty Wallace (2)
10. Brett Bodine; Alan Kulwicki; Greg Sacks; Dick Trickle (1)

Victories

1. Chevrolet (13)
2. Ford (11)
3. Pontiac (3)
4. Buick; Oldsmobile (1)

Poles

1. Chevrolet (11)
2. Ford (8)
3. Pontiac (5)
4. Oldsmobile (2)
5. Buick (1)

1991
Safer at Any Speed

Perhaps it has appeared to be an oversight that this book rarely has mentioned what would seem to be one of the fundamental goals in motorsports: speed.

That has not been an oversight, but rather by design—just as it has been by design that the emphasis in NASCAR Winston Cup racing never has been about speed.

For example, NASCAR in 1991 implemented speed limits on pit road—another step that reduced the opportunity to establish speed records.

From the outset, the Winston Cup Series was designed to be a competition among "stock" cars, which today still somewhat resemble the family sedan and in the sport's infancy *were* indeed the family car in many instances.

NASCAR always has sanely placed safety above speed, and the evolution of its nearly indestructible race cars has made it the safest form of a very dangerous sport. The sanctioning body's emphasis on equalizing the competition also has played a role in the comparative lack of emphasis on speed. NASCAR long ago realized that fans would prefer to watch some 30 cars draft down the backstretch at Talladega, Ala., inches apart at 185 mph than see a lone car capable of running 205 mph—with the rest competing at 200 mph—and winning by several laps.

The relative importance of speeds in the history of Winston Cup racing is further negated by the following:

- Until 1969 there was no uniform method of measuring tracks, thus rendering many of the qualifying and race speeds reported before then meaningless;
- Carburetor restrictor plates, which have been employed periodically since the 1970 Yankee 400 at Michigan International Speedway, often have been used to slow the race cars at those tracks where

speed records most likely would be produced;

- Because caution laps are used in the computation of race speeds, records pertaining to the fastest races are as much, if not more, a product of the relative lack of caution laps as the actual racing speeds.

Regardless, speeds have increased dramatically since Bob Flock captured the pole for the first Winston Cup race in 1949 at Charlotte Speedway at 70.367 mph and Jim Roper won that race with an average speed of 59.88 mph. The increase in speeds has been far from a steady climb, however. On May 7, 1955, Junior Johnson captured the first victory of his career. His average speed at North Carolina's Hickory Speedway, then a dirt track measured at four-tenths of a mile, was 38.723 mph, the slowest winning speed in Winston Cup history. Rex White didn't exactly break the sound barrier when he captured the pole for the March 30, 1959, race at the quarter-mile Bowman Gray Stadium in Winston-Salem, N.C., at a speed of 46.3 mph—the slowest pole-winning speed ever recorded.

Daytona Beach, Fla., has been known as the "Birthplace of Speed" for nearly a century. As the following charts illustrate, that moniker has been appropriate in Winston Cup racing, because every new speed barrier from 100 to 190 mph was reached either at the Beach & Road Course or the 2.5-mile Daytona International Speedway tri-oval.

Qualifying Milestones

* Barrier	** Date	Driver	Car	Speed
100 mph	2-5-50	Joe Littlejohn	Oldsmobile	100.23
110 mph	2-10-52	Pat Kirkwood	Chrysler	110.97
120 mph	2-21-54	Lee Petty	Chrysler	123.41
130 mph	2-27-55	Tim Flock	Chrysler	130.293
140 mph	2-23-58	Paul Goldsmith	Pontiac	140.57
150 mph	2-14-60	*** Fireball Roberts	Pontiac	151.556
160 mph	7-4-62	Banjo Matthews	Pontiac	160.499
170 mph	2-23-64	Paul Goldsmith	Plymouth	174.91
180 mph	2-26-67	Curtis Turner	Chevrolet	180.831
190 mph	2-23-69	**** David Pearson	Ford	190.029

If more than one driver broke the barrier in qualifying, only the fastest at the conclusion of qualifying is listed.

**All dates are the date of the race on the Beach & Road Course or the Firecracker 250 or Daytona 500 at Daytona International Speedway.*

****Cotton Owens won the pole, but Roberts was the fastest qualifier.*

*****Buddy Baker won the pole, but Pearson was the fastest qualifier.*

Bill Elliott, in the Harry Melling-owned Coors Ford Thunderbird, recorded the fastest lap in stock-car racing history—212.809 mph—to win the pole for the 1987 Winston 500 at Talladega, Ala.

Race Milestones

Barrier	Date	Driver	Car	Speed
100 mph	2-7-57	Cotton Owens	Pontiac	101.542
140 mph	2-20-59	Bob Welborn	Chevrolet	143.198
150 mph	2-24-61	Joe Weatherly	Pontiac	152.607
160 mph	2-22-63	Junior Johnson	Chevrolet	164.084
170 mph	2-21-64	Junior Johnson	Dodge	170.778
180 mph	2-19-70	Cale Yarborough	Mercury	183.824

All of those milestones prior to 1959 were recorded at the Beach & Road Course, and those recorded since were achieved at Daytona International Speedway. Note that no race winner in Winston Cup history had averaged even 110 mph until Bob Welborn averaged 143.198 mph in a 100-mile qualifying race for the inaugural Daytona 500 in 1959.

Although no one has averaged 190 mph in a Winston Cup race, the 200 and 210 mph barriers in qualifying were broken at Talladega's 2.66-mile tri-oval—largest closed course in the world—that opened in 1969.

Buddy Baker, driving a Dodge Daytona, was clocked at 200.447 mph in a specially timed—and unofficial—run at Talladega on March 24, 1970, but no one broke the 200 mph barrier in qualifying until Benny Parsons won the pole for the 1982 Winston 500 with a clocking of 200.176 mph in a Pontiac owned by Harry Ranier. By the 1986 Winston 500, every driver who earned a berth in the field based on qualifying speeds (rather than a provisional starting spot) was timed at faster than 200 mph. In fact, Alan Kulwicki and Mark Martin failed to earn spots in the field despite qualifying speeds of more than 201 mph.

Bill Elliott raised the bar with a qualifying run of 212.809 mph—the fastest in NASCAR history—for the 1987 Winston 500.

Since 1990, however, the fastest qualifying speed recorded by a Winston Cup driver was Joe Nemechek's 198.331 mph clocking for the 1999 Winston 500 at Talladega, primarily because carburetor restrictor plates employed at Daytona and Talladega have reduced speeds considerably since Elliott's record run.

Despite those restrictions on speed, Martin averaged 188.354 mph to capture the caution-free Winston 500 on May 10, 1997—the fastest race in Winston Cup history.

1991 in Review

Dale Earnhardt won four races and captured his fifth Winston Cup championship, but Ricky Rudd had a slightly higher Performance Index rating, 733-729. Davey Allison and 51-year-old Harry Gant—who fashioned a four-race winning streak—led the circuit with five victories apiece, and Martin set the pace with five poles.

Most Memorable Race

Rudd crossed the finish line 4.5 seconds ahead of Allison in the Banquet Frozen Foods 300 on the road course at Sonoma, Calif., on June 9. Allison was given the checkered flag and sent to victory lane, however, when NASCAR immediately penalized Rudd for contact with Allison's Ford with one lap remaining. "The best thing I can compare it to is the World Wrestling Federation," Rudd said. "NASCAR makes its own rules."

Most Significant Wreck

J.D. McDuffie, who finished in the top 25 in the Performance Index 16 times from 1966-82, was killed on August 11, when his Pontiac crashed in the fifth turn of the fifth lap in the Budweiser at the Glen on the road course at Watkins Glen, N.Y. McDuffie's car skidded across the grass, hit a wall fronted by tires, flipped, and landed on its roof.

Most Important Off-Track Development

Speed limits on pit road were introduced.

Records & Milestones

Five different manufacturers—Ford, Pontiac, Chevrolet, Oldsmobile, and Buick—won poles to tie a modern record. Five manufacturers previously had won poles on eight occasions in the modern era, but it hasn't happened since. . . . Fourteen drivers won races to tie a modern record set in 1988 and equaled in 1990.

1991 at a Glance

Races:	29
Road:	2
Short Track:	8
Superspeedway:	19
Winners:	14
Pole Winners:	14
Tracks:	16
States:	13

1991 Performance Index Rankings

1. Ricky Rudd (733)
2. Dale Earnhardt (729)
3. Davey Allison (700)
4. Sterling Marlin (659)
5. Ernie Irvan (635)
6. Harry Gant (611)
7. Mark Martin (577)
8. Ken Schrader (565)
9. Bill Elliott; Darrell Waltrip (541)
11. Morgan Shepherd (533)
12. Geoff Bodine (469)
13. Rusty Wallace (465)
14. Alan Kulwicki (445)
15. Michael Waltrip (433)
16. Dale Jarrett (403)
17. Hut Stricklin (401)
18. Terry Labonte (356)
19. Bobby Hamilton (337)
20. Richard Petty (333)
21. Rick Mast (320)
22. Brett Bodine (319)
23. Bobby Hillin Jr. (309)
24. Joe Ruttman (298)
25. Kyle Petty (275)
26. Rick Wilson (268)
27. Jimmy Spencer (258)
28. Ted Musgrave (249)
29. Derrike Cope (232)
30. Chad Little (213)
31. Dave Marcis (164)
32. Lake Speed (119)
33. Mickey Gibbs (116)
34. Dick Trickle (98)
35. Jimmy Hensley (75)
36. Buddy Baker (71)
37. Larry Pearson (64)
38. Phil Barkdoll (46)
39. Greg Sacks (44)
40. Eddie Bierschwale (33)
41. Kenny Wallace (32)
42. Tommy Ellis (29)
43. Robby Gordon (27)
44. Wally Dallenbach Jr.; Irv Hoerr; Bill Sedgwick (21)
47. Jimmy Means (20)
48. Bill Schmitt (17)
49. John Paul Jr. (14)
50. Dorsey Schroeder (13)
51. Tom Kendall (12)
52. Jim Derhaag (10)

1991 Events

Daytona 500 by STP; Daytona Int. Speedway/2.5-mile/500 miles
Ernie Irvan (Chevrolet)/Davey Allison (Ford)

Pontiac Excitement 400; Richmond Int. Raceway/.75-mile/300 m
Dale Earnhardt (Chevrolet)/Davey Allison (Ford)

Goodwrench 500; North Carolina Motor Speedway/1.017-m/500m
Kyle Petty (Pontiac)/Kyle Petty (Pontiac)

Motorcraft Qual. Parts 500; Atl. Motor Speedway/1.522-m/500m
Ken Schrader (Chevrolet)/Alan Kulwicki (Ford)

TranSouth 500; Darlington Raceway/1.366-mile/500 miles
Ricky Rudd (Chevrolet)/Geoff Bodine (Ford)

Valleydale Meats 500; Bristol Int. Raceway/.533-m/267 miles
Rusty Wallace (Pontiac)/Rusty Wallace (Pontiac)

First Union 400; North Wilkesboro Speedway/.625-m/250 miles
Darrell Waltrip (Chevrolet)/Brett Bodine (Buick)

Hanes 500; Martinsville Speedway/.526-mile/263 miles
Dale Earnhardt (Chevrolet)/Mark Martin (Ford)

Winston 500; Talladega Superspeedway/2.66-mile/500 miles
Harry Gant (Oldsmobile)/Ernie Irvan (Chevrolet)

Coca-Cola 600; Charlotte Motor Speedway/1.5-mile/600 miles
Davey Allison (Ford)/Mark Martin (Ford)

Budweiser 500; Dover Downs International Speedway/1-m/500 m
Ken Schrader (Chevrolet)/Michael Waltrip (Pontiac)

Banquet Fr. Foods 300; Sears Pt. Int. Race./2.52-m rd./187 m
Davey Allison (Ford)/Ricky Rudd (Chevrolet)

Champion Spark Plug 500; Pocono Int. Raceway/2.5-m/500 miles
Darrell Waltrip (Chevrolet)/Mark Martin (Ford)

Miller Genuine Draft 400; Michigan Int. Speedway/2-m/400 m
Davey Allison (Ford)/Michael Waltrip (Pontiac)

Pepsi 400; Daytona International Speedway/2.5-mile/400 miles
Bill Elliott (Ford)/Sterling Marlin (Ford)

Miller Genuine Draft 500; Pocono Int. Raceway/2.5-mile/500 m
Rusty Wallace (Pontiac)/Alan Kulwicki (Ford)

Diehard 500; Talladega Superspeedway/2.66-mile/500 miles
Dale Earnhardt (Chevrolet)/Sterling Marlin (Ford)

Budweiser at the Glen; Watkins Glen Int./2.428-m road/219 m
Ernie Irvan (Chevrolet)/Terry Labonte (Oldsmobile)

Champion Spark Plug 400; Michigan Int. Speedway/2-mile/400 m
Dale Jarrett (Ford)/Alan Kulwicki (Ford)

Bud 500; Bristol International Raceway/.533-mile/267 miles
Alan Kulwicki (Ford)/Bill Elliott (Ford)

Heinz Southern 500; Darlington Raceway/1.366-mile/500 miles
Harry Gant (Oldsmobile)/Davey Allison (Ford)

Miller Genuine Draft 400; Richmond Int. Raceway/.75-m/300 m
Harry Gant (Oldsmobile)/Rusty Wallace (Pontiac)

Peak Antifreeze 500; Dover Downs Int. Speedway/1-m/500 miles
Harry Gant (Oldsmobile)/Alan Kulwicki (Ford)

Goody's 500; Martinsville Speedway/.526-mile/263 miles
Harry Gant (Oldsmobile)/Mark Martin (Ford)

Tyson Holly Farms 400; No. Wilkesboro Speedway/.625-m/250 m
Dale Earnhardt (Chevrolet)/Harry Gant (Oldsmobile)

Mello Yello 500; Charlotte Motor Speedway/1.5-mile/500 miles
Geoff Bodine (Ford)/Mark Martin (Ford)

AC Delco 500; North Carolina Motor Speedway/1.017-mile/500 m
Davey Allison (Ford)/Kyle Petty (Pontiac)

Pyroil 500; Phoenix International Raceway/1-mile/312 miles
Davey Allison (Ford)/Geoff Bodine (Ford)

Hardee's 500; Atlanta Motor Speedway/1.522-mile/500 miles
Mark Martin (Ford)/Bill Elliott (Ford)

Victories

1. Davey Allison; Harry Gant (5)
3. Dale Earnhardt (4)
4. Ernie Irvan; Ken Schrader; Rusty Wallace; Darrell Waltrip (2)
8. Geoff Bodine; Bill Elliott; Dale Jarrett; Alan Kulwicki; Mark Martin; Kyle Petty; Ricky Rudd (1)

Poles

1. Mark Martin (5)
2. Alan Kulwicki (4)
3. Davey Allison (3)
4. Geoff Bodine; Bill Elliott; Sterling Marlin; Kyle Petty; Rusty Wallace; Michael Waltrip (2)
10. Brett Bodine; Harry Gant; Ernie Irvan; Terry Labonte; Ricky Rudd (1)

Victories

1. Chevrolet (11)
2. Ford (10)
3. Oldsmobile (5)
4. Pontiac (3)

Poles

1. Ford (18)
2. Pontiac (6)
3. Chevrolet; Oldsmobile (2)
5. Buick (1)

1992 History's Greatest Title Chase

Most Memorable Race

The purpose of a long championship campaign is to identify and reward excellence and consistency.

That's true regardless of the sport, which makes down-to-the-wire pennant races in baseball or points races in the Winston Cup Series a bonus.

There have been truly exciting, down-to-the-wire championship chases in Winston Cup racing—Richard Petty vs. Darrell Waltrip in 1979, for example. But a number of others in which the final margin is minute weren't necessarily that close. Those narrow margins often were the result of a leader who entered the season finale needing to finish 29th, 17th, or whatever—then conservatively achieving that goal—while the runner-up closed the final margin considerably with a victory or a high finish in the finale.

That certainly wasn't the case in 1992, a season that produced the greatest points race in Winston Cup history. The campaign all boiled down to the Hooters 500 on November 15 at Atlanta Motor Speedway.

Few races in Winston Cup history have generated the incredible advance interest the 1992 Hooters 500 did, although that wasn't because of the points race. Despite building a new 12,000-seat grandstand, Atlanta Motor Speedway had exhausted its ticket supply by early August because of an announcement made the previous year: The race would be the final start of Petty's 200-victory career.

In October, as the points race began to tighten and the demand to see Petty's farewell race grew, the speedway arranged to have 18,000 additional bleacher seats shipped to Hampton, Ga., for the race. Those sold

out in a matter of days—before the track could announce their availability or before it had an opportunity to trumpet that the race would mark Jeff Gordon's Winston Cup debut. The 1992 Hooters 500 became *the* landmark event in Winston Cup history: A sport bid farewell to its King, the seven-time Winston Cup champion Petty, and welcomed a possible successor: Gordon, who would win his third Winston Cup title in 1998 at age 27.

Just as significantly, it also produced the greatest finish to a championship showdown in history. A record six drivers entered the finale with a chance to earn Winston Cup racing's greatest prize: Davey Allison, Alan Kulwicki, Bill Elliott, Harry Gant, Kyle Petty, and Mark Martin. Granted, it would take a miracle for Gant, who trailed by 101 points, Kyle Petty (102), or Martin (113) to make up their deficits. But Kulwicki was only 30 points behind Allison, and Elliott trailed by just 40. Allison needed a fifth-place finish—no easy feat—to render the outcome meaningless.

Qualifying yielded few clues. Rick Mast captured the first pole of his career, Martin earned the No. 4 starting spot, and the other championship contenders lined up between 11th and 29th.

King Richard stole the show in the race's early stages, but not intentionally: His STP Pontiac caught fire in a wreck.

"I went out in a blaze, but I forgot the glory part," he said. "I got down to the end of pit road and figured I had better find a firetruck. I drove down beside a firetruck, and I think all those cats wanted to get an autograph, because they didn't bring a fire extinguisher. I sent them back to get a fire extinguisher. They put the fire out, so we were OK."

By the 62nd lap, Elliott had taken the lead in Junior Johnson's Ford. Eleven laps later, it was Kulwicki's turn to establish that his Ford was the other dominant car

"I went out in a blaze, but I forgot the glory part," Richard Petty said after his car caught fire during the 1992 Hooters 500 at Atlanta Motor Speedway. The King's final race was also Jeff Gordon's first and the dramatic culmination of the greatest title chase in Winston Cup history.

in the race. Meanwhile, Allison was running in the top six or seven. By the time anyone could determine how the points race shaped up, a change in position rendered the calculation out of date. It remained that way until the 254th lap, when Ernie Irvan's Chevrolet plowed into Allison's Robert Yates-owned Ford to end Allison's championship dreams.

"That's just the way it goes sometimes. We had some troubles, and we were trying to work our way back up there. We were just trying to run a smart race," Allison said. "I ran over something earlier in the race, and we had to come in and repair the car. We caught a lucky caution flag, and I thought, `All right. We're going to be OK now.' I saw Ernie get loose in turn four and just run out of room. It just wasn't meant to be. It looked like Ernie must have had a flat tire or something. The car just got away from him."

"We gave it all we had," added Larry McReynolds, Allison's crew chief. "We kept overcoming everything that was thrown at us. We almost got a lap down and

luckily caught a caution. We got it fixed and were getting back in the hunt. We were running sixth, and that's where we needed to be running. But it just wasn't meant to be. It was just a racing accident. We don't have any ill feelings against anybody."

The Hooters 500 victory and the Winston Cup title were left to be determined by Elliott and Kulwicki, as the latter said, "as long as we didn't screw anything up."

The dramatic finish was upstaged one final time when, with two laps left, Richard Petty's No. 43 Pontiac returned to the track after undergoing extensive repairs.

"Somehow, he was going to take the checkered flag in his last race. Richard's been doing this for 35 years, and he needed to see the checkered flag in his last race," said Robbie Loomis, the King's crew chief.

Elliott had led five times for 85 laps and Kulwicki twice for two laps before Kulwicki set the pace for 101 consecutive laps. He pitted on the 311th circuit, allowing Elliott to take the lead. Elliott led four laps before he made a gas-only pit and yielded the lead to Terry

Labonte, then led the final 13 laps and beat Kulwicki by 8.06 seconds.

Elliott's victory gave him five more Winston Cup points than Kulwicki, and each driver earned five bonus points for leading a lap. Kulwicki, however, led 103 laps to Elliott's 102 and gained an additional five bonus points for leading the most laps. That gave him the title by a 4,078-4,068 margin—the closest in history. Had Elliott gained the lead on the 310th lap instead of the 311th, he'd have had the five additional bonus points for leading the most laps, and that would have resulted in each driver finishing the season with 4,073 points. The tiebreaker, which has never been used, is to award the title to the driver with the most victories. The Hooters 500 was Elliott's fifth triumph of the year, three more than Kulwicki enjoyed.

"We knew that we needed to pit at 311, and that would clinch it just as long as we finished second. We knew exactly what we had to do, and we did it," said Paul Andrews, Kulwicki's crew chief.

"On the last pit stop, we were about a second and a half ahead of him. I knew I'd led the most laps. I knew he couldn't beat me for the championship unless I screwed up," Kulwicki said. "He probably gambled a little. He got ahead. He won the race. At that point, I knew where I was and could see he was three seconds ahead. The championship was what was important."

Although he lost the war, Elliott was elated about winning the battle.

"Win, lose, or draw, I want to congratulate Alan Kulwicki," Elliott said. "He knew exactly what he had to do, and he came out on top. Tim (Brewer, his crew chief) had tried to tell me on the radio to lead every lap I could. Man, I was trying. I was doing everything I could. To come here and win the last race of the season—and Richard's last race—there was a lot of emotion here today. I think winning Petty's last race is neat. I did everything I could possibly do. I knew if Kulwicki finished one place behind me, I wasn't going to beat him. It was a weird day, totally weird. You can't look back and say if we'd done this and if we'd done that. The ifs are over. This year is history. I gave it everything I had."

So did Kulwicki, who had overcome a seemingly impossible 278-point deficit with six races remaining.

"This is like living a dream," he said. "The car handled real well, and this is the fastest we've ever run at this track. I knew how far I had to go in the race to lead the most laps and, at that point, I knew no one could beat me. I was a little bit safe coming down pit road. I lost first gear in the transmission on our first pit stop, so I had trouble getting out of the pits all day long. I wanted to win the race. We had led quite awhile, but there will be other races. The championship is what I wanted. It's a whole lot better to lose a race by a few seconds than to lose a championship by trying to win the race in the last laps and make a mistake. I knew we had led the most laps and Bill couldn't beat me for the championship unless I screwed up."

If anyone was more relieved than Kulwicki, it was the King.

"It's been a heckuva week, a heckuva year, and a heckuva 35 years," he said. "God doesn't put many people on earth and let them do, accomplish, and play their own game as much as I have."

King Richard bid farewell with a 35th-place finish, and Gordon introduced himself by finishing 31st. In hindsight, perhaps the most memorable scenes were Allison's enthusiastic wave to the crowd after his accident left him in 27th place and Kulwicki's championship celebration, which included his trademark "Polish" victory lap, in which he circled the track in the wrong direction.

"We'll just go back next year and try again," Allison said.

"I wanted to do something memorable other than spewing champagne or standing on top of the car," Kulwicki said. "I wanted to give the fans something to remember me by."

1992 in Review

Allison and Elliott, who won four races in a row early in the year, shared the season lead in victories with five apiece, and Kulwicki set the pace with six poles. The same six drivers who entered the season finale at Atlanta with a chance to capture the Winston Cup championship were the top six in the Performance Index, although the order was different. Elliott posted a season-high 704 rating, followed by Allison (694), Kulwicki (680), Kyle Petty (675), Gant (654), and Martin (606).

Most Significant Wreck

Irvan wasn't particularly apologetic when asked if he felt sorry for Allison after their wreck in the Hooters 500 ended the latter's title hopes. "Davey knocked me in the fence three or four times this year," Irvan said. "I don't feel sorry for Davey. That's part of racing. As far as I'm concerned, I had just as much right to be out there racing as anyone else. We were out there racing our race. If you get tangled up, then you get tangled up."

Most Important Off-Track Development

Rick Hendrick was watching the March 14 Atlanta 300, a NASCAR Busch Series race, from a luxury VIP suite. The 20-year-old Gordon was leading the race while fighting a loose race car, and Hendrick boldly predicted to a companion that the youngster would wreck within 10 laps. But Gordon ended up in victory lane—his first superspeedway win of any kind—and so impressed Hendrick that he immediately began the process of hiring him to drive a Chevrolet for Hendrick Motorsports.

Records & Milestones

Kyle Petty captured the A.C. Delco 500 at the North Carolina Motor Speedway in Rockingham from the pole. He had won the Goodwrench 500 at Rockingam in 1990 and '91, starting from the pole on both occasions. Petty's victory in the A.C. Delco 500 enabled him to become the only driver in history to win a 500-mile race from the pole on the same track three years in a row. In fact, David Pearson, who won at least one 500-mile race from the pole in each season from 1973-76, is the only other driver to win *any* 500-mile race from the pole in as many as three straight seasons.

Nine drivers posted multiple victories—Elliott, Allison, Waltrip (3), Irvan (3), Geoff Bodine (2), Kulwicki (2), Gant (2), Martin (2), and Kyle Petty (2)—to tie a modern record set in 1984. . . . Dave Marcis posted his 22nd consecutive season with a Performance Index rating of 200 or better, the fifth-longest streak in history, and his 25th straight season with a rating of 100 or better. Only two other drivers have recorded longer streaks of seasons with ratings of 100 or better. . . . Tennessee's Bristol International Raceway became the first track in the modern era to replace its asphalt surface with concrete.

1992 at a Glance

Races:	29
Road:	2
Short Track:	8
Superspeedway:	19
Winners:	12
Pole Winners:	14
Tracks:	16
States:	13

1992 Performance Index Rankings

1. Bill Elliott (704)
2. Davey Allison (694)
3. Alan Kulwicki (680)
4. Kyle Petty (675)
5. Harry Gant (654)
6. Mark Martin (606)
7. Terry Labonte (588)
8. Ricky Rudd (579)
9. Morgan Shepherd (553)
10. Geoff Bodine (541)
11. Brett Bodine (527)
12. Sterling Marlin (518)
13. Dale Earnhardt (502)
14. Rusty Wallace (501)
15. Ernie Irvan (498)
16. Darrell Waltrip (492)
17. Ted Musgrave (448)
18. Ken Schrader (444)
19. Derrike Cope (399)
20. Dale Jarrett (397)
21. Dick Trickle (385)
22. Jimmy Hensley (320)
23. Michael Waltrip (298)
24. Richard Petty (278)
25. Bobby Hamilton (245)
26. Rick Mast (235)
27. Hut Stricklin (233)
28. Wally Dallenbach Jr. (223)
29. Greg Sacks (177)
30. Jimmy Spencer (164)
31. Dave Marcis (117)
32. Chad Little (96)
33. Bobby Hillin Jr. (78)
34. Lake Speed (60)
35. Charlie Glotzbach (56)
36. Phil Parsons (35)
37. Buddy Baker (34)
38. Dave Mader III (31)
39. Jim Sauter (29)
40. Phil Barkdoll (28)
41. Dorsey Schroeder (26)
42. Eddie Bierschwale; Bob Schacht (21)
44. Jimmy Means; Mike Potter; Mike Wallace (20)
47. Tom Kendall (17)
48. Bill Sedgwick; Scott Sharp (11)
50. Rich Bickle (5)

1992 Events

Daytona 500 by STP; Daytona Int. Speedway/2.5-mile/500 miles
Davey Allison (Ford)/Sterling Marlin (Ford)

Goodwrench 500; North Carolina Motor Speedway/1.017-m/500m
Bill Elliott (Ford)/Kyle Petty (Pontiac)

Pontiac Excitement 400; Richmond Int. Raceway/.75-mile/300 m
Bill Elliott (Ford)/Bill Elliott (Ford)

Motorcraft 500; Atlanta Motor Speedway/1.522-mile/500 miles
Bill Elliott (Ford)/Mark Martin (Ford)

TranSouth 500; Darlington Raceway/1.366-mile/500 miles
Bill Elliott (Ford)/Sterling Marlin (Ford)

Food City 500; Bristol International Raceway/.533-mile/267 m
Alan Kulwicki (Ford)/Alan Kulwicki (Ford)

First Union 400; North Wilkesboro Speedway/.625-m/250 miles
Davey Allison (Ford)/Alan Kulwicki (Ford)

Hanes 500; Martinsville Speedway/.526-mile/263 miles
Mark Martin (Ford)/Darrell Waltrip (Chevrolet)

Winston 500; Talladega Superspeedway/2.66-mile/500 miles
Davey Allison (Ford)/Ernie Irvan (Chevrolet)

Coca-Cola 600; Charlotte Motor Speedway/1.5-mile/600 miles
Dale Earnhardt (Chevrolet)/Bill Elliott (Ford)

Budweiser 500; Dover Downs International Speedway/1-m/500 m
Harry Gant (Oldsmobile)/Brett Bodine (Ford)

The Save Mart 300; Sears Point Int. Raceway/2.52-m road/187m
Ernie Irvan (Chevrolet)/Ricky Rudd (Chevrolet)

Champion Spark Plug 500; Pocono Int. Raceway/2.5-m/500 miles
Alan Kulwicki (Ford)/Ken Schrader (Chevrolet)

Miller Genuine Draft 400; Michigan Int. Speedway/2-m/400 m
Davey Allison (Ford)/Davey Allison (Ford)

Pepsi 400; Daytona International Speedway/2.5-mile/400 miles
Ernie Irvan (Chevrolet)/Sterling Marlin (Ford)

Miller Genuine Draft 500; Pocono Int. Raceway/2.5-mile/500 m
Darrell Waltrip (Chevrolet)/Davey Allison (Ford)

Diehard 500; Talladega Superspeedway/2.66-mile/500 miles
Ernie Irvan (Chevrolet)/Sterling Marlin (Ford)

Budweiser at the Glen; Watkins Glen Int./2.45-mile road/219m
Kyle Petty (Pontiac)/Dale Earnhardt (Chevrolet)

Champion Spark Plug 400; Michigan Int. Speedway/2-mile/400 m
Harry Gant (Oldsmobile)/Alan Kulwicki (Ford)

Bud 500; Bristol International Raceway/.533-mile/267 miles
Darrell Waltrip (Chevrolet)/Ernie Irvan (Chevrolet)

Mountain Dew Southern 500; Darlington Raceway/1.366-m/500 m
Darrell Waltrip (Chevrolet)/Sterling Marlin (Ford)

Miller Genuine Draft 400; Richmond Int. Raceway/.75-m/300 m
Rusty Wallace (Pontiac)/Ernie Irvan (Chevrolet)

Peak Antifreeze 500; Dover Downs Int. Speedway/1-m/500 miles
Ricky Rudd (Chevrolet)/Alan Kulwicki (Ford)

Goody's 500; Martinsville Speedway/.526-mile/263 miles
Geoff Bodine (Ford)/Kyle Petty (Pontiac)

Tyson Holly Farms 400; No. Wilkesboro Speedway/.625-m/250 m
Geoff Bodine (Ford)/Alan Kulwicki (Ford)

Mello Yello 500; Charlotte Motor Speedway/1.5-mile/500 miles
Mark Martin (Ford)/Alan Kulwicki (Ford)

AC Delco 500; North Carolina Motor Speedway/1.017-mile/500 m
Kyle Petty (Pontiac)/Kyle Petty (Pontiac)

Pyroil 500; Phoenix International Raceway/1-mile/312 miles
Davey Allison (Ford)/Rusty Wallace (Pontiac)

Hooters 500; Atlanta Motor Speedway/1.522-mile/500 miles
Bill Elliott (Ford)/Rick Mast (Oldsmobile)

Victories

1. Davey Allison; Bill Elliott (5)
3. Ernie Irvan; Darrell Waltrip (3)
5. Geoff Bodine; Harry Gant; Alan Kulwicki; Mark Martin; Kyle Petty (2)
10. Dale Earnhardt; Ricky Rudd; Rusty Wallace (1)

Poles

1. Alan Kulwicki (6)
2. Sterling Marlin (5)
3. Ernie Irvan; Kyle Petty (3)
5. Davey Allison; Bill Elliott (2)
7. Brett Bodine; Dale Earnhardt; Mark Martin; Rick Mast; Ricky Rudd;
   Ken Schrader; Rusty Wallace; Darrell Waltrip (1)

Victories

1. Ford (16)
2. Chevrolet (8)
3. Pontiac (3)
4. Oldsmobile (2)

Poles

1. Ford (17)
2. Chevrolet (7)
3. Pontiac (4)
4. Oldsmobile (1)

1993
From Triumphs
To Tragedies

Most Significant Wrecks

Everyone knew that the 1992 Hooters 500 at Atlanta was Richard Petty's swansong.

But no one would have dared speculate that two other principals in that watershed event would soon be leaving as well by losing their lives in 1993.

The first tragedy struck like a bad April Fool's joke: Thirty-nine-year-old Alan Kulwicki was killed in a plane crash along with Mark Brooks and Dan Duncan, executives with Hooters, Kulwicki's sponsor, and pilot Charles Campbell. Their aircraft went down while approaching the airport in Bristol, Tenn., on a foggy April 1 evening.

Kulwicki's "Polish" victory lap at Atlanta just four and a half months earlier—when he'd said he wanted to give the fans a reason to remember him after he had won the closest Winston Cup championship battle in history—had been his last hurrah.

"I'm glad I didn't win the championship last year. I've got plenty of years left to win one," Davey Allison, who in 1992 had become one of only two drivers in history to enter the finale with the points lead and not emerge as the Winston Cup champion, said less than two months later.

Although Allison had won the Pontiac Excitement 400 on March 7 at Richmond, Va., in many ways his wave to the crowd from the wall on pit road at Atlanta after he saw his '92 title hopes end in a crash was also a symbolic farewell gesture.

On July 12, Allison flew short-track legend Red Farmer from his home in Hueytown, Ala., to Talladega Superspeedway in his new helicopter to watch David Bonnett, Neil's son, test his NASCAR Busch Series car. Allison's aircraft was hovering some 20 feet above the track's infield when it crashed. Farmer survived, but Allison died the next morning.

Some seven years after their untimely deaths, one rarely hears Kulwicki's name without hearing Allison's—or vice versa. Although they are inexorably linked in stock-car racing history, they entered the sport from entirely different backgrounds.

Kulwicki was from Wisconsin, earned a degree in mechanical engineering from Wisconsin-Milwaukee, and openly resented his father's lack of support for his career choice.

Allison was to the manor born: son of Bobby Allison, leader of the Alabama Gang and one of the greatest drivers in history.

If Allison and Kulwicki shared common traits, it was probably their work ethic and drive to succeed. Kulwicki turned down lucrative offers to drive for other teams to remain one of the first successful drivers in years to own his team.

No other driver in Kulwicki's seven years in Winston Cup racing spent as much time working on his car. When an eight-inch snowstorm pelted Atlanta Motor Speedway a day before the 1993 Motorcraft 500, only one driver could be found working on his car. Kulwicki spent the day under his Hooters Ford, wearing his racing helmet for protection from the elements.

Davey had spent his formative years learning the ropes in his father's shop, determined to succeed his dad as a Winston Cup champion. That was in sharp contrast to Davey's brother, Clifford, who was killed in a 1992 practice crash at Michigan International Speedway.

"I've always said that it's ironic that Clifford got killed working and Davey got killed playing," Bobby said, "because Davey was always so focused on racing and Clifford was focused on having a good time."

In the wake of his championship, Kulwicki emerged from his protective shell to display a wry sense of humor and a sense of duty. "I want NASCAR, Winston, and everybody in the sport to say they were proud to have Alan Kulwicki represent them as the Winston Cup champion," he said.

Davey always had been outgoing with fans and media. His instant success—the first rookie in the modern era to win two races—together with being the son

of a former Winston Cup champion who was voted NASCAR's Most Popular Driver on six occasions quickly helped the younger Allison secure one of the sport's largest followings.

Kulwicki, the 1986 Rookie of the Year, captured only five victories. But he won 24 poles, twice shared the season lead with six, and ranks among the top 20 in superspeedway poles (17), Grand Slam poles (7), and classic poles (2). From 1986-92, he posted a Performance Index rating of 300 or better each season, finishing 10th in 1990 and third in 1992. His career Performance Index of 3,271 ranks 63rd on the all-time list. But he is one of only 23 drivers to win the Winston Cup title and one of only two to die as the champion.

Kulwicki sported a Mighty Mouse decal on his car, received permission from Ford to carry the phrase "Underbird" (as in underdog) instead of "Thunderbird" on his bumper, and sported Elvis Presley neckwear. When Kulwicki was honored at the NASCAR Winston Cup Awards Banquet at New York's Waldorf-Astoria Hotel af-

ter his 1992 title, the theme song was "My Way," which seemed to fit him as appropriately as it did Frank Sinatra.

Davey was just 32 years old when he was fatally injured, but he already had recorded 19 victories and 14 poles. He ranks among the top 20 in superspeedway victories (14), 500-mile wins (7), superspeedway poles (12), and Grand Slam poles (4).

Allison, the 1987 Rookie of the Year, had at least a 400 Performance Index rating and finished in the top 15 in each of his six full seasons, and he was just beginning to reach his vast potential. In 1991, he shared the season lead with five victories, including the Coca-Cola 600 at Charlotte, and finished third in the Performance Index. A year later, despite serious crashes at Bristol, Charlotte, Long Pond, Pa., and Martinsville, Va., in which he suffered a broken right wrist and shoulder and rib injuries, he again shared the season's leadership with five victories, including the Daytona 500, and had the second-highest Performance Index rating. His career Performance Index of 3,826 ranks 47th on the all-time list.

Alan Kulwicki prepared for a qualifying run that would place him 14th in the starting grid for the 1992 Hooters 500 at Atlanta. Two days later, his second-place finish enabled him to edge race winner Bill Elliott in the closest battle in history for the Winston Cup championship.

"I've got to believe that if Davey was still here, he'd be racing with Jeff Gordon for wins and championships—and beating him," Bobby said when his son was inducted into the National Motorsports Press Association Hall of Fame at Darlington, S.C.

No one would argue.

1993 in Review

Dale Earnhardt captured six races and defeated Rusty Wallace by 80 points to earn his sixth Winston Cup championship. Wallace won a season-high 10 races, and Ken Schrader led the series with six poles. Earnhardt also outdistanced Wallace in the Performance Index, 814-777.

Most Memorable Race

Earnhardt led the Winston 500 at Talladega on May 3 when rain brought out a caution flag with nine laps remaining. The race then was red flagged with two laps to go, and that set the stage for one of the wildest shootouts in history. Earnhardt took the white flag with a slight advantage over Wallace, Mark Martin, and Ernie Irvan. When Earnhardt and Irvan bumped slightly on the final lap, Irvan slipped in front and edged Jimmy Spencer by two car lengths. Dale Jarrett finished third, Earnhardt fourth, and Joe Ruttman fifth. Wallace literally tumbled to sixth. Wallace's Penske Racing South Pontiac flipped wildly end over end through the tri-oval on the last lap, and he suffered a broken wrist and a concussion. "Everybody was driving completely insane, going for as many positions as they could," said Gordon, who finished 11th.

"I would have paid for a seat in the stands to watch," Ruttman added.

Most Important Off-Track Development

A new superspeedway, New Hampshire International Speedway, opened in Loudon. Wallace captured the Slick 50 300 on July 11, the first Winston Cup race held in New England since 1970.

Records & Milestones

Schrader captured six poles without earning a victory. The only other driver to win six poles in a winless season was Kulwicki in 1989. . . . The 1993 season produced only four multiple winners—Wallace, Earnhardt, Martin (5), and Irvan (3). That equaled the four multiple winners in 1974 as the fewest in the modern era.

1993 at a Glance

Races:	30
Road:	2
Short Track:	8
Superspeedway:	20
Winners:	10
Pole Winners:	12
Tracks:	17
States:	14

1993 Performance Index Rankings

1. Dale Earnhardt (814)
2. Rusty Wallace (777)
3. Mark Martin (696)
4. Dale Jarrett (664)
5. Morgan Shepherd (643)
6. Bill Elliott (627)
7. Kyle Petty (595)
8. Ernie Irvan (571)
9. Ken Schrader (534)
10. Jimmy Spencer (521)
11. Ricky Rudd (516)
12. Darrell Waltrip (469)
13. Harry Gant (466)
14. Geoff Bodine (460)
15. Bobby Labonte (441)
16. Terry Labonte (439)
17. Jeff Gordon (420)
18. Brett Bodine (411)
19. Sterling Marlin (403)
20. Michael Waltrip (383)
21. Rick Mast (366)
22. Davey Allison (322)
23. Wally Dallenbach Jr. (307)
24. Bobby Hillin Jr.; Ted Musgrave (285)
26. Hut Stricklin (261)
27. Phil Parsons (246)
28. Kenny Wallace (243)
29. Derrike Cope (230)
30. Lake Speed; Rick Wilson (168)
32. Jimmy Hensley (167)

33. Dick Trickle (154)
34. Greg Sacks (153)
35. Bobby Hamilton (120)
36. Alan Kulwicki (92)
37. Dave Marcis (61)
38. Jeff Purvis (44)
39. Joe Ruttman (41)
40. Jimmy Means (39)
41. Jim Sauter (26)
42. Mike Wallace (25)
43. P.J. Jones (22)
44. Scott Lagasse (17)

1993 Events

Daytona 500 by STP; Daytona Int. Speedway/2.5-mile/500 miles
Dale Jarrett (Chevrolet)/Kyle Petty (Pontiac)

Goodwrench 500; North Carolina Motor Speedway/1.017-m/500m
Rusty Wallace (Pontiac)/Mark Martin (Ford)

Pontiac Excitement 400; Richmond Int. Raceway/.75-mile/300 m
Davey Allison (Ford)/Ken Schrader (Chevrolet)

Motorcraft 500; Atlanta Motor Speedway/1.522-mile/500 miles
Morgan Shepherd (Ford)/Rusty Wallace (Pontiac)

TranSouth 500; Darlington Raceway/1.366-mile/500 miles
Dale Earnhardt (Chevrolet)

Food City 500; Bristol International Raceway/.533-mile/267 m
Rusty Wallace (Pontiac)/Rusty Wallace (Pontiac)

First Union 400; North Wilkesboro Speedway/.625-m/250 miles
Rusty Wallace (Pontiac)/Brett Bodine (Ford)

Hanes 500; Martinsville Speedway/.526-mile/263 miles
Rusty Wallace (Pontiac)/Geoff Bodine (Ford)

Winston 500; Talladega Superspeedway/2.66-mile/500 miles
Ernie Irvan (Chevrolet)/Dale Earnhardt (Chevrolet)

S.M. Supermarkets 300; Sears Pt. Int. Race./2.52-m rd./187 m
Geoff Bodine (Ford)/Dale Earnhardt (Chevrolet)

Coca-Cola 600; Charlotte Motor Speedway/1.5-mile/600 miles
Dale Earnhardt (Chevrolet)/Ken Schrader (Chevrolet)

Budweiser 500; Dover Downs International Speedway/1-m/500 m
Dale Earnhardt (Chevrolet)/Ernie Irvan (Chevrolet)

Champion Spark Plug 500; Pocono Int. Raceway/2.5-m/500 miles
Kyle Petty (Pontiac)/Ken Schrader (Chevrolet)

Miller Genuine Draft 400; Michigan Int. Speedway/2-m/400 m
Ricky Rudd (Chevrolet)/Brett Bodine (Ford)

Pepsi 400; Daytona International Speedway/2.5-mile/400 miles
Dale Earnhardt (Chevrolet)/Ernie Irvan (Chevrolet)

Slick 50 300; New Hampshire Int. Speedway/1.058-m/317 miles
Rusty Wallace (Pontiac)/Mark Martin (Ford)

Miller Genuine Draft 500; Pocono Int. Raceway/2.5-mile/500 m
Dale Earnhardt (Chevrolet)/Ken Schrader (Chevrolet)

Diehard 500; Talladega Superspeedway/2.66-mile/500 miles
Dale Earnhardt (Chevrolet)/Bill Elliott (Ford)

Budweiser at the Glen; Watkins Glen Int./2.45-mile road/221m
Mark Martin (Ford)/Mark Martin (Ford)

Champion Spark Plug 400; Michigan Int. Speedway/2-mile/400 m
Mark Martin (Ford)/Ken Schrader (Chevrolet)

Bud 500; Bristol International Raceway/.533-mile/267 miles
Mark Martin (Ford)/Mark Martin (Ford)

Mountain Dew Southern 500; Darlington Raceway/1.366-m/500 m
Mark Martin (Ford)/Ken Schrader (Chevrolet)

Miller Genuine Draft 400; Richmond Int. Raceway/.75-m/300 m
Rusty Wallace (Pontiac)/Bobby Labonte (Ford)

Splitfire Spark Plug 500; Dover Downs Int. Raceway/1-m/500m
Rusty Wallace (Pontiac)/Rusty Wallace (Pontiac)

Goody's 500; Martinsville Speedway/.526-mile/263 miles
Ernie Irvan (Ford)/Ernie Irvan (Ford)

Tyson Holly Farms 400; No. Wilkesboro Speedway/.625-m/250 m
Rusty Wallace (Pontiac)/Ernie Irvan (Ford)

Mello Yello 500; Charlotte Motor Speedway/1.5-mile/500 miles
Ernie Irvan (Ford)/Jeff Gordon (Chevrolet)

AC Delco 500; North Carolina Motor Speedway/1.017-mile/500 m
Rusty Wallace (Pontiac)/Mark Martin (Ford)

Slick 50 500; Phoenix International Raceway/1-mile/312 miles
Mark Martin (Ford)/Bill Elliott (Ford)

Hooters 500; Atlanta Motor Speedway/1.522-mile/500 miles
Rusty Wallace (Pontiac)/Harry Gant (Chevrolet)

Victories

1. Rusty Wallace (10)
2. Dale Earnhardt (6)
3. Mark Martin (5)
4. Ernie Irvan (3)
5. Davey Allison; Geoff Bodine; Dale Jarrett; Kyle Petty; Ricky Rudd; Morgan Shepherd (1)

Poles

1. Ken Schrader (6)
2. Mark Martin (5)
3. Ernie Irvan (4)
4. Rusty Wallace (3)
5. Brett Bodine; Dale Earnhardt; Bill Elliott (2)
8. Geoff Bodine; Harry Gant; Jeff Gordon; Bobby Labonte; Kyle Petty (1)

Victories

1. Pontiac (11)
2. Ford (10)
3. Chevrolet (9)

Poles

1. Ford (13)
2. Chevrolet (12)
3. Pontiac (4)

1994
The 'Intimidator'

There are millions of Winston Cup fans who despise Dale Earnhardt—and an equal number who idolize him.

But hardly a soul has mixed feelings about the Man in Black, who many believe to be the greatest driver in history. Certainly no driver has been blamed for more crashes *and* still been the center of attention in so many victory-lane celebrations.

And no other driver, from the sport's legends to the out-of-their-league also-rans, ever seemed to turn Winston Cup racing into a Joie Chitwood thrill show as often as Earnhardt, who earned a record-tying seventh Winston Cup crown in 1994.

"If he's leading or running 18th, everybody's watching him, including the competitors. He has an uncanny command of the car and so much savvy. He drives through holes that aren't there," said Richard Childress, who owned the Chevrolets in which Earnhardt won the last six of his seven Winston Cup championships.

"The fact is, you can't be too meek and win out here," Earnhardt said in 1990, when he was on his way to his fourth Winston Cup title. "Rubbing on each other a little, especially at the short tracks, is just part of the game. That doesn't mean you're trying to hurt anybody. You never want to see anybody get hurt, and you sure as heck don't want to knock somebody out of the race. All you're doing is trying to get around him or trying to keep him from getting around you. You've got to be tough when you run this circuit, and I drive to win. It's always been tough on me to lose."

You don't get nicknamed "Ironhead," a tag Earnhardt carried early in his career, or the "Intimidator" by being meek.

A few examples that helped Earnhardt gain those monikers:

- 1984 Talladega 500 at Talladega, Ala: Earnhardt won a 10-car dash to the wire after 16 drivers had swapped the lead on 68 official occasions.

"The fact is, you can't be too meek and win out here," said seven-time Winston Cup champion Dale Earnhardt.

- 1987 Miller High Life 400 at Richmond, Va.: Earnhardt sent Harry Gant's car spinning while they were dueling for second, then beat Geoff Bodine by half a second.
- 1987 TranSouth 500 at Darlington, S.C.: Earnhardt hit the wall with four laps left, but still beat Bill Elliott by nearly three seconds.
- 1987 Valleydale 500 at Bristol, Tenn: Sterling Marlin led until Earnhardt shoved him into the wall midway through the race and went on to take the checkered flag.
- 1987 Summer 500 at Long Pond, Pa.: Earnhardt clipped Alan Kulwicki's car on a last-lap pass and beat him by one second.
- 1993 Coca-Cola 600 at Charlotte: NASCAR penalized Earnhardt for rough driving after he hit Greg Sacks and for speeding on pit road, but the Man in

Black cruised into victory lane.

- 1993 Talladega 500: Earnhardt beat Ernie Irvan to the checkered flag by six inches.
- 1994 Winston Select 500 at Talladega: When the final caution period ended with 22 laps to go, Earnhardt was 11th. Ten laps later, he was third, and he beat Irvan by a car length.
- 1996 Goodwrench 400 at Rockingham, N.C.: Bobby Hamilton held the lead until he was pushed into the wall on the 345th lap by Earnhardt, the eventual winner.
- 1999 Goody's Headache Powder 500 at Bristol: Terry Labonte led the penultimate lap, but Earnhardt sent the leader spinning with a not-so-gentle tap on the final lap, then took the checkered flag.

"If you're not aggressive, you're not going to win. And if you don't win, you don't keep your ride," Earnhardt said.

But make no mistake, Earnhardt never would have equaled Richard Petty's record of seven Winston Cup championships had he not been so adept at bringing his Chevrolet back to the garage in one piece.

Earnhardt captured his first title in 1980 behind the wheel of Rod Osterlund's Chevrolet and became the only driver in history to win the championship just one year after earning Rookie of the Year acclaim.

After suffering through a winless 1981 campaign, Earnhardt posted at least one victory in each of the next 15 years—the fourth-longest streak of that nature in history.

When Earnhardt returned for his second stint with Childress in 1984, he quickly became the dominant driver of his era. He captured at least three races in seven straight seasons (1985-91), and twice during that stretch he captured at least four superspeedway victories in consecutive seasons (in 1986-87 and in 1989-90). In posting his first back-to-back championships in 1986 and 1987, Earnhardt won at least four superspeedway races and at least three 500-mile races each season. In 1987, Earnhardt tied a record set by Lee Petty in 1959 by capturing 11 races without benefit of starting from the pole in any of them.

Earnhardt also won at least four superspeedway races in both 1989 and '90, and in each of those seasons he captured at least four 500-mile triumphs. Only one driver has recorded a longer streak of seasons with at least four victories in 500-mile races, and only Earnhardt has put together three different strings of winning at least three 500-mile races in consecutive seasons—in 1986 and 1987, in 1989 and 1990, and in 1993 and 1994.

After two early victories in 1996, Earnhardt suffered a broken collarbone and a badly bruised sternum in a wreck at Talladega. He was in tears when he had to be replaced early in the next race, the Brickyard 400 at Indianapolis, by Mike Skinner. In his next outing, Earnhardt captured the pole on the road course at Watkins Glen, N.Y., in track-record time, then refused to follow the team's plan to employ a relief driver, finishing a gut-wrenching sixth.

After Earnhardt suffered through a winless 1997 season, he was asked about his chances of earning a record-shattering eighth title.

"Good to great," he said with a rehearsed smile.

How about winning the eighth title in 1998?

"Good to great," he said, now laughing. "The one time I still really enjoy myself is when I'm racing."

No stock-car driver in history has been such a prisoner of his fame as Earnhardt, who has moaned that he "can't even go to the grocery story anymore, and I really used to enjoy that."

Earnhardt now owns a Winston Cup team, and his son, Dale Jr., captured the 1998 and '99 NASCAR Busch Series crowns. Those titles, accomplished in a car owned by Dale Sr., enabled the Earnhardt family to become the first to stretch NASCAR crowns over three generations. Dale's father, Ralph "Ironheart" Earnhardt, won the 1956 title in NASCAR's Late Model Sportsman Division, forerunner of the Busch Series.

Dale earned a stirring victory in the 1998 Daytona 500, then added three more victories after he celebrated his 48th birthday in 1999. Whether Earnhardt is the greatest driver in history is, of course, subject to debate. But if he never wins another race, Earnhardt has established a legacy that certainly puts him on the short list of candidates.

Dale ranks in the top 10 in virtually every Performance Index category and shares the records of seven No. 1 seasons, three consecutive No. 1 seasons (1993-95), and six consecutive top-three campaigns and years with a rating of 700 or better (1986-91). His 13 seasons with a rating of 700 or more, 14 campaigns with a rating of 600 or better, and 20 seasons with a rating of 500 or more each rank second on the all-time list. Among the other categories in which he ranks no worse than second are top-two seasons (9), top-three seasons (10), top-four seasons (12), top-six seasons (14), top-eight seasons (17), top-nine seasons (18), top-11 seasons (19), and 17 consecutive seasons with a rating of 500 or better and consecutive top-14 campaigns (1983-99). His career Performance Index of 14,657 ranks second and is a modern record.

Earnhardt's 74 victories rank sixth on the all-time list, and he is among the top five in Grand Slam wins (25), 500-mile victories (36), superspeedway triumphs (46), and classic victories (8)—three each in the Southern 500 at Darlington and the Coca-Cola 600 and one apiece in the Daytona 500 and the Brickyard 400. Only four drivers have posted more short-track victories than Earnhardt's 27, and his six consecutive triumphs on short tracks in 1987 are the third-longest such streak in history. Earnhardt has won 22 poles and ranks among the top five in poles on road courses (5) and among the top 20 in Grand Slam poles (8), classic poles (2), and superspeedway poles (12).

"I've said many times that I can't believe a boy of modest means from Kannapolis, North Carolina, has accomplished so much and been so blessed," Earnhardt said.

As Lowe's Motor Speedway President Humpy Wheeler aptly said of Earnhardt: "He's one in a million."

1994 in Review

Dale Earnhardt rolled to his record-tying seventh Winston Cup championship and held a commanding 854-678 advantage over Rusty Wallace in the Performance Index. Wallace earned eight victories, twice as many as the runner-up, Earnhardt. Bodine and Irvan shared the leadership in poles with five each.

Most Important Off-Track Development

Indianapolis Motor Speedway decided to welcome the Winston Cup Series to what has been the most hallowed ground in motorsports almost since the inaugural Indianapolis 500 was staged in 1911.

Most Memorable Race

The August 6 Brickyard 400, the most anticipated race in NASCAR history—one for which drivers and fans had pined for decades—turned out to be the best of the year. All of the nearly 300,000 seats were sold the day they went on sale, and more than 70 drivers tried to earn spots in the field. Earnhardt tagged the wall while trying to lead the first lap, but the real fireworks didn't begin until a green-flag restart 100 laps later. Brett Bodine, who has won only one Winston Cup race, was leading, and his older brother, Geoff, was in second. Their cars made contact exiting the third turn, sending Geoff into the wall and also eliminating Dale Jarrett. Jeff Gordon took the lead on the 106th of 160 laps, and only Irvan appeared to have a shot at catching him. But Irvan suffered a flat tire in the waning laps, and Gordon thundered home half a second ahead of Brett for his second Winston Cup victory.

Although Brett was delighted with his second-place finish, Geoff wasn't happy. "He's my brother, but he spun me out," Geoff said. "We've been having some family problems and, unfortunately, he takes it out on the track. But he's still my brother, and I love him."

Brett denied fault in the incident. "We're paid professionals," he said. "Who would do a thing like that?"

Most Significant Wreck

Neil Bonnett won 18 Winston Cup races and 20 poles before he suffered what appeared to be a career-ending head injury in 1990 at Darlington and embarking on a successful broadcasting career. Bonnett began a comeback when he drove in two races in 1993, finishing 34th in the Diehard 500 at Talladega and last in a 42-car field in the season-ending Hooters 500 at Atlanta. Bonnett's ill-fated comeback ended when he was killed in practice at Daytona Beach, Fla., on February 13, just two days after rookie Rodney Orr lost his life in a practice crash at Daytona International Speedway.

Records & Milestones

Only two manufacturers, Ford and Chevrolet, won races. The only other year that happened was 1985. . . . The same two manufacturers were also the only ones to win poles. The only other seasons in which just two makes captured poles were 1984, 1985, and 1995.... Roof flaps were introduced to reduce the possibility of cars becoming airborne.

1994 at a Glance

Races:	31
Road:	2
Short Track:	8
Superspeedway:	21
Winners:	12
Pole Winners:	17
Tracks:	18
States:	15

1994 Performance Index Rankings

1. Dale Earnhardt (854)
2. Rusty Wallace (678)
3. Mark Martin (676)
4. Ricky Rudd (673)
5. Ken Schrader (657)
6. Morgan Shepherd (645)
7. Terry Labonte (629)
8. Jeff Gordon (570)
9. Ernie Irvan (559)
10. Lake Speed (531)
11. Bill Elliott (518)
12. Michael Waltrip (501)
13. Ted Musgrave (493)
14. Sterling Marlin (469)
15. Dale Jarrett (452)
16. Darrell Waltrip (445)
17. Kyle Petty (428)
18. Geoff Bodine (414)
19. Rick Mast (386)
20. Brett Bodine (362)
21. Todd Bodine (352)
22. Bobby Labonte (343)
23. Jimmy Spencer (276)
24. Joe Nemechek (263)
25. Mike Wallace (253)
26. Jeff Burton (246)
27. Hut Stricklin (245)
28. Harry Gant (224)
29. Bobby Hamilton (213)
30. Kenny Wallace (212)
31. Derrike Cope (211)
32. Steve Grissom (206)
33. Wally Dallenbach Jr. (196)
34. Greg Sacks (173)
35. Dick Trickle (140)
36. Jimmy Hensley (108)
37. John Andretti (107)
38. Chuck Bown (86)
39. Ward Burton (85)
40. Dave Marcis (84)
41. Loy Allen Jr. (81)
42. Randy LaJoie (56)
43. Jeremy Mayfield (51)
44. Butch Miller (47)
45. Bobby Hillin Jr. (44)
46. Phil Parsons (30)
47. Joe Ruttman (27)
48. Jimmy Horton (26)
49. Pancho Carter (23)
50. Jeff Green (22)
51. Rich Bickle (15)

1994 Events

Daytona 500; Daytona International Speedway/2.5-m/500 miles
Sterling Marlin (Chevrolet)/Loy Allen Jr. (Ford)

Goodwrench 500; North Carolina Motor Speedway/1.017-m/500m
Rusty Wallace (Ford)/Geoff Bodine (Ford)

Pontiac Excitement 400; Richmond Int. Raceway/.75-mile/300 m
Ernie Irvan (Ford)/Ted Musgrave (Ford)

Purolator 500; Atlanta Motor Speedway/1.522-mile/500 miles
Ernie Irvan (Ford)/Loy Allen Jr. (Ford)

TranSouth Financial 500; Darlington Raceway/1.366-mile/500 m
Dale Earnhardt (Chevrolet)/Bill Elliott (Ford)

Food City 500; Bristol International Raceway/.533-mile/267 m
Dale Earnhardt (Chevrolet)/Chuck Bown (Ford)

First Union 400; North Wilkesboro Speedway/.625-m/250 miles
Terry Labonte (Chevrolet)/Ernie Irvan (Ford)

Hanes 500; Martinsville Speedway/.526-mile/263 miles
Rusty Wallace (Ford)/Rusty Wallace (Ford)

Winston Select 500; Talladega Superspeedway/2.66-m/500 miles
Dale Earnhardt (Chevrolet)/Ernie Irvan (Ford)

S.M. Supermarkets 300; Sears Point Raceway/2.52-m road/187 m
Ernie Irvan (Ford)/Ernie Irvan (Ford)

Coca-Cola 600; Charlotte Motor Speedway/1.5-mile/600 miles
Jeff Gordon (Chevrolet)/Jeff Gordon (Chevrolet)

Budweiser 500; Dover Downs International Speedway/1-m/500 m
Rusty Wallace (Ford)/Ernie Irvan (Ford)

UAW-GM Teamwork 500; Pocono Int. Raceway/2.5-mile/500 miles
Rusty Wallace (Ford)/Rusty Wallace (Ford)

Miller Genuine Draft 400; Michigan Int. Speedway/2-mile/400m
Rusty Wallace (Ford)/Loy Allen Jr. (Ford)

Pepsi 400; Daytona International Speedway/2.5-mile/400 miles
Jimmy Spencer (Ford)/Dale Earnhardt (Chevrolet)

Slick 50 300; New Hampshire Int. Speedway/1.058-m/317 miles
Ricky Rudd (Ford)/Ernie Irvan (Ford)

Miller Genuine Draft 500; Pocono Int. Raceway/2.5-mile/500 m
Geoff Bodine (Ford)/Geoff Bodine (Ford)

Diehard 500; Talladega Superspeedway/2.66-mile/500 miles
Jimmy Spencer (Ford)/Dale Earnhardt (Chevrolet)

Brickyard 400; Indianapolis Motor Speedway/2.5-mile/400 miles
Jeff Gordon (Chevrolet)/Rick Mast (Ford)

Budweiser at the Glen; Watkins Glen Int./2.45-mile road/221m
Mark Martin (Ford)/Mark Martin (Ford)

GM Goodwrench Dealer 400; Michigan Int. Speedway/2-m/400 m
Geoff Bodine (Ford)/Geoff Bodine (Ford)

Goody's 500; Bristol International Raceway/.533-m/267 miles
Rusty Wallace (Ford)/Harry Gant (Chevrolet)

Mountain Dew Southern 500; Darlington Raceway/1.366-m/500 m
Bill Elliott (Ford)/Geoff Bodine (Ford)

Miller Genuine Draft 400; Richmond Int. Raceway/.75-m/300 m
Terry Labonte (Chevrolet)/Ted Musgrave (Ford)

Splitfire Spark Plug 500; Dover Downs Int. Speedway/1-m/500m
Rusty Wallace (Ford)/Geoff Bodine (Ford)

Goody's 500; Martinsville Speedway/.526-mile/263 miles
Rusty Wallace (Ford)/Ted Musgrave (Ford)

Tyson Holly Farms 400; No. Wilkesboro Speedway/.625-m/250 m
Geoff Bodine (Ford)/Jimmy Spencer (Ford)

Mello Yello 500; Charlotte Motor Speedway/1.5-mile/500 miles
Dale Jarrett (Chevrolet)/Ward Burton (Chevrolet)

AC Delco 500; North Carolina Motor Speedway/1.017-mile/500 m
Dale Earnhardt (Chevrolet)/Ricky Rudd (Ford)

Slick 50 500; Phoenix International Raceway/1-mile/312 miles
Terry Labonte (Chevrolet)/Sterling Marlin (Chevrolet)

Hooters 500; Atlanta Motor Speedway/1.522-mile/500 miles
Mark Martin (Ford)/Greg Sacks (Ford)

Victories
1. Rusty Wallace (8)
2. Dale Earnhardt (4)
3. Geoff Bodine; Ernie Irvan; Terry Labonte (3)
6. Jeff Gordon; Mark Martin; Jimmy Spencer (2)
9. Bill Elliott; Dale Jarrett; Sterling Marlin; Ricky Rudd (1)

Poles
1. Geoff Bodine; Ernie Irvan (5)
3. Loy Allen Jr.; Ted Musgrave (3)
5. Dale Earnhardt; Rusty Wallace (2)
7. Chuck Bown; Ward Burton; Bill Elliott; Harry Gant; Jeff Gordon; Sterling Marlin; Mark Martin; Rick Mast; Ricky Rudd; Greg Sacks; Jimmy Spencer (1)

Victories
1. Ford (20)
2. Chevrolet (11)

Poles
1. Ford (25)
2. Chevrolet (6)

1995
Strictly Stock?
Not These Days

When NASCAR founder Bill France Sr. conceived of the Strictly Stock division, the key element was that fans would relate more to competition that matched family sedans than to the exotic, built-for-racing machines that competed in the Indianapolis 500.

Indeed, when Lee Petty became the first driver to crash in a Winston Cup race during the inaugural event on June 19, 1949, he wondered how he'd explain wrecking the family car to his wife.

The bodies of Winston Cup cars in 1995 still resembled the family sedan—if you removed the decals and rainbow-colored paint jobs. But that's about the only similarity—unless your car generates 700 horsepower and lacks such necessities as headlights and taillights.

The evolution of Winston Cup machines has been gradual. It was not uncommon in the early days for drivers to drive their race cars—equipped with a roll bar—to the track, remove the lights, compete, then drive home. The cigarette lighters that were installed in luxury models got ample use during a race. So did the radios—the ones that allowed drivers to listen to music, not today's sophisticated equipment that allows them to communicate with their pit crews.

In 1950, Nash Motor Company became the first manufacturer to enter Winston Cup racing. The equally extinct Hudson Motor Company joined the fray a year later, but that didn't immediately increase the sophistication of the race cars. On March 8, 1951, Frank Mundy let Hertz—or one of its competitors—put him in the driver's seat of a rented Chevrolet and finished 11th in a 100-mile dirt race in Gardena, Calif.

The early changes included adding bracing to the chassis to strengthen suspensions, removing the rear seats, and adding seat belts. Bucket seats followed, and by the time fuel cells replaced gas tanks in the mid-'60s, a Winston Cup stock car was hardly what your local dealer was selling on the showroom floor.

When Chrysler reintroduced its powerful 426 cubic-inch hemi engine in 1964, Paul Goldsmith captured the pole for the Daytona 500 at 174.91 mph, nearly 10 mph faster than the previous year's fastest qualifier, in a hemi-powered Plymouth.

In 1969, Ford unveiled the Torino Talladega, a sleek machine with a large inverted wing in the rear that increased downforce and helped push speeds beyond 200 mph. Chrysler responded by introducing the Dodge Daytona and, a year later, the Plymouth Superbird.

By the 1970s, most Winston Cup teams purchased a chassis built for racing, then added a roll cage and body. By the end of the decade, all bodies were essentially handmade.

Today's engines are limited to 358 cubic inches, but they generate more horsepower than the larger engines of the '60s did, except when reduced by carburetor restrictor plates that have been used periodically since 1970 to temper speeds on certain tracks.

Many veteran drivers consider Bobby Allison's victory in the 1982 Mason-Dixon 500 at Dover, Del., to be among the most significant in history: It was the first achieved by a car with power steering, now standard equipment.

Practically every part in a race car except the hood and trunk are now made by hand. Other than the engine block, the powerplants are built from parts made exclusively for racing. Winston Cup cars during the circuit's 51st season weighed a minimum of 3,400 pounds, more than 1,000 lighter than in the '50s.

To determine its manufacturers' champion, NASCAR currently awards nine points to the winning car in each race, six points to the highest-finishing car by a different manufacturer, and three points to the best finish by a third make. In that scenario, Fords could sweep the top 15 positions and receive nine points. Chevrolets could sweep positions 16-25 and receive six, and a Pontiac that finishes 26th would receive three.

Perhaps a more equitable—and infinitely simpler—method to determine the leading manufacturer is the Manufacturers' Performance Index, which awards the

The No. 22 Pontiac (top) that Fireball Roberts made famous in the early '60s much more closely resembled the family sedan than the STP Pontiac that Richard Petty was driving upon his retirement in 1992.

season title to the brand that wins the most races and uses poles as a tiebreaker.

Although Ford has claimed the most victories and poles—499 of each—in Winston Cup history, Chevrolet has led the Manufacturers' Performance Index on 19 occasions to Ford's 12.

Manufacturers' Performance Index Leaders

1949—Oldsmobile	1966—Dodge	1983—Chevrolet
1950—Oldsmobile	1967—Plymouth	1984—Chevrolet
1951—Oldsmobile	1968—Ford	1985—Chevrolet
1952—Hudson	1969—Ford	1986—Chevrolet
1953—Hudson	1970—Plymouth	1987—Chevrolet
1954—Hudson	1971—Plymouth	1988—Ford
1955—Chrysler	1972—Chevrolet	1989—Chevrolet
1956—Chrysler	1973—Mercury	1990—Chevrolet
1957—Ford	1974—Chevrolet	1991—Chevrolet
1958—Chevrolet	1975—Dodge	1992—Ford
1959—Chevrolet	1976—Chevrolet	1993—Pontiac
1960—Ford	1977—Chevrolet	1994—Ford
1961—Pontiac	1978—Oldsmobile	1995—Chevrolet
1962—Pontiac	1979—Chevrolet	1996—Chevrolet
1963—Ford	1980—Chevrolet	1997—Ford
1964—Ford	1981—Buick	1998—Chevrolet
1965—Ford	1982—Buick	1999—Ford

Seasons Leading the Manufacturers' Performance Index

1. Chevrolet (19)
2. Ford (12)
3. Oldsmobile (4)
4. Hudson; Plymouth; Pontiac (3)
7. Buick; Chrysler; Dodge (2)
10. Mercury (1)

Victories		Poles	
1. Ford	499	1. Ford	499
2. Chevrolet	479	2. Chevrolet	459
3. Plymouth	191	3. Dodge	163
4. Dodge	159	Pontiac	163
5. Pontiac	132	5. Oldsmobile	128
6. Oldsmobile	115	6. Plymouth	126
7. Mercury	96	7. Mercury	104
8. Hudson	79	8. Hudson	69
9. Buick	65	9. Chrysler	51
10. Chrysler	59	10. Buick	50
11. Matador	5	11. Matador	5
12. Lincoln	4	12. Studebaker	4
13. Studebaker	3	13. Lincoln	3
14. Jaguar	1	14. Cadillac	2
Nash	1	15. Jaguar	1

1995 in Review

Jeff Gordon led the Winston Cup Series in both victories (7) and poles (8) and edged Dale Earnhardt by 34 points to capture the Winston Cup title. Earnhardt led the Performance Index with a 789 rating, barely edging Sterling Marlin (784) and Gordon (777).

Most Memorable Race

The start of the Goody's 500 at Bristol, Tenn., on August 26 was delayed 90 minutes because of rain, but it was well worth the wait. The fireworks started on the 32nd lap, when Earnhardt tapped Rusty Wallace into the wall and was sent to the rear of the field as a result. By the 185th lap, Earnhardt also had bumped Derrike Cope and Lake Speed into spins while pushing his way back into the top five. Earnhardt subsequently dropped from first to 12th after a caution flag and was 16th when the last of 15 caution periods for 106 laps ended with 100 of the 500 laps remaining. Earnhardt charged into sixth place on the 469th lap, into fifth three laps later, was fourth in another lap, third in three more, and passed Dale Jarrett—who had yielded the lead to Terry Labonte with 69 laps left—to move into second on the 487th lap. By the time their Chevrolets exited the last of 2,000 turns, Earnhardt was on Labonte's bumper. Earnhardt bumped Labonte with perhaps 50 yards to go and sent him spinning into the wall. Despite that bump, Labonte guided his Hendrick Motorsports Chevrolet across the finish line a car length ahead of Earnhardt to win perhaps the most exciting short-track race in Winston Cup history. An angry Wallace threw a water bottle at Earnhardt at the gas pumps after the race. "I kept having to come through all that traffic," Earnhardt said. "I know Rusty feels bad that he hit the wall, but I don't want to be hit with a water bottle, either."

Most Significant Wreck

Miraculously, Labonte won the Goody's 500 despite the wreck. "Earnhardt got into me. I got into the side of one of those guys, and then I was sideways spinning across the line. I just kept the wheels pointed toward the line the best I could," said Labonte, whose car was hissing and smoking as it entered victory lane.

Most Important Off-Track Development

Speedway Motorsports, Inc., which, under the stewardship of majority stockholder Bruton Smith, owned Charlotte Motor Speedway and Atlanta Motor Speedway, became the first motorsports entity offered on the New York Stock Exchange with an initial public offering on February 24. All of the available stock was sold in less than four hours, and SMI subsequently purchased the Winston Cup tracks at Bristol, Las Vegas, and Sonoma, Calif., and built Texas Motor Speedway.

Records & Milestones

Six drivers won three or more races—Gordon, Earnhardt (5), Mark Martin (4), Bobby Labonte (3), Terry Labonte (3), and Marlin (3)—to tie a modern record set in 1979 and equaled in 1999. . . . Only two manufacturers won poles, Chevrolet and Ford. The only other seasons in which so few manufacturers won poles were 1984, 1985, and 1994.

1995 at a Glance

Races:	31
Road:	2
Short Track:	8
Superspeedway:	21
Winners:	11
Pole Winners:	15
Tracks:	18
States:	15

1995 Performance Index Rankings

1. Dale Earnhardt (789)
2. Sterling Marlin (784)
3. Jeff Gordon (777)
4. Mark Martin (737)
5. Terry Labonte (698)
6. Rusty Wallace (644)
7. Ted Musgrave (607)
8. Ricky Rudd (582)
9. Bobby Labonte (568)
10. Bill Elliott (562)
11. Michael Waltrip (528)
12. Morgan Shepherd (498)
13. Bobby Hamilton (494)
14. Derrike Cope (492)
15. Dale Jarrett (479)
16. John Andretti (379)
17. Geoff Bodine (377)
18. Ken Schrader (367)
19. Ward Burton (351)
20. Darrell Waltrip (338)
21. Joe Nemechek (284)
22. Jimmy Spencer (283)
23. Steve Grissom (277)
24. Rick Mast (268)
25. Jeremy Mayfield (256)
26. Kyle Petty (251)
27. Lake Speed (250)
28. Ricky Craven (248)
29. Dick Trickle (239)
30. Brett Bodine (235)
31. Robert Pressley (214)
32. Hut Stricklin (213)
33. Bobby Hillin Jr. (174)
34. Jeff Burton (173)
35. Mike Wallace (172)
36. Todd Bodine (119)
37. Loy Allen Jr. (75)
38. Randy LaJoie (59)
39. Ernie Irvan (52)
40. Kenny Wallace (47)
41. Dave Marcis (46)
42. Elton Sawyer (31)
43. Wally Dallenbach Jr. (28)
44. Joe Ruttman (26)
45. Ed Berrier (25)
46. Greg Sacks (24)
47. Chad Little (22)
48. Billy Standridge (21)
49. Butch Leitzinger (18)
50. Davy Jones (15)

1995 Events

Daytona 500; Daytona International Speedway/2.5-m/500 miles
Sterling Marlin (Chevrolet)/Dale Jarrett (Ford)

Goodwrench 500; North Carolina Motor Speedway/1.017-m/500m
Jeff Gordon (Chevrolet)/Jeff Gordon (Chevrolet)

Pontiac Excitement 400; Richmond Int. Raceway/.75-mile/300 m
Terry Labonte (Chevrolet)/Jeff Gordon (Chevrolet)

Purolator 500; Atlanta Motor Speedway/1.522-mile/500 miles
Jeff Gordon (Chevrolet)/Dale Earnhardt (Chevrolet)

TranSouth Financial 400; Darlington Raceway/1.366-mile/400 m
Sterling Marlin (Chevrolet)/Jeff Gordon (Chevrolet)

Food City 500; Bristol International Raceway/.533-mile/267 m
Jeff Gordon (Chevrolet)/Mark Martin (Ford)

First Union 400; North Wilkesboro Speedway/.625-m/250 miles
Dale Earnhardt (Chevrolet)/Jeff Gordon (Chevrolet)

Hanes 500; Martinsville Speedway/.526-mile/263 miles
Rusty Wallace (Ford)/Bobby Labonte (Chevrolet)

Winston Select 500; Talladega Superspeedway/2.66-m/500 miles
Mark Martin (Ford)/Terry Labonte (Chevrolet)

S.M. Supermarkets 300; Sears Point Raceway/2.52-m road/186 m
Dale Earnhardt (Chevrolet)/Ricky Rudd (Ford)

Coca-Cola 600; Charlotte Motor Speedway/1.5-mile/600 miles
Bobby Labonte (Chevrolet)/Jeff Gordon (Chevrolet)

Miller Genuine Draft 500; Dover Downs Int. Speedway/1-m/500m
Kyle Petty (Pontiac)/Jeff Gordon (Chevrolet)

UAW-GM Teamwork 500; Pocono Int. Raceway/2.5-m/500 miles
Terry Labonte (Chevrolet)/Ken Schrader (Chevrolet)

Miller Genuine Draft 400; Michigan Int. Speedway/2-m/400 m
Bobby Labonte (Chevrolet)/Jeff Gordon (Chevrolet)

Pepsi 400; Daytona International Speedway/2.5-mile/400 miles
Jeff Gordon (Chevrolet)/Dale Earnhardt (Chevrolet)

Slick 50 300; New Hampshire Int. Speedway/1.058-m/317 miles
Jeff Gordon (Chevrolet)/Mark Martin (Ford)

Miller Genuine Draft 500; Pocono Int Raceway/2.5-m/500 miles
Dale Jarrett (Ford)/Bill Elliott (Ford)

Diehard 500; Talladega Superspeedway/2.66-mile/500 miles
Sterling Marlin (Chevrolet)/Sterling Marlin (Chevrolet)

Brickyard 400; Indianapolis Motor Speedway/2.5-m/400 miles
Dale Earnhardt (Chevrolet)/Jeff Gordon (Chevrolet)

The Bud at the Glen; Watkins Glen Int./2.45-m road/221 miles
Mark Martin (Ford)/Mark Martin (Ford)

GM Goodwrench Dealer 400; Michigan Int. Speedway/2-m/400 m
Bobby Labonte (Chevrolet)/Bobby Labonte (Chevrolet)

Goody's 500; Bristol International Raceway/.533-m/267 miles
Terry Labonte (Chevrolet)/Mark Martin (Ford)

Mountain Dew Southern 500; Darlington Raceway/1.366-m/500 m
Jeff Gordon (Chevrolet)/John Andretti (Ford)

Miller Genuine Draft 400; Richmond Int. Raceway/.75-m/300 m
Rusty Wallace (Ford)/Dale Earnhardt (Chevrolet)

MBNA 500; Dover Downs International Speedway/1-m/500 miles
Jeff Gordon (Chevrolet)/Rick Mast (Ford)

Goody's 500; Martinsville Speedway/.526-mile/263 miles
Dale Earnhardt (Chevrolet)

Tyson Holly Farms 400; No. Wilkesboro Speedway/.625-m/250 m
Mark Martin (Ford)/Ted Musgrave (Ford)

UAW-GM Quality 500; Charlotte Motor Speedway/1.5-mile/500m
Mark Martin (Ford)/Ricky Rudd (Ford)

AC Delco 400; North Carolina Motor Speedway/1.017-mile/400 m
Ward Burton (Pontiac)/Hut Stricklin (Ford)

Dura Lube 500; Phoenix International Raceway/1-m/312 miles
Ricky Rudd (Ford)/Bill Elliott (Ford)

NAPA 500; Atlanta Motor Speedway/1.522-mile/500 miles
Dale Earnhardt (Chevrolet)/Darrell Waltrip (Chevrolet)

Victories
1. Jeff Gordon (7)
2. Dale Earnhardt (5)
3. Mark Martin (4)
4. Bobby Labonte; Terry Labonte; Sterling Marlin (3)
7. Rusty Wallace (2)
8. Ward Burton; Dale Jarrett; Kyle Petty; Ricky Rudd (1)

Poles
1. Jeff Gordon (8)
2. Mark Martin (4)
3. Dale Earnhardt (3)
4. Bill Elliott; Bobby Labonte; Ricky Rudd (2)
7. John Andretti; Dale Jarrett; Terry Labonte; Sterling Marlin; Rick Mast; Ted Musgrave; Ken Schrader; Hut Stricklin; Darrell Waltrip (1)

Victories
1. Chevrolet (21)
2. Ford (8)
3. Pontiac (2)

Poles
1. Chevrolet (17)
2. Ford (13)

1996
The Iceman

When compiling superlatives about Winston Cup drivers in the mid-'90s, NASCAR *Winston Cup Scene's* list included this notation:

Quietest: Terry Labonte.

Perhaps that's how Labonte managed to spend nearly two decades building one of the most consistent records of excellence in Winston Cup history in relative anonymity before the world finally noticed in 1996.

Labonte won the 1980 Southern 500 at Darlington, S.C., at age 23 and added the Winston Cup title four years later. The quiet demeanor that helped the Corpus Christi, Tex., native earn the nickname the "Iceman" virtually enabled him to avoid the limelight until April 14, 1996. When Labonte fired the engine in his Hendrick Motorsports Chevrolet at North Wilkesboro, N.C., that afternoon, it marked his 513th consecutive start, tying the record held by Richard Petty.

In virtually any sport, such records are the province of aging warriors whose best days are behind them, but Labonte proved he was far from over the hill by winning the First Union 400 that afternoon.

"If I'd wrecked the car every third weekend, I'd probably be looking for a job and wouldn't have been able to keep the streak going," said Labonte, whose record streak of consecutive starts had reached 636 by the time the 2000 season dawned. "There's a big difference between being smart and (being) conservative."

Labonte finished the 1996 season by edging teammate Jeff Gordon to become one of only 13 multiple Winston Cup champions. Remarkably, the Iceman finished third in the season's penultimate race, the Dura-Lube 500 at Phoenix, and fifth in the finale, the NAPA 500 at Atlanta, despite a broken left hand suffered when he smacked the wall in practice at Phoenix. The lefthanded Labonte, in obvious pain after clinching the title, said the painkiller "kind of wore off with 100 laps to go."

Labonte hardly seemed a likely candidate to earn a second Winston Cup title when he suffered through four winless campaigns before he landed a ride with Hendrick Motorsports. He then recorded a career-high three victories in 1994 and matched that total in 1995.

"I figured when I won it in '84 that I'd win it again the next year," Labonte recalled upon earning his second crown 12 years later, the longest gap between Winston Cup titles in history. "I think this means more because I realize a lot better now just how difficult it is."

Labonte's 21 victories rank in a 25th-place tie on the all-time list, and his 25 poles rank 20th. He ranks among the top 20 in short-track victories (9), 500-mile triumphs (8), road wins (2), superspeedway poles (12), and short-track victories from the pole (2). He also has a record-tying two poles on road courses in one year (1984) and owns eight road poles, one shy of the record.

Labonte's Performance Index of 12,366, the fifth-highest rating in history, gives a better indication of his multitude of consistently high finishes and his ability not "to wreck the car every third weekend." In each of the last 21 seasons through 1999, he posted a rating of 300 or better and finished no worse than 18th. Only three drivers in history have bettered either of those streaks. Among the host of categories in which Labonte also ranks in the top five are top-seven seasons (13), top-nine campaigns (16), seasons with a rating of 400 or better (20), campaigns with a rating of 500 or better (16), and seasons with a rating of 600 or better (10).

"You have to run hard, but not to the point you get in trouble," he said. "It pays more to lead the last lap."

Not always. While Texas Terry was circling Atlanta Motor Speedway in a float reserved for the 1996 Winston Cup champion, the driver headed for victory lane was his brother, Bobby, who is eight years Terry's junior and could be on his way to matching his brother's accomplishments.

Bobby's Performance Index of 4,100 ranks 41st on the career list, and he is among the top 20 in numerous categories, including superspeedway victories (12), superspeedway poles (16), superspeedway wins from the pole (4), 500-mile victories from the pole

(2), Grand Slam triumphs from the pole (5), and classic poles (3). His 12 victories include the 1995 Coca-Cola 600 at Charlotte, and the 1999 season marked his fourth in a row with at least three superspeedway poles, a streak exceeded only by David Pearson and Bill Elliott.

Before Bobby headed to victory lane and Terry to the champion's float after the 1996 NAPA 500, they made an impromptu, side-by-side victory lap around Atlanta Motor Speedway.

"It was the coolest thing we've ever done together," Bobby said.

And it was enough to stir a tearful response from the Iceman.

"That's probably the first time," Terry said, "I've ever gotten that emotional."

1996 in Review

Terry Labonte edged Gordon, 4,657-4,620, for the Winston Cup championship, but Gordon led the series in both victories (10) and poles (5) for the second year in a row. Gordon also held a narrow 818-812 advantage over Dale Jarrett in the Performance Index. Terry Labonte's 750 Performance Index ranked third.

Most Memorable Race

Gordon edged Jarrett by three car lengths to win the Diehard 500 on July 28 at Talladega, Ala. The fireworks that proceeded the dramatic finish helped make it a great race despite a four-hour rain delay at the outset that reduced the event from 188 laps to 129. On the 117th circuit, just 14 laps after John Andretti had triggered a 15-car pileup, Dale Earnhardt and Sterling Marlin were dueling for the lead when Ernie Irvan's Robert Yates-owned Ford tapped Marlin's Morgan-McClure Chevrolet, which then bumped into Earnhardt's machine. Earnhardt's

Terry Labonte had started a record 636 consecutive races when Winston Cup racing's first 51 years ended. But he'd done more than just start them: He had earned two Winston Cup titles, 21 victories, 25 poles, and posted 16 seasons in the top nine in the Performance Index.

Richard Childress-owned Chevrolet slammed into the wall and was hit by Robert Pressley, Derrike Cope, and Ken Schrader. Earnhardt, who had entered the race only six points out of first place in the Winston Cup standings, suffered a broken collarbone and a fractured sternum. He finished fourth in the season standings, 330 points behind Labonte. "(Irvan) turned into me and (Earnhardt) and wrecked a bunch of cars. He's the one who started the whole thing," Marlin said.

"(Marlin) ran into my right front fender," Irvan said. "You've got to give and take, and (Marlin) didn't do much giving. (Earnhardt) does it all the time. When somebody would go to pass him, he runs almost right into them."

Most Significant Wreck

Elliott's Ford flipped violently after it became airborne on the Talladega backstretch in the Winston Select 500 on April 28. Elliott, winner of 40 Winston Cup races, suffered a broken femur, didn't return to action for more than two months, and is still seeking his first victory since the accident.

Most Important Off-Track Development

NASCAR staged an exhibition race on the road course at Suzuka, Japan, in November. Rusty Wallace won the first NASCAR event ever held in Asia.

Records & Milestones

Jarrett captured the Daytona 500, the Coca-Cola 600, and the Brickyard 400 at Indianapolis to become the third driver to capture three classics in one season. . . . Ted Musgrave won the pole for the September 29 Tyson Holly Farms 400 at North Wilkesboro. That was the fifth pole of Musgrave's career, making him the only driver in the first 51 years of Winston Cup racing who has won that many poles yet has never won a race. . . . The Tyson Holly Farms 400 was the last Winston Cup event at North Wilkesboro Speedway, which played host to at least one Winston Cup race in each of the series' first 48 seasons. . . . R.J. Reynolds Tobacco Company instituted a new bonus plan in which the winner of any race would receive an additional $10,000 if he also emerged as the Winston Cup points leader. . . . President Clinton announced new regulations on tobacco advertising that apparently would end Winston's sponsorship of NASCAR's premier series.

1996 at a Glance

Races:	31
Road:	2
Short Track:	8
Superspeedway:	21
Winners:	11
Pole Winners:	14
Tracks:	18
States:	15

1996 Performance Index Rankings

1. Jeff Gordon (818)
2. Dale Jarrett (812)
3. Terry Labonte (750)
4. Dale Earnhardt (737)
5. Mark Martin (707)
6. Ricky Rudd (612)
7. Rusty Wallace (563)
8. Ernie Irvan (556)
9. Sterling Marlin (553)
10. Jeff Burton (526)
11. Bobby Hamilton (514)
12. Michael Waltrip (502)
13. Bobby Labonte (472)
14. Ken Schrader (469)
15. Jimmy Spencer (468)
16. Ted Musgrave (426)
17. Rick Mast (386)
18. Geoff Bodine (364)
19. Bill Elliott (337)
20. Johnny Benson Jr. (329)
21. Ricky Craven (321)
22. Morgan Shepherd (315)
23. Wally Dallenbach Jr. (288)
24. Lake Speed (279)
25. Jeremy Mayfield (273)
26. Kyle Petty (255)
27. Kenny Wallace (254)
28. Ward Burton (244)
29. John Andretti (210)
30. Hut Stricklin (202)
31. Derrike Cope (184)
32. Bobby Hillin Jr. (160)
33. Darrell Waltrip (153)
34. Joe Nemechek (140)
35. Todd Bodine (134)
36. Dick Trickle (133)
37. Robert Pressley (114)
38. Brett Bodine (108)
39. Steve Grissom (93)
40. Mike Skinner (84)
41. Dave Marcis (59)
42. Mike Wallace (39)
43. Jeff Purvis (33)
44. Chad Little (25)
45. Greg Sacks (22)
46. Elton Sawyer (21)
47. Dorsey Schroeder (17)
48. Butch Leitzinger (10)

1996 Events

Daytona 500; Daytona International Speedway/2.5-m/500 miles
Dale Jarrett (Ford)/Dale Earnhardt (Chevrolet)

Goodwrench 400; North Carolina Motor Speedway/1.017-m/400m
Dale Earnhardt (Chevrolet)/Terry Labonte (Chevrolet)

Pontiac Excitement 400; Richmond Int. Raceway/.75-mile/300 m
Jeff Gordon (Chevrolet)/Terry Labonte (Chevrolet)

Purolator 500; Atlanta Motor Speedway/1.522-mile/500 miles
Dale Earnhardt (Chevrolet)/Johnny Benson Jr. (Pontiac)

TranSouth Financial 400; Darlington Raceway/1.366-mile/400 m
Jeff Gordon (Chevrolet)/Ward Burton (Pontiac)

Food City 500; Bristol International Raceway/.533-mile/267 m
Jeff Gordon (Chevrolet)/Mark Martin (Ford)

First Union 400; North Wilkesboro Speedway/.625-m/250 miles
Terry Labonte (Chevrolet)/Terry Labonte (Chevrolet)

Goody's Head. Powder 500; Martinsville Speedway/.526-m/263 m
Rusty Wallace (Ford)/Ricky Craven (Chevrolet)

Winston Select 500; Talladega Superspeedway/2.66-m/500 miles
Sterling Marlin (Chevrolet)/Ernie Irvan (Ford)

S.M. Supermarkets 300; Sears Point Raceway/2.52-m road/186 m
Rusty Wallace (Ford)/Terry Labonte (Chevrolet)

Coca-Cola 600; Charlotte Motor Speedway/1.5-mile/600 miles
Dale Jarrett (Ford)/Jeff Gordon (Chevrolet)

Miller Genuine Draft 500; Dover Downs Int. Speedway/1-m/500m
Jeff Gordon (Chevrolet)/Jeff Gordon (Chevrolet)

UAW-GM Teamwork 500; Pocono Int. Raceway/2.5-m/500 miles
Jeff Gordon (Chevrolet)/Jeff Gordon (Chevrolet)

Miller Genuine Draft 400; Michigan Int. Speedway/2-mile/400m
Rusty Wallace (Ford)/Bobby Hamilton (Pontiac)

Pepsi 400; Daytona International Speedway/2.5-mile/400 miles
Sterling Marlin (Chevrolet)/Jeff Gordon (Chevrolet)

Jiffy Lube 300; New Hampshire Int. Speedway/1.058-mile/317 m
Ernie Irvan (Ford)/Ricky Craven (Chevrolet)

Miller Genuine Draft 500; Pocono Int. Raceway/2.5-mile/500 m
Rusty Wallace (Ford)/Mark Martin (Ford)

Diehard 500; Talladega Superspeedway/2.66-mile/500 miles
Jeff Gordon (Chevrolet)/Jeremy Mayfield (Ford)

Brickyard 400; Indianapolis Motor Speedway/2.5-mile/400 miles
Dale Jarrett (Ford)/Jeff Gordon (Chevrolet)

The Bud at the Glen; Watkins Glen Int./2.45-m road/221 miles
Geoff Bodine (Ford)/Dale Earnhardt (Chevrolet)

GM Goodwrench Dealer 400; Michigan Int. Speedway/2-m/400 m
Dale Jarrett (Ford)/Jeff Burton (Ford)

Goody's Head. Powder 500; Bristol Motor Speedway/.533-m/267m
Rusty Wallace (Ford)/Mark Martin (Ford)

Mountain Dew Southern 500; Darlington Raceway/1.366-m/500 m
Jeff Gordon (Chevrolet)/Dale Jarrett (Ford)

Miller 400; Richmond International Raceway/.75-m/300 miles
Ernie Irvan (Ford)/Mark Martin (Ford)

MBNA 500; Dover Downs International Speedway/1-m/500 miles
Jeff Gordon (Chevrolet)/Bobby Labonte (Chevrolet)

Hanes 500; Martinsville Speedway/.526-mile/263 miles
Jeff Gordon (Chevrolet)/Bobby Hamilton (Pontiac)

Tyson Holly Farms 400; No. Wilkesboro Speedway/.625-m/250 m
Jeff Gordon (Chevrolet)/Ted Musgrave (Ford)

UAW-GM Quality 500; Charlotte Motor Speedway/1.5-mile/500m
Terry Labonte (Chevrolet)/Bobby Labonte (Chevrolet)

AC Delco 400; North Carolina Motor Speedway/1.017-mile/400 m
Ricky Rudd (Ford)/Dale Jarrett (Ford)

Dura-Lube 500; Phoenix International Raceway/1-m/312 miles
Bobby Hamilton (Pontiac)/Bobby Labonte (Chevrolet)

NAPA 500; Atlanta Motor Speedway/1.522-mile/500 miles
Bobby Labonte (Chevrolet)/Bobby Labonte (Chevrolet)

Victories

1. Jeff Gordon (10)
2. Rusty Wallace (5)
3. Dale Jarrett (4)
4. Dale Earnhardt; Ernie Irvan; Terry Labonte; Sterling Marlin (2)
8. Geoff Bodine; Bobby Hamilton; Bobby Labonte; Ricky Rudd (1)

Poles

1. Jeff Gordon (5)
2. Bobby Labonte; Terry Labonte; Mark Martin (4)
5. Ricky Craven; Dale Earnhardt; Bobby Hamilton; Dale Jarrett (2)
9. Johnny Benson Jr.; Jeff Burton; Ward Burton; Ernie Irvan; Jeremy Mayfield; Ted Musgrave (1)

Victories

1. Chevrolet (17)
2. Ford (13)
3. Pontiac (1)

Poles

1. Chevrolet (17)
2. Ford (10)
3. Pontiac (4)

1997
Only on His Regular Visits To Victory Lane Is Rudd Recognized As a Superstar

Ricky Rudd has never won the Winston Cup championship or even enjoyed a three-victory season.

Rudd has never had a nickname and, in fact, is probably the most anonymous superstar in Winston Cup history.

You didn't realize Rudd was a superstar?

What else would you call someone who strings together 14 consecutive top-12 seasons (1983-96), 16 top-13 seasons in succession (1981-96), and 17 straight top-15 seasons through 1997 to rank second on the all-time list in each of those Performance Index categories?

Still not convinced?

How about 17 consecutive seasons with a rating of 400 or better, the third-longest string in history, or 13 seasons in the top nine? Or a career Performance Index of 11,456, eighth on the all-time list, and a ranking among the top 10 in virtually every Performance Index category?

Perhaps Rudd's remarkable resume has been obscured by the achievement for which he's best known: The 1998 season marked the 16th consecutive year in which Rudd won a race. Only two drivers in history posted longer streaks, Richard Petty (18) and David Pearson (17), and Rudd's 16-season stretch is a modern record.

Rudd maintained that streak in dramatic fashion in 1998 by overcoming heat exhaustion to capture the NAPA AutoCare 500 at Martinsville, Va., then collapsed on his back in victory lane. Yet the Chesapeake, Va., native contends that he never has sacrificed his overall success in order to continue the streak. "We try to win each race," he said. "We've always had the best intentions at each race."

Rudd was 26 when he earned his first victory, which came on the road course at Riverside, Calif., in 1983. Rudd has five victories on road courses, one short of the record; his five road poles rank among the top five in history, and he captured at least one pole on a road course three years in a row (1990-92), a streak bettered only by Darrell Waltrip.

Although Rudd long has been considered a threat to win any time the Winston Cup Series visits a road course, he has accomplished considerably more. Rudd has 20 victories and ranks among the top 25 in poles (23), superspeedway triumphs (11), 500-mile wins (6), and short-track poles (10). Rudd's victory in the 1997 Miller 500 at Dover, Del., gave him at least one superspeedway victory for the seventh year in a row (1991-97), a streak bettered by only five drivers. He then added an exclamation point by capturing the Brickyard 400 at Indianapolis—the biggest victory of his career—later that season.

But, in an age in which Winston Cup drivers are mobbed by autograph seekers wherever they go and often require security guards to get from the garage to the parking lot at race tracks, Rudd remains the anonymous superstar.

Here's proof:

"I can get anywhere I want to go without fans recognizing me," he said in the mid-'90s.

Rudd simply dons a cap that honors another Winston Cup driver—who shall remain nameless in order

While Ricky Rudd's most famous achievement is the modern-record string of 16 consecutive seasons with at least one victory, equally as impressive were his 17 consecutive seasons in the top 15 in the Performance Index, the second-longest such streak ever.

to protect Rudd's privacy—and pulls it down tightly over his forehead. "I can put that cap on after qualifying or a race and walk right through the grandstands to get to my car or wherever I'm going," he said, "and no one will ever recognize me."

Unless, of course, he has to stop in victory lane. Others may have done so more frequently, but few with more amazing regularity.

1997 in Review

Jeff Gordon stumbled home 17th in the season finale, the NAPA 500 at Atlanta Motor Speedway. A runner-up finish in the NAPA 500 by Dale Jarrett and a third-place showing by Mark Martin enabled them to close their final deficits to 14 and 29 points, respectively, in the closest three-way finish in championship history. But it wasn't enough to prevent Gordon from capturing his second Winston Cup title. Gordon earned a season-high 10 victories—winning on 10 different tracks—and edged Martin in the Performance Index, 841-821, with Jarrett third with a 799 rating. Martin and Bobby Labonte each won three poles to share the season lead in that category.

Most Memorable Race

Gordon won the Mountain Dew Southern 500 on August 31 at Darlington, S.C., to become the first driver to capture the same classic three consecutive years. But he had to survive a fierce bumping duel with Jeff Burton in the waning laps before he prevailed by two car lengths. "I'll be honest. I tried to knock the (blank) out of him when he hit me," said Burton, referring to the three times their cars bumped on the penultimate lap. "(Gordon) cut down on me, and I tried to put him in the wall. You can't blame him. He's going for $1 million."

Coupled with his victories in the Daytona 500 and the Coca-Cola 600 at Charlotte, Gordon became the fourth driver to win three classics in one season and the second to win the Winston Million—and the accompanying $1 million bonus from R.J. Reynolds. "I'm blown away," Gordon said after winning the Winston Million in its final year of existence. "You get that checkered flag in your sight, and you'll do just about anything to get there."

The race also featured one of the most bizarre starts in Winston Cup history. Dale Earnhardt became disoriented on the pace lap, scraped the wall in the first turn, bounced off the wall in the second, then missed pit road. He took a slow lap after the rest of the field took the green flag, then departed for a hospital. Extensive tests failed to reveal the cause of the problem.

Most Significant Wreck

Bill Elliott appeared on his way to victory in the Daytona 500 on February 16 until Gordon squeezed Earnhardt into the wall with 10 laps remaining. Earnhardt's car bounced off the wall and left a tire print on Gordon's car. Jarrett then battered Earnhardt's Chevrolet, sending it into a barrel roll. The accident resulted in a caution flag that allowed the three Hendrick Motorsports drivers—Gordon, Terry Labonte, and Ricky Craven—to draft around Elliott on the 195th of 200 laps and finish 1-2-3. "When Jeff, Terry, and Ricky got together, I was history. I knew it. I was a sitting duck," Elliott said.

"That was a break for us," Gordon said.

Most Important Off-Track Development

Two new motorsports palaces, the 1.5-mile Texas Motor Speedway in Fort Worth and the two-mile California Speedway in Fontana, were added to the Winston Cup schedule.

Records & Milestones

Four Winston Cup races were held in North Carolina in 1997, the same number that were staged in Virginia. In each of the first 48 years of Winston Cup racing, North Carolina had the distinction of playing host to more races than any other state. . . . Eighteen drivers captured poles in 1997, a modern record. . . . The 1997 campaign produced a modern-record 10 drivers who won multiple poles: Bobby Labonte, Martin, Geoff Bodine (2), Bobby Hamilton (2), Joe Nemechek (2), Ken Schrader (2), Mike Skinner (2), Kenny Wallace (2), Ernie Irvan (2), and Jarrett (2). . . . Only six races were held on short tracks, the fewest since 1955.

1997 at a Glance

Races:	32
Road:	2
Short Track:	6
Superspeedway:	24
Winners:	11
Pole Winners:	18
Tracks:	19
States:	16

1997 Performance Index Rankings

1. Jeff Gordon (841)
2. Mark Martin (821)
3. Dale Jarrett (799)
4. Jeff Burton (766)
5. Terry Labonte (703)
6. Dale Earnhardt (681)
7. Bobby Labonte (676)
8. Bill Elliott (601)
9. Ken Schrader (503)
10. Ernie Irvan (493)
11. Johnny Benson Jr. (472)
12. Rusty Wallace (470)
13. Kyle Petty (465)
14. Jeremy Mayfield (464)
15. Ricky Rudd (459)
16. Ted Musgrave (435)
17. Bobby Hamilton (425)
18. Geoff Bodine (412)
19. Ricky Craven (410)
20. Michael Waltrip (361)
21. Derrike Cope (351)
22. Sterling Marlin (330)
23. Ward Burton (307)
24. Steve Grissom; Jimmy Spencer (296)
26. Darrell Waltrip (293)
27. John Andretti (267)
28. Joe Nemechek (256)
29. Dick Trickle (235)
30. Rick Mast (210)
31. Brett Bodine (208)
32. Lake Speed (202)
33. Mike Skinner (199)
34. Morgan Shepherd (177)
35. Hut Stricklin (148)
36. Kenny Wallace (146)
37. Chad Little (139)
38. David Green (111)
39. Robby Gordon (99)
40. Wally Dallenbach Jr. (96)
41. Jeff Green (86)
42. Dave Marcis (71)
43. Robert Pressley (33)
44. Kenny Irwin (27)
45. Steve Park (25)
46. Kevin Lepage; Mike Wallace (23)
48. Rick Wilson (21)
49. Bobby Hillin Jr. (20)

1997 Events

Daytona 500; Daytona International Speedway/2.5-m/500 miles
Jeff Gordon (Chevrolet)/Mike Skinner (Chevrolet)

Goodwrench 400; North Carolina Motor Speedway/1.017-m/400m
Jeff Gordon (Chevrolet)/Mark Martin (Ford)

Pontiac Excitement 400; Richmond Int. Raceway/.75-mile/300 m
Rusty Wallace (Ford)

PRIMESTAR 500; Atlanta Motor Speedway/1.522-mile/500 miles
Dale Jarrett (Ford)/Robby Gordon (Chevrolet)

TranSouth Financial 400; Darlington Raceway/1.366-mile/400 m
Dale Jarrett (Ford)/Dale Jarrett (Ford)

Interstate Batteries 500; Texas Motor Speedway/1.5-mile/500m
Jeff Burton (Ford)

Food City 500; Bristol Motor Speedway/.533-mile/267 miles
Jeff Gordon (Chevrolet)/Rusty Wallace (Ford)

Goody's Head. Powder 500; Martinsville Speedway/.526-m/263 m
Jeff Gordon (Chevrolet)/Kenny Wallace (Ford)

S.M. Supermarkets 300; Sears Point Raceway/2.52-m road/186 m
Mark Martin (Ford)/Mark Martin (Ford)

Winston 500; Talladega Superspeedway/2.66-mile/500 miles
Mark Martin (Ford)/John Andretti (Ford)

Coca-Cola 600; Charlotte Motor Speedway/1.5-mile/600 miles
Jeff Gordon (Chevrolet)/Jeff Gordon (Chevrolet)

Miller 500; Dover Downs International Speedway/1-m/500 miles
Ricky Rudd (Ford)/Bobby Labonte (Pontiac)

Pocono 500; Pocono International Raceway/2.5-mile/500 miles
Jeff Gordon (Chevrolet)/Bobby Hamilton (Pontiac)

Miller 400; Michigan Speedway/2-mile/400 miles
Ernie Irvan (Ford)/Dale Jarrett (Ford)

California 500; California Speedway/2-mile/500 miles
Jeff Gordon (Chevrolet)/Joe Nemechek (Chevrolet)

Pepsi 400; Daytona International Speedway/2.5-mile/400 miles
John Andretti (Ford)/Mike Skinner (Chevrolet)

Jiffy Lube 300; New Hampshire Int. Speedway/1.058-mile/317 m
Jeff Burton (Ford)/Ken Schrader (Chevrolet)

Pennsylvania 500; Pocono International Raceway/2.5-mile/500m
Dale Jarrett (Ford)/Joe Nemechek (Chevrolet)

Brickyard 400; Indianapolis Motor Speedway/2.5-m/400 miles
Ricky Rudd (Ford)/Ernie Irvan (Ford)

The Bud at the Glen; Watkins Glen Int./2.45-m road/221 miles
Jeff Gordon (Chevrolet)/Todd Bodine (Chevrolet)

DeVilbiss 400; Michigan Speedway/2-mile/400 miles
Mark Martin (Ford)/Johnny Benson Jr. (Pontiac)

Goody's Head. Powder 500; Bristol Motor Speedway/.533-m/267m
Dale Jarrett (Ford)/Kenny Wallace (Ford)

Mountain Dew Southern 500; Darlington Raceway/1.366-m/500 m
Jeff Gordon (Chevrolet)/Bobby Labonte (Pontiac)

Exide NASCAR Select Bat. 400; Rich. Int. Raceway/.75-m/300 m
Dale Jarrett (Ford)/Bill Elliott (Ford)

CMT 300; New Hampshire International Speedway/1.058-m/317m
Jeff Gordon (Chevrolet)/Ken Schrader (Chevrolet)

MBNA 400; Dover Downs International Speedway/1-m/400 miles
Mark Martin (Ford)/Mark Martin (Ford)

Hanes 500; Martinsville Speedway/.526-mile/263 miles
Jeff Burton (Ford)/Ward Burton (Pontiac)

UAW-GM Quality 500; Charlotte Motor Speedway/1.5-mile/500m
Dale Jarrett (Ford)/Geoff Bodine (Ford)

Diehard 500; Talladega Superspeedway/2.66-mile/500 miles
Terry Labonte (Chevrolet)/Ernie Irvan (Ford)

AC Delco 400; North Carolina Motor Speedway/1.017-mile/400 m
Bobby Hamilton (Pontiac)/Bobby Labonte (Pontiac)

Dura-Lube 500; Phoenix International Raceway/1-m/312 miles
Dale Jarrett (Ford)/Bobby Hamilton (Pontiac)

NAPA 500; Atlanta Motor Speedway/1.54-mile/500 miles
Bobby Labonte (Pontiac)/Geoff Bodine (Ford)

Victories
1. Jeff Gordon (10)
2. Dale Jarrett (7)
3. Mark Martin (4)
4. Jeff Burton (3)
5. Ricky Rudd (2)
6. John Andretti; Bobby Hamilton; Ernie Irvan; Bobby Labonte; Terry Labonte; Rusty Wallace (1)

Poles
1. Bobby Labonte; Mark Martin (3)
3. Geoff Bodine; Bobby Hamilton; Ernie Irvan; Dale Jarrett; Joe Nemechek; Ken Schrader; Mike Skinner; Kenny Wallace (2)
11. John Andretti; Johnny Benson Jr.; Todd Bodine; Ward Burton; Bill Elliott; Jeff Gordon; Robby Gordon; Rusty Wallace (1)

Victories
1. Ford (19)
2. Chevrolet (11)
3. Pontiac (2)

Poles
1. Ford (14)
2. Chevrolet (9)
3. Pontiac (7)

1998
'Wonder Boy'

More than 2,700 drivers have tested their abilities in the world's premier stock-car series.

None of them has made such an assault on the Winston Cup record books as quickly as Jeff Gordon. "I really can't believe this . . . whole career I'm having," Gordon said in victory lane after the 1998 NAPA 500 at Atlanta.

Gordon didn't need to win the NAPA 500 to clinch his third Winston Cup title. He didn't even need to start his Hendrick Motorsports Chevrolet. He already had ensured his third crown before the 1998 season ended when Gordon was 27 years, three months, and four days old.

"I've never put age as a factor because I started racing at such a young age," said Gordon, whose racing career preceded his entry into the first grade. "When I stepped up to sprint cars when I was 13 years old, everybody else was looking at age, and me and my stepdad (John Bickford) were looking at experience, just trying to get experience and using the experience I had in the quarter-midgets, go-karts, and things like that. At first, it was very tough to get the opportunity to showcase that. Once we were given that opportunity, that stepped me about five years ahead of a lot of the guys. From that point on, age never really was a factor to me.

"I don't know too many 13-year-old sprint-car drivers back then or today. Not that I suggest it, either. It scared the heck out of me when I was that age, but I think I grew so much as a race driver because of that. The racing experience I got in an 800-horsepower sprint car at 13 or 14 years old was just awesome. It made me a real race driver."

No other driver captured his *second* Winston Cup championship before turning 30, and the youngest three-time champion before Gordon was Richard Petty, who was 34 years, five months, and 10 days old at the conclusion of the 1971 season, his third of seven championship campaigns.

But his three Winston Cup championships don't begin to measure just how much Gordon—whom seven-time champion Dale Earnhardt nicknamed "Wonder Boy"—has achieved so quickly. Gordon claimed his 49th victory in the 1999 UAW-GM Quality 500 at Lowe's Motor Speedway. Only 10 drivers have won as many races, and the following chart shows the age at which each accomplished his 49th victory:

Driver	Age at 49th Victory	Career Victories
* Jeff Gordon	28 years, 2 months, 7 days	49
Richard Petty	29 years, 4 months, 11 days	200
Ned Jarrett	32 years, 10 months, 25 days	50
David Pearson	34 years, 2 months, 23 days	105
Junior Johnson	34 years, 2 months, 29 days	50
* Darrell Waltrip	35 years, 8 months, 28 days	84
Cale Yarborough	38 years, 5 months, 29 days	83
* Dale Earnhardt	39 years, 9 months, 19 days	74
Bobby Allison	40 years, 3 months, 16 days	85
* Rusty Wallace	42 years, 7 months, 28 days	49
Lee Petty	46 years, 13 days	54

* Active during Winston Cup racing's 51st season in 1999

Gordon's 49 victories have come in 223 starts: a winning percentage of 21.97. If you discount the likes of Marvin Burke, who won his only Winston Cup start, that's the best winning percentage in Winston Cup history. Since Gordon captured the 1994 Coca-Cola 600 at Charlotte for his first Winston Cup victory, his winning percentage has been an incredible 26.92. Logic dictates that he can't continue at that pace. But if he does, based on a yearly schedule of 34 races (the total in 1999), Gordon will equal Petty's record of 200 victories by winning the 19th race of the 2015 season shortly before his 44th birthday.

Gordon's phenomenal success hasn't been achieved merely by winning, however, as much as by *what* he has won.

In 1997, Gordon captured 10 victories, became the only driver to win at least four 500-mile races three years in a row, and won three classic races—the Daytona 500, the Coca-Cola 600 at Concord, N.C., and the Mountain Dew Southern 500 at Darlington, S.C.—on his way to the Winston Million and his second Winston Cup title.

"If this isn't a career year, I don't know what is," Gordon said after clinching the 1997 title in the season finale at Atlanta.

Gordon, however, bettered that performance in 1998, when he tied a modern record with 13 victories, became the only driver in history to win five consecutive superspeedway races, led the circuit in poles for the third time, cruised to his third Winston Cup title, and became the first driver to win three classics in a season a second time. And Gordon's victories in the Coca-Cola 600, the Brickyard 400 at Indianapolis, and the Pepsi Southern 500 gave him three classic victories in two consecutive seasons. His Performance Index of 1,053 marked the only time a driver recorded a season of 1,000 or better in the modern era, and his 79.77 percent of the available total was the best in history.

"I can't believe what we accomplished," Gordon said. "Everything you would want to happen happened. We've had a dream season with the number of wins we've had and the consistency we've had. Somebody asked me to give a highlight of this season. How do you just pick one? This whole year seems like every weekend has been a highlight for us. That's just a year you dream about. This was one of those dream-come-true seasons."

Gordon's magical 1998 campaign enabled him to become the only driver to hold sole possession of the series lead in victories four seasons in a row, earn at least six superspeedway triumphs in four consecutive seasons, or win the same classic (the Southern 500) four years in a row. Gordon also became only the second driver to win two road races from the pole in one season and tied the record of back-to-back seasons with at least seven superspeedway triumphs.

Through the 1999 season, Gordon had a record:

- Five straight seasons in which he held sole possesion of the series lead in victories;
- Six consecutive campaigns with a classic victory;
- Five seasons in a row with at least three 500-mile victories;

- Five consecutive seasons with multiple Grand Slam wins and three seasons in a row with three or more Grand Slam victories;
- Six straight years with at least one superspeedway victory from the pole and three years in a row with a classic win from the pole.

Gordon's 1999 Daytona 500 victory enabled him to become the all-time leader in classic victories (11) and the only driver to win four consecutive classics. In becoming the first driver in the modern era to post five consecutive seasons with seven or more triumphs, Gordon also became the only driver to win five consecutive road races or three consecutive road races from the pole.

In addition to the host of record streaks Gordon had established, he had equaled the following through 1999:

- Five consecutive years with at least three superspeedway victories;
- Seven years in a row with a Grand Slam pole and six straight seasons with a classic pole;
- Three campaigns in a row with a Grand Slam victory from the pole.

Further, Gordon was the last driver in the 20th Century to win four races in a row, three superspeedway races in succession, three consecutive Grand Slam races, three straight 500-mile races, three poles in a row, and three consecutive superspeedway poles. He was also the last driver to win a record-tying three consecutive poles on road courses and had, in fact, posted the three most recent winning streaks of three or more races.

Late in the 1998 season, Gordon professed little knowledge of his significant impact on the record books. "I wasn't aware of that," he said as he was cited a litany of his achievements. "I don't really look at the records and things like that. What we do is try to go out and be competitive every week. There's always something left to accomplish. What drives me is competition, driving into victory lane. It doesn't matter what race it is. I don't look at the records. I like challenging for the wins."

Shortly before Gordon made his Winston Cup debut in the 1992 Hooters 500 at Atlanta, Rick Hendrick said, "Of all the young guys I've seen come along, he's impressed me more than anybody."

Gordon's many critics contend that Hendrick Motorsports is the best team in the sport and consider

As the 21st Century began, Jeff Gordon was on his way to making a prediction that he would "rewrite all the record books" come true.

longtime crew chief Ray Evernham the best in the business. But after Evernham resigned late in the 1999 season, Gordon won his first two starts with Brian Whitesell as his crew chief. And when Gordon joined the team, Hendrick Motorsports had won just five races in the previous three years, had never claimed a championship, and he and Evernham—then a rookie Winston Cup crew chief—were being added as a third team.

Gordon's 11 classic wins include four in the Southern 500, three in the 600-miler at Charlotte, a record-tying two in the Brickyard 400, and two in the Daytona 500. Among the categories in which Gordon already ranks among the top five are road victories (5), superspeedway poles (23), classic poles (9), road poles (3), superspeedway victories from the pole (8), Grand Slam wins from the pole (4), and road victories from the pole (3). He's among the top 10 in superspeedway victories (35), Grand Slam wins (16), 500-mile triumphs (20), Grand Slam poles (8), and 500-mile victories from the pole (4).

Like so many drivers in the modern era, Gordon thinks the ultimate yardstick of his success is championships. "I think it's all about trying to win championships," he said. "I love winning championships."

Gordon's career Performance Index of 5,267 ranks 34th—with a bullet. The 1998 season marked the record-tying third time in a row he had led the Performance Index and the first time in the modern era that a driver had a rating of 800 or better in three consecutive seasons.

"He will rewrite all the record books," Darrell Waltrip told The Atlanta Constitution.

Perhaps the only thing that would stop Gordon's pursuit of 200 victories or seven Winston Cup championships is the lack of hunger that could result from earning a record $9,306,584 in 1998 and more than $30 million through 1999.

"I want to drive for a long, long time, but I don't know if you can put an age or a date on when it's time to quit," he said. "It's certainly not anywhere around the corner for me. I'm not even thinking about it. There's no doubt there's always going to be somebody younger, more talented."

Don't bet on it.

"Jeff Gordon is the best driver of all-time," said rival Winston Cup team owner Felix Sabates. "There's no question in my mind."

1998 in Review

Gordon rolled to his third Winston Cup title and became the first champion in 14 years to hold sole possession of the season leadership in victories (13) and poles (7) and lead the Performance Index, which he accomplished with a 1,053-866 advantage over Mark Martin. Gordon's championship also enabled Hendrick Motorsports to become the only car owner in history to win four consecutive Winston Cup crowns.

Most Memorable Race

In 1986, Earnhardt relinquished the lead in the Daytona 500 when he had to pit for gas with three laps left. In 1990, he held a half-lap lead with half a lap remaining when a flat tire ended his dream. He lost last-lap duels to Dale Jarrett in both 1993 and 1996. Coupled with the fact that Earnhardt had won 70 races and seven Winston Cup championships, his failures in stock-car racing's premier event rivaled those of golf legend Sam Snead and tennis immortal Bjorn Borg, who won everything their sports had to offer except the U.S. Open. Earnhardt must have felt a sense of deja vu in the 40th annual Daytona 500 on February 18, when pole sitter Bobby Labonte scooted from sixth to second, half a car length behind Earnhardt, on the penultimate lap. But John Andretti's spin on the backstretch made that the last green-flag lap and allowed Earnhardt to hold off Labonte's charge and capture stock-car racing's premier event on his 20th try. Earnhardt then took the slowest ride to victory lane in the sport's history. Members of every rival pit crew lined up along pit road to shake his hand as he inched the Richard Childress-owned Chevrolet toward victory lane.

"You don't come that close to winning the Daytona 500 and not feel it," Earnhardt said of his previous failures. "I've said before that it didn't bother me. I lied. It hurt. My eyes watered up in the race car coming to take the checkered."

Labonte was asked a few weeks later who'd have won had there been another green-flag lap. "Somebody who was back in fifth or sixth," he said. "Dale and I would have ended up in the fence somewhere."

Most Significant Wreck

Moments after Gordon passed Rusty Wallace to take the lead with 28 laps left in the Pontiac Excitement 400 at Richmond, Va., on June 6, Wallace clipped Gordon's Chevrolet and sent him spinning into the wall. The sell-out crowd cheered vociferously, but Gordon had the last laugh. He proceeded to record 17 consecutive top-five finishes before finishing seventh and then adding two victories in the final 20 races to run away with the Winston Cup championship. "We didn't have any major catastrophes until Richmond," Gordon said. "I think we were a little upset. I know I was. I think that kind of lit a fire in us. I think we took it up another level."

Most Important Off-Track Development

R.J. Reynolds replaced the Winston Million with the Winston No Bull 5. In the new format, any driver who finished in the top five in any of five designated races could earn a $1 million bonus if he won the next designated race. In its first year, Gordon earned a $1 millon bonus by capturing the Brickyard 400 and another $1 million bonus for winning the Pepsi Southern 500. Jarrett pocketed an extra $1 million for his victory in the Winston 500 at Talladega, Ala.

Records & Milestones

The Winston Cup Series visited 17 states, tying a record set in 1956. . . . The 1.5-mile Las Vegas Motor Speedway joined the Winston Cup circuit.

1998 at a Glance

Races:	33
Road:	2
Short Track:	6
Superspeedway:	25
Winners:	11
Pole Winners:	15
Tracks:	20
States:	17

1998 Performance Index Rankings

1. Jeff Gordon (1,053)
2. Mark Martin (866)
3. Dale Jarrett (790)
4. Rusty Wallace (743)
5. Jeff Burton (742)
6. Bobby Labonte (696)
7. Jeremy Mayfield (659)
8. Terry Labonte (610)
9. Dale Earnhardt (575)
10. John Andretti (549)
11. Bobby Hamilton (520)
12. Sterling Marlin (511)
13. Ken Schrader (491)
14. Bill Elliott; Ernie Irvan (473)
16. Chad Little (448)
17. Jimmy Spencer (427)
18. Michael Waltrip (384)
19. Ward Burton (374)
20. Ted Musgrave (358)
21. Mike Skinner (328)
22. Johnny Benson Jr. (297)
23. Ricky Rudd (290)
24. Kenny Irwin (286)
25. Kenny Wallace (273)
26. Joe Nemechek (271)
27. Geoff Bodine (265)
28. Darrell Waltrip (259)
29. Kevin Lepage (224)
30. Brett Bodine (198)
31. Kyle Petty (189)
32. Dick Trickle (183)
33. Steve Grissom (171)
34. Robert Pressley (159)
35. Todd Bodine (133)
36. Rich Bickle (129)
37. Rick Mast (115)
38. Wally Dallenbach Jr. (106)
39. Derrike Cope (89)
40. Ricky Craven (84)
41. Steve Park (83)
42. Jeff Green (68)
43. David Green (67)
44. Randy LaJoie (65)
45. Lake Speed (53)
46. Buckshot Jones (51)
47. Morgan Shepherd (44)
48. Jerry Nadeau (31)
49. Matt Kenseth (29)
50. Dave Marcis (28)
51. Tom Kendall (27)
52. Dennis Setzer (21)
53. Ron Hornaday Jr. (16)

1998 Events

Daytona 500; Daytona International Speedway/2.5-m/500 miles
Dale Earnhardt (Chevrolet)/Bobby Labonte (Pontiac)

GM Goodwrench Service Plus 400; N.C. Speedway/1.017-m/400m
Jeff Gordon (Chevrolet)/Rick Mast (Ford)

Las Vegas 400; Las Vegas Motor Speedway/1.5-mile/400 miles
Mark Martin (Ford)/Dale Jarrett (Ford)

PRIMESTAR 500; Atlanta Motor Speedway/1.54-mile/500 miles
Bobby Labonte (Pontiac)/John Andretti (Pontiac)

TranSouth Financial 400; Darlington Raceway/1.366-mile/400 m
Dale Jarrett (Ford)/Mark Martin (Ford)

Food City 500; Bristol Motor Speedway/.533-mile/267 miles
Jeff Gordon (Chevrolet)/Rusty Wallace (Ford)

Texas 500; Texas Motor Speedway/1.5-mile/500 miles
Mark Martin (Ford)/Jeremy Mayfield (Ford)

Goody's Head. Powder 500; Martinsville Speedway/.526-m/263 m
Bobby Hamilton (Chevrolet)/Bobby Hamilton (Chevrolet)

Diehard 500; Talladega Superspeedway/2.66-mile/500 miles
Bobby Labonte (Pontiac)/Bobby Labonte (Pontiac)

California 500 by NAPA; California Speedway/2-mile/500 miles
Mark Martin (Ford)/Jeff Gordon (Chevrolet)

Coca-Cola 600; Charlotte Motor Speedway/1.5-mile/600 miles
Jeff Gordon (Chevrolet)/Jeff Gordon (Chevrolet)

MBNA Platinum 400; Dover Downs Int. Speedway/1-m/400 miles
Dale Jarrett (Ford)/Rusty Wallace (Ford)

Pontiac Excitement 400; Richmond Int. Raceway/.75-mile/300 m
Terry Labonte (Chevrolet)/Jeff Gordon (Chevrolet)

Miller Lite 400; Michigan Speedway/2-mile/400 miles
Mark Martin (Ford)/Ward Burton (Pontiac)

Pocono 500; Pocono Raceway/2.5-mile/500 miles
Jeremy Mayfield (Ford)/Jeff Gordon (Chevrolet)

Save Mart/Kragen 350; Sears Point Raceway/1.94-m road/217 m
Jeff Gordon (Chevrolet)/Jeff Gordon (Chevrolet)

Jiffy Lube 300; New Hampshire Int. Speedway/1.058-mile/317 m
Jeff Burton (Ford)/Ricky Craven (Chevrolet)

Pennsylvania 500; Pocono Raceway/2.5-mile/500 miles
Jeff Gordon (Chevrolet)/Ward Burton (Pontiac)

Brickyard 400; Indianapolis Motor Speedway/2.5-m/400 miles
Jeff Gordon (Chevrolet)/Ernie Irvan (Pontiac)

The Bud at the Glen; Watkins Glen Int./2.45-m road/221 miles
Jeff Gordon (Chevrolet)/Jeff Gordon (Chevrolet)

Pepsi 400 by DeVilbiss; Michigan Speedway/2-mile/400 miles
Jeff Gordon (Chevrolet)/Ernie Irvan (Pontiac)

Goody's Head. Powder 500; Bristol Motor Speedway/.533-m/267m
Mark Martin (Ford)/Rusty Wallace (Ford)

Farm Aid on CMT 300; New Hamp. Int. Speedway/1.058-m/317m
Jeff Gordon (Chevrolet)/Jeff Gordon (Chevrolet)

Pepsi Southern 500; Darlington Raceway/1.366-mile/500 miles
Jeff Gordon (Chevrolet)/Dale Jarrett (Ford)

Exide NASCAR Select Batt. 400; Rich. Int. Raceway/.75-m/300m
Jeff Burton (Ford)/Rusty Wallace (Ford)

MBNA Gold 400; Dover Downs International Speedway/1-m/400m
Mark Martin (Ford)/Mark Martin (Ford)

NAPA AutoCare 500; Martinsville Speedway/.526-m/263 miles
Ricky Rudd (Ford)/Ernie Irvan (Pontiac)

UAW-GM Quality 500; Charlotte Motor Speedway/1.5-mile/500m
Mark Martin (Ford)/Derrike Cope (Pontiac)

Winston 500; Talladega Superspeedway/2.66-mile/500 miles
Dale Jarrett (Ford)/Ken Schrader (Chevrolet)

Pepsi 400; Daytona International Speedway/2.5-mile/400 miles
Jeff Gordon (Chevrolet)/Bobby Labonte (Pontiac)

Dura-Lube/Kmart 500; Phoenix International Raceway/1-m/312m
Rusty Wallace (Ford)/Ken Schrader (Chevrolet)

AC Delco 400; North Carolina Speedway/1.017-mile/400 miles
Jeff Gordon (Chevrolet)/Mark Martin (Ford)

NAPA 500; Atlanta Motor Speedway/1.54-mile/500 miles
Jeff Gordon (Chevrolet)/Kenny Irwin (Ford)

Victories

1. Jeff Gordon (13)
2. Mark Martin (7)
3. Dale Jarrett (3)
4. Jeff Burton; Bobby Labonte (2)
6. Dale Earnhardt; Bobby Hamilton; Terry Labonte; Jeremy Mayfield; Ricky Rudd; Rusty Wallace (1)

Poles

1. Jeff Gordon (7)
2. Rusty Wallace (4)
3. Ernie Irvan; Bobby Labonte; Mark Martin (3)
6. Ward Burton; Dale Jarrett; Ken Schrader (2)
9. John Andretti; Derrike Cope; Ricky Craven; Bobby Hamilton; Kenny Irwin; Rick Mast; Jeremy Mayfield (1)

Victories

1. Chevrolet (16)
2. Ford (15)
3. Pontiac (2)

Poles

1. Ford (12)
2. Chevrolet (11)
3. Pontiac (10)

1999
Dale Jarrett:
Late Bloomer

If Harry Gant is considered stock-car racing's ultimate late bloomer, 1999 Winston Cup champion Dale Jarrett isn't far behind.

Through 1995, Jarrett had posted just one season in which he had earned a rating of more than 479 or finished better than 15th in the Performance Index, and he had only four victories to his credit.

In 1996, at age 39, Jarrett became one of only four drivers to win three classics in one season on his way to a four-victory campaign. Only Darel Dieringer, Nelson Stacy, Eddie Gray, and Gant were older when they recorded their first multiple-victory seasons, and only Gant was older than Jarrett when he recorded his first four-victory campaign. Although Gant earned 16 more victories, Dieringer, Stacy, and Gray combined for a total of only one triumph after their initial multiple-victory campaigns.

Jarrett's 1996 campaign—his first with Todd Parrott as crew chief of the Robert Yates-owned Ford—was merely a stepping stone, however.

His 1999 championship campaign was Jarrett's fourth in a row with three or more superspeedway victories, a streak exceeded only by David Pearson and Jeff Gordon. Jarrett also posted his fourth consecutive season with a Performance Index of 700 or better, fourth top-three season in a row, and seventh straight season with at least one superspeedway victory—streaks that rank among the top seven in history. And Jarrett was just 12 days shy of his 43rd birthday when he clinched the Winston Cup championship, which he called "the ultimate goal—as big as it gets in our sport." Only Bobby Allison, who won the 1983 title 13 days before his 46th birthday, was older when he captured his first Winston Cup crown.

"I think I matured as a driver and, hopefully, got smarter on the track," Jarrett said after he clinched the 1999 crown.

Jarrett, whose father, Ned, won the 1961 and '65 Winston Cup titles, became only the second son of a Winston Cup champion to capture the title, joining seven-time champion Richard Petty, whose father, Lee, earned three Winston Cup crowns.

"This sport has been good to the Jarrett family," Dale said. "To become the second father-son team to win a Winston Cup championship is very special to us. I know how much it means to me for my children to accomplish something. My dad has told me a number of times that this would mean more to him than his two championships. I give him a lot of thanks and credit for everything that has happened in my career."

Ironically, Ned retired one year after he won his second crown and just 18 days after his 34th birthday. At the same age, Dale hadn't won a race.

"My dad was one of the few drivers in history ever to retire so young while he was still on top," Jarrett said during lunch at an Italian restaurant in 1998. "Anybody who has been successful in this business has had a long road."

Dale's "long road" to the top may have taken longer than others, but his Hall of Fame resume includes 22 victories, which rank 23rd on the all-time list, and a Performance Index of 6,807, which ranks 25th. His six consecutive years (1993-98) with at least one 500-mile triumph, four consecutive years (1995-98) with at least one Grand Slam pole, and three consecutive years with multiple superspeedway poles (1996-98) all rank among the top 10 streaks in history. Jarrett's five classic victories—a record-tying two in the Brickyard 400, two in the Daytona 500, and one in the Coca-Cola 600—also rank among the top 10, and he's among the top 20 in superspeedway victories (19) and 500-mile wins (8).

1999 in Review

Dale Jarrett won four times and led the Winston Cup Series in both top-five (24) and top-10 finishes (29) to earn the first Winston Cup title for Yates and easily outdistance Bobby Labonte, 990-904, in the Performance Index. Gordon, who had won the two previous

Winston Cup titles, finished sixth in the Performance Index, but still led the circuit in both victories and poles with seven apiece.

Most Memorable Race

In the night race at Bristol Motor Speedway in 1995, Terry Labonte reached the finish line first despite being banged into the wall moments earlier by runner-up Dale Earnhardt. Labonte again appeared to be headed toward victory lane at the Tennessee track on August 28 after he pushed his Hendrick Motorsports Chevrolet from fifth to first in the final five laps. But Earnhardt again clipped Labonte's car on the last lap—this time sending him spinning to an eighth-place finish—on his way to edging Jimmy Spencer for the checkered flag. "Terry got by me, rattled me a little bit. I got back up to him and meant to try to get under him. I didn't by any means mean to wreck him or spin him," said Earnhardt, who was booed lustily.

Terry Labonte, who had lost the lead with 11 laps remaining when Darrell Waltrip's car slammed into his machine during a caution period, was understandably unhappy. "The 66 (Waltrip) just wrecked me when there was oil on the track and the caution was out. Then I passed Earnhardt on the front straightaway, and then he wrecked me," Labonte said. "He never *means* to wreck anybody. It just happens like that."

Most Significant Wreck

On August 20, Ernie Irvan lost control of his car during a practice session at Michigan Speedway and slammed into the retaining wall, suffering a bruised lung and head injuries. Irvan, whose 15 victories included the 1991 Daytona 500, was hospitalized and announced his retirement two weeks later. The accident came five years to the day after Irvan had suffered life-threatening injuries in a practice crash at the same track. "I don't want to retire," he said, "but it's the smart thing."

Most Important Off-Track Development

For the first time, NASCAR packaged television rights for the entire Winston Cup schedule rather than allowing tracks to do so individually. The TV contract, which will begin in the 2001 season, is a six-year deal with NBC, Fox, and TBS worth an estimated $2.4 bil-

lion. Among professional sports entities, the estimated annual bonanza of $400 million trails only the National Football League's TV revenue—NASCAR's reward for being the only sport with improved TV ratings in each year during the '90s. Rights fees for each race will be worth roughly 5.5 times more than the 1999 levels and at least 40 times more than they were at the beginning of the decade. Ironically, when the contract was announced in November, neither Fox nor NBC had televised a Winston Cup race.

Records & Milestones

Billy France relinquished day-to-day control of NASCAR to Mike Helton, NASCAR's Vice President of Competition, who had Chief Operating Officer added to his title. Although France retained the title of president, he said, "I'm out the door." . . . International Speedway Corporation, founded and controlled by the France family, and Roger Penske announced a merger that gave the new company nine Winston Cup tracks—Daytona International Speedway in Daytona Beach, Fla.; Talladega (Ala.) Superspeedway; Darlington (S.C.) Raceway; Watkins Glen (N.Y.) International; Phoenix International Raceway; Homestead-Miami Speedway; Michigan Speedway in Brooklyn; California Speedway in Fontana, and the North Carolina Speedway in Rockingham. . . . When Tony Stewart captured the Exide NASCAR Select Batteries 400 at Richmond, Va., on September 11 and Joe Nemechek won the Dura-Lube/Kmart 500 eight days later at New Hampshire, it marked the first time in the modern era that drivers earned their first victories in consecutive races.

Dodge, which last visited victory lane when Neil Bonnett captured the season-ending Los Angeles Times 500 in 1977, announced it would return to Winston Cup racing in 2001. Ray Evernham, crew chief for the first 47 victories of Gordon's career, will spearhead the Mopar effort. . . . Six drivers captured three or more races—Gordon, Jeff Burton (6), Bobby Labonte (5), Jarrett, Earnhardt (3), and Stewart (3) to equal a modern record set in 1979 and tied in 1995. . . . A record 26 races were held on superspeedways. . . . A modern-record 21 tracks played host to races. . . . The series visited 17 states, tying a record set in 1956 and equaled in 1998.

Ned Jarrett (left) joined his son, Dale, in victory lane after the 1997 PRIMESTAR 500 at Atlanta Motor Speedway, which Dale called a special triumph because it marked the first time he'd captured a race on a track where his father, a two-time Winston Cup champion, also had won.

1999 at a Glance

Races:	34
Road:	2
Short Track:	6
Superspeedway:	26
Winners:	11
Pole Winners:	15
Tracks:	21
States:	17

1999 Performance Index Rankings

1. Dale Jarrett (990)
2. Bobby Labonte (904)
3. Mark Martin (872)
4. Tony Stewart (859)
5. Jeff Burton (829)
6. Jeff Gordon (788)
7. Dale Earnhardt (771)
8. Rusty Wallace (669)
9. Ward Burton (620)
10. Mike Skinner (569)
11. Jeremy Mayfield (544)
12. Terry Labonte (477)
13. Steve Park (463)
14. John Andretti (460)
15. Bobby Hamilton; Ken Schrader (416)
17. Kenny Irwin (404)
18. Wally Dallenbach Jr.; Sterling Marlin (352)
20. Bill Elliott (341)
21. Jimmy Spencer (334)
22. Kenny Wallace (324)
23. Kyle Petty (319)
24. Chad Little (305)
25. Johnny Benson Jr. (294)
26. Michael Waltrip (289)
27. Ricky Rudd (286)
28. Kevin Lepage (276)
29. Elliott Sadler (271)
30. Geoff Bodine (228)
31. Joe Nemechek (214)
32. Ernie Irvan (208)
33. Rick Mast (205)
34. Jerry Nadeau (187)
35. Rich Bickle (159)
36. Ted Musgrave (133)
37. Robert Pressley (115)
38. Darrell Waltrip (102)
39. David Green (100)
40. Hut Stricklin (76)
41. Dale Earnhardt Jr. (70)
42. Brett Bodine (61)
43. Matt Kenseth (52)
44. Dave Marcis (29)
45. Ron Fellows (28)
46. Derrike Cope (27)
47. Ricky Craven (23)
48. Todd Bodine (16)

1999 Events

Daytona 500; Daytona International Speedway/2.5-m/500 miles
Jeff Gordon (Chevrolet)/Jeff Gordon (Chevrolet)

Dura-Lube/Big Kmart 400; N.C. Speedway/1.017-mile/400 miles
Mark Martin (Ford)/Ricky Rudd (Ford)

Las Vegas 400; Las Vegas Motor Speedway/1.5-mile/400 miles
Jeff Burton (Ford)/Bobby Labonte (Pontiac)

Cracker Barrel OCS 500; Atlanta Motor Speedway/1.54-m/500 m
Jeff Gordon (Chevrolet)/Bobby Labonte (Pontiac)

TranSouth Financial 400; Darlington Raceway./1.366-mile/400 m
Jeff Burton (Ford)/Jeff Gordon (Chevrolet)

PRIMESTAR 500; Texas Motor Speedway/1.5-mile/500 miles
Terry Labonte (Chevrolet)/Kenny Irwin (Ford)

Food City 500; Bristol Motor Speedway/.533-mile/267 miles
Rusty Wallace (Ford)/Rusty Wallace (Ford)

Goody's Body Pain 500; Martinsville Speedway/.526-mile/263 m
John Andretti (Pontiac)/Tony Stewart (Pontiac)

Diehard 500; Talladega Superspeedway/2.66-mile/500 miles
Dale Earnhardt (Chevrolet)/Ken Schrader (Chevrolet)

California 500 by NAPA; California Speedway/2-mile/500 miles
Jeff Gordon (Chevrolet)

Pontiac Excitement 400; Richmond Int. Raceway/.75-mile/300 m
Dale Jarrett (Ford)/Jeff Gordon (Chevrolet)

Coca-Cola 600; Lowe's Motor Speedway/1.5-mile/600 miles
Jeff Burton (Ford)/Bobby Labonte (Pontiac)

MBNA Platinum 400; Dover Downs Int. Speedway/1-m/400 miles
Bobby Labonte (Pontiac)/Bobby Labonte (Pontiac)

Kmart 400; Michigan Speedway/2-mile/400 miles
Dale Jarrett (Ford)/Jeff Gordon (Chevrolet)

Pocono 500; Pocono Raceway/2.5-mile/500 miles
Bobby Labonte (Pontiac)/Sterling Marlin (Chevrolet)

Save Mart/Kragen 350; Sears Point Raceway/1.949-m road/218 m
Jeff Gordon (Chevrolet)/Jeff Gordon (Chevrolet)

Pepsi 400; Daytona International Speedway/2.5-mile/400 miles
Dale Jarrett (Ford)/Joe Nemechek (Chevrolet)

Jiffy Lube 300; New Hampshire Int. Speedway/1.058-mile/317 m
Jeff Burton (Ford)/Jeff Gordon (Chevrolet)

Pennyslvania 500; Pocono Raceway/2.5-mile/500 miles
Bobby Labonte (Pontiac)/Mike Skinner (Chevrolet)

Brickyard 400; Indianapolis Motor Speedway/2.5-m/400 miles
Dale Jarrett (Ford)/Jeff Gordon (Chevrolet)

Frontier at the Glen; Watkins Glen Int./2.45-mile road/221 m
Jeff Gordon (Chevrolet)/Rusty Wallace (Ford)

Pepsi 400; Michigan Speedway/2-mile/400 miles
Bobby Labonte (Pontiac)/Ward Burton (Pontiac)

Goody's Head. Powder 500; Bristol Motor Speedway/.533-m/267m
Dale Earnhardt (Chevrolet)/Tony Stewart (Pontiac)

Pepsi Southern 500; Darlington Raceway/1.366-mile/500 miles
Jeff Burton (Ford)/Kenny Irwin (Ford)

Exide NASCAR Sel. Batt. 400; Rich. Int. Raceway/.75-m/300 m
Tony Stewart (Pontiac)/Mike Skinner (Chevrolet)

Dura-Lube/Kmart 500; New Hamp. Int. Speedway/1.058-m/317m
Joe Nemechek (Chevrolet)/Rusty Wallace (Ford)

MBNA Gold 400; Dover Downs International Speedway/1-m/400m
Mark Martin (Ford)/Rusty Wallace (Ford)

NAPA AutoCare 500; Martinsville Speedway/.526-mile/263 miles
Jeff Gordon (Chevrolet)/Joe Nemechek (Chevrolet)

UAW-GM Quality 500; Lowe's Motor Speedway/1.5-m/500 miles
Jeff Gordon (Chevrolet)/Bobby Labonte (Pontiac)

Winston 500; Talladega Superspeedway/2.66-mile/500 miles
Dale Earnhardt (Chevrolet)/Joe Nemechek (Chevrolet)

Pop Secret Micro. Popcorn 400; N.C. Speedway/1.017-m/400 m
Jeff Burton (Ford)/Mark Martin (Ford)

Checker Auto Pts./Dura-Lube 500; Phoenix Int. Race./1-m/312m
Tony Stewart (Pontiac)/John Andretti (Pontiac)

Pennzoil 400; Homestead-Miami Speedway/1.5-mile/400 miles
Tony Stewart (Pontiac)/David Green (Pontiac)

NAPA 500; Atlanta Motor Speedway/1.54-mile/500 miles
Bobby Labonte (Pontiac)/Kevin Lepage (Ford)

Victories
1. Jeff Gordon (7)
2. Jeff Burton (6)
3. Bobby Labonte (5)
4. Dale Jarrett (4)
5. Dale Earnhardt; Tony Stewart (3)
7. Mark Martin (2)
8. John Andretti; Terry Labonte; Joe Nemechek; Rusty Wallace (1)

Poles
1. Jeff Gordon (7)
2. Bobby Labonte (5)
3. Rusty Wallace (4)
4. Joe Nemechek (3)
5. Kenny Irwin; Mike Skinner; Tony Stewart (2)
8. John Andretti; Ward Burton; David Green; Kevin Lepage; Sterling Marlin; Mark Martin; Ricky Rudd; Ken Schrader (1)

Victories
1. Ford (13)
2. Chevrolet (12)
3. Pontiac (9)

Poles
1. Chevrolet (14)
2. Pontiac (10)
3. Ford (9)

Driver Resumes

In case you're skipping around or just can't wait to read your favorite driver's resume, a complete explanation of how to read the Driver Resumes is on page 34.

Legend:
*Won race from pole
m (mile/miles)

MARV ACTON

1971		(104)

CARL ADAMS

1975	(T-24th)	(248)

WELDON ADAMS

1950	(15th)	

GRANT ADCOX

1975		(110)
1976	(20th)	(276)
1978		(166)

MIKE ALEXANDER

1981		(184)
1984		(147)
1988	(24th)	(261)

JOHNNY ALLEN

1956	(13th)	(249)
1957	(7th)	(437)

Poles
Coastal Speedway (.5-mile dirt) (Plymouth)

1958	(24th)	(150)
1960		(141)
1961	(14th)	(333)

Poles
Alabama State Fairgrounds (.5-mile dirt) (Chevrolet)

1962	(24th)	(236)

Victories
Myers Brothers 200; Bowman Gray Stadium (.25-m; 50 miles) (Pontiac)
Poles
Nashville 500; Fairgrounds Speedway (.5-mile) (Pontiac)

LOY ALLEN JR.

1994		

Poles
Daytona 500; Daytona International Speedway (2.5-mile) (Ford)
Purolator 500; Atlanta Motor Speedway (1.522-mile) (Ford)
Miller Genuine Draft 400; Michigan International Speedway (2-m) (Ford)

BOBBY ALLISON

1965		(104)
1966	(10th)	(446)

Victories
* Oxford Plains Speedway (.333-mile; 100 miles) (Chevrolet)
Islip Speedway (.2-mile; 60 miles) (Chevrolet)
* Maryland 200; Beltsville Speedway (.5-mile; 100 miles) (Chevrolet)
Poles
Old Dominion Speedway (.375-mile) (Chevrolet)
* Oxford Plains Speedway (.333-mile) (Chevrolet)
Sandlapper 200; Columbia Speedway (.5-mile dirt) (Chevrolet)
* Maryland 200; Beltsville Speedway (.5-mile) (Chevrolet)

1967	(3rd)	(719)

Victories
* Bowman Gray Stadium (.25-mile; 50 miles) (Chevrolet)
Savannah Speedway (.5-mile dirt; 100 miles) (Chevrolet)
Birmingham Speedway (.625-mile; 100 miles) (Dodge)
Maine 300; Oxford Plains Speedway (.333-mile) (Chevrolet)
American 500; North Carolina Motor Speedway (1-m; 500 m) (Ford)
* Western N.C. 500; Asheville-Weaverville Speed. (.5-m; 250m) (Ford)
Poles
* Bowman Gray Stadium (.25-mile) (Chevrolet)
* Western N.C. 500; Asheville-Weaverville Speedway (.5-mile) (Ford)

Bobby Labonte (left) called the post-race celebration "the coolest thing we've ever done together" after he captured the 1996 NAPA 500 at Atlanta Motor Speedway in the same event in which older brother Terry clinched his second Winston Cup championship.

1968   (8th)   (572)

Victories
Middle Georgia 500; Middle Ga. Raceway (.5625-m; 281m) (Ford)
Islip 300; Islip Speedway (.2-mile; 60 miles) (Chevrolet)

Poles
Wilkes 400; North Wilkesboro Speedway (.625-mile) (Plymouth)
Augusta 200; Augusta Speedway (.5-mile) (Plymouth)

1969   (12th)   (498)

Victories
Alabama 200; Montgomery Speedway (.5-mile; 100 miles) (Plymouth)
Southeastern 500; Bristol Int. Speedway (.5-m; 250 miles) (Dodge)
Gwyn Staley 400; No. Wilkesboro Speedway (.625-m; 250 m) (Dodge)
Capital City 250; Va. State Fairgrounds (.5625-m; 260 m) (Dodge)
Georgia 500; Middle Georgia Raceway (.548-m; 274 miles) (Dodge)

Poles
Virginia 500; Martinsville Speedway (.5-mile) (Dodge)

1970   (2nd)   (1,011)

Victories
Atlanta 500; Atlanta Int. Raceway (1.522-m; 500 miles) (Dodge)
Volunteer 500; Bristol Int. Speedway (.533-m; 267 miles) (Dodge)
Tidewater 300; Langley Field Speedway (.395-mile; 119 m) (Dodge)

Poles
Carolina 500; North Carolina Motor Speedway (1.017-m) (Dodge)
Maryville 200; Smoky Mountain Raceway (.52-mile) (Dodge)
Falstaff 400; Riverside Int. Raceway (2.62-mile road) (Dodge)
Old Dominion 500; Martinsville Speedway (.525-mile) (Dodge)

1971   (3rd)   (993)

Victories
World 600; Charlotte Motor Speedway (1.5-m; 600 miles) (Mercury)
Mason-Dixon 500; Dover Downs Int. Speedway (1-m; 500 m) (Ford)
* Motor State 400; Michigan Int. Speedway (2.04-m; 400m) (Mercury)
* Winston GS 400; River. Int. Raceway (2.62-m rd.; 400m) (Mercury)
* Space City 300; Meyer Speedway (.5-mile; 150 miles) (Dodge)
Myers Brothers 250; Bowman Gray Stadium (.25-mile; 63 m) (Ford)
Yankee 400; Michigan Int. Speedway (2.04-m; 400 miles) (Mercury)
Talladega 500; Alabama Int. Motor Speed. (2.66-m; 500m) (Mercury)
* Southern 500; Darlington Raceway (1.366-m; 500 miles) (Mercury)
National 500; Charlotte Motor Speedway (1.5-mile; 500 m) (Mercury)
* Georgia 500; Middle Georgia Raceway (.548-mile; 274 m) (Ford)

Poles (T-1st)
Hickory 276; Hickory Speedway (.363-mile) (Dodge)
* Motor State 400; Michigan Int. Speedway (2.04-mile) (Mercury)
* Winston GS 400; Riverside Int. Raceway (2.62-m road) (Mercury)
* Space City 300; Meyer Speedway (.5-mile) (Dodge)
Pickens 200; Greenville-Pickens Speedway (.5-mile) (Ford)
West Virginia 500; International Raceway Park (.4375-m) (Ford)
* Southern 500; Darlington Raceway (1.366-mile) (Mercury)
Delaware 500; Dover Downs International Speedway (1-m) (Mercury)
* Georgia 500; Middle Georgia Raceway (.548-mile) (Ford)

1972   (1st)   (962)

Victories (1st)
* Atlanta 500; Atlanta Int. Raceway (1.522-mile; 500 m) (Chevrolet)
* Southeastern 500; Bristol Int. Speedway (.533-m; 267m) (Chevrolet)
Mason-Dixon 500; Dover Downs Int. Speedway (1-m; 500 m) (Chevrolet)
* Volunteer 500; Bristol Int. Speedway (.533-m; 267 m) (Chevrolet)
Northern 300; Trenton Speedway (1.5-mile; 300 miles) (Chevrolet)
Dixie 500; Atlanta International Raceway (1.522-m; 500m) (Chevrolet)

* Nashville 420; Fgds. Speedway (.596-mile; 250 miles) (Chevrolet)
* Southern 500; Darlington Raceway (1.366-m; 500 miles) (Chevrolet)
National 500; Charlotte Motor Speedway (1.5-mile; 500 m) (Chevrolet)
American 500; N.C. Motor Speedway (1.017-m; 500 miles) (Chevrolet)

Poles (1st)
Richmond 500; Richmond Fairgrounds Raceway (.542-mile) (Chevrolet)
* Atlanta 500; Atlanta International Raceway (1.522-m) (Chevrolet)
* Southeastern 500; Bristol Int. Speedway (.533-mile) (Chevrolet)
Virginia 500; Martinsville Speedway (.525-mile) (Chevrolet)
World 600; Charlotte Motor Speedway (1.5-mile) (Chevrolet)
* Volunteer 500; Bristol International Speedway (.533-m) (Chevrolet)
* Nashville 420; Fairgrounds Speedway (.596-mile) (Chevrolet)
* Southern 500; Darlington Raceway (1.366-mile) (Chevrolet)
Capital City 500; Richmond Fairgrounds Raceway (.542-m) (Chevrolet)
Delaware 500; Dover Downs International Speedway (1-m) (Chevrolet)
Old Dominion 500; Martinsville Speedway (.525-mile) (Chevrolet)

1973   (8th)   (521)

Victories
Tuborg 400; Riverside Int. Raceway (2.62-m road; 400 m) (Chevrolet)
* Wilkes 400; North Wilkesboro Speedway (.625-m; 250 m) (Chevrolet)

Poles
Richmond 500; Richmond Fairgrounds Raceway (.542-mile) (Chevrolet)
Gwyn Staley 400; North Wilkesboro Speedway (.625-mile) (Chevrolet)
Firecracker 400; Daytona International Speedway (2.5-m) (Chevrolet)
Talladega 500; Alabama Int. Motor Speedway (2.66-mile) (Chevrolet)
Capital City 500; Richmond Fgds. Raceway (.542-mile) (Chevrolet)
* Wilkes 400; North Wilkesboro Speedway (.625-mile) (Chevrolet)

1974   (5th)   (532)

Victories
* Richmond 500; Richmond Fgds. Raceway (.542-m; 244 m) (Chevrolet)
L.A. Times 500; Ontario Motor Speedway (2.5-m; 500 m) (Matador)

Poles
* Richmond 500; Richmond Fairgrounds Raceway (.542-mile) (Chevrolet)
Gwyn Staley 400; North Wilkesboro Speedway (.625-mile) (Chevrolet)
Music City USA 420; Fairgrounds Speedway (.596-mile) (Chevrolet)

1975   (17th)   (368)

Victories
* Win. West. 500; River. Int. Race. (2.62-m rd.; 500m) (Matador)
Rebel 500; Darlington Raceway (1.366-mile; 500 miles) (Matador)
Southern 500; Darlington Int. Raceway (1.366-m; 500 m) (Matador)

Poles
* Win. West. 500; Riverside Int. Raceway (2.62-m rd.) (Matador)
Tuborg 400; Riverside Int. Raceway (2.62-mile road) (Matador)
Purolator 500; Pocono International Raceway (2.5-mile) (Matador)

1976   (6th)   (581)

Poles
Winston West. 500; Riverside Int. Raceway (2.62-m rd.) (Matador)
Richmond 400; Richmond Fairgrounds Raceway (.542-mile) (Mercury)

1977   (10th)   (454)

1978   (2nd)   (738)

Victories
Daytona 500; Daytona Int. Speedway (2.5-mile; 500 miles) (Ford)
Atlanta 500; Atlanta Int. Raceway (1.522-m; 500 miles) (Ford)
Delaware 500; Dover Downs Int. Speedway (1-m; 500 miles) (Ford)
NAPA National 500; Charlotte Motor Speed. (1.5-m; 500 m) (Ford)
L.A. Times 500; Ontario Motor Speedway (2.5-mile; 500 m) (Ford)

Poles

Rebel 500; Darlington International Raceway (1.366-m) (Ford)

1979   (4th)   (753)

Victories

* Carolina 500; N.C. Motor Speedway (1.017-m; 500 miles) (Ford)
Northwestern Bank 400; N. Wilkesboro Sp. (.625-m; 250 m) (Ford)
Winston 500; Alabama Int. Motor Speedway (2.66-m; 500 m) (Ford)
NAPA River. 400; Riverside Int. Race. (2.62-m rd.; 249m) (Ford)
Capital City 400; Richmond Fgds. Raceway (.542-m; 217 m) (Ford)

Poles

* Carolina 500; North Carolina Motor Speedway (1.017-m) (Ford)
Richmond 400; Richmond Fairgrounds Raceway (.542-mile) (Ford)
Southern 500; Darlington International Raceway (1.366-m) (Ford)

1980   (7th)   (563)

Victories

Mason-Dixon 500; Dover Downs Int. Speedway (1-m; 500 m) (Ford)
Firecracker 400; Daytona Int. Speedway (2.5-mile; 400 m) (Mercury)
Capital City 400; Richmond Fgds. Raceway (.542-m; 217 m) (Ford)
Holly Farms 400; No. Wilkesboro Speedway (.625-m; 250 m) (Ford)

Poles

Northwestern Bank 400; No. Wilkesboro Speedway (.625-m) (Ford)
Atlanta Journal 500; Atlanta Int. Raceway (1.5-mile) (Mercury)

1981   (2nd)   (844)

Victories

Win. West. 500; Riverside Int. Race. (2.62-m rd.; 312m) (Chevrolet)
* Winston 500; Alabama Int. Motor Speed. (2.66-m; 500 m) (Buick)
World 600; Charlotte Motor Speedway (1.5-m; 600 miles) (Buick)
Gabriel 400; Michigan Int. Speedway (2-mile; 400 miles) (Buick)
Win. West. 500; Riverside Int. Race. (2.62-m rd.; 312m) (Buick)

Poles

Daytona 500; Daytona International Speedway (2.5-mile) (Pontiac)
* Winston 500; Alabama Int. Motor Speedway (2.66-mile) (Buick)

1982   (2nd)   (751)

Victories

Daytona 500; Daytona Int. Speedway (2.5-mile; 500 miles) (Buick)
Mason-Dixon 500; Dover Downs Int. Speedway (1-m; 500 m) (Chevrolet)
Van Scoy DM 500; Pocono Int. Raceway (2.5-mile; 500 m) (Buick)
Firecracker 400; Daytona Int. Speedway (2.5-mile; 400 m) (Buick)
Mountain Dew 500; Pocono Int. Raceway (2.5-m; 500 miles) (Buick)
Champion SP 400; Michigan Int. Speedway (2-m; 400 miles) (Buick)
* Wrangler San. 400; Rich. Fgds. Raceway (.542-m; 217m) (Chevrolet)
Atl. Journal 500; Atlanta Int. Raceway (1.522-m; 500 m) (Buick)

Poles

* Wrangler Sanforset 400; Rich. Fgds. Raceway (.542-m) (Chevrolet)

1983   (1st)   (821)

Victories (T-1st)

Richmond 400; Richmond Fgds. Raceway (.542-mile; 217 m) (Chevrolet)
Mason-Dixon 500; Dover Downs Int. Speedway (1-m; 500 m) (Buick)
Van Scoy DM 500; Pocono Int. Raceway (2.5-m; 500 miles) (Buick)
Southern 500; Darlington Int. Raceway (1.366-m; 500 m) (Buick)
Wrangler San. 400; Richmond Fgds. Raceway (.542-m; 217m) (Buick)
Budweiser 500; Dover Downs Int. Speedway (1-mile; 500 m) (Buick)

1984   (6th)   (658)

Victories

W.W. Hodgdon Car. 500; N.C. Motor Speed. (1.017-m; 500m) (Buick)
World 600; Charlotte Motor Speedway (1.5-m; 600 miles) (Buick)

1985   (12th)   (452)

1986   (7th)   (578)

Victories

Winston 500; Alabama Int. Motor Speedway (2.66-m; 500m) (Buick)

1987   (13th)   (466)

Victories

Pepsi Firecracker 400; Daytona Int. Speed. (2.5-m; 400m) (Buick)

Poles

Oakwood Homes 500; Charlotte Motor Speedway (1.5-mile) (Buick)

1988   (25th)   (258)

Victories

Daytona 500; Daytona Int. Speedway (2.5-mile; 500 miles) (Buick)

DAVEY ALLISON

1987   (11th)   (487)

Victories

Winston 500; Alabama Int. Motor Speedway (2.66-m; 500 m) (Ford)
Budweiser 500; Dover Downs Int. Speedway (1-mile; 500 m) (Ford)

Poles

Goodwrench 500; North Carolina Motor Speedway (1.017-m) (Ford)
Pepsi Firecracker 400; Daytona Int. Speedway (2.5-mile) (Ford)
Champion Spark Plug 400; Michigan Int. Speedway (2-m) (Ford)
Southern 500; Darlington International Raceway (1.366-m) (Ford)
AC Delco 500; North Carolina Motor Speedway (1.017-mile) (Ford)

1988   (7th)   (578)

Victories

Champion SP 400; Michigan Int. Speedway (2-mile; 400 m) (Ford)
* Miller HL 400; Richmond Int. Raceway (.75-mile; 300 m) (Ford)

Poles

Winston 500; Alabama Int. Motor Speedway (2.66-mile) (Ford)
Coca-Cola 600; Charlotte Motor Speedway (1.5-mile) (Ford)
* Miller High Life 400; Richmond Int. Raceway (.75-mile) (Ford)

1989   (13th)   (464)

Victories

Winston 500; Talladega Superspeedway (2.66-m; 500 miles) (Ford)
Pepsi 400; Daytona International Speedway (2.5-m; 400 m) (Ford)

Poles

Peak Performance 500; Dover Downs Int. Speedway (1-m) (Ford)

1990   (15th)   (483)

Victories

Valleydale Meats 500; Bristol Int. Race. (.533-m; 267m) (Ford)
Mello Yello 500; Charlotte Motor Speedway (1.5-m; 500 m) (Ford)

1991   (3rd)   (700)

Victories (T-1st)

Coca-Cola 600; Charlotte Motor Speedway (1.5-m; 600 m) (Ford)
Banquet FF 300; Sears Pt. Int. Race. (2.52-m rd.; 187m) (Ford)
Miller Gen. Dr. 400; Michigan Int. Speedway (2-m; 400m) (Ford)
AC Delco 500; N.C. Motor Speedway (1.017-m; 500 miles) (Ford)
Pyroil 500; Phoenix International Raceway (1-m; 312 m) (Ford)

Poles

Daytona 500 by STP; Daytona Int. Speedway (2.5-mile) (Ford)
Pontiac Excitement 400; Richmond Int. Raceway (.75-mile) (Ford)
Heinz Southern 500; Darlington Raceway (1.366-mile) (Ford)

1992   (2nd)   (694)

Victories (T-1st)
Daytona 500 by STP; Daytona Int. Speedway (2.5-m; 500 m) (Ford)
First Union 400; No. Wilkesboro Speedway (.625-m; 250 m) (Ford)
Winston 500; Talladega Superspeedway (2.66-mile; 500 m) (Ford)
* Miller Gen. Dr. 400; Mich. Int. Speedway (2-m; 400m) (Ford)
Pyroil 500; Phoenix Int. Raceway (1-mile; 312 miles) (Ford)

Poles
* Miller Genuine Draft 400; Michigan Int. Speedway (2-m) (Ford)
Miller Genuine Draft 500; Pocono Int. Raceway (2.5-mile) (Ford)

1993   (22nd)   (322)

Victories
Pont. Excitement 400; Richmond Int. Race. (.75-m; 300m) (Ford)

DONNIE ALLISON

1967   (18th)   (282)

1968   (20th)   (294)

Victories
Carolina 500; North Carolina Motor Speedway (1-m; 500 m) (Ford)

Poles
World 600; Charlotte Motor Speedway (1.5-mile) (Ford)

1969   (20th)   (379)

Victories
National 500; Charlotte Motor Speedway (1.5-mile; 500 m) (Ford)

Poles
World 600; Charlotte Motor Speedway (1.5-mile) (Ford)
Motor State 500; Michigan International Speedway (2-m) (Ford)

1970   (14th)   (425)

Victories
Southeastern 500; Bristol Int. Speedway (.533-m; 267 m) (Ford)
World 600; Charlotte Motor Speedway (1.5-mile; 600 miles) (Ford)
Firecracker 400; Daytona Int. Speedway (2.5-mile; 400 m) (Ford)

1971   (22nd)   (305)

Victories
* Winston 500; Ala. Int. Motor Speedway (2.66-m; 500m) (Mercury)

Poles
Virginia 500; Martinsville Speedway (.525-mile) (Mercury)
Rebel 400; Darlington Raceway (1.366-mile) (Mercury)
* Winston 500; Alabama Int. Motor Speedway (2.66-mile) (Mercury)
Firecracker 400; Daytona International Speedway (2.5-m) (Mercury)
Talladega 500; Alabama Int. Motor Speedway (2.66-mile) (Mercury)

1973   (181)

1974   (T-18th)   (289)

Poles
Southeastern 500; Bristol Int. Speedway (.533-mile) (Chevrolet)
Rebel 500; Darlington Raceway (1.366-mile) (Chevrolet)

1975   (205)

Poles
Daytona 500; Daytona International Speedway (2.5-mile) (Chevrolet)
Firecracker 400; Daytona International Speedway (2.5-m) (Chevrolet)

1976   (187)

Victories
National 500; Charlotte Motor Speedway (1.5-mile; 500 m) (Chevrolet)

1977   (14th)   (381)

Victories
Talladega 500; Ala. Int. Motor Speedway (2.66-m; 500m) (Chevrolet)
* American 500; N.C. Motor Speedway (1.017-m; 500 miles) (Chevrolet)

Poles
Daytona 500; Daytona International Speedway (2.5-mile) (Chevrolet)
Carolina 500; North Carolina Motor Speedway (1.017-mile) (Chevrolet)
* American 500; North Carolina Motor Speedway (1.017-m) (Chevrolet)

1978   (15th)   (307)

Victories
Dixie 500; Atlanta Int. Raceway (1.522-mile; 500 miles) (Chevrolet)

1979   (16th)   (375)

Poles
CRC Chem. Rebel 500; Darlington Int. Raceway (1.366-m) (Chevrolet)

1980   (208)

Poles
American 500; North Carolina Motor Speedway (1.017-m) (Chevrolet)

1982   (126)

BILL AMICK

1955

Poles
Arizona State Fairgrounds (1-mile dirt) (Dodge)
Tucson Rodeo Grounds (.5-mile dirt) (Dodge)

1956   (16th)   (188)

1957   (15th)   (226)

Victories
Capitol Speedway (.5-mile dirt; 100 miles) (Ford)

Poles
Norfolk Speedway (.4-mile dirt) (Ford)
Asheville-Weaverville Speedway (.5-mile) (Ford)

1961

Poles
California State Fairgrounds (1-mile dirt) (Pontiac)

JACK ANDERSON

1964   (24th)   (215)

JOHN ANDERSON

1980   (188)

JOHN ANDRETTI

1994   (107)

1995   (16th)   (379)

Poles
Mountain Dew Southern 500; Darlington Raceway (1.366-m) (Ford)

| 1996 | | (210) |
| 1997 | | (267) |

Victories
Pepsi 400; Daytona Int. Speedway (2.5-mile; 400 miles) (Ford)
Poles
Winston 500; Talladega Superspeedway (2.66-mile) (Ford)

| 1998 | (10th) | (549) |

Poles
PRIMESTAR 500; Atlanta Motor Speedway (1.54-mile) (Pontiac)

| 1999 | (14th) | (460) |

Victories
Goody's BP 500; Martinsville Speedway (.526-m; 263m) (Pontiac)
Poles
Checker AP/Dura-Lube 500; Phoenix Int. Race. (1-mile) (Pontiac)

MARIO ANDRETTI

| 1967 | | (126) |

Victories
Daytona 500; Daytona Int. Speedway (2.5-mile; 500 miles) (Ford)

BOB APPERSON

| 1949 | (T-25th) | |

BEN ARNOLD

1969	(16th)	(420)
1970		(292)
1971		(278)
1972	(8th)	(454)

BUDDY ARRINGTON

1964	(T-22nd)	(217)
1965	(20th)	(282)
1966		(136)
1967		(185)
1969		(150)
1970		(186)
1972	(12th)	(383)
1973	(T-12th)	(354)
1974	(25th)	(213)
1975	(20th)	(345)
1976	(T-21st)	(267)
1977	(8th)	(508)
1978	(7th)	(580)

1979	(10th)	(505)
1980	(12th)	(467)
1981	(9th)	(454)
1982	(5th)	(555)
1983	(19th)	(332)
1984		(190)
1985	(18th)	(354)
1986	(23rd)	(258)
1987		(168)

L.D. AUSTIN

1957	(8th)	(368)
1958	(11th)	(291)
1959	(12th)	(284)
1960	(10th)	(265)
1961	(21st)	(233)

DICK BAILEY

| 1959 | | |

Poles
Heidleberg Raceway (.25-mile dirt) (Plymouth)

H.B. BAILEY

| 1965 | | (124) |

BUCK BAKER

| 1950 | (12th) | |

Poles
Martinsville Speedway (.5-mile dirt) (Ford)

| 1951 | (20th) | (107) |
| 1952 | (13th) | (148) |

Victories
* Columbia Speedway (.5-mile dirt; 100 miles) (Hudson)
Poles
Martinsville Speedway (.5-mile dirt) (Hudson)
* Columbia Speedway (.5-mile dirt) (Hudson)

| 1953 | (4th) | (515) |

Victories
Langhorne Speedway (1-mile dirt; 150 miles) (Oldsmobile)
Columbia Speedway (.5-mile dirt; 100 miles) (Oldsmobile)
Southern 500; Darlington Raceway (1.375-mile; 500 miles) (Oldsmobile)
Lakewood Speedway (1-mile dirt; 100 miles) (Oldsmobile)

Poles

Richmond 200; Atlantic Rural Fairgrounds (.5-mile dirt) (Oldsmobile)
Wilson Speedway (5.-mile dirt) (Oldsmobile)
Piedmont Interstate Fairgrounds (.5-mile dirt) (Oldsmobile)
Davenport Speedway (.5-mile dirt) (Oldsmobile)
Wilkes 160; North Wilkesboro Speedway (.625-mile dirt) (Oldsmobile)

1954   (3rd)   (555)

Victories

Wilson Speedway (.5-mile dirt; 100 miles) (Oldsmobile)
Charlotte Speedway (.75-mile dirt; 100 miles) (Oldsmobile)
* Morristown Speedway (.5-mile dirt; 100 miles) (Oldsmobile)
Mid-South 250; Memphis-Arkansas Speed. (1.5-m dt.; 250m) (Oldsmobile)

Poles

Orange Speedway (1-mile dirt) (Oldsmobile)
Columbia Speedway (.5-mile dirt) (Oldsmobile)
Linden Airport (2-mile road) (Oldsmobile)
Santa Fe Speedway (.5-mile dirt) (Oldsmobile)
* Morristown Speedway (.5-mile dirt) (Oldsmobile)
Southern States Fairgrounds (.5-mile dirt) (Oldsmobile)
Southern 500; Darlington Raceway (1.375-mile) (Oldsmobile)

1955   (2nd)   (656)

Victories

Wilkes Co. 160; N. Wilkesboro Speed. (.625-m dirt; 100m) (Oldsmobile)
Charlotte Speedway (.75-mile dirt; 100 miles) (Buick)
* Wilkes 160; N. Wilkesboro Speedway (.625-m dirt; 100m) (Ford)

Poles

Monroe County Fairgrounds (.5-mile dirt) (Chrysler)
* Wilkes 160; North Wilkesboro Speedway (.625-mile dirt) (Ford)

1956   (1st)   (822)

Victories (1st)

Arizona State Fairgrounds (1-mile dirt; 150 miles) (Chrysler)
Lakewood Speedway (1-mile dirt; 100 miles) (Chrysler)
* Langhorne Speedway (1-mile dirt; 150 miles) (Chrysler)
* Richmond 200; Atlantic Rural Fgds. (.5-m dirt; 100 m) (Dodge)
Greenville-Pickens Speedway (.5-mile dirt; 100 miles) (Dodge)
* Orange Speedway (.9-mile dirt; 90 miles) (Chrysler)
* Virginia 500; Martinsville Speedway (.5-m; 250 miles) (Dodge)
Lincoln Speedway (.5-mile dirt; 100 miles) (Dodge)
* New York State Fairgrounds (1-mile dirt; 150 miles) (Chrysler)
Chisholm Speedway (.5-mile dirt; 100 miles) (Chrysler)
Columbia Speedway (.5-mile dirt; 100 miles) (Dodge)
Charlotte Speedway (.75-mile dirt; 100 miles) (Chrysler)
Cleveland County Fairgrounds (.5-m dirt; 100 miles) (Chrysler)
* Wilson Speedway (.5-mile dirt; 100 miles) (Chrysler)

Poles (1st)

Palm Beach Speedway (.5-mile) (Dodge)
* Langhorne Speedway (1-mile dirt) (Chrysler)
* Richmond 200; Atlantic Rural Fairgrounds (.5-m dirt) (Dodge)
Columbia Speedway (.5-mile dirt) (Dodge)
* Orange Speedway (.9-mile dirt) (Chrysler)
* Virginia 500; Martinsville Speedway (.5-mile) (Dodge)
* New York State Fairgrounds (1-mile dirt) (Chrysler)
Memphis-Arkansas Speedway (1.5-mile dirt) (Chrysler)
Road America (4-mile road) (Dodge)
Langhorne Speedway (1-mile dirt) (Chrysler)
Old Dominion 400; Martinsville Speedway (.5-mile) (Chrysler)
* Wilson Speedway (.5-mile dirt) (Chrysler)

1957   (1st)   (767)

Victories (1st)

Orange Speedway (.9-mile dirt; 99 miles) (Ford)
Asheville-Weaverville Speedway (.5-mile dirt; 100 miles) (Chevrolet)
Virginia 500; Martinsville Speedway (.5-mile; 250 miles) (Chevrolet)
Lincoln Speedway (.5-mile dirt; 100 miles) (Chevrolet)
Jacksonville Speedway (.5-mile dirt; 100 miles) (Chevrolet)
Norfolk Speedway (.4-mile dirt; 100 miles) (Chevrolet)
* The Glen 101.2; Watkins Glen Int. (2.3-m road; 101 m) (Chevrolet)
* Columbia Speedway (.5-mile dirt; 100 miles) (Chevrolet)
* Cleveland County Fairgrounds (.5-mile dirt; 100 miles) (Chevrolet)
Greensboro Fairgrounds (.333-mile dirt; 83 miles) (Chevrolet)

Poles (1st)

Greensboro Fairgrounds (.333-mile dirt) (Chevrolet)
Lancaster Speedway (.5-mile dirt) (Chevrolet)
Columbia Speedway (.5-mile dirt) (Chevrolet)
* The Glen 101.2; Watkins Glen International (2.3-m rd.) (Chevrolet)
* Columbia Speedway (.5-mile dirt) (Chevrolet)
* Cleveland County Fairgrounds (.5-mile dirt) (Chevrolet)

1958   (2nd)   (687)

Victories

* Orange Speedway (.9-mile dirt; 99 miles) (Chevrolet)
Southern States Fairgrounds (.5-mile dirt; 100 miles) (Chevrolet)
Gastonia Fairgrounds (.333-mile dirt; 67 miles) (Chevrolet)

Poles

* Orange Speedway (.9-mile dirt) (Chevrolet)
Virginia 500; Martinsville Speedway (.5-mile) (Chevrolet)
Columbia Speedway (.5-mile dirt) (Chevrolet)

1959   (3rd)   (420)

Victories

Greenville-Pickens Speedway (.5-mile dirt; 100 miles) (Chevrolet)

Poles

Concord Speedway (.5-mile dirt) (Chevrolet)
Lakewood Speedway (1-mile dirt) (Chevrolet)
Richmond 200; Atlantic Rural Fairgrounds (.5-mile dirt) (Chevrolet)
Charlotte Fairgrounds (.5-mile dirt) (Chevrolet)

1960   (5th)   (568)

Victories

Rambi Raceway (.5-mile dirt; 100 miles) (Chevrolet)
Southern 500; Darlington Raceway (1.375-m; 500 miles) (Pontiac)

Poles

Charlotte Fairgrounds (.5-mile dirt) (Chevrolet)
Buddy Shuman 250; Hickory Speedway (.4-mile dirt) (Chevrolet)

1961   (8th)   (467)

Victories

Hartsville Speedway (.333-mile dirt; 50 miles) (Chrysler)

Poles

Greenville-Pickens Speedway (.5-mile dirt) (Chrysler)

1962   (12th)   (399)

1963   (5th)   (607)

Victories

Greenville 200; Greenville-Pickens Speedway (.5-mile dirt; 100 miles) (Pontiac)

1964 (9th) (563)

Victories
Valdosta Speedway (.5-mile dirt; 100 miles) (Dodge)
Southern 500; Darlington Raceway (1.375-mile; 500 miles) (Dodge)

1965 (21st) (280)

1966 (13th) (364)

1967 (24th) (232)

1968 (109)

BUDDY BAKER

1960 (101)

1961 (111)

1962 (19th) (312)

1964 (185)

1965 (11th) (477)

1966 (18th) (270)

Poles
Smoky Mountain 200; Smoky Mountain Raceway (.5-m dirt) (Dodge)

1967 (19th) (275)

Victories
National 500; Charlotte Motor Speedway (1.5-mile; 500 m) (Dodge)

1968 (10th) (448)

Victories
World 600; Charlotte Motor Speedway (1.5-m; 600 miles) (Dodge)

Poles
Islip 300; Islip Speedway (.2-mile) (Dodge)
Maine 300; Oxford Plains Speedway (.333-mile) (Dodge)
Dixie 500; Atlanta International Raceway (1.5-mile) (Dodge)
Sandlapper 200; Columbia Speedway (.5-mile dirt) (Dodge)

1969 (19th) (383)

Poles
Daytona 500; Daytona International Speedway (2.5-mile) (Dodge)
Texas 500; Texas International Speedway (2-mile) (Dodge)

1970 (18th) (361)

Victories
Southern 500; Darlington Raceway (1.366-mile; 500 miles) (Dodge)

1971 (8th) (560)

Victories
Rebel 400; Darlington Raceway (1.366-mile; 400 miles) (Dodge)

Poles
Dixie 500; Atlanta International Raceway (1.522-mile) (Dodge)

1972 (13th) (371)

Victories
World 600; Charlotte Motor Speedway (1.5-m; 600 miles) (Dodge)
Texas 500; Texas World Speedway (2-mile; 500 miles) (Dodge)

Poles
Wilkes 400; North Wilkesboro Speedway (.625-mile) (Dodge)

1973 (2nd) (649)

Victories
* World 600; Charlotte Motor Speedway (1.5-m; 600 miles) (Dodge)
Nashville 420; Fairgrounds Speedway (.596-m; 250 miles) (Dodge)

Poles
Daytona 500; Daytona International Speedway (2.5-mile) (Dodge)
Winston 500; Alabama Int. Motor Speedway (2.66-mile) (Dodge)
* World 600; Charlotte Motor Speedway (1.5-mile) (Dodge)
Alamo 500; Texas World Speedway (2-mile) (Dodge)
Motor State 400; Michigan International Speedway (2-m) (Dodge)

1974 (13th) (377)

Poles
Purolator 500; Pocono International Raceway (2.5-mile) (Ford)
Delaware 500; Dover Downs International Speedway (1-m) (Ford)

1975 (6th) (547)

Victories
* Winston 500; Ala. Int. Motor Speedway (2.66-m; 500 m) (Ford)
Talladega 500; Ala. Int. Motor Speedway (2.66-m; 500 m) (Ford)
Dixie 500; Atlanta Int. Raceway (1.522-mile; 500 miles) (Ford)
L.A. Times 500; Ontario Motor Speedway (2.5-mile; 500 m) (Ford)

Poles
Carolina 500; North Carolina Motor Speedway (1.017-mile) (Ford)
Southeastern 500; Bristol Int. Speedway (.533-mile) (Ford)
* Winston 500; Alabama Int. Motor Speedway (2.66-mile) (Ford)

1976 (9th) (477)

Victories
Winston 500; Alabama Int. Motor Speedway (2.66-m; 500 m) (Ford)

Poles
Southeastern 400; Bristol Int. Speedway (.533-mile) (Ford)
Dixie 500; Atlanta International Raceway (1.522-mile) (Ford)

1977 (5th) (625)

1978 (18th) (283)

Poles
Mason-Dixon 500; Dover Downs Int. Speedway (1-mile) (Chevrolet)

1979 (11th) (482)

Victories
* Atlanta 500; Atlanta Int. Raceway (1.522-m; 500 miles) (Oldsmobile)
Gabriel 400; Michigan Int. Speedway (2-mile; 400 miles) (Chevrolet)
Old Dominion 500; Martinsville Speedway (.525-m; 263 m) (Chevrolet)

Poles (1st)
Daytona 500; Daytona International Speedway (2.5-mile) (Oldsmobile)
* Atlanta 500; Atlanta International Raceway (1.522-m) (Oldsmobile)
Southeastern 500; Bristol International Raceway (.533-m) (Chevrolet)
Texas 400; Texas World Speedway (2-mile) (Chevrolet)
Firecracker 400; Daytona International Speedway (2.5-m) (Oldsmobile)
American 500; North Carolina Motor Speedway (1.017-mile) (Chevrolet)
Dixie 500; Atlanta International Raceway (1.522-mile) (Chevrolet)

1980 (14th) (453)

Victories
* Daytona 500; Daytona Int. Speedway (2.5-m; 500 miles) (Oldsmobile)
Winston 500; Alabama Int. Motor Speedway (2.66-m; 500 m) (Oldsmobile)

Poles
* Daytona 500; Daytona International Speedway (2.5-mile) (Oldsmobile)
Atlanta 500; Atlanta International Raceway (1.522-mile) (Oldsmobile)
Talladega 500; Alabama Int. Motor Speedway (2.66-mile) (Oldsmobile)
Champion Spark Plug 400; Michigan Int. Speedway (2-mile) (Chevrolet)
Old Dominion 500; Martinsville Speedway (.525-mile) (Chevrolet)
National 500; Charlotte Motor Speedway (1.5-mile) (Buick)

1981	(17th)	(359)

1982	(20th)	(357)

Poles
CRC Chem. Rebel 500; Darlington Int. Raceway (1.366-m) (Buick)

1983	(16th)	(391)

Victories
Firecracker 400; Daytona Int. Speedway (2.5-mile; 400 m) (Ford)
Poles
World 600; Charlotte Motor Speedway (1.5-mile) (Ford)

1984	(17th)	(379)

Poles
Coca-Cola 500; Atlanta International Raceway (1.522-m) (Ford)

1985	(15th)	(404)

1986	(19th)	(329)

1987	(16th)	(424)

1988	(18th)	(328)

WALTER BALLARD

1971	(12th)	(418)
1972	(7th)	(475)
1973	(10th)	(364)
1974	(16th)	(354)
1975	(16th)	(375)
1976		(110)

EARL BALMER

1964		(118)
1965		(134)
1966		(100)

Victories
Daytona International Speedway (2.5-mile; 100 miles) (Dodge)

STAN BARRETT

1981		(149)

BOB BARRON

1961	(24th)	(202)

LARRY BAUMEL

1970
Poles
Columbia 200; Columbia Speedway (.5-mile dirt) (Ford)

1971		(104)

HERMAN BEAM

1959	(13th)	(276)
1960	(8th)	(294)
1961	(9th)	(441)
1962	(7th)	(470)
1963		(191)

DICK BEATY

1957	(16th)	(219)

JOHNNY BEAUCHAMP

1959		(117)

Victories
Lakewood Speedway (1-mile dirt; 100 miles) (Ford)

1960		(166)

Victories
Nashville 400; Fairgrounds Speedway (.5-mile; 200 miles) (Chevrolet)

JOHNNY BENSON JR.

1996	(20th)	(329)

Poles
Purolator 500; Atlanta Motor Speedway (1.522-mile) (Pontiac)

1997	(11th)	(472)

Poles
DeVilbiss 400; Michigan Speedway (2-mile) (Pontiac)

1998	(22nd)	(297)
1999	(25th)	(294)

GARY BETTENHAUSEN

1974		(118)

TONY BETTENHAUSEN JR.

1974	(24th)	(215)

RICH BICKLE

1998		(129)
1999		(159)

DON BIEDERMAN

1967		(126)

EDDIE BIERSCHWALE

1985		(184)

TERRY BIVINS

1976	(T-21st)	(267)

GENE BLACK

1965		(148)

BUNKIE BLACKBURN

1960		(133)
1962		(162)
1964		(124)

BILL BLAIR

1949	(3rd)	
1950	(7th)	(145)

Victories
Vernon Fairgrounds (.5-mile dirt; 100 miles) (Mercury)

1951	(11th)	(154)
1952	(7th)	(248)

Victories
Lakewood Speedway (1-mile dirt; 100 miles) (Oldsmobile)

Poles
Occoneechee Speedway (1-mile dirt) (Oldsmobile)

1953	(14th)	(176)

Victories
Beach & Road Course (4.1-mile road; 160 miles) (Oldsmobile)

1954	(10th)	(191)

BRETT BODINE

1987		(127)
1988	(21st)	(289)
1989	(17th)	(397)
1990	(13th)	(515)

Victories
First Union 400; N. Wilkesboro Speedway (.625-m; 250 m) (Buick)

Poles
Mello Yello 500; Charlotte Motor Speedway (1.5-mile) (Buick)

1991	(22nd)	(319)

Poles
First Union 400; North Wilkesboro Speedway (.625-mile) (Buick)

1992	(11th)	(527)

Poles
Budweiser 500; Dover Downs International Speedway (1-m) (Ford)

1993	(18th)	(411)

Poles
First Union 400; North Wilkesboro Speedway (.625-mile) (Ford)
Miller Genuine Draft 400; Michigan Int. Speedway (2-m) (Ford)

1994	(20th)	(362)
1995		(235)
1996		(108)
1997		(208)
1998		(198)

GEOFF BODINE

1982	(14th)	(418)

Poles
Firecracker 400; Daytona Int. Speedway (2.5-mile) (Pontiac)
Talladega 500; Alabama Int. Motor Speedway (2.66-mile) (Pontiac)

1983	(21st)	(317)

Poles
Coca-Cola 500; Atlanta International Raceway (1.522-m) (Pontiac)

1984	(8th)	(549)

Victories
Sovran Bank 400; Martinsville Speedway (.526-m; 263 m) (Chevrolet)
Pepsi 420; Nashville Int. Raceway (.596-mile; 250 miles) (Chevrolet)
Win. West. 500; Riverside Int. Race. (2.62-m rd.; 313 m) (Chevrolet)

Poles
Busch 500; Bristol International Raceway (.533-mile) (Chevrolet)
Goody's 500; Martinsville Speedway (.526-mile) (Chevrolet)
W.W. Hodgdon American 500; N.C. Motor Speedway (1.017-m) (Chevrolet)

1985	(6th)	(613)

Poles
Wrangler Sanforset 400; Richmond Fgds. Raceway (.542-m) (Chevrolet)
Goody's 500; Martinsville Speedway (.526-mile) (Chevrolet)
Holly Farms 400; North Wilkesboro Speedway (.625-mile) (Chevrolet)

1986	(10th)	(509)

Victories
Daytona 500; Daytona Int. Speedway (2.5-mile; 500 miles) (Chevrolet)
Budweiser 500; Dover Downs Int. Speedway (1-mile; 500 m) (Chevrolet)

Poles (T-1st)
Valleydale 500; Bristol International Raceway (.533-m) (Chevrolet)
TranSouth 500; Darlington Int. Raceway (1.366-mile) (Chevrolet)
First Union 400; North Wilkesboro Speedway (.625-mile) (Chevrolet)
Coca-Cola 600; Charlotte Motor Speedway (1.5-mile) (Chevrolet)
Miller High Life 500; Pocono Int. Raceway (2.5-mile) (Chevrolet)
Busch 500; Bristol International Raceway (.533-mile) (Chevrolet)
Delaware 500; Dover Downs International Speedway (1-m) (Chevrolet)
Goody's 500; Martinsville Speedway (.526-mile) (Chevrolet)

1987	(14th)	(453)

Poles
Goody's 500; Martinsville Speedway (.526-mile) (Chevrolet)
Winston Western 500; Riverside Int. Raceway (2.62-m rd.) (Chevrolet)

Driver Resumes

1988   (6th)   (590)

Victories
Miller High Life 500; Pocono Int. Raceway (2.5-m; 500 m) (Chevrolet)

Poles
Motorcraft QP 500; Atlanta Int. Raceway (1.522-mile) (Chevrolet)
The Budweiser at the Glen; Watkins Glen Int. (2.428-m r) (Chevrolet)
Checker 500; Phoenix International Raceway (1-mile) (Chevrolet)

1989   (12th)   (497)

Victories
Holly Farms 400; N. Wilkesboro Speedway (.625-m; 250 m) (Chevrolet)

Poles
Pontiac Excitement 400; Richmond Int. Raceway (.75-mile) (Chevrolet)
Pannill Sweatshirts 500; Martinsville Speedway. (.526-m) (Chevrolet)
Champion Spark Plug 400; Michigan Int. Speedway (2-mile) (Chevrolet)

1990   (3rd)   (671)

Victories
* Hanes Activewear 500; Martinsville Sp. (.526-m; 263 m) (Ford)
AC Spark Plug 500; Pocono Int. Raceway (2.5-mile; 500 m) (Ford)
Goody's 500; Martinsville Speedway (.526-m; 263 miles) (Ford)

Poles
TranSouth 500; Darlington Int. Raceway (1.366-mile) (Ford)
* Hanes Activewear 500; Martinsville Speedway (.526-m) (Ford)

1991   (12th)   (469)

Victories
Mello Yello 500; Charlotte Motor Speedway (1.5-m; 500 m) (Ford)

Poles
TranSouth 500; Darlington Raceway (1.366-mile) (Ford)
Pyroil 500; Phoenix International Raceway (1-mile) (Ford)

1992   (10th)   (541)

Victories
Goody's 500; Martinsville Speedway (.526-m; 263 miles) (Ford)
Tyson Holly Farms 400; N. Wilkesboro Sp. (.625-m; 250 m) (Ford)

1993   (14th)   (460)

Victories
S.M. Super. 300; Sears Pt. Int. Race. (2.52-m rd.; 187m) (Ford)

Poles
Hanes 500; Martinsville Speedway (.526-mile) (Ford)

1994   (18th)   (414)

Victories
* Miller Gen. Dr. 500; Pocono Int. Raceway (2.5-m; 500m) (Ford)
* GM Good. Dealer 400; Michigan Int. Speed. (2-m; 400m) (Ford)
Tyson Holly Farms 400; N. Wilkesboro Sp. (.625-m; 250m) (Ford)

Poles (T-1st)
Goodwrench 500; North Carolina Motor Speedway (1.017-m) (Ford)
* Miller Genuine Draft 500; Pocono Int. Raceway (2.5-m) (Ford)
* GM Goodwrench Dealer 400; Michigan Int. Speedway (2-m) (Ford)
Mountain Dew Southern 500; Darlington Raceway (1.366-m) (Ford)
Splitfire Spark Plug 500; Dover Downs Int. Speed. (1-m) (Ford)

1995   (17th)   (377)

1996   (18th)   (364)

Victories
The Bud at the Glen; Watkins Glen Int. (2.45-m rd; 221m) (Ford)

1997   (18th)   (412)

Poles
UAW-GM Quality 500; Charlotte Motor Speedway (1.5-mile) (Ford)
NAPA 500; Atlanta Motor Speedway (1.54-mile) (Ford)

1998   (265)

1999   (228)

TODD BODINE

1994   (21st)   (352)

1995   (119)

1996   (134)

1997

Poles
The Bud at the Glen; Watkins Glen Int. (2.45-mile road) (Chevrolet)

1998   (133)

DAVID RAY BOGGS

1972   (173)

AL BONNELL

1949

Poles
Heidelberg Speedway (.5-mile dirt) (Oldsmobile)

NEIL BONNETT

1976   (144)

Poles
Nashville 420; Nashville Speedway (.596-mile) (Mercury)

1977   (16th)   (340)

Victories
Capital City 400; Richmond Fgds. Raceway (.542-m; 217 m) (Dodge)
L.A. Times 500; Ontario Motor Speedway (2.5-mile; 500 m) (Dodge)

Poles (1st)
Richmond 400; Richmond Fairgrounds Raceway (.542-mile) (Dodge)
Gwyn Staley 400; North Wilkesboro Speedway (.625-mile) (Dodge)
Virginia 500; Martinsville Speedway (.525-mile) (Dodge)
Firecracker 400; Daytona International Speedway (2.5-m) (Dodge)
Delaware 500; Dover Downs International Speedway (1-m) (Dodge)
Old Dominion 500; Martinsville Speedway (.525-mile) (Dodge)

1978   (17th)   (292)

Poles
Richmond 400; Richmond Fairgrounds Raceway (.542-mile) (Dodge)
Carolina 500; North Carolina Motor Speedway (1.017-mile) (Dodge)
Southeastern 500; Bristol International Raceway (.533-m) (Dodge)

1979   (21st)   (284)

Victories
Mason-Dixon 500; Dover Downs Int. Speedway (1-m; 500 m) (Mercury)
Firecracker 400; Daytona Int. Speedway (2.5-mile; 400 m) (Mercury)
Dixie 500; Atlanta Int. Raceway (1.522-mile; 500 miles) (Mercury)

Poles
World 600; Charlotte Motor Speedway (1.5-mile) (Mercury)
Gabriel 400; Michigan International Speedway (2-mile) (Mercury)
Talladega 500; Alabama Int. Motor Speedway (2.66-mile) (Mercury)
NAPA National 500; Charlotte Motor Speedway (1.5-mile) (Mercury)

1980	(11th)	(495)

Victories
Coca-Cola 500; Pocono Int. Raceway (2.5-mile; 500 miles) (Mercury)
Talladega 500; Alabama Int. Motor Speed. (2.66-m; 500 m) (Mercury)

1981	(20th)	(299)

Victories
Southern 500; Darlington Int. Raceway (1.366-m; 500 m) (Ford)
CRC Chemicals 500; Dover Downs Int. Speedway (1-m; 500m) (Ford)
Atlanta Journal 500; Atl. Int. Raceway (1.522-m; 500 m) (Ford)
Poles
World 600; Charlotte Motor Speedway (1.5-mile) (Ford)

1982	(17th)	(391)

Victories
World 600; Charlotte Motor Speedway (1.5-m; 600 miles) (Ford)

1983	(6th)	(611)

Victories
World 600; Charlotte Motor Speedway (1.5-m; 600 miles) (Chevrolet)
Atlanta Journal 500; Atl. Int. Raceway (1.522-m; 500 m) (Chevrolet)
Poles
Northwestern Bank 400; N. Wilkesboro Speedway (.625-m) (Chevrolet)
Valleydale 500; Bristol International Raceway (.533-m) (Chevrolet)
Southern 500; Darlington Int. Raceway (1.366-mile) (Chevrolet)
WW. Hodgdon American 500; N.C. Motor Speedway (1.017-m) (Chevrolet)

1984	(10th)	(532)

1985	(3rd)	(675)

Victories
Carolina 500; N.C. Motor Speedway (1.017-m; 500 miles) (Chevrolet)
Northwestern Bank 400; N. Wilkesboro Sp. (.625-m; 250 m) (Chevrolet)
Poles
Coca-Cola 500; Atlanta International Raceway (1.522-m) (Chevrolet)

1986	(13th)	(438)

Victories
Nationwise 500; N.C. Motor Speedway (1.017-m; 500 miles) (Chevrolet)

1987	(9th)	(536)

1988	(T-14th)	(433)

Victories
Pont. Excite. 400; Richmond Fgds. Race. (.542-m; 217m) (Pontiac)
Goodwrench 500; N.C. Motor Speedway (1.017-m; 500 m) (Pontiac)

1989	(15th)	(430)

KEN BOUCHARD

1988	(22nd)	(274)

RON BOUCHARD

1981	(14th)	(392)

Victories
Talladega 500; Ala. Int. Motor Speedway (2.66-m; 500 m) (Buick)

Poles
Champion Spark Plug 400; Michigan Int. Speedway (2-mile) (Buick)

1982	(8th)	(489)

Poles
Gabriel 400; Michigan International Speedway (2-mile) (Buick)

1983	(14th)	(412)

Poles
Busch Nashville 420; Nashville Int. Raceway (.596-mile) (Buick)

1984	(9th)	(536)

1985	(13th)	(448)

1986		(185)

CHUCK BOWN

1979		(119)

1994		

Poles
Food City 500; Bristol International Raceway (.533-mile) (Ford)

TREVOR BOYS

1983	(25th)	(262)

1984	(18th)	(347)

RICHARD BRICKHOUSE

1968		(119)

1969	(23rd)	(295)

Victories
Talladega 500; Ala. Int. Motor Speedway (2.66-m; 500 m) (Dodge)

DICK BROOKS

1969	(21st)	(366)

1970	(10th)	(488)

1971	(18th)	(364)

1973	(14th)	(332)

Victories
Talladega 500; Ala. Int. Motor Speedway (2.66-m; 500m) (Plymouth)

1974		(144)

1975	(11th)	(457)

1976	(8th)	(505)

1977	(6th)	(575)

1978	(6th)	(582)

1979	(17th)	(359)

1980	(22nd)	(243)

1983	(17th)	(374)

1984	(16th)	(395)

EARL BROOKS

1964		(184)
1967	(22nd)	(254)
1968	(25th)	(213)
1969		(254)
1971		(198)

PERK BROWN

| 1952 | (11th) | (152) |

Poles
Martinsville Speedway (.5-mile dirt) (Hudson)

RICHARD D. BROWN

| 1971 | | (148) |
| 1972 | | (122) |

LAIRD BRUNER

| 1954 | (15th) | (156) |

DARRELL BRYANT

| 1976 | | (106) |

HERSCHEL BUCHANAN

| 1952 | (20th) | (104) |
| 1953 | (20th) | (112) |

BOB BURCHAM

| 1974 | (17th) | (291) |

BOB BURDICK

| 1959 | | (109) |

Poles
Trenton Speedway (1-mile) (Ford)
Columbia Speedway (.5-mile dirt) (Ford)

1961

Victories
Atlanta 500; Atlanta Int. Raceway (1.5-m; 500 miles) (Pontiac)

MARVIN BURKE

1951

Victories
Oakland Stadium (.625-mile dirt; 250 miles) (Mercury)

DICK BURNS

| 1950 | (24th) | |

JEFF BURTON

1994		(246)
1995		(173)
1996	(10th)	(526)

Poles
GM Goodwrench Dealer 400; Michigan Int. Speedway (2-m) (Ford)

| 1997 | (4th) | (766) |

Victories
Interstate Bat. 500; Texas Motor Speedway (1.5-m; 500m) (Ford)
Jiffy Lube 300; New Hamp. Int. Speedway (1.058-m; 317 m) (Ford)
Hanes 500; Martinsville Speedway (.526-mile; 263 miles) (Ford)

| 1998 | (5th) | (742) |

Victories
Jiffy Lube 300; New Hamp. Int. Speedway (1.058-m; 317 m) (Ford)
Exide NASCAR SB 400; Richmond Int. Raceway (.75-m; 300m) (Ford)

| 1999 | (5th) | (829) |

Victories
Las Vegas 400; Las Vegas Motor Speedway (1.5-m; 400 m) (Ford)
TranSouth Finan. 400; Darlington Raceway (1.366-m; 400m) (Ford)
Coca-Cola 600; Lowe's Motor Speedway (1.5-mile; 600 m) (Ford)
Jiffy Lube 300; New Hamp. Int. Speedway (1.058-m; 317 m) (Ford)
Pepsi Southern 500; Darlington Raceway (1.366-m; 500 m) (Ford)
Pop Secret MP 400; N.C. Speedway (1.017-mile; 400 miles) (Ford)

WARD BURTON

1994

Poles
Mello Yello 500; Charlotte Motor Speedway (1.5-mile) (Chevrolet)

| 1995 | (19th) | (351) |

Victories
AC Delco 400; N.C. Motor Speedway (1.017-m; 400 miles) (Pontiac)

| 1996 | | (244) |

Poles
TranSouth Financial 400; Darlington Raceway (1.366-m) (Pontiac)

| 1997 | (23rd) | (307) |

Poles
Hanes 500; Martinsville Speedway (.526-mile) (Pontiac)

| 1998 | (19th) | (374) |

Poles
Miller Lite 400; Michigan Speedway (2-mile) (Pontiac)
Pennsylvania 500; Pocono Raceway (2.5-mile) (Pontiac)

| 1999 | (9th) | (620) |

Poles
Pepsi 400; Michigan Speedway (2-mile) (Pontiac)

RED BYRON

| 1949 | (1st) | |

Victories (T-1st)
Beach & Road Course (4.15-mile road; 166 miles) (Oldsmobile)
Martinsville Speedway (.5-mile dirt; 100 miles) (Oldsmobile)

Poles
Langhorne Speedway (1-mile dirt) (Oldsmobile)

1950	(14th)

Poles
Charlotte Speedway (.75-mile dirt) (Oldsmobile)

SCOTTY CAIN

1957	(23rd)	(145)

WALLY CAMPBELL

1950		

Poles
Langhorne Speedway (1-mile dirt) (Oldsmobile)

BILLY CARDEN

1951	(18th)	(111)

Poles
Asheville-Weaverville Speedway (.5-mile dirt) (Oldsmobile)
Charlotte Speedway (.75-mile dirt) (Oldsmobile)

1956	(20th)	(138)

NEIL CASTLES

1960		(132)
1963		(208)
1964	(11th)	(464)
1965	(5th)	(596)
1966	(8th)	(493)
1967	(9th)	(447)
1968	(15th)	(364)
1969	(5th)	(811)
1970	(6th)	(639)
1971	(25th)	(284)
1972		(102)

TED CHAMBERLAIN

1952	(14th)	(138)

BILL CHAMPION

1968		(118)
1969	(17th)	(399)
1970	(17th)	(363)
1971	(9th)	(503)
1972	(18th)	(320)
1973		(170)

RICHARD CHILDRESS

1973	(17th)	(301)
1974	(22nd)	(259)
1975	(3rd)	(605)
1976	(10th)	(464)
1977	(11th)	(451)
1978	(10th)	(468)
1979	(9th)	(554)
1980	(8th)	(559)
1981		(219)

SARA CHRISTIAN

1949	(8th)

FRANK CHRISTIAN

1949	(T-25th)

NEIL COLE

1951		

Victories
* Thompson Speedway (.5-mile; 100 miles) (Oldsmobile)
Poles
* Thompson Speedway (.5-mile) (Oldsmobile)

1952	(17th)	(118)

RODNEY COMBS

1987		(116)

GENE COMSTOCK

1953	(22nd)	(103)

JIM COOK

1960		

Victories
* California State Fairgrounds (1-mile dirt; 100 miles) (Dodge)
Poles
* California State Fairgrounds (1-mile dirt) (Dodge)

DOUG COOPER

1964	(18th)	(330)
1965	(16th)	(304)
1966		(102)
1967		(109)

DERRIKE COPE

1989		(238)
1990	(18th)	(451)

Victories
Daytona 500; Daytona Int. Speedway (2.5-m; 500 miles) (Chevrolet)
Budweiser 500; Dover Downs Int. Speedway (1-mile; 500 m) (Chevrolet)

1991		(232)
1992	(19th)	(399)
1993		(230)
1994		(211)
1995	(14th)	(492)
1996		(184)
1997	(21st)	(351)
1998		

Poles
UAW-GM Quality 500; Charlotte Motor Speedway (1.5-m) (Pontiac)

DOUG COX

1956		

Poles
Cleveland County Fairgrounds (.5-mile dirt) (Ford)

1958	(20th)	(173)

TOM COX

1962	(9th)	(422)

RICKY CRAVEN

1995		248)
1996	(21st)	(321)

Poles
Goody's HP 500; Martinsville Speedway (.526-mile) (Chevrolet)
Jiffy Lube 300; New Hampshire Int. Speedway (1.058-mile) (Chevrolet)

1997	(19th)	(410)
1998		

Poles
Jiffy Lube 300; New Hampshire Int. Speedway (1.058-mile) (Chevrolet)

CURTIS CRIDER

1960	(20th)	(192)
1961	(19th)	(258)
1962	(8th)	(445)
1963	(11th)	(437)
1964	(4th)	(705)

WALLY DALLENBACH JR.

1992		(223)
1993	(23rd)	(307)
1994	(196)	
1996	(23rd)	(288)
1998		(106)
1999	(T-18th)	(352)

DEAN DALTON

1971		(118)
1972	(16th)	(344)
1973		(185)
1975		(198)

LLOYD DANE

1956	(18th)	(167)

Victories
California State Fairgrounds (1-mile dirt; 100 miles) (Mercury)
Portland Speedway (.5-mile; 125 miles) (Ford)

1957	(T-17th)	(195)

Victories
Eureka Speedway (.625-mile dirt; 125 miles) (Ford)

1961		

Victories
Riverside International Raceway (2.58-m road; 100 miles) (Chevrolet)

JOEL DAVIS

1966		(102)

GEORGE DAVIS

1967		(166)

BILL DENNIS

1970		(175)
1971	(14th)	(398)

Poles
Capital City 500; Richmond Fairgrounds Raceway (.542-m) (Mercury)

BOB DERRINGTON

1964		(159)
1965	(3rd)	(610)

DAREL DIERINGER

1961		(119)

1963 (14th) (412)

Victories
Golden State 400; Riverside Int. Race. (2.7-m rd.; 400m) (Mercury)

1964 (16th) (395)

Victories
Jaycee 300; Augusta Speedway (.5-mile; 150 miles) (Mercury)

Poles
Firecracker 400; Daytona International Speedway (2.5-m) (Mercury)

1965 (10th) (487)

Victories
Daytona International Speedway (2.5-mile; 100 miles) (Mercury)

Poles
Daytona 500; Daytona International Speedway (2.5-mile) (Mercury)

1966 (16th) (340)

Victories
Independent 250; Starlite Speedway (.4-mile dirt; 100 m) (Ford)
Western N.C. 500; Asheville-Weaverville Sp. (.5-m; 250m) (Mercury)
Southern 500; Darlington Raceway (1.375-mile; 500 miles) (Mercury)

1967 (15th) (298)

Victories
* Gwyn Staley 400; N. Wilkesboro Speedway (.625-m; 250m) (Ford)

Poles
Fireball 300; Asheville-Weaverville Speedway (.5-mile) (Ford)
Southeastern 500; Bristol International Speedway (.5-m) (Ford)
* Gwyn Staley 400; North Wilkesboro Speedway (.625-mile) (Ford)
Virginia 500; Martinsville Speedway (.5-mile) (Ford)
Firecracker 400; Daytona International Speedway (2.5-m) (Ford)
Dixie 500; Atlanta International Raceway (1.5-mile) (Ford)

1968 (21st) (263)

Poles
Western N.C. 500; Asheville-Weaverville Speed. (.5-m) (Plymouth)

DICK DIXON

1965 (120)

JOHN DODD JR.

1955 (22nd) (119)

MARK DONOHUE

1973

Victories
Win. West. 500; Riverside Int. Race. (2.62-m rd; 500m) (Matador)

FRED DOVE

1953 (T-17th) (139)

RAY DUHIGG

1952 (9th) (191)

1953 (T-17th) (139)

1954 (23rd)

CLARENCE DeZALIA

1957 (19th) (188)

1958 (T-18th) (183)

BOB DUELL

1958 (130)

Poles
New Bradford Speedway (.333-mile dirt) (Ford)

GERALD DUKE

1960 (150)

GEORGE DUNN

1958 (101)

Poles
Bowman Gray Stadium (.25-mile) (Mercury)

GLENN DUNNAWAY

1949 (11th)

Poles
Hamburg Fairgrounds (.5-mile dirt) (Oldsmobile)

1950 (20th)

CLARK DWYER

1984 (189)

1985 (198)

DALE EARNHARDT

1978 (149)

1979 (8th) (593)

Victories
Southeastern 500; Bristol Int. Raceway (.533-m; 267 m) (Chevrolet)

Poles
NAPA Riverside 400; Riverside Int. Raceway (2.62-m road) (Chevrolet)
Capital City 400; Richmond Fairgrounds Raceway (.542-m) (Chevrolet)
CRC Chemicals 500; Dover Downs Int. Speedway (1-mile) (Chevrolet)
Holly Farms 400; North Wilkesboro Speedway (.625-mile) (Chevrolet)

1980 (1st) (816)

Victories
Atlanta 500; Atlanta Int. Raceway (1.522-m; 500 miles) (Chevrolet)
Valleydale SE 500; Bristol Int. Raceway (.533-m; 267m) (Chevrolet)
Busch Nashville 420; Nashville Int. Race. (.596-m; 250m) (Chevrolet)
Old Dominion 500; Martinsville Speedway (.525-m; 263 m) (Chevrolet)
National 500; Charlotte Motor Speedway (1.5-mile; 500 m) (Chevrolet)

1981 (6th) (568)

1982 (19th) (373)

Driver Resumes

Victories
CRC Ch. Rebel 500; Darlington Int. Race. (1.366-m; 500m) (Ford)

Poles
Coca-Cola 500; Atlanta International Raceway (1.522-m) (Ford)

1983 (8th) (517)

Victories
Busch Nashville 420; Nashville Int. Race. (.596-m; 250m) (Ford)
Talladega 500; Ala. Int. Motor Speedway (2.66-m; 500 m) (Ford)

1984 (4th) (724)

Victories
Talladega 500; Ala. Int. Motor Speedway (2.66-m; 500 m) (Chevrolet)
Atlanta Journal 500; Atl. Int. Raceway (1.522-m; 500 m) (Chevrolet)

1985 (11th) (500)

Victories
Miller HL 400; Richmond Fgds. Raceway (.542-m; 217 m) (Chevrolet)
Valleydale 500; Bristol Int. Raceway (.533-mile; 267 m) (Chevrolet)
* Busch 500; Bristol Int. Raceway (.533-m; 267 miles) (Chevrolet)
Goody's 500; Martinsville Speedway (.526-m; 263 miles) (Chevrolet)

Poles
* Busch 500; Bristol International Raceway (.533-mile) (Chevrolet)

1986 (1st) (778)

Victories
TranSouth 500; Darlington Int. Raceway (1.366-m; 500 m) (Chevrolet)
First Union 400; No. Wilkesboro Speedway (.625-m; 250 m) (Chevrolet)
Coca-Cola 600; Charlotte Motor Speedway (1.5-m; 600 m) (Chevrolet)
Oakwood Homes 500; Charlotte Motor Speed. (1.5-m; 500 m) (Chevrolet)
Atlanta Journal 500; Atl. Int. Raceway (1.522-m; 500 m) (Chevrolet)

Poles
Motorcraft 500; Atlanta International Raceway (1.522-m) (Chevrolet)

1987 (1st) (885)

Victories (1st)
Goodwrench 500; N.C. Motor Speedway (1.017-m; 500 miles) (Chevrolet)
Miller HL 400; Richmond Fgds. Raceway (.542-mile; 217 m) (Chevrolet)
TranSouth 500; Darlington Int. Raceway (1.366-m; 500 m) (Chevrolet)
First Union 400; No. Wilkesboro Speedway (.625-m; 250 m) (Chevrolet)
Valleydale 500; Bristol Int. Raceway (.533-m; 267 miles) (Chevrolet)
Sovran Bank 500; Martinsville Speedway (.526-m; 263 m) (Chevrolet)
Miller American 400; Michigan Int. Speedway (2-m; 400m) (Chevrolet)
Summer 500; Pocono International Raceway (2.5-m; 500 m) (Chevrolet)
Busch 500; Bristol Int. Raceway (.533-mile; 267 miles) (Chevrolet)
Southern 500; Darlington Int. Raceway (1.366-m; 500 m) (Chevrolet)
Wrangler Indigo 400; Richmond Fgds. Race. (.542-m; 217m) (Chevrolet)

Poles
Motorcraft QP 500; Atlanta Int. Raceway (1.522-mile) (Chevrolet)

1988 (3rd) (755)

Victories
Motorcraft QP 500; Atlanta Int. Raceway (1.522-m; 500 m) (Chevrolet)
Pannill Sweatshirts 500; Martinsville Sp. (.526-m; 263m) (Chevrolet)
Busch 500; Bristol International Raceway (.533-m; 267 m) (Chevrolet)

1989 (1st) (730)

Victories
First Union 400; N. Wilkesboro Speedway (.625-m; 250 m) (Chevrolet)
Budweiser 500; Dover Downs Int. Speedway (1-mile; 500 m) (Chevrolet)
Heinz South. 500; Darlington Int. Race. (1.366-m; 500 m) (Chevrolet)
Peak Performance 500; Dover Downs Int. Sp. (1-m; 500 m) (Chevrolet)
Atlanta Journal 500; Atl. Int. Raceway (1.522-m; 500 m) (Chevrolet)

1990 (2nd) (796)

Victories (1st)
Motorcraft QP 500; Atlanta Int. Raceway (1.522-m; 500 m) (Chevrolet)
TranSouth 500; Darlington Int. Raceway (1.366-m; 500 m) (Chevrolet)
Winston 500; Talladega Superspeedway (2.66-mile; 500 m) (Chevrolet)
Miller Gen. Dr. 400; Michigan Int. Speedway (2-m; 400m) (Chevrolet)
Pepsi 400; Daytona International Speedway (2.5-m; 400 m) (Chevrolet)
* Talladega Diehard 500; Talla. Supersp. (2.66-m; 500m) (Chevrolet)
* Heinz South. 500; Darling. Int. Race. (1.366-m; 500m) (Chevrolet)
Miller Gen. Dr. 400; Richmond Int. Raceway (.75-m; 300m) (Chevrolet)
Checker 500; Phoenix Int. Raceway (1-mile; 312 miles) (Chevrolet)

Poles (1st)
* Talladega Diehard 500; Talladega Superspeed. (2.66-m) (Chevrolet)
Budweiser at the Glen; Watkins Glen Int. (2.428-m road) (Chevrolet)
Busch 500; Bristol International Raceway (.533-mile) (Chevrolet)
* Heinz Southern 500; Darlington Int. Raceway (1.366-m) (Chevrolet)

1991 (2nd) (729)

Victories
Pont. Excitement 400; Richmond Int. Race. (.75-m; 300m) (Chevrolet)
Hanes 500; Martinsville Speedway (.526-mile; 263 miles) (Chevrolet)
Diehard 500; Talladega Superspeedway (2.66-m; 500 miles) (Chevrolet)
Tyson Holly Farms 400; N. Wilkesboro Sp. (.625-m; 250m) (Chevrolet)

1992 (13th) (502)

Victories
Coca-Cola 600; Charlotte Motor Speedway (1.5-m; 600 m) (Chevrolet)

Poles
Budweiser at the Glen; Watkins Glen Int. (2.45-mile) (Chevrolet)

1993 (1st) (814)

Victories
TranSouth 500; Darlington Raceway (1.366-m; 500 miles) (Chevrolet)
Coca-Cola 600; Charlotte Motor Speedway (1.5-m; 600 m) (Chevrolet)
Budweiser 500; Dover Downs Int. Speedway (1-m; 500 m) (Chevrolet)
Pepsi 400; Daytona Int. Speedway (2.5-mile; 400 miles) (Chevrolet)
Miller Gen. Dr. 500; Pocono Int. Speedway (2.5-m; 500 m) (Chevrolet)
Diehard 500; Talladega Superspeedway (2.66-m; 500 miles) (Chevrolet)

Poles
Winston 500; Talladega Superspeedway (2.66-mile) (Chevrolet)
Save Mart Super. 300; Sears Pt. Int. Raceway (2.52-m rd) (Chevrolet)

1994 (1st) (854)

Victories
TranSouth Finan. 500; Darlington Raceway (1.366-m; 500m) (Chevrolet)
Food City 500; Bristol Int. Raceway (.533-m; 267 miles) (Chevrolet)
Winston Sel. 500; Talladega Superspeedway (2.66-m; 500m) (Chevrolet)
AC Delco 500; N.C. Motor Speedway (1.017-m; 500 miles) (Chevrolet)

Poles
Pepsi 400; Daytona International Speedway (2.5-mile) (Chevrolet)
Diehard 500; Talladega Superspeedway (2.66-mile) (Chevrolet)

1995 (1st) (789)

Victories
First Union 400; No. Wilkesboro Speedway (.625-m; 250 m) (Chevrolet)
Save Mart Super. 300; Sears Pt. Race. (2.52-m rd.; 186m) (Chevrolet)
Brickyard 400; Indianapolis Motor Speed. (2.5-m; 400 m) (Chevrolet)
Goody's 500; Martinsville Speedway (.526-m; 263 miles) (Chevrolet)
NAPA 500; Atlanta Motor Speedway (1.522-mile; 500 miles) (Chevrolet)

Poles

Purolator 500; Atlanta Motor Speedway (1.522-mile) (Chevrolet)
Pepsi 400; Daytona International Speedway (2.5-mile) (Chevrolet)
Miller Genuine Draft 400; Richmond Int. Raceway (.75-m) (Chevrolet)

1996	(4th)	(737)

Victories

Goodwrench 400; N.C. Motor Speedway (1.017-mile; 400 m) (Chevrolet)
Purolator 500; Atlanta Motor Speedway (1.522-m; 500 m) (Chevrolet)

Poles

Daytona 500; Daytona International Speedway (2.5-mile) (Chevrolet)
The Bud at the Glen; Watkins Glen Int. (2.45-mile road) (Chevrolet)

1997	(6th)	(681)
1998	(9th)	(575)

Victories

Daytona 500; Daytona Int. Speedway (2.5-mile; 500 miles) (Chevrolet)

1999	(7th)	(771)

Victories

Diehard 500; Talladega Superspeedway (2.66-mile; 500 m) (Chevrolet)
Goody's HP 500; Bristol Motor Speedway (.533-m; 267 m) (Chevrolet)
Winston 500; Talladega Superspeedway (2.66-m; 500 miles) (Chevrolet)

RALPH EARNHARDT

1956

Poles

Buddy Shuman 250; Hickory Speedway (.4-mile dirt) (Ford)

1961	(25th)	(197)
1962		(165)

SONNY EASLEY

1976		(111)

RAY ELDER

1969		(124)
1971		(111)

Victories

Motor Trend 500; Riverside Int. Race. (2.62-m rd.; 500m) (Dodge)

1972		(111)

Victories

Golden St. 400; Riverside Int. Race. (2.62-m rd.; 400 m) (Dodge)

HOSS ELLINGTON

1969		(238)

BILL ELLIOTT

1977		(144)
1978	(24th)	(248)
1979	(23rd)	(267)
1980		(197)

1981	(25th)	(266)

Poles

CRC Chem. Rebel 500; Darlington Int. Raceway (1.366-m) (Ford)

1982	(15th)	(407)

Poles

Champion Spark Plug 400; Michigan Int. Speedway (2-mile) (Ford)

1983	(3rd)	(709)

Victories

Win. West. 500; Riverside Int. Race. (2.62-m rd.; 313 m) (Ford)

1984	(1st)	(760)

Victories

* Miller HL 400; Michigan Int. Speedway (2-m; 400 miles) (Ford)
Miller HL 500; Charlotte Motor Speedway (1.5-m; 500 m) (Ford)
WW. Hodgdon Amer. 500; N.C. Motor Sp. (1.017-m; 500 m) (Ford)

Poles (T-1st)

* Miller High Life 400; Michigan Int. Speedway (2-mile) (Ford)
Like Cola 500; Pocono International Raceway (2.5-mile) (Ford)
Champion Spark Plug 400; Michigan Int. Speedway (2-mile) (Ford)
Atlanta Journal 500; Atlanta Int. Raceway (1.522-mile) (Ford)

1985	(1st)	(791)

Victories (1st)

* Daytona 500; Daytona Int. Speedway (2.5-m; 500 miles) (Ford)
Coca-Cola 500; Atlanta Int. Raceway (1.522-m; 500 miles) (Ford)
* TranSouth 500; Darlington Int. Raceway (1.366-m; 500m) (Ford)
* Winston 500; Ala. Int. Motor Speedway (2.66-m; 500 m) (Ford)
Budweiser 500; Dover Downs Int. Speedway (1-mile; 500 m) (Ford)
* Van Scoy DM 500; Pocono Int. Raceway (2.5-mile; 500 m) (Ford)
Miller 400; Michigan Int. Speedway (2-mile; 400 miles) (Ford)
* Summer 500; Pocono Int. Raceway (2.5-mile; 500 miles) (Ford)
* Champion SP 400; Michigan Int. Speedway (2-m; 400 m) (Ford)
* Southern 500; Darlington Int. Raceway (1.366-m; 500 m) (Ford)
Atlanta Journal 500; Atl. Int. Raceway (1.522-m; 500 m) (Ford)

Poles (1st)

* Daytona 500; Daytona International Speedway (2.5-mile) (Ford)
* TranSouth 500; Darlington Int. Raceway (1.366-mile) (Ford)
* Winston 500; Alabama Int. Motor Speedway (2.66-mile) (Ford)
World 600; Charlotte Motor Speedway (1.5-mile) (Ford)
* Van Scoy Dia. Mine 500; Pocono Int. Raceway (2.5-mile) (Ford)
Pepsi Firecracker 400; Daytona Int. Speedway (2.5-mile) (Ford)
* Summer 500; Pocono International Raceway (2.5-mile) (Ford)
Talladega 500; Alabama Int. Motor Speedway (2.66-mile) (Ford)
* Champion Spark Plug 400; Michigan Int. Speedway (2-m) (Ford)
* Southern 500; Darlington Int. Raceway (1.366-mile) (Ford)
Delaware 500; Dover Downs International Speedway (1-m) (Ford)

1986	(4th)	(610)

Victories

Miller American 400; Michigan Int. Speedway (2-m; 400m) (Ford)
Champion SP 400; Michigan Int. Speedway (2-m; 400 miles) (Ford)

Poles

Daytona 500; Daytona International Speedway (2.5-mile) (Ford)
Winston 500; Alabama Int. Motor Speedway (2.66-mile) (Ford)
Talladega 500; Alabama Int. Motor Speedway (2.66-mile) (Ford)
Atlanta Journal 500; Atlanta Int. Raceway (1.522-mile) (Ford)

1987   (2nd)   (682)

Victories
* Daytona 500; Daytona Int. Speedway (2.5-m; 500 miles) (Ford)
* Talladega 500; Ala. Int. Motor Speedway (2.66-m; 500m) (Ford)
Champion SP 400; Michigan Int. Speedway (2-m; 400 miles) (Ford)
Oakwood Homes 500; Charlotte Motor Speed. (1.5-m; 500 m) (Ford)
AC Delco 500; N.C. Motor Speedway (1.017-m; 500 miles) (Ford)
* Atlanta Journal 500; Atl. Int. Raceway (1.522-m; 500m) (Ford)

Poles (1st)
* Daytona 500; Daytona International Speedway (2.5-mile) (Ford)
First Union 400; North Wilkesboro Speedway (.625-mile) (Ford)
Winston 500; Alabama Int. Motor Speedway (2.66-mile) (Ford)
Coca-Cola 600; Charlotte Motor Speedway (1.5-mile) (Ford)
Budweiser 500; Dover Downs International Speedway (1-m) (Ford)
* Talladega 500; Alabama Int. Motor Speedway (2.66-mile) (Ford)
Holly Farms 400; North Wilkesboro Speedway (.625-mile) (Ford)
* Atlanta Journal 500; Atlanta Int. Raceway (1.522-mile) (Ford)

1988   (1st)   (851)

Victories (T-1st)
Valleydale Meats 500; Bristol Int. Race. (.533-m; 267m) (Ford)
Budweiser 500; Dover Downs Int. Speedway (1-mile; 500 m) (Ford)
Pepsi Firecracker 400; Daytona Int. Speed. (2.5-m; 400m) (Ford)
AC Spark Plug 500; Pocono Int. Raceway (2.5-mile; 500 m) (Ford)
* Southern 500; Darlington Int. Raceway (1.366-m; 500 m) (Ford)
Delaware 500; Dover Downs Int. Speedway (1-m; 500 miles) (Ford)

Poles (1st)
Goodwrench 500; North Carolina Motor Speedway (1.017-m) (Ford)
Miller High Life 400; Michigan Int. Speedway (2-mile) (Ford)
Champion Spark Plug 400; Michigan Int. Speedway (2-mile) (Ford)
* Southern 500; Darlington Int. Raceway (1.366-mile) (Ford)
Holly Farms 400; North Wilkesboro Speedway (.625-mile) (Ford)
AC Delco 500; North Carolina Motor Speedway (1.017-mile) (Ford)

1989   (6th)   (610)

Victories
Miller High Life 400; Michigan Int. Speedway (2-m; 400m) (Ford)
AC Spark Plug 500; Pocono Int. Raceway (2.5-mile; 500 m) (Ford)
Autoworks 500; Phoenix Int. Raceway (1-mile; 312 miles) (Ford)

Poles
Miller High Life 400; Richmond Int. Raceway (.75-mile) (Ford)
All Pro Auto Parts 500; Charlotte Motor Speedway (1.5-m) (Ford)

1990   (4th)   (648)

Victories
* Peak Antifreeze 500; Dover Downs Int. Sp. (1-m; 500 m) (Ford)

Poles
Winston 500; Talladega Superspeedway (2.66-mile) (Ford)
* Peak Antifreeze 500; Dover Downs Int. Speedway (1-m) (Ford)

1991   (T-9th)   (541)

Victories
Pepsi 400; Daytona Int. Speedway (2.5-mile; 400 miles) (Ford)

Poles
Bud 500; Bristol International Raceway (.533-mile) (Ford)
Hardee's 500; Atlanta Motor Speedway (1.522-mile) (Ford)

1992   (1st)   (704)

Victories (T-1st)
Goodwrench 500; N.C. Motor Speedway (1.017-m; 500 miles) (Ford)
* Pont. Excite. 400; Richmond Int. Race. (.75-m; 300 m) (Ford)
Motorcraft 500; Atlanta Motor Speedway (1.522-m; 500 m) (Ford)
TranSouth 500; Darlington Raceway (1.366-m; 500 miles) (Ford)
Hooters 500; Atlanta Motor Speedway (1.522-m; 500 miles) (Ford)

Poles
* Pontiac Excitement 400; Richmond Int. Raceway (.75-m) (Ford)
Coca-Cola 600; Charlotte Motor Speedway (1.5-mile) (Ford)

1993   (6th)   (627)

Poles
Diehard 500; Talladega Superspeedway (2.66-mile) (Ford)
Slick 50 500; Phoenix International Raceway (1-mile) (Ford)

1994   (11th)   (518)

Victories
Mt. Dew Southern 500; Darlington Raceway (1.366-m; 500m) (Ford)

Poles
TranSouth Financial 500; Darlington Raceway (1.366-mile) (Ford)

1995   (10th)   (562)

Poles
Miller Genuine Draft 500; Pocono Int. Raceway (2.5-mile) (Ford)
Dura-Lube 500; Phoenix International Raceway (1-mile) (Ford)

1996   (19th)   (337)

1997   (8th)   (601)

Poles
Exide NASCAR Sel. Bat. 400; Richmond Int. Race. (.75-m) (Ford)

1998   (T-14th)   (473)

1999   (20th)   (341)

STICK ELLIOTT

1963	(22nd)	(254)
1965		(109)
1966		(121)

TOMMY ELLIS

1984		(186)
1986	(22nd)	(286)

ERICK ERICKSON

1951	(22nd)	(101)

RAY ERICKSON

1949	(9th)

HERB ESTES

1958		(119)

JOE EUBANKS

1951 (T-23rd)

Poles
Columbia Speedway (.5-mile dirt) (Oldsmobile)

1952 (8th) (206)

1953 (7th) (256)

Poles
Martinsville Speedway (.5-mile dirt) (Hudson)
Central City Speedway (.5-mile dirt) (Hudson)

1954 (5th) (441)

1955 (24th) (112)

1956 (14th) (244)

Poles
Southern States Fairgrounds (.5-mile dirt) (Ford)
Newport Speedway (.5-mile dirt) (Ford)

1958

Victories
Orange Speedway (.9-mile dirt; 99 miles) (Pontiac)

1959 (100)

JIM FIEBELKORN

1951 (19th) (108)

LOU FIGARO

1951 (21st) (105)

Victories
* Carrell Speedway (.5-mile dirt; 100 miles) (Hudson)

Poles
* Carrell Speedway (.5-mile dirt) (Hudson)

BOB FLOCK

1949 (5th)

Victories (T-1st)
* Occoneechee Speedway (1-mile dirt; 200 miles) (Oldsmobile)
Wilkes 200; North Wilkesboro Speedway (.5-m dirt; 100 m) (Oldsmobile)

Poles (1st)
Charlotte Speedway (.75-mile dirt) (Hudson)
* Occoneechee Speedway (1-mile dirt) (Oldsmobile)

1950 (22nd)

1951 (8th) (159)

Victories
Greenville-Pickens Speedway (.5-mile dirt; 100 miles) (Oldsmobile)

Poles
Central City Speedway (.5-mile dirt) (Oldsmobile)

1952

Victories
Asheville-Weaverville Speedway (.5-mile dirt; 100 miles) (Hudson)

FONTY FLOCK

1949 (4th)

1950 (17th)

Victories
Langhorne Speedway (1-mile dirt; 200 miles) (Oldsmobile)

Poles
Martinsville Speedway (.5-mile dirt) (Oldsmobile)
Occoneechee Speedway (1-mile dirt) (Oldsmobile)

1951 (1st) (514)

Victories (1st)
* Occoneechee Speedway (1-mile dirt; 150 miles) (Oldsmobile)
* Wilkes Co. 150; N. Wilkesboro Speed. (.625-m dt.; 94m) (Oldsmobile)
* Bainbridge Speedway (1-mile dirt; 100 miles) (Oldsmobile)
Asheville-Weaverville Speedway (.5-mile dirt; 100 miles) (Oldsmobile)
* Altamont Speedway (.5-mile dirt; 100 miles) (Oldsmobile)
* Dayton Speedway (.5-mile; 100 miles) (Oldsmobile)
* Wilson Speedway (.5-mile dirt; 100 miles (Oldsmobile)
Wilkes 200; No. Wilkesboro Speedway (.625-m dirt; 125 m) (Oldsmobile)

Poles (1st)
Charlotte Speedway (.75-mile dirt) (Oldsmobile)
* Occoneechee Speedway (1-mile dirt) (Oldsmobile)
Arizona State Fairgrounds (1-mile dirt) (Oldsmobile)
* Wilkes Co. 150; No. Wilkesboro Speedway (.625-m dirt) (Oldsmobile)
* Bainbridge Speedway (1-mile dirt) (Oldsmobile)
Heidelberg Speedway (.5-mile dirt) (Oldsmobile)
Monroe County Fairgrounds (.5-mile dirt) (Oldsmobile)
* Altamont Speedway (.5-mile dirt; 100 miles) (Oldsmobile)
Fort Miami Speedway (.5-mile dirt) (Oldsmobile)
Langhorne Speedway (1-mile dirt) (Oldsmobile)
* Dayton Speedway (.5-mile) (Oldsmobile)
* Wilson Speedway (.5-mile dirt) (Oldsmobile)
Carrell Speedway (.5-mile dirt) (Oldsmobile)

1952 (4th) (407)

Victories
* Southern 500; Darlington Raceway (1.25-m; 500 miles) (Oldsmobile)
Occoneechee Speedway (1-mile dirt; 150 miles) (Oldsmobile)

Poles
Dayton Speedway (.5-mile) (Oldsmobile)
Fort Miami Speedway (.5-mile) (Oldsmobile)
Occoneechee Speedway (1-mile dirt) (Oldsmobile)
Charlotte Speedway (.75-mile dirt) (Oldsmobile)
* Southern 500; Darlington Raceway (1.25-mile) (Oldsmobile)
Central City Speedway (.5-mile dirt) (Oldsmobile)
Dayton Speedway (.5-mile) (Oldsmobile)

1953 (5th) (453)

Victories
Raleigh 300; Raleigh Speedway (1-mile; 300 miles) (Hudson)
Wilson Speedway (.5-mile dirt; 100 miles) (Hudson)
Asheville-Weaverville Speedway (.5-m dirt; 100 miles) (Hudson)
Hickory Speedway (.5-mile dirt; 100 miles) (Hudson)

Poles
Powell Motor Speedway (.5-mile dirt) (Oldsmobile)
Southern 500; Darlington Raceway (1.375-mile) (Hudson)
Martinsville Speedway (.5-mile dirt) (Oldsmobile)

1955   (10th)   (306)

Victories
Columbia Speedway (.5-mile dirt; 100 miles) (Chevrolet)
* Mid-South 250; Memphis-Ark. Sp. (1.5-m dirt; 250m) (Chrysler)
* Raleigh Speedway (1-mile; 100 miles) (Chrysler)

Poles
Forsyth County Fairgrounds (.5-mile dirt) (Chrysler)
Fonda Speedway (.5-mile dirt) (Chrysler)
Bay Meadows Speedway (1-mile dirt) (Chrysler)
* Mid-South 250; Memphis-Arkansas Speed. (1.5-m dirt) (Chrysler)
* Raleigh Speedway (1-mile) (Chrysler)
Memphis-Arkansas Speedway (1.5-mile dirt) (Chrysler)

1956

Victories
* Charlotte Speedway (.75-mile dirt; 100 miles) (Chrysler)

Poles
* Charlotte Speedway (.75-mile dirt) (Chrysler)
Palm Beach Speedway (.5-mile) (Chrysler)

TIM FLOCK

1949   (7th)

1950   (6th)   (170)

Victories
Charlotte Speedway (.75-mile dirt; 150 miles) (Lincoln)

Poles
Langhorne Speedway (1-mile dirt) (Lincoln)

1951   (2nd)   (495)

Victories
Lakeview Speedway (.75-mile dirt; 113 miles) (Oldsmobile)
Columbus Speedway (.5-mile dirt; 100 miles) (Oldsmobile)
Fort Miami Speedway (.5-mile dirt; 100 miles) (Oldsmobile)
* Morristown Speedway (.5-mile dirt; 100 miles) (Oldsmobile)
* Columbia Speedway (.5-mile dirt; 100 miles) (Oldsmobile)
Pine Grove Speedway (.5-mile dirt; 100 miles) (Oldsmobile)
Lakewood Speedway (1-mile dirt; 100 miles) (Hudson)

Poles
Beach & Road Course (4.1-mile road) (Lincoln)
Martinsville Speedway (.5-mile dirt) (Oldsmobile)
Dayton Speedway (.5-mile) (Oldsmobile)
* Morristown Speedway (.5-mile dirt) (Oldsmobile)
Greenville-Pickens Speedway (.5-mile dirt) (Oldsmobile)
* Columbia Speedway (.5-mile dirt) (Oldsmobile)

1952   (1st)   (536)

Victories (T–1st)
* Palm Beach Speedway (.5-mile dirt; 100 miles) (Hudson)
Fort Miami Speedway (.5-mile dirt; 100 miles) (Hudson)
Occoneechee Speedway (1-mile dirt; 100 miles) (Hudson)
Motor City 250; Michigan State Fgds. (1-m dirt; 250 m) (Hudson)
* Wine Creek Race Track (.5-mile dirt; 100 miles) (Hudson)
* Monroe Speedway (.5-mile dirt; 100 miles) (Hudson)
Playland Park Speedway (.5-mile dirt; 100 miles) (Hudson)
Monroe County Fairgrounds (.5-mile dirt; 100 miles) (Hudson)

Poles
* Palm Beach Speedway (.5-mile dirt) (Hudson)
Lakewood Speedway (1-mile dirt) (Hudson)
* Wine Creek Race Track (.5-mile) (Hudson)
* Monroe Speedway (.5-mile dirt) (Hudson)

1953   (6th)   (344)

Victories
Hickory Speedway (.5-mile dirt; 100 miles) (Hudson)

Poles
Charlotte Speedway (.75-mile dirt) (Hudson)
Hickory Speedway (.5-mile dirt) (Hudson)
Lakewood Speedway (1-mile dirt) (Hudson)

1954

Poles
Central City Speedway (.5-mile dirt) (Oldsmobile)

1955   (1st)   (771)

Victories (1st)
* Beach & Road Course (4.1-mile road; 160 miles) (Chrysler)
Chisholm Speedway (.5-mile dirt; 100 miles) (Chrysler)
* Langhorne Speedway (1-mile dirt; 150 miles) (Chrysler)
Arizona State Fairgrounds (1-mile dirt; 100 miles) (Chrysler)
Martinsville Speedway (.5-mile dirt; 100 miles) (Chrysler)
Richmond 200; Atlantic Rural Fgds. (.5-m dirt; 100 m) (Chrysler)
Monroe County Fairgrounds (.5-mile dirt; 100 miles) (Chrysler)
* Southern States Fairgrounds (.5-m dirt; 100 miles) (Chrysler)
* Piedmont Interstate Fgds. (.5-mile dirt; 100 miles) (Chrysler)
* Asheville-Weaverville Speedway (.5-m dirt; 100 m) (Chrysler)
* Morristown Speedway (.5-mile dirt; 100 miles) (Chrysler)
* New York State Fairgrounds (1-mile dirt; 100 miles) (Chrysler)
Bay Meadows Speedway (1-mile dirt; 250 miles) (Chrysler)
* Montgomery Speedway (.5-mile; 100 miles) (Chrysler)
* Langhorne Speedway (1-mile dirt; 250 miles) (Chrysler)
Greenville-Pickens Speedway (.5-mile dirt; 100 miles) (Chrysler)
Columbia Speedway (.5-mile dirt; 100 miles) (Chrysler)
* Orange Speedway (1-mile dirt; 100 miles) (Chrysler)

Poles (1st)
* Beach & Road Course (4.1-mile road) (Chrysler)
Columbia Speedway (.5-mile dirt) (Chrysler)
Orange Speedway (1-mile dirt) (Chrysler)
* Langhorne Speedway (1-mile dirt) (Chrysler)
Hickory Speedway (.4-mile dirt) (Chrysler)
State Fairgrounds (.5-mile dirt) (Chrysler)
* Southern States Fairgrounds (.5-mile dirt) (Chrysler)
* Piedmont Interstate Fairgrounds (.5-mile dirt) (Chrysler)
* Asheville-Weaverville Speedway (.5-mile dirt) (Chrysler)
* Morristown Speedway (.5-mile dirt) (Chrysler)
Altamont-Schnectady Fairgrounds (.5-mile dirt) (Chrysler)
* New York State Fairgrounds (1-mile dirt) (Chrysler)
Southern States Fairgrounds (.5-mile dirt) (Chrysler)
Forsyth County Fairgrounds (.5-mile dirt) (Chrysler)
Raleigh Speedway (1-mile) (Chrysler)
* Montgomery Speedway (.5-mile) (Chrysler)
* Langhorne Speedway (1-mile dirt) (Chrysler)
* Orange Speedway (1-mile dirt) (Chrysler)

1956   (9th)   (342)

Victories
* Hickory Speedway (.4-mile dirt; 80 miles) (Chrysler)
* Beach & Road Course (4.1-mile road; 160 miles) (Chrysler)
Wilkes Co. 160; N. Wilkesboro Sp. (.625-m dirt; 100m) (Chrysler)
Road America (4-mile road; 252 miles) (Mercury)

Poles
* Hickory Speedway (.4-mile dirt) (Chrysler)
* Beach & Road Course (4.1-mile road) (Chrysler)
Lakewood Speedway (1-mile dirt) (Chrysler)
Chisholm Speedway (.5-mile dirt) (Ford)
Columbia Speedway (.5-mile dirt) (Ford)

JIMMY FLORIAN

1950   (11th)   (104)

Victories
Dayton Speedway (.5-mile; 100 miles) (Ford)

Poles
Poor Man's 500; Canfield Speedway (.5-mile dirt) (Ford)

GEORGE FOLLMER

1974   (168)

Poles
Tuborg 400; Riverside Int. Raceway (2.62-mile road) (Matador)

ELLIOTT FORBES-ROBINSON

1981   (139)

A.J. FOYT

1964

Victories
Firecracker 400; Daytona Int. Speedway (2.5-mile; 400 m) (Dodge)

1965

Victories
Firecracker 400; Daytona Int. Speedway (2.5-mile; 400 m) (Ford)

1969   (105)

Poles
Motor Trend 500; Riverside Int. Raceway (2.7-mile road) (Ford)

1970

Victories
Motor Trend 500; Riverside Int. Race. (2.62-m rd.; 506m) (Ford)

1971   (160)

Victories
* Miller HL 500; Ontario Motor Speedway (2.5-m; 500 m) (Mercury)
* Atlanta 500; Atlanta Int. Raceway (1.522-m; 500 miles) (Mercury)

Poles
Daytona 500; Daytona International Speedway (2.5-mile) (Mercury)
* Miller High Life 500; Ontario Motor Speedway (2.5-m) (Mercury)
* Atlanta 500; Atlanta International Raceway (1.522-m) (Mercury)

1972   (25th)   (207)

Victories
Daytona 500; Daytona Int. Speedway (2.5-mile; 500 miles) (Mercury)
* Miller HL 500; Ontario Motor Speedway (2.5-m; 500 m) (Mercury)

Poles
Winston Western 500; Riverside Int. Raceway (2.62-m rd.) (Mercury)
* Miller High Life 500; Ontario Motor Speedway (2.5-m) (Mercury)
Texas 500; Texas World Speedway (2-mile) (Mercury)

1976

Poles
Firecracker 400; Daytona International Speedway (2.5-m) (Chevrolet)

1977   (131)

Poles
Winston 500; Alabama Int. Motor Speedway (2.66-mile) (Chevrolet)

LARRY FRANK

1959   (19th)   (201)

1962   (23rd)   (243)

Victories
Southern 500; Darlington Raceway (1.375-m; 500 miles) (Ford)

1963   (151)

1964   (140)

JOE FRASSON

1970   (25th)   (299)

1971   (24th)   (285)

1972   (155)

1973   (162)

1974   (142)

1975   (107)

TOMMY GALE

1977   (125)

1978   (T-21st)   (271)

1979   (24th)   (260)

1980   (17th)   (288)

1981   (19th)   (345)

1982   (24th)   (306)

1983   (121)

HARRY GANT

1979   (20th)   (290)

Poles
Coca-Cola 500; Pocono International Raceway (2.5-mile) (Chevrolet)

1980   (10th)   (527)

1981   (4th)   (620)

Poles
Talladega 500; Alabama Int. Motor Speedway (2.66-mile) (Buick)
Southern 500; Darlington Int. Raceway (1.366-mile) (Pontiac)
Atlanta Journal 500; Atlanta Int. Raceway (1.522-mile) (Pontiac)

1982 (4th) (588)

Victories
Va. National Bank 500; Martinsville Sp. (.525-m; 263m) (Buick)
* National 500; Charlotte Motor Speedway (1.5-m; 500 m) (Buick)

Poles
* National 500; Charlotte Motor Speedway (1.5-mile) (Buick)

1983 (7th) (522)

Victories
TranSouth 500; Darlington Int. Raceway (1.366-m; 500 m) (Buick)

1984 (3rd) (737)

Victories
Like Cola 500; Pocono Int. Raceway (2.5-mile; 500 miles) (Chevrolet)
* Southern 500; Darlington Int. Raceway (1.366-m; 500 m) (Chevrolet)
Delaware 500; Dover Downs Int. Speedway (1-m; 500 miles) (Chevrolet)

Poles
W.W. Hodgdon Carolina 500; N.C. Motor Speedway (1.017-m) (Chevrolet)
World 600; Charlotte Motor Speedway (1.5-mile) (Chevrolet)
* Southern 500; Darlington Int. Raceway (1.366-mile) (Chevrolet)

1985 (5th) (622)

Victories
Sovran Bank 500; Martinsville Speedway (.526-m; 263 m) (Chevrolet)
Delaware 500; Dover Downs Int. Speedway (1-mile; 500 m) (Chevrolet)
Holly Farms 400; No. Wilkesboro Speedway (.625-m; 250m) (Chevrolet)

Poles
Valleydale 500; Bristol International Raceway (.533-m) (Chevrolet)
Miller 500; Charlotte Motor Speedway (1.5-mile) (Chevrolet)
Atlanta Journal 500; Atlanta Int. Raceway (1.522-mile) (Chevrolet)

1986 (14th) (429)

Poles
Summer 500; Pocono International Raceway (2.5-mile) (Chevrolet)
Wrangler Indigo 400; Richmond Fgds. Raceway (.542-mile) (Chevrolet)

1987 (181)

Poles
Valleydale 500; Bristol International Raceway (.533-m) (Chevrolet)

1988 (173)

1989 (8th) (522)

Victories
TranSouth 500; Darlington Int. Raceway (1.366-m; 500 m) (Oldsmobile)

1990 (17th) (474)

Victories
Miller Gen. Dr. 500; Pocono Int. Raceway (2.5-m; 500 m) (Oldsmobile)

1991 (6th) (611)

Victories (T–1st)
Winston 500; Talladega Superspeedway (2.66-m; 500 miles) (Oldsmobile)
Heinz Southern 500; Darlington Raceway (1.366-m; 500 m) (Oldsmobile)
Miller Gen. Dr. 400; Richmond Int. Raceway (.75-m; 300m) (Oldsmobile)
Peak Antifreeze 500; Dover Downs Int. Speed. (1-m; 500m) (Oldsmobile)
Goody's 500; Martinsville Speedway (.526-m; 263 miles) (Oldsmobile)

Poles
Tyson Holly Farms 400; No. Wilkesboro Speedway (.625-m) (Oldsmobile)

1992 (5th) (654)

Victories
Budweiser 500; Dover Downs Int. Speedway (1-m; 500 m) (Oldsmobile)
Champion SP 400; Michigan Int. Speedway (2-m; 400 miles) (Oldsmobile)

1993 (13th) (466)

Poles
Hooters 500; Atlanta Motor Speedway (1.522-mile) (Chevrolet)

1994 (224)

Poles
Goody's 500; Bristol International Raceway (.533-mile) (Chevrolet)

WALSON GARDNER

1968 (100)

DICK GETTY

1957 (22nd) (148)

MICKEY GIBBS

1991 (116)

CHARLIE GLOTZBACH

1967 (168)

1968 (17th) (351)

Victories
* National 500; Charlotte Motor Speedway (1.5-m; 500 m) (Dodge)

Poles
Firecracker 400; Daytona International Speedway (2.5-m) (Dodge)
Southern 500; Darlington Raceway (1.375-mile) (Dodge)
* National 500; Charlotte Motor Speedway (1.5-mile) (Dodge)

1969 (249)

Poles
American 500; North Carolina Motor Speedway (1.017-mile) (Dodge)

1970 (23rd) (313)

Victories
Daytona International Speedway (2.5-mile; 125 miles) (Dodge)
* Yankee 400; Michigan Int. Speedway (2.04-m; 400 miles) (Dodge)

Poles
Rebel 400; Darlington Raceway (1.375-mile) (Dodge)
* Yankee 400; Michigan International Speedway (2.04-m) (Dodge)
National 500; Charlotte Motor Speedway (1.5-mile) (Dodge)
American 500; North Carolina Motor Speedway (1.017-mile) (Dodge)

1971 (269)

Victories
Volunteer 500; Bristol Int. Speedway (.533-m; 267 miles) (Chevrolet)

Poles
World 600; Charlotte Motor Speedway (1.5-mile) (Chevrolet)
National 500; Charlotte Motor Speedway (1.5-mile) (Chevrolet)
American 500; North Carolina Motor Speedway (1.017-mile) (Chevrolet)
Wilkes 400; North Wilkesboro Speedway (.625-mile) (Chevrolet)

1974 (188)

PAUL GOLDSMITH

1956   **(19th)**   **(159)**

Victories
Langhorne Speedway (1-mile dirt; 300 miles) (Chevrolet)

1957   **(10th)**   **(340)**

Victories
Greensboro Fairgrounds (.333-mile dirt; 83 miles) (Ford)
Richmond 200; Atlantic Rural Fgds. (.5-mile dirt; 100 m) (Ford)
Lancaster Speedway (.5-mile dirt; 100 miles) (Ford)
Raleigh 250; Raleigh Speedway (1-mile; 250 miles) (Ford)

Poles
Indian River GC 100; Titusville-Cocoa Speed. (1.6-m rd.) (Chevrolet)
Langhorne Speedway (1-mile dirt) (Ford)
Virginia 500; Martinsville Speedway (.5-mile) (Ford)
Langhorne Speedway (1-mile dirt) (Ford)

1958

Victories
* Beach & Road Course (4.1-mile road; 160 miles) (Pontiac)

Poles
* Beach & Road Course (4.1-mile road) (Pontiac)

1963

Poles
Riverside 500; Riverside Int. Raceway (2.7-mile road) (Pontiac)

1964   **(194)**

Poles
Daytona 500; Daytona International Speedway (2.5-mile) (Plymouth)

1966   **(11th)**   **(414)**

Victories
Daytona International Speedway (2.5-mile; 100 miles) (Plymouth)
* Peach Blossom 500; N.C. Motor Speedway (1-m; 500 m) (Plymouth)
Volunteer 500; Bristol Int. Speedway (.5-m; 250 miles) (Plymouth)

Poles
* Peach Blossom 500; N.C. Motor Speedway (1-mile) (Plymouth)

1967	(14th)	(324)
1968		(154)
1969		(166)

CECIL GORDON

1969	(13th)	(495)
1970	(21st)	(335)
1971	(4th)	(831)
1972	(4th)	(598)
1973	(6th)	(558)
1974	(8th)	(434)
1975	(7th)	(545)
1976	(15th)	(391)
1977	(13th)	(390)

1978		(238)
1979	(25th)	(233)
1980	(19th)	(269)
1981		(146)

JEFF GORDON

1993   **(17th)**   **(420)**

Poles
Mello Yello 500; Charlotte Motor Speedway (1.5-mile) (Chevrolet)

1994   **(8th)**   **(570)**

Victories
* Coca-Cola 600; Charlotte Motor Speedway (1.5-m; 600 m) (Chevrolet)
Brickyard 400; Indianapolis Motor Speedway (2.5-m; 400m) (Chevrolet)

Poles
* Coca-Cola 600; Charlotte Motor Speedway (1.5-mile) (Chevrolet)

1995   **(3rd)**   **(777)**

Victories (1st)
* Goodwrench 500; N.C. Motor Speedway (1.017-m; 500 m) (Chevrolet)
Purolator 500; Atlanta Motor Speedway (1.522-m; 500 m) (Chevrolet)
Food City 500; Bristol Int. Raceway (.533-m; 267 miles) (Chevrolet)
Pepsi 400; Daytona Int. Speedway (2.5-mile; 400 miles) (Chevrolet)
Slick 50 300; New Hamp. Int. Speedway (1.058-m; 317 m) (Chevrolet)
Mt. Dew Southern 500; Darlington Raceway (1.366-m; 500m) (Chevrolet)
MBNA 500; Dover Downs Int. Speedway (1-mile; 500 miles) (Chevrolet)

Poles (1st)
* Goodwrench 500; N.C. Motor Speedway (1.017-mile) (Chevrolet)
Pontiac Excitement 400; Richmond Int. Raceway (.75-mile) (Chevrolet)
TranSouth Financial 400; Darlington Raceway (1.366-mile) (Chevrolet)
First Union 400; North Wilkesboro Speedway (.625-mile) (Chevrolet)
Coca-Cola 600; Charlotte Motor Speedway (1.5-mile) (Chevrolet)
Miller Gen. Draft 500; Dover Downs Int. Speedway (1-m) (Chevrolet)
Miller Genuine Draft 400; Michigan Int. Speedway (2-m) (Chevrolet)
Brickyard 400; Indianapolis Motor Speedway (2.5-mile) (Chevrolet)

1996   **(1st)**   **(818)**

Victories (1st)
Pont. Excitement 400; Richmond Int. Race. (.75-m; 300 m) (Chevrolet)
TranSouth Finan. 400; Darlington Raceway (1.366-m; 400m) (Chevrolet)
Food City 500; Bristol Int. Raceway (.533-m; 267 miles) (Chevrolet)
* Miller Gen. Dr. 500; Dover Downs Int. Sp. (1-m; 500 m) (Chevrolet)
* UAW-GM Teamwork 500; Pocono Int. Raceway (2.5-m; 500m) (Chevrolet)
Diehard 500; Talladega Superspeedway (2.66-m; 500 miles) (Chevrolet)
Mt. Dew Southern 500; Darlington Raceway (1.366-m; 500m) (Chevrolet)
MBNA 500; Dover Downs Int. Speedway (1-mile; 500 miles) (Chevrolet)
Hanes 500; Martinsville Speedway (.526-mile; 263 miles) (Chevrolet)
Tyson Holly Farms 400; N. Wilkesboro Sp. (.625-m; 250 m) (Chevrolet)

Poles (1st)
Coca-Cola 600; Charlotte Motor Speedway (1.5-mile) (Chevrolet)
* Miller Gen. Dr. 500; Dover Downs Int. Speedway (1-m) (Chevrolet)
* UAW-GM Teamwork 500; Pocono Int. Raceway (2.5-mile) (Chevrolet)
Pepsi 400; Daytona International Speedway (2.5-mile) (Chevrolet)
Brickyard 400; Indianapolis Motor Speedway (2.5-mile) (Chevrolet)

Driver, Year (Performance Index ranking)
(Performance Index points)

1997　(1st)　(841)

Victories (1st)

Daytona 500; Daytona Int. Speedway (2.5-mile; 500 miles) (Chevrolet)
Goodwrench 400; N.C. Motor Speedway (1.017-m; 400 miles) (Chevrolet)
Food City 500; Bristol Motor Speedway (.533-mile; 267 m) (Chevrolet)
Goody's HP 500; Martinsville Speedway (.526-mile; 263 m) (Chevrolet)
* Coca-Cola 600; Charlotte Motor Speedway (1.5-m; 600 m) (Chevrolet)
Pocono 500; Pocono Int. Raceway (2.5-mile; 500 miles) (Chevrolet)
California 500; California Speedway (2-mile; 500 miles) (Chevrolet)
The Bud at the Glen; Watkins Glen Int. (2.45-m rd; 221m) (Chevrolet)
Mt. Dew Southern 500; Darlington Raceway (1.366-m; 500m) (Chevrolet)
CMT 300; New Hampshire Int. Speedway (1.058-mile; 317 m) (Chevrolet)

Poles

* Coca-Cola 600; Charlotte Motor Speedway (1.5-mile) (Chevrolet)

1998　(1st)　(1,053)

Victories (1st)

GM Goodwrench Ser. Plus 400; N.C. Speed. (1.017-m; 400m) (Chevrolet)
Food City 500; Bristol Motor Speedway (.533-mile; 267 m) (Chevrolet)
* Coca-Cola 600; Charlotte Motor Speedway (1.5-m; 600 m) (Chevrolet)
* Save Mart/Kragen 350; Sears Pt. Race. (1.94-m rd; 217m)(Chevrolet)
Pennsylvania 500; Pocono Raceway (2.5-mile; 500 miles) (Chevrolet)
Brickyard 400; Indianapolis Motor Speedway (2.5-m; 400m) (Chevrolet)
* The Bud at the Glen; Wat. Glen Int. (2.45-m rd.; 221m) (Chevrolet)
Pepsi 400 by DeVilbiss; Michigan Speedway (2-m; 400 m) (Chevrolet)
* Farm Aid on CMT 300; N.H. Int. Speed. (1.058-m; 317 m) (Chevrolet)
Pepsi Southern 500; Darlington Raceway (1.366-m; 500 m) (Chevrolet)
Pepsi 400; Daytona Int. Speedway (2.5-mile; 400 miles) (Chevrolet)
AC Delco 400; North Carolina Speedway (1.017-m; 400 m) (Chevrolet)
NAPA 500; Atlanta Motor Speedway (1.54-mile; 500 miles) (Chevrolet)

Poles (1st)

California 500 by NAPA; California Speedway (2-mile) (Chevrolet)
* Coca-Cola 600; Charlotte Motor Speedway (1.5-mile) (Chevrolet)
Pontiac Excitement 400; Richmond Int. Raceway (.75-mile) (Chevrolet)
Pocono 500; Pocono Raceway (2.5-mile) (Chevrolet)
* Save Mart/Kragen 350; Sears Pt. Raceway (1.94-m road) (Chevrolet)
* The Bud at the Glen; Watkins Glen Int. (2.45-m road) (Chevrolet)
* Farm Aid on CMT 300; New Hamp. Int. Speedway (1.058-m) (Chevrolet)

1999　(6th)　(788)

Victories (1st)

* Daytona 500; Daytona Int. Speedway (2.5-m; 500 miles) (Chevrolet)
Cracker Barrel OCS 500; Atl. Motor Speed. (1.54-m; 500m) (Chevrolet)
California 500 by NAPA; California Speedway (2-m; 500 m) (Chevrolet)
* Save Mart/Kragen 350; Srs. Pt. Race. (1.949-m rd; 218m)(Chevrolet)
Frontier at the Glen; Watkins Glen Int. (2.45-m rd; 221m)(Chevrolet)
NAPA AutoCare 500; Martinsville Speedway (.526-m; 263 m) (Chevrolet)
UAW-GM Quality 500; Lowe's Motor Speedway (1.5-m; 500 m) (Chevrolet)

Poles (1st)

* Daytona 500; Daytona International Speedway (2.5-mile) (Chevrolet)
TranSouth Financial 400; Darlington Raceway (1.366-mile) (Chevrolet)
Pontiac Excitement 400; Richmond Int. Raceway (.75-mile) (Chevrolet)
Kmart 400; Michigan Speedway (2-mile) (Chevrolet)
* Save Mart/Kragen 350; Sears Pt. Raceway (1.949-m road) (Chevrolet)
Jiffy Lube 300; New Hampshire Int. Speedway (1.058-mile) (Chevrolet)
Brickyard 400; Indianapolis Motor Speedway (2.5-mile) (Chevrolet)

ROBBY GORDON

1997

Poles

PRIMESTAR 500; Atlanta Motor Speedway (1.522-mile) (Chevrolet)

DANNY GRAVES

1957

Victories

* California State Fairgrounds (1-mile dirt; 100 miles) (Chevrolet)

Poles

* California State Fairgrounds (1-mile dirt) (Chevrolet)

1958

Poles

Crown America 500; Riverside Int. Raceway (2.631-m road) (Chevrolet)

EDDIE GRAY

1958

Victories

Crown America 500; River. Int. Race. (2.631-m rd.; 500m) (Ford)

1959

Victories

California State Fairgrounds (1-mile dirt; 100 miles) (Ford)

1961

Victories

Ascot Speedway (.5-mile dirt; 100 miles) (Ford)
California State Fairgrounds (1-mile dirt; 100 miles) (Ford)

Poles

Riverside International Raceway (2.58-mile road) (Ford)

HENLEY GRAY

1965	(22nd)	(258)
1966	(6th)	(551)
1967	(13th)	(364)
1968	(22nd)	(250)
1969	(22nd)	(364)
1970		(184)
1971	(21st)	(312)
1972		(193)
1973	(18th)	(295)
1976		(120)

DAVID GREEN

| 1997 | | (111) |
| 1999 | | (100) |

Poles

Pennzoil 400; Homestead-Miami Speedway (1.5-mile) (Pontiac)

GEORGE GREEN

1957	(25th)	(125)
1959	(25th)	(126)
1962	(T-14th)	(369)

STEVE GRISSOM

1994		(206)
1995	(23rd)	(277)
1997	(T-24th)	(296)
1998		(171)

JOHNNY GRUBB

1950 (18th)

DAN GURNEY

1963		(110)

Victories
Riverside 500; Riverside Int. Raceway (2.7-m road; 500m) (Ford)
Poles
Golden State 400; Riverside Int. Raceway (2.7-mile road) (Ford)

1964	(106)

Victories
Motor Trend 500; Riverside Int. Race. (2.7-m road; 500m) (Ford)

1965

Victories
Motor Trend 500; Riverside Int. Race. (2.7-m road; 500m) (Ford)

1966

Victories
Motor Trend 500; Riverside Int. Race. (2.7-m road; 500m) (Ford)

1968

Victories
* Motor Trend 500; Riverside Int. Race. (2.7-m rd; 500m) (Ford)
Poles
* Motor Trend 500; Riverside Int. Raceway (2.7-mile road) (Ford)

JANET GUTHRIE

1977	(20th)	(288)

ROYCE HAGGERTY

1956

Victories
Portland Speedway (.5-mile; 125 miles) (Dodge)
Poles
Portland Speedway (.5-mile) (Dodge)

JOHNNY HALFORD

1970		(140)

ROGER HAMBY

1978	(T-21st)	(271)
1980		(214)

BOBBY HAMILTON

1991	(19th)	(337)
1992	(25th)	(245)
1993		(120)
1994		(213)
1995	(13th)	(494)
1996	(11th)	(514)

Victories
Dura-Lube 500; Phoenix Int. Raceway (1-m; 312 miles) (Pontiac)
Poles
Miller Genuine Draft 400; Michigan Int. Speedway (2-m) (Pontiac)
Hanes 500; Martinsville Speedway (.526-mile) (Pontiac)

1997	(17th)	(425)

Victories
AC Delco 400; N.C. Motor Speedway (1.017-m; 400 miles) (Pontiac)
Poles
Pocono 500; Pocono International Raceway (2.5-mile) (Pontiac)
Dura-Lube 500; Phoenix International Raceway (1-mile) (Pontiac)

1998	(11th)	(520)

Victories
* Goody's HP 500; Martinsville Speedway (.526-m; 263 m) (Chevrolet)
Poles
* Goody's HP 500; Martinsville Speedway (.526-mile) (Chevrolet)

1999	(T-15th)	(416)

PETE HAMILTON

1968		(146)
1970	(11th)	(472)

Victories
Daytona 500; Daytona Int. Speedway (2.5-m; 500 miles) (Plymouth)
Alabama 500; Ala. Int. Motor Speedway (2.66-m; 500 m) (Plymouth)
Talladega 500; Ala. Int. Motor Speedway (2.66-m; 500m) (Plymouth)
Poles
Motor State 400; Michigan International Speedway (2-m) (Plymouth)

1971	(13th)	(402)

Victories
Daytona International Speedway (2.5-mile; 125 miles) (Plymouth)
Poles
Yankee 400; Michigan International Speedway (2.04-m) (Plymouth)
Texas 500; Texas World Speedway (2-mile) (Plymouth)

FRED HARB

1958	(16th)	(188)
1959		(116)
1960		(167)
1961		(178)
1962		(115)

Driver Resumes

1963		(133)

HAROLD HARDESTY

1956	(25th)	(126)

FERREL HARRIS

1975		(177)
1978	(25th)	(239)

GEORGE HARTLEY

1950	(13th)

BUTCH HARTMAN

1968		(137)
1977		(131)

FRIDAY HASSLER

1967		(195)
1968	(18th)	(298)
1969	(24th)	(291)
1970	(16th)	(404)
1971	(11th)	(424)

Poles
Maryville 200; Smoky Mountain Raceway (.52-mile) (Chevrolet)
Northern 300; Trenton Speedway (1.5-mile) (Chevrolet)

JIMMY HELMS

1965	(18th)	(286)
1966		(116)

HARVEY HENDERSON

1955	(18th)	(134)

JIMMY HENSLEY

1989	

Poles
Goody's 500; Martinsville Speedway (.526-mile) (Chevrolet)

1992	(22nd)	(320)
1993		(167)
1994		(108)

RUSS HEPLER

1957	

Poles
Richmond 200; Atlantic Rural Fairgrounds (.5-m dirt) (Pontiac)

LARRY HESS

1965		(185)

ED HESSERT

1969		(216)

DOUG HEVERON

1986		(106)

ELTON HILDRETH

1953	(16th)	(157)
1954	(20th)	

BRUCE HILL

1975	(13th)	(424)
1976		(182)
1977		(161)
1978		(148)
1979		(122)

BOBBY HILLIN JR.

1983		(164)
1984		(175)
1985	(16th)	(396)
1986	(9th)	(558)

Victories
Talladega 500; Ala. Int. Motor Speedway (2.66-m; 500m) (Buick)

1987	(20th)	(354)
1988	(12th)	(469)
1989	(14th)	(441)
1990	(20th)	(351)
1991	(23rd)	(309)
1993	(T-24th)	(285)
1995		(174)
1996		(160)

GENE HOBBY

1964		(138)

AL HOLBERT

1978		(140)

PAUL DEAN HOLT

1967	(138)
1968	(159)

JIM HUNTER

1967

Poles
East Tennessee 200; Smoky Mountain Raceway (.5-m dirt) (Chevrolet)

JIM HURTUBISE

1966	(201)

Victories
Atlanta 500; Atlanta Int. Raceway (1.5-m; 500 miles) (Plymouth)

DICK HUTCHERSON

1964

Poles
Greenville 200; Greenville-Pickens Speedway (.5-m dirt) (Ford)
Piedmont Interstate Fairgrounds (.5-mile dirt) (Ford)

1965	(2nd)	(982)

Victories
Greenville 200; Greenville-Pickens Sp. (.5-m dirt; 100m) (Ford)
Music City 200; Fairgrounds Speedway (.5-m; 100 miles) (Ford)
Pickens 200; Greenville-Pickens Speed. (.5-m dirt; 100m) (Ford)
* Rambi Raceway (.5-mile dirt; 100 miles) (Ford)
Smoky Mountain Raceway (.5-mile dirt; 100 miles) (Ford)
Augusta Speedway (.5-mile; 100 miles) (Ford)
Moyock 300; Dog Track Speedway (.333-mile; 100 miles) (Ford)
Pennsylvania 200; Lincoln Speedway (.5-mile dirt; 100 m) (Ford)
* Orange Speedway (.9-mile dirt; 101 miles) (Ford)

Poles (T-1st)
Piedmont Interstate Fairgrounds (.5-mile dirt) (Ford)
Tidewater 250; Langley Field Speedway (.4-mile dirt) (Ford)
Cleveland County Fairgrounds (.5-mile dirt) (Ford)
* Rambi Raceway (.5-mile dirt) (Ford)
Valdosta Speedway (.5-mile dirt) (Ford)
Piedmont Interstate Fairgrounds (.5-mile dirt) (Ford)
Sandlapper 200; Columbia Speedway (.5-mile dirt) (Ford)
Capital City 300; Virginia State Fairgrounds (.5-m dirt) (Ford)
* Orange Speedway (.9-mile dirt) (Ford)

1966	(22nd)	(259)

Victories
Southeastern 500; Bristol Int. Speedway (.5-mile; 250 m) (Ford)
* Joe Weatherly 150; Orange Speedway (.9-m dirt; 150 m) (Ford)
Wilkes 400; North Wilkesboro Speedway (.625-mile; 250 m) (Ford)

Poles
* Joe Weatherly 150; Orange Speedway (.9-mile dirt) (Ford)

1967	(5th)	(661)

Victories
* Smoky Mount. 200; Smoky Mount. Race. (.5-m dirt; 100m) (Ford)
Dixie 500; Atlanta International Raceway (1.5-m; 500 m) (Ford)

Poles
Augusta Speedway (.5-mile) (Ford)
Motor Trend 500; Riverside Int. Raceway (2.7-mile road) (Ford)
Greenville 200; Greenville-Pickens Speedway (.5-m dirt) (Ford)
Columbia 200; Columbia Speedway (.5-mile dirt) (Ford)
Carolina 500; North Carolina Motor Speedway (1-mile) (Ford)
* Smoky Mountain 200; Smoky Mountain Raceway (.5-m dirt) (Ford)
Nashville 400; Fairgrounds Speedway (.5-mile) (Ford)
Buddy Shuman 250; Hickory Speedway (.4-mile) (Ford)
Wilkes 400; North Wilkesboro Speedway (.625-mile) (Ford)

SONNY HUTCHINS

1967	(106)

JAMES HYLTON

1966	(2nd)	(756)

Poles
Independent 250; Starlite Speedway (.4-mile dirt) (Dodge)

1967	(2nd)	(826)

Poles
Maine 300; Oxford Plains Speedway (.333-mile) (Dodge)

1968	(4th)	(627)
1969	(3rd)	(919)
1970	(4th)	(937)

Victories
Richmond 500; Virginia State Fgds. (.542-m; 271 miles) (Ford)

Poles
Beltsville 300; Beltsville Speedway (.5-mile) (Ford)

1971	(2nd)	(999)

Poles
Columbia 200; Columbia Speedway (.5-mile) (Ford)

1972	(3rd)	(786)

Victories
Talladega 500; Ala. Int. Motor Speedway (2.66-m; 500 m) (Mercury)

1973	(7th)	(550)
1974	(11th)	(409)
1975	(2nd)	(652)
1976	(12th)	(421)
1977	(9th)	(493)
1978	(20th)	(275)
1979	(14th)	(443)
1980	(15th)	(385)
1981		(226)
1982		(131)

ERNIE IRVAN

1988	(165)

1989   (253)

1990   (11th)   (523)

Victories
Busch 500; Bristol Int. Raceway (.533-mile; 267 miles) (Chevrolet)

Poles
Valleydale Meats 500; Bristol Int. Raceway (.533-mile) (Oldsmobile)
Miller Genuine Draft 500; Pocono Int. Raceway (2.5-mile) (Oldsmobile)
Miller Genuine Draft 400; Richmond Int. Raceway (.75-m) (Chevrolet)

1991   (5th)   (635)

Victories
Daytona 500 by STP; Daytona Int. Speedway (2.5-m; 500 m) (Chevrolet)
Budweiser at the Glen; Wat. Glen Int. (2.428-m rd.; 219m)(Chevrolet)

Poles
Winston 500; Talladega Superspeedway (2.66-mile) (Chevrolet)

1992   (15th)   (498)

Victories
The Save Mart 300; Srs. Pt. Int. Race. (2.52-m rd.; 187m)(Chevrolet)
Pepsi 400; Daytona International Speedway (2.5-m; 400 m) (Chevrolet)
Diehard 500; Talladega Superspeedway (2.66-m; 500 miles) (Chevrolet)

Poles
Winston 500; Talladega Superspeedway (2.66-mile) (Chevrolet)
Bud 500; Bristol International Raceway (.533-mile) (Chevrolet)
Miller Genuine Draft 400; Richmond Int. Raceway (.75-m) (Chevrolet)

1993   (8th)   (571)

Victories
Winston 500; Talladega Superspeedway (2.66-m; 500 miles) (Chevrolet)
* Goody's 500; Martinsville Speedway (.526-m; 263 miles) (Ford)
Mello Yello 500; Charlotte Motor Speedway (1.5-m; 500 miles) (Ford)

Poles
Budweiser 500; Dover Downs International Speedway (1-m) (Chevrolet)
Pepsi 400; Daytona International Speedway (2.5-mile) (Chevrolet)
* Goody's 500; Martinsville Speedway (.526-mile) (Ford)
Tyson Holly Farms 400; No. Wilkesboro Speedway (.625-m) (Ford)

1994   (9th)   (559)

Victories
Pont. Excitement 400; Richmond Int. Race. (.75-m; 300m) (Ford)
Purolator 500; Atlanta Motor Speedway (1.522-m; 500 m) (Ford)
* Save Mart Sup. 300; Sears Pt. Race. (2.52-m rd.; 187m) (Ford)

Poles (T-1st)
First Union 400; North Wilkesboro Speedway (.625-mile) (Ford)
Winston Select 500; Talladega Superspeedway (2.66-mile) (Ford)
* Save Mart Supermark. 300; Sears Pt. Race. (2.52-m rd.) (Ford)
Budweiser 500; Dover Downs International Speedway (1-m) (Ford)
Slick 50 300; New Hampshire Int. Speedway (1.058-mile) (Ford)

1996   (8th)   (556)

Victories
Jiffy Lube 300; New Hamp. Int. Speedway (1.058-m; 317 m) (Ford)
Miller 400; Richmond International Raceway (.75-m; 300m) (Ford)

Poles
Winston Select 500; Talladega Superspeedway (2.66-mile) (Ford)

1997   (10th)   (493)

Victories
Miller 400; Michigan Speedway (2-mile; 400 miles) (Ford)

Poles
Brickyard 400; Indianapolis Motor Speedway (2.5-mile) (Ford)
Diehard 500; Talladega Superspeedway (2.66-mile) (Ford)

1998   (T-14th)   (473)

Poles
Brickyard 400; Indianapolis Motor Speedway (2.5-mile) (Pontiac)
Pepsi 400 by DeVilbiss; Michigan Speedway (2-mile) (Pontiac)
NAPA AutoCare 500; Martinsville Speedway (.526-mile) (Pontiac)

1999   (208)

KENNY IRWIN

1998   (24th)   (286)

Poles
NAPA 500; Atlanta Motor Speedway (1.54-mile) (Ford)

1999   (17th)   (404)

Poles
PRIMESTAR 500; Texas Motor Speedway (1.5-mile) (Ford)
Pepsi Southern 500; Darlington Raceway (1.366-mile) (Ford)

TOMMY IRWIN

1959   (7th)   (311)

Poles
Asheville-Weaverville Speedway (.5-mile) (Ford)

1960   (21st)   (191)

Poles
Columbia Speedway (.5-mile dirt) (Ford)

1961   (18th)   (259)

1962   (157)

1963   (118)

BOBBY ISAAC

1963   (20th)   (307)

1964   (T-20th)   (280)

Victories
Daytona International Speedway (2.5-mile; 100 miles) (Dodge)

1965

Poles
Tidewater 300; Dog Track Speedway (.333-mile) (Ford)

1967   (20th)   (272)

1968   (3rd)   (868)

Victories
Columbia 200; Columbia Speedway (.5-m dirt; 100 miles) (Dodge)
* Dixie 250; Augusta Speedway (.5-mile; 125 miles) (Dodge)
Maryland 300; Beltsville Speedway (.5-mile; 150 miles) (Dodge)

Poles
Richmond 250; Virginia State Fairgrounds (.5-mile dirt) (Dodge)
* Dixie 250; Augusta Speedway (.5-mile) (Dodge)
Smoky Mountain 200; Smoky Mountain Raceway (.5-mile) (Dodge)

1969   (4th)   (900)

Victories (1st)
Daytona International Speedway (2.5-mile; 125 miles) (Dodge)
* Columbia 200; Columbia Speedway (.5-m dirt; 100 miles) (Dodge)
* Hickory 250; Hickory Speedway (.4-mile; 100 miles) (Dodge)
Greenville 200; Greenville-Pickens Sp. (.5-m dirt; 100m) (Dodge)
* Fireball 300; Asheville-Weaverville Sp. (.5-m; 150 m) (Dodge)
* Beltsville 300; Beltsville Speedway (.5-m; 150 miles) (Dodge)
Macon 300; Middle Georgia Raceway (.5-mile; 150 miles) (Dodge)
Maryville 300; Smoky Mountain Raceway (.5-m; 150 miles) (Dodge)
* Pickens 200; Greenville-Pickens Sp. (.5-m dirt; 100m) (Dodge)
* South Boston 100; South Boston Speedway (.375-m; 100m) (Dodge)
* West. N.C. 500; Asheville-Weaverville Sp. (.5-m; 250m) (Dodge)
* Buddy Shuman 250; Hickory Speedway (.4-m; 100 miles) (Dodge)
Sandlapper 200; Columbia Speedway (.5-m dirt; 100 miles) (Dodge)
* Savannah Speedway (.5-mile; 100 miles) (Dodge)
* Augusta Speedway (.5-mile; 100 miles) (Dodge)
Jeffco 200; Jeffco Speedway (.5-mile; 100 miles) (Dodge)
Texas 500; Texas International Speedway (2-m; 500 miles) (Dodge)

Poles (1st)
Cracker 200; Augusta Speedway (.5-mile) (Dodge)
Southeastern 500; Bristol International Speedway (.5-m) (Dodge)
* Columbia 200; Columbia Speedway (.5-mile dirt) (Dodge)
* Hickory 250; Hickory Speedway (.4-mile) (Dodge)
Gwyn Staley 400; North Wilkesboro Speedway (.625-mile) (Dodge)
* Fireball 300; Asheville-Weaverville Speedway (.5-mile) (Dodge)
* Beltsville 300; Beltsville Speedway (.5-mile) (Dodge)
Kingsport 250; Kingsport Speedway (.4-mile) (Dodge)
* Pickens 200; Greenville-Pickens Speedway (.5-m dirt) (Dodge)
North State 200; State Fairgrounds (.5-mile dirt) (Dodge)
Northern 300; Trenton Speedway (1.5-mile) (Dodge)
* South Boston 100; South Boston Speedway (.375-mile) (Dodge)
* Western N.C. 500; Asheville-Weaverville Speed. (.5-m) (Dodge)
* Buddy Shuman 250; Hickory Speedway (.4-mile) (Dodge)
Talladega 500; Alabama Int. Motor Speedway (2.66-mile) (Dodge)
Wilkes 400; North Wilkesboro Speedway (.625-mile) (Dodge)
* Savannah Speedway (.5-mile) (Dodge)
* Augusta Speedway (.5-mile) (Dodge)
Georgia 500; Middle Georgia Raceway (.548-mile) (Dodge)

1970   (1st)   (1,060)

Victories
Beltsville 300; Beltsville Speedway (.5-m; 150 miles) (Dodge)
* Tidewater 300; Langley Field Speedway (.4-mile; 120 m) (Dodge)
Maryville 200; Smoky Mountain Raceway (.52-mile; 104 miles) (Dodge)
Virginia 500; Martinsville Speedway (.525-m; 263 miles) (Dodge)
* Hickory 276; Hickory Speedway (.363-mile; 100 miles) (Dodge)
* Greenville 200; Greenville-Pickens Speed. (.5-m; 100m) (Dodge)
* Thompson 200; Thompson Speedway (.542-mile; 108 miles) (Dodge)
Nashville 420; Fairgrounds Speedway (.596-m; 250 miles) (Dodge)
Sandlapper 200; Columbia Speedway (.5-m dirt; 100 miles) (Dodge)
* Buddy Shuman 276; Hickory Speedway (.363-m; 100 miles) (Dodge)
* Wilkes 400; No. Wilkesboro Speedway (.625-mile; 250 m) (Dodge)

Poles (1st)
Alabama 500; Alabama Int. Motor Speedway (2.66-mile) (Dodge)
Gwyn Staley 400; North Wilkesboro Speedway (.625-mile) (Dodge)
* Tidewater 300; Langley Field Speedway (.4-mile) (Dodge)
World 600; Charlotte Motor Speedway (1.5-mile) (Dodge)
* Hickory 276; Hickory Speedway (.363-mile) (Dodge)
* Greenville 200; Greenville-Pickens Speedway (.5-mile) (Dodge)
Albany-Saratoga 250; Albany-Saratoga Speedway (.362-m) (Dodge)
* Thompson 200; Thompson Speedway (.542-mile) (Dodge)

Schaefer 300; Trenton Speedway (1.5-mile) (Dodge)
Talladega 500; Alabama Int. Motor Speedway (2.66-mile) (Dodge)
* Buddy Shuman 276; Hickory Speedway (.363-mile) (Dodge)
Mason-Dixon 300; Dover Downs Int. Speedway (1-mile) (Dodge)
* Wilkes 400; North Wilkesboro Speedway (.625-mile) (Dodge)

1971   (7th)   (604)

Victories
Greenville 200; Greenville-Pickens Speedway (.5-m; 100m) (Dodge)
* Kingsport 300; Kingsport Speedway (.337-m; 101 miles) (Dodge)
Firecracker 400; Daytona Int. Speedway (2.5-mile; 400 m) (Dodge)
* Old Dominion 500; Martinsville Speedway (.525-m; 263m) (Dodge)

Poles
Gwyn Staley 400; North Wilkesboro Speedway (.625-mile) (Dodge)
Halifax County 100; South Boston Speedway (.357-mile) (Dodge)
* Kingsport 300; Kingsport Speedway (.337-mile) (Dodge)
* Old Dominion 500; Martinsville Speedway (.525-mile) (Dodge)

1972   (15th)   (358)

Victories
* Carolina 500; N.C. Motor Speedway (1.017-m; 500 miles) (Dodge)

Poles
Daytona 500; Daytona International Speedway (2.5-mile) (Dodge)
* Carolina 500; North Carolina Motor Speedway (1.017-m) (Dodge)
Gwyn Staley 400; North Wilkesboro Speedway (.625-mile) (Dodge)
Winston 500; Alabama Int. Motor Speedway (2.66-mile) (Dodge)
Mason-Dixon 500; Dover Downs Int. Speedway (1-mile) (Dodge)
Motor State 400; Michigan International Speedway (2-m) (Dodge)
Firecracker 400; Daytona International Speedway (2.5-m) (Dodge)
Northern 300; Trenton Speedway (1.5-mile) (Dodge)
Talladega 500; Alabama Int. Motor Speedway (2.66-mile) (Dodge)

1973   (25th)   (220)

1974   (136)

BRUCE JACOBI

1975   (22nd)   (299)

DALE JARRETT

1987	(25th)	(185)
1988		(241)
1989		(268)
1990	(21st)	(316)
1991	(16th)	(403)

Victories
Champion SP 400; Michigan Int. Speedway (2-m; 400 miles) (Ford)

1992	(20th)	(397)
1993	(4th)	(664)

Victories
Daytona 500 by STP; Daytona Int. Speedway (2.5-m; 500 m) (Chevrolet)

1994	(15th)	(452)

Victories
Mello Yello 500; Charlotte Motor Speedway (1.5-m; 500 m) (Chevrolet)

1995   (15th)   (479)

Victories

Miller Gen. Draft 500; Pocono Int. Raceway (2.5-m; 500m) (Ford)

Poles

Daytona 500; Daytona International Speedway (2.5-mile) (Ford)

1996   (2nd)   (812)

Victories

Daytona 500; Daytona Int. Speedway (2.5-mile; 500 miles) (Ford)
Coca-Cola 600; Charlotte Motor Speedway (1.5-m; 600 m) (Ford)
Brickyard 400; Indianapolis Motor Speedway (2.5-m; 400m) (Ford)
GM Good. Dealer 400; Michigan Int. Speedway (2-m; 400m) (Ford)

Poles

Mountain Dew Southern 500; Darlington Raceway (1.366-m) (Ford)
AC Delco 400; North Carolina Motor Speedway (1.017-mile) (Ford)

1997   (3rd)   (799)

Victories

PRIMESTAR 500; Atlanta Motor Speedway (1.522-m; 500 m) (Ford)
* TranSouth Fin. 400; Darlington Raceway (1.366-m; 400m) (Ford)
Pennsylvania 500; Pocono Int. Raceway (2.5-mile; 500 m) (Ford)
Goody's HP 500; Bristol Motor Speedway (.533-m; 267 m) (Ford)
Exide NASCAR SB 400; Richmond Int. Race. (.75-m; 300m) (Ford)
UAW-GM Quality 500; Charlotte Motor Speed. (1.5-m; 500m) (Ford)
Dura-Lube 500; Phoenix Int. Raceway (1-mile; 312 miles) (Ford)

Poles

* TranSouth Financial 400; Darlington Raceway (1.366-m) (Ford)
Miller 400; Michigan Speedway (2-mile) (Ford)

1998   (3rd)   (790)

Victories

TranSouth Finan. 400; Darlington Raceway (1.366-m; 400m) (Ford)
MBNA Platinum 400; Dover Downs Int. Speedway (1-m; 400m) (Ford)
Winston 500; Talladega Superspeedway (2.66-m; 500 miles) (Ford)

Poles

Las Vegas 400; Las Vegas Motor Speedway (1.5-mile) (Ford)
Pepsi Southern 500; Darlington Raceway (1.366-mile) (Ford)

1999   (1st)   (990)

Victories

Pont. Excitement 400; Richmond Int. Race. (.75-m; 300m) (Ford)
Kmart 400; Michigan Speedway (2-mile; 400 miles) (Ford)
Pepsi 400; Daytona Int. Speedway (2.5-mile; 400 miles) (Ford)
Brickyard 400; Indianapolis Motor Speedway (2.5-m; 400m) (Ford)

NED JARRETT

1959   (22nd)   (165)

Victories

Rambi Raceway (.5-mile dirt; 100 miles) (Ford)
Charlotte Fairgrounds (.5-mile dirt; 100 miles) (Ford)

1960   (4th)   (628)

Victories

Columbia Speedway (.5-mile dirt; 100 miles) (Ford)
Greenville 200; Greenville-Pickens Sp. (.5-m dirt; 100m) (Ford)
Piedmont Interstate Fairgrounds (.5-m dirt; 100 miles) (Ford)
* Dixie Speedway (.25-mile; 50 miles) (Ford)
Gamecock Speedway (.25-mile dirt; 50 miles) (Ford)

Poles

Richmond 200; Atlantic Rural Fairgrounds (.5-mile dirt) (Ford)
Rambi Raceway (.5-mile dirt) (Ford)
* Dixie Speedway (.25-mile) (Ford)
South Boston Speedway (.25-mile dirt) (Ford)
Capital City 200; Atlantic Rural Fairgrounds (.5-m dirt) (Ford)

1961   (2nd)   (811)

Victories

Alabama State Fairgrounds (.5-mile dirt; 100 miles) (Chevrolet)

Poles

Piedmont Interstate Fairgrounds (.5-mile dirt) (Ford)
Orange Speedway (.9-mile dirt) (Chevrolet)
Columbia Speedway (.5-mile dirt) (Chevrolet)
Pickens 200; Greenville-Pickens Speedway (.5-mile dirt) (Chevrolet)

1962   (3rd)   (816)

Victories

Arclite 200; Columbia Speedway (.5-mile dirt; 100 miles) (Chevrolet)
* Greenville 200; Greenville-Pickens Sp. (.5-m d.; 100m) (Chevrolet)
Piedmont Interstate Fairgrounds (.5-m dirt; 100 miles) (Chevrolet)
* Rambi Raceway (.5-mile dirt; 100 miles) (Chevrolet)
Valdosta Speedway (.5-mile dirt; 100 miles) (Chevrolet)
* Dog Track Speedway (.25-mile dirt; 63 miles) (Chevrolet)

Poles

* Greenville 200; Greenville-Pickens Speed. (.5-m dirt) (Chevrolet)
Rambi Raceway (.5-mile dirt) (Chevrolet)
* Rambi Raceway (.5-mile dirt) (Chevrolet)
* Dog Track Speedway (.25-mile dirt) (Chevrolet)

1963   (2nd)   (875)

Victories

Augusta Speedway (.5-mile dirt; 100 miles) (Ford)
* Southside Speedway (.333-mile; 100 miles) (Ford)
Speedorama 200; Rambi Raceway (.5-mile dirt; 100 miles) (Ford)
Savannah Speedway (.5-mile dirt; 100 miles) (Ford)
Asheville Speedway (.333-mile; 100 miles) (Ford)
Piedmont Interstate Fairgrounds (.5-m dirt; 100 miles) (Ford)
Capital City 300; Atlantic Rural Fgds. (.5-m dirt; 150m) (Ford)
Dog Track Speedway (.25-mile dirt; 75 miles) (Ford)

Poles

South Boston 400; South Boston Speedway (.375-mile) (Ford)
Tar Heel Speedway (.25-mile) (Ford)
* Southside Speedway (.333-mile) (Ford)
Pickens 200; Greenville-Pickens Speedway (.5-mile dirt) (Ford)

1964   (2nd)   (1,091)

Victories (1st)

Textile 250; Concord Speedway (.5-mile dirt; 125 miles) (Ford)
Piedmont Interstate Fairgrounds (.5-m dirt; 100 miles) (Ford)
Columbia 200; Columbia Speedway (.5-m dirt; 100 miles) (Ford)
Tidewater 250; Langley Field Speedway (.4-m dirt; 100 m) (Ford)
Hickory 250; Hickory Speedway (.4-mile dirt; 100 miles) (Ford)
Asheville Speedway (.333-mile; 100 miles) (Ford)
Dixie 400; Atlanta International Raceway (1.5-m; 400 m) (Ford)
Birmingham Raceway (.5-mile; 100 miles) (Ford)
* Old Dominion 400; Old Dominion Speedway (.375-m; 150m) (Ford)
West. N.C. 500; Asheville-Weaverville Sp. (.5-m; 250 m) (Ford)
* Moyock 300; Dog Track Speedway (.333-mile; 100 miles) (Ford)
Old Dominion Speedway (.375-mile; 188 miles) (Ford)
Orange Speedway (.9-mile dirt; 150 miles) (Ford)
* Savannah Speedway (.5-mile dirt; 100 miles) (Ford)
Jacksonville Speedway (.5-mile dirt; 100 miles) (Ford)

Poles

Sunshine 200; Savannah Speedway (.5-mile dirt) (Ford)
Richmond 250; Atlantic Rural Fairgrounds (.5-mile dirt) (Ford)
Valdosta Speedway (.5-mile dirt) (Ford)
* Old Dominion 400; Old Dominion Speedway (.375-mile) (Ford)
* Moyock 300; Dog Track Speedway (.333-mile) (Ford)
Sandlapper 200; Columbia Speedway (.5-mile dirt) (Ford)
Capital City 300; Virginia State Fairgrounds (.5-m dirt) (Ford)
* Savannah Speedway (.5-mile dirt) (Ford)
Jaycee 300; Augusta Speedway (.5-mile) (Ford)

1965   (1st)   (1,162)

Victories (T-1st)

Piedmont Interstate Fairgrounds (.5-m dirt; 100 miles) (Ford)
* Fireball 200; Asheville-Weaverville Sp. (.5-m; 100 m) (Ford)
Orange Speedway (.9-mile dirt; 150 miles) (Ford)
Tidewater 250; Langley Field Speedway (.4-m dirt; 100 m) (Ford)
Cleveland County Fairgrounds (.5-mile dirt; 100 miles) (Ford)
Harris Speedway (.3-mile; 100 miles) (Ford)
* Birmingham 200; Birmingham Raceway (.5-m; 100 miles) (Ford)
Volunteer 500; Bristol Int. Speedway (.5-m; 250 miles) (Ford)
Cleveland County Fairgrounds (.5-mile dirt; 100 miles) (Ford)
Piedmont Interstate Fairgrounds (.5-m dirt; 100 miles) (Ford)
* Beltsville Speedway (.5-mile; 100 miles) (Ford)
Southern 500; Darlington Raceway (1.375-mile; 500 miles) (Ford)
Tidewater 300; Dog Track Speedway (.333-mile; 100 miles) (Ford)

Poles (T-1st)

* Fireball 200; Asheville-Weaverville Speedway (.5-mile) (Ford)
Columbia 200; Columbia Speedway (.5-mile dirt) (Ford)
* Birmingham 200; Birmingham Raceway (.5-mile) (Ford)
Pickens 200; Greenville-Pickens Speedway (.5-mile dirt) (Ford)
Old Dominion Speedway (.375-mile) (Ford)
Smoky Mountain Raceway (.5-mile dirt) (Ford)
Augusta Speedway (.5-mile) (Ford)
* Beltsville Speedway (.5-mile) (Ford)
Old Dominion Speedway (.375-mile) (Ford)

1966   (17th)   (292)

BOBBY JOHNS

1959

Poles

Virginia 500; Martinsville Speedway (.5-mile) (Chevrolet)

1960   (7th)   (307)

Victories

Atlanta 500; Atlanta Int. Raceway (1.5-mile; 500 miles) (Pontiac)

1961   (193)

Poles

Southeastern 500; Bristol Int. Speedway (.5-mile) (Pontiac)

1962   (109)

Victories

Volunteer 500; Bristol Int. Speedway (.5-m; 250 miles) (Pontiac)

1963   (193)

1964   (116)

1965   (24th)   (216)

DICK M. JOHNSON

1969   (137)

JOE LEE JOHNSON

1959   (23rd)   (148)

Victories

Nashville 300; Fairgrounds Speedway (.5-mile; 150 miles) (Chevrolet)

1960   (T-15th)   (207)

Victories

World 600; Charlotte Motor Speedway (1.5-m; 600 miles) (Chevrolet)

JUNIOR JOHNSON

1954

Poles

Mid-South 250; Memphis-Arkansas Speedway (1.5-m dirt) (Cadillac)

1955   (5th)   (385)

Victories

Hickory Speedway (.4-mile dirt; 80 miles) (Oldsmobile)
State Fairgrounds (.5-mile dirt; 100 miles) (Oldsmobile)
* Lincoln Speedway (.5-mile dirt; 100 miles) (Oldsmobile)
Fonda Speedway (.5-mile dirt; 100 miles) (Oldsmobile)
Altamont-Schnectady Fairgrounds (.5-m dirt; 100 miles) (Oldsmobile)

Poles

* Lincoln Speedway (.5-mile dirt) (Oldsmobile)
Columbia Speedway (.5-mile dirt) (Oldsmobile)

1956

Poles

Wilkes Co. 160; No. Wilkesboro Speedway (.625-m dirt) (Pontiac)

1958   (6th)   (403)

Victories

Wilkes Co. 160; No. Wilkesboro Speedway (.625-m; 100 m) (Ford)
Columbia Speedway (.5-mile dirt; 100 miles) (Ford)
New Bradford Speedway (.333-mile dirt; 50 miles) (Ford)
Reading Fairgrounds (.5-mile dirt; 100 miles) (Ford)
Wilkes 160; North Wilkesboro Speedway (.625-mile; 100 m) (Ford)
Lakewood Speedway (1-mile dirt; 150 miles) (Ford)

1959   (5th)   (345)

Victories

Wilson Speedway (.5-mile dirt; 100 miles) (Ford)
Reading Speedway (.5-mile dirt; 100 miles) (Ford)
* Hickory 250; Hickory Speedway (.4-m dirt; 100 miles) (Ford)
Greenville-Pickens Speedway (.5-mile dirt; 100 miles) (Ford)
Wilson Speedway (.5-mile dirt; 100 miles) (Ford)

Poles

* Hickory 250; Hickory Speedway (.4-mile dirt) (Ford)

1960   (6th)   (427)

Victories

Daytona 500; Daytona Int. Speedway (2.5-mile; 500 miles) (Chevrolet)
South Boston Speedway (.25-mile dirt; 38 miles) (Chevrolet)
Buddy Shuman 250; Hickory Speedway (.4-mile dirt; 100 m) (Chevrolet)

Poles
Columbia Speedway (.5-mile dirt) (Dodge)
Gwyn Staley 160; North Wilkesboro Speedway (.625-mile) (Chevrolet)
Asheville-Weaverville Speedway (.5-mile) (Ford)

1961   (4th)   (575)

Victories
* Hickory 250; Hickory Speedway (.4-m dirt; 100 miles) (Pontiac)
Virginia 500; Martinsville Speedway (.5-m; 250 miles) (Pontiac)
Starkey Speedway (.25-mile; 38 miles) (Pontiac)
West. N.C. 500; Asheville-Weaverville Sp. (.5-m; 250m) (Pontiac)
* Southside Speedway (.25-mile; 38 miles) (Pontiac)
South Boston Speedway (.25-mile dirt; 50 miles) (Pontiac)
Greenville-Pickens Speedway (.5-mile dirt; 100 miles) (Pontiac)

Poles (1st)
Speedway Park (.5-mile dirt) (Pontiac)
Greenville 200; Greenville-Pickens Speed. (.5-m dirt) (Pontiac)
Gwyn Staley 400; North Wilkesboro Speedway (.625-mile) (Pontiac)
* Hickory 250; Hickory Speedway (.4-mile dirt) (Pontiac)
Myers Brothers 200; Bowman Gray Stadium (.25-mile) (Pontiac)
Bowman Gray Stadium (.25-mile) (Pontiac)
* Southside Speedway (.25-mile) (Pontiac)
Capital City 250; Atlantic Rural Fgds. (.5-mile dirt) (Pontiac)
Wilkes 320; North Wilkesboro Speedway (.625-mile) (Pontiac)

1962   (21st)   (249)

Victories
National 400; Charlotte Motor Speedway (1.5-m; 400 m) (Pontiac)

Poles
Gwyn Staley 400; North Wilkesboro Speedway (.625-mile) (Pontiac)
Buddy Shuman 250; Hickory Speedway (.4-mile dirt) (Pontiac)

1963   (10th)   (450)

Victories
Daytona International Speedway (2.5-mile; 100 miles) (Chevrolet)
Orange Speedway (.9-mile dirt; 149 miles) (Chevrolet)
* Hickory 250; Hickory Speedway (.4-m dirt; 100 miles) (Chevrolet)
Dixie 400; Atlanta Int. Raceway (1.5-mile; 400 miles) (Chevrolet)
* International 200; Bowman Gray Stadium (.25-m; 50 m) (Chevrolet)
Buddy Shuman 250; Hickory Speedway (.4-mile dirt; 100 m) (Chevrolet)
National 400; Charlotte Motor Speedway (1.5-mile; 400 m) (Chevrolet)

Poles (1st)
Piedmont Interstate Fairgrounds (.5-mile dirt) (Chevrolet)
Asheville-Weaverville Speedway (.5-mile) (Chevrolet)
Atlanta 500; Atlanta International Raceway (1.5-mile) (Chevrolet)
* Hickory 250; Hickory Speedway (.4-mile dirt) (Chevrolet)
World 600; Charlotte Motor Speedway (1.5-mile) (Chevrolet)
Firecracker 400; Daytona Int. Speedway (2.5-mile) (Chevrolet)
Dog Track Speedway (.25-mile dirt) (Chevrolet)
* International 200; Bowman Gray Stadium (.25-mile) (Chevrolet)
Old Dominion 500; Martinsville Speedway (.5-mile) (Chevrolet)

1964   (15th)   (401)

Victories
Daytona International Speedway (2.5-mile; 100 miles) (Dodge)
* Myers Brothers 250; Bowman Gray Stadium (.25-m; 63 m) (Ford)
Starkey Speedway (.25-mile; 50 miles) (Ford)

Poles
Hickory 250; Hickory Speedway (.4-mile dirt) (Ford)
Dixie 400; Atlanta International Raceway (1.5-mile) (Ford)
Western N.C. 500; Asheville-Weaverville Speedway (.5-m) (Ford)
* Myers Brothers 250; Bowman Gray Stadium (.25-mile) (Ford)
Wilkes 400; North Wilkesboro Speedway (.625-mile) (Ford)

1965   (7th)   (564)

Victories (T-1st)
Daytona International Speedway (2.5-mile; 100 miles) (Ford)
* Richmond 250; Va. State Fairgrounds (.5-m dirt; 125 m) (Ford)
* Gwyn Staley 400; N. Wilkesboro Speedway (.625-m; 250m) (Ford)
Southeastern 500; Bristol Int. Speedway (.5-m; 250 m) (Ford)
Rebel 300; Darlington Raceway (1.375-mile; 300 miles) (Ford)
* Bowman Gray Stadium (.25-mile; 50 miles) (Ford)
Hickory 250; Hickory Speedway (.4-mile dirt; 100 miles) (Ford)
* Asheville Speedway (.333-mile; 100 miles) (Ford)
Old Dominion Speedway (.375-mile; 150 miles) (Ford)
Old Bridge 200; Old Bridge Stadium (.5-mile; 100 miles) (Ford)
Myers Brothers 250; Bowman Gray Stadium (.25-mile; 63 m) (Ford)
Old Dominion 500; Martinsville Speedway (.5-mile; 250 m) (Ford)
Wilkes 400; North Wilkesboro Speedway (.625-mile; 250 m) (Ford)

Poles (T-1st)
Motor Trend 500; Riverside Int. Raceway (2.7-mile road) (Ford)
* Richmond 250; Virginia State Fairgrounds (.5-m dirt) (Ford)
Orange Speedway (.9-mile dirt) (Ford)
* Gwyn Staley 400; North Wilkesboro Speedway (.625-mile) (Ford)
Virginia 500; Martinsville Speedway (.5-mile) (Ford)
* Bowman Gray Stadium (.25-mile) (Ford)
* Asheville Speedway (.333-mile) (Ford)
Southern 500; Darlington Raceway (1.375-mile) (Ford)
Buddy Shuman 250; Hickory Speedway (.4-mile dirt) (Ford)

1966

Poles
Western N.C. 500; Asheville-Weaverville Speedway (.5-m) (Ford)
Old Dominion 500; Martinsville Speedway (.5-mile) (Ford)
Wilkes 400; North Wilkesboro Speedway (.625-mile) (Ford)

SLICK JOHNSON

1980   (205)

1982   (141)

PARNELLI JONES

1957

Victories
Kitsap County Airport (.9-mile road; 72 miles) (Ford)

Poles
Eureka Speedway (.625-mile dirt) (Ford)

1958

Victories
* California State Fairgrounds (1-mile dirt; 100 miles) (Ford)

Poles
* California State Fairgrounds (1-mile dirt) (Ford)

1959

Victories
Ascot Stadium (.4-mile dirt; 200 miles) (Ford)

1967

Victories
Motor Trend 500; Riverside Int. Race. (2.7-m road; 500m) (Ford)

1970

Poles

Motor Trend 500; Riverside Int. Raceway (2.62-mile road) (Mercury)

POSSUM JONES

1958

Poles

Columbia Speedway (.5-mile dirt) (Chevrolet)

1960		(134)

REDS KAGLE

1958		(106)

BOBBY KECK

1958	(15th)	(189)
1964		(138)

AL KELLER

1954	(11th)	(189)

Victories

Oglethorpe Speedway (.5-mile dirt; 100 miles) (Hudson)
Linden Airport (2-mile road; 100 miles) (Jaguar)

Poles

Charlotte Speedway (.75-mile dirt) (Hudson)

RON KESELOWSKI

1971		(221)
1972		(197)

JOHN KIEPER

1956	(24th)	(127)

Victories

Portland Speedway (.5-mile; 100 miles) (Oldsmobile)

Poles

Portland Speedway (.5-mile) (Oldsmobile)
Eureka Speedway (.625-mile dirt) (Oldsmobile)
Portland Speedway (.5-mile) (Oldsmobile)

BROWNIE KING

1957	(12th)	(319)
1958	(17th)	(187)

BUB KING

1952	(18th)	(115)
1953	(23rd)	

PAT KIRKWOOD

1952

Poles

Beach & Road Course (4.1-mile road) (Chrysler)

HAROLD KITE

1950

Victories

Beach & Road Course (4.167-mile road; 200 miles) (Lincoln)

ALAN KULWICKI

1986	(16th)	(366)
1987	(19th)	(380)

Poles

Miller High Life 400; Richmond Fgds. Raceway (.542-mile) (Ford)
Wrangler Indigo 400; Richmond Fgds. Raceway (.542-mile) (Ford)
Delaware 500; Dover Downs International Speedway (1-m) (Ford)

1988	(16th)	(363)

Victories

Checker 500; Phoenix International Raceway (1-m; 312 m) (Ford)

Poles

Budweiser 500; Dover Downs International Speedway (1-m) (Ford)
Miller High Life 500; Pocono Int. Raceway (2.5-mile) (Ford)
Busch 500; Bristol International Raceway (.533-mile) (Ford)
Oakwood Homes 500; Charlotte Motor Speedway (1.5-mile) (Ford)

1989	(18th)	(389)

Poles (T-1st)

Motorcraft QP 500; Atlanta Int. Raceway (1.522-mile) (Ford)
Coca-Cola 600; Charlotte Motor Speedway (1.5-mile) (Ford)
Busch 500; Bristol International Raceway (.533-mile) (Ford)
Heinz Southern 500; Darlington Int. Raceway (1.366-mile) (Ford)
AC Delco 500; North Carolina Motor Speedway (1.017-mile) (Ford)
Atlanta Journal 500; Atlanta Int. Raceway (1.522-mile) (Ford)

1990	(10th)	(527)

Victories

AC Delco 500; N.C. Motor Speedway (1.017-m; 500 miles) (Ford)

Poles

Champion Spark Plug 400; Michigan Int. Speedway (2-mile) (Ford)

1991	(14th)	(445)

Victories

Bud 500; Bristol International Raceway (.533-m; 267 m) (Ford)

Poles

Motorcraft QP 500; Atlanta Motor Speedway (1.522-mile) (Ford)
Miller Genuine Draft 500; Pocono Int. Raceway (2.5-mile) (Ford)
Champion Spark Plug 400; Michigan Int. Speedway (2-mile) (Ford)
Peak Antifreeze 500; Dover Downs Int. Speedway (1-mile) (Ford)

1992	(3rd)	(680)

Victories

* Food City 500; Bristol Int. Raceway (.533-m; 267 m) (Ford)
Champion SP 500; Pocono Int. Raceway (2.5-m; 500 miles) (Ford)

Poles (1st)
* Food City 500; Bristol International Raceway (.533-m) (Ford)
First Union 400; North Wilkesboro Speedway (.625-mile) (Ford)
Champion Spark Plug 400; Michigan Int. Speedway (2-mile) (Ford)
Peak Antifreeze 500; Dover Downs Int. Speedway (1-mile) (Ford)
Tyson Holly Farms 400; No. Wilkesboro Speedway (.625-mile) (Ford)
Mello Yello 500; Charlotte Motor Speedway (1.5-mile) (Ford)

BOBBY LABONTE

1993 (15th) (441)

Poles
Miller Genuine Draft 400; Richmond Int. Raceway (.75-m) (Ford)

1994 (22nd) (343)

1995 (9th) (568)

Victories
Coca-Cola 600; Charlotte Motor Speedway (1.5-m; 600 m) (Chevrolet)
Miller Gen. Dr. 400; Michigan Int. Speedway (2-m; 400 m) (Chevrolet)
* GM Goodwrench Deal. 400; Michigan Int. Sp. (2-m; 400m) (Chevrolet)

Poles
Hanes 500; Martinsville Speedway (.526-mile) (Chevrolet)
* GM Goodwrench Dealer 400; Michigan Int. Speedway (2-m) (Chevrolet)

1996 (13th) (472)

Victories
* NAPA 500; Atlanta Motor Speedway (1.522-m; 500 miles) (Chevrolet)

Poles
MBNA 500; Dover Downs International Speedway (1-mile) (Chevrolet)
UAW-GM Quality 500; Charlotte Motor Speedway (1.5-mile) (Chevrolet)
Dura-Lube 500; Phoenix International Raceway (1-mile) (Chevrolet)
* NAPA 500; Atlanta Motor Speedway (1.522-mile) (Chevrolet)

1997 (7th) (676)

Victories
NAPA 500; Atlanta Motor Speedway (1.54-m; 500 miles) (Pontiac)

Poles (T-1st)
Miller 500; Dover Downs International Speedway (1-m) (Pontiac)
Mount. Dew Southern 500; Darlington Raceway (1.366-m) (Pontiac)
AC Delco 400; North Carolina Motor Speedway (1.017-m) (Pontiac)

1998 (6th) (696)

Victories
PRIMESTAR 500; Atlanta Motor Speedway (1.54-m; 500 m) (Pontiac)
* Diehard 500; Talladega Superspeedway (2.66-m; 500 m) (Pontiac)

Poles
Daytona 500; Daytona International Speedway (2.5-mile) (Pontiac)
* Diehard 500; Talladega Superspeedway (2.66-mile) (Pontiac)
Pepsi 400; Daytona International Speedway (2.5-mile) (Pontiac)

1999 (2nd) (904)

Victories
* MBNA Platinum 400; Dover Downs Int. Sp. (1-m; 400m) (Pontiac)
Pocono 500; Pocono Raceway (2.5-mile; 500 miles) (Pontiac)
Pennsylvania 500; Pocono Raceway (2.5-mile; 500 miles) (Pontiac)
Pepsi 400; Michigan Speedway (2-mile; 400 miles) (Pontiac)
NAPA 500; Atlanta Motor Speedway (1.54-m; 500 miles) (Pontiac)

Poles
Las Vegas 400; Las Vegas Motor Speedway (1.5-mile) (Pontiac)
Cracker Barrel OCS 500; Atlanta Motor Speed. (1.54-m) (Pontiac)
Coca-Cola 600; Lowe's Motor Speedway (1.5-mile) (Pontiac)
* MBNA Platinum 400; Dover Downs Int. Speedway (1-m) (Pontiac)
UAW-GM Quality 500; Lowe's Motor Speedway (1.5-mile) (Pontiac)

TERRY LABONTE

1979 (12th) (455)

1980 (9th) (541)

Victories
Southern 500; Darlington Int. Raceway (1.366-m; 500 m) (Chevrolet)

1981 (5th) (591)

Poles
Coca-Cola 500; Atlanta International Raceway (1.522-m) (Buick)
Budweiser NASCAR 400; Texas World Speedway (2-mile) (Buick)

1982 (3rd) (636)

Poles
Va. National Bank 500; Martinsville Speedway (.525-mile) (Chevrolet)
Budweiser 400; Riverside Int. Raceway (2.62-mile road) (Buick)

1983 (5th) (615)

Victories
W.W. Hodgdon Amer. 500; N.C. Motor Sp. (1.017-m; 500 m) (Chevrolet)

Poles
Gabriel 400; Michigan International Speedway (2-mile) (Chevrolet)
Champion Spark Plug 400; Michigan Int. Speedway (2-m) (Chevrolet)
Budweiser 500; Dover Downs International Speedway (1-m) (Chevrolet)

1984 (2nd) (739)

Victories
* Budweiser 400; Riverside Int. Race. (2.62-m rd.; 250m) (Chevrolet)
Busch 500; Bristol Int. Raceway (.533-mile; 267 miles) (Chevrolet)

Poles
* Budweiser 400; Riverside Int. Raceway (2.62-mile road) (Chevrolet)
Winston Western 500; Riverside Int. Raceway (2.62-m rd.) (Chevrolet)

1985 (8th) (535)

Victories
Budweiser 400; Riverside Int. Raceway (2.62-m rd.; 249m) (Chevrolet)

Poles
Carolina 500; North Carolina Motor Speedway (1.017-mile) (Chevrolet)
Budweiser 500; Dover Downs International Speedway (1-m) (Chevrolet)
Nationwise 500; North Carolina Motor Speedway (1.017-m) (Chevrolet)
Winston Western 500; Riverside Int. Raceway (2.62-m rd.) (Chevrolet)

1986 (11th) (491)

Victories
* Goodwrench 500; N.C. Motor Speedway (1.017-m; 500 m) (Oldsmobile)

Poles
* Goodwrench 500; N.C. Motor Speedway (1.017-mile) (Oldsmobile)

1987 (4th) (645)

Victories
Holly Farms 400; North Wilkesboro Speed. (.625-m; 250m) (Chevrolet)

Poles
Miller High Life 500; Pocono Int. Raceway (2.5-mile) (Chevrolet)
Budweiser 400; Riverside Int. Raceway (2.62-mile road) (Chevrolet)
Budweiser at the Glen; Watkins Glen Int. (2.428-m road) (Chevrolet)
Busch 500; Bristol International Raceway (.533-mile) (Chevrolet)

1988   (4th)   (662)

Victories
* First Union 400; N. Wilkesboro Speedway (.625-m; 250m) (Chevrolet)
Poles
* First Union 400; North Wilkesboro Speedway (.625-mile) (Chevrolet)

1989   (7th)   (570)

Victories
Miller High Life 500; Pocono Int. Raceway (2.5-m; 500 m) (Ford)
Talladega Diehard 500; Talladega Super. (2.66-m; 500 m) (Ford)

1990   (7th)   (538)

1991   (18th)   (356)

Poles
Budweiser at the Glen; Watkins Glen Int. (2.428-m road) (Oldsmobile)

1992   (7th)   (588)

1993   (16th)   (439)

1994   (7th)   (629)

Victories
First Union 400; No. Wilkesboro Speedway (.625-m; 250 m) (Chevrolet)
Miller Gen. Dr. 400; Richmond Int. Raceway (.75-m; 300m) (Chevrolet)
Slick 50 500; Phoenix Int. Raceway (1-mile; 312 miles) (Chevrolet)

1995   (5th)   (698)

Victories
Pont. Excitement 400; Richmond Int. Race. (.75-m; 300m) (Chevrolet)
UAW-GM Teamwork 500; Pocono Int. Raceway (2.5-m; 500 m) (Chevrolet)
Goody's 500; Bristol Int. Raceway (.533-mile; 267 miles) (Chevrolet)
Poles
Winston Select 500; Talladega Superspeedway (2.66-mile) (Chevrolet)

1996   (3rd)   (750)

Victories
* First Union 400; N. Wilkesboro Speedway (.625-m; 250m) (Chevrolet)
UAW-GM Quality 500; Charlotte Motor Speed. (1.5-m; 500m) (Chevrolet)
Poles
Goodwrench 400; N.C. Motor Speedway (1.017-mile) (Chevrolet)
Pontiac Excitement 400; Richmond Int. Raceway (.75-mile) (Chevrolet)
* First Union 400; North Wilkesboro Speedway (.625-mile) (Chevrolet)
Save Mart Supermarkets 300; Sears Pt. Race. (2.52-m rd.) (Chevrolet)

1997   (5th)   (703)

Victories
Diehard 500; Talladega Superspeedway (2.66-m; 500 miles) (Chevrolet)

1998   (8th)   (610)

Victories
Pont. Excitement 400; Richmond Int. Race. (.75-m; 300 m) (Chevrolet)

1999   (12th)   (477)

Victories
PRIMESTAR 500; Texas Motor Speedway (1.5-m; 500 miles) (Chevrolet)

ART LAMEY

| 1950 | (T-25th) | |

SHEP LANGDON

| 1959 | (21st) | (172) |

ELMO LANGLEY

1961		(172)
1963		(116)
1964		(124)
1965	(17th)	(289)
1966	(5th)	(552)

Victories
Piedmont Interstate Fairgrounds (.5-m dirt; 100 miles) (Ford)
Old Dominion Speedway (.375-mile; 150 miles) (Ford)
Poles
Hickory 250; Hickory Speedway (.4-mile dirt) (Ford)

1967	(7th)	(539)
1968	(6th)	(608)
1969	(7th)	(667)
1970	(8th)	(598)
1971	(5th)	(664)
1972	(9th)	(449)
1973	(11th)	(360)
1974	(23rd)	(230)
1975	(10th)	(461)

MEL LARSON

| 1957 | | |

Poles
Concord Speedway (.5-mile dirt) (Ford)

| 1960 | | |

Poles
Copper Cup 100; Arizona State Fairgrounds (1-m dirt) (Pontiac)

HARRY LEAKE

| 1961 | | (126) |

KEVIN LEPAGE

| 1998 | | (224) |
| 1999 | | (276) |

Poles
NAPA 500; Atlanta Motor Speedway (1.54-mile) (Ford)

Driver Resumes

DANNY LETNER

1954

Victories
Oakland Stadium (.5-mile dirt; 150 miles) (Hudson)

Poles
Carrell Speedway (.5-mile dirt) (Hudson)

1955

Victories
Tucson Rodeo Grounds (.5-mile dirt; 100 miles) (Oldsmobile)

JIMMIE LEWALLEN

1951	(10th)	(156)
1952	(12th)	(151)
1953	(8th)	(237)
1954	(9th)	(207)
1955	(9th)	(311)

Poles
Columbia Speedway (.5-mile dirt) (Oldsmobile)

PAUL LEWIS

1960	(T-24th)	(171)
1961		(149)
1965	(14th)	(371)

Poles
Harris Speedway (.3-mile) (Ford)

1966	(14th)	(351)

Victories
Smoky Mount. 200; Smoky Mount. Race. (.5-m dirt; 100m) (Plymouth)

1967	(25th)	(207)

RALPH LIGUORI

1952	(22nd)	
1953	(25th)	
1954	(8th)	(221)
1955	(21st)	(123)

DICK LINDER

1950	(T-3rd)	(197)

Victories
Dayton Speedway (.5-mile; 100 miles) (Oldsmobile)
* Hamburg Fairgrounds (.5-mile dirt; 100 miles) (Oldsmobile)
* Vernon Fairgrounds (.5-mile dirt; 100 miles) (Oldsmobile)

Poles (1st)
Dayton Speedway (.5-mile dirt) (Oldsmobile)
Occoneechee Speedway (1-mile dirt) (Oldsmobile)
* Hamburg Fairgrounds (.5-mile dirt) (Oldsmobile)
* Vernon Fairgrounds (.5-mile dirt) (Oldsmobile)
Funk's Speedway (.5-mile dirt) (Oldsmobile)

CHAD LITTLE

1990		(130)
1991		(213)
1997		(139)
1998	(16th)	(448)
1999	(24th)	(305)

JOE LITTLEJOHN

1949	(T-22nd)

1950

Poles
Beach & Road Course (4.167-mile road) (Oldsmobile)

ED LIVINGSTON

1963		(101)

FRED LORENZEN

1960		(166)
1961	(23rd)	(216)

Victories
Grand National 200; Martinsville Speedway (.5-m; 100 m) (Ford)
* Rebel 300; Darlington Raceway (1.375-mile; 300 miles) (Ford)
Festival 250; Atlanta Int. Raceway (1.5-mile; 250 miles) (Ford)

Poles
* Rebel 300; Darlington Raceway (1.375-mile) (Ford)
Volunteer 500; Bristol International Speedway (.5-mile) (Ford)
Old Dominion 500; Martinsville Speedway (.5-mile) (Ford)

1962	(17th)	(347)

Victories
Atlanta 500; Atlanta Int. Raceway (1.5-mile; 500 miles) (Ford)
Augusta Speedway (.5-mile dirt; 100 miles) (Ford)

Poles
Virginia 500; Martinsville Speedway (.5-mile) (Ford)
Rebel 300; Darlington Raceway (1.375-mile) (Ford)
Wilkes 320; North Wilkesboro Speedway (.625-mile) (Ford)

1963	(4th)	(636)

Victories
Atlanta 500; Atlanta Int. Raceway (1.5-mile; 500 miles) (Ford)
World 600; Charlotte Motor Speedway (1.5-m; 600 miles) (Ford)
* Volunteer 500; Bristol Int. Speedway (.5-m; 250 miles) (Ford)
West. N.C. 500; Asheville-Weaverville Sp. (.5-m; 250 m) (Ford)
* Mountaineer 300; W.Va. Int. Speedway (.375-m; 113 m) (Ford)
Old Dominion 500; Martinsville Speedway (.5-mile; 250 m) (Ford)

Poles
Southeastern 500; Bristol International Speedway (.5-m) (Ford)
Gwyn Staley 400; North Wilkesboro Speedway (.625-mile) (Ford)
Rebel 300; Darlington Raceway (1.375-mile) (Ford)
* Volunteer 500; Bristol International Speedway (.5-m) (Ford)
* Mountaineer 300; West Virginia Int. Speedway (.375-m) (Ford)
Southern 500; Darlington Raceway (1.375-mile) (Ford)
Wilkes 400; North Wilkesboro Speedway (.625-mile) (Ford)
Tar Heel Speedway (.25-mile) (Ford)

1964   (17th)   (370)

Victories
Southeastern 500; Bristol Int. Speedway (.5-m; 250 m) (Ford)
* Atlanta 500; Atlanta Int. Raceway (1.5-m; 500 miles) (Ford)
* Gwyn Staley 400; N. Wilkesboro Speedway (.625-m; 250m) (Ford)
* Virginia 500; Martinsville Speedway (.5-m; 250 miles) (Ford)
* Rebel 300; Darlington Raceway (1.375-mile; 300 miles) (Ford)
Volunteer 500; Bristol Int. Speedway (.5-m; 250 miles) (Ford)
* Old Dominion 500; Martinsville Speedway (.5-m; 250 m) (Ford)
National 400; Charlotte Motor Speedway (1.5-mile; 400 m) (Ford)

Poles
Augusta International Speedway (3-mile road) (Ford)
Motor Trend 500; Riverside Int. Raceway (2.7-mile road) (Ford)
* Atlanta 500; Atlanta International Raceway (1.5-mile) (Ford)
* Gwyn Staley 400; North Wilkesboro Speedway (.625-mile) (Ford)
* Virginia 500; Martinsville Speedway (.5-mile) (Ford)
* Rebel 300; Darlington Raceway (1.375-mile) (Ford)
* Old Dominion 500; Martinsville Speedway (.5-mile) (Ford)

1965   (19th)   (285)

Victories
Daytona 500; Daytona Int. Speedway (2.5-mile; 500 miles) (Ford)
Virginia 500; Martinsville Speedway (.5-mile; 250 miles) (Ford)
* World 600; Charlotte Motor Speedway (1.5-m; 600 miles) (Ford)
* National 400; Charlotte Motor Speedway (1.5-m; 400 m) (Ford)

Poles
Rebel 300; Darlington Raceway (1.375-mile) (Ford)
* World 600; Charlotte Motor Speedway (1.5-mile) (Ford)
Dixie 400; Atlanta International Raceway (1.5-mile) (Ford)
Volunteer 500; Bristol International Speedway (.5-mile) (Ford)
Wilkes 400; North Wilkesboro Speedway (.625-mile) (Ford)
* National 400; Charlotte Motor Speedway (1.5-mile) (Ford)

1966   (219)

Victories
Old Dominion 500; Martinsville Speedway (.5-m; 250 m) (Ford)
* American 500; N.C. Motor Speedway (1-mile; 500 miles) (Ford)

Poles
National 500; Charlotte Motor Speedway (1.5-mile) (Ford)
* American 500; North Carolina Motor Speedway (1-mile) (Ford)

1967   (113)

Victories
Daytona International Speedway (2.5-mile; 100 miles) (Ford)

1970

Poles
Dixie 500; Atlanta International Raceway (1.522-mile) (Dodge)

1971   (19th)   (328)

Poles
Carolina 500; North Carolina Motor Speedway (1.017-m) (Plymouth)

1972   (184)

TINY LUND

1956   (17th)   (179)

1957   (11th)   (339)

Poles
Cleveland County Fairgrounds (.5-mile dirt) (Pontiac)
Southern States Fairgrounds (.5-mile dirt) (Pontiac)
Lincoln Speedway (.5-mile dirt) (Pontiac)

1958   (22nd)   (165)

Poles
Gastonia Fairgrounds (.333-mile dirt) (Chevrolet)
Orange Speedway (.9-mile dirt) (Chevrolet)

1959   (14th)   (273)

1961   (148)

1962   (119)

1963   (16th)   (369)

Victories
Daytona 500; Daytona Int. Speedway (2.5-mile; 500 miles) (Ford)

1964   (T-20th)   (280)

1965   (13th)   (376)

Victories
Columbia 200; Columbia Speedway (.5-m dirt; 100 miles) (Ford)

1966   (222)

Victories
Beltsville 200; Beltsville Speedway (.5-mile; 100 miles) (Ford)

Poles
Greenville 200; Greenville-Pickens Speedway (.5-m dirt) (Ford)

1967   (23rd)   (236)

1968   (19th)   (295)

1971   (258)

Victories
Buddy Shuman 276; Hickory Speedway (.363-m; 100 miles) (Chevrolet)
Wilkes 400; North Wilkesboro Speedway (.625-mile; 250 m) (Chevrolet)

CLYDE LYNN

1965   (180)

1966   (12th)   (388)

1967   (8th)   (474)

1968   (7th)   (598)

DAVE MacDONALD

1964   (120)

CHUCK MAHONEY

1950   (10th)   (128)

Poles
Vernon Fairgrounds (.5-mile dirt) (Mercury)

Driver Resumes

LARRY MANNING

1963	(25th)	(219)

SKIP MANNING

1975		(105)
1976	(14th)	(396)
1977	(15th)	(379)
1978		(215)

JOHNNY MANTZ

1950	(16th)

Victories
Southern 500; Darlington Raceway (1.25-m; 500 miles) (Plymouth)

DAVE MARCIS

1968		(142)
1969	(18th)	(386)
1970	(12th)	(451)
1971	(15th)	(393)

Poles
Richmond 500; Richmond Fairgrounds Raceway (.542-mile) (Dodge)
Buddy Shuman 276; Hickory Speedway (.363-mile) (Dodge)

1972	(11th)	(393)
1973	(20th)	(253)
1974	(3rd)	(585)
1975	(4th)	(596)

Victories
Old Dominion 500; Martinsville Speedway (.525-mile; 263 miles) (Dodge)
Poles
Talladega 500; Alabama Int. Motor Speedway (2.66-mile) (Dodge)
Delaware 500; Dover Downs International Speedway (1-m) (Dodge)
American 500; North Carolina Motor Speedway (1.017-mile) (Dodge)
Dixie 500; Atlanta International Raceway (1.522-mile) (Dodge)

1976	(7th)	(508)

Victories
Richmond 400; Richmond Fgds. Raceway (.542-m; 217 miles) (Dodge)
* Talladega 500; Ala. Int. Motor Speedway (2.66-m; 500m) (Dodge)
Dixie 500; Atlanta Int. Raceway (1.522-mile; 500 miles) (Dodge)

Poles
Carolina 500; North Carolina Motor Speedway (1.017-mile) (Dodge)
Atlanta 500; Atlanta International Raceway (1.522-mile) (Dodge)
Gwyn Staley 400; North Wilkesboro Speedway (.625-mile) (Dodge)
Virginia 500; Martinsville Speedway (.525-mile) (Dodge)
Winston 500; Alabama Int. Motor Speedway (2.66-mile) (Dodge)
Mason-Dixon 500; Dover Downs Int. Speedway (1-mile) (Dodge)
* Talladega 500; Alabama Int. Motor Speedway (2.66-mile) (Dodge)

1977	(24th)	(242)
1978	(3rd)	(725)

1979	(19th)	(295)
1980	(13th)	(458)
1981	(10th)	(435)

Poles
Northwestern Bank 400; No. Wilkesboro Speedway (.625-m) (Chevrolet)

1982	(6th)	(513)

Victories
Richmond 400; Richmond Fgds. Raceway (.542-m; 217 miles) (Chevrolet)

1983	(11th)	(445)
1984	(14th)	(432)
1985	(23rd)	(265)
1986	(20th)	(301)
1987	(21st)	(345)
1988		(230)
1989	(24th)	(294)
1990	(23rd)	(266)
1991		(164)
1992		(117)

COO COO MARLIN

1970		(192)
1972	(24th)	(221)
1973	(15th)	(314)
1974	(21st)	(268)
1975	(15th)	(387)
1976	(24th)	(229)
1977	(23rd)	(249)

STERLING MARLIN

1980		(113)
1983	(24th)	(295)
1984		(113)
1986		(143)
1987	(12th)	(483)
1988	(10th)	(540)
1989	(11th)	(507)
1990	(14th)	(498)
1991	(4th)	(659)

Poles
Pepsi 400; Daytona International Speedway (2.5-mile) (Ford)
Diehard 500; Talladega Superspeedway (2.66-mile) (Ford)

1992   (12th)   (518)

Poles

Daytona 500 by STP; Daytona Int. Speedway (2.5-mile) (Ford)
TranSouth 500; Darlington Raceway (1.366-mile) (Ford)
Pepsi 400; Daytona International Speedway (2.5-mile) (Ford)
Diehard 500; Talladega Superspeedway (2.66-mile) (Ford)
Mountain Dew Southern 500; Darlington Raceway (1.366-m) (Ford)

1993   (19th)   (403)

1994   (14th)   (469)

Victories

Daytona 500; Daytona Int. Speedway (2.5-mile; 500 miles) (Chevrolet)

Poles

Slick 50 500; Phoenix International Raceway (1-mile) (Chevrolet)

1995   (2nd)   (784)

Victories

Daytona 500; Daytona Int. Speedway (2.5-mile; 500 miles) (Chevrolet)
TranSouth Finan. 400; Darlington Raceway (1.366-m; 400m) (Chevrolet)
* Diehard 500; Talladega Superspeedway (2.66-m; 500 m) (Chevrolet)

Poles

* Diehard 500; Talladega Superspeedway (2.66-mile) (Chevrolet)

1996   (9th)   (553)

Victories

Winston Sel. 500; Talladega Superspeedway (2.66-m; 500m) (Chevrolet)
Pepsi 400; Daytona Int. Speedway (2.5-mile; 400 miles) (Chevrolet)

1997   (22nd)   (330)

1998   (12th)   (511)

1999   (T-18th)   (352)

Poles

Pocono 500; Pocono Raceway (2.5-mile) (Chevrolet)

MARK MARTIN

1981

Poles

Busch Nashville 420; Nashville Int. Raceway (.596-m) (Pontiac)
Wrangler Sanforset 400; Richmond Fgds. Race. (.542-m) (Pontiac)

1982   (21st)   (338)

1983   (190)

1988   (T-14th)   (433)

Poles

Delaware 500; Dover Downs International Speedway (1-m) (Ford)

1989   (3rd)   (670)

Victories

AC Delco 500; N.C. Motor Speedway (1.017-m; 500 miles) (Ford)

Poles (T-1st)

TranSouth 500; Darlington Int. Raceway (1.366-mile) (Ford)
Valleydale Meats 500; Bristol Int. Raceway (.533-mile) (Ford)
Winston 500; Talladega Superspeedway (2.66-mile) (Ford)
Budweiser 500; Dover Downs International Speedway (1-m) (Ford)
Pepsi 400; Daytona International Speedway (2.5-mile) (Ford)
Talladega Diehard 500; Talladega Superspeedway (2.66-m) (Ford)

1990   (1st)   (800)

Victories

Pont. Excitement 400; Richmond Int. Race. (.75-m; 300m) (Ford)
Champion SP 400; Michigan Int. Speedway (2-m; 400 miles) (Ford)
Tyson Holly Farms 400; N. Wilkesboro Sp. (.625-m; 250 m) (Ford)

Poles

First Union 400; North Wilkesboro Speedway (.625-mile) (Ford)
AC Spark Plug 500; Pocono International Raceway (2.5-m) (Ford)
Goody's 500; Martinsville Speedway (.526-mile) (Ford)

1991   (7th)   (577)

Victories

Hardee's 500; Atlanta Motor Speedway (1.522-mile; 500 m) (Ford)

Poles (1st)

Hanes 500; Martinsville Speedway (.526-mile) (Ford)
Coca-Cola 600; Charlotte Motor Speedway (1.5-mile) (Ford)
Champion Spark Plug 500; Pocono Int. Raceway (2.5-mile) (Ford)
Goody's 500; Martinsville Speedway (.526-mile) (Ford)
Mello Yello 500; Charlotte Motor Speedway (1.5-mile) (Ford)

1992   (6th)   (606)

Victories

Hanes 500; Martinsville Speedway (.526-mile; 263 miles) (Ford)
Mello Yello 500; Charlotte Motor Speedway (1.5-m; 500 m) (Ford)

Poles

Motorcraft 500; Atlanta Motor Speedway (1.522-mile) (Ford)

1993   (3rd)   (696)

Victories

* Bud. at the Glen; Wat. Glen Int. (2.45-m rd.; 221 m) (Ford)
Champion SP 400; Michigan Int. Speedway (2-m; 400 miles) (Ford)
* Bud 500; Bristol Int. Raceway (.533-mile; 267 miles) (Ford)
Mt. Dew Southern 500; Darlington Raceway (1.366-m; 500m) (Ford)
Slick 50 500; Phoenix Int. Raceway (1-mile; 312 miles) (Ford)

Poles

Goodwrench 500; North Carolina Motor Speedway (1.017-m) (Ford)
Slick 50 300; New Hampshire Int. Speedway (1.058-mile) (Ford)
* Budweiser at the Glen; Watkins Glen Int. (2.45-m road) (Ford)
* Bud 500; Bristol International Raceway (.533-mile) (Ford)
AC Delco 500; North Carolina Motor Speedway (1.017-mile) (Ford)

1994   (3rd)   (676)

Victories

* Bud. at the Glen; Wat. Glen Int. (2.45-m rd.; 221 m) (Ford)
Hooters 500; Atlanta Motor Speedway (1.522-m; 500 miles) (Ford)

Poles

* Budweiser at the Glen; Watkins Glen Int. (2.45-m road) (Ford)

1995   (4th)   (737)

Victories

Winston Sel. 500; Talladega Superspeedway (2.66-m; 500m) (Ford)
* The Bud at the Glen; Wat. Glen Int. (2.45-m rd.; 221m) (Ford)
Tyson Holly Farms 400; N. Wilkesboro Sp. (.625-m; 250m) (Ford)
UAW-GM Quality 500; Charlotte Motor Speed. (1.5-m; 500m) (Ford)

Poles

Food City 500; Bristol International Raceway (.533-mile) (Ford)
Slick 50 300; New Hampshire Int. Speedway (1.058-mile) (Ford)
* The Bud at the Glen; Watkins Glen Int. (2.45-m road) (Ford)
Goody's 500; Bristol International Raceway (.533-mile) (Ford)

1996   (5th)   (707)

Poles

Food City 500; Bristol International Raceway (.533-mile) (Ford)
Miller Genuine Draft 500; Pocono Int. Raceway (2.5-mile) (Ford)
Goody's HP 500; Bristol Motor Speedway (.533-mile) (Ford)
Miller 400; Richmond International Raceway (.75-mile) (Ford)

1997   (2nd)   (821)

Victories

* Save Mart Sup. 300; Sears Pt. Race. (2.52-m rd.; 186m) (Ford)
Winston 500; Talladega Superspeedway (2.66-m; 500 miles) (Ford)
DeVilbiss 400; Michigan Speedway (2-mile; 400 miles) (Ford)
* MBNA 400; Dover Downs Int. Speedway (1-mile; 400 miles) (Ford)

Poles (T-1st)

Goodwrench 400; North Carolina Motor Speedway (1.017-m) (Ford)
* Save Mart Supermark. 300; Sears Pt. Race. (2.52-m rd.) (Ford)
* MBNA 400; Dover Downs International Speedway (1-mile) (Ford)

1998   (2nd)   (866)

Victories

Las Vegas 400; Las Vegas Motor Speedway (1.5-m; 400 m) (Ford)
Texas 500; Texas Motor Speedway (1.5-mile; 500 miles) (Ford)
California 500 by NAPA; California Speedway (2-m; 500 m) (Ford)
Miller Lite 400; Michigan Speedway (2-mile; 400 miles) (Ford)
Goody's HP 500; Bristol Motor Speedway (.533-m; 267 m) (Ford)
* MBNA Gold 400; Dover Downs Int. Speedway (1-m; 400 m) (Ford)
UAW-GM Quality 500; Charlotte Motor Speed. (1.5-m; 500m) (Ford)

Poles

TranSouth Financial 400; Darlington Raceway (1.366-mile) (Ford)
* MBNA Gold 400; Dover Downs Int. Speedway (1-mile) (Ford)
AC Delco 400; North Carolina Speedway (1.017-mile) (Ford)

1999   (3rd)   (872)

Victories

Dura-Lube/Big Kmart 400; N.C. Speedway (1.017-m; 400 m) (Ford)
MBNA Gold 400; Dover Downs Int. Speedway (1-mile; 400 m) (Ford)

Poles

Pop Secret Microwave Pop. 400; N.C. Speedway (1.017-m) (Ford)

JIMMY MASSEY

1955   (15th)   (149)

1958

Poles

West. N.C. 500; Asheville-Weaverville Speedway (.5-m) (Pontiac)

1963   (153)

RICK MAST

1989   (132)

1991   (21st)   (320)

1992   (235)

Poles

Hooters 500; Atlanta Motor Speedway (1.522-mile) (Oldsmobile)

1993   (21st)   (366)

1994   (19th)   (386)

Poles

Brickyard 400; Indianapolis Motor Speedway (2.5-mile) (Ford)

1995   (24th)   (268)

Poles

MBNA 500; Dover Downs International Speedway (1-mile) (Ford)

1996   (17th)   (386)

1997   (210)

1998   (115)

Poles

GM Goodwrench Service Plus 400; N.C. Speedway (1.017-m) (Ford)

1999   (205)

BANJO MATTHEWS

1957

Poles

Beach & Road Course (4.1-mile road) (Pontiac)

1960   (23rd)   (180)

1961   (120)

1962

Poles

Atlanta 500; Atlanta International Raceway (1.5-mile) (Pontiac)
Firecracker 250; Daytona Int. Speedway (2.5-mile) (Pontiac)

DICK MAY

1975   (104)

1976   (180)

1977   (138)

1978   (13th)   (354)

1980   (25th)   (224)

1981   (101)

1982   (113)

JEREMY MAYFIELD

1995   (25th)   (256)

1996   (25th)   (273)

Poles

Diehard 500; Talladega Superspeedway (2.66-mile) (Ford)

1997   (14th)   (464)

1998   (7th)   (659)

Victories

Pocono 500; Pocono Raceway (2.5-mile; 500 miles) (Ford)

Poles

Texas 500; Texas Motor Speedway (1.5-mile) (Ford)

1999	(11th)	(544)

ROY MAYNE

1963	(146)
1965	(177)
1966	(222)
1967	(113)
1969	(135)
1970	(212)
1971	(132)

J.D. McDUFFIE

1966	(19th)	(264)
1968	(23rd)	(234)
1969	(14th)	(428)
1970	(22nd)	(322)
1971	(17th)	(378)
1972	(22nd)	(233)
1973	(9th)	(393)
1974	(10th)	(419)
1975	(19th)	(346)
1976	(17th)	(379)
1977	(12th)	(391)
1978	(12th)	(382)

Poles
Delaware 500; Dover Downs International Speedway (1-m) (Chevrolet)

1979	(15th)	(403)
1980	(21st)	(255)
1981	(22nd)	(292)
1982	(25th)	(278)
1983		(107)
1986		(141)

POP McGINNIS

1953	(24th)

HERSHEL McGRIFF

1954	(6th)	(379)

Victories
* Bay Meadows Speedway (1-mile dirt; 250 miles) (Oldsmobile)
Central City Speedway (.5-mile dirt; 100 miles) (Oldsmobile)
* Southern States Fairgrounds (.5-mile dirt; 100 miles) (Oldsmobile)
* Wilkes 160; N. Wilkesboro Speedway (.625-m dirt; 100m) (Oldsmobile)

Poles
Oakland Stadium (.5-mile dirt) (Oldsmobile)
Piedmont Interstate Fairgrounds (.5-mile dirt) (Oldsmobile)
* Bay Meadows Speedway (1-mile dirt) (Oldsmobile)
* Southern States Fairgrounds (.5-mile dirt) (Oldsmobile)
* Wilkes 160; North Wilkesboro Speedway (.625-mile dirt) (Oldsmobile)

1972	(127)

BILL McMAHAN

1964	(147)

WORTH McMILLION

1963	(136)
1964	(203)
1965	(105)

SAM McQUAGG

1965		(202)
1966	(24th)	(249)

Victories
Firecracker 400; Daytona Int. Speedway (2.5-mile; 400 m) (Dodge)

1967	(105)

JIMMY MEANS

1976		(120)
1977	(19th)	(293)
1978	(19th)	(280)
1979		(216)
1980	(16th)	(340)
1981	(21st)	(297)
1982	(9th)	(467)
1983	(18th)	(347)
1984	(24th)	(254)
1985		(207)
1986		(190)
1987		(151)

CHUCK MEEKINS

1956	(112)

STAN MESERVE

1968	(104)

JOE MIHALIC

1976		(135)

BUTCH MILLER

1990	(24th)	(258)

JOE MILLIKAN

1979	(6th)	(603)

Poles
Sun-Drop Music City USA 420; Nash. Int. Race. (.596-m) (Chevrolet)

1980		(146)
1981	(16th)	(364)
1982		(112)

JOEL MILLION

1955	(25th)

CLYDE MINTER

1949	(T-16th)
1950	(19th)
1954	(19th)

RALPH MOODY

1956	(8th)	(434)

Victories
Memphis-Arkansas Speedway (1.5-mile dirt; 250 miles) (Ford)
Old Bridge Stadium (.5-mile; 100 miles) (Ford)
* Piedmont Interstate Fairgrounds (.5-m dirt; 100 miles) (Ford)
Southern States Fairgrounds (.5-mile dirt; 100 miles) (Ford)

Poles
Cleveland County Fairgrounds (.5-mile dirt) (Ford)
Norfolk Speedway (.4-mile dirt) (Ford)
* Piedmont Interstate Fairgrounds (.5-mile dirt) (Ford)
Coastal Speedway (.5-mile dirt) (Ford)
Charlotte Speedway (.75-mile dirt) (Ford)

1957	(115)

Victories
Wilson Speedway (.5-mile dirt; 100 miles) (Ford)

TOMMY MOON

1952

Poles
Hayloft Speedway (.5-mile dirt) (Hudson)

BUD MOORE

1965		(123)

Poles
Greenville 200; Greenville-Pickens Speed. (.5-m. dirt) (Plymouth)

1967		(112)
1968	(24th)	(215)

DOUG MOORE

1964		(171)

LLOYD MOORE

1950	(T-3rd)	(197)

Victories
Funk's Speedway (.5-mile dirt; 100 miles) (Mercury)

1951	(9th)	(158)
1952	(19th)	(105)

ROB MOROSO

1990		(144)

ARDEN MOUNTS

1954	(22nd)

FRANK MUNDY

1949	(13th)
1950	(23rd)
1951	(5th)	(266)

Victories
Columbia Speedway (.5-mile dirt; 100 miles) (Studebaker)
Martinsville Speedway (.5-mile dirt; 100 miles) (Oldsmobile)
* Lakeview Speedway (.75-mile dirt; 113 miles) (Studebaker)

Poles
Southern 500; Darlington Raceway (1.25-mile) (Studebaker)
Lakewood Speedway (1-mile dirt) (Studebaker)
* Lakeview Speedway (.75-mile dirt) (Studebaker)

1956		(110)

TED MUSGRAVE

1991		(249)
1992	(17th)	(448)
1993	(T-24th)	(285)
1994	(13th)	(493)

Poles
Pontiac Excitement 400; Richmond Int. Raceway (.75-mile) (Ford)
Miller Genuine Draft 400; Richmond Int. Raceway (.75-m) (Ford)
Goody's 500; Martinsville Speedway (.526-mile) (Ford)

1995	(7th)	(607)

Poles
Tyson Holly Farms 400; No. Wilkesboro Speedway (.625-m) (Ford)

1996	(16th)	(426)

Poles
Tyson Holly Farms 400; No. Wilkesboro Speedway (.625-m) (Ford)

1997	(16th)	(435)

1998	(20th)	(358)

1999		(133)

BILLY MYERS

1956	(6th)	(470)

Victories
Palm Beach Speedway (.5-mile; 100 miles) (Mercury)
Norfolk Speedway (.4-mile dirt; 100 miles) (Mercury)

Poles
Soldier Field (.5-mile) (Mercury)

1957	(14th)	(249)

GARY B. MYERS

1977		(111)

1978		(173)

JERRY NADEAU

1999		(187)

ED NEGRE

1969		(161)

1971	(20th)	(323)

1972		(188)

1973	(21st)	(240)

1974		(158)

1975	(21st)	(330)

1976	(23rd)	(252)

1977		(163)

NORM NELSON

1955

Victories
* Las Vegas Park Speedway (1-mile dirt; 150 miles) (Chrysler)

Poles
* Las Vegas Park Speedway (1-mile dirt) (Chrysler)

JOE NEMECHEK

1994	(24th)	(263)

1995	(21st)	(284)

1996		(140)

1997		(256)

Poles
California 500; California Speedway (2-mile) (Chevrolet)
Pennsylvania 500; Pocono International Raceway (2.5-m) (Chevrolet)

1998		(271)

1999		(214)

Victories
Dura-Lube/Kmart 500; N.H. Int. Speedway (1.058-m; 317 m) (Chevrolet)

Poles
Pepsi 400; Daytona International Speedway (2.5-mile) (Chevrolet)
NAPA AutoCare 500; Martinsville Speedway (.526-mile) (Chevrolet)
Winston 500; Talladega Superspeedway (2.66-mile) (Chevrolet)

RICK NEWSOM

1973		(114)

1982		(102)

WHITEY NORMAN

1957		(101)

BILL NORTON

1951

Victories
Carrell Speedway (.5-mile dirt; 100 miles) (Mercury)

COTTON OWENS

1950	(21st)	

1957	(21st)	(165)

Victories
Beach & Road Course (4.1-mile road; 160 miles) (Pontiac)

Poles
Southern 500; Darlington Raceway (1.375-mile) (Pontiac)

1958	(10th)	(320)

Victories
Monroe County Fairgrounds (.5-mile dirt; 100 miles) (Pontiac)

Poles
Raleigh 250; Raleigh Speedway (1-mile) (Pontiac)
Alabama State Fairgrounds (.5-mile dirt) (Pontiac)

1959	(2nd)	(511)

Victories
* Capital City 200; Atlantic Rural Fgds. (.5-m d.; 100m) (Ford)

Poles
Piedmont Interstate Fairgrounds (.5-mile dirt) (Pontiac)
* Capital City 200; Atlantic Rural Fgds. (.5-mile dirt) (Ford)

1960	(T-24th)	(171)

Victories
* Piedmont Interstate Fairgrounds (.5-m dirt; 100 m) (Pontiac)

Poles

Daytona 500; Daytona International Speedway (2.5-mile) (Pontiac)
* Piedmont Interstate Fairgrounds (.5-mile dirt) (Pontiac)

1961 (15th) (301)

Victories

Piedmont Interstate Fairgrounds (.5-m dirt; 100 miles) (Pontiac)
Orange Speedway (.9-mile dirt; 99 miles) (Pontiac)
Columbia Speedway (.5-mile dirt; 100 miles) (Pontiac)
* Columbia Speedway (.5-mile dirt; 100 miles) (Pontiac)

Poles

* Columbia Speedway (.5-mile dirt) (Pontiac)
South Boston Speedway (.25-mile dirt) (Pontiac)

1962 (178)

Poles

Piedmont Interstate Fairgrounds (.5-mile dirt) (Pontiac)

1964

Victories

Capital City 300; Virginia State Fgds. (.5-m dirt; 150m) (Dodge)

EDDIE PAGAN

1956 (109)

Victories

* Bay Meadows Speedway (1-mile dirt; 250 miles) (Ford)

Poles

California State Fairgrounds (1-mile dirt) (Ford)
* Bay Meadows Speedway (1-mile dirt) (Ford)

1957 (13th) (284)

Victories

Portland Speedway (.5-mile; 75 miles) (Ford)
* Los Angeles Fairgrounds (.5-mile dirt; 100 miles) (Ford)
Portland Speedway (.5-mile; 100 miles) (Ford)

Poles

* Los Angeles Fairgrounds (.5-mile dirt) (Ford)
Old Dominion 500; Martinsville Speedway (.5-mile) (Ford)

1958 (8th) (357)

Poles

Old Dominion Speedway (.375-mile) (Ford)
Southern 500; Darlington Raceway (1.375-mile) (Ford)

CLYDE PALMER

1956 (103)

MARVIN PANCH

1954 (17th) (142)

Poles

Oakland Stadium (.5-mile dirt) (Dodge)

1955 (20th) (129)

1956 (10th) (284)

Victories

* Montgomery Speedway (.5-mile; 100 miles) (Ford)

Poles

* Montgomery Speedway (.5-mile) (Ford)

1957 (2nd) (644)

Victories

* Willow Springs Speedway (2.5-m dirt road; 150 miles) (Ford)
Concord Speedway (.5-mile dirt; 100 miles) (Ford)
Piedmont Interstate Faigrounds (.5-mile dirt; 100 miles) (Ford)
Southern States Fairgrounds (.5-mile dirt; 100 miles) (Ford)
Memphis-Arkansas Speedway (1.5-mile dirt; 201 miles) (Pontiac)
Lincoln Speedway (.5-mile dirt; 100 miles) (Ford)

Poles

* Willow Springs Speedway (2.5-mile dirt road) (Ford)
Asheville-Weaverville Speedway (.5-mile dirt) (Ford)
Southern States Fairgrounds (.5-mile dirt) (Ford)
Lincoln Speedway (.5-mile dirt) (Ford)

1958 (136)

Poles

Wilson Speedway (.5-mile dirt) (Ford)
Northern 500; Trenton Speedway (1-mile) (Ford)

1960 (111)

1961 (187)

Victories

Daytona 500; Daytona Int. Speedway (2.5-m; 500 miles) (Pontiac)

Poles

Atlanta 500; Atlanta International Raceway (1.5-mile) (Pontiac)

1962 (20th) (292)

1963 (17th) (337)

Victories

Wilkes 400; North Wilkesboro Speedway (.625-mile; 250 m) (Ford)

Poles

Dixie 400; Atlanta International Raceway (1.5-mile) (Ford)
National 400; Charlotte Motor Speedway (1.5-mile) (Ford)

1964 (10th) (561)

Victories

* Bowman Gray Stadium (.25-mile; 50 miles) (Ford)
* Asheville-Weaverville Speedway (.5-mile; 100 miles) (Ford)
Wilkes 400; North Wilkesboro Speedway (.625-mile; 250 m) (Ford)

Poles

Southeastern 500; Bristol Int. Speedway (.5-mile) (Ford)
* Bowman Gray Stadium (.25-mile) (Ford)
* Asheville-Weaverville Speedway (.5-mile) (Ford)
South Boston Speedway (.375-mile) (Ford)
Pickens 200; Greenville-Pickens Speedway (.5-mile dirt) (Ford)

1965 (12th) (448)

Victories

* Atlanta 500; Atlanta Int. Raceway (1.5-m; 500 miles) (Ford)
Dixie 400; Atlanta Int. Raceway (1.5-mile; 400 miles) (Ford)
* Islip Speedway (.2-mile; 50 miles) (Ford)
The Glen 151.8; Watkins Glen Int. (2.3-mile road; 152 m) (Ford)

Poles

* Atlanta 500; Atlanta International Raceway (1.5-mile) (Ford)
Southeastern 500; Bristol International Speedway (.5-m) (Ford)
Firecracker 400; Daytona International Speedway (2.5-m) (Ford)
Old Bridge 200; Old Bridge Stadium (.5-mile) (Ford)
* Islip Speedway (.2-mile) (Ford)

1966	(20th)	(263)

Victories
World 600; Charlotte Motor Speedway (1.5-m; 600 miles) (Plymouth)

RICHIE PANCH

1974	(20th)	(288)
1975		(131)

JIM PARDUE

1960	(11th)	(264)
1961	(7th)	(472)
1962	(T-14th)	(369)

Victories
Southside Speedway (.333-mile; 67 miles) (Pontiac)

1963	(7th)	(539)

Victories
Dog Track Speedway (.25-mile dirt; 63 miles) (Ford)
Poles
Greenville 200; Greenville-Pickens Speedway (.5-m dirt) (Ford)

1964	(6th)	(654)

Poles
Savannah 200; Savannah Speedway (.5-mile dirt) (Plymouth)
World 600; Charlotte Motor Speedway (1.5-mile) (Plymouth)

STEVE PARK

1999	(13th)	(463)

BENNY PARSONS

1969		(100)
1970	(5th)	(649)

Poles
Tidewater 300; Langley Field Speedway (.395-mile) (Ford)

1971	(10th)	(500)

Victories
Halifax Co. 100; South Boston Speedway (.357-m; 100 m) (Ford)

1972	(5th)	(583)
1973	(3rd)	(641)

Victories
Volunteer 500; Bristol Int. Speedway (.533-m; 267 miles) (Chevrolet)

1974	(9th)	(432)
1975	(8th)	(533)

Victories
Daytona 500; Daytona Int. Speedway (2.5-mile; 500 miles) (Chevrolet)
Poles
Virginia 500; Martinsville Speedway (.525-mile) (Chevrolet)
Nashville 420; Nashville Speedway (.596-mile) (Chevrolet)
Capital City 500; Richmond Fairgrounds Raceway (.542-m) (Chevrolet)

1976	(2nd)	(733)

Victories
Mason-Dixon 500; Dover Downs Int. Speedway (1-m; 500 m) (Chevrolet)
Nashville 420; Nashville Speedway (.596-mile; 250 miles) (Chevrolet)
Poles
Music City USA 420; Nashville Speedway (.596-mile) (Chevrolet)
Capital City 400; Richmond Fairgrounds Raceway (.542-m) (Chevrolet)

1977	(4th)	(747)

Victories
Music City USA 420; Nashville Speedway (.596-m; 250 m) (Chevrolet)
Coca-Cola 500; Pocono Int. Raceway (2.5-m; 500 miles) (Chevrolet)
Delaware 500; Dover Downs Int. Speedway (1-m; 500 miles) (Chevrolet)
NAPA National 500; Charlotte Motor Speed. (1.5-m; 500 m) (Chevrolet)
Poles
Nashville 420; Nashville Speedway (.596-mile) (Chevrolet)
Talladega 500; Alabama Int. Motor Speedway (2.66-mile) (Chevrolet)
Capital City 400; Richmond Fairgrounds Raceway (.542-m) (Chevrolet)

1978	(4th)	(701)

Victories
Richmond 400; Richmond Fgds. Raceway (.542-m; 217 miles) (Chevrolet)
Rebel 500; Darlington Int. Raceway (1.366-m; 500 miles) (Chevrolet)
NAPA Riverside 400; River. Int. Race. (2.66-m rd.; 249m) (Chevrolet)
Poles
Gwyn Staley 400; North Wilkesboro Speedway (.625-mile) (Chevrolet)
Coca-Cola 500; Pocono International Raceway (2.5-mile) (Chevrolet)

1979	(5th)	(654)

Victories
Holly Farms 400; No. Wilkesboro Speedway (.625-m; 250 m) (Chevrolet)
L.A. Times 500; Ontario Motor Speedway (2.5-mile; 500 m) (Chevrolet)
Poles
Northwestern Bank 400; No. Wilkesboro Speedway (.625-m) (Chevrolet)

1980	(4th)	(640)

Victories
World 600; Charlotte Motor Speedway (1.5-m; 600 miles) (Chevrolet)
* Gabriel 400; Michigan Int. Speedway (2-m; 400 miles) (Chevrolet)
L.A. Times 500; Ontario Motor Speedway (2.5-mile; 500 m) (Chevrolet)
Poles
CRC Chem. Rebel 500; Darlington Int. Raceway (1.366-m) (Chevrolet)
* Gabriel 400; Michigan International Speedway (2-mile) (Chevrolet)

1981	(12th)	(396)

Victories
Melling Tool 420; Nashville Int. Raceway (.596-m; 250 m) (Ford)
Budweiser NASCAR 400; Texas World Speedway (2-m; 400 m) (Ford)
Wrangler San. 400; Richmond Fgds. Race. (.542-m; 217 m) (Ford)

1982	(12th)	(438)

Poles
Daytona 500; Daytona International Speedway (2.5-mile) (Pontiac)
W.W. Hodgdon Car. 500; N.C. Motor Speedway (1.017-m) (Pontiac)
Winston 500; Alabama Int. Motor Speedway (2.66-mile) (Pontiac)

1983		(245)
1984	(19th)	(340)

Victories
Coca-Cola 500; Atlanta Int. Raceway (1.522-m; 500 miles) (Chevrolet)

Driver Resumes

Driver, Year (Performance Index ranking)
(Performance Index points)

Poles
TranSouth 500; Darlington Int. Raceway (1.366-mile) (Chevrolet)
Miller High Life 500; Charlotte Motor Speedway (1.5-m) (Chevrolet)

1985	(24th)	(216)
1986		(185)

Poles
Champion Spark Plug 400; Michigan Int. Speedway (2-mile) (Oldsmobile)

1987	(17th)	(390)
1988		(221)

PHIL PARSONS

1984	(23rd)	(283)
1985	(21st)	(289)
1986	(25th)	(217)
1987	(15th)	(433)
1988	(8th)	(573)

Victories
Winston 500; Alabama Int. Motor Speedway (2.66-m; 500 m) (Oldsmobile)

1989	(19th)	(381)
1993		(246)

VIC PARSONS

1973		(169)

JIM PASCHAL

1951	(T-13th)	(132)
1952	(15th)	(134)
1953	(9th)	(236)

Victories
Martinsville Speedway (.5-mile dirt; 100 miles) (Dodge)

Poles
Bloomsburg Fairgrounds (.5-mile dirt) (Dodge)

1954	(7th)	(235)

Victories
Martinsville Speedway (.5-mile dirt; 100 miles) (Oldsmobile)

Poles
Wilson Speedway (.5-mile dirt) (Oldsmobile)
Corbin Speedway (.5-mile dirt) (Oldsmobile)

1955	(6th)	(366)

Victories
Orange Speedway (1-mile dirt; 100 miles) (Oldsmobile)
Columbia Speedway (.5-mile dirt; 100 miles) (Oldsmobile)
Southern States Fairgrounds (.5-mile dirt; 100 miles) (Oldsmobile)

Poles
Chisholm Speedway (.5-mile dirt) (Oldsmobile)
Martinsville Speedway (.5-mile dirt) (Oldsmobile)

1956	(5th)	(529)

Victories
Oklahoma State Fairgrounds (.5-mile dirt; 100 miles) (Mercury)

Poles
Monroe County Fairgrounds (.5-mile dirt) (Mercury)

1957	(9th)	(342)
1958		

Victories
* McCormick Field (.25-mile; 38 miles) (Chevrolet)

Poles
* McCormick Field (.25-mile) (Chevrolet)

1960	(19th)	(195)
1961	(11th)	(401)

Victories
Piedmont Interstate Fairgrounds (.5-m dirt; 100 miles) (Pontiac)
Nashville 500; Fairgrounds Speedway (.5-m; 250 miles) (Pontiac)

Poles
West. N.C. 500; Asheville-Weaverville Speedway (.5-m) (Pontiac)

1962	(6th)	(606)

Victories
Southside Speedway (.333-mile; 100 miles) (Pontiac)
Southeastern 500; Bristol Int. Speedway (.5-m; 250 m) (Plymouth)
Nashville 500; Fairgrounds Speedway (.5-m; 250 miles) (Plymouth)
West. N.C. 500; Asheville-Weaverville Sp. (.5-m; 250m) (Plymouth)

1963	(T-8th)	(464)

Victories
* Birmingham Raceway (.5-mile; 100 miles) (Plymouth)
Turkey Day 200; Tar Heel Speedway (.25-mile; 50 miles) (Plymouth)
Bowman Gray Stadium (.25-mile; 50 miles) (Plymouth)
Tar Heel Speedway (.25-mile; 50 miles) (Plymouth)
Nashville 400; Fairgrounds Speedway (.5-m; 200 miles) (Plymouth)

Poles
* Birmingham Raceway (.5-mile) (Plymouth)

1964	(14th)	(426)

Victories
World 600; Charlotte Motor Speedway (1.5-m; 600 miles) (Plymouth)

1965		(106)
1966	(15th)	(346)

Victories
* Gwyn Staley 400; N. Wilkesboro Speed. (.625-m; 250m) (Plymouth)
* Virginia 500; Martinsville Speedway (.5-mile; 250 m) (Plymouth)

Poles
* Gwyn Staley 400; North Wilkesboro Speedway (.625-m) (Plymouth)
* Virginia 500; Martinsville Speedway (.5-mile) (Plymouth)

1967	(4th)	(675)

Victories
Beltsville 200; Beltsville Speedway (.5-m; 100 miles) (Plymouth)
World 600; Charlotte Motor Speedway (1.5-m; 600 miles) (Plymouth)
Asheville 300; Asheville Speedway (.333-m; 100 miles) (Plymouth)
Montgomery Speedway (.5-mile; 100 miles) (Plymouth)

Poles
Birmingham Speedway (.625-mile) (Plymouth)

DICK PASSWATER

1953   (10th)   (233)

Victories
Charlotte Speedway (.75-mile dirt; 113 miles) (Oldsmobile)

JOHNNY PATTERSON

1952   (25th)

DAVID PEARSON

1960   (18th)   (198)

Poles
Gamecock Speedway (.25-mile dirt) (Chevrolet)

1961   (17th)   (266)

Victories
World 600; Charlotte Motor Speedway (1.5-m; 600 miles) (Pontiac)
Firecracker 250; Daytona Int. Speedway (2.5-m; 250 m) (Pontiac)
Dixie 400; Atlanta Int. Raceway (1.5-mile; 400 miles) (Pontiac)

Poles
National 400; Charlotte Motor Speedway (1.5-mile) (Pontiac)

1962   (22nd)   (245)

1963   (6th)   (552)

Poles
Asheville Speedway (.333-mile) (Dodge)
Buddy Shuman 250; Hickory Speedway (.4-mile dirt) (Dodge)

1964   (3rd)   (1,033)

Victories
Richmond 250; Atlantic Rural Fgds. (.5-m dirt; 125 m) (Dodge)
Greenville 200; Greenville-Pickens Sp. (.5-m d.; 100 m) (Dodge)
* Joe Weatherly 150; Orange Speedway (.9-m dirt; 150 m) (Dodge)
Confederate 300; Boyd Speedway (.333-mile; 100 miles) (Dodge)
* Pennsylvania 200; Lincoln Speedway (.5-m dirt; 100 m) (Dodge)
* Rambi Raceway (.5-mile dirt; 100 miles) (Dodge)
Sandlapper 200; Columbia Speedway (.5-m dirt; 100 miles) (Dodge)
* Buddy Shuman 250; Hickory Speedway (.4-m dirt; 100 m) (Dodge)

Poles (1st)
Textile 250; Concord Speedway (.5-mile dirt) (Dodge)
* Joe Weatherly 150; Orange Speedway (.9-mile dirt) (Dodge)
Columbia 200; Columbia Speedway (.5-mile dirt) (Dodge)
Tidewater 250; Langley Field Speedway (.4-mile dirt) (Dodge)
Music City 200; Fairgrounds Speedway (.5-mile) (Dodge)
Birmingham Raceway (.5-mile) (Dodge)
Piedmont Interstate Fairgrounds (.5-mile dirt) (Dodge)
* Pennsylvania 200; Lincoln Speedway (.5-mile dirt) (Dodge)
* Rambi Raceway (.5-mile dirt) (Dodge)
* Buddy Shuman 250; Hickory Speedway (.4-mile dirt) (Dodge)
Old Dominion Speedway (.375-mile) (Dodge)
Orange Speedway; (.9-mile dirt) (Dodge)

1965   (25th)   (213)

Victories
Sandlapper 200; Columbia Speedway (.5-m dirt; 100 miles) (Dodge)
Capital City 300; Virginia St. Fgds. (.5-m dirt; 150 m) (Dodge)

Poles
Cleveland County Fairgrounds (.5-mile dirt) (Dodge)

1966   (1st)   (947)

Victories (1st)
Hickory 250; Hickory Speedway (.4-mile dirt; 100 miles) (Dodge)
Columbia 200; Columbia Speedway (.5-m dirt; 100 miles) (Dodge)
Greenville 200; Greenville-Pickens Sp. (.5-m d.; 100 m) (Dodge)
* Bowman Gray Stadium (.25-mile; 50 miles) (Dodge)
Richmond 250; Virginia State Fgds. (.5-mile dirt; 125 m) (Dodge)
Dog Track Speedway (.333-mile; 100 miles) (Dodge)
Asheville 300; Asheville Speedway (.333-m; 100 miles) (Dodge)
East Tenn. 200; Smoky Mountain Raceway (.5-m dirt; 100m) (Dodge)
* Pickens 200; Greenville-Pickens Sp. (.5-m dirt; 100 miles) (Dodge)
* Bridgehampton Raceway (2.85-mile road; 148 miles) (Dodge)
Fonda Speedway (.5-mile dirt; 100 miles) (Dodge)
Sandlapper 200; Columbia Speedway (.5-m dirt; 100 miles) (Dodge)
Myers Brothers 250; Bowman Gray Stadium (.25-mile; 63 m) (Dodge)
Buddy Shuman 250; Hickory Speedway (.4-m dirt; 100 m) (Dodge)
* Capital City 300; Virginia St. Fgds. (.5-m dirt; 150m) (Dodge)

Poles
Motor Trend 500; Riverside Int. Raceway (2.7-mile road) (Dodge)
Southeastern 500; Bristol International Speedway (.5-m) (Dodge)
* Bowman Gray Stadium (.25-mile) (Dodge)
Piedmont Interstate Fairgrounds (.5-mile dirt) (Dodge)
* Pickens 200; Greenville-Pickens Speedway (.5-m dirt) (Dodge)
* Bridgehampton Raceway (2.85-mile road) (Dodge)
* Capital City 300; Virginia St. Fairgrounds (.5-m dirt) (Dodge)

1967   (11th)   (404)

Victories
Southeastern 500; Bristol Int. Speedway (.5-m; 250 m) (Dodge)
Greenville 200; Greenville-Pickens Sp. (.5-m dirt; 100m) (Dodge)

Poles
Rebel 400; Darlington Raceway (1.375-mile) (Ford)
American 500; North Carolina Motor Speedway (1-mile) (Ford)

1968   (1st)   (1,052)

Victories (T–1st)
Southeastern 500; Bristol Int. Speedway (.5-m; 250 m) (Ford)
Richmond 250; Virginia State Fgds. (.5-mile dirt; 125 m) (Ford)
* Gwyn Staley 400; N. Wilkesboro Speed. (.625-m; 250 m) (Ford)
* Fireball 300; Asheville-Weaverville Sp. (.5-m; 150 m) (Ford)
Rebel 400; Darlington Raceway (1.375-mile; 400 miles) (Ford)
Beltsville 300; Beltsville Speedway (.5-mile; 150 miles) (Ford)
Tidewater 250; Langley Field Speedway (.4-m; 100 miles) (Ford)
* Macon 300; Middle Georgia Raceway (.5-mile; 150 miles) (Ford)
Volunteer 500; Bristol Int. Speedway (.5-m; 250 miles) (Ford)
Nashville 400; Fairgrounds Speedway (.5-mile; 200 miles) (Ford)
Sandlapper 200; Columbia Speedway (.5-m dirt; 100 miles) (Ford)
Myers Brothers 250; Bowman Gray Stadium (.25-mile; 63 m) (Ford)
Western N.C. 500; Asheville-Weaverville Sp. (.5-m; 250m) (Ford)
* Crabber 250; Langley Field Speedway (.4-m; 100 miles) (Ford)
Buddy Shuman 250; Hickory Speedway (.4-mile; 100 miles) (Ford)
Augusta 200; Augusta Speedway (.5-mile; 100 miles) (Ford)

Poles (T–1st)
Hickory 250; Hickory Speedway (.4-mile) (Ford)
Greenville 200; Greenville-Pickens Speedway (.5-m dirt) (Ford)
* Gwyn Staley 400; North Wilkesboro Speedway (.625-mile) (Ford)
Virginia 500; Martinsville Speedway (.5-mile) (Ford)
* Fireball 300; Asheville-Weaverville Speedway (.5-mile) (Ford)
* Macon 300; Middle Georgia Raceway (.5-mile) (Ford)
Smoky Mountain Raceway (.5-mile) (Ford)
Birmingham Speedway (.625-mile) (Ford)
Pickens 200; Greenville-Pickens Speedway (.5-mile dirt) (Ford)

Driver Resumes

Fonda 200; Fonda Speedway (.5-mile dirt) (Ford)
* Crabber 250; Langley Field Speedway (.4-mile) (Ford)
Peach State 200; Jeffco Speedway (.5-mile) (Ford)

1969   (1st)   (1,182)

Victories

Daytona International Speedway (2.5-mile; 125 miles) (Ford)
* Carolina 500; N.C. Motor Speedway (1-mile; 500 miles) (Ford)
Cracker 200; Augusta Speedway (.5-mile; 100 miles) (Ford)
* Richmond 500; Virginia State Fgds. (.5-m; 250 miles) (Ford)
* Tidewater 375; Langley Field Speedway (.4-mile; 150 m) (Ford)
North State 200; State Fairgrounds (.5-m dirt; 100 m) (Ford)
* Thompson 200; Thompson Speedway (.625-mile; 125 miles) (Ford)
Northern 300; Trenton Speedway (1.5-mile; 300 miles) (Ford)
Volunteer 500; Bristol Int. Speedway (.533-m; 267 miles) (Ford)
* Yankee 600; Michigan Int. Speedway (2-mile; 600 miles) (Ford)
Wilkes 400; North Wilkesboro Speedway (.625-mile; 250 m) (Ford)

Poles

Georgia 500; Middle Georgia Raceway (.5-mile) (Ford)
* Carolina 500; North Carolina Motor Speedway (1-mile) (Ford)
Atlanta 500; Atlanta International Raceway (1.5-mile) (Ford)
Greenville 200; Greenville-Pickens Speedway (.5-m dirt) (Ford)
* Richmond 500; Virginia State Fairgrounds (.5-mile) (Ford)
* Tidewater 375; Langley Field Speedway (.4-m; 150 m) (Ford)
Macon 300; Middle Georgia Raceway (.5-mile) (Ford)
Maryville 300; Smoky Mountain Raceway (.5-mile) (Ford)
Mason-Dixon 300; Dover Downs Int. Speedway (1-mile) (Ford)
* Thompson 200; Thompson Speedway (.625-mile) (Ford)
Smoky Mountain 200; Smoky Mountain Raceway (.5-mile) (Ford)
* Yankee 600; Michigan International Speedway (2-mile) (Ford)
Old Dominion 500; Martinsville Speedway (.5-mile) (Ford)
Jeffco 200; Jeffco Speedway (.5-mile) (Ford)

1970   (15th)   (421)

Victories
Rebel 400; Darlington Raceway (1.375-mile; 400 miles) (Ford)
Poles
Southeastern 500; Bristol Int. Speedway (.533-mile) (Ford)
Southern 500; Darlington Raceway (1.366-mile) (Ford)

1971   (253)

Victories
Daytona International Speedway (2.5-mile; 125 miles) (Mercury)
* Southeastern 500; Bristol Int. Speedway (.533-m; 267m) (Ford)
Poles
* Southeastern 500; Bristol Int. Speedway (.533-mile) (Ford)
Greenville 200; Greenville-Pickens Speedway (.5-mile) (Ford)

1972   (6th)   (478)

Victories
* Rebel 400; Darlington Raceway (1.366-mile; 400 miles) (Mercury)
Winston 500; Alabama Int. Motor Speedway (2.66-m; 500 m) (Mercury)
Motor State 400; Michigan Int. Speedway (2-m; 400 miles) (Mercury)
Firecracker 400; Daytona Int. Speedway (2.5-mile; 400 m) (Mercury)
Yankee 400; Michigan Int. Speedway (2-mile; 400 miles) (Mercury)
Delaware 500; Dover Downs Int. Speedway (1-m; 500 miles) (Mercury)

Poles
* Rebel 400; Darlington Raceway (1.366-mile) (Mercury)
Dixie 500; Atlanta International Raceway (1.522-mile) (Mercury)
National 500; Charlotte Motor Speedway (1.5-mile) (Mercury)
American 500; North Carolina Motor Speedway (1.017-mile) (Mercury)

1973   (5th)   (593)

Victories (1st)
* Carolina 500; N.C. Motor Speedway (1.017-m; 500 miles) (Mercury)
Atlanta 500; Atlanta Int. Raceway (1.522-m; 500 miles) (Mercury)
* Rebel 500; Darlington Raceway (1.366-mile; 500 miles) (Mercury)
* Virginia 500; Martinsville Speedway (.525-mile; 263 m) (Mercury)
Winston 500; Alabama Int. Motor Speedway (2.66-m; 500 m) (Mercury)
* Mason-Dixon 500; Dover Downs Int. Speedway (1-m; 500m) (Mercury)
Motor State 400; Michigan Int. Speedway (2-m; 400 miles) (Mercury)
Firecracker 400; Daytona Int. Speedway (2.5-mile; 400 m) (Mercury)
Dixie 500; Atlanta Int. Raceway (1.522-mile; 500 miles) (Mercury)
* Delaware 500; Dover Downs Int. Speedway (1-mile; 500m) (Mercury)
American 500; N.C. Motor Speedway (1.017-m; 500 miles) (Mercury)

Poles (1st)
Winston Western 500; Riverside Int. Raceway (2.62-m rd.) (Mercury)
* Carolina 500; North Carolina Motor Speedway (1.017-m) (Mercury)
* Rebel 500; Darlington Raceway (1.366-mile) (Mercury)
* Virginia 500; Martinsville Speedway (.525-mile) (Mercury)
* Mason-Dixon 500; Dover Downs Int. Speedway (1-mile) (Mercury)
Southern 500; Darlington Raceway (1.366-mile) (Mercury)
* Delaware 500; Dover Downs International Speedway (1-m) (Mercury)
National 500; Charlotte Motor Speedway (1.5-mile) (Mercury)

1974   (4th)   (578)

Victories
Rebel 500; Darlington Raceway (1.366-mile; 450 miles) (Mercury)
* Winston 500; Ala. Int. Motor Speedway (2.66-m; 450 m) (Mercury)
* World 600; Charlotte Motor Speedway (1.5-m; 540 miles) (Mercury)
* Firecracker 400; Daytona Int. Speedway (2.5-m; 400 m) (Mercury)
* Yankee 400; Michigan Int. Speedway (2-mile; 400 miles) (Mercury)
* National 500; Charlotte Motor Speedway (1.5-m; 500 m) (Mercury)
American 500; N.C. Motor Speedway (1.017-m; 500 miles) (Mercury)

Poles (1st)
Winston Western 500; Riverside Int. Raceway (2.62-m rd.) (Mercury)
Daytona 500; Daytona International Speedway (2.5-mile) (Mercury)
Atlanta 500; Atlanta International Raceway (1.522-mile) (Mercury)
* Winston 500; Alabama Int. Motor Speedway (2.66-mile) (Mercury)
Mason-Dixon 500; Dover Downs Int. Speedway (1-mile) (Mercury)
* World 600; Charlotte Motor Speedway (1.5-mile) (Mercury)
Motor State 400; Michigan International Speedway (2-mile) (Mercury)
* Firecracker 400; Daytona International Speedway (2.5-m) (Mercury)
Talladega 500; Alabama Int. Motor Speedway (2.66-mile) (Mercury)
* Yankee 400; Michigan International Speedway (2-mile) (Mercury)
* National 500; Charlotte Motor Speedway (1.5-mile) (Mercury)

1975   (5th)   (562)

Victories
* Mason-Dixon 500; Dover Downs Int. Speedway (1-m; 500m) (Mercury)
Motor State 400; Michigan Int. Speedway (2-m; 400 miles) (Mercury)
Purolator 500; Pocono Int. Raceway (2.5-mile; 500 miles) (Mercury)

Poles (1st)
Rebel 500; Darlington Raceway (1.366-mile) (Mercury)
* Mason-Dixon 500; Dover Downs Int. Speedway (1-mile) (Mercury)
World 600; Charlotte Motor Speedway (1.5-mile) (Mercury)
Champion Spark Plug 400; Michigan Int. Speedway (2-mile) (Mercury)
Southern 500; Darlington International Raceway (1.366-m) (Mercury)
National 500; Charlotte Motor Speedway (1.5-mile) (Mercury)
Los Angeles Times 500; Ontario Motor Speedway (2.5-mile) (Mercury)

1976   **(3rd)**   **(728)**

Victories (1st)

Win. West. 500; Riverside Int. Race. (2.62-m rd.; 500m) (Mercury)
Daytona 500; Daytona Int. Speedway (2.5-mile; 500 miles) (Mercury)
Atlanta 500; Atlanta Int. Raceway (1.522-m; 500 miles) (Mercury)
* Rebel 500; Darlington Int. Raceway (1.366-mile; 500 m) (Mercury)
* World 600; Charlotte Motor Speedway (1.5-m; 600 miles) (Mercury)
* Riverside 400; Riverside Int. Race. (2.62-m rd.; 248m) (Mercury)
Cam2 Motor Oil 400; Michigan Int. Speedway (2-m; 400 m) (Mercury)
* Champion SP 400; Michigan Int. Speedway (2-m; 400 m) (Mercury)
* Southern 500; Darlington Int. Raceway (1.366-m; 500 m) (Mercury)
* L.A. Times 500; Ontario Motor Speedway (2.5-m; 500 m) (Mercury)

Poles (1st)

* Rebel 500; Darlington International Raceway (1.366-m) (Mercury)
* World 600; Charlotte Motor Speedway (1.5-mile) (Mercury)
* Riverside 400; Riverside Int. Raceway (2.62-mile road) (Mercury)
* Champion Spark Plug 400; Michigan Int. Speedway (2-m) (Mercury)
* Southern 500; Darlington Int. Raceway (1.366-mile) (Mercury)
National 500; Charlotte Motor Speedway (1.5-mile) (Mercury)
American 500; North Carolina Motor Speedway (1.017-mile) (Mercury)
* Los Angeles Times 500; Ontario Motor Speedway (2.5-m) (Mercury)

1977   **(7th)**   **(552)**

Victories

Win. West. 500; Riverside Int. Race. (2.62-m rd.; 312 m) (Mercury)
Southern 500; Darlington Int. Raceway (1.366-m; 500 m) (Mercury)

Poles

Rebel 500; Darlington International Raceway (1.366-mile) (Mercury)
World 600; Charlotte Motor Speedway (1.5-mile) (Mercury)
Cam2 Motor Oil 400; Michigan Int. Speedway (2-mile) (Mercury)
Champion Spark Plug 400; Michigan Int. Speedway (2-mile) (Mercury)
NAPA National 500; Charlotte Motor Speedway (1.5-mile) (Mercury)

1978   **(11th)**   **(414)**

Victories

Carolina 500; N.C. Motor Speedway (1.017-m; 500 miles) (Mercury)
Mason-Dixon 500; Dover Downs Int. Speedway (1-m; 500 m) (Mercury)
Firecracker 400; Daytona Int. Speedway (2.5-mile; 400 m) (Mercury)
* Champion SP 400; Michigan Int. Speedway (2-m; 400 m) (Mercury)

Poles

Winston Western 500; Riverside Int. Raceway (2.62-m rd.) (Mercury)
World 600; Charlotte Motor Speedway (1.5-mile) (Mercury)
NAPA Riverside 400; Riverside Int. Raceway (2.62-m road) (Mercury)
Gabriel 400; Michigan International Speedway (2-mile) (Mercury)
* Champion Spark Plug 400; Michigan Int. Speedway (2-m) (Mercury)
Southern 500; Darlington International Raceway (1.366-m) (Mercury)
NAPA National 500; Charlotte Motor Speedway (1.5-mile) (Mercury)

1979   **(187)**

Victories

Southern 500; Darlington Int. Raceway (1.366-m; 500 m) (Chevrolet)

Poles

Winston Western 500; Riverside Int. Raceway (2.62-m rd.) (Mercury)
Champion Spark Plug 400; Michigan Int. Speedway (2-mile) (Chevrolet)

1980   **(220)**

Victories

CRC Ch. Rebel 500; Darlington Int. Race. (1.366-m; 500m) (Chevrolet)

Poles

Winston 500; Alabama Int. Motor Speedway (2.66-mile) (Oldsmobile)

1981

Poles

Mason-Dixon 500; Dover Downs Int. Speedway (1-mile) (Oldsmobile)

1982

Poles

World 600; Charlotte Motor Speedway (1.5-mile) (Buick)
Southern 500; Darlington Int. Raceway (1.366-mile) (Buick)

1983   **(130)**

1984   **(116)**

Poles

Van Scoy Diamond Mine 500; Pocono Int. Raceway (2.5-m) (Chevrolet)

LARRY PEARSON

1989   **(273)**

1990   **(101)**

JACK PENNINGTON

1990   **(119)**

KYLE PETTY

1979   **(101)**

1980   **(23rd)**   **(237)**

1981   **(13th)**   **(395)**

1982   **(23rd)**   **(324)**

1983   **(15th)**   **(393)**

1984   **(21st)**   **(324)**

1985   **(T-9th)**   **(528)**

1986   **(8th)**   **(568)**

Victories

Miller HL 400; Richmond Fgds. Raceway (.542-mile; 217m) (Ford)

1987   **(6th)**   **(580)**

Victories

Coca-Cola 600; Charlotte Motor Speedway (1.5-m; 600 m) (Ford)

1988   **(13th)**   **(457)**

1989   **(22nd)**   **(314)**

1990   **(9th)**   **(533)**

Victories

* Goodwrench 500; N.C. Motor Speedway (1.017-m; 500 m) (Pontiac)

Poles

* Goodwrench 500; N.C. Motor Speedway (1.017-mile) (Pontiac)
Tyson Holly Farms 400; N. Wilkesboro Speedway (.625-m) (Pontiac)

1991   **(25th)**   **(275)**

Victories

* Goodwrench 500; N.C. Motor Speedway (1.017-m; 500 m) (Pontiac)

Poles
* Goodwrench 500; N.C. Motor Speedway (1.017-mile) (Pontiac)
AC Delco 500; North Carolina Motor Speedway (1.017-m) (Pontiac)

1992   (4th)   (675)

Victories
Bud. at the Glen; Watkins Glen Int. (2.45-m rd.; 219m) (Pontiac)
* AC Delco 500; N.C. Motor Speedway (1.017-m; 500 m) (Pontiac)

Poles
Goodwrench 500; N.C. Motor Speedway (1.017-mile) (Pontiac)
Goody's 500; Martinsville Speedway. (.526-mile) (Pontiac)
* AC Delco 500; N.C. Motor Speedway (1.017-mile) (Pontiac)

1993   (7th)   (595)

Victories
Champion SP 500; Pocono Int. Raceway (2.5-mile; 500m) (Pontiac)

Poles
Daytona 500 by STP; Daytona Int. Speedway (2.5-mile) (Pontiac)

1994   (17th)   (428)

1995   (251)

Victories
Miller Gen. Dr. 500; Dover Downs Int. Sp. (1-m; 500m) (Pontiac)

1996   (255)

1997   (13th)   (465)

1998   (189)

1999   (23rd)   (319)

LEE PETTY

1949   (2nd)

Victories
Heidelberg Speedway (.5-mile dirt; 100 miles) (Plymouth)

1950   (1st)   (270)

Victories
Occoneechee Speedway (1-mile dirt; 200 miles) (Plymouth)

1951   (4th)   (373)

Victories
Monroe County Fairgrounds (.5-mile dirt; 100 miles) (Plymouth)

1952   (2nd)   (533)

Victories
Morristown Speedway (.5-mile dirt; 100 miles) (Plymouth)
Central City Speedway (.5-mile dirt; 150 miles) (Plymouth)
Langhorne Speedway (1-mile dirt; 250 miles) (Plymouth)

1953   (2nd)   (640)

Victories
Palm Beach Speedway (.5-mile dirt; 100 miles) (Dodge)
Richmond 200; Atlantic Rural Fgds. (.5-m dirt; 100 m) (Dodge)
Martinsville Speedway (.5-mile dirt; 100 miles) (Dodge)
Louisiana Fairgrounds (.5-mile dirt; 100 miles) (Dodge)
Piedmont Interstate Fairgrounds (.5-m dirt; 100 miles) (Dodge)

1954   (1st)   (613)

Victories
* Beach & Road Course (4.1-mile road; 160 mile) (Chrysler)
Sharon Speedway (.5-mile dirt; 100 miles) (Chrysler)
Monroe County Fairgrounds (.5-mile dirt; 100 miles) (Chrysler)
Grand River Speedrome (.5-mile dirt; 100 miles) (Chrysler)
Southern States Fairgrounds (.5-mile dirt; 100 miles) (Chrysler)
Corbin Speedway (.5-mile dirt; 100 miles) (Chrysler)
* Martinsville Speedway (.5-mile dirt; 100 miles) (Chrysler)

Poles
* Beach & Road Course (4.1-mile road) (Chrysler)
Langhorne Speedway. (1-mile dirt) (Chrysler)
* Martinsville Speedway (.5-mile dirt) (Chrysler)

1955   (3rd)   (581)

Victories
Tri-City Speedway (.5-mile dirt; 100 miles) (Chrysler)
Speedway Park (.5-mile dirt; 100 miles) (Chrysler)
Oglethorpe Speedway (.5-mile dirt; 100 miles) (Chrysler)
Forsyth County Fairgrounds (.5-mile dirt; 100 miles) (Chrysler)
* Airborne Speedway (.5-mile dirt; 100 miles) (Chrysler)
Forsyth County Fairgrounds (.5-mile dirt; 100 miles) (Dodge)

Poles
* Airborne Speedway (.5-mile dirt) (Chrysler)

1956   (4th)   (582)

Victories
Asheville-Weaverville Speedway (.5-mile dirt; 100 miles) (Dodge)
Piedmont Interstate Fairgrounds (.5-m dirt; 100 miles) (Dodge)

Poles
Raleigh 250; Raleigh Speedway (1-mile) (Dodge)

1957   (4th)   (612)

Victories
* Piedmont Interstate Fairgrounds (.5-m dirt; 100 miles) (Oldsmobile)
Old Bridge Stadium (.5-mile; 100 miles) (Oldsmobile)
Asheville-Weaverville Speedway (.5-mile; 100 miles) (Oldsmobile)
* Southern States Fairgrounds (.5-mile dirt; 100 miles) (Oldsmobile)

Poles
* Piedmont Interstate Fairgrounds (.5-mile dirt) (Oldsmobile)
Jacksonville Speedway (.5-mile dirt) (Oldsmobile)
* Southern States Fairgrounds (.5-mile dirt) (Oldsmobile)

1958   (1st)   (853)

Victories (1st)
Concord Speedway (.5-mile dirt; 100 miles) (Oldsmobile)
Wilson Speedway (.5-mile dirt; 100 miles) (Oldsmobile)
Lincoln Speedway (.5-mile dirt; 100 miles) (Oldsmobile)
Buddy Shuman 250; Hickory Speedway (.4-mile dirt; 100 m) (Oldsmobile)
Canadian National Exposition Stadium (.333-m; 33 miles) (Oldsmobile)
Bowman Gray Stadium (.25-mile; 50 miles) (Oldsmobile)
Salisbury Speedway (.625-mile dirt; 100 miles) (Oldsmobile)

Poles
Champion Speedway (.333-mile) (Oldsmobile)
Champion Speedway (.333-mile) (Oldsmobile)
State Line Speedway (.333-mile dirt) (Oldsmobile)
Southern States Fairgrounds (.5-mile dirt) (Oldsmobile)

1959 (1st) (772)

Victories (1st)

Daytona 500; Daytona Int. Speedway (2.5-mile; 500 miles) (Oldsmobile)
Gwyn Staley 160; No. Wilkesboro Speedway (.625-m; 100 m) (Oldsmobile)
Virginia 500; Martinsville Speedway (.5-mile; 250 miles) (Oldsmobile)
Charlotte Fairgrounds (.5-mile dirt; 100 miles) (Oldsmobile)
Lakewood Speedway (1-mile dirt; 150 miles) (Plymouth)
Columbia Speedway (.5-mile dirt; 100 miles) (Plymouth)
Columbia Speedway (.5-mile dirt; 100 miles) (Plymouth)
Buddy Shuman 250; Hickory Speedway (.4-m dirt; 100 m) (Plymouth)
Orange Speedway (.9-mile dirt; 99 miles) (Plymouth)
Asheville-Weaverville Speedway (.5-mile; 100 miles) (Plymouth)
Wilkes 160; North Wilkesboro Speedway (.625-m; 100 m) (Plymouth)

Poles

Bowman Gray Stadium (.25-mile) (Plymouth)
Greenville-Pickens Speedway (.5-mile dirt) (Plymouth)

1960 (3rd) (643)

Victories

Gwyn Staley 160; N. Wilkesboro Speedway (.625-m; 100m) (Plymouth)
Asheville-Weaverville Speedway (.5-mile; 100 miles) (Plymouth)
Orange Speedway (.9-mile dirt; 99 miles) (Plymouth)
Richmond 200; Atlantic Rural Fgds. (.5-m dirt; 100 m) (Plymouth)
* Heidelberg Stadium (.5-mile dirt; 100 miles) (Plymouth)

Poles

Charlotte Fairgrounds (.5-mile dirt) (Plymouth)
International 200; Bowman Gray Stadium (.25-mile) (Plymouth)
* Heidelberg Stadium (.5-mile dirt) (Plymouth)

1961

Victories

Speedway Park (.5-mile dirt; 100 miles) (Plymouth)

Poles

Charlotte Fairgrounds (.5-mile dirt) (Plymouth)

RICHARD PETTY

1959 (17th) (222)

1960 (2nd) (696)

Victories

Charlotte Fairgrounds (.5-mile dirt; 100 miles) (Plymouth)
Virginia 500; Martinsville Speedway (.5-m; 250 miles) (Plymouth)
* Orange Speedway (.9-mile dirt; 99 miles) (Plymouth)

Poles

Orange Speedway (.9-mile dirt) (Plymouth)
* Orange Speedway (.9-mile dirt) (Plymouth)

1961 (T-5th) (526)

Victories

* Richmond 200; Atlantic Rural Fgds. (.5-m dirt; 100m) (Plymouth)
Charlotte Motor Speedway (1.5-mile; 100 miles) (Plymouth)

Poles

* Richmond 200; Atlantic Rural Fgds. (.5-mile dirt) (Plymouth)
World 600; Charlotte Motor Speedway (1.5-mile) (Plymouth)

1962 (2nd) (933)

Victories

Gwyn Staley 400; N. Wilkesboro Speedway (.625-m; 250m) (Plymouth)
Virginia 500; Martinsville Speedway (.5-m; 250 miles) (Plymouth)
Pickens 200; Greenville-Pickens Sp. (.5-m dirt; 100m) (Plymouth)

* Huntsville Speedway (.25-mile; 50 miles) (Plymouth)
Starkey Speedway (.25-mile; 50 miles) (Plymouth)
International 200; Bowman Gray Stadium (.25-m; 50 m) (Plymouth)
* Piedmont Interstate Fairgrounds (.5-m dirt; 100 m) (Plymouth)
Wilkes 320; North Wilkesboro Speedway (.625-m; 200 m) (Plymouth)

Poles

Confederate 200; Boyd Speedway (.333-mile) (Plymouth)
* Huntsville Speedway (.25-mile) (Plymouth)
* Piedmont Interstate Fairgrounds (.5-mile dirt) (Plymouth)
Valdosta Speedway (.5-mile dirt) (Plymouth)

1963 (1st) (1,012)

Victories (1st)

Golden Gate Speedway (.333-mile; 67 miles) (Plymouth)
Piedmont Interstate Fairgrounds (.5-m dirt; 100 miles) (Plymouth)
Asheville-Weaverville Speedway (.5-mile; 100 miles) (Plymouth)
South Boston 400; South Boston Speedway (.375-m; 150m) (Plymouth)
Virginia 500; Martinsville Speedway (.5-m; 250 miles) (Plymouth)
Gwyn Staley 400; N. Wilkesboro Speedway (.625-m; 250m) (Plymouth)
* Columbia 200; Columbia Speedway (.5-m dirt; 100 m) (Plymouth)
* Old Dominion Speedway (.375-mile; 113 miles) (Plymouth)
Birmingham Raceway (.5-mile; 100 miles) (Plymouth)
* Bridgehampton Raceway (2.85-mile road; 100 miles) (Plymouth)
Pickens 200; Greenville-Pickens Sp. (.5-m dirt; 100 m) (Plymouth)
* Sandlapper 200; Columbia Speedway (.5-m dirt; 100 m) (Plymouth)
Tar Heel Speedway (.25-mile; 50 miles) (Plymouth)
South Boston 400; South Boston Speedway (.375-m; 150m) (Plymouth)

Poles

Bowman Gray Stadium (.25-mile) (Plymouth)
* Columbia 200; Columbia Speedway (.5-mile dirt) (Plymouth)
* Old Dominion Speedway (.375-mile) (Plymouth)
Speedorama 200; Rambi Raceway (.5-mile dirt) (Plymouth)
Savannah Speedway (.5-mile dirt) (Plymouth)
* Bridgehampton Raceway (2.85-mile road) (Plymouth)
Nashville 400; Fairgrounds Speedway (.5-mile) (Plymouth)
* Sandlapper 200; Columbia Speedway (.5-mile dirt) (Plymouth)

1964 (1st) (1,097)

Victories

Sunshine 200; Savannah Speedway (.5-m dirt; 100 miles) (Plymouth)
Daytona 500; Daytona Int. Speedway (2.5-m; 500 miles) (Plymouth)
South Boston Speedway (.375-mile; 100 miles) (Plymouth)
* Concord Speedway (.5-mile dirt; 100 miles) (Plymouth)
Music City 200; Fairgrounds Speedway (.5-m; 100 miles) (Plymouth)
Piedmont Interstate Fairgrounds (.5-m dirt; 100 miles) (Plymouth)
* Nashville 400; Fairgrounds Speedway (.5-m; 200 m) (Plymouth)
Mountaineer 500; W.Va. Int. Speedway (.4375-m; 219 miles) (Plymouth)
Harris Speedway (.3-mile; 100 miles) (Plymouth)

Poles

Asheville Speedway (.333-mile) (Plymouth)
* Concord Speedway (.5-mile dirt) (Plymouth)
Confederate 300; Boyd Speedway (.333-mile) (Plymouth)
Bridgehampton Raceway (2.85-mile road) (Plymouth)
Volunteer 500; Bristol International Speedway (.5-m) (Plymouth)
* Nashville 400; Fairgrounds Speedway (.5-mile) (Plymouth)
Southern 500; Darlington Raceway (1.375-mile) (Plymouth)
National 400; Charlotte Motor Speedway (1.5-mile) (Plymouth)

1965 (23rd) (231)

Victories

* Nashville 400; Fairgrounds Speedway (.5-m; 200 m) (Plymouth)
* W.N.C. 500; Asheville-Weaverville Sp. (.5-m; 250 m) (Plymouth)
Buddy Shuman 250; Hickory Speedway (.4-m dirt; 100 m) (Plymouth)
Old Dominion Speedway (.375-mile; 150 miles) (Plymouth)

Poles

* Nashville 400; Fairgrounds Speedway (.5-mile) (Plymouth)
* West. N.C. 500; Asheville-Weaverville Speed. (.5-m) (Plymouth)
Moyock 300; Dog Track Speedway (.333-mile) (Plymouth)
Myers Brothers 250; Bowman Gray Stadium (.25-mile) (Plymouth)
Pennsylvania 200; Lincoln Speedway (.5-mile dirt) (Plymouth)
Old Dominion 500; Martinsville Speedway (.5-mile) (Plymouth)
American 500; North Carolina Motor Speedway (1-mile) (Plymouth)

1966   (4th)   (591)

Victories

* Georgia Cracker 300; Augusta Speedway (.5-m; 150 m) (Plymouth)
* Daytona 500; Daytona Int. Speedway (2.5-mile; 500 m) (Plymouth)
* Rebel 400; Darlington Raceway (1.375-m; 400 miles) (Plymouth)
* Tidewater 250; Langley Field Sp. (.4-m dirt; 100 m) (Plymouth)
* Speedy Morelock 200; Middle Ga. Raceway (.5-m; 100m) (Plymouth)
* Fireball 300; Asheville-Weaverville Sp. (.5-m; 150m) (Plymouth)
* Nashville 400; Fairgrounds Speedway (.5-m; 200 m) (Plymouth)
Dixie 400; Atlanta Int. Raceway (1.5-mile; 400 miles) (Plymouth)

Poles (1st)

* Georgia Cracker 300; Augusta Speedway (.5-mile) (Plymouth)
* Daytona 500; Daytona International Speedway (2.5-m) (Plymouth)
Atlanta 500; Atlanta International Raceway (1.5-mile) (Plymouth)
* Rebel 400; Darlington Raceway (1.375-mile) (Plymouth)
* Tidewater 250; Langley Field Speedway (.4-mile dirt) (Plymouth)
* Speedy Morelock 200; Middle Georgia Raceway (.5-m) (Plymouth)
World 600; Charlotte Motor Speedway (1.5-mile) (Plymouth)
Dog Track Speedway (.333-mile) (Plymouth)
Asheville 300; Asheville Speedway (.333-mile) (Plymouth)
* Fireball 300; Asheville-Weaverville Speedway (.5-m) (Plymouth)
Beltsville 200; Beltsville Speedway (.5-mile) (Plymouth)
Fonda Speedway (.5-mile dirt) (Plymouth)
* Nashville 400; Fairgrounds Speedway (.5-mile) (Plymouth)
Myers Brothers 250; Bowman Gray Stadium (.25-mile) (Plymouth)
Buddy Shuman 250; Hickory Speedway (.4-mile dirt) (Plymouth)

1967   (1st)   (1,130)

Victories (1st)

Augusta 300; Augusta Speedway (.5-mile; 150 miles) (Plymouth)
Fireball 300; Asheville-Weaverville Sp. (.5-m; 150 miles) (Plymouth)
Columbia 200; Columbia Speedway (.5-mile dirt; 100 m) (Plymouth)
* Hickory 250; Hickory Speedway (.4-m dirt; 100 miles) (Plymouth)
Virginia 500; Martinsville Speedway (.5-m; 250 miles) (Plymouth)
* Richmond 250; Virginia State Fgds. (.5-m dirt; 125m) (Plymouth)
Rebel 400; Darlington Raceway (1.375-mile; 400 miles) (Plymouth)
* Tidewater 250; Langley Field Sp. (.4-m dirt; 100 m) (Plymouth)
* Macon 300; Middle Georgia Raceway (.5-m; 150 miles) (Plymouth)
East Tenn. 200; Smoky Mount. Raceway (.5-m dirt; 100m) (Plymouth)
Carolina 500; N.C. Motor Speedway (1-mile; 500 miles) (Plymouth)
* Pickens 200; Greenville-Pickens Sp. (.5-m d.; 100m) (Plymouth)
* Northern 300; Trenton Speedway (1-mile; 300 miles) (Plymouth)
* Fonda Speedway (.5-mile dirt; 100 miles) (Plymouth)
* Islip 300; Islip Speedway (.2-mile; 60 miles) (Plymouth)
* Volunteer 500; Bristol Int. Speedway (.5-m; 250 miles) (Plymouth)
Nashville 400; Fairgrounds Speedway (.5-m; 200 miles) (Plymouth)
* Myers Brothers 250; Bowman Gray Stadium (.25-m; 63m) (Plymouth)
* Sandlapper 200; Columbia Speedway (.5-m dirt; 100 m) (Plymouth)
* Savannah Speedway (.5-mile dirt; 100 miles) (Plymouth)
* Southern 500; Darlington Raceway (1.375-mile; 500 m) (Plymouth)
Buddy Shuman 250; Hickory Speedway (.4-m; 100 miles) (Plymouth)
Capital City 300; Virginia St. Fgds. (.5-m dirt; 150m) (Plymouth)
* Maryland 300; Beltsville Speedway (.5-m; 150 miles) (Plymouth)
* Hillsborough 150; Orange Speedway (.9-m dirt; 150 m) (Plymouth)

Old Dominion 500; Martinsville Speedway (.5-m; 250 m) (Plymouth)
Wilkes 400; North Wilkesboro Speedway (.625-m; 250 m) (Plymouth)

Poles (1st)

* Hickory 250; Hickory Speedway (.4-mile dirt) (Plymouth)
* Richmond 250; Virginia State Fairgrounds (.5-m dirt) (Plymouth)
Beltsville 200; Beltsville Speedway (.5-mile) (Plymouth)
* Tidewater 250; Langley Field Speedway (.4-mile dirt) (Plymouth)
Asheville 300; Asheville Speedway (.333-mile) (Plymouth)
* Macon 300; Middle Georgia Raceway (.5-mile) (Plymouth)
* Pickens 200; Greenville-Pickens Speedway (.5-m dirt) (Plymouth)
Montgomery Speedway (.5-mile) (Plymouth)
* Northern 300; Trenton Speedway (1-mile) (Plymouth)
* Fonda Speedway (.5-mile dirt) (Plymouth)
* Islip 300; Islip Speedway (.2-mile) (Plymouth)
* Volunteer 500; Bristol Int. Speedway (.5-mile) (Plymouth)
* Myers Brothers 250; Bowman Gray Stadium (.25-mile) (Plymouth)
* Sandlapper 200; Columbia Speedway (.5-mile dirt) (Plymouth)
* Savannah Speedway (.5-mile dirt) (Plymouth)
* Southern 500; Darlington Raceway (1.375-mile) (Plymouth)
* Maryland 300; Beltsville Speedway (.5-mile) (Plymouth)
* Hillsborough 150; Orange Speedway (.9-mile dirt) (Plymouth)

1968   (2nd)   (905)

Victories (T-1st)

* Montgomery Speedway (.5-mile; 100 miles) (Plymouth)
Hickory 250; Hickory Speedway (.4-mile; 100 miles) (Plymouth)
Greenville 200; Greenville-Pickens Sp. (.5-m d.; 100m) (Plymouth)
* Asheville 300; Asheville Speedway (.333-m; 100 m) (Plymouth)
Smoky Mountain Raceway (.5-mile; 100 miles) (Plymouth)
Birmingham Speedway (.625-mile; 100 miles) (Plymouth)
Pickens 200; Greenville-Pickens Sp. (.5-m dirt; 100 m) (Plymouth)
Maine 300; Oxford Plains Speedway (.333-m; 100 miles) (Plymouth)
Fonda 200; Fonda Speedway (.5-mile dirt; 100 miles) (Plymouth)
Smoky Mountain 200; Smoky Mountain Race. (.5-m; 100m) (Plymouth)
* South Boston Speedway (.375-mile; 100 miles) (Plymouth)
* Capital City 300; Virginia St. Fgds. (.625-m; 188m) (Plymouth)
* Hillsborough 150; Orange Speedway (.9-m dirt; 150 m) (Plymouth)
Old Dominion 500; Martinsville Speedway (.5-m; 250 m) (Plymouth)
Wilkes 400; North Wilkesboro Speedway (.625-mile) (Plymouth)
American 500; N.C. Motor Speedway (1-mile; 500 miles) (Plymouth)

Poles (T-1st)

* Montgomery Speedway (.5-mile) (Plymouth)
Southeastern 500; Bristol Int. Speedway (.5-mile) (Plymouth)
Columbia 200; Columbia Speedway (.5-mile dirt) (Plymouth)
Beltsville 300; Beltsville Speedway (.5-mile) (Plymouth)
Tidewater 250; Langley Field Speedway (.4-mile) (Plymouth)
* Asheville 300; Asheville Speedway (.333-mile) (Plymouth)
Nashville 400; Fairgrounds Speedway (.5-mile) (Plymouth)
Myers Brothers 250; Bowman Gray Stadium (.25-mile) (Plymouth)
* South Boston Speedway (.375-mile) (Plymouth)
Buddy Shuman 250; Hickory Speedway (.4-mile) (Plymouth)
* Capital City 300; Va. State Fairgrounds (.625-mile) (Plymouth)
* Hillsborough 150; Orange Speedway (.9-mile dirt) (Plymouth)

1969   (2nd)   (1,004)

Victories

Georgia 500; Middle Georgia Raceway (.5-m; 250 miles) (Plymouth)
Motor Trend 500; Riverside Int. Race. (2.7-m rd.; 500 m) (Ford)
Virginia 500; Martinsville Speedway (.5-m; 250 miles) (Ford)
Kingsport 250; Kingsport Speedway (.4-mile; 100 miles) (Ford)
Mason-Dixon 300; Dover Downs Int. Speedway (1-m; 300 m) (Ford)
* Maryland 300; Beltsville Speedway (.5-mile; 150 miles) (Ford)

* Nashville 400; Fairgrounds Speedway (.5-m; 200 miles) (Ford)
Smoky Mountain 200; Smoky Mountain Raceway (.5-m; 100 m) (Ford)
* Myers Brothers 250; Bowman Gray Stadium (.25-m; 63 m) (Ford)
Old Dominion 500; Martinsville Speedway (.5-mile; 250 m) (Ford)

Poles

Alabama 200; Montgomery Speedway (.5-mile) (Plymouth)
* Maryland 300; Beltsville Speedway (.5-mile) (Ford)
* Nashville 400; Fairgrounds Speedway (.5-mile) (Ford)
* Myers Brothers 250; Bowman Gray Stadium (.25-mile) (Ford)
Capital City 250; Virginia State Fairgrounds (.5625-m) (Ford)
Sandlapper 200; Columbia Speedway (.5-mile dirt) (Ford)

1970   (3rd)   (958)

Victories (1st)

Carolina 500; N.C. Motor Speedway (1.017-m; 500 miles) (Plymouth)
* Savannah 200; Savannah Speedway (.5-mile; 100 miles) (Plymouth)
Gwyn Staley 400; N. Wilkesboro Speedway (.625-m; 250m) (Plymouth)
Columbia 200; Columbia Speedway (.5-m dirt; 100 miles) (Plymouth)
Falstaff 400; Riverside Int. Race. (2.62-m rd.; 400m) (Plymouth)
* Kingsport 100; Kingsport Speedway (.337-mile; 100 m) (Plymouth)
Albany-Saratoga 250; Albany-Saratoga Sp. (.362-m; 91m) (Plymouth)
Schaefer 300; Trenton Speedway (1.5-mile; 300 miles) (Plymouth)
* East Tenn. 200; Smoky Mountain Raceway (.52-m; 104m) (Plymouth)
Dixie 500; Atlanta Int. Raceway (1.522-m; 500 miles) (Plymouth)
West Virginia 300; Int. Raceway Park (.4375-m; 131m) (Plymouth)
* Myers Bros. 250; Bowman Gray Stadium (.25-mile; 63m) (Plymouth)
* Halifax Co. 100; South Boston Speed. (.357-m; 100 m) (Plymouth)
* Capital City 500; Virginia St. Fgds. (.542-m; 271m) (Plymouth)
Mason-Dixon 300; Dover Downs Int. Speed. (1-m; 300 m) (Plymouth)
Home State 200; State Fairgrounds (.5-m dirt; 100 m) (Plymouth)
Old Dominion 500; Martinsville Speed. (.525-m; 263 m) (Plymouth)
* Georgia 500; Middle Georgia Raceway (.548-m; 274m) (Plymouth)

Poles

Richmond 500; Virginia State Fairgrounds (.542-mile) (Plymouth)
* Savannah 200; Savannah Speedway (.5-mile) (Plymouth)
* Kingsport 100; Kingsport Speedway (.337-mile) (Plymouth)
* East Tennessee 200; Smoky Mountain Raceway (.52-m) (Plymouth)
Sandlapper 200; Columbia Speedway (.5-mile dirt) (Plymouth)
* Myers Brothers 250; Bowman Gray Stadium (.25-mile) (Plymouth)
* Halifax County 100; South Boston Speedway (.357-m) (Plymouth)
* Capital City 500; Va. State Fairgrounds (.542-m) (Plymouth)
* Georgia 500; Middle Georgia Raceway (.548-mile) (Plymouth)

1971   (1st)   (1,313)

Victories (1st)

Daytona 500; Daytona Int. Speedway (2.5-m; 500 miles) (Plymouth)
Richmond 500; Richmond Fgds. Raceway (.542-m; 271 m) (Plymouth)
Carolina 500; N.C. Motor Speedway (1.017-m; 500 miles) (Plymouth)
Hickory 276; Hickory Speedway (.363-mile; 100 miles) (Plymouth)
Columbia 200; Columbia Speedway (.5-mile; 100 miles) (Plymouth)
Maryville 200; Smoky Mountain Raceway (.52-m; 104 m) (Plymouth)
Gwyn Staley 400; N. Wilkesboro Speedway (.625-m; 250m) (Plymouth)
Virginia 500; Martinsville Speedway (.525-mile; 263 m) (Plymouth)
* Asheville 300; Asheville Speedway (.333-mile; 100 m) (Plymouth)
Pickens 200; Greenville-Pickens Speedway (.5-m; 100 m) (Plymouth)
* Albany-Sara. 250; Albany-Saratoga Sp. (.362-m; 91 m) (Plymouth)
* Islip 250; Islip Speedway (.2-mile; 50 miles) (Plymouth)
Northern 300; Trenton Speedway (1.5-mile; 300 miles) (Plymouth)
* Nashville 420; Fairgrounds Speedway (.596-m; 250 m) (Plymouth)
Dixie 500; Atlanta Int. Raceway (1.522-m; 500 miles) (Plymouth)
West Virginia 500; Int. Raceway Park (.4375-m; 219 m) (Plymouth)
* Sandlapper 200; Columbia Speedway (.51-mile; 102 m) (Plymouth)
Delaware 500; Dover Downs Int. Speedway (1-m; 500 m) (Plymouth)

American 500; N.C. Motor Speedway (1.017-m; 500 miles) (Plymouth)
Capital City 500; Richmond Fgds. Race. (.542-m; 271 m) (Plymouth)
Texas 500; Texas World Speedway (2-mile; 500 miles) (Plymouth)

Poles (T-1st)

Motor Trend 500; Riverside Int. Raceway (2.62-mile road) (Plymouth)
* Asheville 300; Asheville Speedway (.333-mile) (Plymouth)
Mason-Dixon 500; Dover Downs Int. Speedway (1-mile) (Plymouth)
Volunteer 500; Bristol International Speedway (.533-m) (Plymouth)
* Albany-Saratoga 250; Albany-Saratoga Sp. (.362-m) (Plymouth)
* Islip 250; Islip Speedway (.2-mile) (Plymouth)
* Nashville 420; Fairgrounds Speedway (.596-mile) (Plymouth)
Myers Brothers 250; Bowman Gray Stadium (.25-mile) (Plymouth)
* Sandlapper 200; Columbia Speedway (.5-mile) (Plymouth)

1972   (2nd)   (957)

Victories

Win. Wes. 500; Riverside Int. Race. (2.62-m rd.; 500m) (Plymouth)
Richmond 500; Richmond Fgds. Raceway (.542-m; 271 m) (Plymouth)
Gwyn Staley 400; N. Wilkesboro Speedway (.625-m; 250m) (Plymouth)
Virginia 500; Martinsville Speedway (.525-mile; 263 m) (Plymouth)
* Lone Star 500; Texas World Speedway (2-m; 500 miles) (Plymouth)
Capital City 500; Richmond Fgds. Race. (.542-m; 271 m) (Plymouth)
Old Dominion 500; Martinsville Speedway (.525-m; 263m) (Plymouth)
Wilkes 400; North Wilkesboro Speedway (.625-m; 250 m) (Plymouth)

Poles

Golden State 400; Riverside Int. Raceway (2.62-m road) (Plymouth)
* Lone Star 500; Texas World Speedway (2-mile) (Plymouth)
Yankee 400; Michigan International Speedway (2-mile) (Dodge)

1973   (4th)   (633)

Victories

Daytona 500; Daytona Int. Speedway (2.5-mile; 500 miles) (Dodge)
Richmond 500; Richmond Fgds. Raceway (.542-m; 271 miles) (Dodge)
Gwyn Staley 400; No. Wilkesboro Speedway (.625-m; 250 m) (Dodge)
Alamo 500; Texas World Speedway (2-mile; 500 miles) (Dodge)
Capital City 500; Richmond Fgds. Raceway (.542-m; 271 m) (Dodge)
Old Dominion 500; Martinsville Speedway (.525-m; 263 m) (Dodge)

Poles

Tuborg 400; Riverside Int. Raceway (2.62-mile road) (Dodge)
Dixie 500; Atlanta International Raceway (1.522-mile) (Dodge)
American 500; North Carolina Motor Speedway (1.017-mile) (Dodge)

1974   (1st)   (835)

Victories (T-1st)

Daytona 500; Daytona Int. Speedway (2.5-mile; 450 miles) (Dodge)
Carolina 500; N.C. Motor Speedway (1.017-m; 451 miles) (Dodge)
Gwyn Staley 400; North Wilkesboro Speedway (.625-m; 225 m) (Dodge)
Music City USA 420; Fairgrounds Speedway (.596-m; 238 m) (Dodge)
Motor State 400; Michigan Int. Speedway (2-mile; 360 m) (Dodge)
Dixie 500; Atlanta Int. Raceway (1.522-mile; 500 miles) (Dodge)
Purolator 500; Pocono Int. Raceway (2.5-mile; 500 miles) (Dodge)
Talladega 500; Ala. Int. Motor Speedway (2.66-m; 500 m) (Dodge)
* Capital City 500; Richmond Fgds. Race. (.542-m; 271 m) (Dodge)
Delaware 500; Dover Downs Int. Speedway (1-m; 500 miles) (Dodge)

Poles

Volunteer 500; Bristol International Raceway (.533-mile) (Dodge)
Southern 500; Darlington Raceway (1.366-mile) (Dodge)
* Capital City 500; Richmond Fgds. Raceway (.542-mile) (Dodge)
Wilkes 400; North Wilkesboro Speedway (.625-mile) (Dodge)
Old Dominion 500; Martinsville Speedway (.525-mile) (Dodge)
American 500; North Carolina Motor Speedway (1.017-mile) (Dodge)
Los Angeles Times 500; Ontario Motor Speedway (2.5-mile) (Dodge)

1975   (1st)   (910)

Victories (1st)
* Richmond 500; Richmond Fgds. Raceway (.542-m; 271 m) (Dodge)
Southeastern 500; Bristol Int. Speedway (.533-m; 267 m) (Dodge)
* Atlanta 500; Atlanta Int. Raceway (1.522-m; 500 miles) (Dodge)
Gwyn Staley 400; No. Wilkesboro Speedway (.625-m; 250 m) (Dodge)
Virginia 500; Martinsville Speedway (.525-m; 263 miles) (Dodge)
World 600; Charlotte Motor Speedway (1.5-m; 600 miles) (Dodge)
Tuborg 400; Riverside Int. Raceway (2.62-m road; 400 m) (Dodge)
Firecracker 400; Daytona Int. Speedway (2.5-mile; 400 m) (Dodge)
Champion SP 400; Michigan Int. Speedway (2-m; 400 miles) (Dodge)
Delaware 500; Dover Downs Int. Speedway (1-m; 500 miles) (Dodge)
* Wilkes 400; North Wilkesboro Speedway (.625-m; 250 m) (Dodge)
National 500; Charlotte Motor Speedway (1.5-mile; 500 miles) (Dodge)
Volunteer 500; Bristol Int. Speedway (.533-m; 267 miles) (Dodge)

Poles
* Richmond 500; Richmond Fairgrounds Raceway (.542-m) (Dodge)
* Atlanta 500; Atlanta International Raceway (1.522-m) (Dodge)
* Wilkes 400; North Wilkesboro Speedway (.625-mile) (Dodge)

1976   (4th)   (702)

Victories
Carolina 500; N.C. Motor Speedway (1.017-m; 500 miles) (Dodge)
Purolator 500; Pocono Int. Raceway (2.5-mile; 500 miles) (Dodge)
American 500; N.C. Motor Speedway (1.017-m; 500 miles) (Dodge)

Poles
Cam2 Motor Oil 400; Michigan Int. Speedway (2-mile) (Dodge)

1977   (2nd)   (778)

Victories
Carolina 500; N.C. Motor Speedway (1.017-m; 500 miles) (Dodge)
* Atlanta 500; Atlanta Int. Raceway (1.522-mile; 500m) (Dodge)
World 600; Charlotte Motor Speedway (1.5-m; 600 miles) (Dodge)
* NAPA Riverside 400; Riv. Int. Race. (2.62-m rd.; 249m) (Dodge)
Firecracker 400; Daytona Int. Speedway (2.5-mile; 400 m) (Dodge)

Poles
* Atlanta 500; Atlanta International Raceway (1.522-m) (Dodge)
Mason-Dixon 500; Dover Downs Int. Speedway (1-mile) (Dodge)
* NAPA Riverside 400; Riverside Int. Race. (2.62-m rd.) (Dodge)
Wilkes 400; North Wilkesboro Speedway (.625-mile) (Dodge)
Los Angeles Times 500; Ontario Motor Speedway (2.5-m) (Dodge)

1978   (9th)   (568)

1979   (1st)   (873)

Victories
Daytona 500; Daytona Int. Speedway (2.5-mile; 500 miles) (Oldsmobile)
Virginia 500; Martinsville Speedway (.525-m; 263 miles) (Chevrolet)
Champion Sp. Pl. 400; Michigan Int. Speedway (2-m; 400m) (Chevrolet)
CRC Chemicals 500; Dover Downs Int. Speedway (1-m; 500m) (Chevrolet)
American 500; N.C. Motor Speedway (1.017-m; 500 miles) (Chevrolet)

Poles
Volunteer 500; Bristol International Raceway (.533-mile) (Chevrolet)

1980   (3rd)   (657)

Victories
Northwestern Bank 400; N. Wilkesboro Sp. (.625-m; 250m) (Chevrolet)
Music City 420; Nashville Int. Raceway (.596-m; 250 m) (Chevrolet)

1981   (8th)   (521)

Victories
Daytona 500; Daytona Int. Speedway (2.5-mile; 500 miles) (Buick)
Northwestern Bank 400; N. Wilkesboro Sp. (.625-m; 250 m) (Buick)
Champion SP 400; Michigan Int. Speedway (2-m; 400 miles) (Buick)

1982   (7th)   (502)

1983   (4th)   (682)

Victories
W.W. Hodgdon Car. 500; N.C. Motor Sp. (1.017-m; 500 m) (Pontiac)
Winston 500; Ala. Int. Motor Speedway (2.66-m; 500 m) (Pontiac)
Miller HL 500; Charlotte Motor Speedway (1.5-m; 500 m) (Pontiac)

1984   (11th)   (506)

Victories
Budweiser 500; Dover Downs Int. Speedway (1-m; 500 m) (Pontiac)
Pepsi Firecracker 400; Daytona Int. Sp. (2.5-m; 400m) (Pontiac)

1985   (17th)   (382)

1986   (12th)   (451)

1987   (7th)   (553)

1988   (207)

1989   (172)

1990   (147)

1991   (20th)   (333)

1992   (24th)   (278)

ANDY PIERCE

1951

Poles
Carrell Speedway (.5-mile dirt) (Buick)

TOM PISTONE

1959   (4th)   (366)

Victories
Trenton Speedway (1-mile; 150 miles) (Ford)
Richmond 200; Atlantic Rural Fgds. (.5-mile dirt; 100 m) (Ford)

1960   (22nd)   (190)

1965   (198)

Poles
Music City 200; Fairgrounds Speedway (.5-mile) (Ford)

1966   (160)

Poles
Columbia 200; Columbia Speedway (.5-mile dirt) (Ford)
Richmond 250; Virginia State Fairgrounds (.5-mile dirt) (Ford)
East Tennessee 200; Smoky Mountain Raceway (.5-m dirt) (Ford)
Islip Speedway (.2-mile) (Ford)

BLACKIE PITT

1954   (14th)   (173)

1955	(17th)	(144)
1956		(100)

LENNIE POND

1973	(19th)	(286)
1974	(12th)	(380)
1975	(23rd)	(289)
1976	(5th)	(599)
1977		(177)
1978	(8th)	(575)

Victories
Talladega 500; Ala. Int. Motor Speedway (2.66-m; 500 m) (Oldsmobile)

Poles
Virginia 500; Martinsville Speedway (.525-mile) (Chevrolet)
Music City USA 420; Nashville Speedway (.596-mile) (Chevrolet)
Nashville 420; Nashville Speedway (.596-mile) (Chevrolet)
Volunteer 500; Bristol International Raceway (.533-mile) (Oldsmobile)
Old Dominion 500; Martinsville Speedway (.525-mile) (Chevrolet)

1979		(127)
1980	(24th)	(230)
1981		(131)
1982		(128)
1983		(135)
1984		(124)
1985		(164)

BILL POOR

1958	(21st)	(171)

MARVIN PORTER

1957

Victories
Santa Clara Fairgrounds (.5-mile dirt; 100 miles) (Ford)

1960

Victories
California 250; Marchbanks Speedway (1.4-mile; 250 miles) (Ford)

ROBERT PRESSLEY

1995		(214)
1996		(114)
1998		(159)
1999		(115)

BAXTER PRICE

1978		(163)
1979		(145)

BOB PRONGER

1953

Poles
Beach & Road Course (4.1-mile road) (Oldsmobile)

J.T. PUTNEY

1964	(25th)	(214)
1965	(8th)	(553)
1966	(9th)	(458)
1967	(16th)	(294)

BILLY RAFTER

1958	(T-18th)	(183)

KEN RAGAN

1983		(154)

WILBUR RAKESTRAW

1958		(111)

DICK RATHMANN

1951	(16th)	(124)

Poles
Oakland Stadium (.625-mile dirt) (Hudson)
Hanford Motor Speedway (.5-mile dirt) (Hudson)

1952	(5th)	(339)

Victories
Martinsville Speedway (.5-mile dirt; 100 miles) (Hudson)
Langhorne Speedway (1-mile dirt; 150 miles) (Hudson)
Darlington Raceway (1.25-mile; 150 miles) (Hudson)
Dayton Speedway (.5-mile; 100 miles) (Hudson)
Dayton Speedway (.5-mile; 150 miles) (Hudson)

Poles
Poor Man's 500; Canfield Speedway (.5-mile dirt) (Ford)
Motor City 250; Michigan State Fairgrounds (1-mile dirt) (Hudson)

1953	(3rd)	(523)

Victories
Central City Speedway (.5-mile dirt; 100 miles) (Hudson)
International 200; Langhorne Speedway (1-m dirt; 200 m) (Hudson)
Morristown Speedway (.5-mile dirt; 100 miles) (Hudson)
Lincoln City Fairgrounds (.5-mile dirt; 100 miles) (Hudson)
Langhorne Speedway (1-mile dirt; 250 miles) (Hudson)

Poles
Palm Beach Speedway (.5-mile dirt) (Hudson)
Five Flags Speedway (.5-mile dirt) (Hudson)

1954 (4th) (534)

Victories
Oakland Speedway (.5-mile dirt; 125 miles) (Hudson)
Wilkes Co. 160; N. Wilkesboro Speed. (.625-m dirt; 100m) (Hudson)
Santa Fe Speedway (.5-mile dirt; 100 miles) (Hudson)

Poles
Palm Beach Speedway (.5-mile dirt) (Hudson)
Central City Speedway (.5-mile dirt) (Hudson)
Sharon Speedway (.5-mile dirt) (Hudson)
Williams Grove Speedway (.5-mile dirt) (Hudson)

1955 (13th) (183)

Poles
Palm Beach Speedway (.5-mile dirt) (Hudson)
Speedway Park (.5-mile dirt) (Hudson)
Oglethorpe Speedway (.5-mile dirt) (Hudson)

JIM REED

1955 (23rd) (117)

1956 (22nd) (132)

Poles
Willow Springs Speedway (2.5-mile dirt road) (Chevrolet)
Old Bridge Stadium (.5-mile) (Chevrolet)

1958 (12th) (283)

Victories
* Old Bridge Stadium (.5-mile; 100 miles) (Ford)
* Starkey Speedway (.25-mile; 38 miles) (Ford)
Civic Stadium (.25-mile; 25 miles) (Ford)
Wall Stadium (.333-mile; 100 miles) (Ford)

Poles
* Old Bridge Stadium (.5-mile) (Ford)
* Starkey Speedway (.25-mile) (Ford)

1959 (15th) (256)

Victories
Bowman Gray Stadium (.25-mile; 50 miles) (Ford)
Heidelberg Raceway (.25-mile dirt; 50 miles) (Chevrolet)
Southern 500; Darlington Raceway (1.375-mile; 500 miles) (Chevrolet)

Poles
Ascot Stadium (.4-mile dirt) (Chevrolet)

1961 (136)

LEE REITZEL

1961 (126)

BILL REXFORD

1949 (15th)

1950 (2nd) (215)

Victories
Poor Man's 500; Canfield Speedway (.5-m dirt; 100 miles) (Oldsmobile)

1951

Poles
Poor Man's 500; Canfield Speedway (.5-mile dirt) (Oldsmobile)

JACK REYNOLDS

1952 (23rd)

SAM RICE

1949 (T-16th)

TIM RICHMOND

1981 (18th) (353)

1982 (11th) (441)

Victories
Budweiser 400; Riverside Int. Raceway (2.62-m rd.; 250m) (Buick)
Win. West. 500; Riverside Int. Race. (2.62-m rd.; 312m) (Buick)

Poles
Busch 500; Bristol International Raceway (.533-mile) (Buick)

1983 (10th) (460)

Victories
* Like Cola 500; Pocono Int. Raceway (2.5-mile; 500 m) (Pontiac)

Poles
TranSouth 500; Darlington Int. Raceway (1.366-mile) (Pontiac)
* Like Cola 500; Pocono International Raceway (2.5-m) (Pontiac)
Miller High Life 500; Charlotte Motor Speedway (1.5-m) (Pontiac)
Atlanta Journal 500; Atlanta Int. Raceway (1.522-mile) (Pontiac)

1984 (13th) (444)

Victories
Northwest. Bank 400; N. Wilkesboro Sp. (.625-m; 250 m) (Pontiac)

1985 (T-9th) (528)

1986 (2nd) (736)

Victories (1st)
Miller High Life 500; Pocono Int. Raceway (2.5-m; 500 m) (Chevrolet)
Pepsi Firecracker 400; Daytona Int. Speed. (2.5-m; 400m) (Chevrolet)
Summer 500; Pocono Int. Raceway (2.5-mile; 500 miles) (Chevrolet)
* Bud. at the Glen; Watkins Gl. Int. (2.428-m rd.; 219m) (Chevrolet)
* Southern 500; Darlington Int. Raceway (1.366-m; 500 m) (Chevrolet)
Wrangler Indigo 400; Richmond Fgds. Race. (.542-m; 217m) (Chevrolet)
* Win. Wes. 500; Riverside Int. Race. (2.62-m rd.; 312m) (Chevrolet)

Poles (T-1st)
Sovran Bank 500; Martinsville Speedway (.526-mile) (Chevrolet)
Miller American 400; Michigan Int. Speedway (2-mile) (Chevrolet)
* Budweiser at the Glen; Watkins Glen Int. (2.428-m rd.) (Chevrolet)
* Southern 500; Darlington Int. Raceway (1.366-mile) (Chevrolet)
Holly Farms 400; North Wilkesboro Speedway (.625-mile) (Chevrolet)
Oakwood Homes 500; Charlotte Motor Speedway (1.5-mile) (Chevrolet)
Nationwise 500; North Carolina Motor Speedway (1.017-m) (Chevrolet)
* Winston Western 500; Riverside Int. Race. (2.62-m rd.) (Chevrolet)

1987 (160)

Victories
Miller High Life 500; Pocono Int. Raceway (2.5-m; 500 m) (Chevrolet)
Budweiser 400; Riverside Int. Raceway (2.62-m rd.; 249m) (Chevrolet)

Poles
Summer 500; Pocono International Raceway (2.5-mile) (Chevrolet)

JODY RIDLEY

1980	(5th)	(627)
1981	(3rd)	(658)

Victories
Mason-Dixon 500; Dover Downs Int. Speedway (1-m; 500 m) (Ford)

1982	(18th)	(389)
1983		(163)
1984	(25th)	(195)
1986		(151)

CHARLIE ROBERTS

1972	(19th)	(298)
1973	(24th)	(225)

FIREBALL ROBERTS

1950	(9th)	(131)

Victories
Occoneechee Speedway (1-mile dirt; 100 miles) (Oldsmobile)

Poles
Wilkes 200; North Wilkesboro Speedway (.625-mile dirt) (Oldsmobile)

1955

Poles
Southern 500; Darlington Raceway (1.375-mile) (Buick)

1956	(7th)	(443)

Victories
Raleigh 250; Raleigh Speedway (1-mile; 250 miles) (Ford)
Soldier Field (.5-mile; 100 miles) (Ford)
Coastal Speedway (.5-mile dirt; 100 miles) (Ford)
Orange Speedway (.9-mile dirt; 99 miles) (Ford)
Newport Speedway (.5-mile dirt; 100 miles) (Ford)

Poles
Southern States Fairgrounds (.5-mile dirt) (Ford)
Asheville-Weaverville Speedway (.5-mile dirt) (Ford)
Piedmont Interstate Fairgrounds (.5-mile dirt) (Ford)

1957	(3rd)	(619)

Victories
Ind. Riv. GC 100; Titusville-Cocoa Sp. (1.6-m road; 90m) (Ford)
* Wilkes Co. 160; N. Wilkesboro Sp. (.625-m dirt; 100 m) (Ford)
Langhorne Speedway (1-mile dirt; 150 miles) (Ford)
Southern States Fairgrounds (.5-mile dirt; 100 miles) (Ford)
Cleveland County Fairgrounds (.5-mile dirt; 100 miles) (Ford)
Newport Speedway (.5-mile dirt; 100 miles) (Ford)
Newberry Speedway (.5-mile dirt; 100 miles) (Ford)
Concord Speedway (.5-mile dirt; 100 miles) (Ford)

Poles
Wilson Speedway (.5-mile dirt) (Ford)
Orange Speedway (.9-mile dirt) (Ford)
* Wilkes Co. 160; No. Wilkesboro Speedway (.625-m dirt) (Ford)
Wilkes 160; North Wilkesboro Speedway (.625-mile) (Ford)

1958	(13th)	(273)

Victories
Northern 500; Trenton Speedway (1-mile; 500 miles) (Chevrolet)
Raleigh 250; Raleigh Speedway (1-mile; 250 miles) (Chevrolet)
Western N.C. 500; Asheville-Weaverville Sp. (.5-m; 250m) (Chevrolet)
Southern 500; Darlington Raceway (1.375-mile; 500 miles) (Chevrolet)
Alabama State Fairgrounds (.5-mile dirt; 100 miles) (Chevrolet)
Old Dominion 500; Martinsville Speedway (.5-mile; 250 m) (Chevrolet)

1959		(101)

Victories
* Firecracker 250; Daytona Int. Speedway (2.5-m; 250m) (Pontiac)

Poles
Daytona International Speedway (2.5-mile) (Pontiac)
* Firecracker 250; Daytona Int. Speedway (2.5-mile) (Pontiac)
Southern 500; Darlington Raceway (1.375-mile) (Pontiac)

1960		(116)

Victories
Daytona International Speedway (2.5-mile; 100 miles) (Pontiac)
* Dixie 300; Atlanta Int. Raceway (1.5-m; 300 miles) (Pontiac)

Poles (1st)
Rebel 300; Darlington Raceway (1.375-mile) (Pontiac)
World 600; Charlotte Motor Speedway (1.5-mile) (Pontiac)
* Dixie 300; Atlanta International Raceway (1.5-mile) (Pontiac)
Southern 500; Darlington Raceway (1.375-mile) (Pontiac)
National 400; Charlotte Motor Speedway (1.5-mile) (Pontiac)
Atlanta 500; Atlanta International Raceway (1.5-mile) (Pontiac)

1961	(10th)	(432)

Victories
Daytona International Speedway (2.5-mile; 100 miles) (Pontiac)
Marchbanks Speedway (1.4-mile; 250 miles) (Pontiac)

Poles
Daytona 500; Daytona International Speedway (2.5-m) (Pontiac)
Firecracker 250; Daytona Int. Speedway (2.5-mile) (Pontiac)
Festival 250; Atlanta International Raceway (1.5-m) (Pontiac)
Southern 500; Darlington Raceway (1.375-mile) (Pontiac)
Dixie 400; Atlanta International Raceway (1.5-mile) (Pontiac)

1962	(16th)	(364)

Victories
Daytona International Speedway (2.5-mile; 100 miles) (Pontiac)
* Daytona 500; Daytona Int. Speedway (2.5-mile; 500 m) (Pontiac)
Firecracker 250; Daytona Int. Speedway (2.5-m; 250 m) (Pontiac)

Poles
* Daytona 500; Daytona International Speedway (2.5-m) (Pontiac)
Volunteer 500; Bristol International Raceway (.5-m) (Pontiac)
World 600; Charlotte Motor Speedway (1.5-mile) (Pontiac)
Southeastern 500; Bristol Int. Speedway (.5-mile) (Pontiac)
Southern 500; Darlington Raceway (1.375-mile) (Pontiac)
Old Dominion 500; Martinsville Speedway (.5-mile) (Pontiac)
National 400; Charlotte Motor Speedway (1.5-mile) (Pontiac)
Dixie 400; Atlanta International Raceway (1.5-mile) (Pontiac)

1963	(12th)	(432)

Victories
Southeastern 500; Bristol Int. Speedway (.5-mile; 250 m) (Ford)
Firecracker 400; Daytona Int. Speedway (2.5-mile; 400 m) (Ford)
Old Bridge Stadium (.5-mile; 100 miles) (Ford)
Southern 500; Darlington Raceway (1.375-mile; 500 miles) (Ford)

Driver, Year (Performance Index ranking) (Performance Index points)

Poles
Daytona 500; Daytona International Speedway (2.5-mile) (Pontiac)

1964   (198)
Victories
Augusta International Speedway (3-mile road; 510 miles) (Ford)

JACKIE ROGERS

1974	(T-18th)	(289)
1976	(25th)	(222)

SHORTY ROLLINS

1958   (5th)   (415)
Victories
State Line Speedway (.333-mile dirt; 50 miles) (Ford)

JIM ROPER

1949   (20th)
Victories
Charlotte Speedway (.75-mile dirt; 150 miles) (Lincoln)

BOB ROSS

1961
Poles
Marchbanks Speedway (1.4-mile) (Ford)

EARL ROSS

1974   (6th)   (483)
Victories
Old Dominion 500; Martinsville Speedway (.525-mile; 263 miles) (Chevrolet)

JOHN ROSTEK

1960
Victories
Copper Cup 100; Arizona St. Fairgrounds (1-m dirt; 100m) (Ford)
Poles
Empire State 200; Montgomery Air Base (2-mile) (Ford)

RICKY RUDD

1977	(18th)	(326)
1978		(121)
1979	(7th)	(594)
1980		(193)
1981	(7th)	(552)

Poles
Virginia 500; Martinsville Speedway (.525-mile) (Buick)
Melling Tool 420; Nashville Int. Raceway (.596-mile) (Buick)
CRC Chemicals 500; Dover Downs Int. Speedway (1-mile) (Chevrolet)

1982   (13th)   (419)
Poles
CRC Chemicals 500; Dover Downs Int. Speedway (1-mile) (Pontiac)
Old Dominion 500; Martinsville Speedway (.525-mile) (Pontiac)

1983   (9th)   (478)
Victories
Budweiser 400; Riverside Int. Race. (2.62-m road; 250m) (Chevrolet)
Goody's 500; Martinsville Speedway (.525-m; 263 miles) (Chevrolet)
Poles
Daytona 500; Daytona International Speedway (2.5-mile) (Chevrolet)
Richmond 400; Richmond Fairgrounds Raceway (.542-mile) (Chevrolet)
W.W. Hodgdon Carolina 500; N.C. Motor Speedway (1.017-m) (Chevrolet)
Va. National Bank 500; Martinsville Speedway (.525-mile) (Chevrolet)

1984   (7th)   (623)
Victories
Miller HL 400; Richmond Fgds. Raceway (.542-mile; 217 m) (Ford)
Poles (T-1st)
Valleydale 500; Bristol International Raceway (.533-m) (Ford)
Northwestern Bank 400; No. Wilkesboro Speedway (.625-m) (Ford)
Budweiser 500; Dover Downs International Speedway (1-m) (Ford)
Pepsi 420; Nashville International Raceway (.596-mile) (Ford)

1985   (4th)   (651)
Victories
Win. West. 500; Riverside Int. Race. (2.62-m rd.; 312 m) (Ford)

1986   (6th)   (590)
Victories
Sovran Bank 500; Martinsville Speedway (.526-m; 263 m) (Ford)
Delaware 500; Dover Downs Int. Speedway (1-m; 500 miles) (Ford)
Poles
Budweiser 500; Dover Downs International Speedway (1-m) (Ford)

1987   (8th)   (553)
Victories
Motorcraft QP 500; Atlanta Int. Raceway (1.522-m; 500 m) (Ford)
Delaware 500; Dover Downs Int. Speedway (1-m; 500 miles) (Ford)

1988   (11th)   (495)
Victories
The Bud. at the Glen; Wat. Glen Int. (2.428-m rd.; 219m) (Buick)
Poles
Pannill Sweatshirts 500; Martinsville Speedway (.526-m) (Buick)
Budweiser 400; Riverside Int. Raceway (2.62-mile road) (Buick)

1989   (9th)   (520)
Victories
Banquet FF 300; Sears Pt. Int. Race. (2.52-m rd.; 187m) (Buick)

1990   (12th)   (518)
Victories
Budweis. at the Glen; Wat. Glen Int. (2.428-m rd.; 219m) (Chevrolet)
Poles
Pontiac Excitement 400; Richmond Int. Raceway (.75-mile) (Chevrolet)
Banquet FF 300; Sears Point Int. Raceway (2.52-mile rd.) (Chevrolet)

1991   (1st)   (733)
Victories
TranSouth 500; Darlington Raceway (1.366-m; 500 miles) (Chevrolet)

Poles
Banquet FF 300; Sears Point Int. Raceway (2.52-mile rd.) (Chevrolet)

1992 (8th) (579)

Victories
Peak Antifreeze 500; Dover Downs Int. Speed. (1-m; 500m) (Chevrolet)

Poles
The Save Mart 300; Sears Point Int. Raceway (2.52-m rd.) (Chevrolet)

1993 (11th) (516)

Victories
Miller Gen. Dr. 400; Michigan Int. Speedway (2-m; 400m) (Chevrolet)

1994 (4th) (673)

Victories
Slick 50 300; New Hamp. Int. Speedway (1.058-m; 317 m) (Ford)

Poles
AC Delco 500; North Carolina Motor Speedway (1.017-mile) (Ford)

1995 (8th) (582)

Victories
Dura-Lube 500; Phoenix Int. Raceway (1-mile; 312 miles) (Ford)

Poles
Save Mart Super. 300; Sears Point Raceway (2.52-m rd.) (Ford)
UAW-GM Quality 500; Charlotte Motor Speedway (1.5-mile) (Ford)

1996 (6th) (612)

Victories
AC Delco 400; N.C. Motor Speedway (1.017-m; 400 miles) (Ford)

1997 (15th) (459)

Victories
Miller 500; Dover Downs Int. Speedway (1-m; 500 miles) (Ford)
Brickyard 400; Indianapolis Motor Speedway (2.5-m; 400m) (Ford)

1998 (23rd) (290)

Victories
NAPA AutoCare 500; Martinsville Speedway (.526-m; 263 m) (Ford)

1999 (286)

Poles
Dura-Lube/Big Kmart 400; N.C. Speedway (1.017-mile) (Ford)

KEN RUSH

1957 (100)

Poles
Greensboro Fairgrounds (.333-mile dirt) (Ford)

1958

Poles
Lincoln Speedway (.5-mile dirt) (Chevrolet)

JACK RUSSELL

1949 (21st)

JOHNNY RUTHERFORD

1963

Victories
Daytona International Speedway (2.5-mile; 100 miles) (Chevrolet)

1981 (161)

JOE RUTTMAN

1981 (24th) (279)

1982 (16th) (405)

1983 (12th) (434)

Poles
Mason-Dixon 500; Dover Downs Int. Speedway (1-mile) (Buick)
Busch 500; Bristol International Raceway (.533-mile) (Pontiac)

1984 (20th) (339)

Poles
Sovran Bank 500; Martinsville Speedway (.526-mile) (Chevrolet)

1985 (25th) (212)

1986 (15th) (422)

1988 (112)

1991 (24th) (298)

TROY RUTTMAN

1963 (122)

TERRY RYAN

1976 (105)

GREG SACKS

1984 (144)

1985 (20th) (296)

Victories
Pepsi Firecracker 400; Daytona Int. Speed. (2.5-m; 400m) (Chevrolet)

1988 (151)

1990 (210)

Poles
Pepsi 400; Daytona International Speedway (2.5-mile) (Chevrolet)

1992 (177)

1993 (153)

1994 (173)

Poles
Hooters 500; Atlanta Motor Speedway (1.522-mile) (Ford)

ELLIOTT SADLER

1999 (271)

LEON SALES

1950

Victories
Wilkes 200; N. Wilkesboro Speed. (.625-m dirt; 125 m) (Plymouth)

Driver Resumes
Driver, Year (Performance Index ranking)
(Performance Index points)

JIM SAUTER

1986		(103)
1989		(149)

CONNIE SAYLOR

1981		(111)

FRANKIE SCHNEIDER

1952	(21st)	
1957		(120)

Poles
Raleigh 250; Raleigh Speedway (1-mile) (Chevrolet)

1958		

Victories
Old Dominion Speedway (.375-mile; 56 miles) (Chevrolet)

KEN SCHRADER

1985	(14th)	(415)
1986	(21st)	(288)
1987	(10th)	(497)

Poles
TranSouth 500; Darlington Int. Raceway (1.366-mile) (Ford)

1988	(5th)	(634)

Victories
Talla. Diehard 500; Ala. Int. Motor Sp. (2.66-m; 500 m) (Chevrolet)
Poles
Daytona 500; Daytona International Speedway (2.5-mile) (Chevrolet)
TranSouth 500; Darlington Int. Raceway (1.366-mile) (Chevrolet)

1989	(5th)	(616)

Victories
All Pro Auto Parts 500; Char. Motor Speed. (1.5-m; 500m) (Chevrolet)
Poles
Daytona 500; Daytona International Speedway (2.5-mile) (Chevrolet)
Miller High Life 400; Michigan Int. Speedway (2-mile) (Chevrolet)
AC Spark Plug 400; Pocono Int. Raceway (2.5-mile) (Chevrolet)
Autoworks 500; Phoenix International Raceway (1-mile) (Chevrolet)

1990	(8th)	(537)

Poles
Daytona 500; Daytona International Speedway (2.5-mile) (Chevrolet)
Coca-Cola 600; Charlotte Motor Speedway (1.5-mile) (Chevrolet)
AC Delco 500; North Carolina Motor Speedway (1.017-mile) (Chevrolet)

1991	(8th)	(565)

Victories
Motorcraft QP 500; Atl. Motor Speedway (1.522-m; 500 m) (Chevrolet)
Budweiser 500; Dover Downs Int. Speedway (1-mile; 500 m) (Chevrolet)

1992	(18th)	(444)

Poles
Champion Spark Plug 500; Pocono Int. Raceway (2.5-mile) (Chevrolet)

1993	(9th)	(534)

Poles (1st)
Pontiac Excitement 400; Richmond Int. Raceway (.75-mile) (Chevrolet)
Coca-Cola 600; Charlotte Motor Speedway (1.5-mile) (Chevrolet)
Champion Spark Plug 500; Pocono Int. Raceway (2.5-mile) (Chevrolet)
Miller Genuine Draft 500; Pocono Int. Raceway (2.5-mile) (Chevrolet)
Champion Spark Plug 400; Michigan Int. Speedway (2-mile) (Chevrolet)
Mountain Dew Southern 500; Darlington Raceway (1.366-m) (Chevrolet)

1994	(5th)	(657)
1995	(18th)	(367)

Poles
UAW-GM Teamwork 500; Pocono Int. Raceway (2.5-mile) (Chevrolet)

1996	(14th)	(469)
1997	(9th)	(503)

Poles
Jiffy Lube 300; New Hampshire Int. Speedway (1.058-mile) (Chevrolet)
CMT 300; New Hampshire International Speedway (1.058-m) (Chevrolet)

1998	(13th)	(491)

Poles
Winston 500; Talladega Superspeedway (2.66-mile) (Chevrolet)
Dura-Lube/Kmart 500; Phoenix International Raceway (1-m) (Chevrolet)

1999	(T-15th)	(416)

Poles
Diehard 500; Talladega Superspeedway (2.66-mile) (Chevrolet)

TIGHE SCOTT

1977	(21st)	(259)
1978	(14th)	(336)
1979	(18th)	(311)

WENDELL SCOTT

1961		(155)
1962	(11th)	(402)

Poles
Savannah Speedway (.5-mile dirt) (Chevrolet)

1963	(T-8th)	(464)
1964	(7th)	(614)

Victories
Speedway Park (.5-mile dirt; 100 miles) (Chevrolet)

1965	(6th)	(572)
1966	(7th)	(504)
1967	(10th)	(445)
1968	(12th)	(429)
1969	(11th)	(527)
1970	(19th)	(354)
1971		(280)

JOHN SEARS

1966	(3rd)	(598)
1967	(6th)	(654)

Poles
Savannah Speedway (.5-mile dirt) (Ford)

1968	(5th)	(609)
1969	(8th)	(662)
1970	(13th)	(435)

Poles
Home State 200; State Fairgrounds (.5-mile dirt) (Dodge)

1971		(227)
1972	(10th)	(402)

FRANK SECRIST

1960		

Poles
California 250; Marchbanks Speedway (1.4-mile) (Ford)

GEORGE SEEGER

1951	(25th)	
1957		(106)

BILL SEIFERT

1966		(110)
1967	(12th)	(386)
1968	(16th)	(358)
1969	(15th)	(423)
1970		(275)
1971	(23rd)	(286)

LLOYD SHAW

1953		

Poles
International 200; Langhorne Speedway (1-mile dirt) (Jaguar)

MORGAN SHEPHERD

1981	(15th)	(384)

Victories
Virginia 500; Martinsville Speedway (.525-mile; 263 m) (Pontiac)
Poles
Richmond 400; Richmond Fairgrounds Raceway (.542-mile) (Pontiac)

1982	(10th)	(445)

Poles
Busch Nashville 420; Nashville Int. Raceway (.596-mile) (Buick)
Atlanta Journal 500; Atlanta Int. Raceway (1.522-mile) (Buick)

1983	(13th)	(419)
1984		(111)
1985		(147)
1986	(17th)	(332)

Victories
Motorcraft 500; Atlanta Int. Raceway (1.522-mile; 500 m) (Buick)

1987	(18th)	(386)

Poles
Sovran Bank 500; Martinsville Speedway (.526-mile) (Buick)

1988	(23rd)	(266)

Poles
Pontiac Excitement 400; Richmond Fgds. Raceway (.542-m) (Buick)
AC Spark Plug 500; Pocono Int. Raceway (2.5-mile) (Pontiac)

1989	(10th)	(508)

Poles
Budweiser at the Glen; Watkins Glen Int. (2.428-m rd.) (Pontiac)

1990	(5th)	(573)

Victories
Atlanta Journal 500; Atlanta Motor Sp. (1.522-m; 500 m) (Ford)

1991	(11th)	(533)
1992	(9th)	(553)
1993	(5th)	(643)

Victories
Motorcraft 500; Atlanta Motor Speedway (1.522-m; 500 m) (Ford)

1994	(6th)	(645)
1995	(12th)	(498)
1996	(22nd)	(315)
1997		(177)

BILL SHIREY

1970		(116)

BUDDY SHUMAN

1951	(15th)	(125)
1952	(10th)	(170)

Victories
Stamford Park (.5-mile dirt; 100 miles) (Hudson)

GENE SIMPSON

1955	(14th)	(164)

DAVID SISCO

1972		(142)
1973	(16th)	(307)

1974	(7th)	(454)
1975	(18th)	(364)
1976	(18th)	(357)

EDDIE SKINNER

1954	(21st)	
1955	(7th)	(329)

MIKE SKINNER

1997		(199)

Poles
Daytona 500; Daytona International Speedway (2.5-mile) (Chevrolet)
Pepsi 400; Daytona International Speedway (2.5-mile) (Chevrolet)

1998	(21st)	(328)
1999	(10th)	(569)

Poles
Pennsylvania 500; Pocono Raceway (2.5-mile) (Chevrolet)
Exide NASCAR SB 400; Richmond Int. Raceway (.75-mile) (Chevrolet)

ARCHIE SMITH

1949	(T-22nd)

JACK SMITH

1952	(24th)

Poles
Central City Speedway (.5-mile dirt) (Studebaker)

1956	(23rd)	(128)

Victories
Old Dominion 400; Martinsville Speedway (.5-mile; 200 m) (Dodge)

1957	(5th)	(549)

Victories
Concord Speedway (.5-mile dirt; 100 miles) (Chevrolet)
Columbia Speedway (.5-mile dirt; 100 miles) (Chevrolet)
Buddy Shuman 250; Hickory Speedway (.4-m dirt; 100 m) (Chevrolet)
Wilkes 160; North Wilkesboro Speedway (.625-mile; 100 m) (Chevrolet)

Poles
Newberry Speedway (.5-mile dirt) (Chevrolet)
Concord Speedway (.5-mile dirt) (Chevrolet)

1958	(4th)	(439)

Victories
* Greenville-Pickens Speedway (.5-mile dirt; 100 miles) (Chevrolet)
* Bridgehampton Raceway (2.85-mile road; 100 miles) (Chevrolet)

Poles
Champion Speedway (.333-mile) (Chevrolet)
* Greenville-Pickens Speedway (.5-mile dirt) (Chevrolet)
Wilkes County 160; North Wilkesboro Speedway (.625-mile) (Chevrolet)
* Bridgehampton Raceway (2.85-mile road) (Chevrolet)

1959	(9th)	(293)

Victories
* Columbia Speedway (.5-mile dirt; 100 miles) (Chevrolet)
Piedmont Interstate Fairgrounds (.5-m dirt; 100 miles) (Chevrolet)
Charlotte Fairgrounds (.5-mile dirt; 100 miles) (Chevrolet)
Lee Kirby 300; Concord Speedway (.5-m dirt; 150 miles) (Chevrolet)

Poles
* Columbia Speedway (.5-mile dirt) (Chevrolet)
Greenville-Pickens Speedway (.5-mile dirt) (Chevrolet)
Orange Speedway (.9-mile dirt) (Chevrolet)

1960	(17th)	(205)

Victories
Charlotte Fairgrounds (.5-mile dirt; 100 miles) (Chevrolet)
Daytona International Speedway (2.5-mile; 100 miles) (Pontiac)
* Firecracker 250; Daytona Int. Speedway (2.5-m; 250m) (Pontiac)

Poles
Piedmont Interstate Fairgrounds (.5-mile dirt) (Pontiac)
* Firecracker 250; Daytona Int. Speedway (2.5-mile) (Pontiac)
West. N.C. 500; Asheville-Weaverville Speedway (.5-m) (Pontiac)

1961	(12th)	(383)

Victories
Pickens 200; Greenville-Pickens Sp. (.5-m dirt; 100m) (Pontiac)
Volunteer 500; Bristol Int. Speedway (.5-m; 250 miles) (Pontiac)

1962	(4th)	(795)

Victories
Concord Speedway (.5-mile dirt; 100 miles) (Pontiac)
St. Patrick's Day 200; Savannah Sp. (.5-m dirt; 100m) (Pontiac)
Rambi Raceway (.5-mile dirt; 100 miles) (Pontiac)
* Hickory 250; Hickory Speedway (.4-mile dirt; 100 m) (Pontiac)
Asheville Speedway (.4-mile; 100 miles) (Pontiac)

Poles
* Hickory 250; Hickory Speedway (.4-mile dirt) (Pontiac)
South Boston Speedway (.375-mile) (Pontiac)
Sandlapper 200; Columbia Speedway (.5-mile dirt) (Pontiac)
Augusta Speedway (.5-mile dirt) (Pontiac)
Western N.C. 500; Asheville-Weaverville Sp. (.5-mile) (Pontiac)
Starkey Speedway (.25-mile) (Pontiac)
International 200; Bowman Gray Stadium (.25-mile) (Pontiac)

1963	(24th)	(224)

Poles
Birmingham Raceway (.5-mile) (Plymouth)
South Boston 400; South Boston Speedway (.375-mile) (Plymouth)

1964

Poles
Speedway Park (.5-mile dirt) (Plymouth)

LARRY SMITH

1972	(21st)	(283)
1973		(176)

SLICK SMITH

1949	(12th)

1953	(12th)	(181)

Poles
Raleigh 300; Raleigh Speedway (1-mile) (Oldsmobile)

WAYNE SMITH

1965		(172)
1966		(120)
1967		(148)
1969		(136)

BILL SNOWDEN

1949	(10th)	
1951	(7th)	(175)

JOHN SOARES

1954	(18th)	(107)

Victories
Carrell Speedway (.5-mile dirt; 250 miles) (Dodge)

SAM SOMMERS

1977	(17th)	(331)

Poles
Dixie 500; Atlanta International Raceway (1.522-mile) (Chevrolet)

GOBER SOSEBEE

1949	(14th)	

Poles
Beach & Road Course (4.15-mile road) (Oldsmobile)

1951	(17th)	(122)

Poles
Columbus Speedway (.5-mile dirt) (Cadillac)

1952	(16th)	(129)

Victories
Hayloft Speedway (.5-mile dirt; 100 miles) (Chrysler)

1953	(11th)	(194)
1954	(16th)	(151)

Victories
Central City Speedway (.5-mile dirt; 100 miles) (Oldsmobile)
Poles
Wilkes Co. 160; North Wilkesboro Speedway (.625-m dirt) (Oldsmobile)

1958		

Poles
Salisbury Speedway (.625-mile dirt) (Chevrolet)

LAKE SPEED

1980	(18th)	(287)

1981	(23rd)	(287)
1982		(248)
1983	(20th)	(318)
1984	(22nd)	(304)
1985	(7th)	(573)
1986		(100)
1987	(23rd)	(211)
1988	(17th)	(336)

Victories
TranSouth 500; Darlington Int. Raceway (1.366-m; 500 m) (Oldsmobile)

1989	(25th)	(276)
1991		(119)
1993		(168)
1994	(10th)	(531)
1995		(250)
1996	(24th)	(279)
1997		(202)

G.C. SPENCER

1959	(20th)	(190)
1960	(T-15th)	(207)
1961	(13th)	(337)
1962	(18th)	(316)
1963	(19th)	(315)
1964	(T-22nd)	(217)
1965	(4th)	(606)

Poles
Hickory 250; Hickory Speedway (.4-mile dirt) (Ford)

1966	(21st)	(262)
1967	(21st)	(267)
1968		(156)
1969		(242)
1970		(238)
1971		(123)
1977		(100)

JIMMY SPENCER

1989		(168)
1990		(221)
1991		(258)

Driver, Year (Performance Index ranking)
(Performance Index points)

1992		(164)
1993	(10th)	(521)
1994	(23rd)	(276)

Victories
Pepsi 400; Daytona Int. Speedway (2.5-mile; 400 miles) (Ford)
Diehard 500; Talladega Superspeedway (2.66-m; 500 miles) (Ford)

Poles
Tyson Holly Farms 400; No. Wilkesboro Speedway (.625-m) (Ford)

1995	(22nd)	(283)
1996	(15th)	(468)
1997	(T-24th)	(296)
1998	(17th)	(427)
1999	(21st)	(334)

JUNIOR SPENCER

1965		(170)

NELSON STACY

1961	(20th)	(245)

Victories
Southern 500; Darlington Raceway (1.375-mile; 500 miles) (Ford)

1962	(25th)	(222)

Victories
Rebel 300; Darlington Raceway (1.375-mile; 300 miles) (Ford)
World 600; Charlotte Motor Speedway (1.5-m; 600 miles) (Ford)
Old Dominion 500; Martinsville Speedway (.5-mile; 250 m) (Ford)

1963	(21st)	(257)

GWYN STALEY

1955	(11th)	(266)
1956	(12th)	(274)
1957	(T-17th)	(195)

Victories
Coastal Speedway (.5-mile dirt; 100 miles) (Chevrolet)
* New York State Fairgrounds (1-mile dirt; 100 miles) (Chevrolet)
Langhorne Speedway (1-mile dirt; 300 miles) (Chevrolet)

Poles
Buddy Shuman 250; Hickory Speedway (.4-mile dirt) (Chevrolet)
* New York State Fairgrounds (1-mile dirt) (Chevrolet)

CHUCK STEVENSON

1956		

Victories
Willow Springs Speedway (2.5-mile dirt road; 200 miles) (Ford)

TONY STEWART

1999	(4th)	(859)

Victories
Exide NASCAR SB 400; Rich. Int. Race. (.75-m; 300 m) (Pontiac)
Checker AP/Dura-Lube 500; Pho. Int. Race. (1-m; 312m) (Pontiac)
Pennzoil 400; Homestead-Miami Speedway (1.5-m; 400 m) (Pontiac)

Poles
Goody's Body Pain 500; Martinsville Speedway (.526-m) (Pontiac)
Goody's HP 500; Bristol Motor Speedway (.533-mile) (Pontiac)

RAMO STOTT

1972		(132)
1974		(155)
1976		

Poles
Daytona 500; Daytona International Speedway (2.5-mile) (Chevrolet)

BUB STRICKLER

1965		(117)

HUT STRICKLIN

1989	(23rd)	(307)
1990		(239)
1991	(17th)	(401)
1992		(233)
1993		(261)
1994		(245)
1995		(213)

Poles
AC Delco 400; North Carolina Motor Speedway (1.017-mile) (Ford)

1996		(202)
1997		(148)

DON TARR

1968		(125)
1969		(153)
1970		(192)

JESSE JAMES TAYLOR

1951	(T-23rd)	

MARSHALL TEAGUE

1951   (6th)   (201)

Victories

Beach & Road Course (4.1-mile road; 160 miles) (Hudson)
Carrell Speedway (.5-mile dirt; 100 miles) (Hudson)
Arizona State Fairgrounds (1-mile dirt; 150 miles) (Hudson)
Poor Man's 500; Canfield Speedway (.5-m dirt; 100 miles) (Hudson)
* Grand River Speedrome (.5-mile dirt; 100 miles) (Hudson)

Poles

* Grand River Speedrome (.5-mile dirt) (Hudson)
Motor City 250; Michigan State Fairgrounds (1-mile dirt) (Hudson)

1952

Victories

Beach & Road Course (4.1-mile road; 200 miles) (Hudson)
* Speedway Park (.5-mile dirt; 100 miles) (Hudson)

Poles

* Speedway Park (.5-mile dirt) (Hudson)

DAVE TERRELL

1954   (13th)   (180)

1955   (12th)   (228)

DONALD THOMAS

1951   (12th)   (150)

1952   (6th)   (252)

Victories

* Lakewood Speedway (1-mile dirt; 100 miles) (Hudson)

Poles

* Lakewood Speedway (1-mile dirt) (Hudson)

1953   (19th)   (138)

1954   (T-24th)

HANK THOMAS

1966   (140)

HERB THOMAS

1949   (T-16th)

1950   (8th)   (132)

Victories

Martinsville Speedway (.5-mile dirt; 100 miles) (Plymouth)

1951   (3rd)   (461)

Victories

Heidelberg Speedway (.5-mile dirt; 100 miles) (Oldsmobile)
Southern 500; Darlington Raceway (1.25-mile; 500 miles) (Hudson)
Central City Speedway (.5-mile dirt; 100 miles) (Plymouth)
Langhorne Speedway (1-mile dirt; 150 miles) (Hudson)
Charlotte Speedway (.75-mile dirt; 150 miles) (Hudson)
* Occoneechee Speedway (1-mile dirt; 150 miles (Hudson)
* Speedway Park (.5-mile dirt; 100 miles) (Hudson)

Poles

* Occoneechee Speedway (1-mile dirt) (Hudson)
Martinsville Speedway (.5-mile dirt) (Hudson)
Wilkes 200; North Wilkesboro Speedway (.625-mile dirt) (Hudson)
* Speedway Park (.5-mile dirt) (Hudson)

1952   (3rd)   (514)

Victories (T-1st)

* Wilkes Co. 200; N. Wilkesboro Sp. (.625-m dirt; 125m) (Hudson)
Central City Speedway (.5-mile dirt; 150 miles) (Hudson)
Poor Man's 500; Canfield Speedway (.5-m dirt; 100 miles) (Hudson)
Charlotte Speedway (.75-mile dirt; 113 miles) (Hudson)
* Wilson Speedway (.5-mile dirt; 100 miles) (Hudson)
Martinsville Speedway (.5-mile dirt; 100 miles) (Hudson)
* Wilkes 200; N. Wilkesboro Speedway (.625-m dirt; 125m) (Hudson)
* Palm Beach Speedway (.5-mile dirt; 100 miles) (Hudson)

Poles (1st)

* Wilkes Co. 200; No. Wilkesboro Speedway (.625-m dirt) (Hudson)
Langhorne Speedway (1-mile dirt) (Hudson)
Stamford Park (.5-mile dirt) (Hudson)
Morristown Speedway (.5-mile dirt) (Hudson)
Playland Park Speedway (.5-mile dirt) (Hudson)
Asheville-Weaverville Speedway (.5-mile dirt) (Hudson)
Langhorne Speedway (1-mile dirt) (Hudson)
* Wilson Speedway (.5-mile dirt) (Hudson)
* Wilkes 200; North Wilkesboro Speedway (.625-mile dirt) (Hudson)
* Palm Beach Speedway (.5-mile dirt) (Hudson)

1953   (1st)   (691)

Victories (1st)

* Harnett Speedway (.5-mile dirt; 100 miles) (Hudson)
* Wilkes Co. 200; N. Wilkesboro Sp. (.625-m dirt; 125m) (Hudson)
Powell Motor Speedway (.5-mile dirt; 100 miles) (Hudson)
Five Flags Speedway (.5-mile dirt; 100 miles) (Hudson)
* Tri-City Speedway (.5-mile dirt; 100 miles) (Hudson)
Monroe County Fairgrounds (.5-mile dirt; 100 miles) (Hudson)
* Lakewood Speedway (1-mile dirt; 100 miles) (Hudson)
* Rapid Valley Speedway (.5-mile dirt; 100 miles) (Hudson)
Davenport Speedway (.5-mile dirt; 100 miles) (Hudson)
Princess Anne Speedway (.5-mile dirt; 100 miles) (Hudson)
Bloomsburg Fairgrounds (.5-mile dirt; 100 miles) (Hudson)
* Wilson Speedway (.5-mile dirt; 100 miles) (Hudson)

Poles (1st)

* Harnett Speedway (.5-mile dirt) (Hudson)
* Wilkes Co. 200; No. Wilkesboro Speedway (.625-m dirt) (Hudson)
Columbia Speedway (.5-mile dirt) (Hudson)
Hickory Speedway (.5-mile dirt) (Hudson)
Louisiana Fairgrounds (.5-mile dirt) (Hudson)
* Tri-City Speedway (.5-mile dirt) (Hudson)
Morristown Speedway (.5-mile dirt) (Hudson)
* Lakewood Speedway (1-mile dirt) (Hudson)
* Rapid Valley Speedway (.5-mile dirt) (Hudson)
Lincoln City Fairgrounds (.5-mile dirt) (Hudson)
Langhorne Speedway (1-mile dirt) (Hudson)
* Wilson Speedway (.5-mile dirt) (Hudson)

1954   (2nd)   (595)

Victories (1st)

Palm Beach Speedway (.5-mile dirt; 100 miles) (Hudson)
Speedway Park (.5-mile dirt; 100 miles) (Hudson)
* Lakewood Speedway (1-mile dirt; 100 miles) (Hudson)
Orange Speedway (1-mile dirt; 100 miles) (Hudson)
Langhorne Speedway (1-mile dirt; 150 miles) (Hudson)

* Raleigh 250; Raleigh Speedway (1-mile; 250 miles) (Hudson)
* Hickory Speedway (.4-mile dirt; 80 miles) (Hudson)
Williams Grove Speedway (.5-mile dirt; 100 miles) (Hudson)
Piedmont Interstate Fairgrounds (.5-m dirt; 100 miles) (Hudson)
* Asheville-Weaverville Speedway (.5-m dirt; 100 miles) (Hudson)
Southern 500; Darlington Raceway (1.375-mile; 500 miles) (Hudson)
* Langhorne Speedway (1-mile dirt; 250 miles) (Hudson)

Poles (1st)
* Lakewood Speedway (1-mile dirt) (Hudson)
Oglethorpe Speedway (.5-mile dirt) (Hudson)
* Raleigh 250; Raleigh Speedway (1-mile) (Hudson)
* Hickory Speedway (.4-mile dirt) (Hudson)
Monroe County Fairgrounds (.5-mile dirt) (Hudson)
* Asheville-Weaverville Speedway (.5-mile dirt) (Hudson)
Grand River Speedrome (.5-mile dirt) (Hudson)
* Langhorne Speedway (1-mile dirt) (Hudson)

1955   (8th)   (324)

Victories
Palm Beach Speedway (.5-mile dirt; 100 miles) (Hudson)
Raleigh Speedway (1-mile; 100 miles) (Buick)
Southern 500; Darlington Raceway (1.375-mile; 500 miles) (Chevrolet)

Poles
Tri-City Speedway (.5-mile dirt) (Hudson)
Charlotte Speedway (.75-mile dirt) (Buick)

1956   (2nd)   (703)

Victories
Palm Beach Speedway (.5-mile; 100 miles) (Chevrolet)
* Wilson Speedway (.5-mile dirt; 100 miles) (Chevrolet)
Portland Speedway (.5-mile; 100 miles) (Chrysler)
Eureka Speedway (.625-mile dirt; 100 miles) (Chrysler)
* Merced Fairgrounds (.5-mile dirt; 100 miles) (Chrysler)

Poles
* Wilson Speedway (.5-mile dirt) (Chevrolet)
* Merced Fairgrounds (.5-mile dirt) (Chrysler)
Portland Speedway (.5-mile) (Chrysler)

JABE THOMAS

1968	(13th)	(423)
1969	(9th)	(618)
1970	(7th)	(603)
1971	(6th)	(608)
1972	(14th)	(364)
1973	(T-12th)	(354)
1975	(T-24th)	(248)

LARRY THOMAS

1961	(109)	
1962	(13th)	(373)
1963	(18th)	(333)
1964	(8th)	(613)

RONNIE THOMAS

1978	(234)	
1979	(187)	
1980	(20th)	(266)
1981	(130)	
1983	(141)	

JIMMY THOMPSON

1949	(19th)

SPEEDY THOMPSON

1953   (15th)   (168)

Victories
Central City Speedway (.5-mile dirt; 100 miles) (Oldsmobile)
Wilkes 160; No. Wilkesboro Speedway (.625-m dirt; 100m) (Oldsmobile)

1955   (16th)   (148)

Victories
Memphis-Arkansas Speedway (1.5-mile dirt; 300 miles) (Ford)
Martinsville Speedway (.5-mile; 100 miles) (Chrysler)

1956   (3rd)   (642)

Victories
Columbia Speedway (.5-mile dirt; 100 miles) (Dodge)
* Concord Speedway (.5-mile dirt; 100 miles) (Chrysler)
* Hickory Speedway (.4-mile dirt; 80 miles) (Chrysler)
* Charlotte Speedway (.75-mile dirt; 100 miles) (Chrysler)
Southern States Fairgrounds (.5-mile dirt; 100 miles) (Chrysler)
Monroe County Fairgrounds (.5-mile dirt; 100 miles) (Chrysler)
Cleveland County Fairgrounds (.5-mile dirt; 100 miles) (Dodge)
Buddy Shuman 250; Hickory Speedway (.4-m dirt; 100 m) (Chrysler)

Poles
* Concord Speedway (.5-mile dirt) (Chrysler)
* Hickory Speedway (.4-mile dirt) (Chrysler)
Lincoln Speedway (.5-mile dirt) (Dodge)
* Charlotte Speedway (.75-mile dirt) (Chrysler)
Oklahoma State Fairgrounds (.5-mile dirt) (Dodge)
Southern 500; Darlington Raceway (1.375-mile) (Chrysler)
Orange Speedway (.9-mile dirt) (Chrysler)

1957   (6th)   (488)

Victories
* Lancaster Speedway (.5-mile dirt; 100 miles) (Chevrolet)
Southern 500; Darlington Raceway (1.375-mile; 500 miles) (Chevrolet)

Poles
Piedmont Interstate Fairgrounds (.5-mile dirt) (Chevrolet)
Newport Speedway (.5-mile dirt) (Chevrolet)
Memphis-Arkansas Speedway (1.5-mile dirt) (Chevrolet)
* Lancaster Speedway (.5-mile dirt) (Chevrolet)

1958   (3rd)   (532)

Victories
Columbia Speedway (.5-mile dirt; 100 miles) (Chevrolet)
* Piedmont Interstate Fairgrounds (.5-mile dirt; 100 m) (Chevrolet)
* Columbia Speedway (.5-mile dirt; 100 miles) (Chevrolet)
* Richmond 200; Atlantic Rural Fgds. (.5-m dirt; 100 m) (Chevrolet)

Poles (T-1st)
Concord Speedway (.5-mile dirt) (Chevrolet)
* Piedmont Interstate Fairgrounds (.5-mile dirt) (Chevrolet)
Reading Fairgrounds (.5-mile dirt) (Chevrolet)
Buddy Shuman 250; Hickory Speedway (.4-mile dirt) (Chevrolet)
* Columbia Speedway (.5-mile dirt) (Chevrolet)
Rambi Raceway (.5-mile dirt) (Chevrolet)
* Richmond 200; Atlantic Rural Fairgrounds (.5-mile dirt) (Chevrolet)

1959   (8th)   (297)

Poles
Gwyn Staley 160; North Wilkesboro Speedway (.625-mile) (Chevrolet)

1960   (156)

Victories
National 400; Charlotte Motor Speedway (1.5-mile; 400 m) (Ford)
Capital City 200; Atlantic Rural Fgds. (.5-m dirt; 100m) (Ford)

TOMMY THOMPSON

1951

Victories
Motor City 250; Michigan State Fgds. (1-m dirt; 250m) (Chrysler)

DICK TRICKLE

1974		(103)
1989	(20th)	(379)
1990	(22nd)	(278)

Poles
Budweiser 500; Dover Downs Int. Speedway (1-mile) (Pontiac)

1992	(21st)	(385)
1993		(154)
1994		(140)
1995		(239)
1996		(133)
1997		(235)
1998		(183)

E.J. TRIVETTE

1964		(118)
1965	(15th)	(358)
1968		(107)
1969	(10th)	(536)

MAYNARD TROYER

1971		(116)

DONALD TUCKER

1965		(112)

CURTIS TURNER

1949   (6th)

Victories
Langhorne Speedway (1-mile dirt; 200 miles) (Oldsmobile)

Poles
Martinsville Speedway (.5-mile dirt) (Oldsmobile)

1950   (5th)   (185)

Victories (1st)
Langhorne Speedway (1-mile dirt; 150 miles) (Oldsmobile)
Martinsville Speedway (.5-mile dirt; 75 miles) (Oldsmobile)
* Monroe County Fairgrounds (.5-mile dirt; 100 miles) (Oldsmobile)
* Charlotte Speedway (.75-mile dirt; 150 miles) (Oldsmobile)

Poles
* Monroe County Fairgrounds (.5-mile dirt) (Oldsmobile)
* Charlotte Speedway (.75-mile dirt) (Oldsmobile)
Dayton Speedway (.5-mile) (Oldsmobile)
Southern 500; Darlington Raceway (1.25-mile) (Oldsmobile)

1951   (T-13th)   (132)

Victories
Charlotte Speedway (.75-mile dirt; 113 miles) (Nash)
Martinsville Speedway (.5-mile dirt; 100 miles) (Oldsmobile)
Dayton Speedway (.5-mile; 100 miles) (Oldsmobile)

1953   (13th)   (180)

Victories
* Occoneechee Speedway (1-mile dirt; 100 miles) (Oldsmobile)

Poles
* Occoneechee Speedway (1-mile dirt) (Oldsmobile)
Asheville-Weaverville Speedway (.5-mile dirt) (Oldsmobile)
Princess Anne Speedway (.5-mile dirt) (Oldsmobile)

1954   (12th)   (184)

Victories
Columbia Speedway (.5-mile dirt; 100 miles) (Oldsmobile)

Poles
Speedway Park (.5-mile dirt) (Oldsmobile)

1956   (21st)   (134)

Victories
Southern 500; Darlington Raceway (1.375-mile; 500 miles) (Ford)

1957   (24th)   (138)

Poles
Concord Speedway (.5-mile dirt) (Ford)

1958   (14th)   (253)

Victories
Champion Speedway (.333-mile; 50 miles) (Ford)
Lakewood Speedway (1-mile dirt; 100 miles) (Ford)
* Southern States Fairgrounds (.5-mile dirt; 100 miles) (Ford)

Poles
* Southern States Fairgrounds (.5-mile dirt) (Ford)

1959   (24th)   (133)

Victories
* Orange Speedway (.9-mile dirt; 99 miles) (Ford)
Concord Speedway (.5-mile dirt; 100 miles) (Ford)

Poles
* Orange Speedway (.9-mile dirt) (Ford)

1960

Poles
Greenville 200; Greenville-Pickens Speedway (.5-m dirt) (Ford)

1965

Victories
American 500; N.C. Motor Speedway (1-mile; 500 miles) (Ford)

1966	(25th)	(243)

Poles
Volunteer 500; Bristol International Speedway (.5-mile) (Chevrolet)
Dixie 400; Atlanta International Raceway (1.5-mile) (Chevrolet)

1967

Poles
Daytona 500; Daytona International Speedway (2.5-mile) (Chevrolet)

1968		(135)

ROY TYNER

1958	(25th)	(144)
1959	(10th)	(292)
1960		(104)
1964	(13th)	(427)
1965		(152)
1966		(118)
1968	(14th)	(382)
1969		(115)

D.K. ULRICH

1975		(142)
1976	(11th)	(425)
1977	(22nd)	(253)
1978	(16th)	(297)
1979	(13th)	(452)
1981		(140)
1982		(251)
1983	(23rd)	(300)

JOHN UTSMAN

1976		(100)

SHERMAN UTSMAN

1962		(152)

JIM VANDIVER

1970		(184)
1971		(182)
1972		(143)
1973		(157)
1975		(157)

BILLY WADE

1963	(15th)	(375)
1964	(5th)	(657)

Victories
* Fireball Roberts 200; Old Bridge Stadium (.5-m; 100 m) (Mercury)
Bridgehampton Raceway (2.85-mile road; 143 miles) (Mercury)
* Islip Speedway (.2-mile; 60 miles) (Mercury)
* The Glen 151.8; Watkins Glen Int. (2.3-m road; 152 m) (Mercury)

Poles
* Fireball Roberts 200; Old Bridge Stadium (.5-mile) (Mercury)
* Islip Speedway (.2-mile) (Mercury)
* The Glen 151.8; Watkins Glen International (2.3-m rd.) (Mercury)
Mountaineer 500; West Virginia Int. Speedway (.4375-m) (Mercury)
Harris Speedway (.3-mile) (Mercury)

KEN WAGNER

1949

Poles
Wilkes 200; North Wilkesboro Speedway (.5-mile dirt) (Lincoln)

BOB WALDEN

1958		(125)

KENNY WALLACE

1993		(243)
1994		(212)
1996		(254)
1997		(146)

Poles
Goody's Head. Powder 500; Martinsville Speedway (.526-m) (Ford)
Goody's Head. Powd. 500; Bristol Motor Speedway (.533-m) (Ford)

1998	(25th)	(273)
1999	(22nd)	(324)

MIKE WALLACE

1994	(25th)	(253)
1995		(172)

RUSTY WALLACE

1984	(15th)	(404)

1985	(19th)	(327)

1986	(5th)	(603)

Victories
Valleydale 500; Bristol Int. Raceway (.533-m; 267 m) (Pontiac)
Goody's 500; Martinsville Speedway (.526-m; 263 miles) (Pontiac)

1987	(5th)	(634)

Victories
Bud. at the Gl.; Watkins Glen Int. (2.428-m rd.; 219m) (Pontiac)
Win. Wes. 500; Riverside Int. Race. (2.62-m rd.; 312m) (Pontiac)

Poles
Miller American 400; Michigan Int. Speedway (2-mile) (Pontiac)

1988	(2nd)	(826)

Victories (T-1st)
Budweiser 400; Riverside Int. Race. (2.62-m rd.; 249m) (Pontiac)
Miller HL 400; Michigan Int. Speedway (2-m; 400 miles) (Pontiac)
Oakwood Homes 500; Charlotte Motor Sp. (1.5-m; 500m) (Pontiac)
Holly Farms 400; N. Wilkesboro Speedway (.625-m; 250m) (Pontiac)
AC Delco 500; N.C. Motor Speedway (1.017-m; 500 m) (Pontiac)
* Atlanta Journal 500; Atl. Int. Race. (1.522-m; 500m) (Pontiac)

Poles
Goody's 500; Martinsville Speedway (.525-mile) (Pontiac)
* Atlanta Journal 500; Atlanta Int. Raceway (1.522-m) (Pontiac)

1989	(2nd)	(707)

Victories (T-1st)
* Goodwrench 500; N.C. Motor Speedway (1.017-m; 500 m) (Pontiac)
Pont. Excite. 400; Richmond Int. Raceway (.75-m; 300m) (Pontiac)
Valleydale Mts. 500; Bristol Int. Race. (.533-m; 267m) (Pontiac)
Bud. at the Glen; Wat. Glen Int. (2.428-m rd.; 187m) (Pontiac)
Champion SP 400; Michigan Int. Speed (2-m; 400 miles) (Pontiac)
Miller HL 400; Richmond Int. Raceway (.75-mile; 300 m) (Pontiac)

Poles
* Goodwrench 500; N.C. Motor Speedway (1.017-mile) (Pontiac)
First Union 400; North Wilkesboro Speedway (.625-m) (Pontiac)
Banquet FF 300; Sears Pt. Int. Raceway (2.52-m road) (Pontiac)
Miller High Life 500; Pocono Int. Raceway (2.5-mile) (Pontiac)

1990	(6th)	(570)

Victories
Coca-Cola 600; Charlotte Motor Speedway (1.5-m; 600 m) (Pontiac)
Banquet FF 300; Sears Pt. Int. Race. (2.52-m rd. 187m) (Pontiac)

Poles
Checker 500; Phoenix International Raceway (1-mile) (Pontiac)
Atlanta Journal 500; Atlanta Motor Speedway (1.522-m) (Pontiac)

1991	(13th)	(465)

Victories
* Valley. Mts. 500; Bristol Int. Race. (.533-m; 267m) (Pontiac)
Miller Gen. Dr. 500; Pocono Int. Raceway (2.5-m; 500m) (Pontiac)

Poles
* Valleydale Meats 500; Bristol Int. Race. (.533-m) (Pontiac)
Miller Gen. Draft 400; Richmond Int. Raceway (.75-m) (Pontiac)

1992	(14th)	(501)

Victories
Miller Gen. Dr. 400; Richmond Int. Race. (.75-m; 300m) (Pontiac)

Poles
Pyroil 500; Phoenix International Raceway (1-mile) (Pontiac)

1993	(2nd)	(777)

Victories (1st)
Goodwrench 500; N.C. Motor Speedway (1.017-m; 500 m) (Pontiac)
* Food City 500; Bristol Int. Raceway (.533-m; 267 m) (Pontiac)
First Union 400; N. Wilkesboro Speed. (.625-m; 250m) (Pontiac)
Hanes 500; Martinsville Speedway (.526-m; 263 miles) (Pontiac)
Slick 50 300; New Hamp. Int. Speedway (1.058-m; 317m) (Pontiac)
Miller Gen. Dr. 400; Richmond Int. Race. (.75-m; 300m) (Pontiac)
* Splitfire SP 500; Dover Downs Int. Sp. (1-m; 500m) (Pontiac)
Tyson Holly Fms. 400; N. Wilkesboro Sp. (.625-m; 250m) (Pontiac)
AC Delco 500; N.C. Motor Speedway (1.017-m; 500 miles) (Pontiac)
Hooters 500; Atlanta Motor Speedway (1.522-m; 500 m) (Pontiac)

Poles
Motorcraft 500; Atlanta Motor Speedway (1.522-mile) (Pontiac)
* Food City 500; Bristol Int. Raceway (.533-mile) (Pontiac)
* Splitfire SP 500; Dover Downs Int. Speedway (1-mile) (Pontiac)

1994	(2nd)	(678)

Victories (1st)
Goodwrench 500; N.C. Motor Speedway (1.017-m; 500 miles) (Ford)
* Hanes 500; Martinsville Speedway (.526-m; 263 miles) (Ford)
Budweiser 500; Dover Downs Int. Speedway (1-mile; 500 m) (Ford)
* UAW-GM Teamwork 500; Pocono Int. Raceway (2.5-m; 500m) (Ford)
Miller Gen. Dr. 400; Michigan Int. Speedway (2-m; 400 m) (Ford)
Goody's 500; Bristol Int. Raceway (.533-mile; 267 miles) (Ford)
Splitfire SP 500; Dover Downs Int. Speedway (1-m; 500 m) (Ford)
Goody's 500; Martinsville Speedway (.526-m; 263 miles) (Ford)

Poles
* Hanes 500; Martinsville Speedway (.526-mile) (Ford)
* UAW-GM Teamwork 500; Pocono Int. Raceway (2.5-mile) (Ford)

1995	(6th)	(644)

Victories
Hanes 500; Martinsville Speedway (.526-mile; 263 miles) (Ford)
Miller Gen. Dr. 400; Richmond Int. Raceway (.75-m; 300m) (Ford)

1996	(7th)	(563)

Victories
Goody's HP 500; Martinsville Speedway (.526-m; 263 m) (Ford)
Save Mart Super. 300; Sears Pt. Race. (2.52-m rd.; 186m) (Ford)
Miller Gen. Dr. 400; Michigan Int. Speedway (2-m; 400 m) (Ford)
Miller Gen. Dr. 500; Pocono Int. Raceway (2.5-m; 500 m) (Ford)
Goody's HP 500; Bristol Motor Speedway (.533-m; 267 m) (Ford)

1997	(12th)	(470)

Victories
Pont. Excitement 400; Richmond Int. Race. (.75-m; 300m) (Ford)

Poles
Food City 500; Bristol Motor Speedway (.533-mile) (Ford)

1998	(4th)	(743)

Victories
Dura-Lube/Kmart 500; Phoenix Int. Raceway (1-m; 312 m) (Ford)

Poles
Food City 500; Bristol Motor Speedway (.533-mile) (Ford)
MBNA Platinum 400; Dover Downs Int. Speedway (1-mile) (Ford)
Goody's HP 500; Bristol Motor Speedway (.533-mile) (Ford)
Exide NASCAR SB 400; Richmond Int. Raceway (.75-mile) (Ford)

1999   (8th)   (669)

Victories

* Food City 500; Bristol Motor Speedway (.533-m; 267 m) (Ford)

Poles

* Food City 500; Bristol Motor Speedway (.533-mile) (Ford)
Frontier at the Glen; Watkins Glen Int. (2.45-mile road) (Ford)
Dura-Lube/Kmart 500; New Hamp. Int. Speedway (1.058-m) (Ford)
MBNA Gold 400; Dover Downs International Speedway (1-m) (Ford)

DARRELL WALTRIP

1973   (22nd)   (233)

1974   (14th)   (373)

Poles

Nashville 420; Fairgrounds Speedway (.596-mile) (Chevrolet)

1975   (14th)   (421)

Victories

* Music City 420; Nashville Speedway (.596-m; 250 miles) (Chevrolet)
Capital City 500; Richmond Fgds. Raceway (.542-m; 271 m) (Chevrolet)

Poles

Gwyn Staley 400; North Wilkesboro Speedway (.625-mile) (Chevrolet)
* Music City 420; Nashville Speedway (.596-mile) (Chevrolet)

1976   (13th)   (414)

Victories

Virginia 500; Martinsville Speedway (.525-m; 263 miles) (Chevrolet)

Poles

Volunteer 400; Bristol International Speedway (.533-m) (Chevrolet)
Old Dominion 500; Martinsville Speedway (.525-mile) (Chevrolet)
Wilkes 400; North Wilkesboro Speedway (.625-mile) (Chevrolet)

1977   (3rd)   (769)

Victories

Rebel 500; Darlington Int. Raceway (1.366-m; 500 miles) (Chevrolet)
Winston 500; Alabama Int. Motor Speedway (2.66-m; 500 m) (Chevrolet)
Nashville 420; Nashville Speedway (.596-mile; 250 miles) (Chevrolet)
Champion SP 400; Michigan Int. Speedway (2-m; 400 miles) (Chevrolet)
Wilkes 400; North Wilkesboro Speedway (.625-mile; 250 m) (Chevrolet)
Dixie 500; Atlanta International Raceway (1.522-m; 500m) (Chevrolet)

Poles

Music City USA 420; Nashville Speedway (.596-mile) (Chevrolet)
Coca-Cola 500; Pocono International Raceway (2.5-mile) (Chevrolet)
Southern 500; Darlington International Raceway (1.366-m) (Chevrolet)

1978   (5th)   (656)

Victories

Southeastern 500; Bristol Int. Raceway (.533-m; 267 m) (Chevrolet)
Gwyn Staley 400; No. Wilkesboro Speedway (.625-m; 250 m) (Chevrolet)
Virginia 500; Martinsville Speedway (.525-m; 263 miles) (Chevrolet)
World 600; Charlotte Motor Speedway (1.5-m; 600 miles) (Chevrolet)
Coca-Cola 500; Pocono Int. Raceway (2.5-mile; 500 miles) (Chevrolet)
* Capital City 400; Richmond Fgds. Race. (.542-m; 217m) (Chevrolet)

Poles

* Capital City 400; Richmond Fgds. Raceway (.542-mile) (Chevrolet)
Wilkes 400; North Wilkesboro Speedway (.625-mile) (Chevrolet)

1979   (2nd)   (867)

Victories (1st)

Win. West. 500; Riverside Int. Race. (2.62-m rd.; 312 m) (Chevrolet)
CRC Ch. Rebel 500; Darlington Int. Race. (1.366-m; 500m) (Chevrolet)
World 600; Charlotte Motor Speedway (1.5-m; 600 miles) (Chevrolet)
Texas 400; Texas World Speedway (2-mile; 400 miles) (Chevrolet)
* Busch Nashville 420; Nash. Int. Raceway (.596-m; 250m) (Chevrolet)
Talladega 500; Ala. Int. Motor Speedway (2.66-m; 500 m) (Oldsmobile)
Volunteer 500; Bristol Int. Raceway (.533-m; 267 miles) (Chevrolet)

Poles

Virginia 500; Martinsville Speedway (.525-mile) (Chevrolet)
Winston 500; Alabama Int. Motor Speedway (2.66-mile) (Oldsmobile)
Mason-Dixon 500; Dover Downs Int. Speedway (1-mile) (Chevrolet)
* Busch Nashville 420; Nashville Int. Raceway (.596-m) (Chevrolet)
Old Dominion 500; Martinsville Speedway (.525-mile) (Chevrolet)

1980   (6th)   (593)

Victories

* Win. Wes. 500; Riverside Int. Race. (2.62-m rd.; 312m) (Chevrolet)
* Richmond 400; Richmond Fgds. Raceway (.542-m; 217 m) (Chevrolet)
* Virginia 500; Martinsville Speedway (.525-mile; 263 m) (Chevrolet)
W.W. Hodgdon 400; River. Int. Raceway (2.62-m rd.; 249m) (Chevrolet)
CRC Chemicals 500; Dover Downs Int. Speedway (1-m; 500m) (Chevrolet)

Poles

* Winston Western 500; Riverside Int. Race. (2.62-m rd.) (Chevrolet)
* Richmond 400; Richmond Fairgrounds Raceway (.542-mile) (Chevrolet)
Carolina 500; North Carolina Motor Speedway (1.017-mile) (Chevrolet)
* Virginia 500; Martinsville Speedway (.525-mile) (Chevrolet)
Southern 500; Darlington International Raceway (1.366-m) (Chevrolet)

1981   (1st)   (879)

Victories (1st)

Richmond 400; Richmond Fgds. Raceway (.542-m; 217 miles) (Buick)
Carolina 500; N.C. Motor Speedway (1.017-m; 500 miles) (Buick)
* Valleydale 500; Bristol Int. Raceway (.533-m; 267 m) (Buick)
CRC Ch. Rebel 500; Darlington Int. Race. (1.366-m; 500m) (Buick)
* W.W. Hodgdon 400; River. Int. Race. (2.62-m rd.; 249m) (Buick)
Busch Nashville 420; Nash. Int. Raceway (.596-m; 250 m) (Buick)
* Mountain Dew 500; Pocono Int. Raceway (2.5-m; 500 m) (Buick)
* Busch 500; Bristol Int. Raceway (.533-mile; 267 miles) (Buick)
* Old Dominion 500; Martinsville Speedway (.525-m; 263m) (Buick)
* Holly Farms 400; N. Wilkesboro Speedway (.625-m; 250m) (Buick)
* National 500; Charlotte Motor Speedway (1.5-m; 500 m) (Buick)
* American 500; N.C. Motor Speedway (1.017-m; 500 miles) (Buick)

Poles (1st)

Winston Western 500; Riverside Int. Raceway (2.62-m rd.) (Chevrolet)
* Valleydale 500; Bristol International Raceway (.533-m) (Buick)
* W.W. Hodgdon 400; Riverside Int. Raceway (2.62-m rd.) (Buick)
Gabriel 400; Michigan International Speedway (2-mile) (Buick)
* Mountain Dew 500; Pocono International Speedway (2.5-m) (Buick)
* Busch 500; Bristol International Raceway (.533-mile) (Buick)
* Old Dominion 500; Martinsville Speedway (.525-mile) (Buick)
* Holly Farms 400; North Wilkesboro Speedway (.625-mile) (Buick)
* National 500; Charlotte Motor Speedway (1.5-mile) (Buick)
* American 500; North Carolina Motor Speedway (1.017-m) (Buick)
Winston Western 500; Riverside Int. Raceway (2.62-m rd.) (Buick)

1982   (1st)   (768)

Victories (1st)

* Valleydale 500; Bristol Int. Raceway (.533-m; 267 m) (Buick)
Coca-Cola 500; Atlanta Int. Raceway (1.522-m; 500 miles) (Buick)
* Northwest. Bank 400; N. Wilkesboro Sp. (.625-m; 250 m) (Buick)

Winston 500; Alabama Int. Motor Speedway (2.66-m; 500 m) (Buick)
* Cracker Barrel 420; Nash. Int. Raceway (.596-m; 250m) (Buick)
Busch Nashville 420; Nashville Int. Race. (.596-m; 250m) (Buick)
Talladega 500; Alabama Int. Motor Speed. (2.66-m; 500m) (Buick)
Busch 500; Bristol Int. Raceway (.533-mile; 267 miles) (Buick)
CRC Chem. 500; Dover Downs Int. Speedway (1-m; 500 m) (Buick)
* Holly Farms 400; N. Wilkesboro Speedway (.625-m; 250m) (Buick)
Old Dominion 500; Martinsville Speedway (.525-m; 263 m) (Buick)
W.W. Hodgdon Amer. 500; N.C. Motor Sp. (1.107-m; 500m) (Buick)

Poles (1st)
Richmond 400; Richmond Fairgrounds Raceway (.542-mile) (Buick)
* Valleydale 500; Bristol International Raceway (.533-m) (Buick)
* Northwestern Bank 400; N. Wilkesboro Speedway (.625-m) (Buick)
* Cracker Barrel 420; Nashville Int. Raceway (.596-mile) (Buick)
Mason-Dixon 500; Dover Downs Int. Speedway (1-mile) (Buick)
* Holly Farms 400; North Wilkesboro Speedway (.625-mile) (Buick)
Winston Western 500; Riverside Int. Raceway (2.62-m rd.) (Buick)

1983   (2nd)   (818)

Victories (T-1st)
Northwestern Bank 400; N. Wilkesboro Sp. (.625-m; 250m) (Chevrolet)
Va. National Bank 500; Martinsville Sp. (.525-m; 263 m) (Chevrolet)
* Marty Robbins 420; Nashville Int. Race. (.596-m; 250m) (Chevrolet)
Valleydale 500; Bristol Int. Raceway (.533-m; 267 miles) (Chevrolet)
Busch 500; Bristol Int. Raceway (.533-mile; 267 miles) (Chevrolet)
* Holly Farms 400; N. Wilkesboro Speedway (.625-m; 250m) (Chevrolet)

Poles (1st)
* Marty Robbins 420; Nashville Int. Raceway (.596-mile) (Chevrolet)
Budweiser 400; Riverside Int. Raceway (2.62-mile road) (Chevrolet)
Van Scoy Diamond Mine 500; Pocono Int. Raceway (2.5-m) (Chevrolet)
Wrangler Sanforset 400; Richmond Fgds. Raceway (.542-m) (Chevrolet)
Goody's 500; Martinsville Speedway (.525-mile) (Chevrolet)
* Holly Farms 400; North Wilkesboro Speedway (.625-mile) (Chevrolet)
Winston Western 500; Riverside Int. Raceway (2.62-m rd.) (Chevrolet)

1984   (5th)   (667)

Victories (1st)
Valleydale 500; Bristol Int. Raceway (.533-m; 267 miles) (Chevrolet)
TranSouth 500; Darlington Int. Raceway (1.366-m; 500 m) (Chevrolet)
* Coors 420; Nashville Int. Raceway (.596-m; 250 miles) (Chevrolet)
Champion SP 400; Michigan Int. Speedway (2-m; 400 miles) (Chevrolet)
* Wrangler San. 400; Richmond Fgds. Race. (.542-m; 217m) (Chevrolet)
Goody's 500; Martinsville Speedway (.526-m; 263 m) (Chevrolet)
* Holly Farms 400; N. Wilkesboro Speedway (.625-m; 250m) (Chevrolet)

Poles (T-1st)
Miller High Life 400; Richmond Fgds. Raceway (.542-mile) (Chevrolet)
* Coors 420; Nashville International Raceway (.596-mile) (Chevrolet)
* Wrangler Sanforset 400; Richmond Fgds. Race. (.542-m) (Chevrolet)
* Holly Farms 400; North Wilkesboro Speedway (.625-mile) (Chevrolet)

1985   (2nd)   (764)

Victories
World 600; Charlotte Motor Speedway (1.5-m; 600 miles) (Chevrolet)
Wrangler San. 400; Richmond Fgds. Raceway (.542-m; 217m) (Chevrolet)
Nationwise 500; N.C. Motor Speedway (1.017-m; 500 miles) (Chevrolet)

Poles
Miller High Life 400; Richmond Fgds. Raceway (.542-mile) (Chevrolet)
Northwestern Bank 400; No. Wilkesboro Speedway (.625-m) (Chevrolet)
Sovran Bank 500; Martinsville Speedway (.526-mile) (Chevrolet)
Budweiser 400; Riverside Int. Raceway (2.62-mile road) (Chevrolet)

1986   (3rd)   (723)

Victories
* Budweiser 400; Riverside Int. Race. (2.62-m rd.; 249m) (Chevrolet)
Busch 500; Bristol Int. Raceway (.533-mile; 267 miles) (Chevrolet)
Holly Farms 400; No. Wilkesboro Speedway (.625-m; 250 m) (Chevrolet)

Poles
* Budweiser 400; Riverside Int. Raceway (2.62-mile road) (Chevrolet)

1987   (3rd)   (671)

Victories
Goody's 500; Martinsville Speedway (.526-m; 263 miles) (Chevrolet)

1988   (9th)   (555)

Victories
Coca-Cola 600; Charlotte Motor Speedway (1.5-m; 600 m) (Chevrolet)
Goody's 500; Martinsville Speedway (.526-m; 263 miles) (Chevrolet)

Poles
Pepsi Firecracker 400; Daytona Int. Speedway (2.5-mile) (Chevrolet)
Talladega Diehard 500; Ala. Int. Motor Speedway (2.66-m) (Chevrolet)

1989   (4th)   (664)

Victories (T-1st)
Daytona 500; Daytona Int. Speedway (2.5-mile; 500 miles) (Chevrolet)
Motorcraft QP 500; Atlanta Int. Raceway (1.522-m; 500 m) (Chevrolet)
Pannill Sweatshirts 500; Martinsville Sp. (.526-m; 263m) (Chevrolet)
Coca-Cola 600; Charlotte Motor Speedway (1.5-m; 600 m) (Chevrolet)
Busch 500; Bristol Int. Raceway (.533-mile; 267 miles) (Chevrolet)
Goody's 500; Martinsville Speedway (.526-m; 263 miles) (Chevrolet)

1990   (16th)   (481)

1991   (T-9th)   (541)

Victories
First Union 400; No. Wilkesboro Speedway (.625-m; 250m) (Chevrolet)
Champion SP 500; Pocono Int. Raceway (2.5-m; 500 miles) (Chevrolet)

1992   (16th)   (492)

Victories
Miller Gen. Draft 500; Pocono Int. Raceway (2.5-m; 500m) (Chevrolet)
Bud 500; Bristol International Raceway (.533-mile; 267m) (Chevrolet)
Mt. Dew Southern 500; Darlington Raceway (1.366-m; 500m) (Chevrolet)

Poles
Hanes 500; Martinsville Speedway (.526-mile) (Chevrolet)

1993   (12th)   (469)

1994   (16th)   (445)

1995   (20th)   (338)

Poles
NAPA 500; Atlanta Motor Speedway (1.522-mile) (Chevrolet)

1996   (153)

1997   (293)

1998   (259)

1999   (102)

MICHAEL WALTRIP

1986   (18th)   (331)

Driver Resumes
Driver, Year (Performance Index ranking)
(Performance Index points)

1987	(22nd)	(304)
1988	(20th)	(291)
1989	(21st)	(336)
1990	(19th)	(413)
1991	(15th)	(433)

Poles
Budweiser 500; Dover Downs Int. Speedway (1-m; 500 m) (Pontiac)
Miller Genuine Draft 400; Michigan Int. Speedway (2-m) (Pontiac)

1992	(23rd)	(298)
1993	(20th)	(383)
1994	(12th)	(501)
1995	(11th)	(528)
1996	(12th)	(502)
1997	(20th)	(361)
1998	(18th)	(384)
1999		(289)

FRANK WARREN

1966		(134)
1967		(142)
1969		(132)
1970	(24th)	(302)
1971	(16th)	(392)
1972	(23rd)	(224)
1973	(23rd)	(227)
1974	(15th)	(364)
1975	(12th)	(449)
1976	(16th)	(382)
1977	(25th)	(236)
1978	(23rd)	(251)
1979	(22nd)	(273)

AL WATKINS

1956		(116)

BLACKIE WATT

1966		(210)

ART WATTS

1957
Victories
* Portland Speedway (.5-mile; 50 miles) (Ford)
Poles
* Portland Speedway (.5-mile) (Ford)
Portland Speedway (.5-mile) (Ford)
Capitol Speedway (.5-mile dirt) (Ford)
Portland Speedway (.5-mile) (Ford)
Kitsap County Airport (.9-mile road) (Ford)

BOBBY WAWAK

1967		(119)
1976	(19th)	(311)
1982		(122)

JOE WEATHERLY

1956	(15th)	(227)

Poles
Arizona State Fairgrounds (1-mile dirt) (Ford)

1957	(20th)	(169)
1958	(23rd)	(163)

Victories
Nashville 200; Fairgrounds Speedway (.5-mile; 100 miles) (Ford)
Poles
Lakewood Speedway (1-mile dirt) (Ford)

1959	(18th)	(217)
1960	(9th)	(282)

Victories
Hickory 250; Hickory Speedway (.4-mile dirt; 100 miles) (Ford)
Wilson Speedway (.5-mile dirt; 100 miles) (Ford)
Rebel 300; Darlington Raceway (1.375-mile; 300 miles) (Ford)

1961	(T-5th)	(526)

Victories (1st)
Charlotte Fairgrounds (.5-mile dirt; 100 miles) (Ford)
Daytona International Speedway (2.5-mile; 100 miles) (Pontiac)
Charlotte Motor Speedway (1.5-mile; 100 miles) (Pontiac)
* Rambi Raceway (.5-mile dirt; 100 miles) (Pontiac)
Capital City 250; Atlantic Rural Fgds. (.5-m d.; 125m) (Pontiac)
Old Dominion 500; Martinsville Speedway (.5-m; 250 m) (Pontiac)
National 400; Charlotte Motor Speedway (1.5-m; 400 m) (Pontiac)
Southeastern 500; Bristol Int. Speedway (.5-m; 250 m) (Pontiac)
* Orange Speedway (.9-mile dirt; 149 miles) (Pontiac)
Poles
Piedmont Interstate Fairgrounds (.5-mile dirt) (Pontiac)
* Rambi Raceway (.5-mile dirt) (Pontiac)
* Orange Speedway (.9-mile dirt) (Pontiac)

1962	(1st)	(1,049)

Victories (1st)
Daytona International Speedway (2.5-mile; 100 miles) (Pontiac)
Concord Speedway (.5-mile dirt; 100 miles) (Pontiac)
Asheville-Weaverville Speedway (.5-mile; 100 miles) (Pontiac)

* Concord Speedway (.5-mile dirt; 100 miles) (Pontiac)
* Augusta Speedway (.5-mile dirt; 100 miles) (Pontiac)
Augusta Speedway (.5-mile dirt; 100 miles) (Pontiac)
Savannah Speedway (.5-mile dirt; 100 miles) (Pontiac)
Confederate 200; Boyd Speedway (.333-mile; 67 miles) (Pontiac)
Capital City 300; Atlantic Rural Fgds. (.5-m d.; 150m) (Pontiac)

Poles

Concord Speedway (.5-mile dirt) (Pontiac)
Asheville-Weaverville Speedway (.5-mile) (Pontiac)
* Concord Speedway (.5-mile dirt) (Pontiac)
Orange Speedway (.9-mile dirt) (Pontiac)
Arclite 200; Columbia Speedway (.5-mile dirt) (Pontiac)
* Augusta Speedway (.5-mile dirt) (Pontiac)
Augusta Speedway (.5-mile dirt) (Pontiac)

1963	(3rd)	(844)

Victories

Richmond 250; Atlantic Rural Fgds. (.5-m dirt; 125 m) (Pontiac)
Rebel 300; Darlington Raceway (1.375-mile; 300 miles) (Pontiac)
* Orange Speedway (.9-mile dirt; 150 miles) (Pontiac)

Poles

Orange Speedway (.9-mile dirt) (Pontiac)
Old Bridge Stadium (.5-mile) (Pontiac)
Piedmont Interstate Fairgrounds (.5-mile dirt) (Pontiac)
Capital City 300; Atlantic Rural Fairgrounds (.5-m dirt) (Mercury)
Dog Track Speedway (.25-mile dirt) (Mercury)
* Orange Speedway (.9-mile dirt) (Pontiac)

DANNY WEINBERG

1951

Victories

Hanford Motor Speedway (.5-mile dirt; 100 miles) (Studebaker)

1961

Poles

Ascot Speedway (.5-mile dirt) (Ford)

BOB WELBORN

1953	(21st)	(109)
1954	(T-24th)	
1955	(4th)	(401)

Poles

Greenville-Pickens Speedway (.5-mile dirt) (Chevrolet)

1957

Victories

Old Dominion 500; Martinsville Speedway (.5-mile; 250 m) (Chevrolet)

1958	(9th)	(348)

Victories

Champion Speedway (.333-mile; 50 miles) (Chevrolet)
Virginia 500; Martinsville Speedway (.5-mile; 250 miles) (Chevrolet)
* Greensboro Fairgrounds (.333-mile dirt; 50 miles) (Chevrolet)
Bowman Gray Stadium (.25-mile; 38 miles) (Chevrolet)
Rambi Raceway (.5-mile dirt; 100 miles) (Chevrolet)

Poles

* Greensboro Fairgrounds (.333-mile dirt) (Chevrolet)

1959	(11th)	(289)

Victories

* Champion Speedway (.333-mile; 50 miles) (Chevrolet)
Daytona International Speedway (2.5-mile; 100 miles) (Chevrolet)
West. N.C. 500; Asheville-Weaverville Sp. (.5-m; 250 m) (Chevrolet)

Poles (T-1st)

* Champion Speedway (.333-mile) (Chevrolet)
Daytona 500; Daytona International Speedway (2.5-mile) (Chevrolet)
Charlotte Fairgrounds (.5-mile dirt) (Chevrolet)
Rambi Raceway (.5-mile dirt) (Chevrolet)
Charlotte Fairgrounds (.5-mile dirt) (Chevrolet)

1960	(12th)	(254)
1961	(16th)	(274)
1962	(10th)	(406)
1963		(106)

DON WHITE

1966		(194)

JACK WHITE

1949	(T-22nd)

Victories

Hamburg Fairgrounds (.5-mile dirt; 100 miles) (Lincoln)

REX WHITE

1956	(11th)	(282)

Poles

Greenville-Pickens Speedway (.5-mile dirt) (Chevrolet)

1957		(112)

Poles

Old Bridge Stadium (.5-mile) (Chevrolet)

1958	(7th)	(358)

Victories

Champion Speedway (.333-mile; 50 miles) (Chevrolet)
* Asheville-Weaverville Speedway (.5-mile; 100 miles) (Chevrolet)

Poles (T-1st)

Bowman Gray Stadium (.25-mile) (Chevrolet)
* Asheville-Weaverville Speedway (.5-mile) (Chevrolet)
Canadian National Exposition Stadium (.333-mile) (Chevrolet)
Civic Stadium (.25-mile) (Chevrolet)
Monroe County Fairgrounds (.5-mile dirt) (Chevrolet)
Wall Stadium (.333-mile; 100 miles) (Chevrolet)
Nashville 200; Fairgrounds Speedway (.5-mile) (Chevrolet)

1959	(6th)	(330)

Victories

* Music City 200; Fairgrounds Speedway (.5-m; 100 miles) (Chevrolet)
Bowman Gray Stadium (.25-mile; 50 miles) (Chevrolet)
Asheville-Weaverville Speedway (.5-mile; 100 miles) (Chevrolet)
* Bowman Gray Stadium (.25-mile; 50 miles) (Chevrolet)
Old Dominion 500; Martinsville Speedway (.5-mile; 250 m) (Chevrolet)

Poles (T-1st)

Bowman Gray Stadium (.25-mile) (Chevrolet)
* Music City 200; Fairgrounds Speedway (.5-mile) (Chevrolet)
Nashville 300; Fairgrounds Speedway (.5-mile) (Chevrolet)
Western N.C. 500; Asheville-Weaverville Speedway (.5-m) (Chevrolet)
* Bowman Gray Stadium (.25-mile) (Chevrolet)

1960   (1st)   (848)

Victories (1st)

Columbia Speedway (.5-mile dirt; 100 miles) (Chevrolet)
Empire State 200; Montgomery Air Base (2-m; 200 miles) (Chevrolet)
W.N.C. 500; Asheville-Weaverville Speedway (.5-m; 250m) (Chevrolet)
Columbia Speedway (.5-mile dirt; 150 miles) (Chevrolet)
Old Dominion 500; Martinsville Speedway (.5-mile; 250 m) (Chevrolet)
* Wilkes 320; North Wilkesboro Speedway (.625-m; 200 m) (Chevrolet)

Poles

Hickory 250; Hickory Speedway (.4-mile dirt) (Chevrolet)
Nashville 400; Fairgrounds Speedway (.5-mile) (Chevrolet)
* Wilkes 320; North Wilkesboro Speedway (.625-mile) (Chevrolet)

1961   (1st)   (873)

Victories

* Asheville-Weaverville Speedway (.5-mile; 100 miles) (Chevrolet)
Bowman Gray Stadium (.25-mile; 38 miles) (Chevrolet)
Gwyn Staley 400; No. Wilkesboro Speedway (.625-m; 250m) (Chevrolet)
Myers Brothers 200; Bowman Gray Stadium (.25-mile; 50 m) (Chevrolet)
Bowman Gray Stadium (.25-mile; 38 miles) (Chevrolet)
* Buddy Shuman 250; Hickory Speedway (.4-m dirt; 100 m) (Chevrolet)
Wilkes 320; North Wilkesboro Speedway (.625-mile; 200 m) (Chevrolet)

Poles

* Asheville-Weaverville Speedway (.5-mile) (Chevrolet)
Grand National 200; Martinsville Speedway (.5-mile) (Chevrolet)
Virginia 500; Martinsville Speedway (.5-mile) (Chevrolet)
Yankee 500; Norwood Arena (.25-mile) (Chevrolet)
Starkey Speedway (.25-mile) (Chevrolet)
Nashville 500; Fairgrounds Speedway (.5-mile) (Chevrolet)
* Buddy Shuman 250; Hickory Speedway (.4-mile dirt) (Chevrolet)

1962   (5th)   (609)

Victories

Asheville-Weaverville Speedway (.5-mile; 100 miles) (Chevrolet)
Orange Speedway (.9-mile dirt; 99 miles) (Chevrolet)
Richmond 250; Atlantic Rural Fgds. (.5-mile dirt; 125 m) (Chevrolet)
* Bowman Gray Stadium (.25-mile; 50 miles) (Chevrolet)
South Boston Speedway (.375-mile; 100 miles) (Chevrolet)
Sandlapper 200; Columbia Speedway (.5-m dirt; 100 miles) (Chevrolet)
Buddy Shuman 250; Hickory Speedway (.4-mile dirt; 100 m) (Chevrolet)
Dixie 400; Atlanta International Raceway (1.5-m; 400 m) (Chevrolet)

Poles (1st)

Asheville-Weaverville Speedway (.5-mile) (Chevrolet)
St. Patrick's Day 200; Savannah Speedway (.5-mile dirt) (Chevrolet)
* Bowman Gray Stadium (.25-mile) (Chevrolet)
Southside Speedway (.333-mile) (Chevrolet)
Myers Brothers 200; Bowman Gray Stadium (.25-mile) (Chevrolet)
Southside Speedway (.333-mile) (Chevrolet)
Asheville Speedway (.4-mile) (Chevrolet)
Pickens 200; Greenville-Pickens Speedway (.5-mile dirt) (Chevrolet)
Capital City 300; Atlantic Rural Fairgrounds (.5-m dirt) (Chevrolet)

1963   (13th)   (425)

Poles

Golden Gate Speedway (.333-mile) (Chevrolet)
Richmond 250; Atlantic Rural Fairgrounds (.5-mile dirt) (Chevrolet)
Virginia 500; Martinsville Speedway (.5-mile) (Chevrolet)

1964		(110)

REB WICKERSHAM

1963		(113)

DINK WIDENHOUSE

1955	(19th)	(132)

Poles

Wilkes County 160; No. Wilkesboro Speedway (.625-m dirt) (Oldsmobile)

RAYMOND WILLIAMS

1970		(150)
1971		(159)
1972	(17th)	(336)
1973		(141)

ELMER WILSON

1950	(T-25th)	

RICK WILSON

1986	(24th)	(220)
1987		(142)
1988	(19th)	(297)

Poles

Valleydale Meats 500; Bristol Int. Raceway (.533-mile) (Oldsmobile)

1989	(16th)	(400)
1990	(25th)	(248)
1991		(268)
1993		(168)

GLEN WOOD

1958		(128)

Poles

Old Dominion 500; Martinsville Speedway (.5-mile) (Ford)
Wilkes 160; North Wilkesboro Speedway (.625-mile) (Ford)
Lakewood Speedway (1-mile dirt) (Ford)

1959	(16th)	(254)

Poles

Asheville-Weaverville Speedway (.5-mile) (Ford)
Old Dominion 500; Martinsville Speedway (.5-mile) (Ford)
Wilkes 160; North Wilkesboro Speedway (.625-mile) (Ford)

1960		(151)

Victories

* Bowman Gray Stadium (.25-mile; 50 miles) (Ford)
International 200; Bowman Gray Stadium (.25-m; 50 miles) (Ford)
* Bowman Gray Stadium (.25-mile; 50 miles) (Ford)

Poles
Virginia 500; Martinsville Speedway (.5-mile) (Ford)
* Bowman Gray Stadium (.25-mile) (Ford)
* Bowman Gray Stadium (.25-mile) (Ford)
Old Dominion 500; Martinsville Speedway (.5-mile) (Ford)

1961

Poles
Bowman Gray Stadium (.25-mile) (Ford)

1963

Victories
* Bowman Gray Stadium (.25-mile; 50 miles) (Ford)
Poles
Turkey Day 200; Tar Heel Speedway (.25-mile) (Ford)
* Bowman Gray Stadium (.25-mile) (Ford)

1964

Poles
Starkey Speedway (.25-mile) (Ford)

JOHNNY WYNN

| 1966 | | (144) |

CALE YARBOROUGH

1963	(23rd)	(231)
1964	(19th)	(296)
1965	(9th)	(516)

Victories
Valdosta Speedway (.5-mile dirt; 100 miles) (Ford)

| 1966 | (23rd) | (253) |
| 1967 | (17th) | (284) |

Victories
* Atlanta 500; Atlanta Int. Raceway (1.5-m; 500 miles) (Ford)
Firecracker 400; Daytona Int. Speedway (2.5-mile; 400 m) (Ford)
Poles
* Atlanta 500; Atlanta International Raceway (1.5-mile) (Ford)
World 600; Charlotte Motor Speedway (1.5-mile) (Ford)
Old Dominion 500; Martinsville Speedway (.5-mile) (Ford)
National 500; Charlotte Motor Speedway (1.5-mile) (Ford)

| 1968 | (11th) | (439) |

Victories
* Daytona 500; Daytona Int. Speedway (2.5-m; 500 miles) (Mercury)
Atlanta 500; Atlanta Int. Raceway (1.5-mile; 500 miles) (Mercury)
Virginia 500; Martinsville Speedway (.5-mile; 250 miles) (Mercury)
Firecracker 400; Daytona Int. Speedway (2.5-mile; 400 m) (Mercury)
Southern 500; Darlington Raceway (1.375-mile; 500 miles) (Mercury)
Peach State 200; Jeffco Speedway (.5-mile; 100 miles) (Mercury)
Poles
* Daytona 500; Daytona International Speedway (2.5-mile) (Mercury)
Maryland 300; Beltsville Speedway (.5-mile) (Mercury)
Old Dominion 500; Martinsville Speedway (.5-mile) (Mercury)
American 500; North Carolina Motor Speedway (1-mile) (Mercury)

| 1969 | (25th) | (286) |

Victories
Atlanta 500; Atlanta Int. Raceway (1.5-mile; 500 miles) (Mercury)
Motor State 500; Michigan Int. Speedway (2-m; 500 miles) (Mercury)
Poles
Rebel 400; Darlington Raceway (1.375-mile) (Mercury)
Firecracker 400; Daytona International Speedway (2.5-m) (Mercury)
Volunteer 500; Bristol International Speedway (.533-m) (Mercury)
Dixie 500; Atlanta International Raceway (1.5-mile) (Mercury)
Southern 500; Darlington Raceway (1.375-mile) (Mercury)
National 500; Charlotte Motor Speedway (1.5-mile) (Mercury)

| 1970 | (9th) | (492) |

Victories
Daytona International Speedway (2.5-mile; 125 miles) (Mercury)
Motor State 400; Michigan Int. Speedway (2-m; 400 miles) (Mercury)
American 500; N.C. Motor Speedway (1.017-m; 500 miles) (Mercury)
Poles
Daytona 500; Daytona International Speedway (2.5-mile) (Mercury)
Atlanta 500; Atlanta International Raceway (1.522-mile) (Mercury)
Firecracker 400; Daytona International Speedway (2.5-m) (Mercury)
Volunteer 500; Bristol International Speedway (.533-m) (Mercury)

| 1972 | | (134) |
| 1973 | (1st) | (652) |

Victories
* Southeastern 500; Bristol Int. Speedway (.533-m; 267m) (Chevrolet)
* Music City 420; Fairgrounds Speedway (.596-m; 250 m) (Chevrolet)
Southern 500; Darlington Raceway (1.366-mile; 500 miles) (Chevrolet)
National 500; Charlotte Motor Speedway (1.5-mile; 500 m) (Chevrolet)
Poles
* Southeastern 500; Bristol Int. Speedway (.533-mile) (Chevrolet)
* Music City 420; Fairgrounds Speedway (.596-mile) (Chevrolet)
Volunteer 500; Bristol International Speedway (.533-m) (Chevrolet)
Nashville 420; Fairgrounds Speedway (.596-mile) (Chevrolet)
Old Dominion 500; Martinsville Speedway (.525-mile) (Chevrolet)

| 1974 | (2nd) | (801) |

Victories (T-1st)
Win. Wes. 500; Riverside Int. Race. (2.62-m rd.; 500 m) (Chevrolet)
Atlanta 500; Atlanta Int. Raceway (1.522-m; 451 miles) (Chevrolet)
Southeastern 500; Bristol Int. Speedway (.533-m; 240 m) (Chevrolet)
* Virginia 500; Martinsville Speedway (.525-mile; 237 m) (Chevrolet)
Mason-Dixon 500; Dover Downs Int. Speedway (1-m; 450 m) (Chevrolet)
Tuborg 400; Riverside Int. Raceway (2.62-m road; 362 m) (Chevrolet)
Volunteer 500; Bristol Int. Speedway (.533-m; 267 miles) (Chevrolet)
Nashville 420; Fairgrounds Speedway (.596-m; 250 miles) (Chevrolet)
Southern 500; Darlington Raceway (1.366-mile; 500 miles) (Chevrolet)
Wilkes 400; North Wilkesboro Speedway (.625-mile; 250 m) (Chevrolet)
Poles
Carolina 500; North Carolina Motor Speedway (1.017-mile) (Chevrolet)
* Virginia 500; Martinsville Speedway (.525-mile) (Chevrolet)
Dixie 500; Atlanta International Raceway (1.522-mile) (Chevrolet)

| 1975 | (9th) | (517) |

Victories
Carolina 500; N.C. Motor Speedway (1.017-m; 500 miles) (Chevrolet)
Nashville 420; Nashville Speedway (.596-m; 250 miles) (Chevrolet)
American 500; N.C. Motor Speedway (1.017-m; 500 miles) (Chevrolet)

Poles

Motor State 400; Michigan International Speedway (2-m) (Chevrolet)
Old Dominion 500; Martinsville Speedway (.525-mile) (Chevrolet)
Volunteer 500; Bristol International Speedway (.533-m) (Chevrolet)

1976   (1st)   (735)

Victories

Southeastern 400; Bristol Int. Speedway (.533-m; 213 m) (Chevrolet)
Gwyn Staley 400; No. Wilkesboro Speedway (.625-m; 250m) (Chevrolet)
Music City USA 420; Nashville Speedway (.596-m; 250 m) (Chevrolet)
Firecracker 400; Daytona Int. Speedway (2.5-mile; 400 m) (Chevrolet)
Volunteer 400; Bristol Int. Speedway (.533-m; 213 miles) (Chevrolet)
Capital City 400; Richmond Fgds. Raceway (.542-m; 217 m) (Chevrolet)
* Delaware 500; Dover Downs Int. Speedway (1-m; 500 m) (Chevrolet)
Old Dominion 500; Martinsville Speedway (.525-m; 263 m) (Chevrolet)
Wilkes 400; North Wilkesboro Speedway (.625-mile; 250 m) (Chevrolet)

Poles

Purolator 500; Pocono International Raceway (2.5-mile) (Chevrolet)
* Delaware 500; Dover Downs International Speedway (1-m) (Chevrolet)

1977   (1st)   (902)

Victories (1st)

Daytona 500; Daytona Int. Speedway (2.5-mile; 500 miles) (Chevrolet)
Richmond 400; Richmond Fgds. Raceway (.542-m; 217 miles) (Chevrolet)
Gwyn Staley 400; No. Wilkesboro Speedway (.625-m; 250 m) (Chevrolet)
* Southeastern 500; Bristol Int. Speedway (.533-m; 267m) (Chevrolet)
Virginia 500; Martinsville Speedway (.525-mile; 263 miles) (Chevrolet)
Mason-Dixon 500; Dover Downs Int. Speedway (1-m; 500 m) (Chevrolet)
Cam2 Motor Oil 400; Michigan Int. Speedway (2-m; 400 m) (Chevrolet)
* Volunteer 400; Bristol Int. Speedway (.533-m; 213 m) (Chevrolet)
Old Dominion 500; Martinsville Speedway (.525-m; 263 m) (Chevrolet)

Poles

Winston Western 500; Riverside Int. Raceway (2.62-m rd.) (Chevrolet)
* Southeastern 500; Bristol Int. Speedway (.533-mile) (Chevrolet)
* Volunteer 400; Bristol Int. Speedway (.533-m) (Chevrolet)

1978   (1st)   (870)

Victories (1st)

Win. West. 500; Riverside Int. Race. (2.62-m rd.; 312m) (Oldsmobile)
* Winston 500; Ala. Int. Motor Speedway (2.66-m; 500 m) (Oldsmobile)
Music City USA 420; Nashville Speedway (.596-m; 250 m) (Oldsmobile)
Gabriel 400; Michigan International Speedway (2-m; 400m) (Oldsmobile)
Nashville 420; Nashville Speedway (.596-mile; 250 miles) (Oldsmobile)
Volunteer 500; Bristol Int. Raceway (.533-m; 267 miles) (Oldsmobile)
Southern 500; Darlington Int. Raceway (1.366-m; 500 m) (Oldsmobile)
Old Dominion 500; Martinsville Speedway (.525-m; 263 m) (Oldsmobile)
Wilkes 400; North Wilkesboro Speedway (.625-mile; 250 m) (Oldsmobile)
* American 500; N.C. Motor Speedway (1.017-m; 500 miles) (Oldsmobile)

Poles (1st)

Daytona 500; Daytona International Speedway (2.5-mile) (Oldsmobile)
Atlanta 500; Atlanta International Raceway (1.522-mile) (Oldsmobile)
* Winston 500; Alabama Int. Motor Speedway (2.66-mile) (Oldsmobile)
Firecracker 400; Daytona International Speedway (2.5-m) (Oldsmobile)
Talladega 500; Alabama Int. Motor Speedway (2.66-mile) (Oldsmobile)
* American 500; North Carolina Motor Speedway (1.017-m) (Oldsmobile)
Dixie 500; Atlanta International Raceway (1.522-mile) (Oldsmobile)
Los Angeles Times 500; Ontario Motor Speedway (2.5-mile) (Oldsmobile)

1979   (3rd)   (790)

Victories

Richmond 400; Richmond Fgds. Raceway (.542-m; 217 miles) (Oldsmobile)
Sun-Drop MC USA 420; Nashville Int. Race. (.596-m; 250m) (Oldsmobile)
Coca-Cola 500; Pocono Int. Raceway (2.5-mile; 500 miles) (Chevrolet)
NAPA National 500; Charlotte Motor Speed. (1.5-m; 500 m) (Chevrolet)

Poles

Los Angeles Times 500; Ontario Motor Speedway (2.5-mile) (Oldsmobile)

1980   (2nd)   (770)

Victories (1st)

Carolina 500; N.C. Motor Speedway (1.017-m; 500 miles) (Oldsmobile)
* NASCAR 400; Texas World Speedway (2-mile; 400 miles) (Chevrolet)
Champion SP 400; Michigan Int. Speedway (2-mile; 400 m) (Chevrolet)
* Busch Volunteer 500; Bristol Int. Race. (.533-m; 267m) (Chevrolet)
American 500; N.C. Motor Speedway (1.017-m; 500 miles) (Chevrolet)
Atlanta Journal 500; Atl. Int. Raceway (1.522-m; 500 m) (Chevrolet)

Poles (1st)

Valleydale Southeastern 500; Bristol Int. Race. (.533-m) (Chevrolet)
Music City 420; Nashville International Raceway (.596-m) (Chevrolet)
Mason-Dixon 500; Dover Downs Int. Speedway (1-mile) (Chevrolet)
World 600; Charlotte Motor Speedway (1.5-mile) (Chevrolet)
* NASCAR 400; Texas World Speedway (2-mile) (Chevrolet)
Warner W. Hodgdon 400; Riverside Int. Race. (2.62-m rd.) (Chevrolet)
Firecracker 400; Daytona International Speedway (2.5-m) (Chevrolet)
Busch Nashville 420; Nashville Int. Raceway (.596-mile) (Chevrolet)
Coca-Cola 500; Pocono International Raceway (2.5-mile) (Chevrolet)
* Busch Volunteer 500; Bristol Int. Raceway (.533-mile) (Chevrolet)
Capital City 400; Richmond Fairgrounds Raceway (.542-m) (Oldsmobile)
CRC Chemicals 500; Dover Downs Int. Speedway (1-mile) (Chevrolet)
Holly Farms 400; North Wilkesboro Speedway (.625-mile) (Oldsmobile)
Los Angeles Times 500; Ontario Motor Speedway (2.5-mile) (Chevrolet)

1981   (11th)   (411)

Victories

Coca-Cola 500; Atlanta Int. Raceway (1.522-m; 500 miles) (Buick)
* Firecracker 400; Daytona Int. Speedway (2.5-m; 400 m) (Buick)

Poles

Carolina 500; North Carolina Motor Speedway (1.017-mile) (Buick)
* Firecracker 400; Daytona Int. Speedway (2.5-mile) (Buick)

1982   (22nd)   (330)

Victories

W.W. Hodgdon Car. 500; N.C. Motor Speed. (1.017-m; 500m) (Buick)
Gabriel 400; Michigan International Speedway (2-m; 400m) (Buick)
Southern 500; Darlington Int. Raceway (1.366-m; 500 m) (Buick)

Poles

Mountain Dew 500; Pocono International Raceway (2.5-m) (Buick)
W.W. Hodgdon American 500; N.C. Motor Speedway (1.017-m) (Buick)

1983   (22nd)   (308)

Victories

Daytona 500; Daytona Int. Speedway (2.5-m; 500 miles) (Pontiac)
Coca-Cola 500; Atlanta Int. Raceway (1.522-m; 500 miles) (Chevrolet)
Gabriel 400; Michigan Int. Speedway (2-mile; 400 miles) (Chevrolet)
Champion SP 400; Michigan Int. Speedway (2-m; 400 m) (Chevrolet)

Poles

Winston 500; Alabama Int. Motor Speedway (2.66-mile) (Chevrolet)
Firecracker 400; Daytona Int. Speedway (2.5-mile) (Chevrolet)
Talladega 500; Alabama Int. Motor Speedway (2.66-mile) (Chevrolet)

1984   (12th)   (478)

Victories

* Daytona 500; Daytona Int. Speedway (2.5-m; 500 miles) (Chevrolet)
* Winston 500; Alabama Int. Motor Speed. (2.66-m; 500m) (Chevrolet)
Van Scoy DM 500; Pocono Int. Raceway (2.5-mile; 500 miles) (Chevrolet)

Poles (T–1st)
* Daytona 500; Daytona International Speedway (2.5-mile) (Chevrolet)
* Winston 500; Alabama Int. Motor Speedway (2.66-mile) (Chevrolet)
Pepsi Firecracker 400; Daytona Int. Speedway (2.5-mile) (Chevrolet)
Talladega 500; Alabama Int. Motor Speedway (2.66-mile) (Chevrolet)

1985   (22nd)   (273)

Victories
Talladega 500; Ala. Int. Motor Speedway (2.66-m; 500 m) (Ford)
Miller 500; Charlotte Motor Speedway (1.5-m; 500 miles) (Ford)

1986   (194)

Poles
Pepsi Firecracker 400; Daytona Int. Speedway (2.5-mile) (Ford)

1987   (24th)   (195)

1988   (126)

LEE ROY YARBROUGH

1963   (165)

Poles
Augusta Speedway (.5-mile dirt) (Mercury)

1964   (12th)   (447)

Victories
Savannah 200; Savannah Speedway (.5-m dirt; 100 miles) (Plymouth)
Pickens 200; Greenville-Pickens Sp. (.5-m dirt; 100m) (Plymouth)

1965   (126)

1966   (145)

Victories
National 500; Charlotte Motor Speedway (1.5-mile; 500 m) (Dodge)

Poles
Firecracker 400; Daytona International Speedway (2.5-m) (Dodge)
Southern 500; Darlington Raceway (1.375-mile) (Dodge)

1967   (181)

Victories
Daytona International Speedway (2.5-mile; 100 miles) (Dodge)

1968   (9th)   (472)

Victories
* Northern 300; Trenton Speedway (1-mile; 300 miles) (Ford)
Dixie 500; Atlanta International Raceway (1.5-m; 500 m) (Mercury)

Poles
Middle Georgia 500; Middle Georgia Raceway (.5625-mile) (Ford)
Atlanta 500; Atlanta International Raceway (1.5-mile) (Mercury)
Rebel 400; Darlington Raceway (1.375-mile) (Ford)
Carolina 500; North Carolina Motor Speedway (1-mile) (Ford)
* Northern 300; Trenton Speedway (1-mile) (Ford)
Volunteer 500; Bristol International Speedway (.5-mile) (Ford)

1969   (6th)   (724)

Victories
Daytona 500; Daytona Int. Speedway (2.5-mile; 500 miles) (Ford)
Rebel 400; Darlington Raceway (1.375-mile; 400 miles) (Mercury)
World 600; Charlotte Motor Speedway (1.5-m; 600 miles) (Mercury)
Firecracker 400; Daytona Int. Speedway (2.5-mile; 400 m) (Ford)
Dixie 500; Atlanta Int. Raceway (1.5-mile; 500 miles) (Ford)
Southern 500; Darlington Raceway (1.375-mile; 500 miles) (Ford)
American 500; N.C. Motor Speedway (1.017-m; 500 miles) (Ford)

1970   (20th)   (340)

Victories
National 500; Charlotte Motor Speedway (1.5-mile; 500 m) (Mercury)

Poles
Virginia 500; Martinsville Speedway (.525-mile) (Ford)
Nashville 420; Fairgrounds Speedway (.596-mile) (Ford)

1972   (20th)   (288)

DOUG YATES

1960   (14th)   (208)

Poles
Columbia Speedway (.5-mile dirt) (Plymouth)

1961   (22nd)   (217)

1964   (150)

Poles
Jacksonville Speedway (.5-mile dirt) (Plymouth)

BUDDY YOUNG

1969   (209)

EMANUEL ZERVAKIS

1960   (13th)   (238)

Poles
Wilson Speedway (.5-mile dirt) (Chevrolet)

1961   (3rd)   (701)

Victories
Greenville 200; Greenville-Pickens Sp. (.5-m dirt; 100m) (Chevrolet)
Yankee 500; Norwood Arena (.25-mile; 125 miles) (Chevrolet)

Poles
Hartsville Speedway (.333-mile dirt) (Chevrolet)

1962

Legend:
*Won race from pole
m (mile/miles)

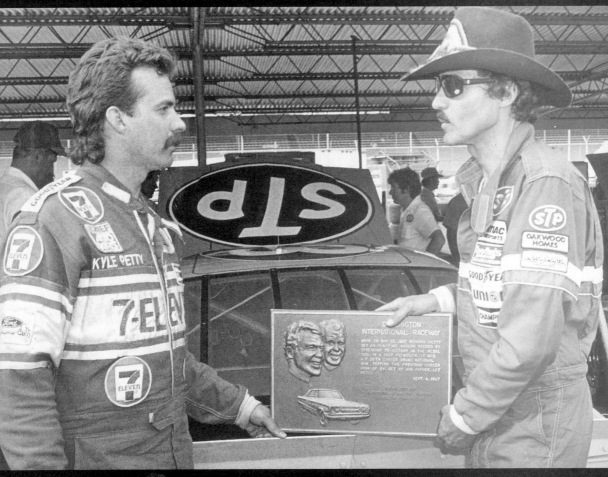

Seven-time Winston Cup champion Richard Petty inherited the throne from his father, Lee, a three-time Winston Cup champ. Kyle (left), Richard's son, didn't win a title during the series' first 51 years, but his eight victories gave the family 262 and make King Richard the only driver to win a Winston Cup race whose father and son can state the same claim.

Miscellaneous Records

NASCAR Winston Cup Champions

1949—Red Byron
1950—Bill Rexford
1951—Herb Thomas
1952—Tim Flock
1953—Herb Thomas
1954—Lee Petty
1955—Tim Flock
1956—Buck Baker
1957—Buck Baker
1958—Lee Petty
1959—Lee Petty
1960—Rex White
1961—Ned Jarrett
1962—Joe Weatherly
1963—Joe Weatherly
1964—Richard Petty
1965—Ned Jarrett
1966—David Pearson
1967—Richard Petty
1968—David Pearson
1969—David Pearson
1970—Bobby Isaac
1971—Richard Petty
1972—Richard Petty
1973—Benny Parsons
1974—Richard Petty
1975—Richard Petty
1976—Cale Yarborough
1977—Cale Yarborough
1978—Cale Yarborough
1979—Richard Petty
1980—Dale Earnhardt
1981—Darrell Waltrip
1982—Darrell Waltrip
1983—Bobby Allison
1984—Terry Labonte
1985—Darrell Waltrip
1986—Dale Earnhardt
1987—Dale Earnhardt
1988—Bill Elliott
1989—Rusty Wallace
1990—Dale Earnhardt
1991—Dale Earnhardt
1992—Alan Kulwicki
1993—Dale Earnhardt
1994—Dale Earnhardt
1995—Jeff Gordon
1996—Terry Labonte
1997—Jeff Gordon
1998—Jeff Gordon
1999—Dale Jarrett

NASCAR Winston Cup Rookies of the Year

1958—Shorty Rollins
1959—Richard Petty
1960—David Pearson
1961—Woodie Wilson
1962—Tom Cox
1963—Billy Wade
1964—Doug Cooper
1965—Sam McQuagg
1966—James Hylton
1967—Donnie Allison
1968—Pete Hamilton
1969—Dick Brooks
1970—Bill Dennis
1971—Walter Ballard
1972—Larry Smith
1973—Lennie Pond
1974—Earl Ross
1975—Bruce Hill
1976—Skip Manning
1977—Ricky Rudd
1978—Ronnie Thomas
1979—Dale Earnhardt
1980—Jody Ridley
1981—Ron Bouchard
1982—Geoff Bodine
1983—Sterling Marlin
1984—Rusty Wallace
1985—Ken Schrader
1986—Alan Kulwicki
1987—Davey Allison
1988—Ken Bouchard
1989—Dick Trickle
1990—Rob Moroso
1991—Bobby Hamilton
1992—Jimmy Hensley
1993—Jeff Gordon
1994—Jeff Burton
1995—Ricky Craven
1996—Johnny Benson Jr.
1997—Mike Skinner
1998—Kenny Irwin
1999—Tony Stewart

Performance Index Records

All-Time Performance Index Rankings

1. Richard Petty (22,321)
2. Dale Earnhardt (14,657)
3. Bobby Allison (14,653)
4. Darrell Waltrip (14,496)
5. Terry Labonte (12,366)
6. Bill Elliott (11,921)
7. David Pearson (11,528)
8. Ricky Rudd (11,456)
9. Cale Yarborough (11,358)
10. Buddy Baker (11,001)
11. James Hylton (9,858)
12. Rusty Wallace (9,679)
13. Dave Marcis (9,612)
14. Benny Parsons (9,344)
15. Mark Martin (9,086)

Performance Index Records

16. Buck Baker (8,565)
17. Kyle Petty (8,206)
18. Geoff Bodine (8,180)
19. Harry Gant (7,802)
20. Ken Schrader (7,447)
21. Sterling Marlin (7,374)
22. Buddy Arrington (7,100)
23. Morgan Shepherd (7,088)
24. Lee Petty (6,691)
25. Dale Jarrett (6,807)
26. Elmo Langley (6,225)
27. Neil Bonnett (5,967)
28. J.D. McDuffie (5,882)
29. Ned Jarrett (5,864)
30. Cecil Gordon (5,601)
31. Jim Paschal (5,552)
32. Dick Brooks (5,375)
33. Michael Waltrip (5,371)
34. Jeff Gordon (5,267)
35. Bobby Isaac (5,163)
36. Ernie Irvan (5,039)
37. Wendell Scott (4,863)
38. Lake Speed (4,660)
39. Neil Castles (4,649)
40. Donnie Allison (4,182)
41. Bobby Labonte (4,100)
42. Bobby Hillin Jr. (4,033)
43. Junior Johnson (3,958)
44. Richard Childress (3,951)
45. Rex White (3,947)
46. G.C. Spencer (3,849)
47. Davey Allison (3,826)
48. Brett Bodine (3,784)
49. John Sears (3,726)
50. Frank Warren (3,724)
51. Joe Weatherly (3,653)
52. Marvin Panch (3,603)
53. Tiny Lund (3,492)
54. Herb Thomas (3,465)
55. Jabe Thomas (3,461)
56. Jimmy Means; Ted Musgrave (3,434)
58. Jimmy Spencer (3,416)
59. Lennie Pond (3,359)
60. Fireball Roberts (3,298)
61. Bobby Hamilton (3,284)
62. Jeff Burton (3,282)
63. Alan Kulwicki (3,271)
64. Jack Smith (3,265)
65. Tim Richmond (3,191)
66. Henley Gray (3,076)
67. Derrike Cope (3,073)
68. Lee Roy Yarbrough (3,065)
69. Fred Lorenzen (2,904)
70. Tim Flock (2,893)
71. Joe Ruttman (2,770)
72. D.K. Ulrich (2,728)
73. Rick Mast (2,703)
74. Speedy Thompson (2,699)
75. Phil Parsons (2,614)
76. Darel Dieringer (2,568)
77. Ron Bouchard (2,522)
78. Dick Trickle (2,455)
79. Bob Welborn (2,450)
80. Ed Negre (2,356)

81. Hut Stricklin (2,349)
82. Jim Pardue (2,348)
83. Jody Ridley (2,338)
84. Bill Champion (2,285)
85. Jeremy Mayfield (2,247)
86. Coo Coo Marlin (2,221)
87. Curtis Turner (2,148)
88. Walter Ballard (2,146)
89. Curtis Crider (2,102)
90. Tommy Gale (2,096)
91. Ward Burton (1,981)
92. Cotton Owens (1,979)
93. Fonty Flock (1,978)
94. Roy Tyner (1,975)
95. John Andretti (1,972)
96. Rick Wilson (1,970)
97. Dick Hutcherson (1,951)
98. Paul Goldsmith (1,950)
99. Bill Seifert (1,894)
100. Charlie Glotzbach (1,763)
101. Friday Hassler (1,755)
102. Johnny Allen (1,729)
103. Dick Rathmann (1,703)
104. Clyde Lynn (1,689)
105. David Sisco (1,676)
106. Herman Beam (1,673)
107. Joe Eubanks (1,659)
108. A.J. Foyt (1,658)
109. Wally Dallenbach Jr. (1,617)
110. Greg Sacks (1,562)
111. Dick May (1,545)
112. Kenny Wallace (1,531)
113. J.T. Putney (1,519)
114. Bobby Johns (1,513)
115. Ben Arnold (1,500)
116. Chad Little (1,487)
117. L.D. Austin (1,441)
118. Joe Nemechek; Larry Thomas (1,428)
120. Johnny Benson Jr. (1,392)
121. Earl Brooks (1,378)
122. Roy Mayne (1,374)
123. E.J. Trivette (1,367)
124. Paul Lewis (1,333)
125. Joe Frasson (1,286)
126. Jim Reed (1,280)
127. Joe Millikan (1,278)
128. Jimmie Lewallen (1,218)
129. Tom Pistone (1,187)
130. Mike Skinner (1,180)
131. Ronnie Thomas (1,154)
132. Emanuel Zervakis (1,135)
133. Pete Hamilton (1,133)
134. Larry Frank (1,118)
135. Bill Blair (1,114)
136. Bobby Wawak (1,101)
137. Skip Manning (1,095)
138. Tommy Irwin (1,094)
139. Billy Wade (1,093)
140. Ricky Craven (1,086)
141. Bruce Hill (1,083)
142. Jim Vandiver (1,077)
143. Steve Grissom; Tighe Scott (1,043)
145. Dean Dalton; Fred Harb (1,022)
147. Hershel McGriff (997)

148. Doug Cooper (863)
149. Tony Stewart (859)
150. Eddie Pagan (855)
151. Gwyn Staley (853)
152. Bob Derrington (850)
153. Bill Dennis (845)
154. Jimmy Hensley (835)
155. Trevor Boys (829)
156. Billy Myers (817)
157. George Green (801)
158. Raymond Williams (786)
159. Lloyd Dane; Sam McQuagg (782)
161. Mike Alexander (770)
162. Gober Sosebee (758)
163. Todd Bodine (754)
164. Glen Wood (749)
165. Donald Thomas (748)
166. Ramo Stott (741)
167. Nelson Stacy (733)
168. Kenny Irwin (717)
169. Tommy Ellis; Brownie King (709)
171. Grant Adcox (693)
172. Wayne Smith (684)
173. H.B. Bailey (648)
174. Charlie Roberts (640)
175. Robert Pressley (635)
176. Stick Elliott (634)
177. Ray Elder (633)
178. Doug Yates (621)
179. Worth McMillion (620)
180. Bobby Keck (605)
181. Jackie Rogers (589)
182. Jimmy Massey (581)
183. Shorty Rollins (577)
184. Slick Johnson (573)
185. Ralph Earnhardt (572)
186. Banjo Matthews; Steve Park (571)
188. Ralph Moody; Jim Sauter (564)
190. Roger Hamby (562)
191. Ron Keselowski; Larry Manning (558)
193. Bill Amick; Ralph Liguori (555)
195. Earl Ross (541)
196. Ferrel Harris (538)
197. Mike Wallace (532)
198. Bunkie Blackburn (529)
199. Kevin Lepage; Frank Mundy (523)
201. Don Tarr (521)
202. Eddie Bierschwale (519)
203. Joe Lee Johnson (508)
204. Larry Pearson (500)
205. Scotty Cain (490)
206. Billy Carden; Larry Smith (489)
208. Dave Terrell (487)
209. Lloyd Moore (484)
210. Richard Brickhouse (478)
211. Ray Duhigg (477)
212. Janet Guthrie; Eddie Skinner (473)
214. Rick Newsom (470)
215. Jim Hurtubise (467)
216. Jimmy Helms (466)
217. Bud Moore (456)
218. Baxter Price (448)
219. Don White (446)
220. Richie Panch (442)

221. Bob Burcham (439)
222. Dan Gurney (437)
223. Blackie Pitt (433)
224. Bill Schmitt (429)
225. Jimmy Thompson (425)
226. Tom Cox; Connie Saylor (422)
228. Chuck Bown (421)
229. Clark Dwyer (417)
230. Slick Smith (408)
231. Sam Sommers (390)
232. Clarence DeZalia; Parnelli Jones (383)
234. Ken Rush (379)
235. Ken Ragan (372)
236. Ted Chamberlain (369)
237. Bob Flock (366)
238. Marty Robbins (365)
239. Bill Rexford (362)
240. Paul Dean Holt (356)
241. Butch Hartman (355)
242. Terry Bivins; Buddy Shuman (353)
244. Earl Balmer (352)
245. Johnny Beauchamp (351)
246. Carl Adams; Bob Cooper (347)
248. Marvin Porter (343)
249. Johnny Rutherford (341)
250. Mel Larson (338)
251. Frankie Schneider (335)
252. Joe Mihalic (334)
253. Jimmy Insolo (332)
254. John Anderson (328)
255. Eddie Gray; Butch Miller (322)
257. Earle Canavan (319)
258. Clyde Minter (318)
259. Gary B. Myers (311)
260. Rich Bickle (308)
261. Shep Langdon (307)
262. Ken Bouchard; Bob Burdick; Fred Dove (303)
265. Jim Cook (300)
266. Bruce Jacobi (299)
267. Hoss Ellington (298)
268. Bill Snowden (293)
269. Richard D. Brown (292)
270. Doug Cox (289)
271. Elton Hildreth; Al Keller (288)
273. Dick Passwater; Marshall Teague (286)
275. Dick Beaty (285)
276. Maurice Petty (281)
277. David Green (278)
278. Johnny Halford; Dick M. Johnson (277)
280. Billy Rafter (272)
281. Possum Jones; Dick Linder; Elliott Sadler (271)
284. David Ray Boggs (269)
285. Jack McCoy (268)
286. Sonny Hutchins (265)
287. Chuck Meekins (263)
288. Danny Letner (257)
289. Al White (256)
290. Ed Hessert (255)
291. Jerry Grant (253)
292. Harvey Henderson (251)
293. Bub King (249)
294. Stan Barrett; Larry Hess (248)
296. Jack Anderson; Herschel Buchanan; Bill Morton (247)
299. Dick Getty (240)

300. Tony Bettenhausen Jr.; Buddy Young (239)
302. Red Byron; Gene Hobby (236)
304. Blackie Watt (235)
305. Bill Widenhouse (233)
306. Ed Livingston; George Seeger (232)
308. Gene Black; Reb Wickersham (230)
310. Rodney Combs (227)
311. Sherman Utsman; Eddie Yarboro (225)
313. Bill Shirey (223)
314. Jimmy Florian (221)
315. Bob Ross (219)
316. Jerry Nadeau (218)
317. Johnny Patterson (216)
318. Don Biederman (211)
319. Gene Comstock; Sonny Easley; Dink Widenhouse (210)
322. Wilbur Rakestraw (208)
323. Randy LaJoie (206)
324. Mario Andretti (205)
325. Gary Balough; Ken Meisenhelder; Arden Mounts (204)
328. Bob Barron (202)
329. Neil Cole (201)
330. Bob Duell; Elliott Forbes-Robinson (200)
332. George Follmer; Don Noel; Terry Ryan (199)
335. Doug Heveron (198)
336. Dick Bown (195)
337. Gordon Johncock; Bill Poor (194)
339. Weldon Adams; Erick Erickson; Reds Kagle; Doug Moore; Junior Spencer (192)
344. Perk Brown (191)
345. Brad Teague; Roscoe Thompson (190)
347. Larry Baumel (189)
348. Mickey Gibbs (188)
349. Al Holbert; Troy Ruttman (187)
351. Art Watts (186)
352. Vic Parsons (185)
353. George Davis (184)
354. Harold Hardesty; Danny Weinberg (183)
356. Jimmy Horton; Johnny Mantz; Clyde Palmer (182)
359. Dave MacDonald (181)
360. Allen Adkins; Whitey Norman; Gene Simpson (179)
363. Jeff Green; John Kieper; Gene White (176)
366. Otis Martin (173)
367. Dean Combs (172)
368. Jim Blomgren (171)
369. Joel Davis; Nace Mattingly; Rob Moroso; Don Oldenberg (170)
373. Harry Leake (169)
374. Jim Robinson (167)
375. Bob Walden (165)
376. Red Farmer; Carl Joiner; Tommy Thompson (162)
379. Joel Million (161)
380. Pappy Hough; Bob Keefe; Bill McMahan; Steve Moore; Dub Simpson (158)
385. Lennie Page (157)
386. Loy Allen Jr.; Laird Bruner (156)
388. Gerald Duke (155)
389. Chuck Mahoney; Swede Savage (154)
391. Ron Hornaday (153)
392. Elmo Henderson; John Soares Jr. (150)
394. Lee Reitzel; John Utsman; Richard White (149)
397. Ed Cole; Glenn Dunnaway; Hank Thomas; Randy Tissot (148)
401. Harvey Hege; Buzz Woodward; Bruce Worrell (147)
404. Travis Tiller (146)
405. John Dodd Jr.; Bud Harless (145)
407. Roy Smith; Johnny Wynn (144)
409. Bill Hollar (143)

410. Joe Booher; Charlie Cregar; Charley Griffith; Bob Perry; Kevin Terris; Al Watkins (141)
416. Johnny Mackison (139)
417. Gary Bettenhausen; Darrell Bryant; Lou Figaro; Ron Hutcherson (138)
421. Bill Elswick; Clarence Lovell (137)
423. Ray Hendrick (136)
424. Glenn Francis; John Lindsay; Bobby Mausgrover (134)
427. Walson Gardner; Pat Kirkwood; Blackie Wangerin (133)
430. Herb Estes; Coleman Lawrence (132)
432. Bobby Waddell (131)
433. Pop McGinnis; Dick Meyer; Bub Strickler (130)
436. George Dunn; Chuck Wahl (128)
438. Ronnie Kohler; Max Ledbetter (127)
440. Robby Gordon; Chuck Hansen (126)
442. Johnny Dodson (125)
443. T.C. Hunt; Sal Tovella (124)
445. Kenny Brightbill; Ewell Weddle (123)
447. Jack Reynolds; Al Unser (121)
449. Dick Dixon; Harry Jefferson; John Soares (120)
452. Phil Barkdoll; Charles Gattalia; Jack Pennington; Herb Tillman (119)
456. Major Melton (118)
457. Norm Nelson; Maynard Troyer (116)
459. Harold Miller; Mike Potter (113)
461. Jimmy Ayers; Donald Tucker (112)
463. Paul Tyler (111)
464. Harold Beal; Jerry Oliver (110)
466. George Alsobrook (109)
467. Jim Fiebelkorn; Woodie Wilson (108)
469. George Althiede; Peck Peckham (107)
471. Bud Farrell; Ed Samples (106)
473. Marv Acton; Stan Meserve (104)
475. Alton Jones; Satch Worley (101)
477. Don Puskarich; Jim Thirkettle (100)
479. John Rostek; Jesse James Taylor (99)
481. Jimmy Crawford; C.H. Dingler; Vic Elford; Ernie Gahan; Brad Noffsinger (98)
486. Bill Foster; Bob Senneker; Don Whittington (97)
489. Jerry Bowman; George Poulos; Barney Shore (96)
492. Steve Christman (95)
493. Iggy Katona; Ned Setzer (94)
495. Lowell Cowell; Jack Harden; Bob Havenmann; Jack Ingram; Harold Kite; Richard Riley (93)
501. Philip Duffie; Roy Hallquist; Junior Miller; Bunk Moore (92)
505. Danny Graves; George Hartley (91)
507. R.L. Combs; Tom Kendall; Bucky Sager; Leon Sales; Ken Spikes (90)
512. Barney Smith; Leonard Tippett (89)
514. Chet Fillip; John Kennedy; Jim Parsley; Jerry Schild; Bill Walker; Shorty York (88)
520. Dick Joslin (87)
521. Ben Hess; Ken Johnson; Ralph Jones; Bobby Myers (86)
525. Dick Gulstrand; Tommy Houston; Harold Smith (85)
528. Pete Stewart; Don Waterman (84)
530. Buck Brigance; Tommy Moon; Don Porter; Fritz Wilson (83)
534. Bill Benson (82)
535. Ed Benedict; Jim Danielson; Bill Ervin; Roz Howard; Lionel Johnson; Matt Kenseth; Dean Roper; Andy Winfree (81)
543. Rick Baldwin; Dave James; Gary Matthews; Bill Morgan (80)
547. Freddy Fryar; Royce Haggerty; Huck Spaulding (79)
550. Don Bailey; Eddie Bradshaw; Ed Brown; Jimmy Lee Capps; Walt Hansgen; Bill Harrison (78)
556. Pete Hazelwood; Jeff Purvis; Pap White (77)
559. Marshall Sargent; Volney Schulze; Russ Truelove (76)
562. Ralph Dyer; Ronnie Hopkins; Dell Pearson; Ernie Shaw; Jack White (75)
567. Jerry Draper; Red Duvall; Ray Hill II; Glenn Jarrett; Bosco Lowe;

Don Reynolds; Bill Ward (74)

574. Dick Smith; Gordon Smith; Roland Wlodyka (73)

577. Bob England; Jimmy Finger; Rick McCray; Bill Stammer; Glenn Steurer (72)

582. Billy Hagan; Gordon Haines; Andy Hampton; Billie Harvey; Frank James (71)

587. Sherman Clark; Jim Delaney; John Dodd; Mark Donohue; Dale Earnhardt Jr.; Ben Gregory; Larry Miller; Clem Proctor; Benny Rakestraw (70)

596. Bill Bowman; Johnny Grubb; Mark Hurley; Eddie Riker; Frank Sessoms; Mark Stahl (69)

602. Randy Baker; Johnny Barnes (68)

604. Tiny Benson; Joe Caspolich; John Findlay; Red Foote; Whitey Gerkin; Dick Kranzler; G.T. Nolan; Dick Skillen; Jerry Wimbish (67)

613. Sara Christian; Ray Erickson; Bob James; John McGinley; Ervin Pruitt; Ernie Young (66)

619. Jack Choquette; Ron Grana; Jeff Hawkins (65)

622. Johnny Anderson; Curley Barker; Mel Bradley; Tommie Elliott; Jack D. McCoy; John McVitty; Pedro Rodriguez; H.G. Rosier; Fred Steinbroner; Dave White (64)

632. Jim Bennett; Bobby Courtwright; Pancho Carter; Dave Dion; Oda Greene; J.C. Hendrix; Irv Hoerr; Don Hume; Bill Hyde; Bob Potter; Tom Sneva; Bill West (63)

644. Jim Cushman; Bud Emra; Norm Palmer; Bobby Unser (62)

648. Paul Connors; Delma Cowart; Larry Flynn; Russ Hepler; Banks Simpson (61)

653. Charlie Baker; Ben Benz; J.V. Hamby; Mack Hanbury; Bob Price; Gary Sain (60)

659. Emory Lewis; Lou Spears; T.A. Toomes (59)

662. Elbert Allen; Jim Bray; Paul Dorrity; Dick Freeman; Lucky Long; Lyle Scott; Dave Watson; Pete Yow (58)

670. Wayne Andrews; Dick Burns; Charlie Chapman; Walt Flinchum; John Meggers (57)

675. June Cleveland; George England; Ray Hughes; Bill Norton; Joe Phipps; Dorsey Schroeder (56)

681. Jim Clark; Gene Cline; Dean Layfield; Bill Miller; Hugh Pearson; Harlan Richardson; Buren Skeen; Jimmy Vaughn (55)

689. Jack Bowsher; Ted Cannady; John DuBoise; Mike Klapak; Bert Robbins (54)

694. Spook Crawford; Darrell Dake; Jim Graham; Joe Jones; Sumner McKnight; Jack Norton; L.D. Ottinger; George Parrish; Joe Schlesser; Louis Weathersbee; Bill Wimble (53)

705. Charles Barrett; Woody Brown; Ray Carter; Larry Esau; Harold Fagan; Ken Fisher; Skip Hudson; Paul Jett; Carl Krueger; Dick Poling; Elton Sawyer (52)

716. Bob Apperson; Buckshot Jones; Dave Mader III; Neil Roberts; Salt Walther (51)

721. Eduardo Dibos; Wimpy Ervin; Kenny Hemphill; Rick Knoop; Gayle Warren (50)

726. Phil Good; John Kenney; Jim McGuirk; Bob Moore; Bob Pronger; Laurent Rioux (49)

732. Eddie Bond; Don Eggert; Joe Fields; Peter Knab; Floyd Powell; Bob Moore II; Charlie Rudolph; Don Sprouse (48)

740. Jim Bown; Bobby Brack; Robert Caswell; Harvey Eakin; Al Elmore; Jack Goodwin; Kevin Housby; Sam Rose; Dorus Wisecraver (47)

749. Fred Bince; Dick Eagan; Ernest Eury; Chuck Huckabee; Art Lamey; Clyde Prickett; Freddy Smith; Dick Walters; Elmer Wilson (46)

758. Jimmy Ingalls; Jeff McDuffie; Howard Phillippi; Ken Wagner (45)

762. Raul Cilloniz; Bud Graham; Jack Holloway; Jim Hunter; Ray Johnstone; Eddie MacDonald; Earl Moss; James Sears (44)

770. Carl Burris; Terry Herman; Dominic Persicketti; Johnny Roberts; Lennie Waldo; Jim Whitt (43)

776. Sonny Black; Clyde Dagit; Jim McElreath; Nestor Peles; Bill Sedgwick (42)

781. Nathan Boutwell; Ray Chaike; Jerry Cranmer; Lou Sherman (41)

785. E.J. Brewer; Bill Butts; Allan Clarke; Tom Dill; Ron Esau; Bob Grossman; Jim Linke; Darryl Sage; Jim Southard; Augie Walackas; Jim Whitman (40)

796. Ivan Baldwin; Norman McGriff; Ken Milligan; James Norton; E.C. Ramsey; Frank Secrist; Bugs Stevens (39)

803. Richard Brownlee; Paul Barrow; Dick Clothier; Bill DeCoster; Bob Dickson; Keith Hamner; Frank Luptow; Roger McCluskey; Charlie Mincey; Bill Moore; Paul Parks; Walt Sprague; Nook Walters (38)

816. Axel Anderson; Dick Cook; Doc Faustina; Leon Fox; Tubby Gonzales; Bill Holland; Bill Irvin; Art Malone; Jack Radtke; Bud Riley; Parks Surrat (37)

827. George Bush; Joe Clark; Paul Pettit; Dub Livingston; Gene Marmor; Mike McGreevey; Jerry Morese; Jackie Oliver; Bob Rauscher; Johnny Steele; Robert Vaughn; Wayne Woodward (36)

839. Chester Barron; Gene Davis; Mel Krueger; Butch Lindley; Joe Bill McGraw; Mario Rossi; Buck Simmons; Pee Wee Wentz; Steve Young (35)

848. Quinton Daniels; Charles Dyer; Marion Edwards; Fred Johnson; Dick Moffitt; Clyde Pittinger; Darvin Randahl; Sam Rice (34)

856. Dick Allwine; Bob Ashbrook; Jack Etheridge; Sonny Fogle; Billy Foster; George Osborne; Dick Simon; Rollin Smith (33)

864. Marvin Copple; Wally Dallenbach; Bobby Fleming; Johnny Gardner; Sam Hawks; Randy Hutchison; Charles Jackson; Joe Kelly; Mike Kempton; Emory Mahon; Bill O'Dell; Jan Opperman; Larry Pollard; John Potter; Bob Ruppert; Jack Russell; Bill Slater; Sam Stanley; Wayne Watercutter (32)

883. Nelson Applegate; Jim Austin; Erwin Blatt; Bill Clinton; Pepper Cunningham; Ronnie Daniel; Dick Jerrett; Jim Reich; Jim Roper; Joel Stowe; Frank Waite (31)

894. Charles Barry; Dan Daughtry; Runt Harris; Red Harvey; Jimmy Mairs; Wes Morgan; George Norton; Eddie Pettyjohn; Charles Prickett; Gene Riniker; Steve Spencer; Chuck Stevenson (30)

906. Buck Barr; Rene Charland; Dick Foley; Al Gross; Don Hall; Ed Massey; Tony Nelson; Graham Shaw; Harold Stockton; Virgil Stockton; G.T. Tallas; Bill Tanner; Carl Tyler (29)

919. John Borneman; Harry Dinwiddie; Ron Fellows; Lloyd Hulette; Kuzie Kuzmanich; Sonny Lanphear; Butch Leitzinger; Joe Merola; Curley Mills; Bo Reeder; Al Self (28)

930. Bill Adams; Lamar Crabtree; Bay Darnell; Bob Dietrich; Ruben Garcia; Chuck Garrett; Vince Giamformaggio; Art Gill; Lee Gordon; Frank Graham; Joe Guide Jr.; Mike James; Amos Johnson; Bill Joslin; Owen Loggins; Clyde Mitchell; Ed Paskovich; Julian Petty; Larry Phillips; Nat Reeder; Ronnie Sanders (27)

951. Mike Batinick; Lefty Bolton; Jim Boyd; Leo Caldwell; Ronnie Chumley; Pat Fay; Pete Frazee; Lamoine Frey; Joe Halton; Dutch Hoag; Armond Holley; Joe Dean Huss; Blaine Kauffman; Joe Littlejohn; Bob McElee; Billy McGinnis; Lloyd Ragon; Bob Riley; Dick Santee; Bob Schacht; John Seeley; Archie Smith; Joe Valente; Bill Vanderhoff; Eddie Van Horn (26)

976. Bruce Atchley; Ed Berrier; Charlie Blanton; Bill Brown; Marvin Burke; Gerald Chamberlain; George Clark; Jack Clarke; James Cox; Willie Crane; Tommie Crozier; George Gallup; Don Hoffman; Jim Ingram; Cal Johnson; Jerry Jolly; Harry LaVois; Buck Smith; Gerald Thompson; J.C. Van Landingham; Don Walker; Jesse White; Bill Whitley (25)

999. Dave Alonzo; Dick Bailey; Max Berrier; Charlie Chamblee; Frank Christian; Bill Claren; Bob Connor; Bob Devine; Randy Dodd; Carson Dyer; Gene Felton; Phil Finney; Cliff Garner; Tubby Harrison; Butch Hirst; Bill Jarlick; Ken Johns; Guy Jones; Al Loquasto; Bill Lutz; Ken Miles; Paul Newkirk; Bill Osborne II; Ansel Rakestraw; John Rezek; Ralph Rose; Walt Schubert; Bill Scott; Les Snow; Pete Torres; Frank Weathers (24)

1030. Joey Arrington; Frank Burnett; Herbert Burns; Danny Byrd; Ray Chase; Johnny Coy Jr.; Jack Donohue; Pee Wee Ellwanger; Buck Fulp; John Gouveia; David Hobbs; Pee Wee Jones; Joe Penland; Walt Price; Carl Renner; Don Simkins; Marvin Sjolin; Otis Skinner; Tommy Wells (23)

1049. Claude Ballot-Lena; Al Brand; Gordon Bracken; Whitey Brainerd; Barry Brooks; Kirk Bryant; Bob Cameron; Bill Chevalier; Gene Coyle; Walt Davis; Henry Ford; Frank Jamison; P.J. Jones; Dick Klank; Bob Korf; Jack Marsh; Bobby Marshman; John Martin; Jack Oldenhage; Nelson Oswald; Bill Smith; Warren Tope; Bill Venturini; Chuck Webb; Bill Whittington (22)

1074. Richard Brown; Terry Byers; Tom Cherry; Jerry Churchill; Bob Dawson; Jim Dimeo; David Ezell; Ronnie Fones; Ron Gautsche; Ernie Gesell; Harry Goularte; Budd Hagelin; Bob Hale; Dick Lawrence; Virgil Livengood; Glenn McDuffie; Dick Miller; Jim Ord; Bill Osborne; Bill Parnell; Ted Rambo; Tommy Ringstaff; John Rogers; Ermon Rush; Dennis Setzer; Billy Standridge; Nero Steptoe; Ernie Stierly; Edgar Wallen; Tim Williamson; Clay Young (21)

1105. Paul Aars; Chuck Blewitt; Ernie Boost; Frank Brantley; John Callis; Leland Colvin; Jack Ely; Lee Faulk; Paul Feldner; Wayne Fielden; Woody Fisher; Fred Frazier; Dick Goode; Jeff Handy; Innes Ireland; Stan Kross; Dick Mitchell; Rocky Moran; Randy Myers; Don O'Dell; Sammy Packard; Steve Peles; Wilbur Pickett; Tommy Riggins; Ed Sczech; Joe Staton; Tom Williams; Doug Wilson (20)

1133. Bernard Alvarez; Gene Austin; George Behlman; Aubrey Boles; Pete Brock; Guy Cork; Herb Crawford; Buddy Helms; Bill Hidden; Al Jacobs; Bud Kutina; Jack Lawrence; Ethel Mobley; Charles Pemberton; Buck Peralta; Bob Reuther; Larry Shurter; Jim Sills; Louise Smith; Ted Swaim; Jim Wilson (19)

1154. Earl Beer; Darin Brassfield; Hal Callentine; Ted Hairfield; Bernie Hentges; Gary Kershaw; Bob Presnell; Jim Rathmann; Jack Rounds; Paul Smith; Ross Surgenor; Dick Stone; Chuck Thompson; Don Tilley (18)

1168. Ken Anderson; George Ashbrook; Bill Bade; Phillips Bell; Gene Blair; Lloyd Chick; Floyd Curtis; John Dineen; Mike Eagan; Bob Greeley; Carl Hammill; Chuck James; Scott Lagasse; Bill Massey; Scott Miller; Budd Olsen; Phil Orr; Nick Rampling; Robert Roeber; Jim Romine; Johnny Sudderth; Jim Watkins; Buzz Wilson; Millard Wright; Cliff Yiskis; Dick Zimmerman (17)

1194. Ed Andrews; Don Angel; Bruce Brantley; Ray Campbell; Billy Cantrell; Ray Fanning; Jack Flynn; Coleman Grant; J.E. Hardie; Ron Hornaday Jr.; Tom Jerris; Byron King; Larry Mann; Jim Murray; Gus Newman; Ed Normi; Steve Pfeifer; Ted Pitcher; Tom Rivers; Sandy Satullo; Jim Tatum; Billy Taylor; Reino Tulonen; Bryant Wallace; Walter Wallace; Al Weber; Donald White; Bob Whitlow; Eldon Yarbrough (16)

1223. John Banks; John Barker; Randy Becker; Fred Bethune; Les Bomar; Jim Byrd; Harold Carmac; Rags Carter; Jack Conley; Don Dahle; Ed DeWolff; Duke DeBrizzi; Yvon DuHamel; Terry Fisher; Rat Garner; Charles Gillman; Jack Goodwin II; Ed Hale; Roy Hall; Rick Hendrick; Hooker Hood; Davy Jones; Hap Jones; Bill Ledbetter; Tracy Leslie; Bill Long; Gene Long; Joe Edd Neubert; Randy Ogden; Billy Oswald; Rod Perry; Bob Rose; Charles Sanchez; Charlie Stone; Ted Sweeney; Roy Trantham; Lou Volk; Claude Wallington; Paul Walton; Gus Wilson (15)

1263. Carl Anderson; Bill Baker; Robert Berrier; Dick Blackwell; Pug Blalock; Leonard Blanchard; John Borden; Len Brown; Ed Camrud; Duane Carter; Ray Clark; Byron Clouse; Hal Cole; Tom Dawson; Pete Diviney; Bob Dugan; Rod Eulenfeld; Bo Fields; Roy Gemberling; Frank Gise; Bobby Greene; Bill Gross; Ed Jackson; Burt Jackson; Jack Kabat; Hoss Kagle; Joe Kilgore; Fred Knapp; Furman Lancaster; Glen Larsen; Sterling Long; Dave Mader; Ken Marriott; Norm McCarthy; Jim Millard; Fred Moore; Walt Mortz; Gary Myers; Rick O'Dell; Bill Olson; Bob Osborne; John Paul Jr.; Bob Pickell; Joe Prismo; Cliff Richmond; Jack Simpson; Bill Stickler; Chuck Stimus; Ward Towers; Dan Warlick; John Wright (14)

1314. Frank Arford; Robert Brown; Andy Buffington; Gordon Campbell; Jerry Carver; Bill Davis; Jim Donovan; Jerry Earl; Howard Elder; Freddie Farmer; Jim Fitzgerald; Nick Fornoro; Alton Haddock; Jim Hendrickson; Joe Hines Jr.; Willard Holt; Chuck Housley; Augie Howerton; John Jennings; Don Johns; Stuart Joyce; Raymond Lewis; Dutch Munsinger; Charles Muscatel; Don Patton; Bill Polich; Frank Price; Leo Ray; Jim Rhoades; Fred Russell; Jerry Smith; Joe Sommers; Lyle Stelter; Don Stives; Gene Tapia; Fred Thompson; Bob Tyrell; Al Wagoner; Ken Warmington (13)

1353. Leo Beiethaupt; Bob Bondurant; Al Bonnell; Bud Boone; Crash Bond; Bill Cheesbourg; Obie Chupp; Bill Cintia; Fuzzy Clifton; Bill Cook; Pappy Crane; Ralph Dutton; Joy Fair; Dick Fellows; Bill Ferrier; Bob Finale; Al Grinnan; Jerry Groh; Dick Hallock; Curley Hatfield; Jim Heath; Marvin Heinis; Cliff Hill; Harland Holmes; Don Israel; Bill Jennings; Bill Jones; Bob Kosiski; George Lewis; Jim Little; Johnny Mock; Elmer Musclow; Joe Nagle; Harry Scott; Sam Speers; Don Strain; Bill Sullivan; Nolan Swift; Herb Trimble; Van Van Wey; Doug Wheeler; Dale Williams; Gifford Wood; Cecil Wray; Ernie Yorton (12)

1398. Will Albright; Roy Bentley; Bill Boldt; Don Branson; Bill Braun; Lynn Carroll; Walt Carver; Bill Cleveland; Fred Cole; Bud Crothers; Reitzel Darner; Sam DiRusso; Huey Dunn; Bud Erb; Len Fanelli; Al Funderburk; Jim Harris; Allen Heath; Claude Holliday; Bob Kennedy II; John Krebs; Tommy Lane; Ted Lee; Albert Lemieux; Keith Lucas; Mike Magill; Jack Marlin; Gary Mathieson; Billy Minter; Burrhead Nantz; Ken Pace; Ellis Pearce; Dean Pelton; Ralph Roberts; Don Rogala; Jim Roland; Buzzy Reutimann; Mike Saathoff; Don Schissler; Charlie Scott; Scott Sharp; Sandy Slack; Ralph Smith; Bob Stanclift; Gene Stokes; Bill Taylor; Johnny Thompson; John Walker; Jimmy Watson; Dick Whalen; Herschel White (11)

1449. Reggie Ausmus; Bob Beck; Bill Bennett; Bruce Blodgett; Pete Boland; Tex Brooks; Hully Bunn; Clarence Burris; Sam Colvin; Chuck Daigh; Joe Deloach; Jim Derhaag; Ernie Derr; Bob Esposito; Wade Fields; John Fite; George Fleming; Tom Francis; Don Gray; Jack Hart; Jake Hatcher; Gary Johnson; Jerry Johnson; Bill Kimmel; Clare Lawicki; Bill Lillenthal; Gene Lovelace; Bill Majot; Bill Mann; Harold Mays; Neil McDonald; Tommy Melvin; Al Metz; Charlie Miller; Dave Mote; Gibb Orr; Harold Painter; Cotton Priddy; Mickey Rorer; John Ross; Robin Schildnecht; Bob Seharns; Eddie Sheeler; John W. Smith; Ray Springer; Jerry Sisco; Len Sutton; Don Taylor; Bill Thurber; Bill Tuten; Tom Usry; Bud Vaughn; Sam Waldrop; Mitch Walker; J.C. White (10)

1504. Thomas Aiken; Chuck Akerblade; Bill Barker; Lee Roy Carrigg; Bob Collins; Vince Cougineri; Hugh Darragh; Mal Delometer; Jack Deniston; Frank Edwards; J.D. Edwards; James Ellis; Curtis Estes; Ed Fiola; Ed Flemke; Dudley Froy; Homer Galloway; J.W. Gentry; Jimmy Griggs; Red Harrelson; Barney Hatchell; Fran Jischke; Lou Johnson; Owen Jones; Frank Katucka; Red Knuter; Larry LeMay; Jim Lamport; Dawson Lechlider; Bobby Lee; Leon Lundy; Paul Magee; Pee Wee Martin; Sam Massey; Bill McDonald; Steve McGrath; Harold Morese; Chuck Neale; Wayne Niedecken; Sam Rider; Hal Ruyle; Red Ryder; Dick Sanford; Ken Seibel; Ralph Sheeler; Bob Slensby; Jack Smith II; Robert Sprague; Willard Starney; Fred Starr; Jim Stewart; Joe Sykes; Al Tasnady; Hildrey Thomas; Ray Throckmorton; Paul Wensink; Buster Whaley; Baldy Wilson; John Winger; Bailey Wynkoop; Jack Zink (9)

1565. Eddie Adams; Fuzzy Anderson; Tommy Andrews; Jim Baker; Russell Bennett; Frank Boylan; Dick Carter; George Cavana; George Combs; Jim Cramblitt; Jack Cumiford; Roxy Dancy; Benny DeRosier; Oliver Dial; Al Disney; Niles Gage; Bud Gardner; Shorty Gibbs; Wally Gore; Herb Gott; Neil Haight; Jack Harrison; Rick Henderson; Fred Hill; Bob Hogle; Bob Hundley; Joe Jernigan; Ed Jordan; Frank Keller; Al Kent; Buddy Krebs; Roland LaRue; Marion Leech; Ed Lenz; Frank Matthews; Jim Mayes; John McDaniel; Allen McMillion; Jack Mulrain; Stan Noble; Bobby Ore; Tom Raley; Cliff Roberts; Bob Sampson; August Sand; Lucky Sawyer; Bob Schwingle; FiFi Scott; Harry Sents; James Shields; Sam Smith; Samuel Smith; Frank Stutts; Frank Thompson; Chet Thompson; Hank Tillman; John Torrese; Hank Trice; Jack Tykarski; Don Vershure; Don Welch; Chub Williams; Harold Wright (8)

1628. Olin Allen; Pete Arnold; Bud Bennett; Leo Bergeron; Fred Boles; Bobby Booth; Jim Bossic; Mike Brown; Johnny Clements; Tommy Coates; Leland Colvin Jr.; Jim Conway; Smokey Cook; Steve Dabb;

Clayton Danello; F.L. Denney; Billy Fritts; Nick Garin; Russ Gemberling; Wayne Gillette; Don Glass; Bill Greever; Buzz Gregory; Al Hager; Jimmy Hailey; Bill Hammersley; Charles Hardiman; Gene Holcomb; Zane Howell; Jake Jacobs; Squirt Johns; Jim Lacy; Hank Lee; Don McLeish; Chuck Mesler; Barney Oldfield; Lee Parris; Goldie Parsons; Frank Powell; Paul Radford; Ken Reeder; Walt Regan; Hassell Reid; Robbie Robinson; Buster Sexton; Frank Smith; Snuffy Smith; Tony Spanos; H.F. Stickleather; Ruben Thrash; Red Untiedt; Dick Vermillion; Harold Wilcox; Doug Wimpy; Whitey Worton (7)

1683. Jack Austin; Gordon Bishop; Bill Bonner; Maudis Brissette; Willard Brooks; Bob Carpenter; Jack Culpepper; Rick DeLewis; Zeke DeRose; Art Dugan; Frank Douglas; Mike Ernest; Bill Galdarisi; Bobby Gerhart; Bob Gould; Stew Hayes; Don Hildreth; Charlie Hill; Morris Hill; Charlie Hoff; Elgin Holmes; Hop Holmes; Fred Hunt; Bill James; James Jones; John Lansaw; Cecil Lassiter; Bill Latham; Leonard Lawrence; Doc Lee; Bill Lone; John Manning; Dick Martin; Buck Mason; V.E. Miller; Johnny Nave; Jess Nelson; Chick Norris; Don Ostendorf; Mike Page; Art Plas; Al Pombo; Don Price; Leo Richards; Bud Rinaldo; Hank Russ; Don Satterfield; Rick Simon; Leland Sewell; Al Stearn; Ken Taylor; Ted Tedrow; Billy Tibbett; Don Tomberlin; Marshall Weatherly; Phil Wendt; Bob Whitmire; Bill Woolkin; Dennis Zimmerman (6)

1742. Bob Anderson; Roger Baldwin; Andy Biddle; Gene Blackburn; Victor Brenzelli; Mason Bright; Jerry Burnett; Paul Bumhaver; Wally Campbell; Don Carr; Mario Caruso; Charles Causey; Paul Clark; Phil Demola; Bud Diamond; Tom Drake; Bubba Farr; Jim Fox; Gene Goodman; Clyde Goons; Bob Greer; Jim Hart; Ted Hauser; Gil Hearne; Jeff Hooker; Lee Humphers; Bob Hurt; Charles Kleber; Max King; Sandy Lynch; Larry Lyndstrom; Larry Marx; Art McBurney; Stan Parnell; Gene Roberts; Frank Ropp; Jim Russell; Bill Schade; Frank Smith II; Ruel Smith; Paul Stanley; Frank Tanner; Rod Turcott; Billy Vee; Bob Walters; David Warren; Charles Weidler; Bob Williams; Bob Wilson (5)

1791. Russell Armentrout; Al Bolinger; Rodney Bruce; Joe Carver; Don Cecchini; Herb Craig; Frank Dagavar; Geoffrey Dessault; Tony DeStafano; Al Farmer; Curt Foss; Wally Gervais; Dick Girvin; Matt Gowan; Walt Hartman; Jack Hauher; Dick Jennette; H.R. Kahl; Gus Linder; Ken Love; Glenn Luce; Lyle Matlock; T.R. Miller; Henry Montgomery; Jack O'Brien; Arthur Page; Sam Pearson; B.E. Renfro; Jack Richardson; Jim Ross; Herbert Scott; Wimpy Sipple; Cy Spencer; Rod Therrian; Marv Thorpe; Chuck Tombs; Pete Toth; Charles Triplett; Dick Turcott; Eli Vukovich; Dick Watson; Fred Weichman; Jim Wesley; Chet Williams; Jack Williams; Bob Wood (4)

1837. Nix Beard; Joe Bellinato; Ronnie Bristow; Cannonball Brown; Ann Bunselmeyer; Bob Carroll; Jim Carrusso; Hank Carruthers; Bill Deakin; O.A. Dean; Bill Delaney; Red Dowdy; Doug Duvall; Bun Emery; Jim Ewing; Johnny Frank; Bud Geiselman; Gene Glover; Lewis Hawkins; Skimp Hersey; Bob Jeffries; Hubert Johnson; Ken Kiser; Joe Kusler; Nick Lari; Herb Legg; Louis Luther; Jack McClure; Herk Moak; Ronny Myers; Keith Olson; Marian Pagan; Tony Pierce; Woody Richmond; Bob Roberts; Dan Rush; Lee Schmidt; Garland Smith; John Smith; Red Tomlinson; Cliff Tyler; Jerome Warren; Ernie Weidler; Vernon West; Keith Wilkinson; Paul Wilson; Ted Wright; Smokey Yunick (3)

1886. Ray Atkinson; Ray Baxter; Joe Bossard; Bill Burton; John Capps; Chauncey Christ; Danny Curley; Gene Darragh; Dick Denise; John Erickson; Bill Faulkner; Herb Gibson; Fred Goad; Ken Goudermoat; Junie Gough; Dick Hagey; Art Hammond; Boyce Hildreth; Herb Hill; Jimmy Ingram; Frank Kapack; Pete Kelly; Al King; Ralph Lyden; Eddie McDonald; Earl Mosbach; Jim Mundy; Harold Nash; Al Neves; Larry Odo; Bill Parks; Paul Phipps; Jug Pierce; Hank Pollard; Macon Powers; Oren Prosser; Buddy Ragsdale; Ken Rauch; Ken Rice; Gene Rose; Rusty Rushton; Bobby Schuyler; Wallace Simpson; Bob Smith; Charles Stark; Jim Thompson; Jack Wade; Charles Williamson; Andy Wilson (2)

1935. Buck Clardy; George Cole; Bob Coleman; Joe Cote; Ray Davis; Roy

Forsythe; Steve Garrett; Richard Hancock; Marshall Harless; Bill Hazel; Lester Hicks; Joe Holder; Henry Jones; Don Kent; Morris Lamb; Irving Leitch; Herb Lewis; Virgil Martin; John McGorrien; Jim McLain; John Montgangelo; Nick Nicolette; Tom Nundy; Hank Ribet; Roscoe Rann; Joe Roletto; Bob Scott; Ace Shearer; Ed Spencer; Richard Spittle; Layman Utsman; Pete Vail; Russ Whitman; J.C. Yarborough (1)

Annual Performance Index Leaders

1949—Red Byron
1950—Lee Petty
1951—Fonty Flock
1952—Tim Flock
1953—Herb Thomas
1954—Lee Petty
1955—Tim Flock
1956—Buck Baker
1957—Buck Baker
1958—Lee Petty
1959—Lee Petty
1960—Rex White
1961—Rex White
1962—Joe Weatherly
1963—Richard Petty
1964—Richard Petty
1965—Ned Jarrett
1966—David Pearson
1967—Richard Petty
1968—David Pearson
1969—David Pearson
1970—Bobby Isaac
1971—Richard Petty
1972—Bobby Allison
1973—Cale Yarborough
1974—Richard Petty
1975—Richard Petty
1976—Cale Yarborough
1977—Cale Yarborough
1978—Cale Yarborough
1979—Richard Petty
1980—Dale Earnhardt
1981—Darrell Waltrip
1982—Darrell Waltrip
1983—Bobby Allison
1984—Bill Elliott
1985—Bill Elliott
1986—Dale Earnhardt
1987—Dale Earnhardt
1988—Bill Elliott
1989—Dale Earnhardt
1990—Mark Martin
1991—Ricky Rudd
1992—Bill Elliott
1993—Dale Earnhardt
1994—Dale Earnhardt
1995—Dale Earnhardt
1996—Jeff Gordon
1997—Jeff Gordon
1998—Jeff Gordon
1999—Dale Jarrett

Performance Index Records

Seasons With a Rating of 1,300 or More
1. Richard Petty (1)

Seasons With a Rating of 1,200 or More
1. Richard Petty (1)

Seasons With a Rating of 1,100 or More
1. Richard Petty (2)
2. Ned Jarrett; David Pearson (1)

Seasons With a Rating of 1,000 or More
1. Richard Petty (5)
2. David Pearson (3)
3. Ned Jarrett (2)
4. Bobby Allison; Jeff Gordon; Bobby Isaac; Joe Weatherly (1)

Seasons With a Rating of 900 or More
1. Richard Petty (10)
2. David Pearson (4)
3. Bobby Allison; James Hylton (3)
5. Bobby Isaac; Ned Jarrett (2)
7. Jeff Gordon; Dick Hutcherson; Dale Jarrett; Bobby Labonte; Joe Weatherly; Cale Yarborough (1)

Seasons With a Rating of 800 or More
1. Richard Petty (12)
2. Bobby Allison; Ned Jarrett (5)
4. Dale Earnhardt; James Hylton; Mark Martin; David Pearson (4)
8. Jeff Gordon; Bobby Isaac; Darrell Waltrip; Cale Yarborough (3)
12. Dale Jarrett; Joe Weatherly; Rex White (2)
15. Buck Baker; Jeff Burton; Neil Castles; Bill Elliott; Cecil Gordon; Dick Hutcherson; Bobby Labonte; Lee Petty; Tony Stewart; Rusty Wallace (1)

Seasons With a Rating of 700 or More
1. Richard Petty (14)
2. Dale Earnhardt (13)
3. Bobby Allison (9)
4. Darrell Waltrip (7)
5. James Hylton; Mark Martin; Cale Yarborough (6)
8. Bill Elliott; Jeff Gordon; Ned Jarrett; David Pearson (5)
12. Dale Jarrett; Rusty Wallace (4)
14. Jeff Burton; Bobby Isaac; Terry Labonte; Benny Parsons (3)
18. Buck Baker; Lee Petty; Joe Weatherly; Rex White (2)
22. Davey Allison; Neil Castles; Curtis Crider; Tim Flock; Harry Gant; Cecil Gordon; Dick Hutcherson; Bobby Labonte; Dave Marcis; Sterling Marlin; Tim Richmond; Ricky Rudd; Jack Smith; Tony Stewart; Herb Thomas; Lee Roy Yarbrough; Emanuel Zervakis (1)

Seasons With a Rating of 600 or More
1. Richard Petty (18)
2. Dale Earnhardt (14)
3. Bill Elliott; Darrell Waltrip (11)
5. Bobby Allison; Terry Labonte; Mark Martin (10)
8. Rusty Wallace (9)
9. James Hylton (8)
10. Benny Parsons; Cale Yarborough (7)
12. Ned Jarrett; Lee Petty (6)
14. Buck Baker; Harry Gant; Jeff Gordon; Dale Jarrett; David Pearson; Ricky Rudd (5)
20. Bobby Isaac (4)
21. Jeff Burton; Bobby Labonte; Elmo Langley; Ken Schrader; John Sears; Jabe Thomas; Rex White (3)

Seasons With a Rating of 500 or More
1. Richard Petty (25)
2. Dale Earnhardt (20)
3. Bobby Allison; Terry Labonte (16)
5. Bill Elliott; Ricky Rudd; Darrell Waltrip (14)
8. Rusty Wallace (12)
9. Mark Martin (11)
10. Benny Parsons; David Pearson (10)
12. Buck Baker; Harry Gant; James Hylton; Lee Petty; Cale Yarborough (9)
17. Sterling Marlin; Ken Schrader (7)
19. Geoff Bodine; Jeff Gordon; Ned Jarrett; Elmo Langley; Kyle Petty; Morgan Shepherd (6)
25. Ernie Irvan; Dale Jarrett; Dave Marcis (5)
28. Buddy Arrington; Buddy Baker; Neil Bonnett; Jeff Burton; Cecil Gordon; Bobby Isaac; Bobby Labonte; Wendell Scott; John Sears; Herb Thomas (4)
38. Davey Allison; Dick Brooks; Neil Castles; Richard Childress; Jim Paschal; Jabe Thomas; Michael Waltrip; Joe Weatherly; Rex White (3)
47. Brett Bodine; Tim Flock; Bobby Hamilton; Dick Hutcherson; Junior Johnson; Alan Kulwicki; Jeremy Mayfield; Marvin Panch; Jim Pardue; Lennie Pond; Dick Rathmann; Tim Richmond; Jody Ridley; Jack Smith; Lake Speed; Speedy Thompson (2)
63. John Andretti; Ron Bouchard; Ward Burton; Bill Champion; Curtis Crider; Bob Derrington; Fonty Flock; Henley Gray; Bobby Hillin Jr.; Fred Lorenzen; Clyde Lynn; Joe Millikan; Ted Musgrave; Cotton Owens; Phil Parsons; J.T. Putney; Fireball Roberts; Mike Skinner; G.C. Spencer; Jimmy Spencer; Tony Stewart; Larry Thomas; E.J. Trivette; Billy Wade; Lee Roy Yarbrough; Emanuel Zervakis (1)

Seasons With a Rating of 400 or More
1. Richard Petty (26)
2. Bobby Allison (21)
3. Dale Earnhardt; Terry Labonte; Darrell Waltrip (20)
6. Ricky Rudd (18)
7. Bill Elliott (16)
8. Rusty Wallace (15)
9. David Pearson (14)
10. Geoff Bodine; James Hylton; Ken Schrader; Cale Yarborough (13)
14. Harry Gant; Mark Martin; Benny Parsons (12)
17. Buck Baker; Buddy Baker; Sterling Marlin (11)
20. Dave Marcis (10)
21. Kyle Petty; Lee Petty; Morgan Shepherd (9)
24. Neil Bonnett; Ernie Irvan; Dale Jarrett; Elmo Langley; Wendell Scott (8)
29. Jeff Gordon (7)
30. Davey Allison; Buddy Arrington; Neil Castles; Richard Childress; Cecil Gordon; Ned Jarrett; Junior Johnson; Bobby Labonte; Jim Paschal; John Sears (6)
40. Dick Brooks; Bobby Hamilton; Ted Musgrave; Tim Richmond; Herb Thomas; Michael Waltrip (5)
46. Ron Bouchard; Jeff Burton; Bobby Isaac; Fireball Roberts; Jabe Thomas; Rex White (4)

52. Brett Bodine; Curtis Crider; Fonty Flock; Tim Flock; Bobby Hillin Jr.; Alan Kulwicki; Jeremy Mayfield; J.D. McDuffie; Marvin Panch; Jim Pardue; Joe Ruttman; Jack Smith; Jimmy Spencer; Speedy Thompson; Joe Weatherly; Lee Roy Yarbrough (3)
68. John Andretti; Ben Arnold; Walter Ballard; Herman Beam; Derrike Cope; Darel Dieringer; Pete Hamilton; Friday Hassler; Dick Hutcherson; Clyde Lynn; Phil Parsons; Lennie Pond; J.T. Putney; Dick Rathmann; Jody Ridley; Lake Speed; D.K. Ulrich; Bob Welborn (2)
86. Johnny Allen; Donnie Allison; Johnny Benson Jr.; Ward Burton; Bill Champion; Tom Cox; Ricky Craven; Bob Derrington; Joe Eubanks; Paul Goldsmith; Henley Gray; Bruce Hill; Kenny Irwin; Chad Little; Fred Lorenzen; Jimmy Means; Joe Millikan; Ralph Moody; Billy Myers; Cotton Owens; Steve Park; Shorty Rollins; Earl Ross; Bill Seifert; David Sisco; Mike Skinner; G.C. Spencer; Tony Stewart; Hut Stricklin; Larry Thomas; E.J. Trivette; Roy Tyner; Billy Wade; Frank Warren; Rick Wilson; Emanuel Zervakis (1)

Seasons With a Rating of 300 or More

1. Richard Petty (28)
2. Bobby Allison; Buddy Baker; Darrell Waltrip (22)
5. Dale Earnhardt; Terry Labonte (21)
7. Ricky Rudd (19)
8. Bill Elliott (18)
9. Geoff Bodine; Rusty Wallace (16)
11. Dave Marcis; Benny Parsons; Kyle Petty; Cale Yarborough (15)
15. James Hylton; David Pearson; Ken Schrader (14)
18. Buck Baker; Sterling Marlin; Mark Martin; Morgan Shepherd (13)
22. Harry Gant (12)
23. Buddy Arrington; Dick Brooks; Michael Waltrip (11)
26. Neil Bonnett; Dale Jarrett; J.D. McDuffie; Lee Petty (10)
30. Cecil Gordon; Elmo Langley; Jim Paschal; Wendell Scott (9)
34. Ernie Irvan; Junior Johnson (8)
36. Davey Allison; Neil Castles; Richard Childress; Jeff Gordon; Bobby Hillin Jr.; Alan Kulwicki; Bobby Labonte (7)
43. Donnie Allison; Brett Bodine; Bobby Hamilton; Bobby Isaac; Ned Jarrett; Ted Musgrave; Tim Richmond; John Sears; Herb Thomas; Jabe Thomas; Rex White (6)
54. Walter Ballard; Ron Bouchard; Tim Flock; Fireball Roberts; Lake Speed; Frank Warren (5)
60. Jeff Burton; Ward Burton; Bill Champion; Derrike Cope; Darel Dieringer; Fonty Flock; Henley Gray; Fred Lorenzen; Rick Mast; Marvin Panch; Jim Pardue; Joe Ruttman; David Sisco; Jack Smith; G.C. Spencer; Jimmy Spencer; Lee Roy Yarbrough (4)
77. John Andretti; Curtis Crider; Paul Goldsmith; Tiny Lund; Clyde Lynn; Jeremy Mayfield; Jimmy Means; Cotton Owens; Phil Parsons; Lennie Pond; Dick Rathmann; Jody Ridley; Bill Seifert; Larry Thomas; Speedy Thompson; D.K. Ulrich; Joe Weatherly; Bob Welborn (3)
95. Johnny Allen; Ben Arnold; Herman Beam; Johnny Benson Jr.; Doug Cooper; Ricky Craven; Wally Dallenbach Jr.; Tommy Gale; Charlie Glotzbach; Pete Hamilton; Friday Hassler; Dick Hutcherson; Paul Lewis; Chad Little; Skip Manning; Coo Coo Marlin; Joe Millikan; Ed Negre; J.T. Putney; Tighe Scott; Mike Skinner; Hut Stricklin; Dick Trickle; E.J. Trivette; Roy Tyner; Billy Wade (2)
121. L.D. Austin; Todd Bodine; Trevor Boys; Tom Cox; Dean Dalton; Bill Dennis; Bob Derrington; Joe Eubanks; George Green; Jimmy Hensley; Bruce Hill; Kenny Irwin; Tommy Irwin; Bobby Johns; Brownie King; Jimmie Lewallen; Dick May; Hershel McGriff; Ralph Moody; Billy Myers; Eddie Pagan; Steve Park; Tom Pistone; Shorty Rollins; Earl Ross; Eddie Skinner; Sam Sommers; Tony Stewart; Kenny Wallace; Bobby Wawak; Raymond Williams; Rick Wilson; Emanuel Zervakis (1)

Seasons With a Rating of 200 or More

1. Richard Petty (32)
2. Buddy Baker; Darrell Waltrip (25)
4. Bobby Allison (23)
5. Dave Marcis (22)
6. Dale Earnhardt; Bill Elliott; Terry Labonte; Ricky Rudd; Cale Yarborough (21)
11. David Pearson; Kyle Petty (19)
13. Benny Parsons; Geoff Bodine (18)
15. Buddy Arrington; James Hylton; J.D. McDuffie; Rusty Wallace (16)
19. Buck Baker; Ken Schrader (15)
21. Harry Gant; Sterling Marlin; Morgan Shepherd; Michael Waltrip (14)
25. Neil Bonnett; Mark Martin; Lake Speed (13)
28. Dick Brooks; Cecil Gordon; Dale Jarrett (12)
31. Donnie Allison; Elmo Langley; Jim Paschal; Lee Petty (11)
35. Ernie Irvan; Wendell Scott; G.C. Spencer; Frank Warren (10)
39. Brett Bodine; Neil Castles; Richard Childress; Bobby Isaac; Junior Johnson; Tiny Lund; Jimmy Means; Jimmy Spencer (9)
47. Derrike Cope; Bobby Hamilton; Bobby Hillin Jr.; Rick Mast; Ted Musgrave; Hut Stricklin (8)
53. Davey Allison; Jeff Gordon; Henley Gray; Ned Jarrett; Alan Kulwicki; Bobby Labonte; Fred Lorenzen; Marvin Panch; Phil Parsons; Joe Ruttman; John Sears; Jack Smith; Jabe Thomas; Rex White (7)
67. Darel Dieringer; Coo Coo Marlin; Lennie Pond; Tim Richmond; Fireball Roberts; Herb Thomas; D.K. Ulrich; Joe Weatherly; Bob Welborn (6)
76. John Andretti; L.D. Austin; Walter Ballard; Ron Bouchard; Jeff Burton; Ward Burton; Tim Flock; Tommy Gale; Jeremy Mayfield; Joe Nemechek; Jim Pardue; Bill Seifert; Dick Trickle; Kenny Wallace; Rick Wilson; Lee Roy Yarbrough (5)
92. Johnny Allen; Ben Arnold; Herman Beam; Johnny Benson Jr.; Bill Champion; Curtis Crider; Wally Dallenbach Jr.; Joe Eubanks; Fonty Flock; Charlie Glotzbach; Friday Hassler; Ed Negre; J.T. Putney; David Sisco; Speedy Thompson (4)
107. Earl Brooks; Ricky Craven; Paul Goldsmith; Steve Grissom; Dick Hutcherson; Jimmie Lewallen; Paul Lewis; Chad Little; Clyde Lynn; Skip Manning; Cotton Owens; Dick Rathmann; Jody Ridley; Tighe Scott; Nelson Stacy; Larry Thomas; Roy Tyner (3)
124. Trevor Boys; Doug Cooper; Larry Frank; Joe Frasson; Roger Hamby; Pete Hamilton; Kenny Irwin; Tommy Irwin; Bobby Johns; Kevin Lepage; Dick May; Roy Mayne; Sam McQuagg; Joe Millikan; Billy Myers; Eddie Pagan; Jim Reed; Charlie Roberts; Jackie Rogers; Greg Sacks; Mike Skinner; Gwyn Staley; Ronnie Thomas; E.J. Trivette; Curtis Turner; Billy Wade; Doug Yates; Emanuel Zervakis (2)
152. Carl Adams; Grant Adcox; Mike Alexander; Bill Amick; Jack Anderson; Bob Barron; Dick Beaty; Tony Bettenhausen Jr.; Terry Bivins; Bill Blair; Todd Bodine; Ken Bouchard; Richard Brickhouse; Bob Burcham; Tom Cox; Dean Dalton; Bill Dennis; Bob Derrington; Hoss Ellington; Stick Elliott; Tommy Ellis; A.J. Foyt; George Green; Janet Guthrie; Ferrel Harris; Jimmy Helms; Jimmy Hensley; Ed Hessert; Bruce Hill; Jim Hurtubise; Bruce Jacobi; Joe Lee Johnson; Slick Johnson; Ron Keselowski; Brownie King; Ralph Liguori; Larry Manning; Hershel McGriff; Worth McMillion; Butch Miller; Ralph Moody; Bud Moore; Frank Mundy; Richie Panch; Steve Park; Dick Passwater; Larry Pearson; Tom Pistone; Robert Pressley; Bill Rexford; Shorty Rollins; Earl Ross; Elliott Sadler; Eddie Skinner; Larry Smith; Sam Sommers; Tony Stewart; Marshall Teague; Dave Terrell; Donald Thomas; Mike Wallace; Blackie Watt; Bobby Wawak; Raymond Williams; Glen Wood; Buddy Young (1)

Seasons With a Rating of 100 or More

1. Richard Petty (34)
2. Buddy Baker (28)
3. Darrell Waltrip (27)
4. Dave Marcis; Cale Yarborough (25)
6. Bobby Allison (24)
7. Bill Elliott; David Pearson; Ricky Rudd (23)
10. Buddy Arrington; Dale Earnhardt (22)
12. Terry Labonte; Kyle Petty (21)
14. Benny Parsons (20)
15. Buck Baker; Geoff Bodine; J.D. McDuffie (18)
18. James Hylton; Sterling Marlin; Morgan Shepherd (17)
21. Harry Gant; Lake Speed; Rusty Wallace (16)
24. Jim Paschal; Ken Schrader (15)
26. Donnie Allison; Neil Bonnett; Elmo Langley; Mark Martin; G.C. Spencer; Michael Waltrip (14)
32. Dick Brooks; Cecil Gordon; Dale Jarrett; Tiny Lund; Lennie Pond; Frank Warren (13)
38. Brett Bodine; Bobby Hillin Jr.; Jimmy Means; Marvin Panch (12)
42. Neil Castles; Ernie Irvan; Lee Petty; Wendell Scott; Jimmy Spencer (11)
47. Henley Gray; Bobby Isaac; Fred Lorenzen; Rick Mast; Fireball Roberts; Dick Trickle; Curtis Turner (10)
54. Richard Childress; Derrike Cope; Bobby Hamilton; Junior Johnson; Ted Musgrave; Hut Stricklin; Rex White; Lee Roy Yarbrough (9)
62. Ned Jarrett; Ed Negre; Joe Ruttman; Jack Smith; Roy Tyner; D.K. Ulrich; Joe Weatherly; Bob Welborn (8)
70. Davey Allison; Darel Dieringer; Tommy Gale; Paul Goldsmith; Jeff Gordon; Alan Kulwicki; Bobby Labonte; Coo Coo Marlin; Dick May; Roy Mayne; Phil Parsons; Tim Richmond; Greg Sacks; John Sears; Herb Thomas; Jabe Thomas; Speedy Thompson; Rick Wilson (7)
88. Johnny Allen; John Andretti; Walter Ballard; Ron Bouchard; Jeff Burton; Bill Champion; Wally Dallenbach Jr.; Joe Eubanks; Tim Flock; Joe Frasson; Charlie Glotzbach; Fred Harb; Bobby Johns; Joe Nemechek; Cotton Owens; Jody Ridley; Bill Seifert; Kenny Wallace (6)
106. L.D. Austin; Herman Beam; Bill Blair; Earl Brooks; Ward Burton; Curtis Crider; Friday Hassler; Bruce Hill; Tommy Irwin; Jimmie Lewallen; Paul Lewis; Chad Little; Jeremy Mayfield; Jim Pardue; Dick Rathmann; Jim Reed; David Sisco; Ronnie Thomas; Jim Vandiver (5)
125. Ben Arnold; Johnny Benson Jr.; Todd Bodine; Doug Cooper; Dean Dalton; Fonty Flock; A.J. Foyt; Larry Frank; Steve Grissom; Clyde Lynn; Skip Manning; Joe Millikan; Tom Pistone; Robert Pressley; J.T. Putney; Wayne Smith; Gober Sosebee; Larry Thomas; E.J. Trivette; Raymond Williams (4)
145. Grant Adcox; Mike Alexander; Earl Balmer; Bunkie Blackburn; Ricky Craven; Ray Elder; Stick Elliott; George Green; Pete Hamilton; Jimmy Hensley; Dick Hutcherson; Worth McMillion; Sam McQuagg; Bud Moore; Lloyd Moore; Eddie Pagan; Blackie Pitt; Tighe Scott; Mike Skinner; Nelson Stacy; Gwyn Staley; Don Tarr; Donald Thomas; Bobby Wawak; Glen Wood; Doug Yates; Emanuel Zervakis (3)
172. Bill Amick; Johnny Beauchamp; Rich Bickle; Trevor Boys; Richard Brickhouse; Richard D. Brown; Herschel Buchanan; Billy Carden; Lloyd Dane; Bill Dennis; Bob Derrington; Ray Duhigg; Clarence DeZalia; Clark Dwyer; Ralph Earnhardt; Tommy Ellis; David Green; Dan Gurney; Roger Hamby; Ferrel Harris; Butch Hartman; Jimmy Helms; Paul Dean Holt; Kenny Irwin; Joe Lee Johnson; Slick Johnson; Bobby Keck; Ron Keselowski; Brownie King; Kevin Lepage; Ralph Liguori; Jimmy Massey; Banjo Matthews; Hershel McGriff; Ralph Moody; Frank Mundy; Billy Myers; Gary B. Myers; Rick Newsom; Richie Panch; Larry Pearson; Baxter Price; Charlie Roberts; Jackie Rogers; Jim Sauter; Buddy Shuman; Larry Smith; Ramo Stott; Dave Terrell; Billy Wade; Mike Wallace (2)
223. Marv Acton; Carl Adams; Jack Anderson; John Anderson; Mario Andretti; H.B. Bailey; Stan Barrett; Bob Barron; Larry Baumel; Dick Beaty; Gary Bettenhausen; Tony Bettenhausen Jr.; Don Biederman; Eddie Bierschwale; Terry Bivins; Gene Black; David Ray Boggs; Ken Bouchard; Chuck Bown; Perk Brown; Laird Bruner; Darrell Bryant; Bob Burcham; Bob Burdick; Scotty Cain; Ted Chamberlain; Neil Cole; Rodney Combs; Gene Comstock; Doug Cox; Tom Cox; Joel Davis; George Davis; Dick Dixon; John Dodd Jr.; Fred Dove; Bob Duell; Gerald Duke; George Dunn; Sonny Easley; Hoss Ellington; Erick Erickson; Herb Estes; Jim Fiebelkorn; Lou Figaro; Bob Flock; Jimmy Florian; George Follmer; Elliott Forbes-Robinson; Walson Gardner; Dick Getty; Mickey Gibbs; Janet Guthrie; Johnny Halford; Harold Hardesty; Harvey Henderson; Larry Hess; Ed Hessert; Doug Heveron; Elton Hildreth; Gene Hobby; Al Holbert; Jim Hurtubise; Sonny Hutchins; Bruce Jacobi; Dick M. Johnson; Possum Jones; Reds Kagle; Al Keller; John Kieper; Bud King; Shep Langdon; Harry Leake; Dick Linder; Ed Livingston; Dave MacDonald; Chuck Mahoney; Larry Manning; Bill McMahan; Chuck Meekins; Stan Meserve; Joe Mihalic; Butch Miller; Doug Moore; Rob Moroso; Jerry Nadeau; Whitey Norman; Clyde Palmer; Steve Park; Vic Parsons; Dick Passwater; Jack Pennington; Bill Poor; Billy Rafter; Ken Ragan; Wilbur Rakestraw; Lee Reitzel; Bill Rexford; Shorty Rollins; Earl Ross; Ken Rush; Johnny Rutherford; Troy Ruttman; Terry Ryan; Elliott Sadler; Connie Saylor; Frankie Schneider; George Seeger; Bill Shirey; Gene Simpson; Eddie Skinner; Slick Smith; Bill Snowden; John Soares; Sam Sommers; Junior Spencer; Tony Stewart; Bub Strickler; Marshall Teague; Hank Thomas; Maynard Troyer; Donald Tucker; John Utsman; Sherman Utsman; Bob Walden; Al Watkins; Blackie Watt; Don White; Reb Wickersham; Dink Widenhouse; Johnny Wynn; Buddy Young (1)

Consecutive Seasons With a Rating of 1,000 Or More

1. Richard Petty	2	(1963-64)
Ned Jarrett	2	(1964-65)
David Pearson	2	(1968-69)

Consecutive Seasons With a Rating of 900 or More

1. Richard Petty	6	(1967-72)
2. Richard Petty	3	(1962-64)
James Hylton	3	(1969-71)
Bobby Allison	3	(1970-72)
5. Ned Jarrett	2	(1964-65)
David Pearson	2	(1968-69)
Bobby Isaac	2	(1969-70)

Consecutive Seasons With a Rating of 800 or More

1. Richard Petty	6	(1967-72)
2. Ned Jarrett	5	(1961-65)
3. Richard Petty	3	(1962-64)
Bobby Isaac	3	(1968-70)
James Hylton	3	(1969-71)
Bobby Allison	3	(1970-72)
Jeff Gordon	3	(1996-98)
Mark Martin	3	(1997-99)
9. Rex White	2	(1960-61)
Joe Weatherly	2	(1962-63)
David Pearson	2	(1968-69)
Richard Petty	2	(1974-75)
Cale Yarborough	2	(1977-78)
Dale Earnhardt	2	(1993-94)

Longest Streaks of Seasons With a Rating Of 700 or More

1.	Richard Petty	6	(1967-72)
	Dale Earnhardt	6	(1986-91)
3.	Ned Jarrett	5	(1961-65)
	Cale Yarborough	5	(1976-80)
	Jeff Gordon	5	(1995-99)
	Mark Martin	5	(1995-99)
7.	James Hylton	4	(1969-72)
	Richard Petty	4	(1974-77)
	Dale Jarrett	4	(1996-99)
10.	Richard Petty	3	(1962-64)
	Bobby Isaac	3	(1968-70)
	Bobby Allison	3	(1970-72)
	Benny Parsons	3	(1976-78)
	Bobby Allison	3	(1981-83)
	Darrell Waltrip	3	(1981-83)
	Bill Elliott	3	(1983-85)
	Dale Earnhardt	3	(1994-96)

Longest Streaks of Seasons With a Rating Of 600 or More

1.	Richard Petty	11	(1967-77)
2.	Bill Elliott	8	(1983-90)
	Mark Martin	8	(1992-99)
4.	James Hylton	7	(1966-72)
	Darrell Waltrip	7	(1981-87)
6.	Ned Jarrett	6	(1960-65)
	Dale Earnhardt	6	(1986-91)
8.	Benny Parsons	5	(1976-80)
	Cale Yarborough	5	(1976-80)
	Dale Earnhardt	5	(1993-97)
	Jeff Gordon	5	(1995-99)

Longest Streaks of Seasons With a Rating Of 500 or More

1.	Richard Petty	19	(1966-84)
2.	Dale Earnhardt	17	(1983-99)
3.	Bill Elliott	13	(1983-95)
	Darrell Waltrip	13	(1977-89)
5.	Mark Martin	11	(1989-99)
6.	Lee Petty	9	(1952-60)
7.	James Hylton	8	(1966-73)
	Cale Yarborough	8	(1973-80)
	Ricky Rudd	8	(1989-96)
10.	Bobby Allison	7	(1978-84)

Longest Streaks of Seasons With a Rating Of 400 or More

1.	Darrell Waltrip	20	(1975-94)
2.	Richard Petty	19	(1966-84)
3.	Ricky Rudd	17	(1981-97)
	Dale Earnhardt	17	(1983-99)
5.	Bill Elliott	14	(1982-95)
	Rusty Wallace	14	(1986-99)
7.	James Hylton	12	(1966-77)
	Bobby Allison	12	(1976-87)
	Terry Labonte	12	(1979-90)
	Mark Martin	12	(1988-99)

Longest Streaks of Seasons With a Rating Of 300 or More

1.	Bobby Allison	22	(1966-87)
	Richard Petty	22	(1966-87)
	Darrell Waltrip	22	(1974-95)
4.	Dale Earnhardt	21	(1979-99)
	Terry Labonte	21	(1979-99)
6.	Bill Elliott	18	(1982-99)
7.	Ricky Rudd	17	(1981-97)
8.	Geoff Bodine	16	(1982-97)
	Rusty Wallace	16	(1984-99)
10.	Benny Parsons	13	(1970-82)
	Sterling Marlin	13	(1987-99)
	Ken Schrader	13	(1987-99)

Longest Streaks of Seasons With a Rating Of 200 or More

1.	Richard Petty	30	(1959-88)
2.	Buddy Baker	24	(1965-88)
3.	Bobby Allison	23	(1966-88)
	Darrell Waltrip	23	(1973-95)
5.	Dave Marcis	22	(1969-90)
6.	Dale Earnhardt	21	(1979-99)
	Terry Labonte	21	(1979-99)
8.	Bill Elliott	19	(1981-99)
	Ricky Rudd	19	(1981-99)
10.	David Pearson	18	(1961-78)
	Kyle Petty	18	(1980-97)
	Geoff Bodine	18	(1982-99)

Longest Streaks of Seasons With a Rating Of 100 or More

1.	Richard Petty	34	(1959-92)
2.	Darrell Waltrip	27	(1973-99)
3.	Buddy Baker	25	(1964-88)
	Dave Marcis	25	(1968-92)
5.	Bobby Allison	24	(1965-88)
6.	Bill Elliott	23	(1977-99)
	Ricky Rudd	23	(1977-99)
8.	Dale Earnhardt	22	(1978-99)
9.	David Pearson	21	(1960-80)
	Terry Labonte	21	(1979-99)
	Kyle Petty	21	(1979-99)

No. 1 Seasons

1. Dale Earnhardt; Richard Petty (7)
3. Bill Elliott; Lee Petty; Cale Yarborough (4)
6. Jeff Gordon; David Pearson (3)
8. Bobby Allison; Buck Baker; Tim Flock; Darrell Waltrip; Rex White (2)
13. Red Byron; Fonty Flock; Bobby Isaac; Dale Jarrett; Ned Jarrett; Mark Martin; Ricky Rudd; Herb Thomas; Joe Weatherly (1)

Top-Two Seasons

1. Richard Petty (13)
2. Dale Earnhardt (9)
3. Lee Petty (7)
4. Bobby Allison; Cale Yarborough (6)
6. Bill Elliott; Darrell Waltrip (5)
8. Buck Baker; James Hylton; Ned Jarrett; Rusty Wallace (4)
12. Tim Flock; Jeff Gordon; Mark Martin; David Pearson; Herb Thomas (3)
17. Dale Jarrett; Rex White (2)
19. Davey Allison; Buddy Baker; Red Byron; Fonty Flock; Dick Hutcherson; Bobby Isaac; Bobby Labonte; Terry Labonte; Sterling Marlin; Cotton Owens; Marvin Panch; Benny Parsons; Bill Rexford; Tim Richmond; Ricky Rudd; Joe Weatherly (1)

Performance Index Records

Top-Three Seasons
1. Richard Petty (15)
2. Dale Earnhardt (10)
3. Lee Petty (9)
4. Bobby Allison; Darrell Waltrip (8)
6. Mark Martin; Cale Yarborough (7)
8. Buck Baker; Bill Elliott; James Hylton (6)
11. Ned Jarrett; David Pearson; Herb Thomas (5)
14. Jeff Gordon; Dale Jarrett; Rusty Wallace (4)
17. Tim Flock; Terry Labonte (3)
19. Davey Allison; Bobby Isaac; Dave Marcis; Benny Parsons; Speedy Thompson; Joe Weatherly; Rex White (2)
26. Buddy Baker; Bill Blair; Geoff Bodine; Neil Bonnett; Red Byron; Richard Childress; Bob Derrington; Fonty Flock; Harry Gant; Dick Hutcherson; Alan Kulwicki; Bobby Labonte; Dick Linder; Sterling Marlin; Lloyd Moore; Cotton Owens; Marvin Panch; Dick Rathmann; Bill Rexford; Tim Richmond; Jody Ridley; Fireball Roberts; Ricky Rudd; John Sears; Emanuel Zervakis (1)

Top-Four Seasons
1. Richard Petty (19)
2. Dale Earnhardt; Lee Petty (12)
4. Bobby Allison; Darrell Waltrip (9)
6. Bill Elliott; James Hylton; Mark Martin (8)
9. Buck Baker; Cale Yarborough (7)
11. Ned Jarrett; David Pearson (6)
13. Dale Jarrett; Terry Labonte; Benny Parsons; Herb Thomas; Rusty Wallace (5)
18. Jeff Gordon (4)
19. Fonty Flock; Tim Flock; Harry Gant; Bobby Isaac; Dave Marcis; Ricky Rudd (3)
25. Davey Allison; Cecil Gordon; Sterling Marlin; Dick Rathmann; Jack Smith; Speedy Thompson; Joe Weatherly; Rex White (2)
33. Buddy Baker; Bill Blair; Geoff Bodine; Neil Bonnett; Jeff Burton; Red Byron; Richard Childress; Curtis Crider; Bob Derrington; Dick Hutcherson; Junior Johnson; Alan Kulwicki; Bobby Labonte; Dick Linder; Fred Lorenzen; Lloyd Moore; Cotton Owens; Marvin Panch; Jim Paschal; Kyle Petty; Tom Pistone; Bill Rexford; Tim Richmond; Jody Ridley; Fireball Roberts; John Sears; G.C. Spencer; Tony Stewart; Bob Welborn; Emanuel Zervakis (1)

Top-Five Seasons
1. Richard Petty (20)
2. Dale Earnhardt; Lee Petty (12)
4. Darrell Waltrip (11)
5. Bobby Allison (10)
6. Buck Baker; Terry Labonte; Mark Martin (9)
9. Bill Elliott; James Hylton; Benny Parsons; David Pearson (8)
13. Rusty Wallace; Cale Yarborough (7)
15. Ned Jarrett (6)
16. Harry Gant; Dale Jarrett; Herb Thomas (5)
19. Fonty Flock; Jeff Gordon (4)
21. Jeff Burton; Tim Flock; Bobby Isaac; Junior Johnson; Dave Marcis; Dick Rathmann; Ricky Rudd; Ken Schrader; Jack Smith; Joe Weatherly; Rex White (3)
32. Davey Allison; Buddy Baker; Neil Castles; Cecil Gordon; Dick Hutcherson; Elmo Langley; Sterling Marlin; Jim Paschal; Jody Ridley; John Sears; Morgan Shepherd; Speedy Thompson (2)
44. Buddy Arrington; Bill Blair; Geoff Bodine; Neil Bonnett; Red Byron; Richard Childress; Curtis Crider; Bob Derrington; Joe Eubanks; Bob Flock; Ernie Irvan; Alan Kulwicki; Bobby Labonte; Dick Linder; Fred Lorenzen; Lloyd Moore; Frank Mundy; Cotton Owens; Marvin Panch; Kyle Petty; Tom Pistone; Lennie Pond; Bill Rexford; Tim Richmond; Fireball Roberts; Shorty Rollins; G.C. Spencer; Tony Stewart; Curtis Turner; Billy Wade; Bob Welborn; Emanuel Zervakis (1)

Top-Six Seasons
1. Richard Petty (20)
2. Dale Earnhardt (14)
3. Bobby Allison; Lee Petty; Darrell Waltrip (12)
6. Bill Elliott; Mark Martin; David Pearson (10)
9. Buck Baker; Terry Labonte; Rusty Wallace (9)
12. James Hylton; Benny Parsons (8)
14. Cale Yarborough (7)
15. Harry Gant; Ned Jarrett (6)
17. Tim Flock; Jeff Gordon; Dale Jarrett; Junior Johnson; Ricky Rudd; Herb Thomas (5)
23. Fonty Flock; Dave Marcis; Jim Paschal; Rex White (4)
27. Buddy Baker; Geoff Bodine; Jeff Burton; Neil Castles; Cecil Gordon; Bobby Isaac; Elmo Langley; Dick Rathmann; Ken Schrader; John Sears; Morgan Shepherd; Jack Smith; Speedy Thompson; Joe Weatherly (3)
41. Davey Allison; Neil Bonnett; Dick Brooks; Dick Hutcherson; Bobby Labonte; Sterling Marlin; Kyle Petty; Jody Ridley; Curtis Turner (2)
50. Buddy Arrington; Bill Blair; Red Byron; Richard Childress; Curtis Crider; Bob Derrington; Joe Eubanks; Bob Flock; Henley Gray; Ernie Irvan; Alan Kulwicki; Dick Linder; Fred Lorenzen; Hershel McGriff; Joe Millikan; Lloyd Moore; Frank Mundy; Billy Myers; Cotton Owens; Marvin Panch; Jim Pardue; Tom Pistone; Lennie Pond; Bill Rexford; Tim Richmond; Fireball Roberts; Shorty Rollins; Earl Ross; Wendell Scott; G.C. Spencer; Tony Stewart; Marshall Teague; Donald Thomas; Jabe Thomas; Billy Wade; Bob Welborn; Lee Roy Yarbrough; Emanuel Zervakis (1)

Top-Seven Seasons
1. Richard Petty (22)
2. Dale Earnhardt (15)
3. Bobby Allison (14)
4. Terry Labonte (13)
5. Lee Petty; Darrell Waltrip (12)
7. Mark Martin; David Pearson (11)
9. Bill Elliott; Rusty Wallace (10)
11. Buck Baker; James Hylton (9)
13. Benny Parsons; Ricky Rudd (8)
15. Harry Gant; Cale Yarborough (7)
17. Tim Flock; Ned Jarrett; Junior Johnson (6)
20. Jeff Gordon; Dale Jarrett; Elmo Langley; Dave Marcis; Jim Paschal; Herb Thomas; Rex White (5)
27. Fonty Flock; Cecil Gordon; Bobby Isaac (4)
30. Davey Allison; Buddy Baker; Bill Blair; Geoff Bodine; Jeff Burton; Neil Castles; Bobby Labonte; Jim Pardue; Kyle Petty; Dick Rathmann; Ken Schrader; Wendell Scott; John Sears; Morgan Shepherd; Jack Smith; Speedy Thompson; Joe Weatherly (3)
47. Buddy Arrington; Neil Bonnett; Dick Brooks; Joe Eubanks; Dick Hutcherson; Sterling Marlin; Jody Ridley; Fireball Roberts; Jabe Thomas; Curtis Turner (2)
57. Johnny Allen; Walter Ballard; Herman Beam; Red Byron; Richard Childress; Curtis Crider; Bob Derrington; Bob Flock; Henley Gray; Ernie Irvan; Tommy Irwin; Bobby Johns; Alan Kulwicki; Dick Linder; Fred Lorenzen; Clyde Lynn; Jeremy Mayfield; Hershel McGriff; Joe Millikan; Lloyd Moore; Frank Mundy; Ted Musgrave; Billy Myers; Cotton Owens; Marvin Panch; Tom Pistone; Lennie Pond; Bill Rexford; Tim Richmond; Shorty Rollins; Earl Ross; David Sisco; Eddie Skinner; Bill Snowden; Lake Speed; G.C. Spencer; Tony Stewart; Marshall Teague; Donald Thomas; Billy Wade; Bob Welborn; Lee Roy Yarbrough; Emanuel Zervakis (1)

Top-Eight Seasons

1. Richard Petty (23)
2. Dale Earnhardt (17)
3. Bobby Allison (16)
4. Terry Labonte (15)
5. Lee Petty; Darrell Waltrip (12)
7. Bill Elliott; Mark Martin; David Pearson; Ricky Rudd; Rusty Wallace (11)
12. Buck Baker (10)
13. James Hylton; Benny Parsons (9)
15. Harry Gant (8)
16. Herb Thomas; Cale Yarborough (7)
18. Tim Flock; Jeff Gordon; Ned Jarrett; Junior Johnson; Elmo Langley; Jim Paschal (6)
24. Cecil Gordon; Dale Jarrett; Dave Marcis; Ken Schrader; Rex White (5)
29. Buddy Baker; Geoff Bodine; Neil Castles; Fonty Flock; Bobby Isaac; Kyle Petty; Wendell Scott; John Sears; Speedy Thompson (4)
38. Davey Allison; Buddy Arrington; Bill Blair; Dick Brooks; Jeff Burton; Joe Eubanks; Ernie Irvan; Bobby Labonte; Jim Pardue; Dick Rathmann; Morgan Shepherd; Jack Smith; Joe Weatherly (3)
51. Herman Beam; Neil Bonnett; Richard Childress; Curtis Crider; Bob Flock; Dick Hutcherson; Clyde Lynn; Sterling Marlin; Lennie Pond; Jody Ridley; Fireball Roberts; Jabe Thomas; Curtis Turner (2)
64. Johnny Allen; Ben Arnold; L.D. Austin; Walter Ballard; Ron Bouchard; Red Byron; Sara Christian; Bob Derrington; Henley Gray; Tommy Irwin; Bobby Johns; Alan Kulwicki; Jimmie Lewallen; Ralph Liguori; Dick Linder; Fred Lorenzen; Jeremy Mayfield; Hershel McGriff; Joe Millikan; Ralph Moody; Lloyd Moore; Frank Mundy; Ted Musgrave; Billy Myers; Cotton Owens; Eddie Pagan; Marvin Panch; Phil Parsons; Tom Pistone; J.T. Putney; Bill Rexford; Tim Richmond; Shorty Rollins; Earl Ross; David Sisco; Eddie Skinner; Bill Snowden; Lake Speed; G.C. Spencer; Tony Stewart; Marshall Teague; Donald Thomas; Larry Thomas; Billy Wade; Bob Welborn; Lee Roy Yarbrough; Emanuel Zervakis (1)

Top-Nine Seasons

1. Richard Petty (24)
2. Dale Earnhardt (18)
3. Bobby Allison; Terry Labonte (16)
5. Darrell Waltrip (14)
6. Ricky Rudd (13)
7. Bill Elliott; Lee Petty (12)
9. Buck Baker; Mark Martin; David Pearson; Rusty Wallace (11)
13. James Hylton; Benny Parsons; Cale Yarborough (10)
16. Harry Gant; Jim Paschal (8)
18. Tim Flock; Elmo Langley; Ken Schrader; Herb Thomas (7)
22. Jeff Gordon; Ned Jarrett; Junior Johnson; Kyle Petty (6)
26. Buddy Baker; Neil Castles; Cecil Gordon; Dale Jarrett; Dave Marcis; Rex White (5)
32. Buddy Arrington; Geoff Bodine; Fonty Flock; Ernie Irvan; Bobby Isaac; Bobby Labonte; Wendell Scott; John Sears; Morgan Shepherd; Jack Smith; Speedy Thompson; Joe Weatherly (4)
44. Davey Allison; Herman Beam; Bill Blair; Neil Bonnett; Dick Brooks; Jeff Burton; Richard Childress; Joe Eubanks; Jimmie Lewallen; Sterling Marlin; Jim Pardue; Dick Rathmann; Fireball Roberts; Jabe Thomas (3)
58. Ron Bouchard; Curtis Crider; Bob Flock; Dick Hutcherson; Clyde Lynn; Lloyd Moore; Lennie Pond; J.T. Putney; Tim Richmond; Jody Ridley; Curtis Turner; Bob Welborn; Lee Roy Yarbrough (2)
71. Johnny Allen; Ben Arnold; L.D. Austin; Walter Ballard; Ward Burton; Red Byron; Bill Champion; Sara Christian; Tom Cox; Bob Derrington; Ray Duhigg; Ray Erickson; Henley Gray; Bobby Hillin Jr.; Tommy Irwin; Bobby Johns; Alan Kulwicki; Ralph Liguori; Dick Linder; Fred Lorenzen; Jeremy Mayfield; J.D. McDuffie; Hershel McGriff; Jimmy Means; Joe Millikan; Ralph Moody; Frank Mundy; Ted Musgrave;

Billy Myers; Cotton Owens; Eddie Pagan; Marvin Panch; Phil Parsons; Tom Pistone; Bill Rexford; Shorty Rollins; Earl Ross; David Sisco; Eddie Skinner; Bill Snowden; Lake Speed; G.C. Spencer; Tony Stewart; Marshall Teague; Donald Thomas; Larry Thomas; Billy Wade; Emanuel Zervakis (1)

Top-10 Seasons

1. Richard Petty (24)
2. Bobby Allison; Dale Earnhardt (18)
4. Terry Labonte (16)
5. Darrell Waltrip (14)
6. Bill Elliott; Ricky Rudd (13)
8. Lee Petty (12)
9. Buck Baker; Mark Martin; Benny Parsons; David Pearson; Rusty Wallace (11)
14. James Hylton; Cale Yarborough (10)
16. Harry Gant (9)
17. Elmo Langley; Jim Paschal; Ken Schrader (8)
20. Tim Flock; Junior Johnson; Herb Thomas (7)
23. Buddy Baker; Geoff Bodine; Jeff Gordon; Ned Jarrett; Dave Marcis; Kyle Petty; Morgan Shepherd (6)
30. Buddy Arrington; Neil Castles; Richard Childress; Fonty Flock; Cecil Gordon; Ernie Irvan; Dale Jarrett; Wendell Scott; John Sears; Rex White (5)
40. Bill Blair; Neil Bonnett; Dick Brooks; Jeff Burton; Bobby Isaac; Bobby Labonte; Jimmie Lewallen; Sterling Marlin; Fireball Roberts; Jack Smith; Speedy Thompson; Joe Weatherly (4)
52. Davey Allison; Herman Beam; Joe Eubanks; Marvin Panch; Jim Pardue; Dick Rathmann; Tim Richmond; Jabe Thomas; Bob Welborn (3)
61. L.D. Austin; Walter Ballard; Ron Bouchard; Curtis Crider; Bob Flock; Dick Hutcherson; Alan Kulwicki; Clyde Lynn; J.D. McDuffie; Lloyd Moore; Cotton Owens; Lennie Pond; J.T. Putney; Jody Ridley; Bill Snowden; Lake Speed; Curtis Turner; Lee Roy Yarbrough (2)
79. Johnny Allen; John Andretti; Ben Arnold; Ward Burton; Red Byron; Bill Champion; Sara Christian; Tom Cox; Bob Derrington; Darel Dieringer; Ray Duhigg; Ray Erickson; Paul Goldsmith; Henley Gray; Bobby Hillin Jr.; Tommy Irwin; Bobby Johns; Ralph Liguori; Dick Linder; Fred Lorenzen; Chuck Mahoney; Jeremy Mayfield; Hershel McGriff; Jimmy Means; Joe Millikan; Ralph Moody; Frank Mundy; Ted Musgrave; Billy Myers; Eddie Pagan; Phil Parsons; Dick Passwater; Tom Pistone; Bill Rexford; Shorty Rollins; Earl Ross; Buddy Shuman; David Sisco; Eddie Skinner; Mike Skinner; G.C. Spencer; Jimmy Spencer; Tony Stewart; Marshall Teague; Donald Thomas; Larry Thomas; E.J. Trivette; Roy Tyner; Billy Wade; Emanuel Zervakis (1)

Top-11 Seasons

1. Richard Petty (25)
2. Dale Earnhardt (19)
3. Bobby Allison (18)
4. Terry Labonte (17)
5. Ricky Rudd (15)
6. Bill Elliott; Darrell Waltrip (14)
8. David Pearson (13)
9. Lee Petty; Cale Yarborough (12)
11. Buck Baker; James Hylton; Mark Martin; Benny Parsons; Rusty Wallace (11)
16. Harry Gant; Elmo Langley; Jim Paschal (9)
19. Buddy Baker; Dave Marcis; Ken Schrader (8)
22. Tim Flock; Junior Johnson; Wendell Scott; Morgan Shepherd; Herb Thomas (7)
27. Geoff Bodine; Neil Castles; Richard Childress; Jeff Gordon; Ernie Irvan; Ned Jarrett; Kyle Petty; Rex White (6)

35. Buddy Arrington; Bill Blair; Neil Bonnett; Dick Brooks; Fonty Flock; Cecil Gordon; Dale Jarrett; Sterling Marlin; John Sears (5)

44. Davey Allison; Jeff Burton; Bobby Isaac; Bobby Labonte; Jimmie Lewallen; Jim Pardue; Tim Richmond; Fireball Roberts; Jack Smith; Speedy Thompson; Joe Weatherly; Bob Welborn (4)

56. L.D. Austin; Herman Beam; Curtis Crider; Joe Eubanks; Marvin Panch; Dick Rathmann; Jabe Thomas (3)

63. Walter Ballard; Ron Bouchard; Bob Flock; Paul Goldsmith; Bobby Hamilton; Dick Hutcherson; Alan Kulwicki; Clyde Lynn; Jeremy Mayfield; J.D. McDuffie; Lloyd Moore; Cotton Owens; Lennie Pond; J.T. Putney; Jody Ridley; Bill Snowden; Lake Speed; Curtis Turner; Lee Roy Yarbrough (2)

82. Johnny Allen; John Andretti; Ben Arnold; Johnny Benson Jr.; Brett Bodine; Perk Brown; Ward Burton; Red Byron; Bill Champion; Sara Christian; Tom Cox; Bob Derrington; Darel Dieringer; Ray Duhigg; Glenn Dunnaway; Ray Erickson; Jimmy Florian; Henley Gray; Pete Hamilton; Friday Hassler; Bobby Hillin Jr.; Tommy Irwin; Bobby Johns; Al Keller; Ralph Liguori; Dick Linder; Fred Lorenzen; Tiny Lund; Chuck Mahoney; Hershel McGriff; Jimmy Means; Joe Millikan; Ralph Moody; Frank Mundy; Ted Musgrave; Billy Myers; Eddie Pagan; Phil Parsons; Dick Passwater; Tom Pistone; Bill Rexford; Shorty Rollins; Earl Ross; Buddy Shuman; David Sisco; Eddie Skinner; Mike Skinner; Gober Sosebee; G.C. Spencer; Jimmy Spencer; Gwyn Staley; Tony Stewart; Marshall Teague; Donald Thomas; Larry Thomas; E.J. Trivette; Roy Tyner; D.K. Ulrich; Billy Wade; Michael Waltrip; Emanuel Zervakis (1)

Top-12 Seasons

1. Richard Petty (26)
2. Bobby Allison (20)
3. Dale Earnhardt; Terry Labonte (19)
5. Ricky Rudd (16)
6. Darrell Waltrip (15)
7. Bill Elliott (14)
8. Buck Baker; Benny Parsons; David Pearson; Cale Yarborough (13)
12. James Hylton; Lee Petty; Rusty Wallace (12)
15. Mark Martin (11)
16. Harry Gant; Elmo Langley; Dave Marcis; Jim Paschal (9)
20. Buddy Arrington; Buddy Baker; Geoff Bodine; Sterling Marlin; Ken Schrader; Wendell Scott; Morgan Shepherd (8)
27. Tim Flock; Junior Johnson; Herb Thomas (7)
30. Neil Castles; Richard Childress; Jeff Gordon; Ernie Irvan; Ned Jarrett; Kyle Petty; Rex White (6)
37. Bill Blair; Neil Bonnett; Dick Brooks; Fonty Flock; Cecil Gordon; Dale Jarrett; Jimmie Lewallen; Fireball Roberts; John Sears; Jack Smith; Bob Welborn (5)
48. Davey Allison; L.D. Austin; Jeff Burton; Bobby Isaac; Bobby Labonte; J.D. McDuffie; Marvin Panch; Jim Pardue; Tim Richmond; Jabe Thomas; Speedy Thompson; Joe Weatherly (4)
60. Walter Ballard; Herman Beam; Curtis Crider; Joe Eubanks; Clyde Lynn; Lennie Pond; Dick Rathmann; Curtis Turner; Michael Waltrip; Lee Roy Yarbrough (3)
70. Ron Bouchard; Bob Flock; Paul Goldsmith; Bobby Hamilton; Bobby Hillin Jr.; Dick Hutcherson; Alan Kulwicki; Jeremy Mayfield; Lloyd Moore; Cotton Owens; J.T. Putney; Jody Ridley; Slick Smith; Bill Snowden; Lake Speed; Gwyn Staley; Donald Thomas (2)
87. Johnny Allen; John Andretti; Ben Arnold; Johnny Benson Jr.; Brett Bodine; Perk Brown; Ward Burton; Red Byron; Bill Champion; Sara Christian; Tom Cox; Bob Derrington; Darel Dieringer; Ray Duhigg; Glenn Dunnaway; Ray Erickson; Jimmy Florian; Henley Gray; Pete Hamilton; Friday Hassler; Tommy Irwin; Bobby Johns; Al Keller; Brownie King; Ralph Liguori; Dick Linder; Fred Lorenzen; Tiny Lund; Chuck Mahoney; Hershel McGriff; Jimmy Means; Joe Millikan; Ralph Moody; Frank Mundy; Ted Musgrave; Billy Myers; Eddie Pagan; Phil Parsons; Dick Passwater; Tom Pistone; Jim Reed; Bill Rexford; Shorty Rollins; Earl Ross; Joe Ruttman; Bill Seifert; Buddy Shuman; David Sisco; Eddie Skinner; Mike Skinner; Gober Sosebee; G.C. Spencer; Jimmy Spencer; Tony Stewart; Marshall Teague; Dave Terrell; Larry Thomas; E.J. Trivette; Roy Tyner; D.K. Ulrich; Billy Wade; Frank Warren; Emanuel Zervakis (1)

Top-13 Seasons

1. Richard Petty (26)
2. Bobby Allison (21)
3. Dale Earnhardt (20)
4. Terry Labonte (19)
5. Ricky Rudd (17)
6. Darrell Waltrip (16)
7. Buck Baker (15)
8. Bill Elliott (14)
9. Benny Parsons; David Pearson; Rusty Wallace; Cale Yarborough (13)
13. James Hylton; Lee Petty (12)
15. Mark Martin (11)
16. Buddy Baker; Harry Gant; Dave Marcis; Jim Paschal (10)
20. Elmo Langley; Kyle Petty; Ken Schrader; Morgan Shepherd (9)
24. Buddy Arrington; Geoff Bodine; Sterling Marlin; Wendell Scott (8)
28. Tim Flock; Cecil Gordon; Junior Johnson; Herb Thomas; Rex White (7)
33. Neil Bonnett; Neil Castles; Richard Childress; Jeff Gordon; Ernie Irvan; Ned Jarrett; Fireball Roberts; John Sears (6)
41. Davey Allison; Bill Blair; Dick Brooks; Fonty Flock; Dale Jarrett; Bobby Labonte; Jimmie Lewallen; Tim Richmond; Jack Smith; Jabe Thomas; Curtis Turner; Bob Welborn (5)
53. L.D. Austin; Herman Beam; Jeff Burton; Bobby Isaac; J.D. McDuffie; Marvin Panch; Jim Pardue; Dick Rathmann; Speedy Thompson; Joe Weatherly (4)
63. Walter Ballard; Ron Bouchard; Curtis Crider; Joe Eubanks; Bobby Hamilton; Clyde Lynn; Lennie Pond; Michael Waltrip; Lee Roy Yarbrough (3)
72. Johnny Allen; Brett Bodine; Bob Flock; Paul Goldsmith; Henley Gray; Pete Hamilton; Bobby Hillin Jr.; Dick Hutcherson; Alan Kulwicki; Tiny Lund; Jeremy Mayfield; Lloyd Moore; Frank Mundy; Ted Musgrave; Cotton Owens; Eddie Pagan; J.T. Putney; Jody Ridley; Slick Smith; Bill Snowden; Lake Speed; G.C. Spencer; Gwyn Staley; Dave Terrell; Donald Thomas; Larry Thomas; Roy Tyner; D.K. Ulrich; Emanuel Zervakis (2)
101. John Andretti; Ben Arnold; Johnny Benson Jr.; Perk Brown; Ward Burton; Red Byron; Bill Champion; Sara Christian; Tom Cox; Bob Derrington; Darel Dieringer; Ray Duhigg; Glenn Dunnaway; Ray Erickson; Jimmy Florian; George Hartley; Friday Hassler; Bruce Hill; Tommy Irwin; Bobby Johns; Al Keller; Brownie King; Ralph Liguori; Dick Linder; Fred Lorenzen; Chuck Mahoney; Dick May; Hershel McGriff; Jimmy Means; Joe Millikan; Ralph Moody; Billy Myers; Steve Park; Phil Parsons; Dick Passwater; Tom Pistone; Jim Reed; Bill Rexford; Shorty Rollins; Earl Ross; Joe Ruttman; Bill Seifert; Buddy Shuman; David Sisco; Eddie Skinner; Mike Skinner; Gober Sosebee; Jimmy Spencer; Tony Stewart; Marshall Teague; E.J. Trivette; Billy Wade; Frank Warren (1)

Top-14 Seasons

1. Richard Petty (26)
2. Bobby Allison (21)
3. Dale Earnhardt (20)
4. Terry Labonte (19)
5. Darrell Waltrip (18)
6. Ricky Rudd (17)
7. Buck Baker; Bill Elliott; Rusty Wallace (15)
10. James Hylton; Benny Parsons; David Pearson; Cale Yarborough (13)
14. Mark Martin; Lee Petty (12)

16. Buddy Baker; Geoff Bodine; Harry Gant; Dave Marcis; Jim Paschal; Ken Schrader (11)
22. Sterling Marlin (10)
23. Elmo Langley; Kyle Petty; Morgan Shepherd (9)
26. Buddy Arrington; Wendell Scott (8)
28. Neil Bonnett; Tim Flock; Cecil Gordon; Ernie Irvan; Junior Johnson; Herb Thomas; Rex White (7)
35. Bill Blair; Dick Brooks; Neil Castles; Richard Childress; Jeff Gordon; Ned Jarrett; Fireball Roberts; John Sears; Jabe Thomas; Curtis Turner (6)
45. Davey Allison; Ron Bouchard; Fonty Flock; Dale Jarrett; Bobby Labonte; Jimmie Lewallen; J.D. McDuffie; Jim Pardue; Tim Richmond; Jack Smith; Bob Welborn (5)
56. L.D. Austin; Herman Beam; Jeff Burton; Joe Eubanks; Bobby Isaac; Marvin Panch; Dick Rathmann; Speedy Thompson; Joe Weatherly (4)
65. Johnny Allen; Walter Ballard; Curtis Crider; Paul Goldsmith; Bobby Hamilton; Bobby Hillin Jr.; Alan Kulwicki; Tiny Lund; Clyde Lynn; Jeremy Mayfield; Lennie Pond; Roy Tyner; Michael Waltrip; Lee Roy Yarbrough (3)
79. Donnie Allison; John Andretti; Brett Bodine; Red Byron; Darel Dieringer; Bob Flock; Henley Gray; Pete Hamilton; Dick Hutcherson; Paul Lewis; Lloyd Moore; Frank Mundy; Ted Musgrave; Billy Myers; Cotton Owens; Eddie Pagan; J.T. Putney; Jody Ridley; Slick Smith; Bill Snowden; Gober Sosebee; Lake Speed; G.C. Spencer; Gwyn Staley; Dave Terrell; Donald Thomas; Larry Thomas; D.K. Ulrich; Emanuel Zervakis (2)
108. Ben Arnold; Johnny Benson Jr.; Perk Brown; Ward Burton; Ted Chamberlain; Bill Champion; Sara Christian; Derrike Cope; Tom Cox; Bill Dennis; Bob Derrington; Ray Duhigg; Glenn Dunnaway; Ray Erickson; Jimmy Florian; George Green; George Hartley; Friday Hassler; Bruce Hill; Tommy Irwin; Bobby Johns; Al Keller; Brownie King; Ralph Liguori; Dick Linder; Fred Lorenzen; Chuck Mahoney; Skip Manning; Dick May; Hershel McGriff; Jimmy Means; Joe Millikan; Ralph Moody; Steve Park; Phil Parsons; Dick Passwater; Tom Pistone; Blackie Pitt; Jim Reed; Bill Rexford; Shorty Rollins; Earl Ross; Joe Ruttman; Tighe Scott; Bill Seifert; Buddy Shuman; Gene Simpson; David Sisco; Eddie Skinner; Mike Skinner; Jimmy Spencer; Tony Stewart; Marshall Teague; E.J. Trivette; Billy Wade; Frank Warren; Doug Yates (1)

Top-15 Seasons

1. Richard Petty (26)
2. Bobby Allison (21)
3. Dale Earnhardt (20)
4. Terry Labonte (19)
5. Ricky Rudd; Darrell Waltrip (18)
7. Bill Elliott (16)
8. Buck Baker; Rusty Wallace (15)
10. James Hylton; David Pearson (14)
12. Benny Parsons; Jim Paschal; Cale Yarborough (13)
15. Buddy Baker; Dave Marcis; Mark Martin; Lee Petty; Ken Schrader (12)
20. Geoff Bodine; Harry Gant (11)
22. Sterling Marlin; Kyle Petty; Morgan Shepherd (10)
25. Elmo Langley (9)
26. Buddy Arrington; Neil Bonnett; Cecil Gordon; Ernie Irvan; Junior Johnson; Wendell Scott (8)
32. Neil Castles; Tim Flock; Dale Jarrett; Herb Thomas; Rex White (7)
37. Davey Allison; Bill Blair; Dick Brooks; Richard Childress; Jeff Gordon; Ned Jarrett; Bobby Labonte; J.D. McDuffie; Fireball Roberts; John Sears; Jabe Thomas; Curtis Turner (6)
49. Ron Bouchard; Fonty Flock; Bobby Isaac; Jimmie Lewallen; Jim Pardue; Tim Richmond; Jack Smith; Speedy Thompson; Joe Weatherly; Bob Welborn (5)
59. L.D. Austin; Herman Beam; Jeff Burton; Joe Eubanks; Bobby Hamilton; Marvin Panch; Dick Rathmann; Michael Waltrip (4)

67. Johnny Allen; Donnie Allison; Walter Ballard; Curtis Crider; Darel Dieringer; Paul Goldsmith; Bobby Hillin Jr.; Alan Kulwicki; Tiny Lund; Clyde Lynn; Jeremy Mayfield; Cotton Owens; Lennie Pond; G.C. Spencer; Roy Tyner; Lee Roy Yarbrough (3)
83. John Andretti; Brett Bodine; Red Byron; Bob Flock; Henley Gray; Pete Hamilton; Dick Hutcherson; Paul Lewis; Skip Manning; Coo Coo Marlin; Lloyd Moore; Frank Mundy; Ted Musgrave; Billy Myers; Eddie Pagan; Phil Parsons; J.T. Putney; Jim Reed; Bill Rexford; Jody Ridley; Joe Ruttman; Bill Seifert; Buddy Shuman; Slick Smith; Bill Snowden; Gober Sosebee; Lake Speed; Jimmy Spencer; Gwyn Staley; Dave Terrell; Donald Thomas; Larry Thomas; E.J. Trivette; D.K. Ulrich; Billy Wade; Frank Warren; Emanuel Zervakis (2)
120. Weldon Adams; Bill Amick; Ben Arnold; Johnny Benson Jr.; Perk Brown; Laird Bruner; Ward Burton; Ted Chamberlain; Bill Champion; Sara Christian; Derrike Cope; Tom Cox; Bill Dennis; Bob Derrington; Ray Duhigg; Glenn Dunnaway; Ray Erickson; Jimmy Florian; George Green; George Hartley; Friday Hassler; Bruce Hill; Tommy Irwin; Bobby Johns; Joe Lee Johnson; Bobby Keck; Al Keller; Brownie King; Ralph Liguori; Dick Linder; Fred Lorenzen; Chuck Mahoney; Jimmy Massey; Dick May; Hershel McGriff; Jimmy Means; Joe Millikan; Ralph Moody; Steve Park; Dick Passwater; Tom Pistone; Blackie Pitt; Shorty Rollins; Earl Ross; Tighe Scott; Gene Simpson; David Sisco; Eddie Skinner; Mike Skinner; Tony Stewart; Marshall Teague; Doug Yates (1)

Top-16 Seasons

1. Richard Petty (26)
2. Bobby Allison; Darrell Waltrip (21)
4. Dale Earnhardt; Terry Labonte (20)
6. Ricky Rudd (18)
7. Bill Elliott (16)
8. Buck Baker; Rusty Wallace (15)
10. James Hylton; Buddy Baker; David Pearson (14)
13. Benny Parsons; Jim Paschal; Cale Yarborough (13)
16. Dave Marcis; Mark Martin; Lee Petty; Ken Schrader (12)
20. Geoff Bodine; Harry Gant (11)
22. Sterling Marlin; Kyle Petty; Morgan Shepherd (10)
25. Neil Bonnett; Elmo Langley (9)
27. Buddy Arrington; Cecil Gordon; Ernie Irvan; Dale Jarrett; Junior Johnson; Wendell Scott; Herb Thomas (8)
34. Dick Brooks; Neil Castles; Tim Flock; Fireball Roberts; Rex White (7)
39. Davey Allison; Bill Blair; Richard Childress; Jeff Gordon; Ned Jarrett; Bobby Labonte; J.D. McDuffie; John Sears; Jabe Thomas; Speedy Thompson; Curtis Turner; Bob Welborn (6)
51. Walter Ballard; Ron Bouchard; Darel Dieringer; Fonty Flock; Bobby Isaac; Alan Kulwicki; Jimmie Lewallen; Jim Pardue; Dick Rathmann; Tim Richmond; Jack Smith; Joe Weatherly (5)
63. Donnie Allison; L.D. Austin; Herman Beam; Jeff Burton; Joe Eubanks; Bobby Hamilton; Bobby Hillin Jr.; Tiny Lund; Ted Musgrave; Marvin Panch; Gober Sosebee; Michael Waltrip; Frank Warren (4)
76. Johnny Allen; John Andretti; Curtis Crider; Paul Goldsmith; Clyde Lynn; Jeremy Mayfield; Cotton Owens; Lennie Pond; J.T. Putney; Joe Ruttman; Bill Seifert; G.C. Spencer; Roy Tyner; D.K. Ulrich; Lee Roy Yarbrough (3)
91. Bill Amick; Ben Arnold; Brett Bodine; Red Byron; Bob Flock; Henley Gray; Pete Hamilton; Friday Hassler; Dick Hutcherson; Paul Lewis; Skip Manning; Coo Coo Marlin; Jimmy Means; Joe Millikan; Lloyd Moore; Frank Mundy; Billy Myers; Eddie Pagan; Phil Parsons; Jim Reed; Bill Rexford; Jody Ridley; Buddy Shuman; David Sisco; Slick Smith; Bill Snowden; Lake Speed; Jimmy Spencer; Gwyn Staley; Dave Terrell; Donald Thomas; Larry Thomas; E.J. Trivette; Billy Wade; Emanuel Zervakis (2)
126. Weldon Adams; Dick Beaty; Johnny Benson Jr.; Perk Brown; Laird Bruner; Ward Burton; Ted Chamberlain; Bill Champion; Sara Christian; Doug Cooper; Derrike Cope; Tom Cox; Dean Dalton; Bill

Performance Index Records

Dennis; Bob Derrington; Ray Duhigg; Glenn Dunnaway; Ray Erickson; Jimmy Florian; George Green; Fred Harb; George Hartley; Elton Hildreth; Bruce Hill; Tommy Irwin; Bobby Johns; Joe Lee Johnson; Bobby Keck; Al Keller; Brownie King; Ralph Liguori; Dick Linder; Chad Little; Fred Lorenzen; Chuck Mahoney; Johnny Mantz; Jimmy Massey; Dick May; Hershel McGriff; Clyde Minter; Ralph Moody; Steve Park; Dick Passwater; Tom Pistone; Blackie Pitt; Sam Rice; Shorty Rollins; Earl Ross; Tighe Scott; Gene Simpson; Eddie Skinner; Mike Skinner; Tony Stewart; Marshall Teague; Rick Wilson; Glen Wood; Doug Yates (1)

Top-17 Seasons

1. Richard Petty (28)
2. Bobby Allison (22)
3. Darrell Waltrip (21)
4. Dale Earnhardt; Terry Labonte (20)
6. Ricky Rudd (18)
7. Buddy Baker; Bill Elliott (16)
9. Buck Baker; David Pearson; Rusty Wallace (15)
12. James Hylton; Benny Parsons; Cale Yarborough (14)
15. Jim Paschal (13)
16. Geoff Bodine; Harry Gant; Dave Marcis; Mark Martin; Lee Petty; Ken Schrader (12)
22. Neil Bonnett; Kyle Petty; Morgan Shepherd (11)
25. Elmo Langley; Sterling Marlin (10)
27. Dick Brooks (9)
28. Buddy Arrington; Cecil Gordon; Ernie Irvan; Dale Jarrett; Junior Johnson; J.D. McDuffie; Wendell Scott; Herb Thomas (8)
36. Neil Castles; Richard Childress; Tim Flock; Jeff Gordon; Ned Jarrett; Fireball Roberts; Rex White (7)
43. Davey Allison; Bill Blair; Fonty Flock; Bobby Labonte; Marvin Panch; John Sears; Jack Smith; Jabe Thomas; Speedy Thompson; Curtis Turner; Bob Welborn (6)
54. Walter Ballard; Ron Bouchard; Darel Dieringer; Bobby Hamilton; Bobby Isaac; Alan Kulwicki; Jimmie Lewallen; Tiny Lund; Ted Musgrave; Jim Pardue; Dick Rathmann; Tim Richmond; Gober Sosebee; Joe Weatherly (5)
68. Donnie Allison; L.D. Austin; Herman Beam; Jeff Burton; Joe Eubanks; Bobby Hillin Jr.; Michael Waltrip; Frank Warren (4)
76. Johnny Allen; John Andretti; Brett Bodine; Bill Champion; Curtis Crider; Paul Goldsmith; Fred Lorenzen; Clyde Lynn; Jeremy Mayfield; Cotton Owens; Lennie Pond; J.T. Putney; Joe Ruttman; Bill Seifert; Lake Speed; G.C. Spencer; Jimmy Spencer; Gwyn Staley; Roy Tyner; D.K. Ulrich; Lee Roy Yarbrough (3)
97. Bill Amick; Ben Arnold; Red Byron; Ray Duhigg; Bob Flock; Henley Gray; Pete Hamilton; Friday Hassler; Dick Hutcherson; Brownie King; Paul Lewis; Skip Manning; Coo Coo Marlin; Jimmy Means; Joe Millikan; Lloyd Moore; Frank Mundy; Billy Myers; Eddie Pagan; Phil Parsons; Blackie Pitt; Jim Reed; Bill Rexford; Jody Ridley; Buddy Shuman; David Sisco; Slick Smith; Bill Snowden; Dave Terrell; Donald Thomas; Larry Thomas; E.J. Trivette; Billy Wade; Emanuel Zervakis (2)
131. Weldon Adams; Dick Beaty; Johnny Benson Jr.; Perk Brown; Laird Bruner; Bob Burcham; Ward Burton; Ted Chamberlain; Sara Christian; Neil Cole; Doug Cooper; Derrike Cope; Tom Cox; Dean Dalton; Lloyd Dane; Bill Dennis; Bob Derrington; Fred Dove; Glenn Dunnaway; Ray Erickson; Jimmy Florian; Tommy Gale; Charlie Glotzbach; George Green; Fred Harb; George Hartley; Elton Hildreth; Bruce Hill; Kenny Irwin; Tommy Irwin; Bobby Johns; Joe Lee Johnson; Bobby Keck; Al Keller; Ralph Liguori; Dick Linder; Chad Little; Chuck Mahoney; Johnny Mantz; Jimmy Massey; Rick Mast; Dick May; Hershel McGriff; Clyde Minter; Ralph Moody; Steve Park; Dick Passwater; Tom Pistone; Sam Rice; Shorty Rollins; Earl Ross; Tighe Scott; Gene Simpson; Eddie Skinner; Mike Skinner; Sam Sommers; Tony Stewart; Hut Stricklin; Marshall Teague; Raymond Williams; Rick Wilson; Glen Wood; Doug Yates (1)

Top-18 Seasons

1. Richard Petty (28)
2. Bobby Allison (22)
3. Terry Labonte; Darrell Waltrip (21)
5. Buddy Baker; Dale Earnhardt (20)
7. Ricky Rudd (19)
8. Bill Elliott; David Pearson (16)
10. Buck Baker; Geoff Bodine; Rusty Wallace (15)
13. James Hylton; Benny Parsons; Ken Schrader; Cale Yarborough (14)
17. Dave Marcis; Jim Paschal (13)
19. Harry Gant; Mark Martin; Lee Petty; Morgan Shepherd (12)
23. Neil Bonnett; Sterling Marlin; Kyle Petty (11)
26. Dick Brooks; Elmo Langley (10)
28. Buddy Arrington (9)
29. Cecil Gordon; Ernie Irvan; Dale Jarrett; Junior Johnson; J.D. McDuffie; Wendell Scott; Herb Thomas (8)
36. Neil Castles; Richard Childress; Tim Flock; Jeff Gordon; Ned Jarrett; Fireball Roberts; Rex White (7)
43. Davey Allison; Donnie Allison; Bill Blair; Fonty Flock; Alan Kulwicki; Bobby Labonte; Marvin Panch; Tim Richmond; John Sears; Jack Smith; Jabe Thomas; Speedy Thompson; Curtis Turner; Michael Waltrip; Joe Weatherly; Bob Welborn (6)
59. Walter Ballard; Ron Bouchard; Darel Dieringer; Bobby Hamilton; Bobby Isaac; Jimmie Lewallen; Tiny Lund; Ted Musgrave; Jim Pardue; Dick Rathmann; Gober Sosebee (5)
70. L.D. Austin; Herman Beam; Brett Bodine; Jeff Burton; Bill Champion; Joe Eubanks; Bobby Hillin Jr.; David Sisco; Lake Speed; G.C. Spencer; Frank Warren (4)
81. Johnny Allen; John Andretti; Curtis Crider; Paul Goldsmith; Henley Gray; Friday Hassler; Fred Lorenzen; Clyde Lynn; Jeremy Mayfield; Jimmy Means; Cotton Owens; Lennie Pond; J.T. Putney; Jody Ridley; Joe Ruttman; Bill Seifert; Jimmy Spencer; Gwyn Staley; Larry Thomas; Roy Tyner; D.K. Ulrich; Lee Roy Yarbrough (3)
103. Bill Amick; Ben Arnold; Red Byron; Doug Cooper; Derrike Cope; Lloyd Dane; Ray Duhigg; Bob Flock; Pete Hamilton; Dick Hutcherson; Tommy Irwin; Brownie King; Paul Lewis; Skip Manning; Coo Coo Marlin; Joe Millikan; Lloyd Moore; Frank Mundy; Billy Myers; Eddie Pagan; Phil Parsons; Blackie Pitt; Jim Reed; Bill Rexford; Tighe Scott; Buddy Shuman; Slick Smith; Bill Snowden; Dave Terrell; Donald Thomas; E.J. Trivette; Billy Wade; Emanuel Zervakis (2)
136. Weldon Adams; Dick Beaty; Johnny Benson Jr.; Trevor Boys; Perk Brown; Laird Bruner; Bob Burcham; Ward Burton; Billy Carden; Ted Chamberlain; Sara Christian; Neil Cole; Tom Cox; Wally Dallenbach Jr.; Dean Dalton; Bill Dennis; Bob Derrington; Fred Dove; Clarence DeZalia; Glenn Dunnaway; Ray Erickson; Jimmy Florian; Tommy Gale; Charlie Glotzbach; George Green; Johnny Grubb; Fred Harb; George Hartley; Jimmy Helms; Harvey Henderson; Elton Hildreth; Bruce Hill; Kenny Irwin; Bobby Johns; Joe Lee Johnson; Bobby Keck; Al Keller; Bub King; Ralph Liguori; Dick Linder; Chad Little; Chuck Mahoney; Johnny Mantz; Jimmy Massey; Rick Mast; Dick May; Hershel McGriff; Clyde Minter; Ralph Moody; Steve Park; Dick Passwater; Tom Pistone; Billy Rafter; Sam Rice; Jackie Rogers; Shorty Rollins; Earl Ross; Gene Simpson; Eddie Skinner; Mike Skinner; John Soares; Sam Sommers; Tony Stewart; Hut Stricklin; Marshall Teague; Raymond Williams; Rick Wilson; Glen Wood; Doug Yates (1)

Top-19 Seasons

1. Richard Petty (28)
2. Buddy Baker (24)
3. Bobby Allison (22)
4. Dale Earnhardt; Terry Labonte; Darrell Waltrip (21)
7. Ricky Rudd (19)
8. Bill Elliott (17)
9. David Pearson; Rusty Wallace (16)

11. Buck Baker; Geoff Bodine; Benny Parsons; Cale Yarborough (15)
15. James Hylton; Dave Marcis; Jim Paschal; Ken Schrader (14)
19. Harry Gant; Sterling Marlin; Mark Martin; Lee Petty; Morgan Shepherd (12)
24. Neil Bonnett; Kyle Petty (11)
26. Buddy Arrington; Dick Brooks; Elmo Langley; J.D. McDuffie (10)
30. Cecil Gordon; Wendell Scott (9)
32. Ernie Irvan; Dale Jarrett; Junior Johnson; Herb Thomas (8)
36. Neil Castles; Richard Childress; Tim Flock; Jeff Gordon; Ned Jarrett; Alan Kulwicki; Fireball Roberts; Michael Waltrip; Rex White (7)
45. Davey Allison; Donnie Allison; Bill Blair; Fonty Flock; Bobby Hamilton; Bobby Labonte; Tiny Lund; Marvin Panch; Tim Richmond; John Sears; Jack Smith; Jabe Thomas; Speedy Thompson; Curtis Turner; Joe Weatherly; Bob Welborn (6)
61. Walter Ballard; Ron Bouchard; Darel Dieringer; Bobby Isaac; Jimmie Lewallen; Fred Lorenzen; Jimmy Means; Ted Musgrave; Jim Pardue; Dick Rathmann; Gober Sosebee; G.C. Spencer (5)
73. L.D. Austin; Herman Beam; Brett Bodine; Jeff Burton; Bill Champion; Curtis Crider; Joe Eubanks; Paul Goldsmith; Bobby Hillin Jr.; Lennie Pond; David Sisco; Lake Speed; Frank Warren (4)
86. Johnny Allen; John Andretti; Ward Burton; Derrike Cope; Henley Gray; Friday Hassler; Clyde Lynn; Jeremy Mayfield; Clyde Minter; Lloyd Moore; Cotton Owens; Phil Parsons; J.T. Putney; Jody Ridley; Joe Ruttman; Bill Seifert; Jimmy Spencer; Gwyn Staley; Donald Thomas; Larry Thomas; Roy Tyner; D.K. Ulrich; Lee Roy Yarbrough (3)
109. Bill Amick; Ben Arnold; Red Byron; Doug Cooper; Lloyd Dane; Ray Duhigg; Clarence DeZalia; Bob Flock; Tommy Gale; Pete Hamilton; Dick Hutcherson; Tommy Irwin; Brownie King; Paul Lewis; Skip Manning; Coo Coo Marlin; Rick Mast; Joe Millikan; Frank Mundy; Billy Myers; Eddie Pagan; Blackie Pitt; Jim Reed; Bill Rexford; Tighe Scott; Buddy Shuman; Slick Smith; Bill Snowden; Dave Terrell; E.J. Trivette; Billy Wade; Rick Wilson; Emanuel Zervakis (2)
142. Weldon Adams; Dick Beaty; Johnny Benson Jr.; Trevor Boys; Perk Brown; Laird Bruner; Bob Burcham; Billy Carden; Ted Chamberlain; Sara Christian; Neil Cole; Tom Cox; Ricky Craven; Wally Dallenbach Jr.; Dean Dalton; Bill Dennis; Bob Derrington; Fred Dove; Glenn Dunnaway; Ray Erickson; Jim Fiebelkorn; Jimmy Florian; Larry Frank; Charlie Glotzbach; George Green; Johnny Grubb; Fred Harb; George Hartley; Jimmy Helms; Harvey Henderson; Elton Hildreth; Bruce Hill; Kenny Irwin; Bobby Johns; Joe Lee Johnson; Bobby Keck; Al Keller; Bub King; Ralph Liguori; Dick Linder; Chad Little; Chuck Mahoney; Johnny Mantz; Jimmy Massey; Dick May; Hershel McGriff; Ralph Moody; Steve Park; Dick Passwater; Tom Pistone; Billy Rafter; Sam Rice; Charlie Roberts; Jackie Rogers; Shorty Rollins; Earl Ross; Gene Simpson; Eddie Skinner; Mike Skinner; John Soares; Sam Sommers; Tony Stewart; Hut Stricklin; Marshall Teague; Jimmy Thompson; Bobby Wawak; Dink Widenhouse; Raymond Williams; Glen Wood; Doug Yates (1)

Top-20 Seasons
1. Richard Petty (29)
2. Buddy Baker (25)
3. Bobby Allison; Darrell Waltrip (22)
5. Dale Earnhardt; Terry Labonte (21)
7. Ricky Rudd (19)
8. Bill Elliott (18)
9. Buck Baker; Dave Marcis; David Pearson; Rusty Wallace (16)
13. Geoff Bodine; James Hylton; Benny Parsons; Cale Yarborough (15)
17. Jim Paschal; Ken Schrader (14)
19. Harry Gant (13)
20. Buddy Arrington; Neil Bonnett; Sterling Marlin; Mark Martin; Lee Petty; Morgan Shepherd (12)
26. Kyle Petty (11)
27. Dick Brooks; Elmo Langley; J.D. McDuffie; Michael Waltrip (10)

31. Cecil Gordon; Dale Jarrett; Marvin Panch; Wendell Scott (9)
35. Donnie Allison; Ernie Irvan; Bobby Isaac; Junior Johnson; Herb Thomas (8)
40. Neil Castles; Richard Childress; Tim Flock; Jeff Gordon; Ned Jarrett; Alan Kulwicki; Tiny Lund; Fireball Roberts; Joe Weatherly; Rex White (7)
50. Davey Allison; Bill Blair; Fonty Flock; Bobby Hamilton; Bobby Hillin Jr.; Bobby Labonte; Ted Musgrave; Tim Richmond; John Sears; Jack Smith; G.C. Spencer; Jabe Thomas; Speedy Thompson; Curtis Turner; Bob Welborn (6)
65. Walter Ballard; Brett Bodine; Ron Bouchard; Curtis Crider; Darel Dieringer; Jimmie Lewallen; Fred Lorenzen; Jimmy Means; Jim Pardue; Dick Rathmann; Gober Sosebee; Lake Speed; Lee Roy Yarbrough (5)
78. L.D. Austin; Herman Beam; Jeff Burton; Bill Champion; Joe Eubanks; Paul Goldsmith; Lennie Pond; Joe Ruttman; David Sisco; Frank Warren (4)
88. Johnny Allen; John Andretti; Ward Burton; Derrike Cope; Henley Gray; Friday Hassler; Clyde Lynn; Jeremy Mayfield; Clyde Minter; Lloyd Moore; Cotton Owens; Phil Parsons; J.T. Putney; Jody Ridley; Bill Seifert; Jimmy Spencer; Gwyn Staley; Donald Thomas; Larry Thomas; Roy Tyner; D.K. Ulrich (3)
109. Bill Amick; Ben Arnold; Johnny Benson Jr.; Herschel Buchanan; Red Byron; Billy Carden; Doug Cooper; Lloyd Dane; Ray Duhigg; Clarence DeZalia; Glenn Dunnaway; Bob Flock; Tommy Gale; Pete Hamilton; Elton Hildreth; Dick Hutcherson; Tommy Irwin; Brownie King; Paul Lewis; Skip Manning; Coo Coo Marlin; Rick Mast; Joe Millikan; Frank Mundy; Billy Myers; Eddie Pagan; Blackie Pitt; Jim Reed; Bill Rexford; Tighe Scott; Buddy Shuman; Slick Smith; Bill Snowden; Dave Terrell; E.J. Trivette; Billy Wade; Rick Wilson; Emanuel Zervakis (2)
147. Weldon Adams; Grant Adcox; Dick Beaty; Trevor Boys; Perk Brown; Laird Bruner; Bob Burcham; Ted Chamberlain; Sara Christian; Neil Cole; Doug Cox; Tom Cox; Ricky Craven; Wally Dallenbach Jr.; Dean Dalton; Bill Dennis; Bob Derrington; Fred Dove; Ray Erickson; Jim Fiebelkorn; Jimmy Florian; Larry Frank; Charlie Glotzbach; George Green; Johnny Grubb; Janet Guthrie; Fred Harb; George Hartley; Jimmy Helms; Harvey Henderson; Bruce Hill; Kenny Irwin; Bobby Johns; Joe Lee Johnson; Bobby Keck; Al Keller; Bub King; Ralph Liguori; Dick Linder; Chad Little; Chuck Mahoney; Johnny Mantz; Jimmy Massey; Dick May; Hershel McGriff; Ralph Moody; Ed Negre; Richie Panch; Steve Park; Dick Passwater; Tom Pistone; Billy Rafter; Sam Rice; Charlie Roberts; Jackie Rogers; Shorty Rollins; Jim Roper; Earl Ross; Greg Sacks; Gene Simpson; Eddie Skinner; Mike Skinner; John Soares; Sam Sommers; Nelson Stacy; Tony Stewart; Hut Stricklin; Marshall Teague; Ronnie Thomas; Jimmy Thompson; Dick Trickle; Bobby Wawak; Dink Widenhouse; Raymond Williams; Glen Wood; Doug Yates (1)

Top-21 Seasons
1. Richard Petty (29)
2. Buddy Baker (25)
3. Bobby Allison; Darrell Waltrip (22)
5. Dale Earnhardt; Terry Labonte (21)
7. Ricky Rudd (19)
8. Bill Elliott (18)
9. Buck Baker; Dave Marcis (17)
11. Geoff Bodine; David Pearson; Rusty Wallace (16)
14. James Hylton; Benny Parsons; Ken Schrader; Cale Yarborough (15)
18. Jim Paschal (14)
19. Buddy Arrington; Neil Bonnett; Harry Gant; Mark Martin (13)
23. Sterling Marlin; Kyle Petty; Lee Petty; Morgan Shepherd (12)
27. Dick Brooks; J.D. McDuffie; Michael Waltrip (11)
30. Cecil Gordon; Dale Jarrett; Elmo Langley (10)
33. Junior Johnson; Marvin Panch; Wendell Scott (9)

Performance Index Records

36. Donnie Allison; Ernie Irvan; Bobby Isaac; G.C. Spencer; Herb Thomas (8)

41. Neil Castles; Richard Childress; Tim Flock; Jeff Gordon; Ned Jarrett; Alan Kulwicki; Tiny Lund; Fireball Roberts; Curtis Turner; Joe Weatherly; Bob Welborn; Rex White (7)

53. Davey Allison; Bill Blair; Brett Bodine; Darel Dieringer; Fonty Flock; Bobby Hamilton; Bobby Hillin Jr.; Bobby Labonte; Jimmy Means; Ted Musgrave; Tim Richmond; John Sears; Jack Smith; Jabe Thomas; Speedy Thompson (6)

68. L.D. Austin; Walter Ballard; Ron Bouchard; Curtis Crider; Jimmie Lewallen; Fred Lorenzen; Cotton Owens; Jim Pardue; Dick Rathmann; Gober Sosebee; Lake Speed; Lee Roy Yarbrough (5)

80. Herman Beam; Jeff Burton; Bill Champion; Derrike Cope; Joe Eubanks; Paul Goldsmith; Henley Gray; Rick Mast; Phil Parsons; Lennie Pond; Joe Ruttman; David Sisco; Jimmy Spencer; Frank Warren (4)

94. Johnny Allen; John Andretti; Ward Burton; Tommy Gale; Friday Hassler; Tommy Irwin; Clyde Lynn; Coo Coo Marlin; Jeremy Mayfield; Clyde Minter; Lloyd Moore; Ed Negre; J.T. Putney; Jody Ridley; Tighe Scott; Bill Seifert; Gwyn Staley; Donald Thomas; Larry Thomas; Roy Tyner; D.K. Ulrich (3)

115. Bill Amick; Ben Arnold; Johnny Benson Jr.; Herschel Buchanan; Red Byron; Billy Carden; Doug Cooper; Ricky Craven; Lloyd Dane; Ray Duhigg; Clarence DeZalia; Glenn Dunnaway; Bob Flock; Pete Hamilton; Elton Hildreth; Dick Hutcherson; Brownie King; Paul Lewis; Ralph Liguori; Skip Manning; Joe Millikan; Frank Mundy; Billy Myers; Eddie Pagan; Blackie Pitt; Jim Reed; Bill Rexford; Buddy Shuman; Eddie Skinner; Mike Skinner; Slick Smith; Bill Snowden; Nelson Stacy; Dave Terrell; Dick Trickle; E.J. Trivette; Billy Wade; Rick Wilson; Emanuel Zervakis (2)

154. Weldon Adams; Grant Adcox; Dick Beaty; Terry Bivins; Todd Bodine; Trevor Boys; Perk Brown; Laird Bruner; Bob Burcham; Ted Chamberlain; Sara Christian; Neil Cole; Doug Cox; Tom Cox; Wally Dallenbach Jr.; Dean Dalton; Bill Dennis; Bob Derrington; Fred Dove; Ray Erickson; Jim Fiebelkorn; Lou Figaro; Jimmy Florian; Larry Frank; Charlie Glotzbach; George Green; Johnny Grubb; Janet Guthrie; Roger Hamby; Fred Harb; George Hartley; Jimmy Helms; Harvey Henderson; Bruce Hill; Kenny Irwin; Bobby Johns; Joe Lee Johnson; Bobby Keck; Al Keller; Bub King; Shep Langdon; Dick Linder; Chad Little; Chuck Mahoney; Johnny Mantz; Jimmy Massey; Dick May; Hershel McGriff; Ralph Moody; Joe Nemechek; Richie Panch; Steve Park; Dick Passwater; Tom Pistone; Bill Poor; Billy Rafter; Sam Rice; Charlie Roberts; Jackie Rogers; Shorty Rollins; Jim Roper; Earl Ross; Jack Russell; Greg Sacks; Frankie Schneider; Gene Simpson; Larry Smith; John Soares; Sam Sommers; Tony Stewart; Hut Stricklin; Marshall Teague; Ronnie Thomas; Jimmy Thompson; Bobby Wawak; Dink Widenhouse; Raymond Williams; Glen Wood; Doug Yates (1)

Top-22 Seasons

1. Richard Petty (29)
2. Buddy Baker (25)
3. Darrell Waltrip (23)
4. Bobby Allison (22)
5. Dale Earnhardt; Terry Labonte (21)
7. Ricky Rudd (19)
8. Bill Elliott; Cale Yarborough (18)
10. Buck Baker; Dave Marcis; David Pearson (17)
13. Geoff Bodine; Rusty Wallace (16)
15. James Hylton; Benny Parsons; Ken Schrader (15)
18. Buddy Arrington; J.D. McDuffie; Jim Paschal (14)
21. Neil Bonnett; Harry Gant; Sterling Marlin; Mark Martin; Kyle Petty; Morgan Shepherd (13)
27. Dick Brooks; Lee Petty; Michael Waltrip (12)
30. Cecil Gordon; Dale Jarrett; Elmo Langley (10)
33. Donnie Allison; Junior Johnson; Marvin Panch; Wendell Scott; G.C. Spencer (9)

38. Richard Childress; Ernie Irvan; Bobby Isaac; Ned Jarrett; Tiny Lund; Herb Thomas (8)

44. Davey Allison; Brett Bodine; Neil Castles; Tim Flock; Jeff Gordon; Henley Gray; Alan Kulwicki; Bobby Labonte; Fireball Roberts; Curtis Turner; Joe Weatherly; Bob Welborn; Rex White (7)

57. Bill Blair; Darel Dieringer; Fonty Flock; Bobby Hamilton; Bobby Hillin Jr.; Jimmy Means; Ted Musgrave; Tim Richmond; John Sears; Jack Smith; Lake Speed; Jabe Thomas; Speedy Thompson (6)

70. L.D. Austin; Walter Ballard; Ron Bouchard; Curtis Crider; Jimmie Lewallen; Fred Lorenzen; Cotton Owens; Jim Pardue; Dick Rathmann; Gober Sosebee; Jimmy Spencer; Frank Warren; Lee Roy Yarbrough (5)

83. Herman Beam; Jeff Burton; Bill Champion; Derrike Cope; Joe Eubanks; Paul Goldsmith; Rick Mast; Phil Parsons; Lennie Pond; Joe Ruttman; David Sisco; D.K. Ulrich (4)

95. Johnny Allen; John Andretti; Johnny Benson Jr.; Ward Burton; Bob Flock; Tommy Gale; Friday Hassler; Dick Hutcherson; Tommy Irwin; Ralph Liguori; Clyde Lynn; Coo Coo Marlin; Jeremy Mayfield; Clyde Minter; Lloyd Moore; Ed Negre; J.T. Putney; Jim Reed; Jody Ridley; Tighe Scott; Bill Seifert; Gwyn Staley; Donald Thomas; Larry Thomas; Dick Trickle; Roy Tyner (3)

121. Bill Amick; Ben Arnold; Herschel Buchanan; Red Byron; Billy Carden; Doug Cooper; Ricky Craven; Lloyd Dane; Ray Duhigg; Clarence DeZalia; Glenn Dunnaway; Pete Hamilton; Elton Hildreth; Brownie King; Paul Lewis; Skip Manning; Joe Millikan; Frank Mundy; Billy Myers; Eddie Pagan; Tom Pistone; Blackie Pitt; Bill Rexford; Buddy Shuman; Eddie Skinner; Mike Skinner; Slick Smith; Bill Snowden; Nelson Stacy; Dave Terrell; E.J. Trivette; Billy Wade; Rick Wilson; Doug Yates; Emanuel Zervakis (2)

156. Weldon Adams; Grant Adcox; Dick Beaty; Terry Bivins; Todd Bodine; Ken Bouchard; Trevor Boys; Earl Brooks; Perk Brown; Laird Bruner; Bob Burcham; Ted Chamberlain; Sara Christian; Neil Cole; Gene Comstock; Doug Cox; Tom Cox; Wally Dallenbach Jr.; Dean Dalton; Bill Dennis; Bob Derrington; John Dodd Jr.; Fred Dove; Stick Elliott; Tommy Ellis; Erick Erickson; Ray Erickson; Jim Fiebelkorn; Lou Figaro; Jimmy Florian; Larry Frank; Dick Getty; Charlie Glotzbach; George Green; Johnny Grubb; Janet Guthrie; Roger Hamby; Fred Harb; George Hartley; Jimmy Helms; Harvey Henderson; Jimmy Hensley; Bruce Hill; Kenny Irwin; Bruce Jacobi; Bobby Johns; Joe Lee Johnson; Bobby Keck; Al Keller; Bub King; Shep Langdon; Dick Linder; Chad Little; Joe Littlejohn; Chuck Mahoney; Johnny Mantz; Jimmy Massey; Dick May; Hershel McGriff; Ralph Moody; Arden Mounts; Joe Nemechek; Richie Panch; Steve Park; Dick Passwater; Bill Poor; Billy Rafter; Sam Rice; Charlie Roberts; Jackie Rogers; Shorty Rollins; Jim Roper; Earl Ross; Jack Russell; Greg Sacks; Frankie Schneider; Gene Simpson; Archie Smith; Larry Smith; John Soares; Sam Sommers; Tony Stewart; Hut Stricklin; Marshall Teague; Ronnie Thomas; Jimmy Thompson; Kenny Wallace; Bobby Wawak; Jack White; Dink Widenhouse; Raymond Williams; Glen Wood (1)

Top-23 Seasons

1. Richard Petty (30)
2. Buddy Baker (25)
3. Darrell Waltrip (23)
4. Bobby Allison (22)
5. Dale Earnhardt; Terry Labonte (21)
7. Ricky Rudd; Cale Yarborough (20)
9. Bill Elliott; Dave Marcis (19)
11. Buck Baker; David Pearson (17)
13. Geoff Bodine; Kyle Petty; Rusty Wallace (16)
16. Buddy Arrington; James Hylton; J.D. McDuffie; Benny Parsons; Ken Schrader (15)
21. Jim Paschal; Morgan Shepherd (14)
23. Neil Bonnett; Harry Gant; Sterling Marlin; Mark Martin; Michael Waltrip (13)

28. Dick Brooks; Lee Petty (12)

30. Elmo Langley (11)

31. Cecil Gordon; Dale Jarrett (10)

33. Donnie Allison; Junior Johnson; Tiny Lund; Marvin Panch; Wendell Scott; G.C. Spencer (9)

39. Richard Childress; Ernie Irvan; Bobby Isaac; Ned Jarrett; Lake Speed; Herb Thomas; Frank Warren; Joe Weatherly (8)

47. Davey Allison; Brett Bodine; Neil Castles; Tim Flock; Jeff Gordon; Henley Gray; Bobby Hillin Jr.; Alan Kulwicki; Bobby Labonte; Fireball Roberts; Jack Smith; Curtis Turner; Bob Welborn; Rex White (7)

61. Bill Blair; Darel Dieringer; Fonty Flock; Bobby Hamilton; Fred Lorenzen; Jimmy Means; Ted Musgrave; Tim Richmond; John Sears; Jimmy Spencer; Jabe Thomas; Speedy Thompson (6)

73. L.D. Austin; Walter Ballard; Ron Bouchard; Curtis Crider; Joe Eubanks; Jimmie Lewallen; Cotton Owens; Jim Pardue; Phil Parsons; Lennie Pond; Dick Rathmann; Gober Sosebee; D.K. Ulrich; Lee Roy Yarbrough (5)

87. Herman Beam; Jeff Burton; Ward Burton; Bill Champion; Derrike Cope; Paul Goldsmith; Coo Coo Marlin; Rick Mast; Ed Negre; Jim Reed; Joe Ruttman; Bill Seifert; David Sisco (4)

100. Johnny Allen; John Andretti; Johnny Benson Jr.; Wally Dallenbach Jr.; Ray Duhigg; Bob Flock; Tommy Gale; Friday Hassler; Dick Hutcherson; Tommy Irwin; Ralph Liguori; Clyde Lynn; Jeremy Mayfield; Clyde Minter; Lloyd Moore; Frank Mundy; J.T. Putney; Jody Ridley; Tighe Scott; Gwyn Staley; Donald Thomas; Larry Thomas; Dick Trickle; Roy Tyner (3)

124. Bill Amick; Ben Arnold; Herschel Buchanan; Red Byron; Billy Carden; Doug Cooper; Ricky Craven; Lloyd Dane; Clarence DeZalia; Glenn Dunnaway; Larry Frank; Charlie Glotzbach; Pete Hamilton; Elton Hildreth; Joe Lee Johnson; Brownie King; Bub King; Paul Lewis; Skip Manning; Joe Millikan; Billy Myers; Eddie Pagan; Tom Pistone; Blackie Pitt; Bill Rexford; Buddy Shuman; Eddie Skinner; Mike Skinner; Slick Smith; Bill Snowden; Nelson Stacy; Hut Stricklin; Dave Terrell; E.J. Trivette; Billy Wade; Rick Wilson; Doug Yates; Emanuel Zervakis (2)

162. Weldon Adams; Grant Adcox; Dick Beaty; Terry Bivins; Todd Bodine; Ken Bouchard; Trevor Boys; Richard Brickhouse; Earl Brooks; Perk Brown; Laird Bruner; Bob Burcham; Scotty Cain; Ted Chamberlain; Sara Christian; Neil Cole; Gene Comstock; Doug Cox; Tom Cox; Dean Dalton; Bill Dennis; Bob Derrington; John Dodd Jr.; Fred Dove; Stick Elliott; Tommy Ellis; Erick Erickson; Ray Erickson; Jim Fiebelkorn; Lou Figaro; Jimmy Florian; Dick Getty; George Green; Steve Grissom; Johnny Grubb; Janet Guthrie; Roger Hamby; Fred Harb; George Hartley; Jimmy Helms; Harvey Henderson; Jimmy Hensley; Bruce Hill; Kenny Irwin; Bruce Jacobi; Bobby Johns; Bobby Keck; Al Keller; Shep Langdon; Dick Linder; Chad Little; Joe Littlejohn; Chuck Mahoney; Johnny Mantz; Jimmy Massey; Banjo Matthews; Dick May; Hershel McGriff; Ralph Moody; Arden Mounts; Joe Nemechek; Richie Panch; Steve Park; Dick Passwater; Bill Poor; Billy Rafter; Jack Reynolds; Sam Rice; Charlie Roberts; Jackie Rogers; Shorty Rollins; Jim Roper; Earl Ross; Jack Russell; Greg Sacks; Frankie Schneider; Gene Simpson; Archie Smith; Larry Smith; John Soares; Sam Sommers; Tony Stewart; Jesse James Taylor; Marshall Teague; Ronnie Thomas; Jimmy Thompson; Kenny Wallace; Bobby Wawak; Jack White; Dink Widenhouse; Raymond Williams; Glen Wood (1)

Top-24 Seasons

1. Richard Petty (31)

2. Buddy Baker (25)

3. Darrell Waltrip (23)

4. Bobby Allison (22)

5. Dale Earnhardt; Terry Labonte; Dave Marcis; Cale Yarborough (21)

9. Bill Elliott; Ricky Rudd (20)

11. Buck Baker (18)

12. David Pearson (17)

13. Geoff Bodine; Benny Parsons; Kyle Petty; Rusty Wallace (16)

17. Buddy Arrington; James Hylton; J.D. McDuffie; Ken Schrader (15)

21. Sterling Marlin; Jim Paschal; Morgan Shepherd (14)

24. Neil Bonnett; Harry Gant; Mark Martin; Michael Waltrip (13)

28. Dick Brooks; Lee Petty (12)

30. Elmo Langley (11)

31. Cecil Gordon; Dale Jarrett (10)

33. Donnie Allison; Junior Johnson; Tiny Lund; Marvin Panch; Wendell Scott; Jack Smith; Lake Speed; G.C. Spencer; Curtis Turner; Frank Warren (9)

43. Richard Childress; Bobby Hillin Jr.; Ernie Irvan; Bobby Isaac; Ned Jarrett; Herb Thomas; Joe Weatherly; Bob Welborn (8)

51. Davey Allison; Brett Bodine; Neil Castles; Tim Flock; Jeff Gordon; Henley Gray; Alan Kulwicki; Bobby Labonte; Jimmy Means; Ted Musgrave; Fireball Roberts; Jimmy Spencer; Jabe Thomas; Rex White (7)

65. Bill Blair; Darel Dieringer; Joe Eubanks; Fonty Flock; Bobby Hamilton; Fred Lorenzen; Coo Coo Marlin; Cotton Owens; Lennie Pond; Tim Richmond; John Sears; Speedy Thompson (6)

78. Johnny Allen; L.D. Austin; Walter Ballard; Ron Bouchard; Curtis Crider; Tommy Gale; Jimmie Lewallen; Rick Mast; Jim Pardue; Phil Parsons; Dick Rathmann; Gober Sosebee; D.K. Ulrich; Lee Roy Yarbrough (5)

92. Herman Beam; Jeff Burton; Ward Burton; Bill Champion; Derrike Cope; Paul Goldsmith; Friday Hassler; Ed Negre; J.T. Putney; Jim Reed; Bill Seifert; David Sisco; Donald Thomas (4)

105. John Andretti; Johnny Benson Jr.; Wally Dallenbach Jr.; Ray Duhigg; Bob Flock; Dick Hutcherson; Tommy Irwin; Paul Lewis; Ralph Liguori; Clyde Lynn; Jeremy Mayfield; Clyde Minter; Lloyd Moore; Frank Mundy; Jody Ridley; Tighe Scott; Gwyn Staley; Larry Thomas; Dick Trickle; Roy Tyner; Rick Wilson (3)

126. Bill Amick; Ben Arnold; Herschel Buchanan; Red Byron; Billy Carden; Doug Cooper; Ricky Craven; Lloyd Dane; Clarence DeZalia; Glenn Dunnaway; Larry Frank; Charlie Glotzbach; Steve Grissom; Pete Hamilton; Elton Hildreth; Kenny Irwin; Bobby Johns; Joe Lee Johnson; Brownie King; Bub King; Chad Little; Skip Manning; Joe Millikan; Billy Myers; Joe Nemechek; Eddie Pagan; Tom Pistone; Blackie Pitt; Bill Rexford; Charlie Roberts; Buddy Shuman; Eddie Skinner; Mike Skinner; Slick Smith; Bill Snowden; Nelson Stacy; Hut Stricklin; Dave Terrell; E.J. Trivette; Billy Wade; Doug Yates; Emanuel Zervakis (2)

168. Carl Adams; Weldon Adams; Grant Adcox; Mike Alexander; Bob Barron; Dick Beaty; Tony Bettenhausen Jr.; Terry Bivins; Todd Bodine; Ken Bouchard; Trevor Boys; Richard Brickhouse; Earl Brooks; Perk Brown; Laird Bruner; Bob Burcham; Dick Burns; Scotty Cain; Ted Chamberlain; Sara Christian; Neil Cole; Gene Comstock; Doug Cox; Tom Cox; Dean Dalton; Bill Dennis; Bob Derrington; John Dodd Jr.; Fred Dove; Stick Elliott; Tommy Ellis; Erick Erickson; Ray Erickson; Jim Fiebelkorn; Lou Figaro; Jimmy Florian; Joe Frasson; Dick Getty; George Green; Johnny Grubb; Janet Guthrie; Roger Hamby; Fred Harb; George Hartley; Jimmy Helms; Harvey Henderson; Jimmy Hensley; Bruce Hill; Bruce Jacobi; Bobby Keck; Al Keller; John Kieper; Shep Langdon; Dick Linder; Joe Littlejohn; Chuck Mahoney; Johnny Mantz; Jimmy Massey; Banjo Matthews; Dick May; Pop McGinnis; Hershel McGriff; Sam McQuagg; Butch Miller; Ralph Moody; Bud Moore; Arden Mounts; Richie Panch; Steve Park; Dick Passwater; Bill Poor; Billy Rafter; Jack Reynolds; Sam Rice; Jackie Rogers; Shorty Rollins; Jim Roper; Earl Ross; Jack Russell; Greg Sacks; Frankie Schneider; Gene Simpson; Archie Smith; Larry Smith; John Soares; Sam Sommers; Tony Stewart; Jesse James Taylor; Marshall Teague; Ronnie Thomas; Jimmy Thompson; Kenny Wallace; Bobby Wawak; Jack White; Dink Widenhouse; Raymond Williams; Glen Wood (1)

Performance Index Records

Top 25 Seasons

1. Richard Petty (31)
2. Buddy Baker (25)
3. Bobby Allison; Darrell Waltrip (23)
5. Cale Yarborough (22)
6. Dale Earnhardt; Bill Elliott; Terry Labonte; Dave Marcis (21)
10. Ricky Rudd (20)
11. Buck Baker; David Pearson (18)
13. Kyle Petty (17)
14. Buddy Arrington; Geoff Bodine; J.D. McDuffie; Benny Parsons; Rusty Wallace (16)
19. James Hylton; Ken Schrader (15)
21. Sterling Marlin; Jim Paschal; Morgan Shepherd (14)
24. Neil Bonnett; Harry Gant; Mark Martlin; Michael Waltrip (13)
28. Dick Brooks; Lee Petty (12)
30. Cecil Gordon; Dale Jarrett; Elmo Langley (11)
33. Lake Speed; Curtis Turner; Frank Warren (10)
36. Donnie Allison; Bobby Isaac; Junior Johnson; Tiny Lund; Marvin Panch; Wendell Scott; Jack Smith; G.C. Spencer (9)
44. Neil Castles; Richard Childress; Bobby Hillin Jr.; Ernie Irvan; Ned Jarrett; Herb Thomas; Joe Weatherly; Bob Welborn (8)
52. Davey Allison; Brett Bodine; Tim Flock; Jeff Gordon; Henley Gray; Bobby Hamilton; Alan Kulwicki; Bobby Labonte; Jimmy Means; Ted Musgrave; Fireball Roberts; Joe Ruttman; Jimmy Spencer; Jabe Thomas; Rex White (7)
67. Bill Blair; Darel Dieringer; Joe Eubanks; Fonty Flock; Fred Lorenzen; Coo Coo Marlin; Cotton Owens; Phil Parsons; Lennie Pond; Tim Richmond; John Sears; Speedy Thompson (6)
79. Johnny Allen; L.D. Austin; Walter Ballard; Ron Bouchard; Curtis Crider; Tommy Gale; Jimmie Lewallen; Rick Mast; Jeremy Mayfield; Jim Pardue; Dick Rathmann; Gober Sosebee; D.K. Ulrich; Lee Roy Yarbrough (5)
93. Herman Beam; Johnny Benson Jr.; Jeff Burton; Ward Burton; Bill Champion; Derrike Cope; Paul Goldsmith; Friday Hassler; Paul Lewis; Ralph Liguori; Ed Negre; J.T. Putney; Jim Reed; Jody Ridley; Bill Seifert; David Sisco; Donald Thomas; Roy Tyner; Rick Wilson (4)
112. John Andretti; Wally Dallenbach Jr.; Ray Duhigg; Bob Flock; George Green; Dick Hutcherson; Tommy Irwin; Clyde Lynn; Clyde Minter; Lloyd Moore; Frank Mundy; Tighe Scott; Nelson Stacy; Gwyn Staley; Larry Thomas; Dick Trickle (3)
128. Bill Amick; Ben Arnold; Trevor Boys; Earl Brooks; Herschel Buchanan; Red Byron; Billy Carden; Doug Cooper; Ricky Craven; Lloyd Dane; Clarence DeZalia; Glenn Dunnaway; Larry Frank; Joe Frasson; Charlie Glotzbach; Steve Grissom; Pete Hamilton; Elton Hildreth; Kenny Irwin; Bobby Johns; Joe Lee Johnson; Brownie King; Bub King; Chad Little; Skip Manning; Dick May; Joe Millikan; Billy Myers; Joe Nemechek; Eddie Pagan; Tom Pistone; Blackie Pitt; Bill Rexford; Charlie Roberts; Jackie Rogers; Buddy Shuman; Eddie Skinner; Mike Skinner; Slick Smith; Bill Snowden; Hut Stricklin; Dave Terrell; E.J. Trivette; Billy Wade; Kenny Wallace; Doug Yates; Emanuel Zervakis (2)
175. Carl Adams; Weldon Adams; Grant Adcox; Mike Alexander; Jack Anderson; Bob Apperson; Bob Barron; Dick Beaty; Tony Bettenhausen Jr.; Terry Bivins; Todd Bodine; Ken Bouchard; Richard Brickhouse; Perk Brown; Laird Bruner; Bob Burcham; Dick Burns; Scotty Cain; Ted Chamberlain; Sara Christian; Frank Christian; Neil Cole; Gene Comstock; Doug Cox; Tom Cox; Dean Dalton; Bill Dennis; Bob Derrington; John Dodd Jr.; Fred Dove; Ralph Earnhardt; Stick Elliott; Tommy Ellis; Erick Erickson; Ray Erickson; Jim Fiebelkorn; Lou Figaro; Jimmy Florian; A.J. Foyt; Dick Getty; Johnny Grubb; Janet Guthrie; Roger Hamby; Fred Harb; Harold Hardesty; Ferrel Harris; George Hartley; Jimmy Helms; Harvey Henderson; Jimmy Hensley; Bruce Hill; Bruce Jacobi; Bobby Keck; Al Keller; John Kieper; Art Lamey; Shep Langdon; Dick Linder; Joe Littlejohn; Chuck Mahoney; Larry Manning; Johnny Mantz; Jimmy Massey; Banjo Matthews; Pop McGinnis; Hershel McGriff; Sam McQuagg; Butch Miller; Joel Million; Ralph Moody; Bud Moore; Arden Mounts; Richie Panch; Steve Park; Dick Passwater; Johnny Patterson; Bill Poor; Billy Rafter; Jack Reynolds; Sam Rice; Shorty Rollins; Jim Roper; Earl Ross; Jack Russell; Greg Sacks; Frankie Schneider; George Seeger; Gene Simpson; Archie Smith; Larry Smith; John Soares; Sam Sommers; Tony Stewart; Jesse James Taylor; Marshall Teague; Ronnie Thomas; Jimmy Thompson; Mike Wallace; Bobby Wawak; Jack White; Dink Widenhouse; Raymond Williams; Elmer Wilson; Glen Wood (1)

Consecutive No. 1 Seasons

1. Cale Yarborough	3	(1976-78)
Dale Earnhardt	3	(1993-95)
Jeff Gordon	3	(1996-98)
4. Buck Baker	2	(1956-57)
Lee Petty	2	(1958-59)
Rex White	2	(1960-61)
Richard Petty	2	(1963-64)
David Pearson	2	(1968-69)
Richard Petty	2	(1974-75)
Darrell Waltrip	2	(1981-82)
Bill Elliott	2	(1984-85)
Dale Earnhardt	2	(1986-87)

Consecutive Top-Two Seasons

1. Buck Baker	4	(1955-58)
2. Lee Petty	3	(1952-54)
Richard Petty	3	(1962-64)
Ned Jarrett	3	(1963-65)
Richard Petty	3	(1967-69)
Cale Yarborough	3	(1976-78)
Bobby Allison	3	(1981-83)
Darrell Waltrip	3	(1981-83)
Dale Earnhardt	3	(1989-91)
Dale Earnhardt	3	(1993-95)
Jeff Gordon	3	(1996-98)
12. Lee Petty	2	(1949-50)
Tim Flock	2	(1951-52)
Herb Thomas	2	(1953-54)
Lee Petty	2	(1958-59)
Rex White	2	(1960-61)
James Hylton	2	(1966-67)
David Pearson	2	(1968-69)
Richard Petty	2	(1971-72)
Richard Petty	2	(1974-75)
Bill Elliott	2	(1984-85)
Dale Earnhardt	2	(1986-87)
Bill Elliott	2	(1987-88)
Rusty Wallace	2	(1988-89)
Rusty Wallace	2	(1993-94)

Longest Streaks of Top-Three Seasons

1. Buck Baker	6	(1954-59)
Richard Petty	6	(1967-72)
Dale Earnhardt	6	(1986-91)
4. Ned Jarrett	5	(1961-65)
Cale Yarborough	5	(1976-80)
6. Herb Thomas	4	(1951-54)
Lee Petty	4	(1952-55)
Jeff Gordon	4	(1995-98)
Dale Jarrett	4	(1996-99)

10. Lee Petty	3	(1958-60)
Richard Petty	3	(1962-64)
Bobby Allison	3	(1970-72)
Bobby Allison	3	(1981-83)
Darrell Waltrip	3	(1981-83)
Bill Elliott	3	(1983-85)
Darrell Waltrip	3	(1985-87)
Dale Earnhardt	3	(1993-95)
Mark Martin	3	(1997-99)

Longest Streaks of Top-Four Seasons

1. Lee Petty	12	(1949-60)
Richard Petty	12	(1966-77)
3. Buck Baker	7	(1953-59)
James Hylton	7	(1966-72)
5. Ned Jarrett	6	(1960-65)
Bill Elliott	6	(1983-88)
Dale Earnhardt	6	(1986-91)
8. Cale Yarborough	5	(1976-80)
9. Herb Thomas	4	(1951-54)
Dale Earnhardt	4	(1993-96)
Jeff Gordon	4	(1995-98)
Dale Jarrett	4	(1996-99)

Longest Streaks of Top-Five Seasons

1. Lee Petty	12	(1949-60)
Richard Petty	12	(1966-77)
3. Buck Baker	8	(1953-60)
4. James Hylton	7	(1966-72)
Darrell Waltrip	7	(1981-87)
Mark Martin	7	(1993-99)
7. Ned Jarrett	6	(1960-65)
Bill Elliott	6	(1983-88)
Dale Earnhardt	6	(1986-91)
10. Richard Petty	5	(1960-64)
Benny Parsons	5	(1976-80)
Cale Yarborough	5	(1976-80)

Longest Streaks of Top-Six Seasons

1. Lee Petty	12	(1949-60)
Richard Petty	12	(1966-77)
3. Darrell Waltrip	11	(1977-87)
4. Buck Baker	8	(1953-60)
Bill Elliott	8	(1983-90)
Mark Martin	8	(1992-99)
7. James Hylton	7	(1966-72)
8. Ned Jarrett	6	(1960-65)
Dale Earnhardt	6	(1986-91)
10. Richard Petty	5	(1960-64)
David Pearson	5	(1972-76)
Benny Parsons	5	(1976-80)
Cale Yarborough	5	(1976-80)
Rusty Wallace	5	(1986-90)
Dale Earnhardt	5	(1993-97)
Jeff Gordon	5	(1995-99)

Longest Streaks of Top-Seven Seasons

1. Lee Petty	12	(1949-60)
Richard Petty	12	(1966-77)
3. Darrell Waltrip	11	(1977-87)
Mark Martin	11	(1989-99)
5. Buck Baker	8	(1953-60)
James Hylton	8	(1966-73)
Bill Elliott	8	(1983-90)
8. Bobby Allison	7	(1978-84)
9. Ned Jarrett	6	(1960-65)
David Pearson	6	(1972-77)
Dale Earnhardt	6	(1986-91)

Longest Streaks of Top-Eight Seasons

1. Lee Petty	12	(1949-60)
Richard Petty	12	(1966-77)
3. Darrell Waltrip	11	(1977-87)
Mark Martin	11	(1989-99)
5. Buck Baker	9	(1953-61)
6. James Hylton	8	(1966-73)
Bill Elliott	8	(1983-90)
8. Herb Thomas	7	(1950-56)
Bobby Allison	7	(1978-84)
10. Ned Jarrett	6	(1960-65)
David Pearson	6	(1972-77)
Benny Parsons	6	(1975-80)
Dale Earnhardt	6	(1986-91)
Jeff Gordon	6	(1994-99)

Longest Streaks of Top-Nine Seasons

1. Richard Petty	18	(1966-83)
2. Darrell Waltrip	13	(1977-89)
3. Lee Petty	12	(1949-60)
4. Bill Elliott	11	(1983-93)
Mark Martin	11	(1989-99)
6. Buck Baker	9	(1953-61)
Benny Parsons	9	(1972-80)
8. James Hylton	8	(1966-73)
Cale Yarborough	8	(1973-80)
10. Herb Thomas	7	(1950-56)
Elmo Langley	7	(1966-72)
Bobby Allison	7	(1978-84)
Dale Earnhardt	7	(1993-99)

Longest Streaks of Top-10 Seasons

1. Richard Petty	18	(1966-83)
2. Darrell Waltrip	13	(1977-89)
3. Lee Petty	12	(1949-60)
4. Benny Parsons	11	(1970-80)
Bill Elliott	11	(1983-93)
Mark Martin	11	(1989-99)
7. Buck Baker	9	(1953-61)
Bobby Allison	9	(1976-84)
9. James Hylton	8	(1966-73)
Cale Yarborough	8	(1973-80)

Longest Streaks of Top-11 Seasons

1. Richard Petty	18	(1966-83)
2. Darrell Waltrip	13	(1977-89)
Bill Elliott	13	(1983-95)
4. Lee Petty	12	(1949-60)
5. Benny Parsons	11	(1970-80)
Terry Labonte	11	(1980-90)
Mark Martin	11	(1989-99)
8. James Hylton	10	(1966-75)
9. Buck Baker	9	(1953-61)
Cale Yarborough	9	(1973-81)
Bobby Allison	9	(1976-84)
Dale Earnhardt	9	(1983-91)

Performance Index Records

Longest Streaks of Top-12 Seasons

1. Richard Petty	19	(1966-84)
2. Ricky Rudd	14	(1983-96)
3. Bill Elliott	13	(1983-95)
Benny Parsons	13	(1970-82)
Darrell Waltrip	13	(1977-89)
6. Lee Petty	12	(1949-60)
Buck Baker	12	(1953-64)
James Hylton	12	(1966-77)
Terry Labonte	12	(1979-90)
10. Bobby Allison	11	(1976-86)
Mark Martin	11	(1989-99)

Longest Streaks of Top-13 Seasons

1. Richard Petty	19	(1966-84)
2. Dale Earnhardt	17	(1983-99)
3. Ricky Rudd	16	(1981-96)
4. Darrell Waltrip	14	(1976-89)
5. Buck Baker	13	(1952-64)
Benny Parsons	13	(1970-82)
Bill Elliott	13	(1983-95)
8. Lee Petty	12	(1949-60)
James Hylton	12	(1966-77)
Bobby Allison	12	(1976-87)
Terry Labonte	12	(1979-90)

Longest Streaks of Top-14 Seasons

1. Richard Petty	19	(1966-84)
2. Dale Earnhardt	17	(1983-99)
3. Darrell Waltrip	16	(1974-89)
Ricky Rudd	16	(1981-96)
5. Rusty Wallace	14	(1986-99)
6. Buck Baker	13	(1952-64)
Benny Parsons	13	(1970-82)
Bill Elliott	13	(1983-95)
9. Lee Petty	12	(1949-60)
James Hylton	12	(1966-77)
Bobby Allison	12	(1976-87)
Terry Labonte	12	(1979-90)
Mark Martin	12	(1988-99)

Longest Streaks of Top-15 Seasons

1. Richard Petty	19	(1966-84)
2. Ricky Rudd	17	(1981-97)
Dale Earnhardt	17	(1983-99)
4. Darrell Waltrip	16	(1974-89)
5. Buck Baker	15	(1950-64)
6. Bill Elliott	14	(1982-95)
Rusty Wallace	14	(1986-99)
8. Benny Parsons	13	(1970-82)
9. Lee Petty	12	(1949-60)
James Hylton	12	(1966-77)
Bobby Allison	12	(1976-87)
Terry Labonte	12	(1979-90)
Mark Martin	12	(1988-99)

Longest Streaks of Top-16 Seasons

1. Darrell Waltrip	21	(1974-94)
2. Richard Petty	19	(1966-84)
3. Ricky Rudd	17	(1981-97)
Dale Earnhardt	17	(1983-99)
5. Bill Elliott	14	(1982-95)
Rusty Wallace	14	(1986-99)

Longest Streaks of Top-17 Seasons

7. Buck Baker	13	(1952-64)
Benny Parsons	13	(1970-82)
9. Lee Petty	12	(1949-60)
James Hylton	12	(1966-77)
Bobby Allison	12	(1976-87)
Terry Labonte	12	(1979-90)
Mark Martin	12	(1988-99)

1. Bobby Allison	22	(1966-87)
Richard Petty	22	(1966-87)
3. Darrell Waltrip	21	(1974-94)
4. Ricky Rudd	17	(1981-97)
Dale Earnhardt	17	(1983-99)
6. Bill Elliott	14	(1982-95)
Rusty Wallace	14	(1986-99)
8. Buck Baker	13	(1952-64)
Benny Parsons	13	(1970-82)
10. Lee Petty	12	(1949-60)
James Hylton	12	(1966-77)
Terry Labonte	12	(1979-90)
Mark Martin	12	(1988-99)

Longest Streaks of Top-18 Seasons

1. Bobby Allison	22	(1966-87)
Richard Petty	22	(1966-87)
3. Darrell Waltrip	21	(1974-94)
Terry Labonte	21	(1979-99)
5. Ricky Rudd	17	(1981-97)
Dale Earnhardt	17	(1983-99)
7. Geoff Bodine	14	(1984-97)
Bill Elliott	14	(1982-95)
Rusty Wallace	14	(1986-99)
10. Buck Baker	13	(1952-64)
Benny Parsons	13	(1970-82)
Ken Schrader	13	(1987-99)

Longest Streaks of Top-19 Seasons

1. Bobby Allison	22	(1966-87)
Richard Petty	22	(1966-87)
3. Darrell Waltrip	21	(1974-94)
Dale Earnhardt	21	(1979-99)
Terry Labonte	21	(1979-99)
6. Buddy Baker	17	(1965-81)
Ricky Rudd	17	(1981-97)
Bill Elliott	17	(1982-98)
9. Rusty Wallace	16	(1984-99)
10. Geoff Bodine	14	(1984-97)

Longest Streaks of Top-20 Seasons

1. Buddy Baker	24	(1965-88)
2. Bobby Allison	22	(1966-87)
Richard Petty	22	(1966-87)
Darrell Waltrip	22	(1974-95)
5. Dale Earnhardt	21	(1979-99)
Terry Labonte	21	(1979-99)
7. Bill Elliott	18	(1982-99)
8. Ricky Rudd	17	(1981-97)
9. Rusty Wallace	16	(1984-99)
10. Buck Baker	15	(1950-64)
James Hylton	15	(1966-80)

Longest Streaks of Top-21 Seasons

1.	Buddy Baker	24		(1965-88)
2.	Bobby Allison	22		(1966-87)
	Richard Petty	22		(1966-87)
	Darrell Waltrip	22		(1974-95)
5.	Dale Earnhardt	21		(1979-99)
	Terry Labonte	21		(1979-99)
7.	Bill Elliott	18		(1982-99)
8.	Buck Baker	17		(1950-66)
	Ricky Rudd	17		(1981-97)
10.	Geoff Bodine	16		(1982-97)
	Rusty Wallace	16		(1984-99)

Longest Streaks of Top-22 Seasons

1.	Buddy Baker	24		(1965-88)
2.	Darrell Waltrip	23		(1973-95)
3.	Bobby Allison	22		(1966-87)
	Richard Petty	22		(1966-87)
5.	Dale Earnhardt	21		(1979-99)
	Terry Labonte	21		(1979-99)
7.	Bill Elliott	18		(1982-99)
8.	Buck Baker	17		(1950-66)
	Ricky Rudd	17		(1981-97)
10.	Geoff Bodine	16		(1982-97)
	Rusty Wallace	16		(1984-99)

Longest Streaks of Top-23 Seasons

1.	Richard Petty	29		(1959-87)
2.	Buddy Baker	24		(1965-88)
3.	Darrell Waltrip	23		(1973-95)
4.	Bobby Allison	22		(1966-87)
5.	Dale Earnhardt	21		(1979-99)
	Terry Labonte	21		(1979-99)
7.	Ricky Rudd	18		(1981-98)
	Bill Elliott	18		(1982-99)
9.	Buck Baker	17		(1950-66)
10.	Geoff Bodine	16		(1982-97)
	Rusty Wallace	16		(1984-99)

Longest Streaks of Top-24 Seasons

1.	Richard Petty	29		(1959-87)
2.	Buddy Baker	24		(1965-88)
3.	Darrell Waltrip	23		(1973-95)
4.	Bobby Allison	22		(1966-87)
5.	Dale Earnhardt	21		(1979-99)
	Terry Labonte	21		(1979-99)
7.	Dave Marcis	19		(1969-87)
8.	Buck Baker	18		(1950-67)
	Ricky Rudd	18		(1981-98)
	Bill Elliott	18		(1982-99)

Longest Streaks of Top-25 Seasons

1.	Richard Petty	29		(1959-87)
2.	Buddy Baker	24		(1965-88)
3.	Bobby Allison	23		(1966-88)
	Darrell Waltrip	23		(1973-95)
5.	Dale Earnhardt	21		(1979-99)
	Terry Labonte	21		(1979-99)
7.	Dave Marcis	19		(1969-87)
	Bill Elliott	19		(1981-99)
9.	Buck Baker	18		(1950-67)
	Ricky Rudd	18		(1981-98)

Victory Records

Victories

1.	Richard Petty	200
2.	David Pearson	105
3.	Bobby Allison	85
4.	Darrell Waltrip	84
5.	Cale Yarborough	83
6.	Dale Earnhardt	74
7.	Lee Petty	54
8.	Junior Johnson	50
	Ned Jarrett	50
10.	Jeff Gordon	49
	Rusty Wallace	49
12.	Herb Thomas	48
13.	Buck Baker	46
14.	Bill Elliott	40
15.	Tim Flock	39
16.	Bobby Isaac	37
17.	Fireball Roberts	33
18.	Mark Martin	31
19.	Rex White	28
20.	Fred Lorenzen	26
21.	Jim Paschal	25
	Joe Weatherly	25
23.	Dale Jarrett	22
24.	Terry Labonte	21
	Benny Parsons	21
	Jack Smith	21
27.	Ricky Rudd	20
	Speedy Thompson	20
29.	Davey Allison	19
	Buddy Baker	19
	Fonty Flock	19
32.	Geoff Bodine	18
	Neil Bonnett	18
	Harry Gant	18
35.	Marvin Panch	17
	Curtis Turner	17
37.	Ernie Irvan	15
38.	Dick Hutcherson	14
	Lee Roy Yarbrough	14
40.	Dick Rathmann	13
	Tim Richmond	13
42.	Bobby Labonte	12
43.	Jeff Burton	11
44.	Donnie Allison	10
45.	Paul Goldsmith	9
	Cotton Owens	9
	Bob Welborn	9
48.	Kyle Petty	8
49.	Darel Dieringer	7
	A.J. Foyt	7
	Jim Reed	7
	Marshall Teague	7
53.	Sterling Marlin	6
54.	Dan Gurney	5
	Alan Kulwicki	5
	Tiny Lund	5
	Dave Marcis	5
	Ralph Moody	5
59.	Lloyd Dane	4
	Bob Flock	4

Charlie Glotzbach	4	
Eddie Gray	4	
Pete Hamilton	4	
Parnelli Jones	4	
Hershel McGriff	4	
Eddie Pagan	4	
Ken Schrader	4	
Morgan Shepherd	4	
Nelson Stacy	4	
Billy Wade	4	
Glen Wood	4	
72. Bill Blair	3	
Bobby Hamilton	3	
Dick Linder	3	
Frank Mundy	3	
Gwyn Staley	3	
Tony Stewart	3	
78. John Andretti	2	
Johnny Beauchamp	2	
Red Byron	2	
Derrike Cope	2	
Ray Elder	2	
James Hylton	2	
Bobby Johns	2	
Joe Lee Johnson	2	
Al Keller	2	
Elmo Langley	2	
Danny Letner	2	
Billy Myers	2	
Jim Pardue	2	
Tom Pistone	2	
Marvin Porter	2	
Gober Sosebee	2	
Jimmy Spencer	2	
Emanuel Zervakis	2	
96. Johnny Allen	1	
Bill Amick	1	
Mario Andretti	1	
Earl Balmer	1	
Brett Bodine	1	
Ron Bouchard	1	
Richard Brickhouse	1	
Dick Brooks	1	
Bob Burdick	1	
Marvin Burke	1	
Ward Burton	1	
Neil Cole	1	
Jim Cook	1	
Mark Donohue	1	
Joe Eubanks	1	
Lou Figaro	1	
Jimmy Florian	1	
Larry Frank	1	
Danny Graves	1	
Royce Haggerty	1	
Bobby Hillin Jr.	1	
Jim Hurtubise	1	
John Kieper	1	
Harold Kite	1	
Paul Lewis	1	
Johnny Mantz	1	
Jeremy Mayfield	1	
Sam McQuagg	1	

Lloyd Moore	1
Norm Nelson	1
Joe Nemechek	1
Bill Norton	1
Phil Parsons	1
Dick Passwater	1
Lennie Pond	1
Bill Rexford	1
Jody Ridley	1
Shorty Rollins	1
Jim Roper	1
Earl Ross	1
John Rostek	1
Johnny Rutherford	1
Greg Sacks	1
Leon Sales	1
Frankie Schneider	1
Wendell Scott	1
Buddy Shuman	1
John Soares	1
Lake Speed	1
Chuck Stevenson	1
Donald Thomas	1
Tommy Thompson	1
Art Watts	1
Danny Weinberg	1
Jack White	1

Annual Victory Leaders

1949—Red Byron (2)
      Bob Flock (2)
1950—Curtis Turner (4)
1951—Fonty Flock (8)
1952—Tim Flock (8)
      Herb Thomas (8)
1953—Herb Thomas (12)
1954—Herb Thomas (12)
1955—Tim Flock (18)
1956—Buck Baker (14)
1957—Buck Baker (10)
1958—Lee Petty (7)
1959—Lee Petty (11)
1960—Rex White (6)
1961—Joe Weatherly (9)
1962—Joe Weatherly (9)
1963—Richard Petty (14)
1964—Ned Jarrett (15)
1965—Ned Jarrett (13)
      Junior Johnson (13)
1966—David Pearson (15)
1967—Richard Petty (27)
1968—David Pearson (16)
      Richard Petty (16)
1969—Bobby Isaac (17)
1970—Richard Petty (18)
1971—Richard Petty (21)
1972—Bobby Allison (10)
1973—David Pearson (11)
1974—Richard Petty (10)
      Cale Yarborough (10)
1975—Richard Petty (13)
1976—David Pearson (10)
1977—Cale Yarborough (9)
1978—Cale Yarborough (10)

1979—Darrell Waltrip (7)
1980—Cale Yarborough (6)
1981—Darrell Waltrip (12)
1982—Darrell Waltrip (12)
1983—Bobby Allison (6)
      Darrell Waltrip (6)
1984—Darrell Waltrip (7)
1985—Bill Elliott (11)
1986—Tim Richmond (7)
1987—Dale Earnhardt (11)
1988—Bill Elliott (6)
      Rusty Wallace (6)
1989—Rusty Wallace (6)
      Darrell Waltrip (6)
1990—Dale Earnhardt (9)
1991—Davey Allison (5)
      Harry Gant (5)
1992—Davey Allison (5)
      Bill Elliott (5)
1993—Rusty Wallace (10)
1994—Rusty Wallace (8)
1995—Jeff Gordon (7)
1996—Jeff Gordon (10)
1997—Jeff Gordon (10)
1998—Jeff Gordon (13)
1999—Jeff Gordon (7)

Seasons Recording Most Victories *

1. Richard Petty (7)
2. Darrell Waltrip (6)
3. Jeff Gordon (5)
4. David Pearson; Rusty Wallace; Cale Yarborough (4)
7. Bill Elliott Herb Thomas (3)
9. Bobby Allison; Davey Allison; Buck Baker; Dale Earnhardt; Tim Flock; Ned Jarrett; Lee Petty; Joe Weatherly (2)
17. Red Byron; Bob Flock; Fonty Flock; Harry Gant; Bobby Isaac; Junior Johnson; Tim Richmond; Curtis Turner; Rex White (1)
* Including ties

Longest Streaks of Seasons With a Victory

1. Richard Petty	18	(1960-77)
2. David Pearson	17	(1964-80)
3. Ricky Rudd	16	(1983-98)
4. Darrell Waltrip	15	(1975-89)
Dale Earnhardt	15	(1982-96)
6. Rusty Wallace	14	(1986-99)
7. Lee Petty	13	(1949-61)
Cale Yarborough	13	(1973-85)
9. Buck Baker	10	(1952-61)
Bobby Allison	10	(1966-75)
Bill Elliott	10	(1983-92)

Longest Streaks of Seasons With Multiple Victories

1. Richard Petty	18	(1960-77)
2. Cale Yarborough	13	(1973-85)
3. Bobby Allison	10	(1966-75)
Darrell Waltrip	10	(1977-86)
5. Lee Petty	9	(1952-60)
Dale Earnhardt	9	(1983-91)
7. David Pearson	8	(1971-78)
8. Bobby Allison	7	(1978-84)
9. Herb Thomas	6	(1951-56)
Jack Smith	6	(1957-62)

Fred Lorenzen	6	(1961-66)
David Pearson	6	(1964-69)
Benny Parsons	6	(1976-81)
Bill Elliott	6	(1984-89)
Rusty Wallace	6	(1986-91)
Davey Allison	6	(1987-92)
Jeff Gordon	6	(1994-99)

10 Consecutive Victories

Richard Petty

8/12/67—Myers Brothers 250; Bowman Gray Stadium
8/17/67—Sandlapper 200; Columbia Speedway
8/25/67—Savannah Speedway
9/4/67—Southern 500; Darlington Raceway
9/8/67—Buddy Shuman 250; Hickory Speedway
9/10/67—Capital City 300; Virginia State Fairgrounds
9/15/67—Maryland 300; Beltsville Speedway
9/17/67—Hillsborough 150; Orange Speedway
9/24/67—Old Dominion 500; Martinsville Speedway
10/1/67—Wilkes 400; North Wilkesboro Speedway

Five Consecutive Victories

Bobby Allison

5/30/71—World 600; Charlotte Motor Speedway
6/6/71—Mason-Dixon 500; Dover Downs International Speedway
6/13/71—Motor State 400; Michigan International Speedway
6/20/71—Winston Golden State 400; Riverside Int. Raceway
6/23/71—Space City 300; Meyer Speedway

Richard Petty

7/14/71—Albany-Saratoga 250; Albany-Saratoga Speedway
7/15/71—Islip 250; Islip Speedway
7/18/71—Northern 300; Trenton Speedway
7/24/71—Nashville 420; Fairgrounds Speedway
8/1/71—Dixie 500; Atlanta International Raceway

Four Consecutive Victories

Billy Wade

7/10/64—Fireball Roberts 200; Old Bridge Stadium
7/12/64—Bridgehampton Raceway
7/15/64—Islip Speedway
7/19/64—The Glen 151.8; Watkins Glen International

David Pearson

4/3/66—Hickory 250; Hickory Speedway
4/7/66—Columbia 200; Columbia Speedway
4/9/66—Greenville 200; Greenville-Pickens Speedway
4/11/66—Bowman Gray Stadium

David Pearson

5/5/68—Fireball 300; Asheville-Weaverville Speedway
5/11/68—Rebel 400; Darlington Raceway
5/17/68—Beltsville 300; Beltsville Speedway
5/18/68—Tidewater 250; Langley Field Speedway

Cale Yarborough

9/12/76—Capital City 400; Richmond Fairgrounds Raceway
9/19/76—Delaware 500; Dover Downs International Speedway
9/26/76—Old Dominion 500; Martinsville Speedway
10/3/76—Wilkes 400; North Wilkesboro Speedway

Darrell Waltrip

9/27/81—Old Dominion 500; Martinsville Speedway
10/4/81—Holly Farms 400; North Wilkesboro Speedway
10/11/81—National 500; Charlotte Motor Speedway
11/1/81—American 500; North Carolina Motor Speedway

Dale Earnhardt
3/29/87—TranSouth 500; Darlington International Raceway
4/5/87—First Union 400; North Wilkesboro Speedway
4/12/87—Valleydale 500; Bristol International Raceway
4/26/87—Sovran Bank 500; Martinsville Speedway

Harry Gant
9/1/91—Heinz Southern 500; Darlington Raceway
9/7/91—Miller Genuine Draft 400; Richmond Int. Raceway
9/15/91—Peak Antifreeze 500; Dover Downs Int. Speedway
9/22/91—Goody's 500; Martinsville Speedway

Bill Elliott
3/1/92—Goodwrench 500; North Carolina Motor Speedway
3/8/92—Pontiac Excitement 400; Richmond Int. Raceway
3/15/92—Motorcraft 500; Atlanta Motor Speedway
3/29/92—TranSouth 500; Darlington Raceway

Mark Martin
8/8/93—Budweiser at the Glen; Watkins Glen International
8/15/93—Champion Spark Plug 400; Michigan Int. Speedway
8/28/93—Bud 500; Bristol International Raceway
9/5/93—Mountain Dew Southern 500; Darlington Raceway

Jeff Gordon
7/26/98—Pennsylvania 500; Pocono Raceway
8/1/98—Brickyard 400; Indianapolis Motor Speedway
8/9/98—The Bud at the Glen; Watkins Glen International
8/16/98—Pepsi 400 by DeVilbiss; Michigan Speedway

Three Consecutive Victories

Herb Thomas
9/8/51—Central City Speedway
9/15/51—Langhorne Speedway
9/23/51—Charlotte Speedway

Dick Rathmann
5/4/52—Langhorne Speedway
5/10/52—Darlington Raceway
5/18/52—Dayton Speedway

Herb Thomas
6/27/54—Williams Grove Speedway
7/3/54—Piedmont Interstate Fairgrounds
7/4/54—Asheville-Weaverville Speedway

Buck Baker
5/13/56—Orange Speedway
5/20/56—Virginia 500; Martinsville Speedway
5/27/56—Lincoln Speedway

Fireball Roberts
4/7/57—Wilkes County 160; North Wilkesboro Speedway
4/14/57—Langhorne Speedway
4/19/57—Southern States Fairgrounds

Junior Johnson
6/5/58—Columbia Speedway
6/12/58—New Bradford Speedway
6/15/58—Reading Fairgrounds

Junior Johnson
8/13/61—Western N.C. 500; Asheville-Weaverville Speedway
8/18/61—Southside Speedway
8/27/61—South Boston Speedway

Richard Petty
8/15/62—Starkey Speedway
8/18/62—International 200; Bowman Gray Stadium
8/21/62—Piedmont Interstate Fairgrounds

Richard Petty
4/21/63—Virginia 500; Martinsville Speedway
4/28/63—Gwyn Staley 400; North Wilkesboro Speedway
5/2/63—Columbia 200; Columbia Speedway

Richard Petty
4/30/66—Rebel 400; Darlington Raceway
5/7/66—Tidewater 250; Langley Field Speedway
5/10/66—Speedy Morelock 200; Middle Georgia Raceway

Richard Petty
7/13/67—Fonda Speedway
7/15/67—Islip 300; Islip Speedway
7/23/67—Volunteer 500; Bristol International Speedway

Bobby Allison
10/29/67—American 500; North Carolina Motor Speedway
11/5/67—Western N.C. 500; Asheville-Weaverville Speedway
* 11/12/67—Middle Georgia 500; Middle Georgia Raceway

David Pearson
8/8/68—Sandlapper 200; Columbia Speedway
8/10/68—Myers Brothers 250; Bowman Gray Stadium
8/18/68—Western N.C. 500; Asheville-Weaverville Speedway

Richard Petty
9/15/68—Hillsborough 150; Orange Speedway
9/22/68—Old Dominion 500; Martinsville Speedway
9/29/68—Wilkes 400; North Wilkesboro Speedway

Bobby Isaac
4/3/69—Columbia 200; Columbia Speedway
4/6/69—Hickory 250; Hickory Speedway
4/8/69—Greenville 200; Greenville-Pickens Speedway

Richard Petty
9/13/70—Capital City 500; Virginia State Fairgrounds
9/20/70—Mason-Dixon 300; Dover Downs International Speedway
9/30/70—Home State 200; State Fairgrounds

Richard Petty
3/7/71—Richmond 500; Richmond Fairgrounds Raceway
3/14/71—Carolina 500; North Carolina Motor Speedway
3/21/71—Hickory 276; Hickory Speedway

Richard Petty
4/15/71—Maryville 200; Smoky Mountain Raceway
4/18/71—Gwyn Staley 400; North Wilkesboro Speedway
4/25/71—Virginia 500; Martinsville Speedway

Bobby Allison
7/9/72—Volunteer 500; Bristol International Speedway
7/16/72—Northern 300; Trenton Speedway
7/23/72—Dixie 500; Atlanta International Raceway

David Pearson
4/15/73—Rebel 500; Darlington Raceway
4/29/73—Virginia 500; Martinsville Speedway
5/6/73—Winston 500; Alabama International Motor Speedway

Richard Petty
7/28/74—Dixie 500; Atlanta International Raceway
8/4/74—Purolator 500; Pocono International Raceway
8/11/74—Talladega 500; Alabama International Motor Speedway

Richard Petty
3/16/75—Southeastern 500; Bristol International Speedway
3/23/75—Atlanta 500; Atlanta International Raceway
4/6/75—Gwyn Staley 400; North Wilkesboro Speedway

David Pearson
5/30/76—World 600; Charlotte Motor Speedway
6/13/76—Riverside 400; Riverside International Raceway
6/20/76—Cam2 Motor Oil 400; Michigan International Speedway

Bobby Allison
9/5/83—Southern 500; Darlington International Raceway
9/11/83—Wrangler Sanforset 400; Richmond Fgds. Raceway
9/18/83—Budweiser 500; Dover Downs International Speedway

Dale Earnhardt
8/22/87—Busch 500; Bristol International Raceway
9/6/87—Southern 500; Darlington International Raceway
9/13/87—Wrangler Indigo 400; Richmond Fairgrounds Raceway

Rusty Wallace
10/9/88—Oakwood Homes 500; Charlotte Motor Speedway
10/16/88—Holly Farms 400; North Wilkesboro Speedway
10/23/88—AC Delco 500; North Carolina Motor Speedway

Rusty Wallace
4/4/93—Food City 500; Bristol International Raceway
4/18/93—First Union 400; North Wilkesboro Speedway
4/25/93—Hanes 500; Martinsville Speedway

Rusty Wallace
6/5/94—Budweiser 500; Dover Downs International Speedway
6/12/94—UAW-GM Teamwork 500; Pocono International Raceway
6/19/94—Miller Genuine Draft 400; Michigan Int. Speedway

Jeff Gordon
9/15/96—MBNA 500; Dover Downs International Speedway
9/22/96—Hanes 500; Martinsville Speedway
9/29/96—Tyson Holly Farms 400; North Wilkesboro Speedway

Jeff Gordon
11/1/98—AC Delco 400; North Carolina Speedway
11/8/98—NAPA 500; Atlanta Motor Speedway
2/14/99—Daytona 500; Daytona International Speedway
* 1968 season

Dirt Victories

1.	Lee Petty	42
2.	Herb Thomas	41
3.	Buck Baker	40
4.	Tim Flock	34
5.	Ned Jarrett	33
6.	Richard Petty	31
7.	Junior Johnson	24
8.	David Pearson	23
9.	Speedy Thompson	17
10.	Fonty Flock	15
	Joe Weatherly	15
12.	Jack Smith	14
13.	Curtis Turner	13
14.	Fireball Roberts	12
15.	Dick Rathmann	10
16.	Dick Hutcherson	8
	Cotton Owens	8
18.	Rex White	7
19.	Bobby Isaac	6
	Jim Paschal	6
21.	Marvin Panch	5
	Marshall Teague	5
23.	Bob Flock	4
	Paul Goldsmith	4
	Hershel McGriff	4
	Ralph Moody	4
27.	Eddie Gray	3
	Frank Mundy	3
	Gwyn Staley	3
30.	Bill Blair	2
	Lloyd Dane	2

	Parnelli Jones	2
	Danny Letner	2
	Dick Linder	2
	Eddie Pagan	2
	Gober Sosebee	2
	Bob Welborn	2
	Lee Roy Yarbrough	2
39.	Bobby Allison	1
	Bill Amick	1
	Johnny Beauchamp	1
	Marvin Burke	1
	Red Byron	1
	Jim Cook	1
	Darel Dieringer	1
	Joe Eubanks	1
	Lou Figaro	1
	Danny Graves	1
	Al Keller	1
	Elmo Langley	1
	Paul Lewis	1
	Fred Lorenzen	1
	Tiny Lund	1
	Lloyd Moore	1
	Billy Myers	1
	Norm Nelson	1
	Bill Norton	1
	Jim Pardue	1
	Dick Passwater	1
	Tom Pistone	1
	Marvin Porter	1
	Jim Reed	1
	Bill Rexford	1
	Shorty Rollins	1
	Jim Roper	1
	John Rostek	1
	Leon Sales	1
	Wendell Scott	1
	Buddy Shuman	1
	John Soares	1
	Donald Thomas	1
	Tommy Thompson	1
	Danny Weinberg	1
	Jack White	1
	Cale Yarborough	1
	Emanuel Zervakis	1

Longest Streaks of Seasons With a Dirt Victory

1.	Lee Petty	13	(1949-61)
2.	Buck Baker	10	(1952-61)
3.	Richard Petty	9	(1960-68)
4.	Herb Thomas	7	(1950-56)
	Ned Jarrett	7	(1959-65)
6.	Jack Smith	6	(1957-62)
	David Pearson	6	(1964-69)
8.	Fonty Flock	4	(1950-53)
	Tim Flock	4	(1950-53)
	Jim Paschal	4	(1953-56)
	Speedy Thompson	4	(1955-58)
	Junior Johnson	4	(1958-61)
	Cotton Owens	4	(1958-61)
	Joe Weatherly	4	(1960-63)

Victory Records

Five Consecutive Dirt Victories

Richard Petty
4/30/67—Richmond 250; Virginia State Fairgrounds
5/20/67—Tidewater 250; Langley Field Speedway
6/8/67—East Tennessee 200; Smoky Mountain Raceway
6/24/67—Pickens 200; Greenville-Pickens Speedway
7/13/67—Fonda Speedway

Four Consecutive Dirt Victories

David Pearson
7/21/64—Pennsylvania 200; Lincoln Speedway
8/7/64—Rambi Raceway
8/21/64—Sandlapper 200; Columbia Speedway
9/11/64—Buddy Shuman 250; Hickory Speedway

Ned Jarrett
9/20/64—Orange Speedway
10/9/64—Savannah Speedway
11/8/64—Jacksonville Speedway
2/27/65—Piedmont Interstate Fairgrounds

Richard Petty
8/17/67—Sandlapper 200; Columbia Speedway
8/25/67—Savannah Speedway
9/10/67—Capital City 300; Virginia State Fairgrounds
9/17/67—Hillsborough 150; Orange Speedway

Three Consecutive Dirt Victories

Herb Thomas
9/8/51—Central City Speedway
9/15/51—Langhorne Speedway
9/23/51—Charlotte Speedway

Herb Thomas
2/7/54—Palm Beach Speedway
3/7/54—Speedway Park
3/21/54—Lakewood Speedway

Herb Thomas
6/27/54—Williams Grove Speedway
7/3/54—Piedmont Interstate Fairgrounds
7/4/54—Asheville-Weaverville Speedway

Fireball Roberts
4/7/57—Wilkes County 160; North Wilkesboro Speedway
4/14/57—Langhorne Speedway
4/19/57—Southern States Fairgrounds

Junior Johnson
6/5/58—Columbia Speedway
6/12/58—New Bradford Speedway
6/15/58—Reading Fairgrounds

Lee Petty
5/29/60—Orange Speedway
6/5/60—Richmond 200; Atlantic Rural Fairgrounds
7/10/60—Heidelberg Stadium

David Pearson
3/10/64—Richmond 250; Atlantic Rural Fairgrounds
3/28/64—Greenville 200; Greenville-Pickens Speedway
4/12/64—Joe Weatherly 150; Orange Speedway

David Pearson
4/3/66—Hickory 250; Hickory Speedway
4/7/66—Columbia 200; Columbia Speedway
4/9/66—Greenville 200; Greenville-Pickens Speedway

David Pearson
6/9/66—East Tennessee 200; Smoky Mountain Raceway
6/25/66—Pickens 200; Greenville-Pickens Speedway
7/14/66—Fonda Speedway

David Pearson
8/18/66—Sandlapper 200; Columbia Speedway
9/9/66—Buddy Shuman 250; Hickory Speedway
9/11/66—Capital City 300; Virginia State Fairgrounds

Bobby Isaac
4/3/69—Columbia 200; Columbia Speedway
4/8/69—Greenville 200; Greenville-Pickens Speedway
6/21/69—Pickens 200; Greenville-Pickens Speedway

Short-Track Victories

1. Richard Petty	107	
2. Darrell Waltrip	47	
3. Bobby Allison	31	
Cale Yarborough	31	
5. Dale Earnhardt	27	
David Pearson	27	
7. Bobby Isaac	26	
8. Rusty Wallace	22	
9. Rex White	19	
10. Junior Johnson	18	
11. Jim Paschal	17	
12. Ned Jarrett	15	
13. Fred Lorenzen	12	
14. Lee Petty	10	
15. Jeff Gordon	9	
Terry Labonte	9	
17. Geoff Bodine	8	
Benny Parsons	8	
19. Mark Martin	6	
Marvin Panch	6	
Bob Welborn	6	
22. Harry Gant	5	
Dick Hutcherson	5	
Jim Reed	5	
Fireball Roberts	5	
26. Davey Allison	4	
Ernie Irvan	4	
Ricky Rudd	4	
Jack Smith	4	
Joe Weatherly	4	
Glen Wood	4	
32. Neil Bonnett	3	
Darel Dieringer	3	
Dale Jarrett	3	
Tiny Lund	3	
Dave Marcis	3	
37. Buck Baker	2	
Buddy Baker	2	
Jeff Burton	2	
Bill Elliott	2	
Tim Flock	2	
Alan Kulwicki	2	
Eddie Pagan	2	
Dick Rathmann	2	
Tim Richmond	2	
Herb Thomas	2	
Curtis Turner	2	
Billy Wade	2	

49. Johnny Allen	1
Donnie Allison	1
John Andretti	1
Johnny Beauchamp	1
Brett Bodine	1
Neil Cole	1
Lloyd Dane	1
Fonty Flock	1
Jimmy Florian	1
Charlie Glotzbach	1
Paul Goldsmith	1
Royce Haggerty	1
Bobby Hamilton	1
James Hylton	1
Bobby Johns	1
Joe Lee Johnson	1
John Kieper	1
Elmo Langley	1
Dick Linder	1
Ralph Moody	1
Billy Myers	1
Jim Pardue	1
Kyle Petty	1
Earl Ross	1
Frankie Schneider	1
Morgan Shepherd	1
Nelson Stacy	1
Tony Stewart	1
Speedy Thompson	1
Art Watts	1
Emanuel Zervakis	1

Longest Streaks of Seasons With a Short-Track Victory

1. Darrell Waltrip	15	(1975-89)
2. Richard Petty	14	(1962-75)
3. Bobby Allison	9	(1966-74)
4. Cale Yarborough	8	(1973-80)
Rusty Wallace	8	(1991-98)
6. Dale Earnhardt	7	(1985-91)
7. Rex White	5	(1958-62)
Jeff Gordon	5	(1995-99)
9. Lee Petty	4	(1957-60)
Fred Lorenzen	4	(1963-66)
David Pearson	4	(1966-69)
Bobby Isaac	4	(1968-71)
Benny Parsons	4	(1976-79)

Eight Consecutive Short-Track Victories

Richard Petty
7/15/67—Islip 300; Islip Speedway
7/23/67—Volunteer 500; Bristol International Speedway
7/29/67—Nashville 400; Fairgrounds Speedway
8/12/67—Myers Brothers 250; Bowman Gray Stadium
9/8/67—Buddy Shuman 250; Hickory Speedway
9/15/67—Maryland 300; Beltsville Speedway
9/24/67—Old Dominion 500; Martinsville Speedway
10/1/67—Wilkes 400; North Wilkesboro Speedway

Cale Yarborough
8/29/76—Volunteer 500; Bristol International Speedway
9/12/76—Capital City 400; Richmond Fairgrounds Raceway
9/26/76—Old Dominion 500; Martinsville Speedway
10/3/76—Wilkes 400; North Wilkesboro Speedway

2/27/77—Richmond 400; Richmond Fairgrounds Raceway
3/27/77—Gwyn Staley 400; North Wilkesboro Speedway
4/17/77—Southeastern 500; Bristol International Speedway
4/24/77—Virginia 500; Martinsville Speedway

Six Consecutive Short-Track Victories

Dale Earnhardt
3/8/87—Miller High Life 400; Richmond Fairgrounds Raceway
4/5/87—First Union 400; North Wilkesboro Speedway
4/12/87—Valleydale 500; Bristol International Raceway
4/26/87—Sovran Bank 500; Martinsville Speedway
8/22/87—Busch 500; Bristol International Raceway
9/13/87—Wrangler Indigo 400; Richmond Fairgrounds Raceway

Five Consecutive Short-Track Victories

Bobby Isaac
5/15/70—Beltsville 300; Beltsville Speedway
5/18/70—Tidewater 300; Langley Field Speedway
5/28/70—Maryville 200; Smoky Mountain Raceway
5/31/70—Virginia 500; Martinsville Speedway
6/20/70—Hickory 276; Hickory Speedway

Four Consecutive Short-Track Victories

Rex White
9/25/60—Old Dominion 500; Martinsville Speedway
10/2/60—Wilkes 320; North Wilkesboro Speedway
3/5/61—Asheville-Weaverville Speedway
4/3/61—Bowman Gray Stadium

Darrell Waltrip
4/17/83—Northwestern Bank 400; North Wilkesboro Speedway
4/24/83—Virginia National Bank 500; Martinsville Speedway
5/7/83—Marty Robbins 420; Nashville International Raceway
5/21/83—Valleydale 500; Bristol International Raceway

Three Consecutive Short-Track Victories

Rex White
5/24/59—Music City 200; Fairgrounds Speedway
6/27/59—Bowman Gray Stadium
6/28/59—Asheville-Weaverville Speedway

Junior Johnson
5/2/65—Southeastern 500; Bristol International Speedway
5/15/65—Bowman Gray Stadium
5/29/65—Asheville Speedway

David Pearson
5/5/68—Fireball 300; Asheville-Weaverville Speedway
5/17/68—Beltsville 300; Beltsville Speedway
5/18/68—Tidewater 250; Langley Field Speedway

David Pearson
6/27/68—Nashville 400; Fairgrounds Speedway
8/10/68—Myers Brothers 250; Bowman Gray Stadium
8/18/68—Western N.C. 500; Asheville-Weaverville Speedway

Bobby Isaac
10/17/69—Savannah Speedway
10/19/69—Augusta Speedway
11/2/69—Jeffco 200; Jeffco Speedway

Richard Petty
8/11/70—West Virginia 300; International Raceway Park
8/28/70—Myers Brothers 250; Bowman Gray Stadium
8/29/70—Halifax County 100; South Boston Speedway

Richard Petty
4/15/71—Maryville 200; Smoky Mountain Raceway
4/18/71—Gwyn Staley 400; North Wilkesboro Speedway
4/25/71—Virginia 500; Martinsville Speedway

Richard Petty
7/14/71—Albany-Saratoga 250; Albany-Saratoga Speedway
7/15/71—Islip 250; Islip Speedway
7/24/71—Nashville 420; Fairgrounds Speedway

Darrell Waltrip
4/2/78—Southeastern 500; Bristol International Raceway
4/16/78—Gwyn Staley 400; North Wilkesboro Speedway
4/23/78—Virginia 500; Martinsville Speedway

Cale Yarborough
6/3/78—Music City USA 420; Nashville Speedway
7/15/78—Nashville 420; Nashville Speedway
8/26/78—Volunteer 500; Bristol International Raceway

Darrell Waltrip
5/8/82—Cracker Barrel 420; Nashville International Raceway
7/10/82—Busch Nashville 420; Nashville Int. Raceway
8/28/82—Busch 500; Bristol International Raceway

Darrell Waltrip
9/9/84—Wrangler Sanforset 400; Richmond Fairgrounds Raceway
9/23/84—Goody's 500; Martinsville Speedway
10/14/84—Holly Farms 400; North Wilkesboro Speedway

Rusty Wallace
10/16/88—Holly Farms 400; North Wilkesboro Speedway
3/26/89—Pontiac Excitement 400; Richmond Int. Raceway
4/9/89—Valleydale Meats 500; Bristol International Raceway

Rusty Wallace
4/4/93—Food City 500; Bristol International Raceway
4/18/93—First Union 400; North Wilkesboro Speedway
4/25/93—Hanes 500; Martinsville Speedway

Superspeedway Victories

1.	Richard Petty	56
2.	David Pearson	51
3.	Cale Yarborough	48
4.	Bobby Allison	47
5.	Dale Earnhardt	46
6.	Bill Elliott	37
7.	Jeff Gordon	35
8.	Darrell Waltrip	32
9.	Mark Martin	21
	Rusty Wallace	21
11.	Dale Jarrett	19
12.	Buddy Baker	17
13.	Neil Bonnett	15
14.	Davey Allison	14
	Fireball Roberts	14
16.	Harry Gant	13
	Fred Lorenzen	13
18.	Bobby Labonte	12
	Benny Parsons	12
	Lee Roy Yarbrough	12
21.	Ricky Rudd	11
22.	Terry Labonte	10
23.	Donnie Allison	9
	Jeff Burton	9
25.	Ernie Irvan	8
	Junior Johnson	8
27.	Geoff Bodine	7

28.	A.J. Foyt	6
	Sterling Marlin	6
	Kyle Petty	6
	Tim Richmond	6
	Joe Weatherly	6
33.	Bobby Isaac	5
	Herb Thomas	5
35.	Pete Hamilton	4
	Marvin Panch	4
	Ken Schrader	4
38.	Buck Baker	3
	Fonty Flock	3
	Charlie Glotzbach	3
	Paul Goldsmith	3
	Alan Kulwicki	3
	Morgan Shepherd	3
	Nelson Stacy	3
45.	Derrike Cope	2
	Darel Dieringer	2
	Bobby Hamilton	2
	Ned Jarrett	2
	Dave Marcis	2
	Jim Paschal	2
	Jack Smith	2
	Jimmy Spencer	2
	Tony Stewart	2
	Speedy Thompson	2
	Curtis Turner	2
	Rex White	2
57.	John Andretti	1
	Mario Andretti	1
	Earl Balmer	1
	Ron Bouchard	1
	Richard Brickhouse	1
	Dick Brooks	1
	Bob Burdick	1
	Ward Burton	1
	Larry Frank	1
	Bobby Hillin Jr.	1
	Jim Hurtubise	1
	Dick Hutcherson	1
	James Hylton	1
	Bobby Johns	1
	Joe Lee Johnson	1
	Tiny Lund	1
	Johnny Mantz	1
	Jeremy Mayfield	1
	Sam McQuagg	1
	Joe Nemechek	1
	Phil Parsons	1
	Lee Petty	1
	Tom Pistone	1
	Lennie Pond	1
	Marvin Porter	1
	Dick Rathmann	1
	Jim Reed	1
	Jody Ridley	1
	Johnny Rutherford	1
	Greg Sacks	1
	Lake Speed	1
	Bob Welborn	1

Longest Streaks of Seasons With A Superspeedway Victory

1. David Pearson	13	(1968-80)
Cale Yarborough	13	(1973-85)
3. Richard Petty	12	(1966-77)
4. Dale Earnhardt	11	(1986-96)
5. Bill Elliott	9	(1984-92)
6. Fred Lorenzen	7	(1961-67)
Benny Parsons	7	(1975-81)
Bobby Allison	7	(1978-84)
Mark Martin	7	(1989-95)
Ricky Rudd	7	(1991-97)
Dale Jarrett	7	(1993-99)

Longest Streaks of Seasons With Multiple Superspeedway Victories

1. Cale Yarborough	13	(1973-85)
2. Bobby Allison	7	(1978-84)
3. Bill Elliott	6	(1984-89)
Jeff Gordon	6	(1994-99)
5. David Pearson	5	(1972-76)
Richard Petty	5	(1973-77)
7. Fireball Roberts	4	(1960-63)
Dale Earnhardt	4	(1993-96)
Dale Jarrett	4	(1996-99)
10. Fred Lorenzen	3	(1963-65)
Darrell Waltrip	3	(1977-79)
Neil Bonnett	3	(1979-81)

Five Consecutive Superspeedway Victories

Jeff Gordon
7/26/98—Pennsylvania 500; Pocono Raceway
8/1/98—Brickyard 400; Indianapolis Motor Speedway
8/16/98—Pepsi 400 by DeVilbiss; Michigan Speedway
8/30/98—Farm Aid on CMT 300; New Hampshire Int. Speedway
9/6/98—Pepsi Southern 500; Darlington Raceway

Four Consecutive Superspeedway Victories

Herb Thomas
5/29/54—Raleigh 250; Raleigh Speedway
9/6/54—Southern 500; Darlington Raceway
8/20/55—Raleigh Speedway
9/5/55—Southern 500; Darlington Raceway

Bobby Allison
8/15/71—Yankee 400; Michigan International Speedway
8/22/71—Talladega 500; Alabama International Motor Speedway
9/6/71—Southern 500; Darlington Raceway
10/10/71—National 500; Charlotte Motor Speedway

David Pearson
3/18/73—Carolina 500; North Carolina Motor Speedway
4/1/73—Atlanta 500; Atlanta International Raceway
4/15/73—Rebel 500; Darlington Raceway
5/6/73—Winston 500; Alabama International Motor Speedway

Bill Elliott
3/17/85—Coca-Cola 500; Atlanta International Raceway
4/14/85—TranSouth 500; Darlington International Raceway
5/5/85—Winston 500; Alabama International Motor Speedway
5/19/85—Budweiser 500; Dover Downs International Speedway

Three Consecutive Superspeedway Victories

Bobby Allison
5/30/71—World 600; Charlotte Motor Speedway
6/6/71—Mason-Dixon 500; Dover Downs International Speedway
6/13/71—Motor State 400; Michigan International Speedway

Richard Petty
10/17/71—Delaware 500; Dover Downs International Speedway
10/24/71—American 500; North Carolina Motor Speedway
12/12/71—Texas 500; Texas World Speedway

David Pearson
6/24/73—Motor State 400; Michigan International Speedway
7/4/73—Firecracker 400; Daytona International Speedway
7/22/73—Dixie 500; Atlanta International Raceway

Richard Petty
7/28/74—Dixie 500; Atlanta International Raceway
8/4/74—Purolator 500; Pocono International Raceway
8/11/74—Talladega 500; Alabama International Motor Speedway

Bill Elliott
10/11/87—Oakwood Homes 500; Charlotte Motor Speedway
10/25/87—AC Delco 500; North Carolina Motor Speedway
11/22/87—Atlanta Journal 500; Atlanta International Raceway

Dale Earnhardt
3/18/90—Motorcraft Quality Parts 500; Atlanta Int. Raceway
4/1/90—TranSouth 500; Darlington International Raceway
5/6/90—Winston 500; Talladega Superspeedway

Bill Elliott
3/1/92—Goodwrench 500; North Carolina Motor Speedway
3/15/92—Motorcraft 500; Atlanta Motor Speedway
3/29/92—TranSouth 500; Darlington Raceway

Rusty Wallace
6/5/94—Budweiser 500; Dover Downs International Speedway
6/12/94—UAW-GM Teamwork 500; Pocono International Raceway
6/19/94—Miller Genuine Draft 400; Michigan Int. Speedway

Jeff Gordon
11/1/98—AC Delco 400; North Carolina Speedway
11/8/98—NAPA 500; Atlanta Motor Speedway
2/14/99—Daytona 500; Daytona International Speedway

Grand Slam Victories

1. David Pearson	26
2. Dale Earnhardt	25
3. Richard Petty	24
Cale Yarborough	24
5. Bobby Allison	22
6. Bill Elliott	16
Jeff Gordon	16
8. Darrell Waltrip	15
9. Fred Lorenzen	12
10. Buddy Baker	10
Fireball Roberts	10
Lee Roy Yarbrough	10
13. Dale Jarrett	9
14. Junior Johnson	8
15. Neil Bonnett	7
16. Mark Martin	6
Joe Weatherly	6
18. Donnie Allison	5
Harry Gant	5
Bobby Labonte	5
Benny Parsons	5

22. Davey Allison	4
A.J. Foyt	4
Ernie Irvan	4
Sterling Marlin	4
Marvin Panch	4
Rusty Wallace	4
28. Buck Baker	3
Jeff Burton	3
Bobby Isaac	3
Morgan Shepherd	3
Nelson Stacy	3
Herb Thomas	3
34. Geoff Bodine	2
Darel Dieringer	2
Charlie Glotzbach	2
Pete Hamilton	2
Ned Jarrett	2
Terry Labonte	2
Jim Paschal	2
Tim Richmond	2
Ricky Rudd	2
Ken Schrader	2
Jack Smith	2
Speedy Thompson	2
46. John Andretti	1
Mario Andretti	1
Earl Balmer	1
Bob Burdick	1
Derrike Cope	1
Fonty Flock	1
Larry Frank	1
Paul Goldsmith	1
Jim Hurtubise	1
Dick Hutcherson	1
Bobby Johns	1
Joe Lee Johnson	1
Tiny Lund	1
Johnny Mantz	1
Dave Marcis	1
Sam McQuagg	1
Kyle Petty	1
Lee Petty	1
Dick Rathmann	1
Jim Reed	1
Johnny Rutherford	1
Greg Sacks	1
Lake Speed	1
Jimmy Spencer	1
Curtis Turner	1
Bob Welborn	1
Rex White	1

Longest Streaks of Seasons With a Grand Slam Victory

1. Cale Yarborough	10	(1976-85)
2. David Pearson	7	(1968-74)
3. Fireball Roberts	6	(1958-63)
Jeff Gordon	6	(1994-99)
5. Fred Lorenzen	5	(1961-65)
Lee Roy Yarbrough	5	(1966-70)
David Pearson	5	(1976-80)
Bobby Allison	5	(1980-84)
Dale Earnhardt	5	(1986-90)
Mark Martin	5	(1991-95)
Dale Earnhardt	5	(1992-96)
Bobby Labonte	5	(1995-99)

Five Consecutive Grand Slam Victories

Lee Roy Yarbrough

5/10/69—Rebel 400; Darlington Raceway
5/25/69—World 600; Charlotte Motor Speedway
7/4/69—Firecracker 400; Daytona International Speedway
8/10/69—Dixie 500; Atlanta International Raceway
9/1/69—Southern 500; Darlington Raceway

Four Consecutive Grand Slam Victories

David Pearson

2/15/76—Daytona 500; Daytona International Speedway
3/21/76—Atlanta 500; Atlanta International Raceway
4/11/76—Rebel 500; Darlington International Raceway
5/30/76—World 600; Charlotte Motor Speedway

Three Consecutive Grand Slam Victories

Bobby Allison

7/23/72—Dixie 500; Atlanta International Raceway
9/4/72—Southern 500; Darlington Raceway
10/8/72—National 500; Charlotte Motor Speedway

David Pearson

4/7/74—Rebel 500; Darlington Raceway
5/26/74—World 600; Charlotte Motor Speedway
7/4/74—Firecracker 400; Daytona International Speedway

Dale Earnhardt

3/28/93—TranSouth 500; Darlington Raceway
5/30/93—Coca-Cola 600; Charlotte Motor Speedway
7/3/93—Pepsi 400; Daytona International Speedway

Jeff Gordon

11/8/98—NAPA 500; Atlanta Motor Speedway
2/14/99—Daytona 500; Daytona International Speedway
3/14/99—Cracker Barrel OCS 500; Atlanta Motor Speedway

Classic Victories

Driver	Brickyard 400	Daytona 500	Southern 500	World 600	Total
1. Jeff Gordon	2	2	4	3	11
2. Bobby Allison		3	4	3	10
Richard Petty		7	1	2	10
4. Cale Yarborough		4	5		9
5. Dale Earnhardt	1	1	3	3	8
6. David Pearson		1	3	3	7
Darrell Waltrip		1	1	5	7
8. Buddy Baker		1	1	3	5
Bill Elliott		2	3		5
Dale Jarrett	2	2		1	5
11. Buck Baker			3		3
Neil Bonnett			1	2	3
Fred Lorenzen		1		2	3
Fireball Roberts		1	2		3
Herb Thomas			3		3
Lee Roy Yarbrough		1	1	1	3
17. Davey Allison		1		1	2
Jeff Burton			1	1	2
Harry Gant			2		2
Sterling Marlin		2			2
Marvin Panch		1		1	2
Benny Parsons		1		1	2
Jim Paschal				2	2
Nelson Stacy			1	1	2
25. Donnie Allison				1	1
Mario Andretti		1			1
Geoff Bodine		1			1
Derrike Cope		1			1
Darel Dieringer			1		1
Fonty Flock			1		1
A.J. Foyt		1			1
Larry Frank			1		1
Pete Hamilton		1			1
Ernie Irvan		1			1
Ned Jarrett			1		1
Joe Lee Johnson				1	1
Junior Johnson		1			1
Bobby Labonte				1	1
Terry Labonte			1		1
Tiny Lund		1			1
Johnny Mantz			1		1
Mark Martin			1		1
Kyle Petty				1	1
Lee Petty		1			1
Jim Reed			1		1
Tim Richmond			1		1
Ricky Rudd	1				1
Speedy Thompson			1		1
Curtis Turner		1			1
Rusty Wallace				1	1

Four Consecutive Classic Victories

Jeff Gordon

5/24/98—Coca-Cola 600; Charlotte Motor Speedway
8/1/98—Brickyard 400; Indianapolis Motor Speedway
9/6/98—Pepsi Southern 500; Darlington Raceway
2/14/99—Daytona 500; Daytona International Speedway

Three Consecutive Classic Victories

Lee Roy Yarbrough

2/23/69—Daytona 500; Daytona International Speedway
5/25/69—World 600; Charlotte Motor Speedway
9/1/69—Southern 500; Darlington Raceway

David Pearson

2/15/76—Daytona 500; Daytona International Speedway
5/30/76—World 600; Charlotte Motor Speedway
9/6/76—Southern 500; Darlington International Raceway

Dale Jarrett

2/18/96—Daytona 500; Daytona International Speedway
5/26/96—Coca-Cola 600; Charlotte Motor Speedway
8/3/96—Brickyard 400; Indianapolis Motor Speedway

Jeff Gordon

9/1/96—Mountain Dew Southern 500; Darlington Raceway
2/16/97—Daytona 500; Daytona International Speedway
5/25/97—Coca-Cola 600; Charlotte Motor Speedway

500-Mile Victories

1. Richard Petty		38
2. Bobby Allison		37
3. Dale Earnhardt		36
4. Cale Yarborough		34
5. Bill Elliott		27
6. David Pearson		26
7. Darrell Waltrip		24
8. Jeff Gordon		20
9. Rusty Wallace		14
10. Neil Bonnett		12
Harry Gant		12
12. Buddy Baker		11
Mark Martin		11
14. Terry Labonte		9
Benny Parsons		9
16. Dale Jarrett		8
17. Davey Allison		7
Donnie Allison		7
Bobby Labonte		7
Lee Roy Yarbrough		7
21. Geoff Bodine		6
Ricky Rudd		6
23. A.J. Foyt		5
Dan Gurney		5
Ernie Irvan		5
Fred Lorenzen		5
Kyle Petty		5
Tim Richmond		5
Fireball Roberts		5
30. Sterling Marlin		4
Ken Schrader		4
32. Buck Baker		3
Pete Hamilton		3
Morgan Shepherd		3
Herb Thomas		3
36. Jeff Burton		2
Derrike Cope		2
Bobby Isaac		2
Alan Kulwicki		2
Dave Marcis		2
Marvin Panch		2
Curtis Turner		2

43. Mario Andretti   1
Ron Bouchard   1
Richard Brickhouse   1
Dick Brooks   1
Bob Burdick   1
Darel Dieringer   1
Mark Donohue   1
Ray Elder   1
Fonty Flock   1
Larry Frank   1
Charlie Glotzbach   1
Paul Goldsmith   1
Eddie Gray   1
Bobby Hillin Jr.   1
Jim Hurtubise   1
Dick Hutcherson   1
James Hylton   1
Ned Jarrett   1
Bobby Johns   1
Junior Johnson   1
Parnelli Jones   1
Tiny Lund   1
Johnny Mantz   1
Jeremy Mayfield   1
Phil Parsons   1
Lee Petty   1
Lennie Pond   1
Jim Reed   1
Jody Ridley   1
Lake Speed   1
Jimmy Spencer   1
Nelson Stacy   1
Speedy Thompson   1

Longest Streaks of Seasons With a 500-Mile Victory

1. Cale Yarborough   13   (1973-85)
2. Richard Petty   12   (1966-77)
3. David Pearson   9   (1972-80)
4. Bobby Allison   7   (1978-84)
5. Benny Parsons   6   (1975-80)
Darrell Waltrip   6   (1977-82)
Dale Earnhardt   6   (1986-91)
Dale Jarrett   6   (1993-98)
9. Fred Lorenzen   5   (1962-66)
Mark Martin   5   (1991-95)
Jeff Gordon   5   (1995-99)

Six Consecutive 500-Mile Victories

Bill Elliott
3/17/85—Coca-Cola 500; Atlanta International Raceway
4/14/85—TranSouth 500; Darlington International Raceway
5/5/85—Winston 500; Alabama International Motor Speedway
5/19/85—Budweiser 500; Dover Downs International Speedway
6/9/85—Van Scoy Diamond Mine 500; Pocono Int. Raceway
7/21/85—Summer 500; Pocono International Raceway

Five Consecutive 500-Mile Victories

David Pearson
3/18/73—Carolina 500; North Carolina Motor Speedway
4/1/73—Atlanta 500; Atlanta International Raceway
4/15/73—Rebel 500; Darlington Raceway
5/6/73—Winston 500; Alabama International Motor Speedway
6/3/73—Mason-Dixon 500; Dover Downs International Speedway

Four Consecutive 500-Mile Victories

Richard Petty
10/17/71—Delaware 500; Dover Downs International Speedway
10/24/71—American 500; North Carolina Motor Speedway
12/12/71—Texas 500; Texas World Speedway
1/23/72—Winston Western 500; Riverside Int. Raceway

Three Consecutive 500-Mile Victories

Bobby Allison
8/22/71—Talladega 500; Alabama International Motor Speedway
9/6/71—Southern 500; Darlington Raceway
10/10/71—National 500; Charlotte Motor Speedway

Richard Petty
7/28/74—Dixie 500; Atlanta International Raceway
8/4/74—Purolator 500; Pocono International Raceway
8/11/74—Talladega 500; Alabama International Motor Speedway

Bobby Allison
5/16/82—Mason-Dixon 500; Dover Downs International Speedway
6/13/82—Van Scoy Diamond Mine 500; Pocono Int. Raceway
7/25/82—Mountain Dew 500; Pocono International Raceway

Bill Elliott
10/11/87—Oakwood Homes 500; Charlotte Motor Speedway
10/25/87—AC Delco 500; North Carolina Motor Speedway
11/22/87—Atlanta Journal 500; Atlanta International Raceway

Rusty Wallace
10/9/88—Oakwood Homes 500; Charlotte Motor Speedway
10/23/88—AC Delco 500; North Carolina Motor Speedway
11/20/88—Atlanta Journal 500; Atlanta International Raceway

Dale Earnhardt
3/18/90—Motorcraft Quality Parts 500; Atlanta Int. Raceway
4/1/90—TranSouth 500; Darlington International Raceway
5/6/90—Winston 500; Talladega Superspeedway

Bill Elliott
3/1/92—Goodwrench 500; North Carolina Motor Speedway
3/15/92—Motorcraft 500; Atlanta Motor Speedway
3/29/92—TranSouth 500; Darlington Raceway

Jeff Gordon
7/28/96—Diehard 500; Talladega Superspeedway
9/1/96—Mountain Dew Southern 500; Darlington Raceway
9/15/96—MBNA 500; Dover Downs International Speedway

Jeff Gordon
11/8/98—NAPA 500; Atlanta Motor Speedway
2/14/99—Daytona 500; Daytona International Speedway
3/14/99—Cracker Barrel OCS 500; Atlanta Motor Speedway

Road Victories

1. Bobby Allison   6
Richard Petty   6
Rusty Wallace   6
4. Jeff Gordon   5
Dan Gurney   5
Tim Richmond   5
Ricky Rudd   5
Darrell Waltrip   5
9. Mark Martin   4
David Pearson   4
11. Geoff Bodine   3
Tim Flock   3
Ernie Irvan   3
Cale Yarborough   3

15. Ray Elder	2	
Parnelli Jones	2	
Terry Labonte	2	
Marvin Panch	2	
Fireball Roberts	2	
Marshall Teague	2	
Billy Wade	2	
22. Davey Allison	1	
Buck Baker	1	
Bill Blair	1	
Red Byron	1	
Lloyd Dane	1	
Darel Dieringer	1	
Mark Donohue	1	
Dale Earnhardt	1	
Bill Elliott	1	
A.J. Foyt	1	
Paul Goldsmith	1	
Eddie Gray	1	
Al Keller	1	
Harold Kite	1	
Cotton Owens	1	
Benny Parsons	1	
Kyle Petty	1	
Lee Petty	1	
Jack Smith	1	
Chuck Stevenson	1	

Consecutive Seasons With a Road Victory

1. Dan Gurney	4	(1963-66)
Rusty Wallace	4	(1987-90)
3. Darrell Waltrip	3	(1979-81)
Ricky Rudd	3	(1988-90)
Mark Martin	3	(1993-95)
Jeff Gordon	3	(1997-99)
7. Marshall Teague	2	(1951-52)
Tim Flock	2	(1955-56)
Richard Petty	2	(1969-70)
Ray Elder	2	(1971-72)
David Pearson	2	(1976-77)
Terry Labonte	2	(1984-85)
Tim Richmond	2	(1986-87)
Ernie Irvan	2	(1991-92)

Five Consecutive Road Victories

Jeff Gordon

8/10/97—The Bud at the Glen; Watkins Glen International
6/28/98—Save Mart/Kragen 350; Sears Point Raceway
8/9/98—The Bud at the Glen; Watkins Glen International
6/27/99—Save Mart/Kragen 350; Sears Point Raceway
8/15/99—Frontier at the Glen; Watkins Glen International

Three Consecutive Road Victories

David Pearson

1/18/76—Winston Western 500; Riverside Int. Raceway
6/13/76—Riverside 400; Riverside International Raceway
1/16/77—Winston Western 500; Riverside Int. Raceway

Tim Richmond

8/10/86—Budweiser at the Glen; Watkins Glen International
11/16/86—Winston Western 500; Riverside Int. Raceway
6/21/87—Budweiser 400; Riverside International Raceway

Rusty Wallace

8/10/87—Budweiser at the Glen; Watkins Glen International
11/8/87—Winston Western 500; Riverside Int. Raceway
6/12/88—Budweiser 400; Riverside International Raceway

Victories From the Pole Records

Victories From the Pole

1. Richard Petty	61	
2. David Pearson	37	
3. Darrell Waltrip	24	
4. Bobby Allison	20	
Bobby Isaac	20	
6. Herb Thomas	19	
7. Tim Flock	17	
8. Cale Yarborough	15	
9. Bill Elliott	14	
10. Buck Baker	13	
11. Jeff Gordon	11	
Ned Jarrett	11	
Junior Johnson	11	
Fred Lorenzen	11	
15. Fonty Flock	10	
16. Rusty Wallace	8	
17. Mark Martin	7	
Speedy Thompson	7	
Rex White	7	
20. Marvin Panch	6	
Lee Petty	6	
22. Jack Smith	5	
Curtis Turner	5	
Joe Weatherly	5	
25. Buddy Baker	4	
Dick Hutcherson	4	
Bobby Labonte	4	
Terry Labonte	4	
Jim Paschal	4	
Tim Richmond	4	
Fireball Roberts	4	
32. Geoff Bodine	3	
Dale Earnhardt	3	
A.J. Foyt	3	
Hershel McGriff	3	
Cotton Owens	3	
Kyle Petty	3	
Billy Wade	3	
Glen Wood	3	
40. Davey Allison	2	
Donnie Allison	2	
Harry Gant	2	
Charlie Glotzbach	2	
Paul Goldsmith	2	
Ernie Irvan	2	
Dick Linder	2	
Eddie Pagan	2	
Jim Reed	2	
Marshall Teague	2	
Bob Welborn	2	
51. Neil Cole	1	
Jim Cook	1	

Darel Dieringer	1
Lou Figaro	1
Bob Flock	1
Danny Graves	1
Dan Gurney	1
Bobby Hamilton	1
Dale Jarrett	1
Parnelli Jones	1
Alan Kulwicki	1
Dave Marcis	1
Sterling Marlin	1
Ralph Moody	1
Frank Mundy	1
Norm Nelson	1
Benny Parsons	1
Gwyn Staley	1
Donald Thomas	1
Art Watts	1
Lee Roy Yarbrough	1

Longest Streaks of Seasons With a Victory From the Pole

1. Richard Petty	13	(1960-72)
2. Darrell Waltrip	7	(1978-84)
3. David Pearson	6	(1971-76)
Jeff Gordon	6	(1994-99)
5. Buck Baker	5	(1954-58)
Rex White	5	(1958-62)
Bobby Isaac	5	(1968-72)
Bobby Allison	5	(1971-75)
9. Herb Thomas	4	(1951-54)
Ned Jarrett	4	(1962-65)
Fred Lorenzen	4	(1963-66)

Four Consecutive Victories From the Pole

Richard Petty
8/12/67—Myers Brothers 250; Bowman Gray Stadium
8/17/67—Sandlapper 200; Columbia Speedway
8/25/67—Savannah Speedway
9/4/67—Southern 500; Darlington Raceway

Darrell Waltrip
9/27/81—Old Dominion 500; Martinsville Speedway
10/4/81—Holly Farms 400; North Wilkesboro Speedway
10/11/81—National 500; Charlotte Motor Speedway
11/1/81—American 500; North Carolina Motor Speedway

Three Consecutive Victories From the Pole

Richard Petty
4/30/66—Rebel 400; Darlington Raceway
5/7/66—Tidewater 250; Langley Field Speedway
5/10/66—Speedy Morelock 200; Middle Georgia Raceway

Richard Petty
7/13/67—Fonda Speedway
7/15/67—Islip 300; Islip Speedway
7/23/67—Volunteer 500; Bristol International Speedway

Bobby Allison
6/13/71—Motor State 400; Michigan International Speedway
6/20/71—Winston Golden State 400; Riverside Int. Raceway
6/23/71—Space City 300; Meyer Speedway

Dirt Victories From the Pole

1. Herb Thomas	18
2. Richard Petty	16
3. Tim Flock	13
4. Buck Baker	11
5. Fonty Flock	7
Speedy Thompson	7
7. David Pearson	6
8. Junior Johnson	5
Lee Petty	5
Curtis Turner	5
Joe Weatherly	5
12. Dick Hutcherson	4
Ned Jarrett	4
14. Hershel McGriff	3
Cotton Owens	3
Jack Smith	3
17. Bobby Isaac	2
Dick Linder	2
Eddie Pagan	2
Marshall Teague	2
21. Jim Cook	1
Lou Figaro	1
Bob Flock	1
Danny Graves	1
Parnelli Jones	1
Ralph Moody	1
Frank Mundy	1
Norm Nelson	1
Fireball Roberts	1
Gwyn Staley	1
Donald Thomas	1
Bob Welborn	1
Rex White	1

Consecutive Seasons With a Dirt Victory From The Pole

1. Buck Baker	5	(1954-58)
Richard Petty	5	(1960-64)
3. Herb Thomas	4	(1951-54)
4. Speedy Thompson	3	(1956-58)
Cotton Owens	3	(1959-61)
Joe Weatherly	3	(1961-63)
Dick Hutcherson	3	(1965-67)
Richard Petty	3	(1966-68)
9. Tim Flock	2	(1951-52)
Marshall Teague	2	(1951-52)
Lee Petty	2	(1954-55)
Tim Flock	2	(1955-56)
Eddie Pagan	2	(1956-57)
Jack Smith	2	(1958-59)
Curtis Turner	2	(1958-59)

Three Consecutive Dirt Victories From The Pole

Richard Petty
8/17/67—Sandlapper 200; Columbia Speedway
8/25/67—Savannah Speedway
9/17/67—Hillsborough 150; Orange Speedway

Short-Track Victories From the Pole

1. Richard Petty — 36
2. Darrell Waltrip — 18
3. Bobby Isaac — 17
4. Bobby Allison — 12
5. David Pearson — 10
6. Ned Jarrett — 7
7. Junior Johnson — 6
   Rex White — 6
   Cale Yarborough — 6
10. Fred Lorenzen — 5
11. Marvin Panch — 4
   Jim Paschal — 4
   Rusty Wallace — 4
14. Glen Wood — 3
15. Tim Flock — 2
   Terry Labonte — 2
   Jim Reed — 2
   Billy Wade — 2
19. Davey Allison — 1
   Buck Baker — 1
   Geoff Bodine — 1
   Neil Cole — 1
   Darel Dieringer — 1
   Dale Earnhardt — 1
   Bill Elliott — 1
   Fonty Flock — 1
   Bobby Hamilton — 1
   Ernie Irvan — 1
   Alan Kulwicki — 1
   Mark Martin — 1
   Art Watts — 1
   Bob Welborn — 1

Consecutive Seasons With a Short-Track Victory From the Pole

1. Richard Petty — 10 — (1962-71)
2. Darrell Waltrip — 7 — (1978-84)
3. Rex White — 5 — (1958-62)
4. Bobby Isaac — 4 — (1968-71)
   Bobby Allison — 4 — (1971-74)
6. Ned Jarrett — 3 — (1963-65)
   Junior Johnson — 3 — (1963-65)
8. Fred Lorenzen — 2 — (1963-64)
   Marvin Panch — 2 — (1964-65)
   Bobby Allison — 2 — (1966-67)
   David Pearson — 2 — (1968-69)
   Cale Yarborough — 2 — (1973-74)
   Richard Petty — 2 — (1974-75)
   Rusty Wallace — 2 — (1993-94)

Three Consecutive Short-Track Victories From the Pole

Richard Petty

7/14/71—Albany-Saratoga 250; Albany-Saratoga Speedway
7/15/71—Islip 250; Islip Speedway
7/24/71—Nashville 420; Fairgrounds Speedway

Superspeedway Victories From the Pole

1. David Pearson — 19
2. Bill Elliott — 13
3. Cale Yarborough — 9
4. Jeff Gordon — 8
5. Richard Petty — 7
6. Bobby Allison — 6
   Fred Lorenzen — 6
8. Buddy Baker — 4
   Bobby Labonte — 4
   Rusty Wallace — 4
11. A.J. Foyt — 3
   Kyle Petty — 3
   Fireball Roberts — 3
   Darrell Waltrip — 3
15. Donnie Allison — 2
   Geoff Bodine — 2
   Dale Earnhardt — 2
   Fonty Flock — 2
   Harry Gant — 2
   Charlie Glotzbach — 2
   Mark Martin — 2
   Tim Richmond — 2
23. Davey Allison — 1
   Paul Goldsmith — 1
   Bobby Isaac — 1
   Dale Jarrett — 1
   Terry Labonte — 1
   Dave Marcis — 1
   Sterling Marlin — 1
   Marvin Panch — 1
   Benny Parsons — 1
   Jack Smith — 1
   Herb Thomas — 1
   Lee Roy Yarbrough — 1

Consecutive Seasons With a Superspeedway Victory From the Pole

1. Jeff Gordon — 6 — (1994-99)
2. David Pearson — 5 — (1972-76)
3. Fred Lorenzen — 3 — (1964-66)
   Cale Yarborough — 3 — (1976-78)
   Kyle Petty — 3 — (1990-92)
6. Fireball Roberts — 2 — (1959-60)
   Richard Petty — 2 — (1966-67)
   Cale Yarborough — 2 — (1967-68)
   Bobby Allison — 2 — (1971-72)
   A.J. Foyt — 2 — (1971-72)
   Cale Yarborough — 2 — (1980-81)
   Bill Elliott — 2 — (1984-85)
   Bill Elliott — 2 — (1987-88)
   Rusty Wallace — 2 — (1988-89)
   Rusty Wallace — 2 — (1993-94)
   Bobby Labonte — 2 — (1995-96)
   Mark Martin — 2 — (1997-98)
   Bobby Labonte — 2 — (1998-99)

Victories From the Pole Records

Grand Slam Victories From the Pole

1. David Pearson — 8
2. Bill Elliott — 6
3. Fred Lorenzen — 5
   Richard Petty — 5
5. Jeff Gordon — 4
   Cale Yarborough — 4
7. Bobby Allison — 3
   Buddy Baker — 3
   Fireball Roberts — 3
10. Harry Gant — 2
11. Dale Earnhardt — 1
   Fonty Flock — 1
   A.J. Foyt — 1
   Charlie Glotzbach — 1
   Dale Jarrett — 1
   Bobby Labonte — 1
   Marvin Panch — 1
   Tim Richmond — 1
   Jack Smith — 1
   Rusty Wallace — 1
   Darrell Waltrip — 1

8. Buddy Baker — 3
   A.J. Foyt — 3
   Kyle Petty — 3
   Darrell Waltrip — 3
12. Donnie Allison — 2
   Dale Earnhardt — 2
   Harry Gant — 2
   Bobby Labonte — 2
   Fred Lorenzen — 2
   Tim Richmond — 2
18. Geoff Bodine — 1
   Fonty Flock — 1
   Charlie Glotzbach — 1
   Paul Goldsmith — 1
   Dan Gurney — 1
   Bobby Isaac — 1
   Terry Labonte — 1
   Dave Marcis — 1
   Sterling Marlin — 1
   Marvin Panch — 1
   Fireball Roberts — 1

Consecutive Seasons With a Grand Slam Victory From the Pole

1. David Pearson — 3 — (1972-74)
   Jeff Gordon — 3 — (1997-99)
3. Fireball Roberts — 2 — (1959-60)
   Fred Lorenzen — 2 — (1964-65)
   Richard Petty — 2 — (1966-67)
   Cale Yarborough — 2 — (1967-68)
   Bobby Allison — 2 — (1971-72)
   Bill Elliott — 2 — (1987-88)

Classic Victories From the Pole

1. Bill Elliott — 4
   Jeff Gordon — 4
3. David Pearson — 3
4. Bobby Allison — 2
   Buddy Baker — 2
   Richard Petty — 2
   Cale Yarborough — 2
8. Dale Earnhardt — 1
   Fonty Flock — 1
   Harry Gant — 1
   Fred Lorenzen — 1
   Tim Richmond — 1
   Fireball Roberts — 1

Consecutive Seasons With a Classic Victory From the Pole

1. Jeff Gordon — 3 — (1997-99)
2. Richard Petty — 2 — (1966-67)
   Bobby Allison — 2 — (1971-72)
   Bill Elliott — 2 — (1987-88)

500-Mile Victories From the Pole

1. Bill Elliott — 11
2. David Pearson — 10
3. Cale Yarborough — 7
4. Bobby Allison — 6
5. Richard Petty — 5
6. Jeff Gordon — 4
   Rusty Wallace — 4

Consecutive Seasons With a 500-Mile Victory From the Pole

1. David Pearson — 4 — (1973-76)
2. Kyle Petty — 3 — (1990-92)
3. Richard Petty — 2 — (1966-67)
   Cale Yarborough — 2 — (1967-68)
   Bobby Allison — 2 — (1971-72)
   A.J. Foyt — 2 — (1971-72)
   Bill Elliott — 2 — (1987-88)
   Rusty Wallace — 2 — (1988-89)
   Rusty Wallace — 2 — (1993-94)
   Jeff Gordon — 2 — (1995-96)

Road Victories From the Pole

1. Mark Martin — 4
2. Jeff Gordon — 3
   Darrell Waltrip — 3
4. Bobby Allison — 2
   Tim Flock — 2
   David Pearson — 2
   Richard Petty — 2
   Tim Richmond — 2
9. Buck Baker — 1
   Paul Goldsmith — 1
   Dan Gurney — 1
   Ernie Irvan — 1
   Terry Labonte — 1
   Marvin Panch — 1
   Lee Petty — 1
   Jack Smith — 1
   Billy Wade — 1

Three Consecutive Road Victories From The Pole

Jeff Gordon

6/28/98—Save Mart/Kragen 350; Sears Point Raceway
8/9/98—The Bud at the Glen; Watkins Glen International
6/27/99—Save Mart/Kragen 350; Sears Point Raceway

Pole Records

Poles

1. Richard Petty — 123
2. David Pearson — 113
3. Cale Yarborough — 69
4. Darrell Waltrip — 59
5. Bobby Allison — 58
6. Bill Elliott — 49
   Bobby Isaac — 49
8. Buck Baker — 45
   Junior Johnson — 45
10. Mark Martin — 39
    Herb Thomas — 39
12. Buddy Baker — 38
    Tim Flock — 38
14. Geoff Bodine — 37
15. Rex White — 36
16. Ned Jarrett — 35
17. Fonty Flock — 33
18. Fireball Roberts — 32
19. Fred Lorenzen — 31
20. Jeff Gordon — 30
21. Rusty Wallace — 26
22. Terry Labonte — 25
23. Alan Kulwicki — 24
    Ricky Rudd — 24
25. Ken Schrader — 23
    Jack Smith — 23
27. Dale Earnhardt — 22
    Ernie Irvan — 22
29. Dick Hutcherson — 21
    Marvin Panch — 21
31. Neil Bonnett — 20
    Benny Parsons — 20
33. Speedy Thompson — 19
34. Bobby Labonte — 18
    Lee Petty — 18
    Joe Weatherly — 18
37. Donnie Allison — 17
    Harry Gant — 17
39. Curtis Turner — 16
40. Davey Allison — 14
    Dave Marcis — 14
    Tim Richmond — 14
    Glen Wood — 14
44. Dick Rathmann — 13
45. Charlie Glotzbach — 12
    Jim Paschal — 12
47. Lee Roy Yarbrough — 11
48. Sterling Marlin — 10
    Cotton Owens — 10
50. Darel Dieringer — 9
    A.J. Foyt — 9
52. Paul Goldsmith — 8
    Kyle Petty — 8
54. Dale Jarrett — 7
    Morgan Shepherd — 7
    Bob Welborn — 7
57. Ward Burton — 6
    Tiny Lund — 6
    Eddie Pagan — 6
60. Bill Amick — 5
    Brett Bodine — 5

Joe Eubanks — 5
Bobby Hamilton — 5
Dick Linder — 5
Hershel McGriff — 5
Ralph Moody — 5
Ted Musgrave — 5
Joe Nemechek — 5
Tom Pistone — 5
Lennie Pond — 5
Jim Reed — 5
Billy Wade — 5
Art Watts — 5
74. John Andretti — 4
    James Hylton — 4
    Rick Mast — 4
    Mike Skinner — 4
    Gober Sosebee — 4
79. Johnny Allen — 3
    Loy Allen Jr. — 3
    Ron Bouchard — 3
    Ricky Craven — 3
    Bob Flock — 3
    Pete Hamilton — 3
    Kenny Irwin — 3
    Parnelli Jones — 3
    John Kieper — 3
    Banjo Matthews — 3
    Frank Mundy — 3
    Jim Pardue — 3
    Joe Ruttman — 3
    Marshall Teague — 3
93. Johnny Benson Jr. — 2
    Bob Burdick — 2
    Red Byron — 2
    Billy Carden — 2
    Danny Graves — 2
    Dan Gurney — 2
    Friday Hassler — 2
    Tommy Irwin — 2
    Bobby Johns — 2
    Mel Larson — 2
    Jeremy Mayfield — 2
    Ken Rush — 2
    Greg Sacks — 2
    John Sears — 2
    Gwyn Staley — 2
    Tony Stewart — 2
    Kenny Wallace — 2
    Michael Waltrip — 2
    Doug Yates — 2
    Emanuel Zervakis — 2
113. Dick Bailey — 1
     Larry Baumel — 1
     Bill Blair — 1
     Todd Bodine — 1
     Al Bonnell — 1
     Chuck Bown — 1
     Perk Brown — 1
     Jeff Burton — 1
     Wally Campbell — 1
     Neil Cole — 1
     Jim Cook — 1
     Derrike Cope — 1
     Doug Cox — 1

Pole Records

Bill Dennis	1
Bob Duell	1
George Dunn	1
Glenn Dunnaway	1
Ralph Earnhardt	1
Lou Figaro	1
Jimmy Florian	1
George Follmer	1
Robby Gordon	1
Eddie Gray	1
David Green	1
Royce Haggerty	1
Jimmy Hensley	1
Russ Hepler	1
Jim Hunter	1
Possum Jones	1
Al Keller	1
Pat Kirkwood	1
Elmo Langley	1
Kevin Lepage	1
Danny Letner	1
Jimmie Lewallen	1
Paul Lewis	1
Joe Littlejohn	1
Chuck Mahoney	1
Jimmy Massey	1
J.D. McDuffie	1
Joe Millikan	1
Tommy Moon	1
Bud Moore	1
Billy Myers	1
Norm Nelson	1
Andy Pierce	1
Bob Pronger	1
Bill Rexford	1
Bob Ross	1
John Rostek	1
Frankie Schneider	1
Wendell Scott	1
Frank Secrist	1
Lloyd Shaw	1
Slick Smith	1
Sam Sommers	1
G.C. Spencer	1
Jimmy Spencer	1
Ramo Stott	1
Hut Stricklin	1
Donald Thomas	1
Dick Trickle	1
Ken Wagner	1
Danny Weinberg	1
Dink Widenhouse	1
Rick Wilson	1

Annual Pole Leaders

1949—Bob Flock (2)
1950—Dick Linder (5)
1951—Fonty Flock (12)
1952—Herb Thomas (10)
1953—Herb Thomas (11)
1954—Herb Thomas (8)
1955—Tim Flock (18)
1956—Buck Baker (13)
1957—Buck Baker (6)
1958—Speedy Thompson (7)
    Rex White (7)
1959—Bob Welborn (5)
    Rex White (5)
1960—Fireball Roberts (6)
1961—Junior Johnson (9)
1962—Rex White (9)
1963—Junior Johnson (9)
1964—David Pearson (12)
1965—Dick Hutcherson (9)
    Ned Jarrett (9)
    Junior Johnson (9)
1966—Richard Petty (15)
1967—Richard Petty (18)
1968—David Pearson (12)
    Richard Petty (12)
1969—Bobby Isaac (19)
1970—Bobby Isaac (13)
1971—Bobby Allison (9)
    Richard Petty (9)
1972—Bobby Allison (13)
1973—David Pearson (8)
1974—David Pearson (11)
1975—David Pearson (7)
1976—David Pearson (8)
1977—Neil Bonnett (6)
1978—Cale Yarborough (8)
1979—Buddy Baker (7)
1980—Cale Yarborough (14)
1981—Darrell Waltrip (11)
1982—Darrell Waltrip (7)
1983—Darrell Waltrip (7)
1984—Bill Elliott (4)
    Ricky Rudd (4)
    Darrell Waltrip (4)
    Cale Yarborough (4)
1985—Bill Elliott (11)
1986—Geoff Bodine (8)
    Tim Richmond (8)
1987—Bill Elliott (8)
1988—Bill Elliott (6)
1989—Alan Kulwicki (6)
    Mark Martin (6)
1990—Dale Earnhardt (4)
1991—Mark Martin (5)
1992—Alan Kulwicki (6)
1993—Ken Schrader (6)
1994—Geoff Bodine (5)
    Ernie Irvan (5)
1995—Jeff Gordon (8)
1996—Jeff Gordon (5)
1997—Bobby Labonte (3)
    Mark Martin (3)
1998—Jeff Gordon (7)
1999—Jeff Gordon (7)

Seasons Recording Most Poles *

1. David Pearson (6)
2. Bill Elliott; Jeff Gordon; Richard Petty; Darrell Waltrip (4)
6. Junior Johnson; Mark Martin; Herb Thomas; Rex White; Cale Yarborough (3)
11. Bobby Allison; Buck Baker; Geoff Bodine; Bobby Isaac; Alan Kulwicki (2)
16. Buddy Baker; Neil Bonnett; Dale Earnhardt; Bob Flock; Fonty Flock; Tim Flock; Dick Hutcherson; Ernie Irvan; Ned Jarrett; Bobby Labonte; Dick Linder; Tim Richmond; Fireball Roberts; Ricky Rudd; Ken Schrader; Speedy Thompson; Bob Welborn (1)

Including ties

Longest Streaks of Seasons With a Pole

1. David Pearson	20		(1963-82)
2. Richard Petty	18		(1960-77)
3. Darrell Waltrip	13		(1974-86)
4. Cale Yarborough	12		(1973-84)
Bill Elliott	12		(1984-95)
Mark Martin	12		(1988-99)
7. Bobby Allison	11		(1966-76)
8. Buck Baker	10		(1952-61)
Geoff Bodine	10		(1982-91)
10. Lee Petty	8		(1954-61)
Rex White	8		(1956-63)
Junior Johnson	8		(1959-66)
Terry Labonte	8		(1981-88)
Rusty Wallace	8		(1987-94)

Longest Streaks of Seasons With Multiple Poles

1. Richard Petty	16		(1960-75)
2. David Pearson	14		(1966-79)
3. Darrell Waltrip	11		(1975-85)
4. Bill Elliott	10		(1984-93)
5. Buck Baker	9		(1952-60)
6. Geoff Bodine	8		(1984-91)
7. Junior Johnson	7		(1960-66)
Bobby Allison	7		(1970-76)
9. Herb Thomas	6		(1951-56)
Rex White	6		(1958-63)
Ned Jarrett	6		(1960-65)
Fred Lorenzen	6		(1961-66)
Cale Yarborough	6		(1973-78)

Note: All dates in the Pole Records section are race dates, not necessarily actual qualifying dates.

Five Consecutive Poles

Bobby Allison
* 8/26/72—Nashville 420; Fairgrounds Speedway
* 9/4/72—Southern 500; Darlington Raceway
9/10/72—Capital City 500; Richmond Fairgrounds Raceway
9/17/72—Delaware 500; Dover Downs International Speedway
9/27/72—Old Dominion 500; Martinsville Speedway

Cale Yarborough
5/10/80—Music City 420; Nashville International Raceway
5/18/80—Mason-Dixon 500; Dover Downs Int. Speedway
5/25/80—World 600; Charlotte Motor Speedway
* 6/1/80—NASCAR 400; Texas World Speedway
6/8/80—Warner W. Hodgdon 400; Riverside Int. Raceway

Bill Elliott
* 6/9/85—Van Scoy Diamond Mine 500; Pocono Int. Raceway
7/4/85—Pepsi Firecracker 400; Daytona Int. Speedway
* 7/21/85—Summer 500; Pocono International Raceway
7/28/85—Talladega 500; Alabama Int. Motor Speedway
* 8/11/85—Champion Spark Plug 400; Mich. Int. Speedway

Four Consecutive Poles

Herb Thomas
7/10/53—Morristown Speedway
* 7/12/53—Lakewood Speedway
* 7/22/53—Rapid Valley Speedway
7/26/53—Lincoln City Fairgrounds

Tim Flock
* 7/10/55—Asheville-Weaverville Speedway
* 7/15/55—Morristown Speedway
7/29/55—Altamont-Schnectady Fairgrounds
* 7/30/55—New York State Fairgrounds

Rex White
7/18/58—Canadian National Exposition Stadium
7/19/58—Civic Stadium
7/25/58—Monroe County Fairgrounds
7/26/58—Wall Stadium

Richard Petty
* 8/12/67—Myers Brothers 250; Bowman Gray Stadium
* 8/17/67—Sandlapper 200; Columbia Speedway
* 8/25/67—Savannah Speedway
* 9/4/67—Southern 500; Darlington Raceway

Bobby Allison
* 6/13/71—Motor State 400; Michigan Int. Speedway
* 6/20/71—Winston Golden St. 400; Riverside Int. Raceway
* 6/23/71—Space City 300; Meyer Speedway
6/26/71—Pickens 200; Greenville-Pickens Speedway

Darrell Waltrip
* 9/27/81—Old Dominion 500; Martinsville Speedway
* 10/4/81—Holly Farms 400; North Wilkesboro Speedway
* 10/11/81—National 500; Charlotte Motor Speedway
* 11/1/81—American 500; North Carolina Motor Speedway

Three Consecutive Poles

Fonty Flock
* 4/15/51—Occoneechee Speedway
4/22/51—Arizona State Fairgrounds
* 4/29/51—Wilkes County 150; North Wilkesboro Speedway

Fonty Flock
6/1/52—Fort Miami Speedway
6/8/52—Occoneechee Speedway
6/15/52—Charlotte Speedway

Herb Thomas
7/11/52—Morristown Speedway
7/20/52—Playland Park Speedway
8/15/52—Asheville-Weaverville Speedway

Curtis Turner
* 8/9/53—Occoneechee Speedway
8/16/53—Asheville-Weaverville Speedway
8/23/53—Princess Anne Speedway

Buck Baker
* 4/22/56—Langhorne Speedway
* 4/29/56—Richmond 200; Atlantic Rural Fairgrounds
5/5/56—Columbia Speedway

Ralph Moody
8/22/56—Norfolk Speedway
* 8/23/56—Piedmont Interstate Fairgrounds
8/25/56—Coastal Speedway

Glen Wood
10/12/58—Old Dominion 500; Martinsville Speedway
10/19/58—Wilkes 160; North Wilkesboro Speedway
10/26/58—Lakewood Speedway

Pole Records

Rex White
8/9/59—Nashville 300; Fairgrounds Speedway
8/16/59—Western N.C. 500; Asheville-Weaverville Speedway
* 8/21/59—Bowman Gray Stadium

Joe Weatherly
* 10/29/61—Orange Speedway
+ 11/5/61—Concord Speedway
+ 11/12/61—Asheville-Weaverville Speedway

Jack Smith
8/12/62—Western N.C. 500; Asheville-Weaverville Speedway
8/15/62—Starkey Speedway
8/18/62—International 200; Bowman Gray Stadium

Richard Petty
* 4/30/66—Rebel 400; Darlington Raceway
* 5/7/66—Tidewater 250; Langley Field Speedway
* 5/10/66—Speedy Morelock 200; Middle Georgia Raceway

Richard Petty
5/22/66—World 600; Charlotte Motor Speedway
5/29/66—Dog Track Speedway
6/2/66—Asheville 300; Asheville Speedway

Richard Petty
* 7/13/67—Fonda Speedway
* 7/15/67—Islip 300; Islip Speedway
* 7/23/67—Volunteer 500; Bristol International Speedway

David Pearson
* 6/2/68—Macon 300; Middle Georgia Raceway
6/6/68—Smoky Mountain Raceway
6/8/68—Birmingham Speedway

Bobby Isaac
6/19/69—Kingsport 250; Kingsport Speedway
* 6/21/69—Pickens 200; Greenville-Pickens Speedway
6/26/69—North State 200; State Fairgrounds

Bobby Isaac
7/7/70—Albany-Saratoga 250; Albany-Saratoga Speedway
* 7/9/70—Thompson 200; Thompson Speedway
7/12/70—Schaefer 300; Trenton Speedway

Richard Petty
7/11/71—Volunteer 500; Bristol International Speedway
7/14/71—Albany-Saratoga 250; Albany-Saratoga Speedway
7/15/71—Islip 250; Islip Speedway

Cale Yarborough
* 10/22/78—American 500; North Carolina Motor Speedway
11/5/78—Dixie 500; Atlanta International Raceway
11/19/78—Los Angeles Times 500; Ontario Motor Speedway

Cale Yarborough
7/4/80—Firecracker 400; Daytona International Speedway
7/12/80—Busch Nashville 420; Nashville Int. Raceway
7/27/80—Coca-Cola 500; Pocono International Raceway

Cale Yarborough
9/7/80—Capital City 400; Richmond Fairgrounds Raceway
9/14/80—CRC Chemicals 500; Dover Downs Int. Speedway
9/21/80—Holly Farms 400; North Wilkesboro Speedway

Ricky Rudd
2/20/83—Daytona 500; Daytona International Speedway
2/27/83—Richmond 400; Richmond Fairgrounds Raceway
3/13/83—Warner W. Hodgdon Car. 500; N.C. Motor Speedway

Geoff Bodine
4/6/86—Valleydale 500; Bristol International Raceway
4/13/86—TranSouth 500; Darlington International Raceway
4/20/86—First Union 400; North Wilkesboro Speedway

Tim Richmond
9/28/86—Holly Farms 400; North Wilkesboro Speedway
10/5/86—Oakwood Homes 500; Charlotte Motor Speedway
10/19/86—Nationwise 500; North Carolina Motor Speedway

Bill Elliott
5/3/87—Winston 500; Alabama International Motor Speedway
5/24/87—Coca-Cola 600; Charlotte Motor Speedway
5/31/87—Budweiser 500; Dover Downs International Speedway

Jeff Gordon
5/26/96—Coca-Cola 600; Charlotte Motor Speedway
* 6/2/96—Miller Gen. Dr. 500; Dover Downs Int. Speedway
* 6/16/96—UAW-GM Teamwork 500; Pocono Int. Raceway

* Won race
+ 1962 Season

Dirt Poles

1.	Buck Baker	37
	Herb Thomas	37
3.	Tim Flock	31
4.	Fonty Flock	26
	Richard Petty	26
6.	Ned Jarrett	22
7.	David Pearson	19
8.	Junior Johnson	18
9.	Speedy Thompson	17
10.	Joe Weatherly	16
11.	Dick Hutcherson	15
12.	Dick Rathmann	13
13.	Jack Smith	12
	Lee Petty	12
15.	Curtis Turner	11
16.	Rex White	8
17.	Cotton Owens	7
	Fireball Roberts	7
19.	Tiny Lund	6
	Marvin Panch	6
	Jim Paschal	6
22.	Joe Eubanks	5
	Hershel McGriff	5
	Ralph Moody	5
	Bob Welborn	5
26.	Bill Amick	4
	Bobby Isaac	4
	Dick Linder	4
29.	Bob Flock	3
	Eddie Pagan	3
	Tom Pistone	3
	Gober Sosebee	3
	Marshall Teague	3
34.	Johnny Allen	2
	Red Byron	2
	Buddy Baker	2
	Billy Carden	2
	Paul Goldsmith	2
	Parnelli Jones	2
	Mel Larson	2
	Frank Mundy	2
	Jim Pardue	2
	Ken Rush	2
	John Sears	2
	Gwyn Staley	2
	Doug Yates	2
	Emanuel Zervakis	2

48. Bobby Allison	1
Dick Bailey	1
Larry Baumel	1
Bill Blair	1
Al Bonnell	1
Perk Brown	1
Bob Burdick	1
Wally Campbell	1
Jim Cook	1
Doug Cox	1
Bob Duell	1
Glenn Dunnaway	1
Ralph Earnhardt	1
Lou Figaro	1
Jimmy Florian	1
Danny Graves	1
Russ Hepler	1
Jim Hunter	1
James Hylton	1
Tommy Irwin	1
Possum Jones	1
Al Keller	1
John Kieper	1
Elmo Langley	1
Danny Letner	1
Jimmie Lewallen	1
Chuck Mahoney	1
Tommy Moon	1
Bud Moore	1
Norm Nelson	1
Andy Pierce	1
Jim Reed	1
Bill Rexford	1
Wendell Scott	1
Lloyd Shaw	1
G.C. Spencer	1
Donald Thomas	1
Ken Wagner	1
Art Watts	1
Danny Weinberg	1
Dink Widenhouse	1
Glen Wood	1
Lee Roy Yarbrough	1

Longest Streaks of Seasons With a Dirt Pole

1. Richard Petty	11		(1960-70)
2. Buck Baker	10		(1952-61)
3. Tim Flock	7		(1950-56)
Junior Johnson	7		(1959-65)
5. Herb Thomas	6		(1951-56)
Ned Jarrett	6		(1960-65)
7. Lee Petty	5		(1957-61)
Cotton Owens	5		(1958-62)
Dick Rathmann	5		(1951-55)
10. Fonty Flock	4		(1950-53)
Jim Paschal	4		(1953-56)
Rex White	4		(1960-63)
David Pearson	4		(1963-66)
Dick Hutcherson	4		(1964-67)

Four Consecutive Dirt Poles

Herb Thomas
7/10/53—Morristown Speedway
* 7/12/53—Lakewood Speedway
* 7/22/53—Rapid Valley Speedway
7/26/53—Lincoln City Fairgrounds

Tim Flock
* 7/10/55—Asheville-Weaverville Speedway
* 7/15/55—Morristown Speedway
7/29/55—Altamont-Schnectady Fairgrounds
* 7/30/55—New York State Fairgrounds

Three Consecutive Dirt Poles

Fonty Flock
* 4/15/51—Occoneechee Speedway
4/22/51—Arizona State Fairgrounds
* 4/29/51—Wilkes County 150; North Wilkesboro Speedway

Fonty Flock
6/1/52—Fort Miami Speedway
6/8/52—Occoneechee Speedway
6/15/52—Charlotte Speedway

Herb Thomas
7/11/52—Morristown Speedway
7/20/52—Playland Park Speedway
8/17/52—Asheville-Weaverville Speedway

Curtis Turner
* 8/9/53—Occoneechee Speedway
8/16/53—Asheville-Weaverville Speedway
8/23/53—Princess Anne Speedway

Buck Baker
* 4/22/56—Langhorne Speedway
* 4/29/56—Richmond 200; Atlantic Rural Fairgrounds
5/5/56—Columbia Speedway

Ralph Moody
8/22/56—Norfolk Speedway
* 8/23/56—Piedmont Interstate Fairgrounds
8/25/56—Coastal Speedway

Joe Weatherly
* 10/29/61—Orange Speedway
+ 11/5/61—Concord Speedway
2/25/62—Concord Speedway

Richard Petty
5/2/63—Columbia 200; Columbia Speedway
7/7/63—Speedorama 200; Rambi Raceway
7/10/63—Savannah Speedway

Joe Weatherly
9/8/63—Capital City 300; Atlantic Rural Fairgrounds
9/24/63—Dog Track Speedway
* 9/27/63—Orange Speedway

David Pearson
6/26/64—Piedmont Interstate Fairgrounds
* 7/21/64—Pennsylvania 200; Lincoln Speedway
* 8/7/64—Rambi Raceway

Dick Hutcherson
* 9/18/66—Joe Weatherly 150; Orange Speedway
3/25/67—Greenville 200; Greenville-Pickens Speedway
4/6/67—Columbia 200; Columbia Speedway

Pole Records

Richard Petty
* 8/17/67—Sandlapper 200; Columbia Speedway
* 8/25/67—Savannah Speedway
* 9/17/67—Hillsborough 150; Orange Speedway
* *Won race*
+ *1962 Season*

Short-Track Poles

1.	Richard Petty	68
2.	Darrell Waltrip	35
3.	Bobby Allison	34
4.	Bobby Isaac	30
5.	David Pearson	28
	Rex White	28
7.	Junior Johnson	21
	Cale Yarborough	21
9.	Fred Lorenzen	15
10.	Geoff Bodine	14
11.	Ned Jarrett	13
	Mark Martin	13
	Glen Wood	13
14.	Rusty Wallace	11
15.	Benny Parsons	10
	Ricky Rudd	10
17.	Neil Bonnett	9
	Jack Smith	9
19.	Ernie Irvan	8
	Marvin Panch	8
21.	Bill Elliott	7
	Buddy Baker	7
	Alan Kulwicki	7
24.	Jim Paschal	6
25.	Darel Dieringer	5
	Dale Earnhardt	5
	Harry Gant	5
	Terry Labonte	5
	Dave Marcis	5
	Ted Musgrave	5
	Lennie Pond	5
32.	Buck Baker	4
	Fonty Flock	4
	Jeff Gordon	4
	Dick Hutcherson	4
	Lee Petty	4
	Fireball Roberts	4
	Morgan Shepherd	4
	Billy Wade	4
	Lee Roy Yarbrough	4
41.	Tim Flock	3
	James Hylton	3
	Jim Reed	3
	Tim Richmond	3
	Art Watts	3
46.	Davey Allison	2
	Donnie Allison	2
	Brett Bodine	2
	Bobby Hamilton	2
	Bobby Johns	2
	John Kieper	2
	Bobby Labonte	2
	Eddie Pagan	2
	Kyle Petty	2
	Tom Pistone	2
	Joe Ruttman	2
	Tony Stewart	2
	Curtis Turner	2
	Kenny Wallace	2
	Joe Weatherly	2
61.	Johnny Allen	1
	Bill Amick	1
	Ron Bouchard	1
	Chuck Bown	1
	Ward Burton	1
	Neil Cole	1
	Ricky Craven	1
	Bill Dennis	1
	George Dunn	1
	Charlie Glotzbach	1
	Paul Goldsmith	1
	Royce Haggerty	1
	Friday Hassler	1
	Jimmy Hensley	1
	Tommy Irwin	1
	Paul Lewis	1
	Dick Linder	1
	Jimmy Massey	1
	Joe Millikan	1
	Billy Myers	1
	Joe Nemechek	1
	Ken Schrader	1
	Mike Skinner	1
	Jimmy Spencer	1
	Herb Thomas	1
	Speedy Thompson	1
	Bob Welborn	1
	Rick Wilson	1

Longest Streaks of Seasons With a Short-Track Pole

1.	Darrell Waltrip	12	(1974-85)
2.	Richard Petty	10	(1962-71)
3.	Bobby Allison	9	(1966-74)
4.	Rex White	7	(1957-63)
	Junior Johnson	7	(1960-66)
6.	Fred Lorenzen	5	(1961-65)
	Bobby Isaac	5	(1968-72)
	Benny Parsons	5	(1975-79)
9.	Glen Wood	4	(1958-61)
	Cale Yarborough	4	(1967-70)
	David Pearson	4	(1968-71)
	Ricky Rudd	4	(1981-84)
	Geoff Bodine	4	(1984-87)

Five Consecutive Short-Track Poles

Richard Petty
* 5/10/66—Speedy Morelock 200; Middle Georgia Raceway
5/29/66—Dog Track Speedway
6/2/66—Asheville 300; Asheville Speedway
* 6/12/66—Fireball 300; Asheville-Weaverville Speedway
6/15/66—Beltsville 200; Beltsville Speedway

Richard Petty
7/11/71—Volunteer 500; Bristol International Speedway
* 7/14/71—Albany-Saratoga 250; Albany-Saratoga Speedway
* 7/15/71—Islip 250; Islip Speedway
* 7/24/71—Nashville 420; Fairgrounds Speedway
8/6/71—Myers Brothers 250; Bowman Gray Stadium

Bobby Allison
4/30/72—Virginia 500; Martinsville Speedway
* 7/9/72—Volunteer 500; Bristol International Speedway
* 8/26/72—Nashville 420; Fairgrounds Speedway
9/10/72—Capital City 500; Richmond Fairgrounds Raceway
9/24/72—Old Dominion 500; Martinsville Speedway

Cale Yarborough
5/10/80—Music City 420; Nashville International Raceway
7/12/80—Busch Nashville 420; Nashville Int. Raceway
* 8/23/80—Busch Volunteer 500; Bristol Int. Raceway
9/7/80—Capital City 400; Richmond Fairgrounds Raceway
9/21/80—Holly Farms 400; North Wilkesboro Speedway

Darrell Waltrip
* 9/27/81—Old Dominion 500; Martinsville Speedway
* 10/4/81—Holly Farms 400; North Wilkesboro Speedway
2/21/82—Richmond 400; Richmond Fairgrounds Raceway
* 3/14/82—Valleydale 500; Bristol International Raceway
* 4/18/82—Northwestern Bank 400; No. Wilkesboro Speedway

Geoff Bodine
9/8/85—Wrangler Sanforset 400; Richmond Fgds. Raceway
9/22/85—Goody's 500; Martinsville Speedway
9/29/85—Holly Farms 400; North Wilkesboro Speedway
4/6/86—Valleydale 500; Bristol International Raceway
4/20/86—First Union 400; North Wilkesboro Speedway

Four Consecutive Short-Track Poles

Rex White
7/18/58—Canadian National Exposition Stadium
7/19/58—Civic Stadium
7/26/58—Wall Stadium
8/10/58—Nashville 200; Fairgrounds Speedway

Richard Petty
* 9/8/74—Capital City 500; Richmond Fairgrounds Raceway
9/22/74—Wilkes 400; North Wilkesboro Speedway
9/29/74—Old Dominion 500; Martinsville Speedway
* 2/23/75—Richmond 500; Richmond Fairgrounds Raceway

Lennie Pond
4/23/78—Virginia 500; Martinsville Speedway
6/3/78—Music City USA 420; Nashville Speedway
7/15/78—Nashville 420; Nashville Speedway
8/26/78—Volunteer 500; Bristol International Raceway

Darrell Waltrip
9/11/83—Wrangler Sanforset 400; Richmond Fgds. Raceway
9/25/83—Goody's 500; Martinsville Speedway
* 10/2/83—Holly Farms 400; North Wilkesboro Speedway
2/26/84—Miller High Life 400; Richmond Fgds. Raceway

Three Consecutive Short-Track Poles

Rex White
8/9/59—Nashville 300; Fairgrounds Speedway
8/16/59—Western N.C. 500; Asheville-Weaverville Speedway
* 8/21/59—Bowman Gray Stadium

Rex White
5/4/62—Southside Speedway
6/16/62—Myers Brothers 200; Bowman Gray Stadium
6/22/62—Southside Speedway

Jack Smith
8/12/62—Western N.C. 500; Asheville-Weaverville Speedway
8/15/62—Starkey Speedway
8/18/62—International 200; Bowman Gray Stadium

Marvin Panch
3/22/64—Southeastern 500; Bristol International Speedway
* 3/30/64—Bowman Gray Stadium
* 4/11/64—Asheville-Weaverville Speedway

Richard Petty
5/19/67—Beltsville 200; Beltsville Speedway
6/2/67—Asheville 300; Asheville Speedway
* 6/6/67—Macon 300; Middle Georgia Raceway

David Pearson
4/7/68—Hickory 250; Hickory Speedway
* 4/21/68—Gwyn Staley 400; North Wilkesboro Speedway
4/28/68—Virginia 500; Martinsville Speedway

Richard Petty
5/17/68—Beltsville 300; Beltsville Speedway
5/18/68—Tidewater 250; Langley Field Speedway
* 5/31/68—Asheville 300; Asheville Speedway

David Pearson
* 6/2/68—Macon 300; Middle Georgia Raceway
6/6/68—Smoky Mountain Raceway
6/8/68—Birmingham Speedway

Bobby Isaac
3/16/69—Cracker 200; Augusta Speedway
3/23/69—Southeastern 500; Bristol International Speedway
* 4/6/69—Hickory 250; Hickory Speedway

David Pearson
* 5/17/69—Tidewater 375; Langley Field Speedway
6/1/69—Macon 300; Middle Georgia Raceway
6/5/69—Maryville 300; Smoky Mountain Raceway

Bobby Isaac
10/5/69—Wilkes 400; North Wilkesboro Speedway
* 10/17/69—Savannah Speedway
* 10/19/69—Augusta Speedway

Bobby Isaac
* 6/27/70—Greenville 200; Greenville-Pickens Speedway
7/7/70—Albany-Saratoga 250; Albany-Saratoga Speedway
* 7/9/70—Thompson 200; Thompson Speedway

Cale Yarborough
* 5/12/73—Music City 420; Fairgrounds Speedway
7/8/73—Volunteer 500; Bristol International Speedway
8/25/73—Nashville 420; Fairgrounds Speedway
Won race

Superspeedway Poles

1.	David Pearson	58
2.	Cale Yarborough	46
3.	Bill Elliott	42
4.	Buddy Baker	29
5.	Jeff Gordon	23
	Richard Petty	23
7.	Mark Martin	22
	Ken Schrader	22
9.	Geoff Bodine	21
	Fireball Roberts	21
11.	Bobby Allison	18
12.	Alan Kulwicki	17
13.	Bobby Labonte	16
14.	Donnie Allison	15
	Bobby Isaac	15
	Darrell Waltrip	15
17.	Fred Lorenzen	14

18.	Ernie Irvan	13
	Rusty Wallace	13
20.	Davey Allison	12
	Dale Earnhardt	12
	Harry Gant	12
	Terry Labonte	12
24.	Neil Bonnett	11
	Charlie Glotzbach	11
26.	Sterling Marlin	10
	Benny Parsons	10
28.	Dave Marcis	9
	Tim Richmond	9
	Ricky Rudd	9
31.	A.J. Foyt	7
	Dale Jarrett	7
33.	Marvin Panch	6
	Kyle Petty	6
	Lee Roy Yarbrough	6
36.	Ward Burton	5
	Junior Johnson	5
38.	John Andretti	4
	Darel Dieringer	4
	Rick Mast	4
	Joe Nemechek	4
42.	Loy Allen Jr.	3
	Brett Bodine	3
	Fonty Flock	3
	Bobby Hamilton	3
	Pete Hamilton	3
	Kenny Irwin	3
	Cotton Owens	3
	Mike Skinner	3
	Curtis Turner	3
51.	Johnny Benson Jr.	2
	Ron Bouchard	2
	Ricky Craven	2
	Paul Goldsmith	2
	Banjo Matthews	2
	Jeremy Mayfield	2
	Greg Sacks	2
	Morgan Shepherd	2
	Michael Waltrip	2
60.	Buck Baker	1
	Bob Burdick	1
	Jeff Burton	1
	Derrike Cope	1
	Tim Flock	1
	Robby Gordon	1
	David Green	1
	Friday Hassler	1
	Dick Hutcherson	1
	Kevin Lepage	1
	J.D. McDuffie	1
	Frank Mundy	1
	Eddie Pagan	1
	Jim Pardue	1
	Lee Petty	1
	Bob Ross	1
	John Rostek	1
	Joe Ruttman	1
	Frankie Schneider	1
	Frank Secrist	1
	Jack Smith	1

Slick Smith	1
Sam Sommers	1
Ramo Stott	1
Hut Stricklin	1
Herb Thomas	1
Speedy Thompson	1
Dick Trickle	1
Bob Welborn	1

Longest Streaks of Seasons With A Superspeedway Pole

1.	Bill Elliott	12	(1984-95)
2.	David Pearson	11	(1972-82)
3.	Richard Petty	7	(1971-77)
	Cale Yarborough	7	(1978-84)
	Jeff Gordon	7	(1993-99)
6.	Fred Lorenzen	6	(1961-66)
	Alan Kulwicki	6	(1987-92)
	Mark Martin	6	(1988-93)
9.	Fireball Roberts	5	(1959-63)
	Darrell Waltrip	5	(1979-83)
	Ernie Irvan	5	(1990-94)
	Bobby Labonte	5	(1995-99)
	Mark Martin	5	(1995-99)

Longest Streaks of Seasons With Multiple Superspeedway Poles

1.	David Pearson	7	(1972-78)
2.	Cale Yarborough	5	(1980-84)
	Bill Elliott	5	(1984-88)
4.	Fireball Roberts	4	(1959-62)
	Fred Lorenzen	4	(1963-66)
	Cale Yarborough	4	(1967-70)
	Bobby Labonte	4	(1996-99)
8.	Bobby Allison	3	(1971-73)
	Richard Petty	3	(1972-74)
	Buddy Baker	3	(1973-75)
	Cale Yarborough	3	(1974-76)
	Darrell Waltrip	3	(1979-81)
	Ken Schrader	3	(1988-90)
	Dale Jarrett	3	(1996-98)

Eight Consecutive Superspeedway Poles

Bill Elliott

5/26/85—World 600; Charlotte Motor Speedway
* 6/9/85—Van Scoy Diamond Mine 500; Pocono Int. Raceway
7/4/85—Pepsi Firecracker 400; Daytona Int. Speedway
* 7/21/85—Summer 500; Pocono International Raceway
7/28/85—Talladega 500; Alabama Int. Motor Speedway
* 8/11/85—Champion Spark Plug 400; Mich. Int. Speedway
* 9/1/85—Southern 500; Darlington International Raceway
9/15/85—Delaware 500; Dover Downs International Speedway

Five Consecutive Superspeedway Poles

Fireball Roberts

* 7/31/60—Dixie 300; Atlanta International Raceway
9/5/60—Southern 500; Darlington Raceway
10/16/60—National 400; Charlotte Motor Speedway
10/30/60—Atlanta 500; Atlanta International Raceway
2/26/61—Daytona 500; Daytona International Speedway

David Pearson

* 5/5/74—Winston 500; Alabama Int. Motor Speedway
5/19/74—Mason-Dixon 500; Dover Downs Int. Speedway
* 5/26/74—World 600; Charlotte Motor Speedway
6/16/74—Motor State 400; Michigan Int. Speedway
* 7/4/74—Firecracker 400; Daytona Int. Speedway

Four Consecutive Superspeedway Poles

Fireball Roberts

7/4/61—Firecracker 250; Daytona International Speedway
7/9/61—Festival 250; Atlanta International Raceway
9/4/61—Southern 500; Darlington Raceway
9/17/61—Dixie 400; Atlanta International Raceway

Fireball Roberts

9/3/62—Southern 500; Darlington Raceway
10/14/62—National 400; Charlotte Motor Speedway
10/28/62—Dixie 400; Atlanta International Raceway
2/24/63—Daytona 500; Daytona International Speedway

Three Consecutive Superspeedway Poles

Fred Lorenzen

5/8/65—Rebel 300; Darlington Raceway
* 5/23/65—World 600; Charlotte Motor Speedway
6/13/65—Dixie 400; Atlanta International Raceway

Richard Petty

3/27/66—Atlanta 500; Atlanta International Raceway
* 4/30/66—Rebel 400; Darlington Raceway
5/22/66—World 600; Charlotte Motor Speedway

David Pearson

9/3/73—Southern 500; Darlington Raceway
* 9/16/73—Delaware 500; Dover Downs Int. Speedway
10/7/73—National 500; Charlotte Motor Speedway

Cale Yarborough

* 10/22/78—American 500; North Carolina Motor Speedway
11/5/78—Dixie 500; Atlanta International Raceway
11/19/78—Los Angeles Times 500; Ontario Motor Speedway

Cale Yarborough

5/18/80—Mason-Dixon 500; Dover Downs Int. Speedway
5/25/80—World 600; Charlotte Motor Speedway
* 6/1/80—NASCAR 400; Texas World Speedway

Bill Elliott

5/3/87—Winston 500; Alabama International Motor Speedway
5/24/87—Coca-Cola 600; Charlotte Motor Speedway
5/31/87—Budweiser 500; Dover Downs International Speedway

Geoff Bodine

* 8/21/94—GM Goodwrench Dealer 400; Mich. Int. Speedway
9/1/94—Mountain Dew Southern 500; Darlington Raceway
9/18/94—Splitfire Spark Pl. 500; Dover Downs Int. Speed.

Jeff Gordon

5/26/96—Coca-Cola 600; Charlotte Motor Speedway
* 6/2/96—Miller Gen. Dr. 500; Dover Downs Int. Speedway
* 6/16/96—UAW-GM Teamwork 500; Pocono Int. Raceway
* Won race

Grand Slam Poles

1. David Pearson — 31
2. Cale Yarborough — 24
3. Fireball Roberts — 21
4. Bill Elliott — 17
5. Buddy Baker — 16
6. Fred Lorenzen — 12
   Richard Petty — 12

8. Bobby Allison		10
	Geoff Bodine	10
	Jeff Gordon	10
11. Donnie Allison		9
12. Dale Earnhardt		8
	Harry Gant	8
	Bobby Labonte	8
	Ken Schrader	8
16. Charlie Glotzbach		7
	Alan Kulwicki	7
18. Neil Bonnett		6
	Mark Martin	6
20. Davey Allison		5
	Junior Johnson	5
	Sterling Marlin	5
	Marvin Panch	5
	Tim Richmond	5
	Darrell Waltrip	5
26. Darel Dieringer		4
	Dale Jarrett	4
	Benny Parsons	4
	Lee Roy Yarbrough	4
30. A.J. Foyt		3
	Bobby Isaac	3
	Curtis Turner	3
	Rusty Wallace	3
34. Loy Allen Jr.		2
	John Andretti	2
	Ward Burton	2
	Fonty Flock	2
	Kenny Irwin	2
	Dave Marcis	2
	Banjo Matthews	2
	Cotton Owens	2
	Ricky Rudd	2
	Greg Sacks	2
	Mike Skinner	2
45. Buck Baker		1
	Johnny Benson Jr.	1
	Brett Bodine	1
	Derrike Cope	1
	Paul Goldsmith	1
	Robby Gordon	1
	Ernie Irvan	1
	Terry Labonte	1
	Kevin Lepage	1
	Rick Mast	1
	Frank Mundy	1
	Joe Nemechek	1
	Eddie Pagan	1
	Jim Pardue	1
	Kyle Petty	1
	Morgan Shepherd	1
	Jack Smith	1
	Sam Sommers	1
	Ramo Stott	1
	Speedy Thompson	1
	Bob Welborn	1

Pole Records

Longest Streaks of Seasons With a Grand Slam Pole

1. David Pearson	7	(1972-78)
Jeff Gordon	7	(1993-99)
3. Bill Elliott	6	(1984-89)
Fred Lorenzen	6	(1961-66)
5. Fireball Roberts	5	(1959-63)
6. Cale Yarborough	4	(1967-70)
Donnie Allison	4	(1968-71)
Ken Schrader	4	(1987-90)
Dale Jarrett	4	(1995-98)
Bobby Labonte	4	(1996-99)

Six Consecutive Grand Slam Poles

Cale Yarborough
7/4/69—Firecracker 400; Daytona Int. Speedway
8/10/69—Dixie 500; Atlanta International Raceway
9/1/69—Southern 500; Darlington Raceway
10/12/69—National 500; Charlotte Motor Speedway
2/22/70—Daytona 500; Daytona International Speedway
3/29/70—Atlanta 500; Atlanta International Raceway

Five Consecutive Grand Slam Poles

Fireball Roberts
* 7/31/60—Dixie 300; Atlanta International Raceway
9/5/60—Southern 500; Darlington Raceway
10/16/60—National 400; Charlotte Motor Speedway
10/30/60—Atlanta 500; Atlanta International Raceway
2/26/61—Daytona 500; Daytona International Speedway

Four Consecutive Grand Slam Poles

Fireball Roberts
7/4/61—Firecracker 250; Daytona International Speedway
7/9/61—Festival 250; Atlanta International Raceway
9/4/61—Southern 500; Darlington Raceway
9/17/61—Dixie 400; Atlanta International Raceway

Fireball Roberts
9/3/62—Southern 500; Darlington Raceway
10/14/62—National 400; Charlotte Motor Speedway
10/28/62—Dixie 400; Atlanta International Raceway
2/24/63—Daytona 500; Daytona International Speedway

Richard Petty
* 2/27/66—Daytona 500; Daytona International Speedway
3/27/66—Atlanta 500; Atlanta International Raceway
* 4/30/66—Rebel 400; Darlington Raceway
5/22/66—World 600; Charlotte Motor Speedway

David Pearson
9/3/73—Southern 500; Darlington Raceway
10/7/73—National 500; Charlotte Motor Speedway
2/17/74—Daytona 500; Daytona International Speedway
3/24/74—Atlanta 500; Atlanta International Raceway

Bill Elliott
* 4/14/85—TranSouth 500; Darlington Int. Raceway
5/26/85—World 600; Charlotte Motor Speedway
7/4/85—Pepsi Firecracker 400; Daytona Int. Speedway
* 9/1/85—Southern 500; Darlington International Raceway

Three Consecutive Grand Slam Poles

Fred Lorenzen
5/8/65—Rebel 300; Darlington Raceway
* 5/23/65—World 600; Charlotte Motor Speedway
6/13/65—Dixie 400; Atlanta International Raceway

Buddy Baker
11/4/79—Dixie 500; Atlanta International Raceway
* 2/17/80—Daytona 500; Daytona International Speedway
3/16/80—Atlanta 500; Atlanta International Raceway
* Won race

Classic Poles

Driver	Brickyard 400	Daytona 500	Southern 500	World 600	Total
1. David Pearson		1	6	6	13
2. Fireball Roberts		3	5	2	10
3. Jeff Gordon	3	1		5	9
4. Bill Elliott		3	2	3	8
5. Cale Yarborough		4	1	2	7
6. Buddy Baker		4		2	6
Richard Petty		1	3	2	6
Ken Schrader		3	1	2	6
9. Bobby Allison		1	3	1	5
10. Davey Allison		1	2	1	4
Donnie Allison		2		2	4
12. Neil Bonnett			1	2	3
Harry Gant			2	1	3
Dale Jarrett		1	2		3
Bobby Labonte		1	1	1	3
16. Geoff Bodine		1		1	2
Dale Earnhardt		1	1		2
Fonty Flock		2			2
Charlie Glotzbach		1		1	2
Ernie Irvan	2				2
Bobby Isaac		1		1	2
Junior Johnson			1	1	2
Alan Kulwicki		1		1	2
Fred Lorenzen		1		1	2
Sterling Marlin		1	1		2
Cotton Owens		1	1		2
Curtis Turner		1	1		2
Darrell Waltrip			2		2
29. Loy Allen Jr.		1			1
John Andretti		1			1
Buck Baker		1			1
Darel Dieringer		1			1
A.J. Foyt		1			1
Paul Goldsmith		1			1
Kenny Irwin		1			1
Mark Martin				1	1
Rick Mast	1				1
Frank Mundy		1			1
Eddie Pagan		1			1
Jim Pardue				1	1
Benny Parsons		1			1
Kyle Petty		1			1
Tim Richmond		1			1
Ricky Rudd		1			1
Mike Skinner		1			1
Ramo Stott		1			1
Speedy Thompson			1		1
Bob Welborn		1			1
Lee Roy Yarbrough		1		1	1

Longest Streaks of Seasons With a Classic Pole

1. David Pearson	6		(1973-78)
Jeff Gordon	6		(1994-99)
3. Fireball Roberts	5		(1959-63)
4. Cale Yarborough	4		(1967-70)
Bill Elliott	4		(1985-88)
6. Ken Schrader	3		(1988-90)
Bobby Labonte	3		(1997-99)
8. Fonty Flock	2		(1952-53)
Richard Petty	2		(1966-67)
Donnie Allison	2		(1968-69)
Bobby Allison	2		(1971-72)
Buddy Baker	2		(1979-80)
Davey Allison	2		(1987-88)
Dale Jarrett	2		(1995-96)

Five Consecutive Classic Poles

Fireball Roberts

9/4/61—Southern 500; Darlington Raceway
* 2/18/62—Daytona 500; Daytona International Speedway
5/27/62—World 600; Charlotte Motor Speedway
9/3/62—Southern 500; Darlington Raceway
2/24/63—Daytona 500; Daytona International Speedway

Four Consecutive Classic Poles

Bill Elliott

* 2/17/85—Daytona 500; Daytona International Speedway
5/26/85—World 600; Charlotte Motor Speedway
* 9/1/85—Southern 500; Darlington International Raceway
2/16/86—Daytona 500; Daytona International Speedway

Three Consecutive Classic Poles

Fireball Roberts

6/19/60—World 600; Charlotte Motor Speedway
9/5/60—Southern 500; Darlington Raceway
2/26/61—Daytona 500; Daytona International Speedway

David Pearson

9/3/73—Southern 500; Darlington Raceway
2/17/74—Daytona 500; Daytona International Speedway
* 5/26/74—World 600; Charlotte Motor Speedway
* *Won race*

Road Poles

1. Darrell Waltrip	9
2. Terry Labonte	8
David Pearson	8
4. Richard Petty	6
5. Bobby Allison	5
Dale Earnhardt	5
Ricky Rudd	5
8. Mark Martin	4
9. Buck Baker	3
Tim Flock	3
Paul Goldsmith	3
Jeff Gordon	3
13. Geoff Bodine	2
A.J. Foyt	2
Dan Gurney	2
Fred Lorenzen	2
Tim Richmond	2
Rusty Wallace	2
Cale Yarborough	2

20. Todd Bodine	1
George Follmer	1
Danny Graves	1
Eddie Gray	1
Dick Hutcherson	1
Ernie Irvan	1
Junior Johnson	1
Parnelli Jones	1
Pat Kirkwood	1
Joe Littlejohn	1
Banjo Matthews	1
Marvin Panch	1
Lee Petty	1
Bob Pronger	1
Jim Reed	1
Morgan Shepherd	1
Jack Smith	1
Gober Sosebee	1
Billy Wade	1
Art Watts	1

Consecutive Seasons With a Road Pole

1. Darrell Waltrip	4		(1980-83)
2. Richard Petty	3		(1971-73)
Ricky Rudd	3		(1990-92)
Mark Martin	3		(1993-95)
5. Tim Flock	2		(1955-56)
Buck Baker	2		(1956-57)
Paul Goldsmith	2		(1957-58)
Richard Petty	2		(1963-64)
Bobby Allison	2		(1970-71)
David Pearson	2		(1973-74)
Bobby Allison	2		(1975-76)
David Pearson	2		(1978-79)
Terry Labonte	2		(1984-85)
Darrell Waltrip	2		(1985-86)
Geoff Bodine	2		(1987-88)
Dale Earnhardt	2		(1992-93)
Jeff Gordon	2		(1998-99)

Three Consecutive Road Course Poles

Bobby Allison

* 1/19/75—Winston Western 500; Riverside Int. Raceway
6/8/75—Tuborg 400; Riverside International Raceway
1/18/76—Winston Western 500; Riverside Int. Raceway

David Pearson

1/22/78—Winston Western 500; Riverside Int. Raceway
6/11/78—NAPA Riverside 400; Riverside Int. Raceway
1/14/79—Winston Western 500; Riverside Int. Raceway

Darrell Waltrip

1/11/81—Winston Western 500; Riverside Int. Raceway
* 6/14/81—Warner W. Hodgdon 400; Riverside Int. Raceway
11/22/81—Winston Western 500; Riverside Int. Raceway

Darrell Waltrip

11/21/82—Winston Western 500; Riverside Int. Raceway
6/5/83—Budweiser 400; Riverside International Raceway
11/20/83—Winston Western 500; Riverside Int. Raceway

Jeff Gordon

* 6/28/98—Save Mart/Kragen 350; Sears Point Raceway
* 8/9/98—The Bud at the Glen; Watkins Glen International
* 6/27/99—Save Mart/Kragen 350; Sears Point Raceway
* *Won race*

Tracks
State–Number of Winston Cup races held
City–track name (track distance/type) (years of races) total races

Sites of Winston Cup Races During the 20th Century

A complete state-by-state listing of the 169 tracks that played host to Winston Cup races during the sport's first 51 years follows. Beside each state is the number of Winston Cup races that were held in that state from 1949-99. Each track's listing begins with the city in which the track is located, followed by the name of the track, the distance of the track, a notation if the track was dirt or a road course, the years in which it staged Winston Cup races, and the number of races held at that facility. Tracks that underwent name changes are listed by the name the facility used during its last year of Winston Cup racing.

ALABAMA-80

* Birmingham—Birmingham Speedway (1958, 1961, 1963-65, 1967-68)	8
Birmingham—Dixie Speedway (.25-mile) (1960)	1
Huntsville—Huntsville Speedway (.25-mile) (1962)	1
Mobile—Lakeview Speedway (.75-mile dirt) (1951)	2
Montgomery—Chisholm Speedway (.5-mile dirt) (1955-56)	2
Montgomery—Montgomery Speedway (.5-mile) (1955-56, 1967-69)	5
** Talladega—Talladega Superspeedway (2.66-mile) (1969-99)	61

* Known as the Alabama State Fairgrounds, a .5-mile dirt track, for its race in 1958 and its race in 1961; as Birmingham Raceway, a .5-mile track, for its four races from 1963-65, and as Birmingham Speedway, a .625-mile track, when it held a race in 1967 and another in '68.

** Known as Alabama International Motor Speedway for the 39 races it held from 1969-88.

ARIZONA-17

Phoenix—Arizona State Fairgrounds (1-mile dirt) (1951, 1955-56, 1960)	4
Phoenix—Phoenix International Raceway (1-mile) (1988-99)	12
Tucson—Tucson Rodeo Grounds (.5-mile dirt) (1955)	1

ARKANSAS-5

LeHi—Memphis-Arkansas Speedway (1.5-mile dirt) (1954-57)	5

CALIFORNIA-100

Eureka—Eureka Speedway (.625-mile dirt) (1956-57)	2
Fontana—California Speedway (2-mile) (1997-99)	3
Gardena—Carrell Speedway (.5-mile dirt) (1951, 1954)	4
Hanford—Hanford Speedway (.5-mile dirt) (1951)	1
Hanford—Marchbanks Speedway (1.4-mile) (1960-61)	2
Lancaster—Willow Springs Speedway (2.5-mile dirt road) (1956-57)	2
* Los Angeles—Ascot Stadium (1959, 1961)	2
Los Angeles—Los Angeles Fairgrounds (.5-mile dirt) (1957)	1
Merced—Merced Fairgrounds (.5-mile dirt) (1956)	1
** Oakland—Oakland Stadium (1951, 1954)	3
Ontario—Ontario Motor Speedway (2.5-mile) (1971-72, 1974-80)	9
*** Riverside—Riverside International Raceway (1958, 1961, 1963-88)	48
Sacramento—California State Fairgrounds (1-mile dirt) (1956-61)	6
Sacramento—Capitol Speedway (.5-mile dirt) (1957)	1
San Jose—Santa Clara Fairgrounds (.5-mile dirt) (1957)	1
San Mateo—Bay Meadows Speedway (1-mile dirt) (1954-56)	3
**** Sonoma—Sears Point Raceway (1989-99)	11

* Measured as a 4-mile dirt track for its race in 1959 and as a .5-mile dirt track for its race in '61.
** A .625-mile dirt track for its race in 1951 and a .5-mile dirt track for its two races in 1954.
*** Measured as a 2.631-mile road course for its race in 1958, as a 2.58-mile road course for its race in '61, as a 2.7-mile road course for its eight races from 1963-69, and as a 2.62-mile road course for its 38 races from 1970-88.
**** Known as Sears Point International Raceway for its five races from 1989-93; measured as a 2.52-mile road course for its nine races from 1989-97 and as a 1.94-mile road course for its races in '98 and '99.

CANADA-2

Niagara Falls—Stamford Park (.5-mile dirt) (1952)	1
Toronto—Canadian National Exposition Stadium (.333-mile) (1958)	1

CONNECTICUT-3

* Thompson—Thompson Speedway (1951, 1969, 1970)	3

* Measured as a .5-mile track for its race in 1951, as a .625-mile track for its race in '69, and as a .542-mile track for its race in '70.

DELAWARE-60

Dover—Dover Downs International Speedway (1-mile) (1969-99)	60

FLORIDA-132

* Daytona Beach—Beach & Road Course (1949-58)	10
Daytona Beach—Daytona International Speedway (2.5-mile) (1959-99)	105
Homestead—Homestead-Miami Speedway (1.5-mile) (1999)	1
Jacksonville—Speedway Park (.5-mile dirt) (1951-52, 1954-55, 1961, 1964-65)	6
Pensacola—Five Flags Speedway (.5-mile dirt) (1953)	1
Tampa—Golden Gate Speedway (.333-mile) (1963)	1
Titusville—Titusville-Cocoa Speedway (1.6-mile road) (1957)	1
** West Palm Beach—Palm Beach Speedway (1952-56)	7

* Measured as a 4.15-mile road course for its race in 1949, as a 4.167-mile road course for its race in '50, and as a 4.1-mile road course for its eight races from 1951-58.
** A .5-mile dirt track for its five races from 1952-55 and a .5-mile track for its two races in '56.

GEORGIA-140

Augusta—Augusta International Speedway (3-mile road) (1964)	1
* Augusta—Augusta Speedway (1962-69)	12
Augusta—Hayloft Speedway (.5-mile dirt) (1952)	1
Atlanta—Lakewood Speedway (1-mile dirt) (1951-54, 1956, 1958-59)	11
Columbus—Columbus Speedway (.5-mile dirt) (1951)	1
** Hampton—Atlanta Motor Speedway (1960-99)	81
Jefferson—Jeffco Speedway (.5-mile) (1968-69)	2
Macon—Central City Speedway (.5-mile dirt) (1951-54)	7
*** Macon—Middle Georgia Raceway (1966-71)	9
Savannah—Oglethorpe Speedway (.5-mile dirt) (1954-55)	1
**** Savannah—Savannah Speedway (1962-64, 1967, 1969-70)	10
Valdosta—Valdosta Speedway (.5-mile dirt) (1962, 1964-65)	3

* A .5-mile dirt track for the four races it held in 1962 and '63 and a .5-mile track for the eight races it held from 1964-69.
** Known as Atlanta International Raceway for the 62 races it held from 1960 through the first race of the 1990 season; measured at 1.5 miles for the 21 races it held from 1960-69, at 1.522 miles for the 55 races it held from 1970 through the first race of the 1997 season, and at 1.54 miles for the second race it held in 1997 and its four races in '98 and '99.
*** Measured as a .5-mile track for its race in 1966 and its race in '67, as a .5625-mile track for its first race in '68, as a .5-mile track for its second race in '68 and the two races it held in '69, and as a .548-mile track for the three races it held from 1969-71.
**** A .5-mile dirt track for the eight races it held from 1962-64 and in '67 and a .5-mile track for its race in 1969 and its race in '70.

ILLINOIS-2

Chicago—Soldier Field (.5-mile) (1956)	1
Willow Springs—Santa Fe Speedway (.5-mile dirt) (1954)	1

INDIANA-8

Indianapolis—Indianapolis Motor Speedway (2.5-mile) (1994-99)	6
South Bend—Playland Park Speedway (.5-mile dirt) (1952)	1
Winchester—Funk's Speedway (.5-mile dirt) (1950)	1

IOWA-1

Davenport—Davenport Speedway (.5-mile dirt) (1953)	1

KENTUCKY-1
Corbin—Corbin Speedway (.5-mile dirt) (1954)   1

LOUISIANA-1
Shreveport—Louisiana Fairgrounds (.5-mile dirt) (1953)   1

MAINE-3
Oxford—Oxford Plains Speedway (.333-mile) (1966-68)   3

MARYLAND-10
Beltsville—Beltsville Speedway (.5-mile) (1965-70)   10

MASSACHUSETTS-1
Norwood—Norwood Arena (.25-mile) (1961)   1

MICHIGAN-66
* Brooklyn—Michigan Speedway (1969-99)   61
Detroit—Michigan State Fairgrounds (1-mile dirt) (1951-52)   2
Grand Rapids—Grand River Speedrome (.5-mile dirt) (1951, 1954)   2
Monroe—Monroe Speedway (.5-mile dirt) (1952)   1

Known as Michigan International Speedway for the 55 races it held from 1969-96; measured at two miles for the two races it held in 1969 and its first race in '70; at 2.04 miles for its second race in 1970 and its two races in 1971, and at two miles for the 55 races it held from 1972-99.

NEBRASKA-1
North Platte—Lincoln City Fairgrounds (.5-mile dirt) (1953)   1

NEVADA-3
Las Vegas—Las Vegas Motor Speedway (1.5-mile) (1998-99)   2
Las Vegas—Las Vegas Park Speedway (1-mile dirt) (1955)   1

NEW HAMPSHIRE-10
Loudon—New Hampshire International Speedway (1.058-mile) (1993-99) 10

NEW JERSEY-21
Belmar—Wall Stadium (.333-mile) (1958)   1
Linden—Linden Airport (2-mile road) (1954)   1
Morristown—Morristown Speedway (.5-mile dirt) (1951-55)   5
Old Bridge—Old Bridge Stadium (.5-mile) (1956-58, 1963-65)   6
* Trenton—Trenton Speedway (1958-59, 1967-72)   8

Measured at one mile for the four races it held from 1958-68; measured at 1.5 miles for the four races it held from 1969-72.

NEW YORK-55
* Altamont—Altamont-Schnectady Fairgrounds (.5-mile dirt) (1951, 1955) 2
Bridgehampton—Bridgehampton Raceway (2.85-m rd.) (1958, 1963-64, 1966) 4
Buffalo—Civic Stadium (.25-mile) (1958)   1
Busti—State Line Speedway (.333-mile dirt) (1958)   1
Fonda—Fonda Speedway (.5-mile dirt) (1955, 1966-68)   4
Hamburg—Hamburg Fairgrounds (.5-mile dirt) (1949-50)   2
Islip—Islip Speedway (.2-mile) (1964-68, 1971)   6
Malta—Albany-Saratoga Speedway (.362-mile) (1970-71)   2
Montgomery—Montgomery Air Base (2-mile) (1960)   1
Owego—Wine Creek Race Track (.5-mile) (1952)   1
Plattsburg—Airborne Speedway (.5-mile dirt) (1955)   1
Rochester—Monroe County Fairgrounds (.5-mile dirt) (1950-56, 1958) 8
Syracuse—New York State Fairgrounds (1-mile dirt) (1955-57)   3
Vernon—Vernon Fairgrounds (.5-mile dirt) (1950)   2
** Watkins Glen—Watkins Glen International (1957, 1964-65, 1986-99) 17

Known as Altamont Speedway for the race it held in 1951.

Measured as a 2.3-mile road course for its three races in 1957, '64 and '65; as a 2.428-mile road course for its six races from 1986-91, and as a 2.45-mile road course for the eight races it held from 1992-99.

NORTH CAROLINA-481
* Asheville Speedway—Asheville (1962-68, 1971)   8
Asheville—McCormick Field (.25-mile) (1958)   1
Charlotte—Charlotte Speedway (.75-mile dirt) (1949-56)   12
** Charlotte—Charlotte Fairgrounds (.5-mile dirt) (1954-61)   17
*** Concord—Lowe's Motor Speedway (1.5-mile) (1960-99)   82
Concord—Concord Speedway (.5-mile dirt) (1956-59, 1962, 1964)   12
Fayetteville—Champion Speedway (.333-mile) (1958-59)   4
Gastonia—Gastonia Fairgrounds (.333-mile dirt) (1958)   1
Greensboro—Greensboro Fairgrounds (.333-mile dirt) (1957-58)   3
Harris—Harris Speedway (.3-mile) (1964-65)   2
**** Hickory—Hickory Speedway (1953-71)   35
High Point—Tri-City Speedway (.5-mile dirt) (1953, 1955)   2
***** Hillsborough—Orange Speedway (1949-68)   32
Jacksonville—Jacksonville Speedway (.5-mile dirt) (1957, 1962)   2
Monroe—Starlite Speedway (.4-mile dirt) (1966)   1
****** Moyock—Dog Track Speedway (1962-66)   7
******* North Wilkesboro—North Wilkesboro Speedway (1949-96) 93
Raleigh—Raleigh Speedway (1-mile) (1953-58)   7
Raleigh—State Fairgrounds (.5-mile dirt) (1955, 1969-70)   3
Randleman—Tar Heel Speedway (.25-mile) (1963)   3
******** Rockingham—North Carolina Speedway (1965-99)   69
Salisbury—Salisbury Speedway (.625-mile dirt) (1958)   1
Shelby—Cleveland County Fairgrounds (.5-mile dirt) (1956-57, 1965) 6
Spring Lake—Harnett Speedway (.5-mile dirt) (1953)   1
********* Weaverville—Asheville-Weaverville Speedway (1951-69) 34
Wilson—Wilson Speedway (.5-mile dirt) (1951-54, 1956-60)   12
Winston-Salem—Bowman Gray Stadium (.25-mile) (1958-71)   29
Winston-Salem—Forsyth County Fairgrounds (.5-mile dirt) (1955)   2

Measured as a .4-mile track for its race in 1962 and as a .333-mile track for the seven races it held from 1963-68 and in '71.

Known as Southern States Fairgrounds for the 11 races it held from 1954-58.

Known as Charlotte Motor Speedway for the 80 races it held from 1960-98.

****Measured as a .5-mile dirt track for its two races in 1953; as a .4-mile dirt track for the 24 races it held from 1954-67; as a .4-mile track for the five races it held from 1967-69, and as a .363-mile track for the four races it held in 1970 and '71.****

*****Known as Occoneechee Speedway for the eight races it held from 1949-53; measured as a 1-mile dirt track for the 11 races it held from 1949-55 and as a .9-mile dirt track for the 21 races it held from 1956-68; spelling of city's name was changed from Hillsboro to Hillsborough during the 1965 season.*****

******Measured as a .25-mile dirt track for the three races it held in 1962 and '63 and as a .333-mile track for the four races it held from 1964-66.******

*******Measured as a .5-mile dirt track for its race in 1949, as a .625-mile dirt track for the 13 races it held from 1950 through its first race in '57, and as a .625-mile track for the 79 races it held from its second race in 1957 through 1996.*******

********Known as the North Carolina Motor Speedway for its 65 races from 1966-97; measured as a one-mile track for the eight races it held from 1965 through its first race in 1969; measured as a 1.017-mile track for the 61 races it held from the second race of 1969 through 1999.********

*********Measured as a .5-mile dirt track for the seven races it held from 1951 through its first race in '57 and as a .5-mile track for the 27 races it held from its second race in 1957 through 1969.*********

OHIO-13
Bainbridge—Bainbridge Speedway (1-mile dirt) (1951)   1
Canfield—Canfield Speedway (.5-mile dirt) (1950-52)   3
Columbus—Powell Motor Speedway (.5-mile dirt) (1953)   1
Dayton—Dayton Speedway (.5-mile) (1950-52)   6
Toledo—Fort Miami Speedway (.5-mile dirt) (1951-52)   2

OKLAHOMA–1

Oklahoma City—Oklahoma State Fairgrounds (.5-mile dirt) (1956)   1

OREGON–7

Portland—Portland Speedway (.5-mile) (1956-57)   7

PENNSYLVANIA–79

Bloomsburg—Bloomsburg Fairgrounds (.5-mile dirt) (1953)   1
Langhorne—Langhorne Speedway (1-mile dirt) (1949-57)   17
* Long Pond—Pocono Raceway (1974-99)   44
Mechanicsburg—Williams Grove Speedway (.5-mile dirt) (1954)   1
New Bradford—New Bradford Speedway (.333-mile dirt) (1958)   1
New Oxford—Lincoln Speedway (.5-mile dirt) (1955-58, 1964-65)   7
** Pittsburgh—Heidelberg Raceway (1949, 1951, 1959-60)   4
*** Reading—Reading Speedway (.5-mile dirt) (1958-59)   2
Shippenville—Pine Grove Speedway (.5-mile dirt) (1951)   1
Sharon—Sharon Speedway (.5-mile dirt) (1954)   1

Known as Pocono International Raceway for the 40 races it held from 1974-97.
**Known as Heidelberg Speedway, a .5-mile dirt track, for the three races it held in 1949, '51 and '60; measured as a .25-mile dirt track for the race it held in 1959.*
***Known as Reading Fairgrounds for its 1958 race.*

SOUTH CAROLINA–201

* Columbia—Columbia Speedway (1951-71)   43
** Darlington—Darlington Raceway (1950-99)   91
*** Greenville—Greenville-Pickens Speedway (1951, 1955-56, 1958-71)   29
Hartsville—Hartsville Speedway (.333-mile dirt) (1961)   1
Lancaster—Lancaster Speedway (.5-mile dirt) (1957)   2
Myrtle Beach—Coastal Speedway (.5-mile dirt) (1956-57)   2
Myrtle Beach—Rambi Raceway (.5-mile dirt) (1958-65)   9
Newberry—Newberry Speedway (.5-mile dirt) (1957)   1
Spartanburg—Piedmont Interstate Fairgrounds (.5-mile dirt) (1953-66) 22
Sumter—Gamecock Speedway (.25-mile dirt) (1960)   1

Measured as a .5-mile dirt track for the 41 races it held from 1951-70, as a .5-mile track for its first race in 1971, and as a .51-mile track for its second race in '71.
**Known as Darlington International Raceway for the 31 races it held from the second race of 1975 through 1990; measured at 1.25 miles for its five races from 1950-53, at 1.375 miles for its 27 races from 1954 through its first race in 1970, and at 1.366 miles for the 59 races it held from its second race in 1970 through 1999.*
***Measured as a .5-mile dirt track for the 26 races it held from 1951-69 and as a .5-mile track for the three races it held in 1970 and '71.*

SOUTH DAKOTA–1

Rapid City—Rapid Valley Speedway (.5-mile dirt) (1953)   1

TENNESSEE–139

* Bristol—Bristol Motor Speedway (1961-99)   78
Chattanooga—Boyd Speedway (.333-mile) (1962, 1964)   2
** Kingsport—Kingsport Speedway (1969-71)   3
*** Maryville—Smoky Mountain Raceway (1965-71)   12
**** Nashville—Nashville International Raceway (1958-84)   42
Newport—Newport Speedway (.5-mile dirt) (1956-57)   2

Known as Bristol International Speedway for the 34 races it held from 1961-77 and as Bristol International Raceway for the 37 races it held from 1978-96; measured as a .5-mile track for the 17 races it held from 1961 through its first race of 1969 and as a .533-mile track for the 61 races it held from its second race in 1969 through 1999.
**Measured as a .4-mile track for its race in 1969 and as a .337-mile track for its race in 1970 and its race in '71.*
***Measured as a .5-mile dirt track for the five races it held from 1965-67, as a .5-mile track for the four races it held in 1968 and '69, and as a .52-mile track for the three races it held in 1970 and '71.*

****Known as Fairgrounds Speedway for the 15 races it held from 1958-69 and as Nashville Speedway for the eight races it held from 1975-78; measured as a .5-mile track for the 15 races it held from 1958-69 and as a .596-mile track for the 27 races it held from 1970-84.*

TEXAS–12

* College Station—Texas World Speedway (2-mile) (1969, 1971-73, 1979-81)   8
Fort Worth—Texas Motor Speedway (1.5-mile) (1997-99)   3
Houston—Meyer Speedway (.5-mile) (1971)   1

Known as Texas International Speedway for its race in 1969.

VIRGINIA–226

* Hampton—Langley Field Speedway (1964-70)   9
Manassas—Old Dominion Speedway (.375-mile) (1958, 1963-66)   7
** Martinsville—Martinsville Speedway (1949-99)   102
Norfolk—Norfolk Speedway (.4-mile dirt) (1956-57)   2
Norfolk—Princess Anne Speedway (.5-mile dirt) (1953)   1
*** Richmond—Richmond Fairgrounds Raceway (1953, 1955-88)   64
Richmond—Richmond International Raceway (.75-mile) (1988-99)   23
**** Richmond—Southside Speedway (1961-63)   4
Roanoke—Starkey Speedway (.25-mile) (1958, 1961-62, 1964)   4
***** South Boston—South Boston Speedway (1960-64, 1968-71)   10

* A .4-mile dirt track for the four races it held from 1964-67 and a .4-mile track for the five races it held from 1968-70.*
**Measured as a .5-mile dirt track for the 12 races it held from 1949 through its first race of 1955, as a .5-mile track for the 30 races it held from its second race in 1955 through 1969, as a .525-mile track for the 28 races it held from 1970-83, and as a .526-mile track for the 32 races it held from 1984-99.*
***Known as the Atlantic Rural Fairgrounds for the 16 races it held in 1953 and from 1955 through its first race in 1964 and as the Virginia State Fairgrounds for the 13 races it held from its second race in 1964 through 1970; measured as a .5-mile dirt track for the 24 races it held from 1953 through its first race in 1968, as a .625-mile track for its second race in 1968, as a .5-mile track for its first race in 1969, as a .5625-mile track for its second race in '69, and as a .542-mile track for the 37 races it held from 1970-88.*
****Measured as a .25-mile dirt track for its race in 1961 and as a .333-mile track for the three races it held in 1962 and '63.*
*****Measured as a .25-mile dirt track for the race it held in 1960 and its race in '61, as a .375-mile track for the six races it held in 1962-69, and as a .357-mile track for the race it held in 1970 and its race in '71.*

WASHINGTON–1

Bremerton—Kitsap County Airport (.9-mile road) (1957)   1

WEST VIRGINIA–4

* Ona—International Raceway Park (1963-64, 1970-71)   4

Known as West Virginia International Speedway for its race in 1963 and its race in '64; measured as a .375-mile track for its race in 1963 and as a .4375-mile track for its three races from 1964-71.

WISCONSIN–1

Elkhart Lake—Road America (4-mile road) (1956)   1

If someone had visited Atlanta Motor Speedway in 1960 and never returned until today, he or she might have a difficult time believing it's the same track.

Acknowledgments

So much of the information in this book was compiled during more than a quarter of a century that I spent as a motorsports journalist and publicist that it is virtually impossible to thank all of the sources who contributed.

I acquired considerable knowledge that became part of this book from the more than 100 books, thousands of newspaper and magazine articles, and news releases I've read about NASCAR Winston Cup racing. Conducting and attending hundreds of news conferences certainly contributed to the information, as did the countless race telecasts I've watched or broadcasts I've heard. Particularly important were thousands of interviews and conversations, as many casual as formal, with motorsports personalities.

So while it isn't feasible to list everyone whose aid and cooperation during those 27 years helped make this book possible, I'd be remiss if I didn't thank some of the more obvious contributors.

First, I'd like to thank longtime Martinsville (Va.) Speedway executives Dick Thompson and the late Clay Earles for their role in helping introduce a novice motorsports reporter to scores of people in stock-car racing and helping him learn the ropes. Similar thanks go to former publicists Bobby Batson and Bob Latford, while a special acknowledgment goes to Bob Myers and Bob Moore, veteran motorsports reporters who were always helpful years ago despite working for competing publications. The many publicists who have helped promote the sport throughout its history, particularly those with NASCAR, the R.J. Reynolds' Tobacco Company's Sports Marketing Enterprises, the Winston Cup facilities, and the manufacturers, also were invaluable in providing information.

Although the research material in this book reveals hundreds of differences in opinion about historical facts and often reaches contradictory conclusions about correct statistics and data than the books that follow, I nevertheless found these to be helpful reference sources: the *NASCAR Winston Cup Series Media Guide* and its predecessors, *Winston Cup Official NASCAR Record Book and Press Guide*; *NASCAR Record Book and Press Guide*; *NASCAR Record Book*, and *NASCAR Stock Car Racing Record Book*, and *The Stock Car Racing Encyclopedia*, edited by Peter Golenbock and Greg Fielden and published by Macmillan.

While I'd like to thank everyone in motorsports who has been kind enough to give me a few minutes or hours of their time—or in many cases, a great deal more—during the past 27 years, I'd particularly like to acknowledge Donnie Allison, Buddy Arrington, Buck Baker, Buddy Baker, Brett Bodine, Geoff Bodine, Jeff Burton, Richard Childress, Derrike Cope, Dale Earnhardt, Bill Elliott, A.J. Foyt, Charlie Glotzbach, Jeff Gordon, Janet Guthrie, Rick Hendrick, Dale Inman, Dale Jarrett, Ned Jarrett, Junior Johnson, Bobby Labonte, Terry Labonte, Mark Martin, Larry McReynolds, Ralph Moody, Benny Parsons, Lee Petty, Maurice Petty, Ricky Rudd, Rusty Wallace, Darrell Waltrip, Glen Wood, Leonard Wood, Cale Yarborough, Smokey Yunick and, although they aren't quoted in this book, Dick Trickle and motorsports marketing executive Skipper Burns—if, for no other reason, their friendship.

And I wish the following were still around to thank: Davey Allison, Neil Bonnett, Tim Flock, Bobby Isaac, Alan Kulwicki, J.D. McDuffie, and Tim Richmond.

I'd also like to thank Bruton Smith, chairman of the board of Speedway Motorsports, Inc., for his guidance and those many bull sessions in which he shared tales of the past, and especially Humpy Wheeler, President of Lowe's Motor Speedway, who, for a quarter of a century, always has been helpful and such a wonderful source of inspiration.

I'd also like to thank Don Boykin, Assistant Managing Editor/Sports of *The Atlanta Journal-Constitution* and the help provided by David Davidson of his staff. Boykin gratefully arranged access to his newspapers' archives and gave me permission to use them—an extremely valuable reference source in helping me locate hard-to-find information that I needed. Thanks to Richard Hallman, those newspapers' chief archivist, and Kathryn Pease, John Jackson, Betty Darden, and Lauren Colburn of his staff for their assistance in my quest.

I'm especially grateful to the *Martinsville Bulletin*, *Roanoke Times*, *Gastonia Gazette*, Louisville *Courier-Journal*, *The Sporting News*, and Atlanta Motor Speedway for providing me with jobs that enabled me to immerse myself in the great sport of auto racing.

Finally, there are several special acknowledgements:

- To Gene Granger, probably NASCAR's premier historian, for providing me with copies of any of NASCAR's original Winston Cup race reports that I didn't already have. Because media coverage of Winston Cup racing often was so inadequate in its early years, this book—and particularly its accuracy—couldn't have been possible without him.
- To Bobby Allison and Richard Petty, once bitter rivals who share a common bond: perhaps the two most accessible, down-to-earth superstars—not a term to be used loosely—in the history of sports. Both of them went far and above the call of duty in being so generous to me with the greatest gift of all: their valuable time.
- To Atlanta Motor Speedway President and General Manager Ed Clark for allowing me access to the speedway's archives and granting permission to use Atlanta Motor Speedway's photo library and to former speedway photographer Ted McMahan and his fine staff for taking so many wonderful pictures.
- To Tom Morgan and Liz McGhee for their wonderful design of the book.
- To David Bull, my editor and publisher, and his right-hand man, Skylar Browning, for their support—and considerable effort—in making this project a reality.
- To Scott Anderson of the Richard Petty Driving Experience and Valerie Sowers for serving as sounding boards throughout the progress of this book, and additional thanks to Valerie for her love, support, and faith in this project.
- And, finally, to David Pearson, not only for his time, but for his role in making this book a reality, when several years ago he and I were arguing over a minute detail from 1964 and I cited information provided in two different sources.

"You need to get another book," he told me.

Here it is, David.

Richard Sowers

About the Author

Richard Sowers is the former Executive Director of Public Relations at Atlanta Motor Speedway and has been an editor and writer for various sports publications, including *The Sporting News*. During his career Richard has compiled extensive statistical records of numerous sports and is one of a handful of people to have a copy of all the original NASCAR race reports—documents that NASCAR itself no longer has. This is Richard's first book about motorsports.

Front cover photos:
From left to right: Top: Richard Petty in 1960 (photo by Don Hunter); Lee Petty in 1959; Jeff Gordon and Bobby Labonte lead the pack around Atlanta Motor Speedway; Bottom: Fireball Roberts in 1964; David Pearson in 1976, and Darrell Waltrip and Dale Earnhardt in 1997, all courtesy of Atlanta Motor Speedway.

Back Cover photo: Rusty Wallace and Dale Earnhardt Jr. pace the field at the start of the Martinsville race in April 2000 (Nigel Kinrade).

Spine photo: Tim Flock on Daytona Beach in 1955, courtesy of Atlanta Motor Speedway.